CONFIDENCE IN BATTLE, INSPIRATION IN PEACE

THE UNITED STATES ARMY CHAPLAINCY 1945–1975

By

Rodger R. Venzke

University Press of the Pacific
Honolulu, Hawaii

Confidence in Battle, Inspiration in Peace:
The United States Army Chaplaincy 1945-1975

by
Rodger R. Venzke

ISBN: 1-4102-1129-0

Copyright © 2004 by University Press of the Pacific

Reprinted from the 1985 edition

University Press of the Pacific
Honolulu, Hawaii
http://www.universitypressofthepacific.com

FOREWORD

This volume is one of a series of five prepared by various authors, designed to be useful and instructive regarding the long history of the United States Army Chaplaincy. The emphasis throughout is on how chaplains did their ministry in the contexts of both war and peace. The series seeks to present as full and as balanced an account as limitations of space and research time permit. The bibliography in each volume offers opportunities for further research leading to detailed studies, articles, monographs, and perhaps even volumes regarding persons, developments, and events of the periods concerned. No attempt has been made to express any specific point of view or to make policy recommendations. The contents of each volume represent the work of the individual author and do not represent the official view of the United States government.

The author of this volume is Chaplain Rodger R. Venzke, a Regular Army chaplain of the Lutheran Church—Missouri Synod. Chaplain Venzke, a native of Wisconsin, was Pastor of a civilian congregation in Frazee, Minnesota, prior to his entry on active duty in 1963. He has served at Fort Bliss, Texas; Walter Reed Army Medical Center, Washington, D.C.; the Staff and Faculty, US Army Chaplain Center and School, Fort Wadsworth, Staten Island, N.Y. and overseas, in Vietnam and Germany. He has earned and received the Master of Science Degree from Long Island University, New York, and the Master of Sacred Theology Degree from New York Theological Seminary, New York. He has been awarded the Meritorious Service Medal and the Army Commendation Medal.

ORRIS E. KELLY
Chaplain (Major General) US Army
Chief of Chaplains

. . . to the American Soldier
and the Guardian of his Faith

PREFACE

There are some obvious dangers in writing a history of recent events, not least of which is the great availability of critics. Researching, writing, and evaluating the events of centuries long past, after all, only receive an honest appraisal from others who have done the same, an exercise of scholars matching sources. The recording of recent events, however, pits the author's words against the memories of those who are still alive and well.

Author Ingrid Bengis struggled with that problem in her article "Truth or Honesty" (*New York Times,* 26 November 1973, p. 31). When a woman who appeared in one of her books objected that she should have been portrayed "the way I am," the writer replied: "But I have. I've tried to show the essence of you, according to my own perceptions." "But your perceptions are different from my perceptions," protested the woman. "That's exactly the point," replied the writer.

In a sense, the same could be said of my approach to the past 30 years of the United States Army Chaplaincy. Along with the other four who have labored on volumes covering preceding eras, I was asked to produce an objective, readable account, focusing on the ministry of the Army chaplaincy within an established, limited space. Unquestionably, the most difficult of those guidelines, especially for the period from 2 September 1945 to the "present," was the element of objectivity—attempting to deal with the subject material apart from personal reflections or feelings. For someone not only living in the era, but also working within the institution, this is somewhat like attempting to describe the architecture of a house while sitting in the living room, absorbed with the structure's atmosphere as a home. Others within the "house" will rightfully conclude: "But you didn't mention . . .," "That's not exactly the way it was . . .," saying essentially, "Your perceptions are different from my perceptions." I can only reply also, "That's exactly the point." Future historians will be able to be more coldly objective regarding this period of the chaplaincy, but they, in turn, will be disadvantaged because they were not there and did not personally experience the milieu in which many of the events took place. For them, hopefully, this limited volume may help to recapture some of that mood as well as the facts of those of us who lived and served during this period as chaplains in the Unitel States Army.

I am particularly grateful to those many individuals who helped to contribute to the following pages. Most of that gratitude goes to the chaplains, both retired and on active duty, who shared their experiences through questionnaires, personal and recorded interviews, and correspondence, including material from their personal files. Appreciation is also extended to the personnel at the National Archives, the West Point Military Academy Library, the U.S. Army Military History Research Center, the U.S. Army War College Library, and the General Commission on Chaplains and Armed Forces Personnel. Various individuals in the Office of the Army Chief of Chaplains were most gracious in answering my persistent questions, as were the personnel at the U.S. Army Reserve Components and Personnel Administration Center.

But special laurels are reserved for those at the U.S. Army Chaplain Center and School, without whose support and work this volume would not have been possible: the Commandant, Chaplain (COL) Chester R. Lindsey, the Librarian, Chaplain (COL) Dick J. Oostenink, USAR, and the proofreaders and "bosses," Chaplain (COL) William E. Paul, Jr., and Chaplain (LTC) James H. Young. Finally, included among that latter group are those wonderful people who toiled to make it all legible: Patricia L. O'Connell, who transcribed the recorded interviews, and Charlesetta L. Sizemore, Constance C. Hanlon, Anna M. Buther, and Joseph S. De Fazio of the Chaplain School Composing Room.

Fort Wadsworth, New York   Rodger R. Venzke
15 May 1975   Chaplain (MAJ), USA

CONTENTS

CHAPTER I

In the Aftermath of World War

GIVING THANKS FOR PEACE

The second day of September 1945 was a Sunday, and it seemed as if the battleship *Missouri,* anchored in Tokyo Bay, momentarily became the pulpit in a world cathedral. The brief, 20-minute ceremony was like a great liturgy of peace, and the homily was delivered by Douglas Mac-Arthur:

> . . . We have had our last chance. If we do not now devise some greater and more equitable system Armageddon will be at our door. The problem basically is theological and involves a spiritual recrudescence and improvement of human character that will synchronize with our almost matchless advance in science, art, literature and all material and cultural developments of the past two thousand years. It must be of the spirit if we are to save the flesh. . . .[1]

One reporter mused how, as the surrender document was signed, "the sun burst through low-hanging clouds as a shining symbol to a ravaged world now done with war." [2] Unfortunately, it was not our "last chance," for the world seemed nowhere near being "done with war."

For that moment in time, however, the slow and agonizing death of world war seemed to awaken again America's spiritual convictions. Four months earlier, when Colonel General Gustav Jodl, Chief of Staff of the German Army, surrendered to the Allies in a little red schoolhouse in Reims, France, President Truman proclaimed:

> . . . For the triumph of spirit and of arms which we have won, and for its promise to peoples everywhere who join us in the love of freedom, it is fitting that we, as a nation, give thanks to Almighty God, who has strengthened us and given us the victory. Now, therefore, I

See footnotes at end of chapter.

Harry S. Truman, President of the United States of America, do hereby appoint Sunday, May 13, 1945, to be a day of prayer. . . .[3]

Of course, the more than 9,000 Army chaplains who had shared in the sufferings of World War II offered their prayers of thanksgiving for V–E and V–J Days in severely contrasting circumstances. Luther D. Miller, an Episcopalian who had just become the Army's Chief of Chaplains in April, joined his Navy counterpart at a service held in the White House. Shortly afterwards he led the nation in prayer over a world-wide radio network.[4] On the other hand, Albert G. Wildman, United Presbyterian, had just participated in the burial of 184 victims of the Wobbelin Concentration Camp at Hagenow, Germany, and simply noted at the end of his diary account for 8 May: "V–E Day! Thanks be to God." [5] But an account which best exemplified the mixture of great sorrow and joy was noted at the end of one chaplain's monthly report:

> The Service of Thanksgiving for final Victory held at this Post was an unforgettable experience. Early that morning we learned that "it was finished" at last, and at the commanding officer's suggestion special devotions were arranged for 10:30 A.M.
>
> At the nine o'clock news broadcast the loss of the U.S.S. *Indianapolis* was announced. My oldest son was an ensign aboard her. I had reason to be grateful that the next hour had to be spent in arranging the details of the service and listing so many things for which we all could offer our deep and joyful gratitude. Something told me at the time that my son's name would not be on the small list of survivors, and at first I feared it would be hard to head a service of thanksgiving. But the very work of preparing the service brought home to me the wonderful realization that the very hour of loss was even more an hour of thanksgiving, for "it is well with the child!"
>
> The news of our bereavement spread through the hospital and I think every officer, nurse, and enlisted man that could be spared from duty, and every patient that could get out of bed, was present at the service. Their unspoken understanding was like a deep, quiet tide bearing me along, and I believe that nowhere that day was God worshipped with fuller hearts or deeper reverence.[6]

"I ain't good enough to pray much," said one soldier to his chaplain. "But tonight I'm not asking for nothing, I'm just saying thanks." Sick and wounded left their beds to kneel in prayer as chapel bells chimed the news. "Arranged for Prayer and Thanksgiving Services every half-hour from 2 p.m. to 8 p.m.," noted one chaplain. "More than 1500 men attended these services." On troop ships and shell-scarred fields, in dis-

See footnotes at end of chapter.

tant and long-since-forgotten places, in humble and great houses of worship, gratitude to God was the keynote.[7]

Emotions at the end of the War ranged from idealism to bitterness. Representative Jennings Randolph of West Virginia, a member of the General Commission on Army and Navy Chaplains (the General Commission), introduced a bill in Congress calling for a new cabinet position for a "Department of Peace."[8] Others said V-E and V-J Days should be succeeded by "V-W Day—Victory over War."[9] Some Army chaplains, however, being no less human than those they served, expressed a continuing rage against the former enemies. In his letter to the editor of a periodical, one told the doubtfully humorous story of a Mexican laborer who, after his boss raised a pick handle at him, finally replied, "Me savvy! Me savvy!" Then he continued:

> The Jap is neither a Christian nor a gentleman. He interprets our language of the Prince of Peace as stupidity and weakness. . . . The Japs were beginning to understand when we pulverized their homeland with thousands of B–29's. . . . But they really did "savvy" the atomic bomb. . . .[10]

Ironically, the previous issue of the same periodical had carried this brief note:

> Chaplain Masao Yamada, Congregationalist minister, serving with the 442nd Infantry Regimental Combat Team, has recently been awarded the Legion of Merit. The chaplain is one of three American chaplains of Japanese ancestry in the United States Army.[11]

RETURNING TO CIVILIAN LIFE

For most chaplains the end of the War was an anxious and traumatic time, not unlike that experienced by other military personnel. The overwhelming desire to go home was mingled with the uncertainty of what, if anything, awaited them. *Time* magazine reported that "many a young ex-chaplain was beset by misgivings. Misgiving No. 1 he shared with mustered out Americans of every sort . . . 'Will I get a job?' . . . Misgiving No. 2 they also had in common with their brother veterans: 'How can I get along with civilians?' "[12]

There was a strange mixture too of the anxiety over acceptance and the conviction that their experiences had been a priceless asset to their ministry. Chaplain Ben W. Sinderson, Disciples of Christ, wrote:

See footnotes at end of chapter.

> We chaplains know the future we face. The ministers in civilian pastorates are entrenched; we are outsiders. We have no ill feelings in this matter; it is just one of those things. Our peace-loving public will soon forget everything connected with the war, even the sacrifice of human lives. The chaplain may be looked upon as a militant, dangerous to the Peace. His military career won't count for much in the average church. . . . In some respects we will have been on a detour; we are now back on the main highway, changed, different, wiser—and better able to do a job, if we had one!
>
> In many ways, I have passed 'beyond'—beyond being quizzed about my orthodoxy, beyond denominational bickering and in-institutional self sufficiency. . . .
>
> So the chaplain's future is none too clear or certain. . . .[13]

The last monthly reports of many of those leaving active duty were filled with phrases that searched for expression of experiences now gone: "Many blessings that cannot be valued in money" . . . "Nothing I would trade for these months and years" . . . "The happiest and most fruitful years of my ministry" . . . "Rich in experience and Christian service" . . . "I depart with keen regret" . . . "My faith in prayer has been confirmed over and over again" . . . "I am grateful to God for every day of my service as a chaplain" . . . "It has been a privilege to be a soldier-minister." [14]

Nevertheless, the Office of the Chief of Chaplains (OCCH) was swamped with so many requests for release from active duty that it somewhat sternly reminded these men that the "point system," which established priorities according to length of service overseas and in combat, applied to them like every other officer.[15] Aware of the drastic effect of a mass exodus, it attempted to encourage waivers of eligibility for release and agreements to continue on duty until at least 30 June 1947.[16]

By mid-1946 even General Eisenhower, then the Army's Chief of Staff, was attempting to discourage the rapid departure of chaplains:

> . . . today, with the fighting over, the need for their continued service is undiminished. Our soldiers the world over, with more time on their hands, anxious to go home and conscious of the problems facing them on return to civil life, are urgently in need of the counsel of these men who served them so well in battle. . . .
>
> It is my earnest endeavor to release as rapidly as possible every individual not actually required in accomplishing the Army's mission.
>
> In the meantime, I must repeat, the opportunity for service by the Army Chaplain is as great, or greater, than it has ever been.[17]

See footnotes at end of chapter.

The statistical reports of separations published by the OCCH indicated the immensity of the problem. From V–J Day to 31 December 1945, 2,106 had returned to civilian life. Within 6 months the figure had grown to 5,807, leaving 2,334 on active duty.[18] The number of Army Chaplains continued to drop until it leveled at exactly 1,100 in service at the end of 1947.[19]

A variety of efforts were made to smooth the transition to civilian life. The American Lutheran Church, for example, established a $50,000 fund for returning chaplains to enjoy either a year's recuperation or study.[20] The Army Navy Chaplains' Association (the Chaplains' Association) began publishing a series of articles to assist them in readjustment.[21] Similarly, the General Commission ran a series on churches' responses to the question: "What has your denomination done to assure its returning chaplains that they shall not have to suffer in civilian life for their sacrifice in the chaplaincy?"[22]

For 161 of them, the sacrifice was simply marked by a plain white cross or Star of David and they were not to return at all.[23] For others, even though they remained in service, there was no organization or church to replace what they had lost. Robert P. Taylor, Baptist, destined to become the Air Force's Chief of Chaplains in 1962, survived the Bataan Death March and nearly 4 years in a Japanese prison camp. When he returned, he discovered that his wife, who thought he had died, was remarried.[24]

CONTINUING THE UNIQUE MINISTRY

During a brief moment immediately following World War II, some Protestant chaplains, returning to civilian life or not, became irate over a public suggestion that most of them had been less than top quality. Brigadier General Harry H. Vaughn, then military aide to President Truman, had been invited to speak to the Women's Auxiliary of the Alexandria (Virginia) Westminster Presbyterian Church in early September 1945. It was apparently as shocking to Vaughn as it was to the chaplains when his remarks appeared in a national magazine.

> I don't know why a minister can't be a regular guy, but unfortunately some of them are not. You have to give the Roman Church credit. When the War Department requests a bishop to supply 20 priests for chaplains, he looks over his diocese and picks out the 20 best men. Frequently a Protestant [minister] does not have a

---

See footnotes at end of chapter.

church at that moment or is willing to go on vacation for about three years.[25]

The General Commission, registering a protest with General Vaughn as well as the President, labeled the remarks as "highly offensive and prejudicial." [26] The President quickly replied:

> . . . The highly controversial remarks attributed to General Vaughn—whether authentic or unauthentic—in nowise represent my views. General Vaughn was speaking in a private capacity in his own church. . . . Any views which he may have expressed were therefore his own, not mine. I completely disassociate myself from them.
>
> No one regrets more than I that misunderstanding and misrepresentation should have occurred. . . .[27]

While the General's remarks may have been "offensive," it is hard to believe that they were totally "prejudicial." He not only was a member of the church, he had served as an elder and later taught a teenage Bible class; two of his students were influenced by him to enter Protestant ministries. He had probably taught them from his own Bible which bore the following hand-written note on the fly leaf:

> To Harry H. Vaughn,
> friend, comrade, advisor, military aide: read it, act on it, and you will be as you always have, fundamentally right.
> Harry S. Truman [28]

For those who remained on active duty, either temporarily during the days of occupation or so long as to endure two more wars in Asia, the immediate tasks were as totally varied as the areas of assignment. Some Army clergymen, like Leigh O. Wright, Presbyterian, made so many ocean crossings as transport chaplains they must have considered themselves more fit for the Navy. Chaplain Wright reported in the fall of 1946 that he had recently made his eighty-sixth trip across the Atlantic. Eighty-two of those were on the *Queen Mary*.[29] With those in similar duty on the Pacific was Robert T. Handy, American Baptist. The young men who joined in his Bible study groups on those long voyages must have enjoyed a rare privilege—Chaplain Handy was later to become a professor at Union Theological Seminary.[30]

Whether destined to become a seminary professor or not, many chaplains during and after the War were apparently heavily engaged in the recruitment of future clergymen. Already in 1944 so many reports of possible candidates for the ministry had arrived at the OCCH that a

---

See footnotes at end of chapter.

Memorandum was sent out requesting specific information about these men which could be relayed to the various denominations.[31] At the Army Air Forces' Lowry Field in Denver, for example, 17 future candidates had formed their own "Embryo Ministers' Association." [32]

In less than 2 years, responding to the Memorandum from the Chief, chaplains had sent in the names of nearly 4,000 potential clergymen.[33] By 1948, Selective Service reports indicated that 8,973 veterans were studying to become ministers in Protestant colleges, 231 were enrolled in Catholic seminaries, and 16 were in Jewish schools with the intention of becoming rabbis.[34]

SERVING AMONG THE GERMAN WAR CRIMINALS

One of the most unique ministries performed in the very early days of the occupation was announced rather sensationally by the *New York Times* on V–J Day:

NAZIS GET RELIGION IN WAIT FOR TRIALS

Calls For Bibles and Services by U.S. Chaplains Increase, America Jailer Says

NUREMBERG, Germany, Sept 1 (AP) About half of the Nazi leaders held here for war crimes trials are professing an interest in religion. . . .

Adolf Hitler's henchmen have Bibles in their cells, many of them say long prayers and they keep United States Army chaplains busy holding church services. . . .[35]

Chaplain Carl R. Eggers, 1st Battalion, 26th Infantry, had initially worked with the prisoners at Nuremberg. On 12 November 1945, he introduced his fellow Missouri Synod Lutheran chaplain, Henry F. Gerecke, newly assigned to the 6850th Internal Security Detachment, to the 21 defendants.[36] Chaplain Sixtus R. O'Connor was to be his Roman Catholic counterpart. Together with Dr. G. M. Gilbert, the prison psychologist, they were the only American officers on the staff who could speak German.[37] Colonel Burton C. Andrus, Commandant of the Nuremberg Prison from May 1945 to October 1946, commented later: "We had two of the finest chaplains a prison commandant could have been given." [38]

The names of the prisoners still recall the historic ethical struggle of the Allies to fix the responsibility for the unspeakable atrocities. Chaplain Gerecke was to minister to Goering, von Ribbentrop, Keitel, Frick, Funk, Schacht, Doenitz, Raeder, Schirach, Sauckel, Speer, Neurath and

See footnotes at end of chapter.

Fritzche. Chaplain O'Connor served Kaltenbrunner, Frank, von Papen, and Seyss-Inquart. Prisoners Hess, Rosenberg, Streicher, and Jodl refused to align themselves with a chaplain and never attended worship services.[39]

Of the three chaplains who became intimately acquainted with these men, Gerecke apparently shared more of his experiences with the public than the others. While his reflections, coupled with those of other writers, give us insights to the spiritual convictions of the famous defendants, his openness in discussing his ministry was not without objection. In turning down a request to print his accounts in a denominational youth magazine, a spokesman for the OCCH explained:

> The objection was based on the ground that the manuscript revealed intimate confidences which were deserving of the secrecy of the confessional. The War Department discourages anything that would possibly suggest to men that chaplains did not zealously guard intimate knowledge and confidence.[40]

Nevertheless, Gerecke did publish his experiences in a journal of the Chaplains' Association. He introduced the article by saying:

> Remember, friends, this report is unofficial and has no connection with any report that may come from the War Department. These are my personal observations and feelings about the men on trial at Nuremberg.[41]

Initially, Chaplain Gerecke apparently had his doubts about the effectiveness of his ministry there. "When I put my request for his services to the Chaplain-General," wrote the Commandant, "Gerecke was told that the decision was completely up to him. 'How,' Gerecke asked himself at the time, 'can a humble preacher from a Missouri farm make any impression on the disciples of Adolph Hitler?' " [42] Despite this hesitancy, he soon found many of them open to his ministry.

Sauckel, he reported, was his first communicant. He prayed regularly with Chaplain Gerecke, often ending with: "God be merciful to me, a sinner." Fritzche, von Schirach and Speer were given Communion after instruction by Gerecke in Luther's Catechism. Keitel, Gerecke wrote, "asked me to convey his thanks to the Christian people of America for sending a chaplain to them." The former Chief of Staff is quoted as having said to the chaplain after one private Communion service: "You have helped me more than you know. May Christ, my Saviour, stand by me all the way. I shall need him so much." Ribbentrop, who apparently was cool toward the chaplain at first, later became involved in a discussion of how one could be patriotic and a Christian at the same time.[43]

See footnotes at end of chapter.

In December 1945 Frank shared some of his feeling regarding the Catholic chaplain with the prison psychologist.

> I am glad that you and Pater Sixtus, at least, still come to talk to me.—You know, Pater Sixtus is such a wonderful man. If you could say "virgin" about a man, you would say it about him—so delicate, so sympathetic, so maidenly—you know what I mean.—And religion is such a comfort—my only comfort now. I look forward to Christmas now like a little child. . . .[44]

Streicher, among those who rejected the chaplains' ministry, told the doctor:

> The chaplain left some leaflets here for me to read, but I don't put any stock in that stuff. I'm quite a philosopher myself, you know. I've often thought about this business about God creating the universe. I always ask myself, if God made everything, who made God? You see, you can go crazy thinking about that. And all that stuff about Christ—the Jew who was the Son of God—I don't know. It sounds like propaganda.[45]

Rosenberg, who had once been a Lutheran, told Gerecke he had no need of his services and lightly remarked that he thought it was nice if anyone could be so simple as to accept the story of the Cross as the chaplain spoke of it.[46]

Of all the prisoners, Hermann Goering seemed to trouble Gerecke the most. Goering was always the first to the little chapel, sat in front and sang louder than anyone.[47] He told the chaplain, however, that he was only doing him a favor "because as ranking man of the group, if I attend the others will follow suit." [48] Once, when the psychologist ended a session with Goering because it was time for chapel services, the former leader scoffed, "Prayers, hell! It's just a chance to get out of this damn cell for a half hour." [49] Privately he told Gerecke that, while not an atheist, he rejected Lutheranism. He would only admit a belief in Almighty Power but scoffed at Christianity.[50]

O'Connor and Gerecke convinced the authorities to allow the prisoners' families to visit while the judges were in closed session. During this time, the chaplains became particularly close to the children.[51] One day, when little Edda Goering was left with Gerecke, he asked her, "Do you ever say your prayers?" "I pray every night," she replied. "And how do you pray?" the chaplain asked. "I kneel down by my bed and look to heaven and ask God to open my daddy's heart and let Jesus in." [52]

The intensity of the bond which grew between the chaplains and the prisoners was demonstrated in the spring of 1946. A rumor had spread

---

See footnotes at end of chapter.

that Gerecke, already 54 and away from home 2½ years, was going to be relieved. A letter was written to Mrs. Gerecke in St. Louis, signed by all 21 defendants, asking her to understand how much they benefited from him for 6 months and how deeply they needed him for the future. Gerecke's wife immediately wrote him and told him he must stay.[53]

For the prisoners who were eventually condemned to death, the time was set for midnight, 15 October 1946. "Fr. O'Connor and Chaplain Gerecke were untiringly moving from condemned cell to condemned cell," reported the Commandant. "Prayers were now taking on a new meaning, a new urgency." [54] At 2030 hours Gerecke visited Goering who had requested Communion. But since he still refused to make a confession of Christian faith, the chaplain, following his denominational convictions, refused to give him the sacrament. Two hours later Gerecke was quickly summoned again—only to find that Goering had taken a concealed cyanide capsule. The chaplain knelt beside him trying to get some response, but it was too late. In his own way Goering had cheated his enemies out of the final victory.[55]

Gerecke's refusal to give Communion to Goering met with some criticism. One author later wrote:

> When Hitler ordered that the men implicated in the plot of the 20th of July, 1944, should be denied the consolations of religion before their execution, the world was horrified at his inhumanity; from the minister of a Christian Church one might reasonably have expected a higher degree of Christian charity.
>
> There are perhaps no lines in the English language more moving than those of the old ballad:
>
> *"Between the stirrup and the ground*
> *He mercy sought and mercy found,—"*
>
> Certainly there are none more expressive of the grace of God freely offered even to the most miserable of sinners. That mercy was refused by the prison chaplain, as far as it lay in his power to refuse it, to Hermann Göring.[56]

Even Chaplain Gerecke struggled with that decision. "If I blundered in my approach to reach this man's heart and soul with the meaning of the Cross of Jesus," he wrote, "then I'm very sorry and I hope a Christian world will forgive me." [57]

The chaplains walked the "last mile" with each of the condemned that night. "I put my trust in Christ," Ribbentrop told Gerecke, "I'll see you again." Keitel said to the chaplain, just before his execution, "I thank you and those who sent you, with all my heart." [58]

See footnotes at end of chapter.

The excutions were finally finished. "It was a little after 3 in the morning. The chaplains went into separate cells for personal prayers and private devotions," wrote Gerecke. "Then we waited for several hours before returning to the execution chamber for prayer." [59]

Apparently the Allies had determined that some additional, symbolic act was necessary. The bodies of the executed were secretly taken to Dachau and incinerated in the ovens of the concentration camp. [60]

Such Nazi-built concentration camps, scattered throughout Germany and Austria, vividly remained in the memories of those who had accompanied the liberating units. By way of example, Chaplain Edward L.R. Elson, Presbyterian, had made an official survey of the imprisoned clergy at Dachau. The results, later included as part of the War Crimes Board material, indicated there had been 2,448 Christian ministers in the camp but that only 1,100 were still living on the day of the camp's liberation. [61] Chaplain Albert Wildman was serving as 8th Infantry Division Chaplain in May of 1945 when that unit opened the gates of two camps near the town of Wobbelin. Along with the 2,500 captives who were found barely alive were several hundred unburied bodies and five common graves containing the remains of 261. Before the bodies were removed, all of the citizens of Wobbelin and ten leading citizens of Schwerin were required to view the horrors. Included among them, under the supervision of the chaplain, was the pastor of St. Paul's Parish in Schwerin. The pastor later dictated a six-page report in which he repeatedly struggled, like the judges at Nuremberg, with the ethical question of the ultimate responsibility for such atrocities.

The citizens of the area were required to dig graves for new cemeteries and reverently transpose the bodies from the camp. Each grave was marked by a Christian Cross or Jewish Star of David constructed by the villagers. The chief magistrates of the towns were then directed to have prepared permanent stone markers for each of the cemeteries with the following inscription, written by Chaplain Wildman:

> Here lie the bodies of (number) victims of Nazi atrocity from Poland, Russia, Greece, Czechoslovakia, Belgium, Holland, and Germany, who died of starvation and brutality in the Wobbelin Concentration Camp. Buried (date) under supervision of the 8th Infantry Division, U.S. Army, by whom the surviving prisoners of the camp were liberated
> God is our Refuge and Strength. [62]

See footnotes at end of chapter.

MINISTERING TO THE JAPANESE WAR CRIMINALS

General of the Army Douglas MacArthur, Supreme Commander for the Allied Powers in the Far East, had issued a charter on 19 January 1946 for an international tribunal to try major war criminals among the former Japanese leaders. The trial of the most prominent opened in Tokyo on 3 May and 28 defendants faced the long and arduous court proceedings that lasted until November 1948. Two of the defendants died during that period and one was declared unfit to stand trial. Of the 25 who remained at the time of sentencing, 7 were executed, 16 received life imprisonment, and 2 were imprisoned for specific periods.[63]

During the trial the defendants were held in the Sugamo military prison in Tokyo. The most famous of the group, Tojo Hideki, former Prime Minister and Minister of War, had unsuccessfully attempted suicide on the day of his arrest.

To provide a ministry for these men was even more of a challenge than that faced at Nuremberg. Among the many Army chaplains who served in some capacity at Sugamo were DeWitt C. Clemens, Methodist, and Francis P. Scott, Roman Catholic. Obviously, however, there were language and religious barriers that prevented the type of deeply personal ministry experienced by the chaplains at Nuremberg.

Since 90 percent of the prisoners were Buddhist, a request was made to the Japanese government for a Buddhist priest who could be employed as a civilian chaplain. On 14 February 1946, Chaplain Clemens and other prison officials interviewed an applicant named Sninsho Hanayama. Satisfied that he would be able to provide the ministry they sought for the prisoners, they informed him that he could begin his work the following week. "Thus I became, so to say, a voluntary prisoner at Sugamo," wrote Hanayama in the introduction of his book, *The Way of Deliverance,* in which he later detailed his experiences.[64]

Hanayama admitted that the American request for a chaplain had actually embarrassed Japanese authorities "since they had never before concerned themselves with religion." He noted in contrast the sentiment expressed by President Roosevelt on the first page of a copy of the New Testament and Psalms given him by one of the Army chaplains:

> As Commander-in-Chief I take pleasure in commending the reading of the Bible to all who serve in the armed forces of the United States. Throughout the centuries men of many faiths and diverse origins have found in the Sacred Book words of wisdom, counsel and inspiration. It is a fountain of strength and now, as

See footnotes at end of chapter.

always, an aid in attaining the highest aspirations of the human soul.

Reflecting on those words, Hanayama wrote:

> The act of the President in officially making this recommendation to think on spiritual things filled me with admiration. And knowing that all Americans serving in the Pacific went to the front with this Bible in their pockets, I felt as though cold perspiration were running down my spine. For how many of *our* supreme commanders had taught their subordinates the importance of having religious faith? In this point alone it can be said that we were beaten before we started. And I thought to myself then how strange that now I should be called upon to preach the truth and the need for faith to these very leaders.[65]

The few Christian prisoners held at Sugamo during the various trials in Tokyo were ministered to by both U.S. Army chaplains via interpreters and Hanayama. Former Captain Masao Nishizawa, who had commanded the Yokohama Prisoner of War (POW) Camp during the War, wrote a stirring letter to his two children just before his execution. In the conclusion he noted:

> Lastly, one more thing I want to say to you is that you must always study the words of God well. Those words will be taught you by your mother and other people. Then, you will be able to see a glorious Japan, which though I want to see it I cannot behold. . . .
>
> Praying to God the Father, in Heaven, that you may grow up blessed by the mercy and protection of Jesus Christ, the redeemer of human sins—Amen.[66]

The 64-year-old Tojo, considered the chief war criminal by many Americans, was actually converted from Shintoism to Buddhism largely through the concerned ministry of Hanayama. One of Tojo's cousins, also a Buddhist priest, supplied the customary special name for the former leader's tombstone: *Eishoin shakuji Komyoro Koji*—"By Buddha's Grace, All Sins Committed While Living are Absolved."[67]

Chaplain Carl J. Bergstrom, General Conference Baptist, attended some of the trials of the Japanese War Criminals. His thoughts seemed to reflect the sentiments of many of those who had worked closely with the prisoners. As he listened to the proceedings he began to regret that the United States had not sent them missionaries instead of scrap iron and oil.[68]

Apparently this kind of ministry held a special and perhaps morbid fascination for some chaplains. One, stationed at the Philippine Deten-

See footnotes at end of chapter.

tion and Rehabilitation Center, complained in a letter to the Chief of Chaplains that he had not been allowed to visit Roman Catholic prisoners at Luzon POW Camp No. 1. Responding to the inquiry that resulted, his supervisory chaplain claimed that the writer, whose primary responsibility for ministry was to the prison guards, wanted to attend every execution of a prisoner and annoint every body regardless of faith. The senior chaplain further indicated that the spiritual needs of the prisoners were more than adequately met by the services of a Japanese Roman Catholic priest and the other chaplains assigned.[69]

For the most part, however, the long and extremely trying pastorates of those who served the condemned was a torturous experience which even the memory of the crimes committed could not ease. Thirty years later, retired Chaplain Oscar W. Schoech, Missouri Synod Lutheran, who had also served at Sugamo in Tokyo, reflected succinctly:

> There were many things in connection with the numerous executions which I witnessed which I did not care to put into writing and I am grateful that time has erased many of these things from my memory.[70]

SERVING OTHER PRISONERS OF WAR

Although it was less spectacular, the ministry of many U.S. Army chaplains among the thousands of lesser-known captives, both in the United States and abroad, may have been more significant. When Italy surrendered in September 1943, Chaplain Wallace M. Hale, Southern Baptist, was Division Chaplain of the 88th "Blue Devil" Division in the Mediterranean Theater of Operations. Along with four other chaplains, he set out to bring a "rebirth of religion" among the 300,000 German prisoners under the command of the 88th. Although Chaplain Oscar H. Reinboth, Missouri Synod Lutheran, was the only one who spoke German fluently, they managed to locate and enlist the aid of former German clergymen among the prisoners. Attendance at worship services ran as high as 70 percent of those able to attend. "Typical of the new spirit in the German prisoners," Chaplain Hale wrote, "was an incident at the stockade high in the Alps near Merano. An American-appointed chaplain posted the traditional Wehrmacht chaplain's sign outside his tent. It read 'Kriegspfarrer,' or 'War Clergyman.' The next morning he found that the word 'War' had been crossed out and in its place was written 'Peace.'"[71]

See footnotes at end of chapter.

Connie A. DeBruin, Reformed Church of America, and Phillip J. Schroeder, Missouri Synod Lutheran, were among the many chaplains who served German prisoners in the United States. Along with inmate clergymen, DeBruin ministered to 6,400 captives at Fort Custer, Michigan. Schroeder, who later became a professor at Concordia Theological Seminary in St. Louis, had started a "Little POW Seminary" during his 2 years of work with prisoners at Fort Lewis, Washington.[72]

In the various occupied islands of the Pacific at the end of the War, chaplains were sent into prison camps to supervise the treatment of Japanese soldiers and conduct services for those who were Christian. Among the prisoners in the four large camps covered by Chaplain William V. O'Connor, Roman Catholic, was the Japanese general who formerly commanded the island. "I'm interested in Christianity," he told O'Connor through an interpreter. When asked why, the general speculated that there would have been no war if all men were Christians. Chaplain O'Connor acknowledged that as a possibility but pointed out that Christians also had been known to fight one another. "But if *you* had been good Christians," retorted the general, in reference to Americans who had exploited the Japanese in earlier days, "there would have been no war!" [73]

In Europe chaplains often were overwhelmed by the response of liberated allies. One Roman Catholic chaplain extended a casual invitation to a Polish-speaking soldier to attend a weekday Mass in the attic of a German farmhouse. When the chaplain arrived he was amazed to find the place jammed. Italians, French, Austrians, Belgians, Hollanders, Ukranians—nearly 350 of them joined American soldiers and sang their native hymns with great enthusiasm. For some, it had been the first opportunity for public worship in 6 years.[74]

WORKING WITH THE OCCUPATION FORCES IN EUROPE

Chaplain Winfred L. Kingen, Disciples of Christ, with the 862nd Engineer Aviation Battalion, supervised the construction of the first American-type chapel in Germany. Erected on Lechfeld Airfield from a variety of war ruin materials, it was dedicated on 9 December 1945. "This new chapel," he wrote, "stands as a living symbol of one of the corner-stones of any new world of lasting peace which we are striving to build here in the heart of war-torn and ravaged Europe." [75]

The unspeakable sufferings endured from the war in Europe were no more vivid than in the lives of remaining Jews. Chaplain Wolf Gunther

---

See footnotes at end of chapter.

Plaut, 104th Infantry Division, conducted Germany's first public Jewish service since 1938 in the remains of Cologne's synagogue on Roon Street a little over a month before the Nazi surrender. He described it as "an unforgettable experience. Ragged, half-starved Jews, their spirits barely kindled, stood next to their more fortunate co-religionists from America." All of them cried unashamedly and "were swept up in an immense wave of gratitude that the reign of evil was coming to an end and that even in the land of terror the spirit of the Eternal People would not be quenched forever." [76] By August, General Eisenhower appointed Rabbi Judah Nadich, the senior Jewish Chaplain at Supreme Headquarters Allied Powers Europe, as Consultant on Jewish Problems. Nadich, who later wrote about his experiences in his book, *Eisenhower and the Jews,* paved the way for the Office of Jewish Advisor—a position first occupied by Federal Judge Simon Rifkind. The Office coordinated the various efforts to aid Jewish displaced persons from October 1945 to December 1949.[77]

For the most part, Jewish Army chaplains were the first contact between displaced persons and their own people in the outside world. Besides the burial of the "liberated dead," they worked daily among the chaos, confusion and disorganization of the living, attempting to bring some semblance of order along with material and spiritual assistance. "Where is my family?," was a common, anguished plea. Army rabbis worked day and night attempting to reunite loved ones. They established synagogues and organized soldiers to assist with orphans. One group of children from Buchenwald was evacuated immediately to Palestine through the work of Jewish chaplains. By the spring of 1946, ten Jewish chaplains had been recruited and assigned specifically to solve the problems of displaced persons. Actually, it simply meant that the work which was already in full swing now had official status and could be done on a full-time basis.[78]

By the summer of 1946, thousands of refugees poured into Austria attempting to flee persecution in Poland. They had hoped that by passing through the American zone they might move on to Palestine with little difficulty, but the camps in Austria could no longer contain them. They were sent into Germany, by whatever rail transportation was available, accompanied by a chaplain who served as escort, interpreter and liaison officer. The experiences of those men are captured by one who recalled:

> How vivid are my recollections of these transports. A thousand
> people—men, pregnant women, and children, all crowded together
> in thirty box cars on a miserable, rainy day. Twenty-four hours try-

See footnotes at end of chapter.

ing to bring some measure of comfort and solace to these weary travellers, some of whom were on the road for three months. Whenever the train came to a stop the chaplain . . . would dash from car to car, thus attempting to assure the people that they were not alone. Here was a "pastor" in the true sense of the word, serving a congregation on wheels—a bar of chocolate to a crying child, milk for a pregnant woman, hot coffee for a shivering old man, frantic search at midnight for a doctor to deliver a baby. Twenty-four hours into which were crowded innumerable experiences, even to leading a sunrise worship in a corner of a box-car and joining in the singing of groups of youngsters whose spirits could not be dampened.[79]

Chaplain George Vida took special interest in his Jewish fellowmen who suffered as displaced persons and eventually, because of his involvement and personal expertise in several languages, was assigned to work closely with Bartley C. Crum, head of the Anglo-American Commission of Inquiry on Palestine. In 1967, Vida authored a book which outlined his experiences: *From Doom to Dawn* (Jonathan David Publishers, New York).

For most of the chaplains with the occupation forces in Europe, the keynote seemed to be set by Episcopal Bishop Henry Knox Sherrill, former World War I chaplain and head of the Army-Navy Commission for Episcopal Chaplains as well as Chairman of the General Commission. "The problem the victor in the European war must now face," he said, "is the fact that they must live with the Germans and therefore it is to our interest to establish relations as soon as possible with people who can build a new nation. . . . In my opinion, we must hold out a hand to the churches in Germany." [80]

One of the immediate difficulties faced by chaplains, however, was the existence of non-fraternization regulations. Despite their existence, many chaplains began organizing German youth groups. In September 1945, the Seventh Army gave official direction to chaplains to participate in such activities even though it was in clear violation of the non-fraternization policy.[81] Apparently this confusion resulted in some embarrassing incidents prior to an alteration of the regulations. Early in 1946, the president of the "American Women's Unit for War Relief, Inc.," wrote to the Secretary of War, Robert Patterson, and inclosed a newspaper article that claimed some U.S. Army chaplains had been arrested and threatened with court marial for "collaborating with the enemy." The OCCH replied for the Secretary and explained:

See footnotes at end of chapter.

Similar reports of some unfortunate episodes during the early days of the occupation of Germany by American forces have appeared in a number of publications. However, it is believed that these refer to happenings during the early period of occupation. It seems probable that the same is true of the circumstances referred to in the clipping attached to your letter and that the recent modification of the non-fraternization policy would prevent the repetition of any such incident.[82]

Despite these difficulties, the youth programs were an apparent success. Chaplains of one division reported that in 3 months 30,000 had attended movies, 25,000 had participated in sports, and 8,000 attended Christmas parties—all sponsored by chaplains and aided by American troops.[83] The groups, in some cases, developed into "Youth for Christ" organizations which were particularly strong in Frankfurt, Munich, Berlin, and Nuremberg. Teenage American soldiers, and eventually American dependents, joined with German youth in what was called a "training ground of Christian democrary in Europe."[84]

As was mentioned earlier, some of the first contacts between American chaplains and German clergymen were made in POW camps. Many German pastors had been drafted during the War and served as regular soldiers or medical assistants. Through the efforts of American chaplains, who provided literature and facilities, these clergy began to resume their original professions. Seminars and seminaries were organized and a variety of welfare activities for hospitals, orphanages, kindergartens and youth-recreational groups became joint efforts of Army chaplains and national clergy.[85] When American units moved into Austria, an "Ecclesiastical Affairs Branch" was formed and continued until January 1947. Its primary purpose was to restore freedom of religion and public worship by releasing former clergymen who had been in confinement, assisting in the repair of buildings, and supplying materials. It also became an agency to render assistance to Austrian civilians with housing, clothing, fuel, and medical supplies.[86] One chaplain in Germany established weekly lectures for local pastors on the general topic of American church life. "Realizing that many and drastic changes lie ahead for the Evangelical Church in Germany," he said, "it is their desire to learn all they can of the workings of American Protestant Churches."[87]

In the midst of all the activities by chaplains who were attempting to restore religious life in Europe, there was also the lonely duty of tending to those soldiers who had fallen in battle. Chaplain Theodore

Pfeiffer, Presbyterian USA, was among those who served with the American graves Registration Command. He and his fellow chaplains performed countless committal services and answered the continual flow of mail from the next of kin of many of the 150,000 Americans buried in the 37 military cemeteries throughout Europe. They were moved by the great kindnesses shown by many local civilians in Holland, France and Belgium who visited the graves, adorned them with flowers and knelt to offer prayers. For the most part, however, the task was the lonely vigil described by one chaplain:

> One of our principal duties is to go to the cemeteries three or four times a week for prayers for American soldiers, whose bodies have been recovered from various battle grounds throughout Europe. They have been brought from many places to rest among their own. The chaplains stand alone with the Commanding Officer of the cemetery, prayers and requiems are recited by the chaplains, and a final salute is given. There are no mourners. Only God knows that America is giving her final tribute to her heroic dead.[88]

Ironically, one of the great leaders of American soldiers during the War was killed in a vehicle accident only a few months after the War had ended. General George S. Patton joined his fallen comrades whose places were now marked by endless rows of white crosses and Stars of David. Chaplain Edwin R. Carter, Congregationalist, Deputy Staff Chaplain of the European Theater of Operations, and Chaplain Loren T. Jenks, Disciples of Christ, conducted the funeral services in Christ Church, Heidelberg, on 23 December 1945. On the following day, Christmas Eve, Chaplain Carter held the committal service in the American Military cemetery near Luxembourg.[89]

Immediately following the War, the reaction of the German people to the activities of American Army chaplains was generally one of favorable surprise. Chaplain Leslie V. Barnes, Roman Catholic, observed:

> The spectacle of churches filled with soldiers on their knees in prayer, the Armies of men in uniform assisting by thousands at colorful field Masses, others assembled in great Cathedrals at services in Thanksgiving—all made profound impressions on people indoctrinated with the gospel of hate.[90]

One chaplain set up his office in a storeroom formerly occupied by the Wehrmacht. He placed a portable altar in the front window with an open Bible and a large card inscribed with John 3:16 in German. The display attracted a great deal of attention from those who passed by and one individual remarked through an interpreter: "The Nazis told us that

---

See footnotes at end of chapter.

there was nothing to religion, and here the American Army comes bringing the very words of Jesus." [91] A Catholic chaplain reported that groups of Germans would watch in amazement as American troops came in large numbers to Confession and Holy Communion. "It seems as though the complete absence of official repression at Divine Services," he said, "was something they could not entirely grasp." [92]

Nevertheless, even chaplains sometimes experienced a reluctance on the part of German citizens to see them in any other way than as former adversaries. When fellow Methodists Alfred M. Ellison and Clovis G. Childers attended a German church service in Bad Kissingen, Chaplain Ellison noted: "During the singing of the choir and the great music of Brahms and Bach and others, I felt the sting of being an enemy. Chaplain Childers and I took our seats but the church members carefully avoided sitting near us until nearly all seats were taken." [93]

To provide a type of police force for the U.S. area of occupation in Germany, the United States Constabulary was formed under the command of Major General Ernest Harmon. Comparable to a division with three brigades, they were made up of a variety of units previously involved in the invasion. Dressed in olive-drab uniforms, combat boots, striped helmet liners and yellow scarves, they made regular patrols in jeeps and armored cars painted yellow, blue and red. In February 1946 the chaplain section for the Constabulary was established with Charles P. Malumphy, Roman Catholic, as Staff Chaplain. "I want the best chaplains for this outfit," General Harmon told Chaplain Malumphy. "I want you to get them and I'll do all I can to help them in their work, but they must work." [94]

The Constabulary had to confront the normal problems inherent in occupation forces. With the danger of battle past, chaplains began to notice a slow change in the attitude of American troops. "Interest in chapel has dropped almost to the 'cold storage' point," reported Chaplain Vern A. Slater, General Conference Baptist. "Last month I held 12 worship services with 430 attending. . . . Immorality, drunkenness, and indifference are taking a heavy toll of our young men." [95] By the end of 1946, the House Military Affairs Committee of the U.S. Congress was releasing a third draft of a report that sharply criticized the policies of the U.S. Army of occupation in the European Theater. One Army chaplain had given a statement to representatives of the committee complaining that the Army in Europe virtually condoned immorality and gave little stress to recreational and religious activities. The committee, in turn,

See footnotes at end of chapter.

publicly commended the role played by chaplains in their attempt to retain a high standard of morality.[96]

In the spring of 1947, a commission of 14 clergymen was appointed by the War Department to survey the problems and conditions of the American occupation of Germany and Austria. Their report indicated a need for stronger support of chaplains who were trying to change some of the bad examples set by American soldiers who, they believed, were giving discredit to the United States and democracy in general.[97] Although the introduction of American military dependents to Europe, which began in April 1946, slowly tempered such problems, as late as August 1948 a corporal addressed the following comments to the Chief of Chaplains. His letter hinted that even chaplains were not producing the kind of change he desired:

> Today, as never before, we are in need of some real honest to goodness chaplains in the army of occupation that are interested in the men enough to do some good. I have no complaint to make against the chaplains we have in the service and as far as I know they are all men of excellent reputation and are doing all within their power to combat sin and the devil, but when you go to church and there are perhaps a dozen there, then I am wondering if something is not drastically wrong somewhere. . . . Isn't there someway that all the chaplains can be awakened to the great need of these soldiers? . . . Isn't there someway that I may help in a greater way?[98]

Chaplain James B. Murphy, Roman Catholic, answering for the Chief, said in part:

> Unfortunately, my young friend, you have had to witness a revolution in the social order and to endure the fears, uncertainty and disappointment so often attendant upon disaster. You can be sure that we, along with other men of good will, are aware of the perils of the day. Our efforts may seem weak and our purposes sometimes uncertain, but confident of God's power we yet press forward in doing His will.[99]

With the relaxation of the non-fraternization policy there came an increase in application for German-American marriages. The resultant counseling and interpretation of regulations fell largely upon the chaplains. Invariably, the delays caused by endless paper work as well as the restrictive quota system for foreign spouses to enter the United States resulted in soldiers being shipped home without their wives. The practical and emotional problems inherent in that situation consumed much of

---

See footnotes at end of chapter.

the time and energy of the occupation chaplains. By the last half of
1948, since the quota system of the War Brides Act was scheduled to expire on 28 December, the number of marriages increased sharply.[100] Chaplain Charles P. Carlson, Presbyterian, serving with the 7720th European
Command Replacement Depot in that year, was particularly impressed
by the number of soldiers who returned to Europe with the intention of
marrying German girls they had met on their previous tour.

> Each shipment brings five to twenty men who convey this to the
> chaplain. It is believed that these men are sincere for they have had
> a time of separation to think it over. . . . from three to a dozen men
> come to the office of the chaplain and inform him that they have
> come back to locate, provide for, and make permanent arrangements
> for children they have sired and left behind. . . . These men are to
> be regarded very highly, for they have come back, oftentimes at a
> great sacrifice, to right the wrong they committed.[101]

The continual arrival of more and more dependents in Europe
made it necessary to draw many chaplains from troop units to provide
spiritual ministries to the American military communities springing up
throughout Germany.[102] One of those chaplains arrived to find two American wives valiantly struggling every Sunday morning to clean and organize
the main hall of the officers' club for Sunday School. With their help he
was able to move the classes to the local community school, establish a
Bible Class for teacher-training, and in 5 months build the largest American community Sunday School in Germany.[103]

A vigorous chapel-building program was also initiated for the American communities—some from the ground up and others from rehabili-
tated buildings. In 8 years approximately 270 such structures were
serving as the center of American religious activities in communities now
equipped with commissaries, post exchanges, administrative offices, and
various other public service buildings.[104] While many of the Army
churches conformed to a standard design, some employed uniquely sym-
bolical material. Chaplain Cloma A. Huffman, Christian Congregational,
supervised the transformation of an old German artillery stable into a
chapel at Heilbronn. Three symbolic stones were mounted in the base
of the altar. One, dating back to the 13th century with 400-year-old
engravings, came from the badly damaged Saint Kilian's Evangelical
Church. The congregation donated the stone in appreciation for the
contributions of American soldiers for the reconstruction of their church.
Another came from Saint Augustine's Roman Catholic Church;

See footnotes at end of chapter.

together with Saint Kilian's it was virtually destroyed during 1944 bombing raids but had since been rebuilt. The third stone came from the Stuttgart Jewish Synagogue which SS troops had demolished in 1938; the stone was among those for which members of the congregation had risked their lives—hiding and secretly burying fragments as precious symbols of their faith. The three stones uniquely represented the cooperation of the major faiths as well as the new found friendship of the German people.[105]

"The community chaplain," wrote Chaplain John B. Youngs, Bible Presbyterian, "enjoys a position much like that of the civilian pastor." As such, those chaplains ministered to soldiers and their families, as well as to civilian workers and local German churches, developing and supervising a variety of organizations and programs.[106] Chaplain Paul J. Maddox, Southern Baptist, Staff Chaplain for the European Command from July 1946 to July 1950, maintained that there was no greater opportunity for ministry in the chaplaincy. By 1948, more than 125 religious schools had been established and more than 2,000,000 people were helped annually through civic action programs. "Chaplains have been a living witness," said Maddox, "that the purpose of the United States is not to exploit the conquered but to help them regain faith in life and in the living God."[107]

While the total efforts and effects of what is commonly called "Civic Action" are almost impossible to measure, the contribution of a single chaplain in that area gives some hint of the immensity of the work. When Chaplain Herman H. Heuer, Missouri Synod Lutheran, was reassigned to the Headquarters from one of the brigades in the Constabulary in 1947, a reporter for the unit newspaper wrote: "The only people glad to see him go were the APO clerks." In a matter of a few months, Chaplain Heuer had received and distributed 592 charity parcels representing approximately 20,000 pounds of "warmth and comfort."[108]

While the occupation of Europe slowly changed the lives of American soldiers stationed there, as well as the ministry of their chaplains, the memories of the long and agonizing War remained. One chaplain mused:

> It was my privilege recently to make a trip by jeep back through the Siegfried line sector where our 76th Infantry Division fought . . . "Death Valley" and Echternach Hill were quiet and peaceful under a bright fall sun. The beauty of God's handiwork already obscured many of the horrible seats of war. But could I ever forget the trails in blood, the whine and roar of shells, the pain and torture of mangled bodies, the weary, miserable soldiers that those

scenes caused to stir again within my mind? Never! I could only
thank God those days were over, and earnestly pray that mankind
will tune their hearts to God's message of love and peace.[109]

Chaplain Thomas L. Doyle, Methodist, with the 120th Station Hospital
in Bayreuth, wrote in 1948:

> The continuing ministry of the chaplain will always be needed
> whether in peace or war. We must have something that goes deeper
> than peace pacts and societies . . . a religion that will change
> not only the heart of mankind, but create justice, loyalty and free-
> dom and thus build a happier and better world where truth and
> righteousness dwell.[110]

SERVING THE OCCUPATION FORCES IN THE FAR EAST

Army chaplains with the occupation units in Japan entered their
work with such fervor that their first chapel, constructed from war
wreckage materials, was dedicated a mere 15 days after the signing of
the peace treaty.[111] More significant, however, is the fact that in late
November 1945, over 80 Army and Navy chaplains gathered in the Red
Cross Building in Tokyo to form an organization for "the discussion of
common problems and inspiration." Originally meeting under the leadership of the Eighth Army Chaplain, Yandell S. Beans, Disciples of Christ,
they elected Chaplain Hudson B. Phillips, Northern Baptist, as their
temporary chairman.[112] It was this group—later to become the "Tokyo-
Yokohama Chapter of the Army-Navy Chaplains' Association"—which
became influential not only in coordinating pastoral activities but also
in providing a common voice on the various issues of occupation.

On 17 December 1946, Phillips and two other chaplains—William
Nern, Roman Catholic, and Morris Adler, Jewish—met with General
MacArthur as representatives of the chaplains' group. Their report on
the meeting indicated MacArthur's commitment to a strong western
religious influence in Japan.

> He expressed conviction earnestly that there can be no hope for
> the world apart from the teachings of religion and the attitudes it
> fosters. The collapse of Japan has created a spiritual vacuum which
> Christian leadership should seek to fill with Christian values and
> sentiments. Shintoism never struck deep roots in the daily life of the
> Japanese. In a sense it was no religion at all. It was a political
> device which the government used for its own purposes. It was
> artificially stimulated and maintained by deliberate design. That is
> why it has been abolished. What saved the situation in the Philip-

See footnotes at end of chapter.

pines was the Christianization and Democracy of the inhabitants four centuries ago. . . . His plan and hope was that through Christianity and Democracy the Japanese would be tamed.[113]

The determination of MacArthur to bring the combination of Christianity and democracy to Japan was emphasized repeatedly during his command. Early in 1946 he invited four prominent American Christian leaders to Japan—men who had influential positions in organizations representing the missionary activities of U.S. churches. Their assignment was to meet with Japanse Christian leaders, as well as Emperor Hirohito, and determine what the Church at large could do to help rebuild the country.[114] By the late 1940's MacArthur encouraged a mass distribution of Bibles in Japan. He referred to efforts in this program as a "demonstration of practical Christianity" which met the "heart-needs" of the Japanese by giving them the Scriptures "which reveal the knowledge of God and His love through Jesus Christ." [115] As late as 1950 he commented to a visiting American churchman: "Please send ten missionaries for every one you now have in Japan. We must have ten thousand Christian missionaries and a million Bibles to complete the occupation of this land." [116] It's no wonder that one chaplain in Japan referred to the General in a letter by saying, "He has done more than any other man to further Christianity in Japan." [117]

MacArthur's conviction that democracy and Christianity were inseparable necessities for the rebirth of Japan was readily accepted by many chaplains. The Eighth Army Chaplain in late 1946 stressed to the chaplains' organization that foremost in their duties was the presentation of western civilization, American democracy, and the Christian faith to the people of Japan.[118]

During the early days of occupation, MacArthur was equally concerned with the increasing problems of morale among American troops. He told his chaplains he was convinced that such problems would become more difficult and serious with the passing of time; homesickness would become intensified, and grumbling and complaints would be heard everywhere. Although he felt that such difficulties were to be expected among occupation forces, he bolstered his chaplains by maintaining that during the War "the Command in the Pacific won to an unequalled degree the religious and spiritual interest of the troops. There was six times more religious attendance than in any other theater." [119]

What troubled the chaplains was the phenomenal increase in houses of prostitution. On 11 January 1946, with the unanimous approval of

See footnotes at end of chapter.

the 88 military clergymen present, the chaplains' organization drafted a lengthy letter to the Commander-in-Chief, U.S. Army Forces in the Pacific, under the subject title: "Repression of Prostitution." They stated that they were "strongly of the conviction that prostitution as it relates to the U.S. Occupation Forces in Japan is producing moral degradation that is exceptionally widespread and unusually ruinous to the character of American troops." The letter contained many recommendations. Among them were disciplinary action against officers who advertise houses of prostitution; discontinuance of the practice of labeling "acceptable" houses; emphasis to troops on the moral issues, not just the physical dangers of promiscuity; establishment of lecture and interview periods by chaplains for all in-coming troops; and, above all, the declaration of all houses of prostitution as being "off limits." [120]

The first acknowledgment of the letter came nearly a month later with a restricted communication signed for the Commander-in-Chief by an assistant adjutant. It thanked the chaplains' organization for its "excellent report" and promised action. Interestingly, the reply noted that a Memorandum from the Supreme Commander to the Imperial Japanese Government—dated 10 days after the chaplains' letter—had directed the abolition of licensed prostitution in the country.[121] Then, on 31 March, a two-page letter was published and distributed to "All Army Chaplains on Duty in Japan." On the bottom was the familiar bold autograph without a signature block: "Douglas MacArthur." Whether or not he was personally aware of their January letter is unclear. With no reference to it whatsoever, he wrote in part:

> . . . I have . . . received letters from American homes expressing grave concern and deep distress over published reports suggestive of an existing widespread promiscuous relationship between members of the occupying forces and Japanese women of immoral character.
>
> . . . To protect the members of our occupying forces as far as possible from influences of evil, houses of prostitution and of ill repute have been placed off limits . . . . Every effort furthermore is being made to increase the opportunities for educational advancement and interesting and healthy recreation for soldiers when off duty. It is not sufficient, however, that we take such diversionary measures in the solution of a problem which has confronted armies of occupation throughout military history. We must, in addition, exert strong and direct moral leadership over the members of the occupying forces, to the end that the underlying moral fiber remain undiminished in strength. Such moral leadership devolves, in large

---

See footnotes at end of chapter.

measure, upon the corps of chaplains working in close understanding and cooperation with all unit commanders. . . .[122]

While the chaplains were pleased with the content of the letter, some were disturbed that it had been released to the press without reference to their original correspondence. "The open letter of General MacArthur," protested the Eighth Army Chaplain in a Memorandum to the Chief of Staff, "produces the impression that the chaplains at this late date have to be called upon to fulfill their duty." [123]

In May 1946 the Chief of Chaplains asked all chaplains in occupation zones to provide publicity about their ministries in an attempt to counteract the emphasis in the press on the issue of promiscuity.[124] As late as November, however, the Veterans of Foreign Wars complained that servicemen were returning to the States as physical, mental, moral, and social wrecks infected with venereal disease. They called on the President and the War Department to allow chaplains to have a greater voice in the choice of entertainment for those in occupation areas.[125] Much like the situation in Europe, the issue of immorality seemed to subside only after the influx of American dependents into Japan.[126]

Despite the publicity given to the bad examples of some of the occupation troops, there were contributions and services given by many soldiers that unfortunately received less notice. By mid-1946, reports to the Chief of Chaplains indicated that occupation personnel had contributed thousands of dollars for the repair and, in some cases, construction of churches, seminaries and orphanages. Nippon Union Theological Seminary in Tokyo was one recipient of such help.[127] "The G.I.s of the Army of Occupation," reported one American-clergy observer, "have won many of the Japanese people." It was his opinion that, for the most part, American soldiers had conducted themselves "with a decent respect for the feelings of others. The situation is so much better than the people of Japan had dared to expect that hatred has largely dissipated." [128]

Establishing a precedent for continuing liaison and cooperation with local churches, the chaplains' organization in Tokyo invited a Japanese Christian minister to their initial meeting. In his address to the group he asked them to publicize the special 1945 Christmas services at which the famous Toyohiko Kagawa was to speak and a choir, composed of both Japanese and Americans, was to present portions of Handel's "Messiah." [129]

In Utsunomiya, occupation troops repaired an old church building, erasing the ugly scars of bombing, installing new windows and replacing

See footnotes at end of chapter.

the flooring. It was filled twice every day with Japanese who came to hear the Christian message. A sign in front bore the unique name in Japanese and English: "GI Gospel Mission." [130]

When Chaplain William J. Reiss, Missouri Synod Lutheran, arrived in Hokkaido in August 1974, a Mr. Kosaku Nao served as his interpreter and Mrs. Nao as his chapel organist. Reiss later discovered, to his surprise, that Nao was in fact a fellow Lutheran minister who had served on the mainland before the War. They became close friends and worked together supporting new missionary efforts in the country. Over 2 decades later, the humble interpreter became the president of the subsequently-formed Japan Lutheran Church. [131]

Chaplain Francis L. Sampson, Roman Catholic, also stationed in Japan, commented on the people of the country by writing: "The Japanese are in their way a wonderful people . . . and those who become Christians do not do so by half measure." [132] That was a sentiment with which most chaplains and American missionaries thoroughly agreed.

There were on occasion, of course, incidents which marred this relationship. In 1948, for example, there was considerable correspondence between the OCCH, the Methodist Board of Missions and the Far East Command chaplains involving a single situation in which a Japanese Christian woman was ridiculed by some Americans for her religious devotion. The incident helped to emphasize the meaning of General MacArthur's warning: "One misdeed may overshadow a thousand good deeds." [133]

For the most part, however, a cooperative spirit between the occupation forces and the Japanese prevailed. It was a spirit beautifully captured in a letter received by Chaplain Peter E. Cullom, Southern Baptist, in October 1947:

> Our most respectable and dear Chaplain Cullom:
> It was this spring that you came to this Ashiya as a chaplain of the U.S. occupation forces. About half a year since then, you preached the gospel of merciful Christ earnestly for us stray sheep ever since the defeat. . . .
> We firmly believe it is these deeds of yours that will be a corner stone, the ground work of good will between yours and our country. . . .
>
> Yours in Christ
> Ashiya Baptest [sic] Church [134]

American religious endeavors among the Japanese continued for some time to be associated with U.S. political ideals. As late as 1950, for

See footnotes at end of chapter.

example, a chaplain with the 25th Division Artillery in Nara, Honshu, Japan, was commenting on his good chapel attendance and added: "I believe we are selling the ideals of democracy to the Japanese people to the degree that we uphold the standards of righteousness." [135] In the same year, retired Admiral William F. Halsey accepted a position as a regional chairman in a $10,000 campaign for the international Christian University in Japan. In accepting, the noted former leader wrote: "It is very apparent that the Japanese associate Democracy with Christianty. It is therefore fitting that a nonsectarian Christian college be established to spread this philosophy." [136]

Many of the initial efforts of Army chaplains with occupation units in Japan were directed and guided by Chaplain Frank P. MacKenzie, Presbyterian U.S., Far East Command Chaplain. During his leadership, as in the European occupation, the ministry of chaplains slowly changed from duty with specific units to local parish service within military communities.[137] The number of Army dependents and American civilian personnel continued to grow after MacKenzie's retirement in 1948 and became even more a part of the chaplains' ministry under his successor, Roy H. Parker, Southern Baptist. Chapel Centers, constructed to provide facilities for all ages in various programs, were credited for vast increases in attendance at chapel activities. A report to the Secretary of the Army in 1951 indicated the Center at the General Headquarters in Tokyo had increased activities from 20 to 234 per month during the previous 2 years. Attendance rates during the same period shot up from 1,800 to over 15,000.[138] Reflecting on those days, Chaplain Duncan N. Naylor, Presbyterian U.S., recalled:

> As Protestant chaplain at Nasugbu Beach Chapel, Yokohama, Japan, I developed the first totally rounded chapel program of my chapel ministry—men, women, youth, benevolent giving and projects, as well as worship and Sunday School. The chapel became the activity center of the housing area.[139]

By 1952, it was reported that Chaplain Alexander J. Turner, Southern Baptist, serving at the Grant Heights Chapel in Tokyo, had the distinction of conducting both the largest Sunday school and largest allied adult worship services in the world. His average Sunday service attendance was nearly 700.[140]

Chaplains with the occupation forces in the Far East also made early use of the Armed Forces Radio Network. Shortly after the arrival of U.S. troops, Chaplain Amos P. Bailey, Methodist, presented the first Christian broadcast from Tokyo since 1941. A weekly schedule, including daily devotions and Sunday services, was beamed throughout Japan and as far away as China and Okinawa.[141]

The Commander-in-Chief of the Army Forces in the Pacific had a vast range of responsibility following the War and the great number of men under his command included a group of Philippine Scouts. When authority was granted for the appointment of Philippine soldiers as officers in the Army of the United States, approval was given also, though contrary to a previous provision, for the appointment of not more than ten Philippine chaplains. On 13 November 1946, three national clergymen—Nataneal Depano, Methodist, Eligio B. A. Hernandez, Presbyterian (United Evangelical Church), Eusebio M. Taguined, Roman Catholic—were appointed with the restriction that their ministry would be conducted only among the Scouts.[142]

While the occupation units in Japan received most of the attention, there were also many U.S. troops and their chaplains serving in those Far Eastern places whose names most Americans had forgotten. Among them was a 25,000-square-mile peninsula known as Korea; like Germany, it lay divided by the occupation forces of the Soviet Union and the United States. In the American sector, the U.S. Army Military Government in Korea (USAMGIK) set out to build a nation for an impoverished people. Besides those serving various occupation units there, twelve Army chaplains, assigned to USAMGIK, worked directly with the Military Provincial Governors in the separate, established provinces. A senior chaplain at the time reported:

> I find here a unique opportunity for far-reaching service. A new civilization is being built. The American Military Governor and his key officers are men of serious purpose, high vision and exceptional ability. They seem to have the confidence and support of the Korean people. They are steadily implementing the program of government throughout the southern half of Korea, replacing the machinery of Japanese despotism with democratic processes, and preparing the Korean people for self-government and independence. My work . . . gives me an important part in this great enterprise.[143]

All of the chaplains in Korea, including those with USAMGIK, came under the supervision of the XXIV Corps Chaplain, Vernon P. Jaeger, American Baptist. In late 1947 he was succeeded briefly by George F. Rixey, Methodist, who had served as Deputy Chief of Chaplains during most of World War II, and afterwards as an Assistant Inspector General.

See footnotes at end of chapter.

When Rixey retired in early 1948 to become the Executive Secretary of the Chaplains' Association, he was succeeded by Chaplain Peter C. Schroeder, United Lutheran.[144]

Despite optimistic reports on the progress in Korea, there was a growing concern that a conflict might lie ahead. In 1948, Dr. Hyungki Lew, a leading educator and author of the country, warned a world mission conference in Chautaugua, New York, that Korea was a land in which Christianity and Communism were "in a life and death fight." While he praised the hard work of U.S. occupation personnel and American missionaries, he maintained that they were being "out-talked" by the Communists.[145] Border incidents were frequent and some Koreans looked with fear on the announcement of an early withdrawal of all U.S. forces except for a small advisory group. Despite those apprehensions, the exodus took place at the end of June 1949.[146] As if by prophecy, a Communist invasion would return U.S. soldiers to battle a mere 12 months later—less than 5 years after the expressed hope that the world was done with war.

What first came to a head on the battlefields of Korea was a growing antagonism between two political systems, an antagonism that had started decades earlier. Soviet Communism versus Western democracy was always far more than an argument between politicians or a simple disagreement on the more efficient form of government. The deep chasm between them was formed by a variance in their very philosophies of man. Preached with a religious enthusiasm, Soviet Communism made bold advances following World War II. It was not surprising, therefore, that this considered threat to democracy caused concern among many Americans over the defense and continuance of their old ideals. To a certain extent, that concern was instrumental in developing new trends in the United States Army Chaplaincy.

FOOTNOTES

CHAPTER I

[1] *New York Times,* 2 September 1945, p. 3.

[2] *Ibid.,* p. 1.

[3] *Ibid.,* 9 May 1945, p. 5.

[4] *Circular Letter,* Headquarters Army Service Forces, Office of the Chief of Chaplains, (hereafter referred to as *Circular Letter*), No. 301, 1 October 1945, p. 2.

[5] Diary of Albert C. Wildman, [8 May 1945], US Army Chaplain Center and School Archives, Ft. Wadsworth, NY. (hereafter referred to as USACHCS).

[6] *Circular Letter,* No. 305, 1 February 1946, p. 2.

[7] *Ibid.,* No. 302, 1 November 1945, p. 2.

[8] Jennings Randolph, "Time for a Department of Peace," *The Chaplain*, March 1946, pp. 14–15.

[9] Jacob S. Payton, "Toward a Lasting Peace," *Ibid.*, September 1945, p. 26.

[10] L. L. Bowles to editor, *Ibid.*, January 1946, p. 43.

[11] *Ibid.*, December 1945, p. 47.

[12] "Refresher Course," *Time*, 14 January 1946, p. 52.

[13] Ben W. Sinderson to editor, *The Chaplain*, November 1945, p. 40.

[14] *Circular Letter*, No. 303, 1 December 1945, p. 3; No. 305, 1 February 1946, pp. 2–3.

[15] "The War Department had planned discharges according to a point system, worked out before the Japanese defeat, to reward length and arduous service; but soon after Japan's surrender it announced that the point system would be submerged and all men with two years' service would be released forthwith" (Russell F. Weigley, *History of the United States Army* [New York: Macmillan Co., 1967], p. 486).

[16] *Circular Letter*, No. 302, 1 November 1945, p. 3.

[17] Dwight D. Eisenhower to Dr. Hazen, *The Chaplain*, April 1946, cover.

[18] *Circular Letter*, No. 305, 1 February 1946, p. 4; No. 312, 1 September 1946, p. 4.

[19] Office of Chief of Chaplains, file M–9, (U.S. Army Chaplains on Active Duty on 31 December for 1941 through 1952), USACHCS.

[20] *Circular Letter*, No. 298, 1 July 1945, p. 3.

[21] For example see Ellwood C. Nance, "What War Service is Doing to Ministers in Uniform," *Army and Navy Chaplain*, October–November 1945, p. 34.

[22] *The Chaplain*, January 1946, p. 27.

[23] *Circular Letter*, No. 314, 1 November 1946, pp. 3–4.

[24] Billy Keith, *Days of Anguish, Days of Hope* (Garden City, NY: Doubleday & Co., 1972), pp. 212–213.

[25] "Uncensored Dope," *Time*, 10 September 1945, p. 20.

[26] Edwin F. Lee to Harry S. Truman, *The Chaplain*, December 1945, cover.

[27] Harry S. Truman to Edwin F. Lee, *Ibid.*, February 1946, p. 3.

[28] Frank B. Gigliotti, "Christian, Soldier, Friend," *Ibid.*, May–June 1950, pp. 22–23.

[29] *Ibid.*, September 1946, p. 16.

[30] Robert T. Handy, Historical Questionnaire, 17 November 1973, USACHCS.

[31] Memorandum, Chief of Chaplains, To All Chaplains, Subj: "Candidates For The Ministry," 1 December 1944 (*Circular Letter*, file, USACHCS).

[32] *Circular Letter*, No. 297, 1 June 1945, p. 2.

[33] Edward A. Simon, "The Influence of the American Protestant Churches on the Development of the Structure and Duties of the Army Chaplaincy, 1914–1962" (STM diss., Princeton Theological Seminary, Princeton, NJ, 1963), pp. 116–117.

[34] *The Chaplain*, November 1948, pp. 44–45.

[35] *New York Times*, 2 September 1945, p. 16.

[36] Henry F. Gerecke, "Assignment With the International Tribunal As Spiritual Advisor," *Army and Navy Chaplain*, July–August 1947, p. 2.

[37] G. M. Gilbert, *Nuremberg Diary* (New York: A Signet Book by the New American Library, 1947), p. 10.

[38] Burton C. Andrus, *I Was The Nuremberg Jailer* (New York: Coward-McCann, 1969), pp. 108–109.

[39] *Ibid.*

[40] Matthew H. Imrie, OCCH, to Alfred P. Klausler, "Walther League Messenger," 22 April 1947, Records of the Army Chief of Chaplains, Record Group 247 (hereafter referred to as RG 247), file 000.76, National Archives, Washington, D.C. (hereafter referred to as NA).

[41] Gerecke, "Assignment With Tribunal," p. 2.

[42] Andrus, *Nuremberg Jailer*, p. 109.

[43] Gerecke, "Assignment With Tribunal," p. 3.

[44] Gilbert, *Nuremberg Diary*, p. 81.

[45] *Ibid.*, p. 87.

[46] Robert Cecil, *The Myth of the Master Race: Alfred Rosenberg and Nazi Ideology* (New York: Dodd Mead & Co., 1972), pp. 229–230.

[47] Andrus, *Nuremberg Jailer*, p. 137.

[48] Gilbert, *Nuremberg Diary*, p. 60.

[49] *Ibid.*, p. 125.

[50] Andrus, *Nuremberg Jailer*, pp. 185–186.

[51] Gerecke, "Assignment With Tribunal," p. 5.

[52] Andrus, *Nuremberg Jailer*, p. 189.

[53] *Ibid.*, pp. 188–189.

[54] *Ibid.*, p. 182.

[55] Gerecke, "Assignment With Tribunal," p. 20.

[56] Charles Bewley, *Hermann Göring and the Third Reich* (Toronto: Devin-Adair Co., 1962), pp. 503–504.

[57] Gerecke, "Assignment With Tribunal," p. 20.

[58] Andrus, *Nuremberg Jailer*, pp. 194–195.

[59] Gerecke, "Assignment With Tribunal," p. 25.

[60] Cecil, *Myth of the Master Race*, p. 230.

[61] Edward L. R. Elson to Rodger R. Venzke, 1 May 1974, USACHCS.

[62] Albert C. Wildman, Historical Questionnaire, 22 October 1973, and attached Headquarters, 8th Infrantry Division to Commanding General, Second British Army, Subj: "Concentration Camp at Wobbelin, Germany," 13 May 1945, USACHCS.

[63] *New York Times*, 12 November 1948, p. 1; *Encyclopedia Britannica*, 1972 ed., s.v. "War Crimes."

[64] Shinsho Hanayama, *The Way of Deliverance: Three Years With the Condemned Japanese War Criminals*, trans. Harrison Collins (New York: Charles Scribner's Sons, 1950), p. XIII.

[65] *Ibid.*, pp. XIV–XV.

[66] *Ibid.*, p. 110.

[67] *Ibid.*, pp. 197–224; *New York Times*, 10 September 1947, p. 13; 24 December 1948, p. 2.

[68] Ronald Wiley and Robert McNeil, "A History of the Baptist General Conference Chaplaincy Program" (Bethel Theological Seminary, St. Paul, MN, 1968), p. 57.

[69] Edwin J. Duffy to Luther D. Miller, 12 August 1946; Harold O. Prudell to Edwin J. Duffy, 13 September 1946; James C. Bean to Harold O. Prudell, 9 October 1946, RG 247, file 000.3 RM, NA.

[70] Oscar W. Schoech to Rodger R. Venzke, 30 April 1973, USACHCS.

[71] Wallace M. Hale, "U.S. Chaplains Revive Religion Among German PW's," *Army and Navy Chaplain*, January–February 1946, pp. 10–11.

[72] "More From Behind the Barbed Wire," *Ibid.*, July–August 1946, pp. 27–28; Philip J. Schroeder to Rodger R. Venzke, 17 April 1973, USACHCS.

[73] William V. O'Connor, Recorded Interview, 29 October 1973, USACHCS.

[74] *Circular Letter*, No. 299, 1 August 1945, p. 4.

[75] Vincent J. Murphy to Charles I. Carpenter, 21 December 1945, and accompanying report "Construction of the First Chapel in Germany," RG 247, file 000.76, NA.

[76] Louis Barish, ed., *Rabbis in Uniform: The Story of the American Jewish Military Chaplain* (New York: Jonathan David Publishers, 1962), pp. 242–245.

[77] *Army and Navy Journal*, 15 September 1945, p. 88; Herman Dicker, "The U.S. Army and Jewish Displaced Persons," *The Chicago Jewish Forum* 19, no. 4 (Summer 1961): pp. 290–298.

[78] Ralph H. Blumenthal, "Jewish Chaplains as Liaison Officers for G–5 with Jewish D.P. Camps," *The Contribution of Chaplains to the Occupation European Command* (Paul J. Maddox, ed., Chief of Chaplains European Command, 1 March 1948), p. 43, USACHCS.

[79] *Ibid.*, p. 45.

[80] *New York Times*, 23 May 1945, p. 5.

[81] Oliver J. Frederikson, *The American Military Occupation of Germany 1945–1953* (Headquarters, U.S. Army, Europe: Historical Division, 1953), p. 130, U.S. Army Military History Research Collection, Carlisle Barracks, PA.

[82] Frances Coleman to Robert Patterson, 19 February 1946, and attached article; Roy J. Honeywell to Frances Coleman, 7 March 1946, RG 247, file 211, NA.

[83] *Circular Letter*, No. 309, 1 June 1946, p. 2.

[84] John B. Youngs, "The Community or Post Chaplain," *Contribution of Chaplains to Occupation*, p. 12.

[85] Delvin E. Ressel, "Liaison Between the Protestant Chaplains and the German Churches," *Ibid.*, p. 38.

[86] Roman J. Nuwer and Mert M. Lampson, "United States Forces Austria," *Ibid.*, p. 50.

[87] *Circular Letter*, No. 306, 1 March 1946, p. 2.

[88] Theodore Pfeiffer, "The Chaplains in American Graves Registration Command, European Area," *Contribution of Chaplains to Occupation*, p. 24.

[89] *The Chaplain*, March 1946, p. 47.

[90] Leslie V. Barnes, "Relationship of the Catholic Army Chaplain to the Local Germany Clergy," *Contribution of Chaplains to Occupation*, p. 41.

[91] *Circular Letter*, No. 300, 1 September 1945, p. 4.

[92] *Ibid.*, No. 304, 1 January 1946, p. 2.

[93] *The Chaplain*, May 1946, p. 44.

[94] James W. Sosebee, "Experiences of a Unit Constabulary Chaplain," *Contribution of Chaplains to Occupation*, p. 34; *The Chaplain*, March 1949, pp. 7–16.

[95] Wiley and McNeil, "History of Baptist G.C. Chaplaincy," p. 54.

[96] *Army and Navy Journal*, 4 January 1947, pp. 421 & 423.

[97] *Army and Navy Chaplain*, July–August 1947, p. 15.

[98] Glenn W. Morrow to Army Chief of Chaplains, 8 August 1948, RG 247, file 000.3, NA.

[99] James B. Murphy to Glenn W. Morrow, 30 August 1948, *Ibid.*

[100] Frederikson, *Military Occupation of Germany*, p. 110; Vincent E. Nelson, "The Post Staging Area Chaplain," *Contribution of Chaplains to Occupation*, p. 5.

[101] Charles P. Carlson, "The Chaplain in a Replacement Depot," *Contribution of Chaplains to Occupation*, p. 22..

[102] Frederikson, *Military Occupation of Germany*, p. 110.

[103] John B. Youngs, "The Community or Post Chaplain," *Contribution of Chaplains to Occupation*, pp. 11–12.

[104] Frederickson, *Military Occupation of Germany*, pp. 110, 123–124, 166.

[105] *Military Chaplain*, January 1954, p. 30.

[106] *The Chaplain*, January 1949, pp. 7–9.

[107] *Army and Navy Journal*, 18 June 1949, p. 1197.

[108] *Army and Navy Chaplain*, April–May 1948, p. 8.

[109] Wiley and McNeil, "History of Baptist G.C. Chaplaincy," p. 54.

[110] Thomas L. Doyle, "The Experiences of a Hospital Chaplain in the European Command," *Contribution of Chaplains to Occupation*, p. 20.

[111] *The Chaplain*, July 1946, p. 45.

[112] Minutes of Army and Navy Chaplains' Meeting, Tokyo, 27 November 1945, USACHCS.

[113] *Ibid.*, 8 January 1946.

[114] *Circular Letter*, No. 304, 1 January 1946, p. 2.

[115] Douglas MacArthur to Alfred A. Kunz, 8 December 1949, RG 247, file 461, NA.

[116] Tom Watson, Jr., *T. J. Bach, A Voice for Missions* (Chicago: Moody Press, 1965), p. 168.

[117] *Ibid.*, p. 167.

[118] *Army and Navy Journal*, 7 December 1946, p. 337.

[119] Minutes Chaplains' Meeting, Tokyo, 8 January 1946, USACHCS.

[120] Tokyo-Yokohama Chapter of Army and Navy Chaplains' Association to Supreme Commander for Allied Powers, Subj: "Repression of Prostitution," 11 January 1946, *Ibid.*

[121] General Headquarters, U.S. Forces, Pacific, to Secretary, Tokyo-Yokohama Chapter Army Navy Chaplains' Association, 18 February 1946, *Ibid.*

[122] Douglas MacArthur to All Army Chaplains On Duty In Japan, 31 March 1946, *Ibid.*

[123] Memorandum, Thomas F. Reilly, Eighth Army Office of the Chaplain to Chief of Staff Eighth Army, n.d., *Ibid.*

[124] *Circular Letter*, No. 308, 1 May 1946, p. 3.

[125] *New York Times*, 18 November 1946, p. 5.

[126] William J. Reiss, Recorded Interview, 27 October 1973, USACHCS.

[127] *Circular Letter*, No. 309, 1 June 1946, p. 2.

[128] *Ibid.*, No. 310, 1 July 1946, p. 3.

[129] Minutes Chaplains' Meeting, Toyko, 27 November 1945, USACHCS.

[130] *Circular Letter*, No. 309, 1 June 1946, p. 3.

[131] Reiss. Recorded Interview.

[132] Francis L. Sampson, *Look Out Below* (Washington, D.C.: The Catholic University Press, 1958), p. 180.

[133] Garland E. Hopkins to Luther D. Miller, 6 August 1948; Luther D. Miller to Garland E. Hopkins and Roy H. Parker, 20 August 1948; Roy H. Parker to Luther D. Miller and William C. Shure and Garland E. Hopkins, 6 September 1948; Garland E. Hopkins to Luther D. Miller, 24 September 1948, RG 247, file 000.3 RM, NA.

[134] *Military Chaplain*, July 1950, p. 25.

[135] *The Chaplain*, January–February 1950, p. 47.

[136] *Ibid.*, March–April 1950, p. 46.

[137] See *Army and Navy Journal*, 9 November 1946, p. 245.

[138] Roy H. Parker to Secretary of the Army, 27 August 1951, RG 247, file 319.1, NA.

[139] Duncan N. Naylor, Historical Questionnaire, 26 October 1973, USACHCS.

[140] *The Chaplain*, January–February 1952, p. 48.

[141] See *The Chaplain*, January 1946, p. 45; Minutes Chaplains' Meeting, Tokyo, 8 January 1946, USACHCS.

[142] Messages, The Adjutant General (TAG) to Commander in Chief Army Forces Pacific (CINCAFPAC), 16 April 1946; CINCAFPAC to TAG, 5 July 1946; CINCAFPAC to TAG, 14 September 1946; Office Memorandum Col. Atkinson to Col. Ryan, 16 September 1946; War Department Procurement Branch (Col. Atkinson) to CINCAFPAC, 18 September 1946; Memorandum, Roy H. Parker to Col. Atkinson, 13 November 1946, RG 247, file 210.1, NA.

[143] *Circular Letter*, No. 309, 7 June 1946, p. 3.

[144] *Ibid.*, No. 299, 1 August 1945, p. 2.

[145] *The Chaplain*, December 1948, p. 13.

[146] See *Army and Navy Journal*, 25 June 1949, p. 1250; 2 July 1949, p. 1278.

CHAPTER II

Shifting From Guard to the Backfield

REACTING TO THE MOODS OF THE TIMES

"Communism is one of the most acute issues of our day," began a January 1950 article in a chaplain-oriented periodical. "It claims to be the one way of salvation for human society but stands opposed to Christianity at essential points. . . . Christians are called upon not only to set forth the principles of Christ but also to apply them to the whole social life of man." [1] To fully understand some of the developments in the Army Chaplaincy between World War II and the conflict in Korea, one must attempt to recapture some of that ideological mood which permeated America for nearly 2 decades.

On the one hand, Americans desperately wanted to be done with war. They looked with favor on the rapid dismantling of the gigantic military machine. In the 2 years following V–J Day, the U.S. Army dropped in strength by nearly seven million men. By the beginning of 1950 it numbered just 630,000. It continued to drop until only 591,500 remained on the eve of the Korean War. [2]

On the other hand, fear and mistrust of the Soviet Union and Communism in general kindled a strong animosity in the United States which grew hotter each year. The hostility was fed by Communist advances in 1947 and 1948. American military supplies and advisors were sent to aid Greece in its fight against Communist guerrillas. The 1948 Communist coup in Czechoslovakia gave further credence to the reality of a "Red Threat." The most shocking challenge came, however, with the Soviet blockade of isolated Berlin. The United States and Britain responded with a massive air lift and the Allied Powers formed the North Atlantic Treaty Organization in an attempt to discourage the Russian advance. Meanwhile, a Communist take-over in China drove America's wartime friends, Chiang Kai-shek and his followers, to Taiwan (Formosa).

See footnotes at end of chapter.

What came to be known as the "Cold War" grew hotter with the September 1949 announcement that the Russians had exploded their first atomic bomb. President Truman, in laying the cornerstone for the new United Nations building in New York, called on the organization to help control atomic weapons. At the same time, however, the U.S. stepped up its own work on a greater weapon—the hydrogen bomb. Many believed a confrontation was imminent and that it might, in fact, spell the end of human civilization.

Added to this fear was a suspicion of others that grew from the clandestine activities of the Communist Party throughout the world. As a result, patriotism in the United States was no longer simply pro-American. It had become vehemently anti-Communist.

With all their diversity, U.S. citizens held a common respect for religion and stood appalled at the boldness of Communist atheism. The mood of America was reinforced by the 1947 "Freedom Train." Threading its way from Philadelphia through all 48 states in a 1-year, 33,000 mile journey, the train's seven red-white-and-blue cars carried 113 original documents from American history. Thousands of citizens had their first opportunity to see the precious foundatons of American democracy and were encouraged to recognize, among other things, "the close relationship between our religious beliefs and our democratic ideals." [3]

Where was the United States Army Chaplaincy to fit in that kind of national climate? Roy J. Honeywell, in his book *Chaplains of the United States Army,* made an interesting comment on the role of chaplains during the American Revolution:

> It has been said that the chaplains were governed by two objectives—to save souls and to defend American liberties. There are many indications that the latter was not considered wholly subordinate in value.[4]

The disputed primacy of those same values was again debated by chaplains following World War II. One chaplain, for example, wrote in October 1945:

> . . . Chaplains are not in the Army because government is primarily interested in the saving of men's souls. The chaplain shares the mission of all other arms of the service to strengthen the will to victory. . . . Religion can and does make souls strong for battle. . . .[5]

Another chaplain reacted strongly against that sentiment and declared that "chaplains are not in uniform to preach and teach religious and

---

See footnotes at end of chapter.

moral values to insure military triumph. I am primarily interested," he insisted, "in the saving of men's souls." [6]

If there was an alignment with either of those opinions, the attitude that the chaplaincy must play a major role in defending American liberties seemed to carry more weight. In 1946, Francis Cardinal Spellman called chaplains: "Soldiers in the midst of war on the homefront." He told them that all their achievements during World War II would "fade and die unless you continue to preserve and protect America against aggression of enemies within her borders." [7] At the 1948 convention of the Chaplains Association of the Army and Navy, men like John Foster Dulles and James Forrestal voiced similar opinions.[8] At the same convention, "chaplains of every faith" were given "an opportunity to ask for devine guidance for the unfortunate, misled people of Russia." [9]

In early 1950, President Truman appointed a representative civilian committee to study and promote religion and welfare in the U.S. Armed Forces. At the conclusion of their work, just before the invasion in Korea, a committee staff member declared:

> Of the ministerial group, no part of it has a more significant role to play in the struggle for a decent and more tolerable world than those who minister to the moral and spiritual needs of the members of the armed forces and their dependents.[10]

Any criticism today against the chaplaincy and its programs of those years, should be tempered with an understanding of that mood. It was amid that kind of developing milieu that its leadership sought new directions.

SEEKING AN INFLUENTIAL ROLE

The nomination of Luther D. Miller, Episcopalian, to the rank of brigadier general and Army Chief of Chaplains was confirmed by the U.S. Senate on 11 April 1945. His predecessor, Chaplain (Major General) William R. Arnold, Roman Catholic, who had led the Army's chaplains for the previous 8 years—longer than any man to hold the office of Chief of Chaplains—was designated to serve briefly as an Assistant Inspector General in the Office of the Inspector General of the Army. Together with his former Deputy Chief, Chaplain George F. Rixey, Methodist, Arnold assumed the new, temporary task of serving as an inspector of affairs dealing with the Chaplain Corps and religious mat-

See footnotes at end of chapter.

ters.[11] Arnold and Rixey had supervised the largest number of Army chaplains ever to serve on active duty and had emphasized, obviously, their pastoral ministry to soldiers on the battlefield. It was a ministry that sought divine protection and comfort for those who faced the horror of war.

Miller, who was promoted to major general 8 months after his appointment as Chief, set a different focus for Army chaplains following the War. In an article for a military periodical in 1947, he described post-War chaplains as influential military instructors in Bible-based morality. He believed that moral training was a prerequisite for a continuing democracy and saw future chaplains as educators who would help build a stronger citizenry. "Consequently," he concluded, "the Army chaplain is no longer playing guard; he is in the backfield." [12] The most immediate and practical element of Chaplain Miller's philosophy appeared in another article of the same issue:

> The new weekly Army publication, known as *The Chaplain's Hour* made its debut on 12 Sept. [1947] . . . the eight page first issue of the Chaplain's Hour contains material for a lecture on citizenship and morality. Such lectures are to be given throughout the Army by chaplains as a regular feature wherever troops are stationed.[13]

SUPPORTING UNIVERSAL MILITARY TRAINING

"The Chaplain's Hour," later called "Character Guidance," had evolved in conjunction with another concept known as "Universal Military Training" (UMT). UMT was a long-discussed, theoretical plan to provide military training for all of the nation's youth and thus produce a citizen army ready to fight whenever called. As envisioned by President Truman, however, the military phase was merely incidental. He seemed concerned mainly with an overall improvement of America's young men. The President wanted the program in order "to develop skills that could be used in civilian life, to raise the physical standards of the nation's manpower, to lower the illiteracy rate, to develop citizenship responsibilities, and to foster the moral and spiritual welfare of our young people." [14]

Chaplain Miller had appeared before the Post-War Military Policy Committee of the House of Representatives in mid-1945 to endorse the UMT proposal. Apparently receptive to the President's concept, he declared himself "thoroughly convinced" that "the proposed program of universal military training could serve to support and extend the efforts

---

See footnotes at end of chapter.

of the home, the church, and the community to enrich the character of our youth." [15]

In reality, UMT never got beyond planning and testing stages despite the high-level interest. The hesitation to rebuild a large Army following the War, despite the Communist threat, made it difficult to gain popular support. When the Korean War suddenly required a larger Army, the necessary rapidity of the buildup negated the establishment of such a new concept. It was not until 1951 that Congress finally passed the Universal Military Training and Selective Service Act. Even then, the bill simply endorsed the plan in principle and never implemented it. [16]

Early in 1946, however, when high-level politicians supported the theory, the War Department made plans for an experimental UMT unit to be activated at Fort Knox, Kentucky. The initial proposal envisioned a group of roughly 800 men, all under the age of 19, to train for 1 year. Brigadier General John M. Devine was selected as the unit's commander. [17] When the plans for the unit were sent to the OCCH for comment, Chaplain Harold O. Prudell, Roman Catholic, in the Plans and Programs Division, made several suggestions. Among them was the presentation of specially prepared lectures by chaplains on topics related to citizenship and morality. [18] Perhaps because of the fact that chaplains had been making similar presentations to soldiers for years, the suggestion was adopted. [19] Various elements for the experimental unit were passed out for detail work and this new portion of the project was given to the Army Chaplain School. Eventually, in October 1946, the "buck" stopped with Chaplain Martin H. Scharlemann, Missouri Synod Lutheran, an instructor at the School. Along with his normal duties at the Chaplain School, he was assigned the additional task of preparing what was called simply, "Citizenship and Morality Talks." [20]

Amazingly, within a matter of weeks Scharlemann prepared an entire outline of a proposed series as well as a few complete sample lectures. His work was staffed back to the OCCH through a relatively new organization called "The U.S. Army Chaplain Board." [21]

INSTRUCTING THE ARMY IN MORALITY

It was during this same period that the growing concern among the high command about the increase of venereal disease in the Army, especially among occupation troops, was extremely prevalent. Apparently determined to offer some practical solution to the problem,

See footnotes at end of chapter.

Chaplain Miller submitted Scharlemann's work to a VD-control committee chairman in the War Department. The Chief's accompanying letter suggested a broader use of the lectures than originally planned. He said he would make the lectures available to all chaplains, who could present them during unit training periods throughout the Army. "It is believed that these lectures, delivered once a week," he wrote, "will be of inestimable value and benefit to all Regular Army personnel and trainees in the development of a moral and spiritual background upon which to develop the deeper aspects of morale." [22]

The suggestion, it appears, received some top level attention. On 24 January 1947, Secretary of War Robert Patterson addressed a five-page, restricted letter to the Chief of Chaplains entitled, "Discipline and Venereal Disease." "Present annual venereal disease incidence rates within the Army are higher than at any time in the past thirty years," it began. Outlining his method of attack, the Secretary described the chaplains' role in the war against social disease by authorizing the new lecture program:

> The Corps of Chaplains bears a special responsibility for the moral and spiritual welfare of troops. To aid the chaplain in meeting this responsibility, commanding officers will allocate appropriate periods in the regular training schedule for instruction in citizenship and morality which all personnel will attend. This instruction will be prepared in the Office of the Chief of Chaplains . . .[23]

Within a month, Chaplain Miller informed his supervisory chaplains throughout the world of this "significant opportunity" which "contemplates a weekly lecture by the chaplain to all personnel." At the same time, obviously aware that the success or failure of the program now rested with individual unit chaplains who had to give the lectures, Miller strongly directed:

> . . . . whenever a chaplain habitually fails to give a reasonably creditable presentation of these lectures, he [is to] be promptly substituted by a chaplain who can do so. Consistent failure to adequately present these lectures should be reason for reclassification.[24]

For the next 5 years, Chaplain Scharlemann was busy producing discourses on citizenship and morality. He wrote 88 lectures; 60 of them were eventually published in six volumes under the general title, "Duty–Honor–Country." [25]

LECTURING FROM FORT KNOX TO THE MARIANAS

The UMT experimental unit came into being at Fort Knox in January 1947. The first group, made up of 664 volunteers, was organized into a four-company battalion and given 6 months of training. Three chaplains joined the unit's staff: Morris E. Eson, Jewish, Charles J. Murphy, Roman Catholic, and Maury Hundley, Jr., Disciples of Christ. At the beginning of the trainees' fifth week, immediately following a series of lectures on "Military Sanitation," the chaplains began delivering Scharlemann's talks on "The Moral and Religious Aspects of Citizenship." The series included such topics as "Purity in Thought, Word and Deed," "Marriage as a Sacred Institution," "The Ten Commandments," and "Grounds for Moral Conduct." [26] Before the series went into publication, Scharlemann's manuscripts were sent directly from his typewriter to the UMT chaplains on the platform.[27]

The extremely heavy emphasis on moral and religious training for the Knox volunteers was quite evident. Although chapel attendance was never mandatory, it was encouraged so strongly that only one of the 664 chose not to attend. Following a practice that became policy for the unit, "an hour's study in general ethics was arranged for his benefit." [28] The whole tenor of the chaplains' deep influence is reflected in the remarks of Chaplain Murphy as printed in the post's newspaper on 8 March 1947:

> In UMT you are more than a body to be bayonetted or bulleted. You are more than organized flesh to be set in the wake of some rolling barrage. You are more than an animated sandbag. You are first, last and always a religious animal; and UMT will not let you forget it.[29]

Along with other members of the staff, the chaplains were further involved as publicity agents for the experiment. They escorted high-ranking clergymen, who were regularly invited to inspect the program, and spoke extensively at public gatherings in support of the plan.[30]

Even though UMT was never implemented on a national scale, the chaplains' heavy involvement as its salesmen during those early days of experimentation became food for later critics of the chaplaincy. Looking at the Fort Knox Experiment 2 decades later, one author maintained that it provided evidence for the conjecture that chaplains were little more than publicity agents for a military establishment.[31]

See footnotes at end of chapter.

Although Universal Military Training did not survive, the chaplain's new task as an instructor in morality throughout the Army was firmly planted. Chaplains Murphy and Hundley had given Scharlemann's first six lectures to the UMT volunteers in 25-minute periods—one period per week for 6 weeks. As others were written, the training was increased to 50 minutes and the cadre were included in the audience. A short time later, the Third Armored Division, also at Fort Knox, began to include the lectures in their training.[32] By April 1947, copies of the citizenship and morality talks had been distributed to all chaplains on active duty.[33]

With the advent of 1948, the offices of the Chief of Chaplains and the Army Surgeon General cooperated in producing and releasing a 40-minute motion picture entitled, "Miracle of Living." More than 1,400 civilian educators and clergymen in the Washington, D.C. area were invited to view the new training film which emphasized the moral aspects in the fight against venereal disease.[34] By the end of the year, a Department of the Army Memorandum directed the establishment of Character Guidance Councils at all commands, to include units of battalion size or larger. The councils were "to aid commanders of all echelons in implementing the character guidance programs." [35] They were not only to help enhance the quality of instruction but also to suggest ways to apply the material, in practical terms, to the daily life of the soldier.

In some instances, despite the talented work put into the program, occasional publicity efforts seemed to border on naivete. The following item, for example, was printed in a December 1948 Circular Letter from the OCCH; from the perspective of several decades, it's hard to believe that the item was taken as seriously as intended.

CONVERSATION IN OFFICE
CHIEF OF CHAPLAINS

"Good morning, Chaplain," said the infantry colonel, "What are my chances of getting a set of the 'Chaplain's Hour'? I heard some of them in Europe and thought they were mighty fine."

"It's good to hear your high opinion of the 'Chaplain's Hour,' Colonel. They represent a tremendous amount of hard work, in fact, the job is still under way at the Chaplain School in Carlisle. What do you want the lectures for,—your files?"

"Yes. I wish to familiarize myself with them. Incidentally, I plan to use some of the material on my kids. You know, Chaplain, there's some mighty good stuff in those lectures."

See footnotes at end of chapter.

"How were the talks received overseas? Did the men like them? Did the chaplains get them across?"

"The men were really interested. And the chaplains did a good job, too, that is, all but one chaplain. He had the reputation of being a 'ball of fire,' but he would show up fifteen minutes late and wind up ten minutes ahead of time. He seemed to have the idea that he gained popularity by making the lectures as short as possible. The other chaplains, however, took them seriously and did a swell job. . . ." [36]

In the spring of 1949, the Chaplain Section of the Marianas—Bonins Command in the Pacific proudly announced that it was the first to complete 52 continuous weeks of Citizenship and Morality lectures with a total attendance of over 190,000.[37] Such attendance reports were to become the norm for chaplains for many years to come.

REFINING THE INFLUENTIAL ROLE

The Chaplain's Hour might appear at first glance to have been a program simply designed to give the chaplain a role in UMT or a voice against the immoral aspects of venereal disease. A closer study, however, reveals its strong anti-Communism flavor in keeping with the mood of that day. Early lectures included such topics as "The Meaning of Citizenship," "The Citizen and His Religion," and "The Citizen and His Worship." In Lecture No. 22, "My Right to the Truth," the following paragraph appears under "Poisoning the Minds of Men":

> At the present time the philosophy of Communism is "on the loose" in the world, poisoning men's souls against their own governments and against the truth. According to Communism everything must start with the belief that all other systems of economy are wrong, that the salvation of the world can be effected only by extending the "partnership of workers" to the ends of the earth. Communism is a system of thought with a vicious purpose which denies my right to the truth by insisting that it alone is truth.[38]

"The Character Guidance Program has deservedly occupied much of the chaplains' time," said a 1949 annual report from the Chief of Chaplains to the Secretary of the Army. The report declared that the program was fulfilling the purpose for which it was designed—"to develop the individual's sense of responsibility and to counteract alien philosophies."[39]

Chaplain Miller's original concept of teaching morality, as based in the Bible, was particularly strong in the early days and throughout the

See footnotes at end of chapter.

1950's when Moody Bible Institute films often supplemented the lectures.[40] When the task of preparing the material was eventually passed to the Army Chaplain Board, myriads of new techniques, including the proposal for the publication of a comic book, were tested and in some cases sent to the field for actual use.[41] Impossible as it must have been to evaluate the results of those early efforts, chaplains at higher levels of command made various claims, including taking the credit for a "drastic reduction in the Army prison population and the incidence of courts martial." [42]

During the next 25 years the program took on as many changes as it did various titles. It was known successively as "The Chaplain's Hour," "Character Guidance Instruction," "Our Moral Heritage Series," and "Human Self Development." It progressed from stilted lectures against promiscuity and Communism to open group discussions on such topics as drug abuse and race relations. By the 1970's the program had evolved all the way from its original classroom-lecture atmosphere to an incentive-producing plan for the involvement of soldiers in community action.

The most significant challenge to the Character Guidance Program came in 1968 with a complaint from the Washington, D.C., Office of the American Civil Liberties Union. Maintaining that certain religious elements in the mandatory instruction violated the rights guaranteed soldiers under the First Amendment, the complaint precipitated considerable study, correspondence, and policy statements.[43] The dispute resulted in an interesting, official emphasis on the delineation of chaplain duties. On 24 April 1969, the OCCH disseminated technical guidelines which noted, in part:

> . . . acceptable instruction within the Character Guidance Program depends on the instructor's good judgment and the attitude he brings to his role. Since some chaplains have on occasion not clearly distinguished their staff officer/instructor role in the Character Guidance Program from their role as clergymen in the Army's religious programs, it is important to reiterate the necessity for chaplains to avoid 'preaching' in Character Guidance instruction and to avoid any presentation that gives the appearance of a religious indoctrination session. . . . [44]

With the vast change in national attitudes since 1947, there came in 1971 a discontinuance of the program's mandatory instruction for all units except those in Basic and Advanced Individual Training.[45] The most modern Army-wide emphasis is "to confront individual and local social needs" with "actions to enrich the social environment." [46] Perhaps as such it is fulfilling even more the original intention of Chaplain Miller—taking the chaplain out of the guard position and placing him in the influential backfield.

DISPOSING OF WAR SURPLUS

In the history of most organizations, the struggle to establish new and influential programs is often accompanied by the daily drudgery of more mundane tasks. While the chaplaincy was concerned about its role in moral and ideological instruction following World War II, for example, it was also forced, along with other branches, into the gigantic post-War activity of property disposal.

A War Department press release in April 1946 announced that agents of the War Assets Administration had been instructed to advertise and sell surplus chapels. The action came as a result of numerous letters to the OCCH regarding the possibility of making such purchases. [47]

There were 1,532 Army chapels in use in the United States at the close of the War. The vast majority of them, resembling wood-frame New England churches, seated roughly 350 people. [48] By October 1949, nearly half of those chapels had been sold to local civilian congregations. Surprisingly, they netted less than $930,000 for the War Assets Administration—an average of roughly $1,400 per chapel. [49] Within a year, because of the Korean War and the renewed expansion of the Army, nearly 180 chapels, previously boarded-up on inactivated installations, were reconditioned, refurnished and opened once more to military congregations. [50]

At the beginning of 1948, the Chief of Chaplains also announced that over one million Army-issue portions of the Scriptures had been distributed, free of charge, to religious, educational and civic institutions. [51] That disposal, however, had not been without controversy. An April 1946 article in *The Christian Advocate* had claimed that the Army had so many surplus Bibles on hand that it was burning them. The article started a flood of protests and inquiries to the OCCH—many of which came via offices of U.S. senators. An investigation located the source of the rumor with a chaplain's assistant who had been serving at the Indiantown Gap Military Reservation in Pennsylvania during the process of inactivation. The assistant said that he had asked his chaplain what

See footnotes at end of chapter.

was to be done with the large surplus of Bibles and Testaments on the post. "I think," stated the assistant, "that his reply was, 'I guess we will have to burn them.' I suggested that I could dispose of them in civilian churches. He accepted my proposal and gave me permission to take all I wanted." The Chief of Chaplains was happy to announce that, as far as he was able to determine, no Bibles had been burned during the disposal process; *The Christian Advocate* published a correction of their original article 3 months later.[52]

At the same time in which the large reduction in America's military strength necessitated concentration on the dismantling process, new directions in organization and administration were changing the configuration of the Army Chaplaincy.

ESTABLISHING THE AIR FORCE CHAPLAINCY

The National Security Act of 1947 provided for a "National Military Establishment" with three military services, the Army, the Navy, and the Air Force, under the general supervision of a new Secretary of Defense—James Forrestal, former Secretary of the Navy. To eliminate some of the confusion in the lines of authority, an amendment to the act was passed in 1949 converting the National Military Establishment into an executive department renamed the "Department of Defense." The separate services were reduced from executive departments to military departments within the Department of Defense and a chairman's position, without vote, was added to the formerly established Joint Chiefs of Staff.[53]

The significance of the new organization to the Army Chaplaincy was in the transformation of the former Army Air Corps or Army Air Forces (AAF) into a separate, new military service—the United States Air Force. The change became effective on 26 September 1947 with "Transfer Order No. 1," the first official order of Secretary of Defense Forrestal.[54]

When the Army was organized in 1942 into Service Forces, Ground Forces and Air Forces, a chaplain had been assigned as a liaison officer in the OCCH with the title of "Air Chaplain." Chaplain Charles I. Carpenter, Methodist, served as Air Chaplain through most of the War and was succeeded briefly in 1945 by Chaplain Gynther Storaasli, American Lutheran. Carpenter returned to the job at the end of that

---

See footnotes at end of chapter.

year when Storaasli was appointed Commandant of the Chaplain School.[55]

Chaplains who had served in the AAF hoped to be organized into a separate Air Force Chaplaincy. Since, however, the original "Army-Air Force Agreements" discouraged parallel branches in the two services, Chief of Chaplains Luther Miller opposed the idea. But Carpenter and others pursued the goal, emphasizing the need for identity with the personnel they were to serve. When a concession was made by assigning additional, separate duties to the Air Chaplain, the Air Force suggested that the job at least be accorded the rank of brigadier general. But the Army disapproved that recommendation also.

Finally, in mid-1948, General Carl Spaatz, U.S. Air Force Chief of Staff, asked Chaplain Carpenter to give him a briefing on his recommendation for a separate chaplain service. The immensity of the study had to be summarized on one sheet of paper—a common requirement of General Spaatz in regard to any briefing. Chaplain Daniel B. Jorgensen, author of *Air Force Chaplains 1947-1960,* described what happened:

> General Spaatz cordially greeted his Air Chaplain, and he listened attentively to the summary. There was an awkward moment of silence. Then the General said, "Chaplain, it's already been decided. My mind is made up. There will be no separate chaplaincy for the Air Force. In fact, I have a conference at 11 o'clock with Chaplain Miller, of the Army, to work out the details."
>
> Carpenter left with a burning sense of defeat. To Col. Charles Maylon he said, "It looks like we lost this one."
>
> But, at 1:15 that afternoon, he received another call from the office of General Spaatz, "The general wants to see you, and bring that paper with you." He picked up the summary and hurried back.
>
> General Spaatz took the sheet of paper, folded it so that Carpenter's signature would not show, and placed it under the glass on his desk top. "I'll need that," he explained. "Another conference at three with Chaplain Miller. I've changed my mind. The Air Force will have its own chaplains." [56]

Precisely what happened to change the general's mind is only a matter of speculation today. The irony is that the historic decision to have an Air Force Chaplaincy apparently was influenced more by the plan's main opponent than by its principal advocate.

Chaplain Carpenter was designated the first Chief of Air Force Chaplains on 11 June 1948, nearly a year before the branch came into existence. The actual "Transfer Order No. 35," allowing Army chaplains

---

See footnotes at end of chapter.

to enter the new Air Force Chaplaincy, was issued by Secretary of Defense Louis Johnson on 10 May 1949, and stipulated that all transfers had to be completed by 26 July. By that date, 458 chaplains on active duty and 573 Reserve chaplains on inactive status had transferred from the Army and officially formed the United States Air Force Chaplaincy. The following day Chaplain Carpenter was promoted to the rank of major general.[57]

MINISTERING TO THE VETERAN

Another chaplain service came into existence only a few years prior to that of the Air Force. On 15 June 1945, the Reverend Crawford W. Brown, Episcopalian, a former Army chaplain, was appointed the first Director of the Chaplaincy Service of the Veterans Administration. Somewhat like his counterpart in the Air Force, Brown was initially made the head of a service that didn't officially exist. A letter from the Administrator of the Veterans Administration announced the establishment of the service 2 months later. Six months passed, however, before another letter authorized the appointment of VA chaplains. By 1947 Brown had guided the growth of the new service from 11 to 226 full-time chaplains, assisted by 115 part-time chaplains.[58]

Although there has never been any official connection between the U.S. VA Chaplaincy Service and that of the Armed Forces, a close liaison has been maintained throughout the years. General Omar Bradley, who was Veterans Administrator at the time, asserted in an October 1946 speech:

> The question of getting the veteran back into the church and congregation is one of the most important facing the country today. Religion is the basis upon which we place everything else, and unless we have a solid foundation upon which to work we may go astray as a nation.[59]

The reasoning of many Army chaplains at the end of the War was very similar. One chaplain, who was serving in a convalescent hospital, devised a small card which he sent to the hometown churches of returning veterans:

> This is to inform you that the undersigned received an honorable discharge from the Army of the United States, as of this date. We would appreciate your cooperation in helping him in his adjustment to civilian life.[60]

The chaplain received hundreds of replies from churches that were grateful for his personal concern.

See footnotes at end of chapter.

REVIEWING THE MINISTRY AT WEST POINT

While new chaplaincy services were in the making, there was a brief effort by the Army to regain one chaplain position it had lost many years before—Cadet Chaplain for the United States Military Academy at West Point. Apparently encouraged by the Chief of Chaplains, a detailed, eleven-page study of the matter was prepared by the Staff Judge Advocate under the direction of the Assistant Chief of Staff, G–1, in February 1945. The study concluded that the office of Cadet Chaplain had been occupied by a military chaplain prior to 1896 primarily because the position also required duties performed as a member of the faculty. When the office was opened to all clergy solely for the job as chaplain, however, it was assumed to be a civilian position.

The study recommended that if there was a desire to detail a Regular Army Chaplain as Cadet Chaplain, steps should be taken to change legislation to clearly allow such a change. Chief of Chaplains Miller approved that suggestion but the plan was never implemented. A later, in-house note in the OCCH indicated that it would take at least 4 years to bring about such legislation, and that the change might wrongfully suggest to the public some disfavor of the incumbent civilian appointee.[61]

Only 9 months before that study, on 4 June 1944, the Post Chapel at West Point, designed to meet the worship needs of Protestant non-cadet personnel, had been dedicated. Chaplain John P. Fellows, Methodist, who had served as the first "Post Chaplain" starting in August 1943, was succeeded in October 1946 by Chaplain Ralph H. Pugh, Northern Baptist. An additional position as "Assistant Post Chaplain" was opened in 1957.[62]

Although the Army's official attempt to regain the influential position of Cadet Chaplain was laid aside, other voices were beginning to be heard regarding West Point. In 1946 military chaplains, line officers, and enlisted men who were members of the denomination influenced the General Assembly of the Presbyterian Church in the USA to recommend that the curriculum at the academy include training on the responsibility of commanders for the moral and spiritual welfare of their men.[63] The overture was based on the charge that a great number of commanding officers had failed to adequately support the work of their chaplains during World War II.[64]

Meanwhile, the fact that the civilian position as Cadet Chaplain had long been dominated by appointees from the Episcopal Church began

See footnotes at end of chapter.

to draw critical comments. By 1954, the United Lutheran Church in America adopted a recommendation calling for Congress to rotate the appointment among other denominations.[65] Four years later, the Military Chaplains Association charged that there was "calculated and unwarranted discrimination against other denominations" in the appointment of Protestant cadet chaplains, and it recommended Congressional legislation to correct the matter.[66] The tide was somewhat reduced by the 1959 appointment of Theodore C. Speers, former pastor of the Central Presbyterian Church in New York City, as Cadet Chaplain. Speers, however, was the fourth Presbyterian to have served in the position.[67] After his death in 1964, he was succeeded by James D. Ford, a minister of the Lutheran Church in America.[68]

ADVISING AND COORDINATING FOR BETTER SERVICE

The United States Army Chaplain Board, referred to in the discussion on Character Guidance, was activated at Fort Oglethorpe, Georgia, in October 1945, at the U.S. Army Chaplain School. Originally such "boards" were authorized, under a 1944 Army regulation, to advise chiefs of branches on subjects normally referred to them and to make recommendations for improvements in the service of the branch. In June 1945, the Army Chaplain Board became a Class II Installation and separated from the school, which moved to Carlisle Barracks, Pennsylvania. When Fort Oglethorpe was closed in January 1947, the Board also moved, and made its new home at Fort George G. Meade in Maryland.[69]

To many of the chaplains who remained in service following the War, the mere mention of a "board" seemed to be a potential threat to their active duty status. Attempting to clarify the duties of the new Army Chaplain Board to the chaplains in the field, the OCCH somewhat wryly announced in 1947: "Contrary to a misunderstanding, which seems to be rather widespread, the Chaplain Board has nothing to do with the integration of chaplains into the Regular Army." [70] The announcement further outlined six sample subject areas normally referred to the Board— such things as testing new items of supply and equipment, determining operating techniques, and providing liaison with other branches.[71] Throughout the years, chaplains assigned to the Board have dealt with a vast diversity of projects ranging all the way from producing training films to making recommendations on the number of bedrooms in military housing. Some of their work, such as the production of the motion picture, "The Bridge" (a brief history of the Army Chaplaincy), has been of such high quality that it merited awards from organizations like the Freedoms Foundation of Valley Forge, Pennsylvania.[72]

Perhaps due in part to the additional formation of chaplain services for the Air Force and the Veterans Administration, in 1949 a Reserve chaplain wrote to General Vaughn, President Truman's military aide. He asked the general's assistance in bringing to the attention of the President a proposal for the appointment of a "Coordinator of Religious Activities in the United States Armed Forces and Federal Agencies." The idea called for one office to supervise and coordinate chaplain services in the Army, Navy, Air Force, Veterans Administration, federal penal institutions, the U.S. military academies, and "others that may be added."

General Vaughn sent the proposal to Chaplain Miller for comment. Miller replied that "all the objectives it aims to accomplish are already satisfied." He further warned that "the establishment of a super-bureau might give the impression of a national regimentation of religious life in all these services." [73]

An agency was formed later that year, however, to at least assist in coordinating the chaplain branches of the three Armed Forces. Just before the retirement of Chaplain Miller from his position as Army Chief of Chaplains, the Secretary of Defense established the Armed Forces Chaplains Board. Composed of the three Chiefs of Chaplains, who were to rotate annually as chairman, and one additional member from each of the services, the board held its first meeting on 11 August 1949. Its primary responsibilities continue to be in the area of unifying policies on manpower, supply, and relationships with civilian churches. Because the Army is the oldest of the three services, the Chief of Chaplains for that service was appointed the first chairman.[74] He was Roy H. Parker, Southern Baptist. The former Far East Command Chaplain had been appointed as Chaplain Miller's successor and promoted to major general on 1 August 1949.[75]

DEVELOPING BETTER TRAINING

In July 1945, roughly 2 months before the end of the War, the United States Army Chaplain School had moved to Fort Oglethorpe, Georgia—its fourth new home since the beginning of the conflict. Even then the move proved to be temporary. Exactly 12 months later it was moved

See footnotes at end of chapter.

again. Carlisle Barracks, Pennsylvania, became the eleventh "new home" for the Army Chaplain School since its establishment in 1918.

During The War, clergy students were rushed through a 1 month basic course that attempted to orient them to the Army before they were shipped to various battlefields throughout the world. When peace returned, the pace at the School slowed and the course was extended to 3 months. The new emphasis was to give the fledgling chaplain "a picture of his peacetime job and its many opportunities." [76]

Among the eight-man faculty—which included the Commandant and his Deputy—was Chaplain Scharlemann, author of the Citizenship and Morality Talks. With his colleagues, Scharlemann helped revamp the curriculum of the school and revitalize its instruction. At the same time he was given the responsibility, along with $10,000, to establish a library for the school. [77]

The first class to graduate from the 3 month course had 55 students and received their diplomas from Chief of Chaplains Miller on 1 May 1946. [78] Three days earlier, the School's Commandant, Chaplain Gynther Storaasli, had delivered his farewell remarks to the class. Storaasli, who had served briefly as Air Chaplain before assuming the job as Commandant, left a deep impression of his spiritual concern on most of those who served with him. The conclusion to his farewell remarks captured some of his philosophy of the chaplaincy:

> In bidding you farewell and Godspeed—I would leave just this one thought with you. In my Opening Address, I called to your remembrance the fact that in view of your high calling, God, and not man, is your real Commanding Officer, regardless of what your military position may be.
>
> I would like to carry that thought a little further and make this parting suggestion: In the performance of all the varied duties you henceforth will be called upon to perform, be not primarily concerned about the efficiency rating your military commander may give you, but the efficiency rating God will give you. Make this thought your chief concern: What in God's opinion is and will be my efficiency index?
>
> With that as your chief worry and concern, you will never need "be dismayed what'ere betide" for "God will take care of you." [79]

The character Storaasli displayed in public before the students and faculty at the Chaplain School was consistent with that in his private life. It was unknown to most of his colleagues, for example, that he refused an award offered to him by the Chief of Chaplains for the accomplishments at the School during the period of transition. Remarks from his letter to Chaplain Miller clearly display the honest approach he took toward his work:

> According to the dictates of my own conscience. . . . I have not done anything as Commandant of the School to warrant an award of any kind. When I make the above statement, I am not governed by any false modesty, nor am I setting up any false front. . . .
>
> Much as I might like, for reasons of personal vanity, to claim credit for what has been accomplished in the School during the time I have served as Commandant, honesty forbids my "reaping where I have not sowed."
>
> We endeavor to impress upon all Student Chaplains the necessity to be ruggedly honest with oneself and in one's relations with the personnel one serves. And I would be preaching one rule of life for others and practicing another were I to succumb to the temptation to accept an award which I have honestly not earned.[80]

In the same letter he recommended nine other men—ranging from a lieutenant colonel to a corporal—as individuals who ought to receive awards such as the one offered to him.

Shortly after the School moved to Carlisle Barracks, a resident course of instruction was opened for Reserve and National Guard chaplains. In 1947 approximately 60 Reservists and an equal number of Guard chaplains graduated from the three sessions held for them during the year.[81] At the same time, non-resident training through extension courses was also initiated for Reserve and National Guard chaplains; the Army Chaplain Board assumed responsibility for preparing the material.[82]

Thirty-seven of the highest-ranking administrative chaplains gathered at the School in November 1947. The meeting, which Storaasli called "the most successful conference of chaplains in my 28 years," provided an opportunity to share methods of operation and study plans for future cooperation between the services.[83] The meeting was undoubtedly instrumental in the makeup of the Advanced Conference Course held at the School in the fall of 1948. The single-subject seminar on counseling was the first course at the Army Chaplain School taught by civilian lecturers and the first attended jointly by Army, Army Air Forces, and Navy chaplains. Most of the Advanced Course instruction at the School was under the direction of Chaplain Robert J. Sherry, Roman Catholic, who served as Deputy Commandant from July 1946 to April 1950.[84]

On the occasion of its 30th anniversary in 1948, the Army Chaplain School was referred to by a national news magazine as "one of the service's

See footnotes at end of chapter.

toughest." Describing the lives of both basic and advanced students, the reporter wrote: "From the time they enter the School's red-brick building and stack their gear in the single cot-filled dorm, they live under strict military discipline." The same article announced the School's plan to soon begin using a relatively new training aid—television.[85]

Chaplain Arthur C. Piepkorn, Missouri Synod Lutheran, succeeded Chaplain Storaasli as Commandant on 1 March 1948. The academic brilliance of Chaplain Piepkorn became obvious to every new student who entered the School. Often they passed on the apocryphal story about one of his four daughters asking Mrs. Peipkorn questions from a homework assignment. When the Commandant's wife suggested that the girl ask her father, the daughter replied, "I don't want to know that much about it!"[86]

Piepkorn was transferred to become the Army Chaplain Board's president in October 1950. Two years later he left active duty to assume a professorship at Concordia Seminary in St. Louis—a position he held until his death in 1973.[87] Among his various writings was a "Statement of the Legality and Constitutionality of the Chaplaincy," delivered originally as an address at a conference at Fort Leonard Wood, Missouri, in 1963. The document became a guideline for others studying in that area.[88]

Even after the establishment of a separate Air Force Chaplaincy, chaplains of that service continued to receive their training at the Army Chaplain School until July 1953. As a matter of fact, recommendations were made in 1950, by both the Armed Forces Chaplains Board and the President's Committee on Religion and Welfare in the Armed Forces, to establish a unified school for chaplains in all three services under Army administration. The recommendation was disapproved, however, by the Under Secretary of the Navy, who maintained that the primary function of a chaplain school should be to familiarize chaplains with their specific branch of service.[89] The Navy, consequently, established its own chaplain school in conjunction with the General Line School at Newport, Rhode Island, in 1951.[90]

Economy and interservice understanding were among the arguments for a unified chaplain school. The fact was, however, that even the Army and Air Force had found it difficult to train together for more than 3 years. A certain amount of friction developed between Army traditions and the approaches of the new Air Force Chaplaincy. Similarly, while the Army insisted that the Air Force carry more of the financial load at the School, the Air Force Chief of Chaplains insisted on more of a voice

See footnotes at end of chapter.

in the School's policies. It was largely because agreements could not be reached in such areas that the Air Force pulled out of the Army Chaplain School. On 1 July 1953 they established a USAF Chaplain Training Program as part of the Officer Basic Military Course at Lackland Air Force Base, Texas.[91] An official United States Air Force Chaplain School was established at Lackland on 1 June 1960 and moved, 6 years later, to Maxwell Air Force Base, Alabama.[92]

PREPARING QUALIFIED ASSISTANTS

The matter of attempting to secure a special corps of enlisted assistants for chaplains had been debated for many years. Although enlisted assistants had been working with chaplains during and after World War II, they were for the most part clerk-typists who had never received any chaplain-oriented, specialized training. It was no secret that individuals assigned to work with chaplains were often soldiers who suffered problems on other jobs. Many commanders seemed to reason that their chaplains would not only tolerate malcontents—they might even be able to reform them. Any qualified individual assigned to a chaplain would often request a transfer because of the lack of promotion opportunities. As a result, chaplains often found themselves without an assistant or spending an inordinate amount of time on in-house counseling.[93]

Manpower cuts following the War complicated the matter further. Authorizations were gained to employ civilians in an attempt to fill chaplain assistant vacancies. In some cases, members of the Women's Army Corps (WAC) were used as assistants, Sunday school teachers, and organists.[94]

A study prepared in the OCCH in September 1949 recommended that assistants be secured and assigned on the basis of one or more of the following:

(1) Completition of a special course of instruction at the Army Chaplain School;

(2) Demonstrated ability from on-the-job-training (OJT) for a period of not less than 90 days;

(3) Civilian training or experience in religion or music and OJT for not less than 60 days.[95]

At the same time, however, a letter from the Deputy Chief of Chaplains to the Executive Secretary of the Military Chaplains Association said that, based on studies to that date, the Chief of

Chaplains was "disinclined to recommend the formation of an Enlisted Corps for Chaplains." Instead, his approach was to train men already qualified in the Personnel and Administration Career Field and to have the letter "C" added to their MOS (Military Occupational Speciality).[96] In this way, an individual soldier could at least be designated as a "Qualified Chaplain's Assistant." [97]

A program of instruction was instituted at the Army Chaplain School in 1950—the first enlisted training program at the School in its 32-year history. Sixty-nine Air Force students, who were to be designated as "Welfare Specialists," were the first graduates. As with subsequent classes for Army personnel, the class contained a small percentage of women students.[98]

The Chaplain School continued its training program for Personnel Specialists to qualify them for chaplains' assistants until 1954. Two years later, the program was reinstated at Fort Dix, New Jersey, and Fort Ord, California. It was not until the early 1960's, however, that a distinct MOS was granted to chaplains' assistants. As a consequence, on 11 September 1967, a more complete and detailed course of instruction was re-opened at the Chaplain School and graduates were awarded the special MOS of 71M20.[99]

EVALUATING THE CHAPLAIN'S SIGNIFICANT ROLE

President Truman's Committee on Religion and Welfare in the Armed Forces was appointed in 1950 to evaluate the military chaplaincy program—but not without some opposition. When the House Appropriations Subcommittee reviewed Defense Department budget requirements, one U.S. Representative questioned the projected need for $100,000 to finance the President's special study group. "I thought the Chaplains' Corps was organized to look after the religious welfare of the Armed Forces," he protested. "Now we have another committee appointed to look after the Chaplains' Corps. I have not seen any records of the Chaplains' Corps to indicate that they were not doing a good job. . . ." [100]

Even though the appointment of the Committee was approved, the objection of the Representative was probably correct. There was very little criticism of the chaplaincy following the War. As a matter of fact, the results of the Committee's study seemed predetermined far before they even went to work. An editorial in a magazine of the General

Commission on Army and Navy Chaplains, printed 9 months before the Committee submitted their report, said: "All of us who know the fine record and significant role of chaplains in the three branches of the service welcome the recognition this study indicates." [101]

The Committee obliged such anticipation and their eventual, 43-page report spoke in glowing terms of the past devotion and future significance of military chaplains. "The importance of the work of the chaplain is today recognized as never before in the history of the Armed Forces," it stated. "Because of the world's unprecedented awareness of the need for spiritual vitality, the importance of the work of the chaplaincy has reached an unparalleled peak." [102]

The sentiment of that report, sprinkled with the philosophy that chaplains were defenders of American democracy, was repeated by successive Army Chiefs of Staff:

> A good chaplain in the Army is worth more than his weight in gold. . . . The world is experiencing as it always has after a great war, an era of doubt, confusion and fear. We can only travel forward with the guidance of eternal truth. It is the job of chaplains and their civilian counterparts to supply that guidance today.[103]
>
> —Dwight D. Eisenhower
>
> The young men in our Army today must look to their chaplain as a true guide and leader on the road to success and accomplishment. For without the essential strengthening of our basic moral creeds we can never hope to achieve our goal.[104]
>
> —Omar Bradley
>
> The Chaplain Corps has always reinforced the spiritual strength of our servicemen and has been one of their greatest sources of confidence in battle and inspiration in peace. In its service to our Army, the Chaplain Corps performs an indispensable role in our Nation's security.[105]
>
> —J. Lawton Collins

During the 1947 Easter Sunrise Service at Walter Reed Army Medical Center, Chief of Chaplains Luther Miller could look from his pulpit far across the crowd of more than 3,000 people gathered in the Rose Garden and see a lone figure on the balcony atop the Administration Building. There, outside the hospital home he had occupied since 1941, was the venerable leader of the Army's past— 86-year-old General of the Army John J. Pershing. One wonders if both these men may have pondered for a moment on what had taken place during the previous 30 years. It was, after all, under Pershing's direction that the Army Chaplaincy had matured—that there even was such an

See footnotes at end of chapter.

office as Chief of Chaplains or an institution called the Army Chaplain School. The aged general, in surveying the chaplains who jointly conducted the service that day, may well have recalled his own words: "Their usefulness in the maintenance of morale, through religious counsel and example, has now become a matter of history. . . ." [106]

Luther Miller retired in 1949 to become Canon Precentor at the Washington Cathedral—his first civilian pulpit since graduating from Chicago Theological Seminary in 1917. During his 31 years in the Army Chaplaincy he had become the personal friend of many officers who, in later years, rose to become the Army's leaders. Even after his complete retirement in 1961, he was a regular visitor at Walter Reed, where he continued his ministry among those with whom he had served. Outliving many of his contemporaries, he not only participated in the funeral service of General Pershing, but also at the internment of such notables as Robert P. Patterson, Charles Summerall, Donald Quarles, and George C. Marshall.[107] At his own death, on 27 April 1972, one reporter said he was best remembered for the moving benediction he delivered at the funeral of Dwight D. Eisenhower: "His battles are all fought and his victories are all won. He lies down to rest a while, awaiting the bugler's call." [108]

A year before his death, Miller's friends cooperated in having a keystone carved in the ceiling of the vesting room of the Washington Cathedral's War Memorial Chapel. Honoring Chaplain Miller, it holds a Bible, chaplain's emblem, a star (representing his rank), his personal flag, and a cross.[109] More lasting still, perhaps, was the tenor he had set for Army chaplains following the great War. His emphasis on their positions as influential instructors of morality and builders of a stronger citizenry was based on his sincere conviction "that as Christ went before His disciples into Galilee, so He is leading us on in the creation of a better world of Christian brotherhood and peace." [110]

"If we had a responsibility during the war," Chaplain Miller once wrote, "it is an even greater responsibility during the peace; if we had a duty to end a wrong that was, we have a duty now to start a right that ought to be. Your religious and military mission is to strive to inspire men to live their best. The thrill of being a chaplain is not gone with the silencing of guns." [111]

Unfortunately, it had been a brief and tension-filled period of peace. Less than a year after his retirement, chaplains again would have to follow their men through the tragic horrors of the battlefield.

See footnotes at end of chapter.

FOOTNOTES

CHAPTER II

[1] "Christianity and Communism: An Analysis by Members of the Faculty of Garrett Biblical Institute," *The Chaplain*, January–February 1950, pp. 9–12.

[2] Russell F. Weigley, *History of the United States Army* (New York: Macmillan Co., 1967), p. 486; *Army and Navy Journal*, 16 August 1947, p. 1330; 29 October 1949, p. 224; 24 June 1950, p. 1168.

[3] Publicity on "Freedom Train" as quoted in *Circular Letter*, Army Service Forces, Office of the Chief of Chaplains (hereafter referred to as *Circular Letter*), No. 327, 1 December 1947, p. 3.

[4] Roy J. Honeywell, *Chaplains of the United States Army* (Washington, D.C.: Office of the Chief of Chaplains, 1958), p. 71.

[5] James L. McBride, "The Chaplain's Handicap," *The Chaplain*, October 1945, p. 31.

[6] Alfred G. Belles to editor, *The Chaplain*, December 1945, p. 43.

[7] *New York Times*, 25 October 1946, p. 48.

[8] See *Ibid.*, 12 May 1948, p. 2; *The Chaplain*, August 1948, pp. 7–12.

[9] *New York Times*, 25 April 1948, p. 17.

[10] Sherwood Gates, "The Strength of America," *The Chaplain*, July–August 1950, pp. 27–28; For information on the Committee see January–February 1950, p. 25; The President's Committee on Religion and Welfare in the Armed Forces made their study during the first half of 1950. While the report was being written, the Korean War was in progress. The report, entitled *The Military Chaplaincy*, was published on 1 October 1950.

[11] *Circular Letter*, No. 296, 1 May 1945, p. 1; No. 299, 1 August 1945, p. 2.

[12] Luther D. Miller, "The Chaplains in the Army," *Army and Navy Journal*, 20 September 1947, pp. 49 & 74.

[13] *Ibid.*, p. 63.

[14] Weigley, *History of Army*, p. 499.

[15] Luther D. Miller, "Moral Effect of Military Service," *Army and Navy Chaplain*, July–August 1945, p. 11.

[16] Weigley, *History of Army*, pp. 497–500.

[17] *Army and Navy Journal*, 30 November 1946, p. 307.

[18] Harold O. Prudell, Historical Questionnaire, 30 October 1973, US Army Chaplain Center and School Archives, Ft. Wadsworth, NY (hereafter referred to as USACHCS).

[19] See entries "Post Schools," and "Morality and Citizenship Lectures," Volume III.

[20] Martin H. Scharlemann, Historical Questionnaire, 4 October 1973, USACHCS.

[21] Charles E. Brown, Jr. to Office of the Chief of Chaplains and inclosures, 8 November 1946, Records of the Army Chief of Chaplains, Record Group 247 (hereafter referred to as RG 247), file 726, National Archives, Washington, D.C. (hereafter referred to as NA).

[22] Memorandum, Luther D. Miller to Director of Personnel and Administration, War Department General Staff, Subj: "Supplemental Material for Brochure on VD Control Display," 10 December 1946, *Ibid.*

[23] Robert P. Patterson to Chief of Chaplains, Subj: "Discipline and Venereal Disease," 24 January 1947, *Ibid.*

[24] Luther D. Miller to James C. Bean, Subj: "Supervision of Chaplain Lectures Program," 13 February 1947, *Ibid.*

[25] Scharlemann, Questionnaire, USACHCS.

[26] Matthew H. Imrie, "The Fort Knox Experiment," *Army and Navy Chaplain*, April–May 1947, pp. 2–6, 32.

[27] Maury Hundley, Recorded Interview, 8 November 1973, USACHCS.

[28] Imrie, "Fort Knox Experiment," p. 4.

[29] As quoted in John M. Swomley, Jr. *The Military Establishment* (Boston: Beacon Press, 1964), p. 200.

[30] Hundley, Interview, USACHCS.

[31] See Swomley, *Military Establishment*, pp. 125, 199–201.

[32] Maury Hundley to Rodger R. Venzke, 2 September 1973, USACHCS.

[33] *Circular Letter*, No. 319, Addenda, 1 April 1947, p. 3.

[31] *Army and Navy Journal,* 28 February 1948, p. 683.

[35] DA Memorandum, No. 600–900–1, 7 October 1948, *Circular Letter,* file, USACHCS.

[36] *Circular Letter,* No. 339, 1 December 1948, pp. 4–5.

[37] *Army and Navy Journal,* 9 April 1949, p. 931.

[38] "My Right to the Truth" (Lecture 22), *The Chaplain's Hour,* p. 6, USACHCS.

[39] "Report of the Chaplain Corps, Department of the Army" (fiscal year 1 July 1948–30 June 1949) to Secretary of the Army, 14 September 1949, RG 247, file 319.1, NA.

[40] "Chaplains Activities" (Semi-Annual report) to Secretary of the Army, 12 June 1950, *Ibid.; The Chaplain,* May–June 1950, pp. 11–14.

[41] See *Army Information Digest,* October 1959, pp. 3–6; James H. O'Neill to The Chaplain Board, 5 October 1950; James B. Murphy to Philip Copp, 17 August 1951 and 1 October 1951; Philip Copp to James B. Murphy, 29 November 1951; Charles J. Murphy to James B. Murphy, 17 December 1952, RG 247, file 461, NA.

[42] *Office of the Chief of Chaplains: Summary of Major Events and Problems, 1 July 1959 to 30 June 1960* (Washington, D.C.: Department of the Army), p. 53.

[43] See *Office of the Chief of Chaplains: Historical Review, 1 July 1968–30 June 1969* (Washington, D.C.: Department of the Army), pp. 72–87.

[44] *Ibid.,* p. 86.

[45] *Monthly Newsletter,* Department of the Army, Office of the Chief of Chaplains, 1 August 1971, p. 3.

[46] *Ibid.,* 1 July 1972, p. 6.

[47] Press Release, War Department, 18 April 1946, as quoted in *Circular Letter,* Chief of Chaplains, No. 309, Addenda, 1 May 1946, p. 1.

[48] *Military Chaplain,* October–November 1948, pp. 23–24.

[49] Roy H. Parker to Karl L. Darkey, 31 October 1949, RG 247, file 631, NA.

[50] Press Release, Department of Defense, No. 1105–50, 2 September 1950, *Ibid.*

[51] *Army and Navy Journal,* 24 January 1948, p. 539.

[52] Roy J. Honeywell to Roy L. Smith, 11 June 1946; S. W. Hollingsworth, Jr. to Chief of Chaplains, 31 July 1946; Luther D. Miller to Kenneth Wherry, 28 August 1946, RG 247, file 201.2, NA.

[53] *American Military History,* ed. Maurice Matloff (Washington, D.C.: DA Office of the Chief of Military History, 1969), pp. 531–533.

[54] *Army and Navy Journal,* 4 October 1947, p. 105; 3 January 1948, p. 451.

[55] Daniel B. Jorgensen, *Air Force Chaplains 1947–1960* (Washington, D.C.: Government Printing Office, 1961 [?]), pp. 3–7; *The Chaplain,* May–June 1969, pp. 12–13.

[56] Jorgensen, *Air Force Chaplains,* pp. 6–7.

[57] *Ibid.,* pp. 7–8.

[58] *The Chaplain,* May–June 1967, p. 30; June 1963, pp. 40–47.

[59] *New York Times,* 24 October 1946, p. 33.

[60] *Circular Letter,* No. 298, Addenda, 1 July 1945, p. 1.

[61] Memorandum For The Judge Advocate General, Subj: "Appointment or detail of a Regular Army chaplain as chaplain at the United States Military Academy," 3 February 1945; Luther D. Miller to Legislative and Liaison Division, The Pentagon, and inclosures, 7 April 1947; Homer W. Jones to Director, P & A Div., 21 April 1947; John B. Murphy to TJAG thru Chief of Chaplains, 28 April 1947; Patrick J. Ryan to TJAG, 2 May 1947; J. W. Huyssoon to Chief of Chaplains, and inclosures, 8 May 1947; in-house note, n.d., signed "H" attached to above correspondence, RG 247 file 210.1, NA.

[62] Martha Rogers, *History of the Post Chapel, United States Military Academy,* revised William Blewett (West Point, NY: USMA, 1967).

[63] Edward A. Simon, "The Influence of the American Protestant Churches on the Development of the Structure and Duties of the Army Chaplaincy, 1914–1962" (S.T.M. diss.: Princeton Theological Seminary, Princeton, NJ, 1963), pp. 117–118.

[64] *New York Times,* 26 May 1946, pp. 1 & 2.

[65] *Ibid.,* 12 October 1954, p. 25.

[66] *Ibid.,* 25 April 1958, p. 15.

[67] See *Ibid.,* 29 April 1959, p. 35; *Frontlines,* October 1959, p. 2.

[68] See *Frontlines,* November 1964, p. 6; *The Chaplain,* December 1965, p. 50.

[69] *Circular Letter,* No. 320, Addenda, 1 May 1947, p. 1.

[70] *Ibid.*, p. 2.

[71] *Ibid.*, p. 1.

[72] *OCCH Historical Review 1 July 1965–31 December 1966,* pp. 285–286; *1 July 1968–30 June 1969,* p. 119.

[73] Cecil B. Lawton to Harry H. Vaughn, 22 March 1949; Memorandum, Harry H. Vaughn to Chief of Chaplains, 26 March 1949; Luther D. Miller to Harry H. Vaughn, 1 April 1949, RG 247, file 211, NA.

[74] *Army and Navy Journal,* 23 July 1949, p. 1372; *The Chaplain,* November-December 1949, p. 44; November-December 1950, p. 44; OCCH to Secretary of the Army (Semi-Annual Report), 16 January 1950, RG 247, file 319.1; Report of Armed Forces Chaplain Board to Secretary of Defense, 17 January 1950, RG 247, file 211, NA.

[75] *Army and Navy Journal,* 16 July 1949, p. 1321; 6 August 1949, p. 1411.

[76] *Ibid.,* 4 May 1946, p. 1060.

[77] Scharlemann, Questionnaire, USACHCS.

[78] *Circular Letter,* No. 308, 1 May 1946, p. 2.

[79] Gynther Storaasli, "Farewell Remarks of Commandant to Graduating Class," 29 August 1946, p. 3, US Army Chaplain School, file "Historical Events" 370.7, USACHCS.

[80] Gynther Storaasli to Luther D. Miller, 7 January 1947, RG 247, file 200.6, NA.

[81] *The Chaplain,* April 1947, p. 14; *Army and Navy Journal,* 16 August 1947, p. 1341.

[82] *Army and Navy Chaplain,* January–February 1948, pp. 6–7; *The Chaplain,* November 1948, p. 41.

[83] *Army and Navy Journal,* 8 November 1947, p. 247; 22 November 1947, p. 324.

[84] "69th Advanced Conference Course," *Military Chaplain,* October–November 1948, p. 14.

[85] "Army Sermon Service," *Newsweek,* 22 March 1948, p. 84.

[86] Story from personal experience of author while attending Chaplain School, 1959.

[87] *Army, Navy & Air Force Journal,* 17 November 1951, p. 351.

[88] Document first distributed by Walter G. McLeod, 11 December 1963, Ft. Leonard Wood, MO, USACHCS.

[89] Jorgensen, *Air Force Chaplains,* pp. 95–96; *The Military Chaplaincy,* (A Report to the President by the President's Committee on Religion and Welfare in the Armed Forces, 1 October 1950), pp. 40–42.

[90] *The Chaplain,* July–August 1951, pp. 45–46.

[91] Jorgensen, *Air Force Chaplains,* p. 96.

[92] Ike C. Barnett, "The United States Air Force Chaplain School," *The Chaplain,* February 1963, pp. 2–6; July–August 1966, p. 48.

[93] *Military Chaplaincy,* (President's Committee), p. 26.

[94] *Circular Letter,* No. 308, 1 May 1946; No. 309, Addenda, 1 May 1946, p. 1; No. 313, 1 October 1946, p. 2.

[95] Earl D. Compton to J. F. Leiblich (Mil. Pers. Mgt. Grp.), 1 September 1949, RG 247, file 221, NA.

[96] James H. O'Neill to George F. Rixey, 1 November 1949, *Ibid.*

[97] *Military Chaplaincy,* (President's Committee), p. 26.

[98] Honeywell, *Army Chaplains,* p. 318; *Army, Navy & Air Force Journal,* 21 January 1950, p. 547.

[99] See Honeywell, *Army Chaplains,* p. 319; *Religious Support Manual: ST 16–159* (Ft. Hamilton, NY: US Army Chaplain School, 15 April 1973), USACHCS; *OCCH Historical Review 1 January 1967–30 June 1968,* p. 115.

[100] Representative Engle (R–Mich) as quoted in *Army, Navy & Air Force Journal,* 28 January 1950, p. 563.

[101] *The Chaplain,* January–February 1950, p. 25.

[102] *Military Chaplaincy,* (President's Committee), p. 19.

[103] *Circular Letter,* No. 310, 1 July 1946, p. 3.

[104] *Army and Navy Journal,* 30 July 1949, p. 1376.

[105] *Ibid.,* 13 May 1950, p. 988.

[106] *Military Chaplaincy,* (President's Committee), p. 13; See also *Army and Navy Journal* 19 April 1947, p. 840; See Volume III, index, "Pershing."

[107] Casper Nannes, "A Visit With Chaplain Luther D. Miller," *The Chaplain*, March–April 1969, pp. 9–12; See also references under individual names in B. C. Mossman and M. W. Stark, *The Last Salute: Civil and Military Funerals, 1921–1969* (Washington, D.C.: Government Printing Office, 1971); Personal experience of author while serving at Walter Reed Army Medical Center, 1966–1968.

[108] *Washington Post*, 30 April 1972, p. 14.

[109] *Ibid.*

[110] *New York Times*, 20 April 1946, p. 11.

[111] *The Chaplain*, January 1947, p. 39.

CHAPTER III

Warring Ideologies—
The Battle for Korea

RETURNING TO THE BATTLEFIELD

In the morning hours of 5 July 1950, the antagonism of the world-adversaries came to a head near Osan, South Korea. Soviet-supported North Korean troops met face to face with U.S. soldiers—the first contingent of a United Nations' force. Shortly after 0800, as the surrounding hills trembled with the roar of battle, the first American fell dead. Before it would end, 33,628 more would die.[1] "It was a war between two differing ideologies," said one author. "All ethical standards of western civilization were scorned by the Communists."[2]

For most Army chaplains it would mean an all-too-soon end to the relative comfort of garrison duty and the parish-like ministries in occupation zones or the United States. Again the altar would be the hood of a jeep, a jagged stump, or an ammunition crate; the pews would be sand bags or the simple bare ground. The faces in the congregations would be dirty, weary, fear-filled—many of the chaplains' young charges would die in their arms before they could even learn their names. The well-planned services and intricate counselings would give way to whatever hope and comfort could be gleaned from Holy Writ at the spur of the moment. All this because the philosophy chaplains had warned about in citizenship lectures had suddenly become a living enemy on a battlefield, testing the strength of their spiritual muscles.

Regrettably, there is no way in which the ministry of the hundreds of chaplains who served in Korea could be adequately recounted in this limited space. Hopefully, however, the few examples cited will give some composite picture of how religious convictions, permeating their commonness, led many of them to uncommon deeds and sacrifices.

See footnotes at end of chapter.

64

Annexed to Japan in 1910, Korea had made various attempts toward independence, generally ignored by the rest of the world. Later independence leaders attempted to establish a government-in-exile with Syngman Rhee as President. Unable to unite the various factions of the group, Rhee moved to the U.S., hoping to gain Korean freedom through diplomacy.

World War II had restored hope to those who sought Korean sovereignty; the Cairo Conference of 1943 and the Potsdam Proclamation of 1945 promised them independence. The promise was complicated, however, by the Russian declaration of war against Japan a mere 25 days before their formal surrender. A hasty Allied agreement set the 38th degree of latitude across Korea as a dividing line between American and Russian areas of responsibility: Japanese forces north of the line surrendered to Soviet units; south of the line, to U.S. units. This seemingly innocent arrangement spelled the beginning of future problems since the Russians considered the 38th Parallel a permanent delineation between occupation zones. The United Nations called for free elections, but because the Soviets would not allow them to be held above the Parallel they were held only in the south. On 15 August 1948 the Republic of Korea was formed with Syngman Rhee as President. The Soviets responded by establishing the Democratic People's Republic of Korea in the north less than a month later.

This strange turn of events made the small land a dangerous contact point between the world powers—touching like bare wires in a global circuitry. By the time the Soviet troops left North Korea in the fall of 1948, that country had a formidable army, heavily armed and Russian-equipped. U.S. units, with the exception of 500 advisors, left South Korea in June 1949, but their military influence was far less impressive.[3]

In May 1950 Senator Tom Connally of Texas, then chairman of the Senate Foreign Relations Committee, warned of a possible Communist invasion of South Korea.[4] Many agreed, but few expected the attempt so soon. One month later, on 25 June, a massive drive by North Korean Army (NKA) units, supported by tanks, rumbled across the 38th Parallel and headed straight for Seoul, the southern capital.

The U.N. Security Council promptly condemned the attack and called on member nations to assist the South. President Truman quickly ordered General MacArthur to use U.S. air and sea power in the Far East in support of the Republic of Korea (ROK) Army.

Despite this response, Seoul fell on 28 June and MacArthur informed the President that the ROK Army could not repell the invasion with air

---

See footnotes at end of chapter.

and sea support alone. As a consequence, on 30 June 1950, President Truman authorized the use of U.S. Far East ground forces.

Unfortunately, those forces—four divisions in the thinly-populated Eighth Army—were understrength and poorly equipped. Nevertheless, the first organization tapped was Major General William F. Dean's 24th Infantry Division. Dean ordered his units to Korea via available air and sea transportation. Lieutenant Colonel Charles B. Smith and his 1st Battalion of the 21st Regiment were to lead the way. Smith's "battalion" consisted of two understrength infantry companies augmented by a recoilless rifle platoon and a mortar platoon—just over 400 men. This meager group, destined to be the first U.S. ground unit to face battle in Korea, was named after the commander—"Task Force Smith." [5]

MINISTERING TO THE FIRST IN COMBAT

Chaplain Carl R. Hudson, Southern Baptist, had been assigned to the 21st Regiment only a few weeks earlier. He was looking forward to a relaxed tour of garrison duty in Kyushu, Japan, hardly expecting combat duty. When alerted, even the men of Smith's unit anticipated only a brief skirmish and a quick return to Japan. The chaplain, a doctor, and a few aid men were ordered to accompany them.

In the early morning hours of 1 July, they drove through a monsoon rain storm to Itazuke Air Base. Although their first flight to South Korea was aborted because of ground fog, their second attempt landed them safely at Pusan, on the southern end of the peninsula. Later that evening they boarded trains for an uncomfortable ride north—made less enjoyable by the limited rations they had brought with them. Their morale was high, however, as they pulled into Taejon the next morning. There Colonel Smith was briefed by Brigadier General John H. Church, who headed MacArthur's survey party, and representatives of the Korean Military Advisory Group (KMAG). Smith also had a chance to go forward and survey the area near Osan.

Moving on to P'yongt'aek, the unit was joined by a battery of the 52nd Field Artillery Battalion. They commandeered old U.S. Army trucks from some retreating ROK soldiers and finally reached a pre-chosen hill north of Osan in the morning darkness of 5 July. Shell holes and a few burning huts indicated the enemy was near. The men dug in and set up their artillery.

It was raining at daybreak, so Chaplain Hudson wandered with a few men to the foot of the hill, found an abandoned hut, and went in to

---

See footnotes at end of chapter.

prepare some breakfast. Shortly after they entered, Hudson heard the noise of an approaching vehicle. He innocently glanced out the door and was momentarily stunned—staring directly at him was a North Korean tank. Dashing through the hut and out the back door, he and the others hurled themselves into a ditch as the tank's machine gun riddled the shack. The tank, followed by others, rumbled on south and the chaplain and his companions scrambled for their unit on top of the hill. Even before they reached the top, the U.S. howitzer and mortar crews opened up on the tank column. Their fire power had little effect, however, and most of the tanks continued right past their position. Following the tanks came an incredible convoy of NKA trucks, estimated at nearly 6-miles long. Hordes of enemy soldiers dismounted and began attacking the tiny U.S. group in an attempt to encircle the hill.

As the battle raged, U.S. casualties began to fall by the scores. Chaplain Hudson dashed through the rain and mud consoling the dying, praying with the wounded, and assisting the aid men. With the passing of each hour, however, the situation began to appear hopeless.

By noon, Hudson had worked his way to Colonel Smith. The commander told him he had sent a messenger south for help but that unless aid came quickly they would have to retreat. Meanwhile, the foul weather prevented any hope of air support.

By mid-afternoon, after 7 tortuous and valiant hours of combat, with no relief in sight, communications knocked out, and ammunition nearly gone, Smith decided to lead his remaining men out. The few undamaged vehicles were used to transport some of the wounded. Chaplain Hudson and others walked and ran assisting other wounded, but many of the severely injured and all of the dead had to be abandoned.

Hudson's group rushed south through the night and most of the next day attempting to make contact with the forward element of the 34th Regiment, scheduled to augment them. They waded streams and rice paddies, climbed hills, sloshed through rain and mud, resting only 5 or 10 minutes each hour. Hudson and the doctor circulated among the bedraggled men trying to instill some courage and hope. "Many prayers, both audible and silent, we uttered that night." Sections of the retreating unit met at various points and it became clear that only about 250 of them had escaped. When they finally met the 34th, more vehicles were secured. "We were never so glad to see those men and have rides as on that day," said Hudson.[6]

See footnotes at end of chapter.

Among the early arrivals in the 34th Regiment was Chaplain Elwood L. Temple, Presbyterian USA. Arriving with the rest of the 21st Regiment were Chaplains John L. Gilman, Roman Catholic, and Gerhardt W. Hyatt, Missouri Synod Lutheran. Hyatt, a native of Saskatchewan, Canada, who served as a transport chaplain at the end of World War II, became the Army's Chief of Chaplains more than 20 years later.[7]

These first few men, leading the long line of Army chaplains who were to serve in Korea, encountered the enemy and faced death many more times in the months that followed. After a brief rest and first aid for his blistered and swollen feet, Hudson was returned to 13 months of combat. "I think some of the best times were under extreme disadvantages like these," he said. "I didn't have to hold services then— but I wanted to. The men and officers knew this. They appreciated it and came in large numbers." [8]

Beginning with Hudson, many chaplains felt compelled to instruct their men regarding the ideological conflict. "I was always glad of the opportunity to explain the workings and effects of Communism as compared to the life and blessings of being an American," he later wrote. "We saw all the horrors of war and misery caused by Communism. I am still glad God called me to serve our men in Korea. I would do it again." [9]

RENDERING THE HIGHEST DEVOTION

General Dean did his best to slow the Communist advance while other U.S. and U.N. forces were being readied for shipment to Korea. He sent one unit after another to meet the enemy in their persistent drive south. Meanwhile, responding to a U.N. request, President Truman appointed General MacArthur Commander in Chief of the United Nations Command.[10]

"Dean's Delay," as it was called, was nearly suicidal. Every effort was met by seemingly endless streams of the NKA. One of the first heavy battles raged for 5 days (16–20 July 1950) near Taejon and the Kum River. Among the men involved were those of the 19th Infantry Regiment. Herman G. Felhoelter, Roman Catholic, was one of their chaplains. He had written his mother 4 days earlier:

> Don't worry, Mother. God's will be done. I feel so good to know
> the power of your prayers accompanying me. I am not comfortable

in Korea (that is impossible here) but I am happy in the thought that I can help some souls who need help. Keep your prayers going upward. . . . [11]

Felhoelter was just north of Taejon on 16 July, making his way up a hill across the Kum River with roughly 100 other men. They were carrying nearly 30 wounded while attempting to escape the enemy force that overpowered them. Felhoelter, who had been in the Army from 1944 to 1946 and returned in 1948, was now in the unenviable home of a military congregation—the battlefield.

The Korean conflict already contained those physical and psychological elements of every war—deafening noise, rampant confusion, overwhelming fear and fatigue, and indescribable carnage. Intermingled with it also were those inexplicable acts of self-sacrifice by common men who sought no special recognition or personal honor.

By the time Felhoelter's group reached the top of the hill, it was obvious they could not continue carrying the injured and still escape the advancing North Koreans. The chaplain convinced a medical officer to leave with the others while he remained behind with the wounded. Several minutes later from a distance, a sergeant turned and stared through binoculars at the pitiful group they had left behind. He watched in unbelief as enemy soldiers overcame the suffering men and murdered them all—including the chaplain praying over them. Only 11 days after American soldiers had entered the fight, the first Army chaplain lay dead on the battlefield. The next day would have been Herman Felhoelter's 37th Birthday. Posthumously he was awarded the Distinguished Service Cross. [12]

The bloody battle for Taejon ended on 20 July with North Korean forces attacking the 24th Division on three sides and invading the city. Even General Dean, injured and separated from his men, was eventually captured and subsequently spent nearly 3 years in a North Korean prison camp. His division was eventually relieved by the arriving 25th Infantry and 1st Cavalry Divisions. A few days later, the 24th, supplemented with raw recruits and commanded by General Church, moved to the southwest to meet a sweeping move along the coast by an NKA division. [13]

During the fighting south of Taejon and along the southwest perimeter, Chaplains Carrol G. Chaphe, Methodist, and Edward S. Dorsey, Roman Catholic, were cut off from their units—a harrowing

See footnotes at end of chapter.

experience endured by many chaplains during the course of the War. It took Chaphe 3 days and Dorsey 4 days to get back to friendly ground. Chaplain Chaphe, a veteran of World War II, was wounded in the course of one battle. "We were slapped by one wing of the Red drive on Chinju," he said from his hospital bed in Tokyo. "Our casualties were heavier than the medics could handle, but they kept working and I gave them a hand. . . . A light mortar dropped in ten feet from me, and they're still picking out the metal. When the medics repair this leg I'm going right back to those boys." [14]

Also wounded was Chaplain Arthur E. Mills, Advent Christian, with the 8th Regiment of the 1st Cavalry Division. He had overheard the remark of an officer that a group of wounded might have to be abandoned on the field as the unit withdrew from a heavy assault. Mills, who had served in World War II, quickly responded: "This is the way we did it in the last war!" He jumped into a jeep and sped off under enemy fire. Despite the fact that he too was hit, Chaplain Mills returned with a jeep-load of men. Besides the Purple Heart, he was awarded the Silver Star—his second for combat bravery. [15]

An occasional lighter moment broke some of the tension in those early days of fighting. With portions of the 25th Division on a train heading toward the front was the Division Chaplain, Mitchell W. Phillips, Disciples of Christ. Phillips was no stranger to Korea since he had served there during the occupation. When his train stopped for fuel, he heard the anguished cries of a refugee whose wife was about to give birth to a child. Phillips jumped from the train and assisted in delivering the baby as the mother lay alongside a road. Even though the father wanted to name the child after the chaplain, Phillips convinced him otherwise and dashed back to the train just as it was leaving. [16]

Among the chaplains of the 35th Regiment of the same division, which was attempting to stop a Communist drive near Sangju, was Byron D. Lee, Nazarene. The 33-year-old minister became a chaplain in 1944, a year after graduating from his demonination's Northwest College and Seminary in Nampa, Idaho. He had served in the European Theater in World War II and, prior to that time, had enlisted service in the Minnesota National Guard. As his regiment pulled back from an assault on Hamch'ang, enemy planes spotted the convoy in which Lee was moving, swooped down, and strafed the scattering soldiers. Lee was mortally wounded. It was only the 25th of July and already the second Army chaplain had been killed in action. [17]

Every contact with the enemy seemed to result in catastrophe. What remained of U.S. and ROK units, now designated as the Eighth Army, struggled to hold a daily-decreasing piece of South Korea. Their commander, Lieutenant General Walton H. Walker, designated leader of all U.N. ground forces, announced his intention to hold the line at whatever the cost. Four days after Chaplain Lee's death, General Walker gave his famous "defend or die" speech at the 25th Division's command post.[18] Unfortunately, there were more withdrawals. Ultimately the entire U.N. force, now augmented by units from the United Kingdom, occupied only a small area behind what was called the "Pusan Perimeter." The fragile line stretched a mere 60 miles from Taegu to the eastern coast and 90 miles south, partially along the Naktong River, to the Tsushima Strait. Squeezed into that tiny, southeastern edge of Korea, U.N. troops struggled to hold the North Korean advance.

RECALLING THE RESERVES

The Communist invasion in Korea caught much of the U.S. Army off guard. The Chaplains' Branch was no exception. Roy H. Parker, a Southern Baptist graduate of William Jewell Academy, had been serving as Chief of Chaplains for less than a year. But the 60-year-old major general had been a chaplain since 1918 and both he and his Deputy, James H. O'Neil, Roman Catholic, were combat veterans of World War II. Chaplain Parker was also well versed on the Korean situation, having served as Far East Command Chaplain under General MacArthur before his appointment as Chief of Chaplains.[19]

The primary difficulty in facing the emergency was a lack of sufficient manpower. The formation of the Air Force Chaplaincy during the previous year had cut the number of Army chaplains on active duty from over 1,200 to roughly 775. Worse, yet, a Reduction in Force (RIF) went into effect at the end of 1949. A January 1950 Memorandum in the Office of the Chief of Chaplains (OCCH) announced, with inappropriate terminology, that the Branch "was given the opportunity to participate on a voluntary basis" in the separation of non-Regular chaplains.[20]

Chaplain William J. Reiss, Missouri Synod Lutheran, who had worked for Chaplain Parker in the Far East, was serving in the OCCH at that time. Reiss recalled the pressure from the Department of the Army's Personnel people to reduce chaplain strength to 700 by July. Chaplains with low efficiency reports were encouraged to revert to an inactive

See footnotes at end of chapter.

Reserve status and some were literally forced out under the RIF. The number of chaplains assigned to administrative positions was reduced, the Associate Advance Course at the Chaplain School was eliminated, and the number of chaplains authorized to study at civilian schools was cut by two thirds. Virtually every position considered a luxury was done away with to free the remaining men for troop assignments. Many commanders, for that matter, were encouraged to make use of civilian auxiliary chaplains. But the sudden outbreak of the Korean War and the subsequent buildup of the U.S. Armed Forces required a complete reversal. Overnight the Chaplain Branch was told to raise their strength to roughly 950.[21]

"Parker was so confident that we could get this by volunteers," said Reiss, "that he said we wouldn't force anybody to come into the Service." With obvious embarrassment, personnel in the OCCH began sending letters to many of the men they had just forced off of active duty. "We waited a couple of weeks," recalled Reiss, "and we got one response." In essence, the one Reservist said he would like to return but he was in the midst of a church-building program.[22]

There was no recourse but to initiate an involuntary recall. Besides those who were already being activated with Reserve and National Guard units, 240 company grade Chaplain Reservists were individually ordered to active duty. Letters of protest poured into the Chief's Office, but the situation required the recall and virtually no exceptions could be granted. "Those were rough days," said Chaplain Reiss. "But the men who came in did a tremendous job." [23]

The call for an increase, however, didn't end there. Try as it might through involuntary recalls and denominational recruitment, the OCCH could never meet the rising authorized ceiling. Within a year of the North Korean invasion, U.S. Army chaplain strength rose from 706 to 1,208. But the authorized strength by then was 1,331. On 9 September 1951 they had 1,398 against 1,464 authorized. A month later the Office reported that 1,448—16 less than the number authorized—were on duty. The report told the Secretary of the Army, "[this is] the closest we have come to attaining full strength." [24]

Attempting to meet the illusive, constantly growing authorized number, the OCCH started new processing procedures and planned new training programs. Clergymen who applied for appointments were allowed to process centrally with the Department of the Army, rather than through the long chain of Army echelons from their local area to Washington. This cut the time involved from as much as 6 months to no more than

60 days.[25] Plans were also begun, although not implemented until 1954, to allow seminary students to train at the Chaplain School as probationary second lieutenants; an automatic promotion to first lieutenant and eligibility for active duty would follow their ordination.[26] Eventually, facing a 1953 authorized strength of 1,618—nearly 200 above the actual strength—the OCCH convinced the Department of the Army to allow company grade Reserve chaplains to volunteer for a 1-year tour of active duty (as opposed to the normal 3-year period).[27]

During this time, occasional accusations were being made that American clergymen had become apathetic to the needs of soldiers in battle. In most cases, however, apathy was not the problem. Many former chaplains were bitter after being "Johnsonized"—a term applied to the RIF under Secretary of Defense Louis Johnson. Others, who were veterans of World War II and had volunteered to return to active duty, held Reserve ranks that were too high for the troop-duty vacancies.[28] Meanwhile, many religious bodies were making valiant and sacrificial efforts to help. One of the noblest examples was a "self-imposed draft" at various Jewish rabbinical schools from which entire graduating classes volunteered for the chaplaincy.[29] Boston's Roman Catholic Archbishop, Richard J. Cushing, typical of denominational leaders who strongly encouraged their clergy to volunteer, declared: "Mass must be said within the sound of the cannon. From now on, our priests will have less freedom and more work and can no longer afford to be spiritual millionaires while our men are dying in Korea." [30]

Whether nobly concerned for American soldiers or unwillingly recalled to active duty, however, few chaplains had a real desire to be in another war—especially one which, at least in the beginning, appeared so hopeless. "When we were getting the pants knocked off us and we got down to that Pusan Perimeter," said Reiss, "nobody wanted to go to Korea!" [31]

PRAYING WITH THE DEFEATED AND THE VICTORIOUS

The Army Chaplaincy was 175 years old on 29 July 1950. Shaken by the gloomy reports from Korea, a crowd of 3,000 gathered in New York City's Central Park to attend a special ceremony for the occasion. Following musical tributes, the main speaker, Bernard M. Baruch, extolled the clergymen in uniform. "Although few monuments have been dedicated to the corps," he said, "its brave men have left their own monu-

---

See footnotes at end of chapter.

ment in courage on the battlefield." Referring to Chaplain Felhoelter's death, he added: "War brings out all the harshest forms of materialism, yet incidents like this prove that men in war can express the noblest forms of spiritualism." [32]

Despite such laudatory phrases, few of the chaplains thousands of miles away considered themselves heroic. Human as the men they served, their spiritual concerns seemed to grow with the desperateness of the situation. Donald F. Carter, Progressive Brethren, was among the many chaplains in the bleak surroundings of the Pusan Perimeter. He was ministering among the men of the 8th Cavalry Regiment (Infantry), 1st Cavalry Division. "Cooks and clerks were pressed into service as riflemen as the situation became desperate," he remembered. "There was talk that we might be pushed into the sea. . . . Through fear and uncertainy many men talked to me about spiritual things." [33]

As was often the case in such circumstances, an uncommon brotherhood began to grow and frequently breached long-established walls. A Jewish chaplain, for example, movingly described the breadth of his ministry:

> . . . I find most of my work with men of Protestant and Catholic faiths. Moving about clearing stations, mobile hospitals, rest centers, and reserve units, . . . one cannot merely seek his own fellow worshippers. Every boy is equally important—and a smile looks as good on anyone. We forget that we are this faith or another and emphasize the common denominator of fellowship. When they bring them in on a litter covered with mud, blood-soaked, with fear and shock in their faces, you can't tell what they are until you look at their dog tags. To serve such men is my privilege. [34]

While General Walker shifted his reserves from one point to another, constantly struggling to hold the fragile line, MacArthur ordered rapid preparations for a bold move—an amphibious assault on Inch'on, 200 miles northwest of Pusan. MacArthur directed that preparations be made in one month and a frantic pace was set toward that goal.

Meanwhile, General Walker attempted an offensive assault on Chinju on his western front. The 1st Provisional Marine Brigade and the 5th Regimental Combat Team were attached to the 25th Infantry Division for the counterattack. The operation was titled "Task Force Kean" after Major General William B. Kean, the Division Commander. Ironically, the planned offensive met headlong with an attack devised by the North Koreans in the same area and at the same time. With the 5th RCT

See footnotes at end of chapter.

were Chaplains Darrell F. Joachim, Disciples of Christ, Francis A. Kapica, Roman Catholic, and Dick J. Oostenink, Christian Reformed.

The Task Force made a brief penetration into the NKA positions, but was forced to withdraw after a week of heavy fighting in stifling summer heat. Chaplains Joachim and Oostenink managed to get back with most of their men, but part of Kapica's battalion was decimated near Pongam-ni. As the battalion commander was trying to make his way to those men, he met Chaplain Kapica returning with his jeep loaded with wounded soldiers. The chaplain told him they were all he was able to find before pulling out himself.[35] Although Task Force Kean gained no ground, it had inadvertently stopped a heavy NKA attack. More important, it momentarily boosted the battered morale of U.S. troops who, for the first time, had taken some offensive action.

A short time later, near the end of August, a breakthrough across the Naktong River by the North Koreans was nearly disastrous for Walker's Eighth Army. In the evening of 31 August, Chaplain Lewis B. Sheen, Episcopalian, had gone forward to hold services for B Company, 9th Regiment, 25th Infantry Division, occupying a hill near the river roughly 15 miles northwest of Masan. In the darkness, Sheen and the other men could hear sounds of people crossing the river below them. Squinting into the night, they made out a long line of enemy troops approaching. A devastating 4-day battle followed. Chaplain Sheen managed to lead one group of soldiers back to friendly ground.[36]

Adding to the troubles of the rapid preparations for the Inch'on landing, a typhoon roared in from the Sea of Japan during the first days of September. Chaplain John W. Handy, Jr., Methodist, with the 24th Regiment of the 25th Infantry Division, was shipwrecked between Pusan and Sasebo, Japan, for 3 days and nights. For most people, this would have been "the last straw." Handy had previously been cut off from his unit during a front-line engagement—an experience identical to one he had gone through at the Battle of St. Lo in World War II. But Handy described the event as an "opportunity to lean heavily on the 'power of prayer' for my own salvation and in so doing, to strengthen others to face these dangers." [37]

There were many possibilities that could have made the Inch'on landing a disaster. Fortunately, however, the major offensive movement, beginning on 15 September, was a complete success. Following heavy naval and air bombardment, nearly 70,000 U.S. and ROK troops with the 7th Infantry Division, 1st Marine Division, and support units poured into the area in a combined element designated as the X Corps. It was later described as "one of the great strategic strokes of history." [38]

The X Corps Chaplain at the time of the invasion was Frank A. Tobey, American Baptist. Tobey, who had both enlisted and commissioned experience before becoming a chaplain in 1938, was assigned as the Eighth Army Chaplain 4 months later. Chaplain Tobey became Chief of Chaplains in 1958. [39]

The Inch'on landing, breaking the rear positions of the NKA, brought a long-desired relief for Walker's Army and allowed them to make their first successful assaults from the south. Chaplain Carter, with lead elements of the 1st Cavalry Division, remembered the sudden stillness as the enemy pulled back:

> . . . men looked at each other with wonder. The enemy was just gone! Then the company was ordered to assemble and the weary soldiers began to tumble into the defile where we were waiting. Such shouting and exultation and laughter followed with men beating each other on the back, hugging and dancing in joy and release from tension. The chaplain was included in this spontaneous demonstration. What an experience this was, and what a revelation of the pent-up emotions that burst into expression at such a time as this. [40]

After regrouping, the units moved north at a rapid pace. Carter was separated from his gear and his assistant for 2 days while moving with the infantry. He described himself as "a vagabond with my beloved men."

> There was walking, talking, sharing "C" rations with whoever had something to spare, rides on tanks, jeeps, and trucks always in the northward movement to catch the enemy. Eventually my faithful assistant "found" me and a more normal way of life was resumed.
> Looking back upon that adventure I realize that I had been favored with a glimpse of the real life of that most noble group of men, the combat soldiers. I had experienced just a little bit of their joys and sorrows, victories and frustrations and hopes and fears. I am a better minister of God today because of those days. [41]

The Marines, spearheading the drive in the north, liberated Seoul—a victory as important psychologically as it was strategically. Anxious to broadcast the news, MacArthur announced the liberation 2 days before the city was actually secured. Freeing the city, for that matter, had not

---

See footnotes at end of chapter.

been easy. Total Marines killed, wounded, and missing during the 6-day fight was 1,482.[42]

INFLUENCING KOREAN RELIGIOUS ATTITUDES

General MacArthur's conviction that the spiritual condition of nations affected their ultimate history again became evident. Returning President Rhee to the National Assembly Hall in the Government House of the capital, the general began his address before a large crowd gathered inside: "Mr. President: By the grace of a merciful Providence our forces . . . have liberated this ancient capital city of Korea." He went on to speak of the U.N.'s "righteous wrath," referred to a "spiritual revulsion against Communism," and concluded by leading the assembly in a recitation of the Lord's Prayer.[43]

One month later, Chaplain Vernon P. Jaeger, American Baptist, published an article that not only assumed an imminent victory, but also predicted a Christian conversion of the nation:

> Just as in Japan, so also in Korea the winning of the war by the Americans and their allies caused the people to realize that their way of life was apparently in error. Now they were interested to inquire into Christianity because it seemed that there was a definite link between the military success of the United States and the religious beliefs that the people of that nation hold.[44]

Actually most Koreans claimed no religious affiliation, but there was still some truth in Jaeger's evaluation. Roman Catholic missionaries had brought Christianity to Korea in the 1700's; Protestant missionaries followed in the late 1800's. The 1950 War, however, brought the first significant impression of western religions on the nation.

Even common citizens recognized the religious aspects attached to the conflict. On the one hand, U.S. forces were regularly accompanied by chaplains and many openly participated in religious worship. American soldiers seemed naturally drawn to civic action projects and charitable causes. On the other hand, Communist forces took pride in denouncing such acts, publicly persecuting missionaries, and degrading houses of worship. When the Roman Catholic Bishop of Seoul returned to his church, for example, he was shocked by the filth inside. Religious pictures had been slashed and obscene drawings covered the walls. The life-size crucifix from above the altar lay smashed on the floor, covered with human waste. In its place hung a picture of Joseph Stalin.[45]

See footnotes at end of chapter.

Obviously, not all American soldiers gave the impression of living saints—far from it. But there were concerted efforts by many of them to impress Koreans with what they considered important. Two American missionaries, Methodist William E. Shaw and Roman Catholic George M. Carroll, attached to the Eighth Army as auxiliary chaplains, began early work to create a ROK Chaplain Corps. One U.S. Army chaplain said regarding that venture: "It is my conviction that out of the present carnage, expensive though it is in both life and money, the cause of Christ will be advanced and that Korea . . . will be a citadel of strength for both democracy and Christianity in the Orient." [46]

The Army Chaplaincy of the Republic of Korea was officially established on 11 April 1951. For some time, however, ROK chaplains were simply civilian volunteers who served without pay. Only with the supplies given by U.S. military chaplains and the aid from the Cooperative for American Remittance to Everywhere, Inc. (C.A.R.E.), were the chaplains able to survive and perform their duties. Not until 1958, when the ROK Army had become the second largest in the free world, did the first Korean chaplain receive a commission as an army officer. [47]

Despite those shaky beginnings, however, a seed had been planted. Just before the end of the War, the Chief of ROK Chaplains, addressing a graduating class at the Chaplain Training School in Taegu, asserted: "The War has given us a spiritual revival." [48]

Among the chaplains who came ashore during the Inch'on landing was a Presbyterian named Harold Voelkel—a man whose ministry among the Koreans was to become one of the most remarkable in history. Voelkel was a civilian missionary in Seoul at the time of the Communist invasion. Shortly after his evacuation to Japan, he met Chaplain Ivan L. Bennett, Southern Baptist, the Far East Command Chaplain. Because of Voelkel's knowledge of the Korean language, Bennett invited him to serve as a civilian auxiliary chaplain among ROK troops. As it turned out, however, his most significant ministry was among North Koreans.

Soon after the liberation of Seoul, Chaplain Voelkel learned of a large number of enemy POW's held in a nearby prison and decided to visit them; there his impressive work began. Serving first at Inch'on, later at P'yongyang, and ultimately on the island of Koje-do, over the months Voelkel's work brought him in contact with nearly 150,000 North Koreans. He sought out Christians among them, established Bible

See footnotes at end of chapter.

Institutes (a type of Christian-laymen's school), and conducted hundreds of evangelistic services often attended by thousands. Many considered Voelkel's ministry as one of the influences that ultimately convinced some 60,000 North Korean prisoners not to return to the Communist state following the War. Over 160 of them became Christian ministers and served in the South as pastors, Bible teachers, seminary professors, and chaplains in the armed forces. Years after his somewhat off-hand visit to the prison in Inch'on, Voelkel's name was affixed in honor to a large Christian high school in that city—a school built through the efforts of former North Korean POW's. In 1961, the continued effect of this one chaplain's ministry was recognized by the President of the Republic of Korea who personally decorated Voelkel for his contributions to the welfare of the Korean people.[49]

Among other U.S. civilian clergy who served in various ways as chaplains in the War was Father Patrick O'Connor, a correspondent for the National Catholic Welfare Conference News Service. One author said that O'Connor "very likely celebrated Mass for more soldiers than did any military chaplain in Korea." [50] Although the priest, like many chaplains, spoke out against Communist efforts to destroy religion, when asked if he considered the conflict a Holy War, he replied: "Hardly as yet. Many of our side are just as materialistic as are [the] Communists. It is futile and fragile to fight one form of materialism with another." Criticizing many U.S. commanders as "noncommittal or merely sentimental about religion," he added: "They encourage well-publicized charities, assistance to orphans, and graveside religious display. It's not enough and it's not all as straightforward as it might be." [51]

Nevertheless, threaded as they often were with human error and selfish concerns, that open display of U.S. religious attitudes and those acts of charitable assistance left a mark on "The Land of the Morning Calm."

SERVING THE ARMY ON THE MOVE

Trying to describe briefly the movements of U.N. forces during the months following the Inch'on landing is like trying to describe a yo-yo while in use. Chaplain William E. Paul, Jr., United Lutheran, offloaded at Inch'on on 15 September with the 328th Ordnance Ammunition Battalion. His subsequent travels over the Korean terrain give some picture of the rapid changes in the War's front.

See footnotes at end of chapter.

Chaplain Paul and his unit, providing support to the 7th Infantry Division, moved southeast to hook up with Walker's Eighth Army. He eventually continued all the way to Pusan—over 200 miles away. By the latter part of October, however, he participated in an amphibious landing at Wonsan, 300 miles north on the eastern coast of North Korea. From there he marched to Hamhung but, because of the Chinese intervention, moved south to Hungnam and proceeded, again by sea, nearly to Pusan. Once more he moved north. In the process he was reassigned to the 24th Infantry Division Artillery. Hospitalized with the flu and delayed in locating points along the way, it took him 17 days to get to the unit. Even when he finally left Korea in September 1951, it took him 20 days via Japan, by ship and aircraft, to return to the States.[52]

The U.N. forces that broke out of the Pusan Perimeter and drove north in the fall of 1950, met heavy resistance before they hooked up with the X Corps north of Osan in late September. Like a hammer meeting an anvil, however, the two forces crushed the NKA units caught in between. One of the fastest drives from the south was made by the ROK 3rd Division which pushed up the east coast and arrived within 5 miles of the 38th Parallel on the last day of the month.

There was some debate whether to cross the Parallel because of concern over possible reactions from China and Russia. After receiving no replies to calls for surrender, however, the U.N. forces pushed on into North Korea. ROK troops, often without adequate supplies and frequently moving on bare feet, made an incredible dash north and captured the port city of Wonsan, 75 miles north of the Parallel, by 10 October. Walker's Eighth Army moved across the border on the west and captured the North Korean capital, P'yongyang, by mid-October. On the 26th of that month, X Corps troops made a mass amphibious landing almost due east, at Wonsan, on the opposite coast.[53]

Meanwhile, a massive airborne drop was made by the 187th Airborne Regiment near Sukch'on and Such'on, north of P'yongyang. MacArthur had hoped they could rescue American prisoners who, it was assumed, would be moved northward and, at the same time, cut off North Korean officials and enemy troops. Among the paratrooper-chaplains were Francis L. Sampson, Roman Catholic, and Holland Hope, Methodist. Both were seasoned combat veterans of World War II. Sampson, as a matter of fact, twice survived capture by the Germans following airborne jumps in Europe.

Chaplain Hope, suffering from a fractured vertebra he incurred from the jump, was accompanying the 187th Regimental Combat Team. Hearing that men of "I" Company in the 3rd Battalion had been cut off, Hope, a recognized marksman, organized a rescue force from "L" Company. Following the chaplain, the men fought their way in to recover the dead and wounded. For this feat, Chaplain Hope was later awarded the Silver Star, the Purple Heart, and one additional, unprecedented award for a chaplain—the Combat Infantryman's Badge.[54]

Despite MacArthur's hopes, unfortunately, the major objectives of the airborne operation were lost. Many of the NKA had already retreated farther north. Far more tragic, 73 American prisoners were found murdered in one of the great atrocities of the War.[55]

Sampson and Hope eventually moved south to P'yongyang and, while there, helped minister to POW's. Sampson collected rosaries from his men for use by the NKA Catholic prisoners. Later he wrote, "I was struck by the strange twist wars can make of things. These Christians had been forced into the Communist army; now here they were using the rosaries belonging to the men they had been shooting at only a few days ago." [56]

Chaplain Sampson, who became Chief of Chaplains in 1967, was the momentary victim of a common plight in the War—someone stole his jeep. Undaunted by the experience, he announced to some British Catholics, after serving Mass at a neighboring English tank unit: "Now if any of you men can procure a jeep for me, from any source of your choice, I will give that man a jug of soluble coffee, a bottle of wine, and absolution." In 20 minutes, a British sergeant delivered a new vehicle. It not only had the previous markings painted out, but also a fresh new "Chaplain" sign emblazoned on the front.[57]

Chaplain Joseph A. Dunne, Roman Catholic, replaced Sampson in the 187th Regiment when the latter returned to Japan. While Sampson, an avid tennis player, was temporarily serving at the Tokyo Hospital Annex, he met and became good friends with another player named Yuri Rostovorov. Counter Intelligence Corps (CIC) agents soon informed the chaplain that his friend was, in fact, the Chief of the Russian Secret Police in Japan. They wanted Sampson to regularly report his conversations with the Russian, but the chaplain refused such an arrangement as being totally inappropriate for a clergyman. The friendship continued with the CIC's knowledge and word came one day that Chaplain Dunne, seriously wounded by a land mine in Korea, had

See footnotes at end of chapter.

been brought to the Tokyo hospital. Rostovorov asked to join Sampson in a visit to the wounded priest and, while there, was obviously moved by Dunne's quiet composure to severe pain. "A little over a year later," wrote Sampson, "the Washington department of the CIC arranged a meeting between Rostovorov and myself. He had found his way into the democratic camp, and . . . he told about the deep impression Father Dunne's Christ-like suffering had made upon him." [58]

SUFFERING UNDER THE CHINESE INTERVENTION

Americans had become optimistic about the War when the U.N. forces seemed to be finishing their work. Many U.S. units anticipated withdrawal to Japan. What appeared to be the end of the fighting, however, was actually only the beginning of some of the bloodiest in Korea. The sudden change came with an unexpected intervention by Chinese Communist Forces (CCF), who crossed the Manchurian border and led a new offensive against the U.N. lines.

Initial fighting between the U.S. and CCF forces began near Unsan, roughly 60 miles north of P'yongyang. During the first days of November, the 8th Regiment of the 1st Cavalry Division, especially the 3rd Battalion, suffered heavy losses. Chaplain Emil J. Kapaun, Roman Catholic, a veteran of the Burma-India Theater in World War II, was with them. Years before, Kapaun had confided to a high school friend in Kansas that he wanted more than anything to be a martyr. Asked once why he refused to wear gloves while working in a farming harvest, he replied: "I want to feel some of the pain our Lord felt when he was nailed to the cross." [59]

Kapaun had served in the 1st Cavalry for some time and suffered through early defeats with fellow Chaplains Donald Carter, Arthur Mills, and Julius B. Gonia, Baptist, who replaced the wounded Mills. Carter remembered how Kapaun found a bicycle after losing his jeep in the early days "and covered our units as few other chaplains I know." [60]

The chaplains of the 8th Regiment agreed to rotate among the battalions; near the first of November, Chaplain Carter, living with the 3rd Battalion held in reserve, exchanged places with his friend, Kapaun, in the 1st Battalion. Carter wanted the priest to "enjoy a day or so" away from the tension where the heaviest attack was expected. Ironically, it was the 3rd Battalion that received the full force of the Chinese assault and Kapaun's martyrdom started to be a reality in the evening of 2 November 1950. [61]

See footnotes at end of chapter.

The battalion was nearly wiped out during the severe battle. CCF soldiers captured Kapaun while he was with a group of over 50 wounded he had helped gather in an old dugout. Ordered to leave many of those for whom he had risked his life, Kapaun and a few ambulatory wounded were forced to crawl through the battlefield and were later imprisoned. For 6 months, under the most deprived conditions, he fought Communist indoctrination among the men, ministered to sick and dying, and literally stole food from the enemy in trying to keep his fellow soldiers alive. Eventually, suffering from a blood clot, pneumonia, and dysentery, he died there on 23 May 1951.[62]

Kapaun became one of the popular heroes of the Korean War and was referred to as "the man whose story best sums up the glory of the Chaplain Corps." [63] At a memorial service honoring Kapaun in 1954, Chief of Chaplains Patrick J. Ryan, Roman Catholic, relayed the feelings of former prisoners:

> Men said of him that for a few minutes he could invest a seething hut with the grandeur of a cathedral. He was filled with the spirit of Christ. In that spirit he was able to inspire others so that they could go on living—when it would have been easier for them to die.[64]

In the citation for the Legion of Merit, posthumously awarded to Chaplain Kapaun, were references to the "courageous actions" of a man who "considered no menial task beneath him." [65]

Chaplain Kapaun was the first of several Army chaplains who suffered in captivity. A mere 2 days after his capture, another chaplain fell into the hands of the Chinese. Kenneth C. Hyslop, Northern Baptist, was with the men of the 19th Regiment, 24th Infantry Division, who were attempting to stop the Communist drive south of Unsan near Anju. The 6-year veteran of Army service received the Bronze Star earlier for remaining with wounded who were cut off and eventually leading them back to friendly lines. Hyslop was captured on 4 November. Primarily because of internal injuries as a result of mistreatment by his captors, he died of starvation 38 days later on 12 December.[66]

In November the War's front became somewhat lopsided. While the Eighth Army was along the Ch'ongch'on River on the west coast, elements of the 7th Infantry Division in the X Corps had penetrated all the way to the Yalu River on the east. The Chinese in the west temporarily drew behind a screen of the NKA. MacArthur, meanwhile, had ordered bombing raids on the Yalu bridges in an attempt to prevent Chinese reinforcements from entering Korea from Manchuria.

Despite the entry of Chinese forces into the war, the Eighth Army resumed its advance toward the Yalu on 24 November. The next day, the Chinese opened an offensive of far greater strength than their initial attack, forcing the Eighth Army into a deep withdrawal. The 2nd Infantry Division, last to leave the Ch'ongch'on River, attempted to withdraw over a road that led through a narrow pass bordered by high hills south of the town of Kunu-ri.

Chaplain John J. Murphy, Roman Catholic, was with the 68th AAA Battalion as they passed through the 2nd Division and down the pass—surprisingly without serious incident. Murphy recalled seeing "Oriental soldiers" in the hills as they moved through the defile; he and the others were assured that they were probably ROK troops. Shortly after his unit left the pass, however, the "Oriental soldiers," actually Chinese forces, opened up with a heavy barrage on their main targets now entering the draw and, on 30 November, one of the worst battles of the War raged in the area. Chaplains John E. Gannon, Baptist, Samuel R. Simpson, Methodist, and James C. Carroll, Roman Catholic, were in the 38th Regiment of the 2nd Division. During the course of the battle the unit lost nearly 50 percent of its men. Simpson was a 44-year-old veteran of World War II. In a convoy trying to rush a Chinese roadblock set up on the 2nd Division's withdrawal route, he was cut down by enemy fire.[67] On the very same day, Chaplain Wayne H. Burdue, Disciples of Christ, with the 2nd Combat Engineer Battalion, was taken prisoner by the Communist forces. Burdue was 39 years old and had first entered the Army in 1942. Later reports indicated that he died in prison on 31 July 1951.[68] Chaplains Simpson and Burdue were just two of the nearly 4,000 casualties of the tragic ambush at Kunu-ri.

Twenty-three years later, while Chaplain Carroll was serving as Post Chaplain at Ford Hood, Texas, he received a letter from a retired sergeant. What the sergeant lacked in English grammar and spelling was more than compensated for by his moving message.

> Dear Sir:
> You are proberly the only chaplin in the hold Army that I can remember his name. . . .
> To let you know who I am, I was the one that jumped on you when we were ambushed at Conrea Pass. . . .

You sure did have a great influence on my life that day in Korea. I have never forgot how cool and collective you were when everybody was getting killed all around us. You said "the Lord is with us and will get us out of this mess" which he did. You were the calmiest person that I have every known.

After Korea, I started trying to find out in my own mind why you were so cool that day. Well I found it sometime late. I became a Christian. I am a Deacon and Sunday School Superintendant of my Church. Thanks very much . . . [69]

Three days before the Kunu-ri engagement, other Chinese forces hit the X Corps far to the northeast where sub-zero temperatures covered the land with ice and snow. MacArthur ordered a withdrawal by the Corps to the port at Hungnam for evacuation. Unfortunately, an envelopment by the Chinese forced the units in the Changjin (Chosin) Reservoir area to fight their way out to the evacuation points.

Chaplain Martin C. Hoehn, Roman Catholic, serving with a portion of the 31st Regiment of the 7th Infantry Division, was later awarded the Silver Star for his heroic service and encouragement to the wounded.[70] In the same unit, Chaplain James W. Conner, Episcopalian, was lost in the fierce fighting. The former priest to churches in Puerto Rico was listed as missing on 1 December 1950—exactly 2 years from the date of his entry on active duty. Chaplain Conner was never found and was eventually declared as "Presumed Dead." [71]

A Navy chaplain, serving the Marines in the area, wrote a magazine article later in which he accused the 31st Regiment of cowardice. He claimed that some 400 soldiers had feigned wounds and frostbite in order to be evacuated—leaving the 1st Marine Division completely cut off. The article gained publicity in other periodicals and the Department of the Army issued a public denial of the story. A personal letter, presumably of protest, was sent to the chaplain from the Secretary of the Navy. Although the accuracy of the chaplain's accusation may never be known, the reports indicated that the wounded from the 31st continued firing at the enemy while lying on trucks awaiting evacuation.[72]

In the same action, the day after Chaplain Conner was lost, Chaplain Lawrence F. Brunnert, Roman Catholic, in a sister unit, part of the 32nd Regiment was taken prisoner near the infamous Changjin Reservoir. Repatriated prisoners testified to Brunnert's devoted, though brief, service after his capture. He was the last U.S. Army chaplain taken prisoner in Korea and, tragically like the three who preceded him, he also died in captivity. Returned prisoners indicated that he died of wounds on 20 December 1950.[73]

For 6 days the 1st Marine Division fought southward from the Reservoir. Finally, on 9 December, a relief column from the 3rd Infantry Division met them outside of Hungnam. The immense evacuation had already begun. The Air Force and Navy moved 110,000 troops, 98,000 refugees, 350,000 tons of cargo, and 18,000 vehicles out of the area by Christmas Eve.[74]

The cost in lives caused by the Chinese intervention had been extremely high. The extent of those casualties can be measured somewhat by the tragic realization that six U.S. Army chaplains, nearly half of those who died in Korea, were lost in that 1-month period—four of them within 3 days.

MIXING SWEAT AND BLOOD WITH KOREAN SOIL

When Chaplain Frederick H. Ogilvie, Southern Baptist, reported for duty with the 7th Infantry Division, it appeared as though the Division's Chaplain Section was preparing for the Olympics. Ogilvie was a former Baylor University football star. He joined Chaplains Benton S. Wood, Christian Science, former captain of the Harvard swimming team; James M. Bragan, Baptist, and John W. Betzold, Orthodox Presbyterian, outstanding baseball players; Martin Hoehn, a talented skier, and Division Chaplain Maurice E. Powers, Roman Catholic, a boxer.[75] For the moment, however, it appeared as if none of them were on a winning team.

Chaplain Betzold, like many others, had once stood on the banks of the Yalu River, but during the bitter 1950 winter he was moving south in the rapid "bug out," as the soldiers called it. A land mine destroyed a communications truck near the head of his column. Betzold rushed forward with the others, fearing the worst for the driver. They spotted him, clothes in tatters, calmly searching the brush by the road. "I've found it!" he suddenly shouted to the stunned observers, as he held up a piece of wood with a few strings hanging limp. They were the shattered remains of his beloved guitar. "His humor saved the day for us," Betzold said; then he added soulfully, "at least that part of it." [76]

The incident seemed characteristic of the winter mood into which scores of chaplains tried to bring the spirit of Hanukkah and Christmas like a smile on the face of tragedy. The victorious had again become the defeated in a sudden twist of events. Somewhat symbolic of the course

See footnotes at end of chapter.

of the War, General Walker was suddenly killed in a freak accident. He died while driving to the front to decorate a group of soldiers— including his own son—when his jeep collided with a ROK Army truck.[77]

U.S. emotions were straining at what some were beginning to call a "pointless war." It was difficult for many to accept the political expediency of limited action in which thousands of Americans were giving their lives. The "U.S. Fighting Man" was chosen as *Time* magazine's "Man of the Year." "It was not a role the American had sought either as an individual or as a nation," said the periodical. "The U.S. fighting man was not civilization's crusader, but destiny's draftee." [78] A chaplain working in a replacement depot said that many of the religious conversions at his station were based on fear—"Who would not be scared to face those ruthless and godless communists?" [79] Meanwhile, General MacArthur's disagreement with the policy-makers' conduct of the War was becoming increasingly apparent.

By this time, Chaplain Ivan Bennett, in his dual capacity as Far East and U.N. Command Chaplain, was supervising nearly 270 chaplains representing a variety of nations. Frank Tobey, as Eighth Army Chaplain, was the senior cleric in Korea. Interestingly, 67 of his chaplains were civilians—seven U.S. auxiliary chaplains (former missionaries) and 60 ROK chaplain-volunteers.[80] Beginning in late January and into the spring of 1951, they joined their men once more in the regaining of formerly occupied ground.

Lieutenant General Matthew Ridgway, Walker's replacement, launched several attacks and reoccupied Seoul by 16 March. To block an NKA withdrawal route, the 187th Regimental Combat Team made another airborne assault—this time at Munsan, nearly 175 miles below the area they had captured 6 months earlier. It was during this operation that Chaplian Joseph Dunne, whose quiet composure to pain had influenced Chaplain Sampson's Russian friend, was seriously wounded. Dunne, who was later retired for disability, received the Silver Star for his heroic service in the area.[81]

On 5 April near Chunchon, almost due west of Munsan, Chaplain Leo P. Craig, Roman Catholic, was vesting for afternoon Mass at the 99th Field Artillery Battalion of the 1st Cavalry Division. An exploding land mine injured a soldier about 70 yards away and Craig, shedding his vestments, rushed with some others to aid the man. As they knelt beside the soldier, someone stepped on a second mine and Chaplain Craig, along with seven others, was killed by the blast. The former Cincinnati priest had died after less than 2 years in the Army. By the next morning, when prayers were being recited over the chaplain's body by the Division Chaplain, Harold Prudell, the story of Craig's death was being filed in a news story by the priest-correspondent, Patrick O'Connor.[82]

Six days later, despite their knowledge of some of the disagreements involved, many Americans were stunned by a brief announcement released by President Truman through his press secretary. "With deep regret," it began, "I have concluded that General of the Army Douglas MacArthur is unable to give his wholehearted support to the policies of the United States Government and of the United Nations in matters pertaining to his official duties. . . . I have, therefore, relieved General MacArthur of his commands and have designated Lt. Gen. Matthew B. Ridgway as his successor. . . ."[83]

Chaplain Francis Sampson described Ridgway as a "soldier's soldier" and compared him to Washington at Valley Forge "who met the supreme test in one of his country's darkest hours."[84] Meanwhile, Lieutenant General James A. Van Fleet was rushed from the States to assume Ridgeway's former job.

Obviously, many chaplains were becoming increasingly, if not wearily, familiar with the Korean terrain. Because of the constantly changing front and the rapid movement of units, some chaplains had to travel more than 50 miles between the elements of their "congregations." A chaplain reported that to get to one of his units required flying for 1 hour, riding a boat for 1½ hours, and driving a jeep for another ½ hour. The constant traveling, however, brought many of them in contact with the needs of the local people and inspired their involvement in soliciting and distributing supplies from Stateside churches.[85]

Two Communist offensives during the last of April and the middle of May resulted in heavy casualties for both sides along the 38th Parallel. On 18 May, Chaplain Carl P. Oberleiter, American Lutheran, with the 5th Regiment, 1st Cavalry Division, had stopped by the Command Post of Lieutenant Colonel Richard L. Irby's 2nd Battalion near Uijongbu. Irby, who was about to confer with the division commander at the time, noticed Oberleiter's jeep move onto the shoulder of a road to by-pass another vehicle when suddenly it detonated a land mine. Shrapnel ripped into the chaplain, severing an arm above the elbow. After evacuation, Oberleiter nearly died but, through the concerted efforts primarily of an Army nurse, he managed to survive. After spending months in military

---

See footnotes at end of chapter.

hospitals, he was retained on active duty, despite his handicap—due in part to his obvious morale-building influence on other patients. The cheerful chaplain, however, shared a different reason with the soldiers. While dwelling in subconsciousness, he told them, he had presented himself at the gates of heaven and dutifully turned over his "201 File" (Personnel Records) for inspection. After the review, unfortunately, he was refused admittance and sent "below." Once more the file was perused and again the chaplain told that he didn't qualify for entrance. Asking in frustration where he could possibly go, he was told: "Generally in such cases, we simply retain them on active duty." [86]

Chaplain Leonard F. Stegman, Roman Catholic, and David M. Reardon, Reformed, were awarded Silver Stars for their brave services on 20 May with the 15th Regiment, 3rd Infantry Division. Both had left an aid station to assist in evacuating the wounded from the field under intense enemy fire. Reardon, who was wounded in the process, refused to leave until the last man was recovered. He commented in a later acceptance of a civilian award: "My thoughts of those days are fresh with memories of splendid and heroic acts of my comrades whose sweat and blood is mixed with the soil of Korea." [87]

Enemy advances were soon spent and General Van Fleet began pushing back across the Parallel. On 27 May the 19th and 21st Regiments of the 24th Infantry Division flanked a Communist-held hill near the border. Chaplain John J. Murphy, now with the 19th Regiment, had spent some previous time with fellow Catholic Francis X. Coppens of the 21st Regiment. When Murphy attempted to contact his friend by field phone on the 28th, he was shocked to hear that Coppens had been killed the night before. Communist forces had stormed down the hill on the side held by the 21st Regiment; Coppens and Chaplain John B. Youngs, Bible Presbyterian, were occupying the same tent at the time. As machine gun fire riddled the canvas, Youngs dashed out for cover under a vehicle. Coppens, however, who had been quietly reciting his rosary, was cut down by the fire. Although the Massachusetts' priest had been on active duty from 1945 to 1947, his second tour had just begun on September 30, 1950. Chaplain Coppens was the tenth U.S. Army chaplain-victim of a war that was less than 1-year old. [88]

SERVING IN A STALEMATE

By late June 1951, a Soviet-proposed Cease Fire brought a lull to the fighting and the first negotiations between the sides. Unfortunately, the time was primarily spent strengthening positions along the line that snaked roughly along the Imjin River on the west to a point about 40 miles above the parallel on the east. The U.N. particularly fortified its hold near the "Iron Triangle" (Chorwon—Kumhwa—P'yonggang) on the central front. Clashes between the sides broke out regularly even while the talks were being held.

Chaplain John A. DeVeaux, Sr., African Methodist, was conducting services for the war dead one day at an Inch'on cemetery during the July–August lull. A South Korean, pointing to the stars above some of the graves, remarked: "I had no idea that you Americans have lost so many generals." "Those aren't generals," replied DeVeaux. "They're soldiers of the Jewish faith—men of all ranks who died for the cause. The Star of David is the symbol of their religion, as the cross is of the Christian faith." [89]

During the previous months, many U.S. troops had picked up orphan boys who lost their parents in the War. The homeless children were fed and clothed by the soldiers and referred to as their "mascots." In August, the 1st Cavalry Division Commander, who was concerned about the welfare of these youngsters, asked Chaplain Prudell to see to it that they were properly cared for. Prudell organized "Operation Mascot" by which 43 boys were given medical examinations, fed, and transported to various orphanges. Unfortunately, two of the little fellows "escaped" and hitch-hiked their way—over 100 miles—back to the only home they knew. Once more they had to be transported back to the orphanages for which the 1st Cavalry soldiers alone had contributed more than $1,600. [90]

Chief of Chaplains Roy Parker, who visited the battle-torn country in August, quoted a letter from a Korea-based chaplain in a report to the Secretary of the Army near the end of the month. "We are all praying that an armistice can be negotiated here," wrote the chaplain, but added his discouragement over the Communists use of the talks for propaganda purposes. "We can ill afford to lose the caliber of men we have lost here," he continued. "Perhaps this is not quite properly expressed as any price which assures freedom is worthwhile. But at the same time, it hurts to lose such good men." [91]

As the negotiations deteriorated into little more than formal name-calling and completely broke off near the end of August, the fighting rose again to full crescendo. Names like "The Punch Bowl," "Bloody Ridge," and "Heartbreak Ridge" became common as the news media tried to describe the coveted, rugged terrain commanding the area for which thousands of men gave their lives. Chaplain Parker quoted the 7th Infantry Division Chaplain in his September report to the Secretary of the Army:

> We are still engaged against an implacable and staunch foe, but if morale ever won a war our men will win this conflict. We are in excellent shape and the new chaplains . . . have already demonstrated eagerness, cooperation, zeal for the welfare of the men, and a fine cooperative religious interest in everything, notwithstanding the rigors and lack of amenities. . . .[92]

At about the same time the OCCH received a narrative from Korea entitled, "Diary Notes From the Chaplain," written by Chaplain Wendell F. Byrd, Church of God, 13th Combat Engineer Battalion. Among the pages were comments of thankfulness for the blessings of being an American. He had written that his faith had been increased by his nation's work to keep men free and then, commenting about American soldiers, added:

> To me there is something fascinating about the courage of men who can go out through mines facing enemy fire on dangerous missions and raids, then come back to their tents or foxholes and stomach a good meal in a cheerful mood.[93]

One month later, on 27 October, Chaplain Byrd was enjoying some time off during a new lull in the War—hunting pheasants with a Korean interpreter. With tragic irony, the 10-year veteran of Army service tripped a concealed land mine and was killed instantly.[94]

U.N. forces had managed to inch forward over the difficult ground. The Communists called for a resumption of the armistice negotiations and discussions opened again in late October 1951 at Panmunjom, southeast of Kaesong, near the 38th Parallel. The little village, which rested in "No Man's Land" between the lines, became the center of the world's attention.

By that time, the Korean War had become increasingly unpopular in the U.S. and some chaplains, like the soldiers they served, were emotionally torn by the issues. Adamantly refusing to declare all of the sacrifice of no value, they were frustrated over the little gain that seemed to be resulting from it. As if to remind them of the ideological struggle at stake, however, a Navy chaplain, who had served with the Marines in battle, lashed out at American attitudes. "They ask questions as if it [the war] had no special significance or relationship to themselves or the

---

See footnotes at end of chapter.

interests of our country and our way of life." Korea, he insisted, "is a segment of a world-wide struggle for the preservation of our way of life." [95]

While the talks at Panmunjom dragged on, minor skirmishes between patrols and front-line elements continued. It was, perhaps, easier during this time for chaplains to locate the units they served, but no less difficult or dangerous for them to get there. One chaplain had to use a 2,200-foot cable tramway to transport his field organ and altar kit part of the way up a hill to one group. He and his assistant carried the equipment on their backs the rest of the way. Another estimated that he traveled between 1,500 to 2,000 miles a month to provide counseling and religious services for his men. [96]

Concentrating much of their efforts at aid stations and hospitals, many of them empathized with the suffering of their comrades. Chaplain Paul W. Bare, Methodist, was over 50 years old when he concluded: "The world is in flames, I just couldn't sit it out as a civilian." [97] Quietly he moved through a front-line hospital late one night and grieved over the misery about him. He repeated prayers and Psalms for a young Tennessee boy who had lost both his legs. He bent down to embrace a 17-year-old, wounded for the second time, who clung to him like a child to his father in the dark. He helped another, whose shoulder was ripped and torn, to concentrate on the blessing of life rather than his handicap. He stopped by an old sergeant who wept for his lost men and prayed with him till he was calmed. Hundreds were suffering and dying as the negotiations continued. [98]

Some outside viewers thought the Cease Fire meant that no conflict was taking place. One chaplain was amused by a radio reporter's efforts to pre-record artillery fire so that he could overlap it as a background on his recording of the chaplain's worship service. Actual firing was carried on so close during the service that the back blasts from the guns kept blowing out the candles in the chapel tent. [99]

During the stalemate in March 1952, elements of the 40th Infantry Division were occupying positions on the central front. Among the men assigned was Episcopal Chaplain Robert M. Crane. The 40th Division was a National Guard unit that had relieved the 24th Infantry Division little more than a month before. Although Crane, like many of the men he served, had had previous Army experience, his second tour had begun only 12 months earlier. He spent most of that time in Japan where the two National Guard divisions, the 40th and the 45th, trained and provided security while high-level commanders debated over sending

See footnotes at end of chapter.

them into combat. When the units were finally shipped to Korea, however, they quickly demonstrated their effectiveness.[100]

On 11 March Chaplain Crane had just concluded a worship service for a unit of the 160th Infantry Regiment near Kumsong, North Korea. As he was leaving the area, an incoming artillery round nearly scored a direct hit on his jeep. The blast beside the road mortally wounded him. Robert Crane was the last U.S. Army chaplain to be killed in action in Korea. Nearly a year later the final Army chaplain casualty was added to the list when fellow Episcopalian Kenneth C. Wilson, 54th Quartermaster Battalion, died of non-battle causes on 23 January 1953. There was tragic similarity between Crane's loss and the sacrifices of the Minutemen-chaplains of the American Revolution—dying among citizen-soldiers who struggled to protect the independence of a tiny and, to many people, unimportant nation.[101]

The men of the 40th Division collected over $5,000 during worship services to help build a Robert Crane Memorial Chapel in northern Honshu, Japan, where the chaplain had expressed an interest in serving as a missionary after the War. The same division contributed more than $29,000 toward relief work in Korea during their service there. Their contributions were typical of thousands of dollars donated by American servicemen around the world for Korean relief, particularly among war orphans, in drives often sponsored by Army chaplains.[102]

In April 1952 Far East Command Chaplain Ivan Bennett left for the States with the intention of retiring. He was succeeded by Chaplain James T. Wilson, Methodist, former Third Army Chaplain. Because of an October 1952 reorganization which made the Far East Command a joint command, Wilson became the first Staff Chaplain of the newly organized Army Forces, Far East. Shortly after Bennett arrived on the west coast, he learned that he had been nominated by the President as the next Chief of Chaplains, to replace retiring Roy Parker. After confirmation by the Senate and promotion to major general, the 60-year-old Bennett assumed the leadership role on 28 May.[103]

Chaplain Bennett's ingenuity for getting things done at high command levels was seldom flashy but generally effective. Early in the Korean conflict, for example, he was determined to publish a combined English-Korean hymnbook for use in the war zone. Chaplain Steve P. Gaskins, Jr., Methodist, serving as the project officer, was frustrated by constant refusals from the responsible officers to grant necessary funds for printing. Bennett, understanding the psychology of staff officers,

See footnotes at end of chapter.

went to General MacArthur and invited him to autograph a pre-written foreword to the book. The general obligingly signed the document. With a clever grin, Bennett visited the man holding the "purse strings" and suggested it would be nice to have a hymnbook to go with the general's foreword. Chagrined, the officer admitted, "O.K., Chaplain, you've got me again." [104]

Some of the chaplain's talents were obviously inherited by his children—Dr. Ivan L. Bennett, Jr., was appointed Deputy Director of Science and Technology by President Johnson in 1966 and his brother, Major General John C. Bennett, became the commander of Fort Carson, Colorado, and the 4th Infantry Division in 1970.[105]

SURVIVING WITH DETERMINATION

Just as General Mark W. Clark arrived in May 1952 to replace General Ridgway as the U.N. Commander, an embarrassing incident took place at the large POW camp on the island of Koje-do. Brigadier General Francis T. Dodd, the camp commander, was captured and held hostage by his own prisoners. Brigadier General Charles F. Colson secured Dodd's release by making a statement tantamount to an admission of mistreatment of prisoners—providing the Communist negotiators at Panmunjom with a powerful propaganda tool. Clark eventually ordered Brigadier General Haydon Boatner to the scene and order was final restored.

Much of the camp's disturbance began over discussions by the negotiators regarding the right of POW's to choose whether or not to be repatriated. When screening processes for that purpose were first attempted, staunch Communist prisoners violently objected, refused to be questioned, and punished those who admitted a desire to remain in South Korea.[106]

Civilian Auxiliary Chaplain Harold Voelkel recalled the difficult struggles of the Christian prisoners during this period. Hard-core Communist leaders literally controlled some of the compounds and dealt ruthlessly with those who refused to remain loyal. Many were murdered by their fellow prisoners; a large portion of the victims were faithful attendees at Voelkel's services and Bible classes. Like the Christians in ancient persecutions, however, their faith only strengthened under the pressure. One group drew up a declaration of their willingness to die rather than return to Communist North Korea, individually signed the

See footnotes at end of chapter.

document with their own blood, and presented it to Chaplain Voelkel. Within days, Christians in every compound presented similar blood petitions to the chaplain. One of these petitions was later given to visiting Evangelist Billy Graham who, in turn, presented it to the President on a subsequent visit to the White House.[107]

The fervor with which many Koreans grasped Christianity after conversion amazed American observers. Chaplain Viggo Aronsen, American Lutheran, discovered that six ROK sergeants serving with the 10th Field Artillery Battalion, 3rd Infantry Division, were actually ordained Presbyterian ministers. Aronsen supplied a field altar and other supplies for them and was astounded at the results.

> What happened thereafter was a minor miracle. After the initial English-GI service on Sunday, these ROKs (great people) set up for Christian worship in the same location. Believe it or not, the hills emptied and people came in by the hundreds (conservatively, more than 500) . . . . Our own worship services in combat were tremendous experiences throughout the 3d Div Arty, but when it came to the Korean Christians we couldn't hold a candle to what they accomplished in the same sector.[108]

Attacks and counterattacks continued to take the lives of men as the jagged hills north of the Parallel repeatedly changed hands and the negotiations again deteriorated. The intensity of the fighting was reflected in the medal-citations awarded to many chaplains during the period. Chaplain Peter D. Van Dyke, Episcopalian, was awarded the Silver Star for his services in the 17th Regiment, 7th Infantry Division, on 3 July. During intense enemy fire, he left his position in a rear-area aid station and dashed about the battlefield ministering to wounded and dying, encouraging those still fighting, and aiding the litter bearers. As the unit was forced to withdraw, he remained on the field until all of the wounded were evacuated—personally carrying out the last man.[109]

Chaplain Michael T. Morgan, Roman Catholic, with the "Puerto Rico Regiment" (65th) of the 3rd Infantry Division, was in the midst of battle so often that the men jokingly insisted the enemy intensified their fire whenever he arrived. In one inadvertent move he nearly became a chaplain for the NKA. On his way to the front to conduct services, he had stopped to examine a burned-out Communist tank when suddenly he noticed a soldier some distance away waving for him to come back. Glancing in the other direction, he could see enemy soldiers about 100 yards away staring at him incredulously. "You know, Father," said his

---

See footnotes at end of chapter.

driver, "I think we're on the wrong road." Quickly jumping in their jeep they sped back to the friendly side.[110]

By October 1952 the Panmunjom talks had broken down again and the whole war issue was the hottest political topic in the U.S. Dwight D. Eisenhower, promising to bring a conclusion to the agony, was elected President in November and visited Korea before his inauguration. But the War continued through its third bitter winter as the new Chief of Chaplains, Ivan Bennett, asked religious leaders for more chaplains. By then, 175 Army chaplains had received 218 decorations in Korea, including 22 Silver Stars.[111] Chaplain William H. Weitzel, Episcopalian, had even received the Marine Commendation Medal with "V" device for his voluntary work among front-line Marines while assigned to an Army ordnance unit.[112]

It was obvious by now that the chaplains in Korea were facing a different ministry than those in World War II. While the fearful environment of the battlefield was the same, the attitude and morale of the soldier—deeply affected by the debates over the value of his sacrifice—had slowly changed. Severely wounded on the battlefield with the bodies of his friends lay the idealism of many soldiers. The interminable, on-again, off-again negotiations while blood was continually shed over the same terrain, made many feel like little more than political pawns.[113]

Fortunately, perhaps due in part to the death of Joseph Stalin on 5 March 1953, the Communist position softened somewhat. Surprisingly, at the end of that month, they agreed to a previous proposal by General Clark to exchange sick and wounded prisoners while resuming the talks. Operation "Little Switch" in April returned 684 U.N. personnel and 6,670 Communists. With the 149 Americans came the stories of many deaths—including those of the four chaplains who would never return.[114]

But the political-football aspect continued in a war that seemed to refuse to die. ROK President Syngman Rhee would not agree to a divided Korea and the subsequent discussions among the allies became as difficult as those with the enemy. General Clark later remarked, "Never, it seemed to me, was it more thoroughly demonstrated that winning a satisfactory peace, even a temporary one, is more difficult than winning a war." [115]

Beginning in April 1953, and reaching its peak in June and July, renewed fighting, mostly against CCF forces, tested the abilities of Lieutenant General Maxwell D. Taylor, who had replaced Van Fleet as Eighth Army Commander in February. Chaplain Parker C. Thompson, Southern Baptist, was among many who would have sworn that the War

---

See footnotes at end of chapter.

was nowhere near an end. Serving from November 1952 until May 1953 in the 7th Regiment, 3rd Infantry Division, and then in the 10th Combat Engineer Battalion, he was wounded three times and suffered a severe back injury during those 6 months. In one of his awards for combat bravery, he was cited for giving his armored vest to one of the wounded he was helping to evacuate. First used extensively in the latter part of the War, the vest was considered the most important possession of the infantry soldier next to his weapon.[116]

The intensity of the last 4 months of the War is reflected by the statistics: the combined total of dead, wounded, and missing from both sides was more than 200,000, and the artillery rounds expended by them during the same period totalled an incredible 8½ million.[117]

For organizing the evacuation of the wounded under withering fire—personally carrying many of them himself—Chaplain Cormac A. Walsh, Roman Catholic, 180th Regiment, 45th Infantry Division, received his third Silver Star. That incident took place only 2 days before the negotiations resumed for the last time, and 9 days before the final Armistice was eventually signed on 27 July 1953.[118] Like some horrible monster dying after one final, violent convulsion, the Korean War had come to an end. For a moment, in the tension-filled silence that followed, only the quiet utterances of thanksgiving drifted with the smoke toward heaven.

One author of the period had written:

> The man least attuned to what Bernhardi has called "the biological necessity" of war, and than whom there is non deeper enmeshed in it, is the chaplain. By vocation he is committed to an optimism of the spirit which believes and preaches that a man is capable of settling his differences by means other than war. Yet he accepts the commission to walk in the midst of it, to work in the thick of it, and to pray for the successful prosecution of it.[119]

To many people, perhaps, it was an inconsistent philosophy. To most chaplains it was an inescapable call to instill an ancient conviction: "Whither shall I go from Thy Spirit: or whither shall I flee from Thy presence? If I ascend up into heaven, Thou art there: if I make my bed in hell, behold, Thou art there." [120] To that end, scores of them had shed their blood, 13 had given their lives, and hundreds were committed to a continuing ministry among American soldiers.

See footnotes at end of chapter.

FOOTNOTES

CHAPTER III

[1] Harry J. Middleton, *The Compact History of the Korean War* (New York: Hawthorne Books, 1965), p. 17; R. Ernest Dupuy and Trevor N. Dupuy, *The Encyclopedia of Military History* (New York: Harper & Row, 1970), p. 1219.

[2] Dupuy and Dupuy, *Military History,* p. 1219.

[3] Roy E. Appleman, *South to the Naktong, North to the Yalu* (Washington, D.C.: DA Office of the Chief of Military History, 1961), pp. 1–18; Dupuy and Dupuy, *Military History,* p. 1209; *Encyclopedia Americana,* 1962 ed., s.v. "Korea."

[4] *Army, Navy and Air Force Journal,* 6 May 1950, p. 971.

[5] Dupuy and Dupuy, *Military History,* pp. 1209–1210; *Army, Navy and Air Force Journal,* 27 June 1953, p. 1306.

[6] Carl R. Hudson to Patrick H. Hyde, 10 May 1970, U.S. Army Chaplain Center and School Archives, Ft. Wadsworth, NY (hereafter referred to as USACHCS); Appleman, *Naktong to Yalu,* pp. 57–76; Dupuy and Dupuy, *Military History,* p. 1210; *Army, Navy and Air Force Journal,* 27 June 1953, p. 1306.

[7] Hudson to Hyde, 10 May 1970, USACHCS; Biographical Sketch of Gerhardt W. Hyatt, USACHCS; Telephone interviews of Gerhardt W. Hyatt and Carl R. Hudson, 10 October 1974, USACHCS.

[8] Hudson to Hyde, 10 May 1970, USACHCS.

[9] *Ibid.*

[10] Dupuy and Dupuy, *Military History,* p. 1210.

[11] *Military Chaplain,* April 1951, p. 14.

[12] *New York Times,* 31 July 1950, p. 15; 14 April 1951, p. L–3; Appleman, *Naktong to Yalu,* p. 143; *Army, Navy and Air Force Journal,* 25 July 1953, p. 1456; 12 August 1950, p. 1353; *Military Chaplain,* October 1953, pp. 1–3; Personnel Records of Herman G. Felhoelter, U.S. Army Reserve Components Personnel and Administration Center, St. Louis, MO (hereafter referred to as USARCPAC).

[13] Appleman, *Naktong to Yalu,* pp. 146–181.

[14] "The Church in Uniform," *Time,* 4 August 1950, p. 68; "Chaplain Heroes," *Newsweek,* 30 October 1950, p. 75; "Chaplains in Korea," *The Chaplain,* November–December 1950, pp. 35–37.

[15] *Army, Navy and Air Force Journal,* 2 September 1950, p. 17; "Chaplains in Korea," *The Chaplain,* November–December 1950, pp. 35–37; "Chaplain Heroes," *Newsweek,* 30 October 1950, p. 75.

[16] *Army, Navy and Air Force Journal,* 19 August 1950, p. 1379.

[17] Personnel Records of Byron D. Lee, USARCPAC; *The Chaplain,* May–June 1951, p. 47; *Military Chaplain,* October 1953, pp. 1–3; "Chaplain Heroes," *Newsweek,* 30 October 1950, p. 75.

[18] Appleman, *Naktong to Yalu,* pp. 207–208.

[19] *Army, Navy and Air Force Journal,* 16 July 1949, p. 1321; 6 August 1949, p. 1411; 24 September 1949, p. 90; *The Chaplain,* November–December 1949, p. 2.

[20] Memorandum For The Record, OCCH, 11 January 1950; Report of the Chaplain Corps, Department of the Army for fiscal year 1 July 1948–30 June 1949; Semi-Annual Report OCCH to Secretary of the Army, 12 June 1950, Records of the Army Chief of Chaplains, Record Group 247 (hereafter referred to as RG 247), file 319.1, National Archives, Washington, D.C. (hereafter referred to as NA).

[21] William J. Reiss, Recorded Interview, 27 October 1973; *OCCH Summary of Major Events and Problems, 25 June 1950–8 September 1951,* p. 2, USACHCS.

[22] Reiss, Recorded Interview, 27 October 1973, USACHCS.

[23] *Ibid.; New York Times,* 19 September 1950, p. 1.

[24] Report of OCCH to Secretary of the Army, 25 October 1951, RG 247, file 319.1, NA; *OCCH Summary of Major Events and Problems, 25 June 1950–8 September 1951,* p. 1, USACHCS.

[25] Memorandum OCCH to MG Anthony C. McAuliffe, 19 July 1951, RG 247, file 210.455, NA; OCCH Report to Secretary of the Army, 24 April 1952, RG 247, file 319.1, NA.

[26] Report of OCCH to Secretary of the Army, 24 April 1952, RG 247, file 319.1, NA; *OCCH Summary of Major Events and Problems, 25 June 1950–8 September 1951*, pp. 2–3; *Army, Navy and Air Force Journal*, 10 April 1954, p. 960; *Military Chaplain*, January 1954, p. 24.

[27] OCCH to Assistant Chief of Staff, G1, 11 December 1952, RG 247, file 210.455, NA; *New York Times*, 17 March 1953, p. 16.

[28] See "Our Servicemen Need Chaplains," *Christian Century*, 8 April 1953, p. 405; subsequent letters to editor 22 April 1953, p. 484; 13 May 1953, pp. 577–578.

[29] *New York Times*, 9 November 1950, p. 28; 13 January 1951, p. 17; 8 June 1952, p. 59.

[30] *Ibid.*, 2 August 1950, p. 23.

[31] Reiss, Recorded Interview, 27 October 1973, USACHCS.

[32] *New York Times*, 31 July 1950, p. 4.

[33] Donald F. Carter, Historical Questionnaire, 28 December 1973, USACHCS.

[34] *Military Chaplain*, October 1950, p. 9.

[35] Dick J. Oostenink, Personal Interview, 18 October 1974, USACHCS; Appleman, *Naktong to Yalu*, p. 283.

[36] Appleman, *Naktong to Yalu*, pp. 447–448.

[37] John W. Handy, Jr., Historical Questionnaire, 24 October 1973, USACHCS.

[38] Dupuy and Dupuy, *Military History*, p. 1212; see also Appleman, *Naktong to Yalu*, pp. 488–514.

[39] Frank A. Tobey, Historical Questionnaire, 4 October 1973, USACHCS.

[40] Carter, Historical Questionnaire, 28 December 1973, USACHCS.

[41] *Ibid.*

[42] Appleman, *Naktong to Yalu*, pp. 541 & 515–541.

[43] *Ibid.*, p. 537.

[44] Vernon P. Jaeger, "Experiences in Korea," *Military Chaplain*, October 1950, pp. 1–2.

[45] Albert C. Wildman, "Christianity in Korea," *Military Chaplain*, October 1950, pp. 6–8; Francis L. Sampson, *Look Out Below* (Washington, D.C.: Catholic University of America Press, 1958), p. 184.

[46] Wildman, "Christianity in Korea," *Military Chaplain*, October 1950, pp. 6–8.

[47] "Chaplains for the ROKs," *Time*, 1 June 1953, p. 60; *The Chaplain*, June 1958, p. 43; *New York Times*, 18 June 1953, p. 38.

[48] "Chaplains For The ROKs," *Time*, 1 June 1953, p. 60.

[49] Harold Voelkel, *Behind Barbed Wire in Korea* (Grand Rapids, MI: Zondervan Publishing House, 1953), pp. 5–32; Harold Voelkel to Rodger R. Venzke, 14 April 1973, USACHCS.

[50] Melvin B. Voorhees, *Korean Tales* (New York: Simon & Schuster, 1952), p. 118.

[51] *Ibid.*, p. 122.

[52] William E. Paul, Jr., Historical Questionnaire, 6 April 1974, USACHCS.

[53] See Appleman, *Naktong to Yalu*, pp. 542–653.

[54] Holland Hope, Historical Questionnaire, 16 January 1974, USACHCS; Sampson, *Look Out Below*, p. 185; Appleman, *Naktong to Yalu*, pp. 654–666.

[55] Appleman, *Naktong to Yalu*, pp. 661–663.

[56] Sampson, *Look Out Below*, p. 187.

[57] *Ibid.*, pp. 191–192.

[58] *Ibid.*, pp. 193–195.

[59] Arthur Tonne, *The Story of Chaplain Kapaun: Patriot Priest of the Korean Conflict* (Emporia, KA: Didde Publishers, 1954), pp. 35–36; Appleman, *Naktong to Yalu*, pp. 702–707.

[60] Donald F. Carter to Rodger R. Venzke, 21 September 1973, USACHCS.

[61] *Ibid.*

[62] Personnel Records of Emil J. Kapaun, USARCPAC, indicate conflicting reports from returned prisoners as to actual date of Kapaun's death in May 1951, but official date accepted is the latest of those reported.

[63] Thomas J. Fleming, "God's Warriors," *This Week*, 26 March 1967, p. 23; See also Eugene Kinkead, *In Every War But One* (New York: W. W. Norton Co., 1959), p. 152.

[64] *The Chaplain*, December 1954, p. 47.

[65] *Army, Navy and Air Force Journal*, 13 November 1954, p. 312; See also *New York Times*, 15 February 1954, p. 7; 7 February 1954, p. 32.

[66] Personnel Records of Kenneth C. Hyslop, USARCPAC, indicate conflicting reports from returned prisoners as to actual date of Hyslop's death, but official date accepted is the latest of those reported.

[67] John J. Murphy, Personal Interview, 31 October 1974, USACHCS; James C. Carroll, Historical Questionnaire, 25 October 1973, and accompanying letters, USACHCS; See also *The Chaplain,* July–August 1951, p. 1; Dupuy and Dupuy, *Military History,* p. 1213.

[68] *Military Chaplain,* October 1953, pp. 1–3; *The Chaplain,* December 1953, p. 44.

[69] Arlen D. Dieus to James C. Carroll, 12 February 1973, Carroll Questionnaire file, USACHCS.

[70] Ivan L. Bennett to Chief of Chaplains, Subj: "Recommendation for B'NAI B'RITH Award," 16 November 1951, RG 247, file 200.6, NA; *Army, Navy and Air Force Journal,* 24 March 1951, p. 814; See also Dupuy and Dupuy, *Military History,* pp. 1213–1214.

[71] Personnel file of James W. Conner, OCCH; *Military Chaplain,* October 1953, pp. 1–3.

[72] *Army, Navy and Air Force Journal,* 31 March 1951, p. 840; *New York Times,* 14 June 1951, p. 8.

[73] *Military Chaplain,* October 1953, pp. 1–3; See also *The Catholic Chaplains Memorial Chapel, Columban Fathers, Seoul, Korea* (Program of Dedication Day Ceremonies and Events, 4 November 1953), s.v. "Chaplain (1st Lt) Lawrence F. Brunnert," RG 247, file 200.6, NA; Personnel file of Lawrence F. Brunnert, OCCH.

[74] Dupuy and Dupuy, *Military History,* pp. 1213–1214.

[75] *Army, Navy and Air Force Journal,* 17 March 1951, p. 787.

[76] John W. Betzold, Historical Questionnaire, 4 December 1973, USACHCS.

[77] *Army, Navy and Air Force Journal,* 30 December 1950, p. 470.

[78] As quoted in *Ibid.,* p. 482; See also quote of editorial from *Mansfield, Ohio, News Journal* in 27 January 1951, p. 574.

[79] Ronald Wiley and Robert McNeil, "A History of the Baptist General Conference Chaplaincy Program" (Historical Research Project, Bethel Theological Seminary, St. Paul, MN, 1968), p. 66.

[80] *Army, Navy and Air Force Journal,* 10 March 1951, p. 760.

[81] *New York Times,* 27 May 1954, p. 5.

[82] Personnel file on Leo P. Craig, USACHCS; For sample of O'Connor's story on Craig see "Fr. Craig Killed in Korea While Ministering to Wounded Soldiers," *Paterson, New Jersey, News* 27 April 1951.

[83] *Army, Navy and Air Force Journal,* 14 April 1951, p. 908.

[84] Sampson, *Look Out Below,* p. 190.

[85] See *The Chaplain,* January–February 1951, p. 48; March–April 1951, pp. 45–46 & 48.

[86] Telephone interviews of Carl P. Oberleiter, Aurora, CO, 1 November 1974, and MG Richard L. Irby, Virginia Military Institute, 8 November 1974, USACHCS.

[87] Leonard F. Stegman, Historical Questionnaire, 1 November 1973, and accompanying documents, USACHCS; General Orders 91, Hq, 3d Infantry Division, 10 April 1911; General Orders 347, Hq, 3d Infantry Division, 10 August 1951; David M. Reardon to Roy H. Parker, 8 February 1952, RG 247, file 200.6, NA.

[88] John J. Murphy, Personal Interview, 8 November 1974, USACHCS; see also *Catholic Memorial Chapel,* s.v. "Chaplain (Capt) Francis X. Coppens," RG 247, file 200.6, NA; Personnel file of Francis X. Coppens, OOCH.

[89] *The Chaplain,* July–August 1951, p. 2.

[90] Harold O. Prudell, Historical Questionnaire, 30 October 1973, USACHCS.

[91] Roy H. Parker to The Secretary of the Army, 27 August 1951, RG 247, file 319.1, NA.

[92] Roy H. Parker to The Secretary of the Army, 25 September 1951, RG 247, file 319.1, NA.

[93] *The Chaplain,* March–April 1952, p. 21.

[94] Personnel Records of Wendell F. Byrd, USARCPAC; Telephone interview of William Brooks, Church of God Prophecy, Cleveland, TN, who passed on information received from mother and sister of Wendell F. Byrd in same city, 27 September 1974; See also *Military Chaplain,* October 1953, pp. 1–3.

[95] *New York Times,* 27 December 1951, p. 3.

[96] Roy H. Parker, "Religion at Work," *The Chaplain,* January–February 1952, p. 10; Albert C. Wildman, "The Work of Chaplains in Korea," *The Chaplain,* March–April 1952, pp. 28–29.

[97] *New York Times,* 6 May 1951, p. 65.

[98] "A Chaplain Writes Home," *Pacific Stars and Stripes* as quoted in *The Chaplain,* May–June 1952, pp. 9–11; See also Paul W. Bare, "Front Line Chaplain," *Military Chaplain,* October 1952, pp. 14–15.

[99] Albert C. Wildman, "The Work of Chaplains in Korea," *The Chaplain,* March–April 1952, pp. 28–29.

[100] See Walter G. Hermes, *Truce Tent and Fighting Front* (Washington, D.C.: DA Office of the Chief of Military History, 1966), pp. 202–204.

[101] Personnel Records of Robert M. Crane, USARCPAC; *New York Times,* 20 March 1952, p. 6; *The Chaplain,* September–October 1952, p. 48; *Military Chaplain,* October 1953, pp. 1–3; Personnel file of Kenneth C. Wilson, OCCH.

[102] *The Chaplain,* November–December 1952, p. 16; *Military Chaplain,* April 1953, p. 28; See also *The Chaplain,* March–April 1952, p. 47.

[103] *Army, Navy and Air Force Journal,* 12 April 1942, p. 1005; *The Chaplain,* July–August 1952, p. 48; Reiss, Recorded Interview, 27 October 1973, USACHCS.

[104] Steve P. Gaskins to Rodger R. Venzke, 2 July 1974, USACHCS.

[105] *Journal of the Armed Forces,* 19 November 1966, p. 19; *The Chaplain,* May–June 1971, p. 57.

[106] Hermes, *Truce Tent and Fighting Front,* pp. 233–262.

[107] Voelkel, *Behind Barbed Wire,* pp. 27–30; Voelkel to Rodger R. Venzke, 14 April 1973, USACHCS.

[108] Viggo O. Aronsen, Historical Questionnaire, 12 October 1973, USACHCS.

[109] Citation, Award of the Silver Star Medal, Chaplain Peter D. Van Dyke, n.d. (for action on 3 July 1952 with Hq, 17th Infantry Regiment, 7th Infantry Division), RG 247, file 200.6, NA.

[110] *Military Chaplain,* October 1952, p. 29.

[111] *Newsweek,* 3 November 1952, pp. 68–69.

[112] *The Chaplain,* November–December 1952, p. 48.

[113] "Are the Churches Failing Our GI's?" *Military Chaplain,* April 1953, pp. 4–6.

[114] Dupuy and Dupuy, *Military History,* p. 1219; Hermes, *Truce Tent and Fighting Front,* p. 514.

[115] Mark W. Clark, *From the Danube to the Yalu* (New York: Harper & Brothers, 1954), p. 257.

[116] St. Louis Globe Democrat, 19 January 1954, p. 6; Parker C. Thompson, Personal interview, 29 October 1974, USACHCS; For discussion on armored vests see Hermes, *Truce Tent and Fighting Front, p.* 372.

[117] Hermes, *Truce Tent and Fighting Front,* p. 477.

[118] *New York Times,* 25 February 1955, p. 3.

[119] Timothy J. Mulvey, *These Are Your Sons* (New York: McGraw Hill, 1952) p. 151.

[120] Psalm 139:7–8, KJV.

Responding to the Strategic Opportunities

LACKING EARLY UNITY AGAINST DISCRIMINATION

In the fall of 1951 Chaplain John F. Orzel, Roman Catholic, officiated at a unique funeral in Arlington National Cemetery for a Korean War casualty. The family of the deceased, Sergeant John R. Rice, intended to have him buried at Sioux City, Iowa, but they were barred from using a municipal cemetery. The President of the United States directly intervened in the case and ordered Sergeant Rice's committal to be conducted at Arlington. Only one factor of Sergeant Rice's life had been the' basis for this unusual situation—he was a Winnebago Indian.[1]

Army chaplains had witnessed American racial and ethnic prejudice for years. Unfortunately, like their civilian counterparts, most of them seemed preoccupied with other issues. A group of seminary professors who taught elective courses on ministry in the military labeled the chaplaincy in 1953: "a strategic opportunity for a spiritual ministry." Of course, in the mood of that time, they were speaking of the "ideological and spiritual" struggle with Communism rather than with the festering, indigenous social problems in the United States. It was as if the "strategic opportunity" for chaplains was always thought of in terms of protecting American soldiers from foreign political influence rather than from erroneous U.S. attitudes.[2]

Army chaplains didn't ignore the issue of prejudice, but they did fail to recognize the "strategic opportunity" to unite and organize their efforts against the problem. Individual "prophets" were common. Just as World War II ground to a halt, Chaplain Jacob W. Beck, Presbyterian, boldly attacked the popular American practice of degrading Japanese and further reprimanded his nation for its attitudes toward blacks.

See footnotes at end of chapter.

Praising the willing sacrifice and the passion to minister to fellowmen in the name of Christ by both Japanese and blacks, Beck wrote that only when he had done the same, "then I shall consider myself their equals in the Faith. But, only when I can measure up to the stature of Jesus Christ, will I dare to presume I am in a position to judge the Negro and the Japanese—and then I shall be so near to the heart of my God and Savior that I will know better!" [3]

Six months later, Chaplain Charles E. Byrd, Baptist, accused the U.S. of "The World's Biggest Problem"—segregation and discrimination against blacks. The War, he insisted, had in no way been a struggle between the "holy" and the "unholy" but, if anything, between the "bad" and the "worse." "We are aware as never before," he wrote, reminding readers of the Nazi philosophy they had just fought, "that individual and social institutions stand under the judgment of the God of history whose judgment demands the disgarding of the doctrine of the 'master race' in any form." [4]

In July 1947 former Chaplain Ira Freeman, Southern Baptist, protested American unwillingness to accept veterans of all races with equal honor. "I Am Intolerant Toward Intolerance," he wrote, challenging his fellow veterans to set an example against discrimination in the country. [5]

Occasionally an individual chaplain not only proclaimed an anti-prejudice philosophy but also sought some practical resolution. Chaplain Melvin J. Friesen, Northern Baptist, wrote to the Army Chief of Staff in January 1947 and detailed what he called "intolerable conditions" for Philippine Scouts augmented into the U.S. Army. Friesen sent copies of his letter to the Chief of Chaplains and his congressman. Unfortunately, his single voice against the alleged wrongs resulted mostly in attacks on his personal effectiveness. "The writer's talent," countered Friesen's commanding general to the chaplain's complaint, "is better developed in the field of crusader than in the more prosaic field of hard work and encouragement of his men in meeting the actualities of life." [6]

Symbolic of these early individual protests is a single sentence found hidden in the minutes of the Tokyo-Yokohama chaplains' meeting for 11 December 1945:

> Chaplain Hall raised his voice to object to discrimination against Negro troops. [7]

See footnotes at end of chapter.

No explanatory or resultant discussion was recorded by the group's secretary. In much the same way, the single voices of chaplains against racial prejudice went by largely without notice, further comment, or practical result.

In one case from that period of history, however, involving a former Army chaplain, the issue of discrimination was recognized as a strategic opportunity for ministry. World War II chaplain-veteran Grant Reynolds, Congregational, while serving as a New York official, led a group of black civilians which was organized in 1947 as "The Committee Against Jim Crow in Military Service and Training." In retrospect, some historians have credited the committee with influencing President Truman to issue his executive order on 26 July 1948 for "equality of treatment and opportunity" in the Armed Forces.[8] Unfortunately, it took more than 3 years for the Department of the Army to completely respond by doing away with all-black units; General Ridgway gained authority to inactivate the last one (24th Regiment, 25th Infantry Division) on the battlefields of Korea in late 1951. Members of the unit, which had been established by law in 1866, were integrated like other blacks into a variety of formerly all-white organizatons.[9]

But problems of racial tension and discriminaton plagued the Army and the nation for many years to come. A few black chaplains, like John W. Handy, United Methodist, John A. DeVeaux, Sr., African Methodist, and Mitchell C. Johnson, United Church of Christ, managed to rise in rank and position. In many cases, however, it was neither their race nor their prestige but their compassionate, pastoral concern which led to better understanding. In 1951, for example, Chaplain Johnson stood on the hood of a jeep one night facing an angry mob of black soldiers who had commandeered tanks from the motor pool at Fort Polk, Louisiana. They were determined to take by force what had been denied them through discrimination both on and off post. Johnson "delivered an impromptu sermon directed at both offenders and offended," managed to avert what could have been a bloody confrontation, and opened the way for a command policy to "unlock" post facilities to all soldiers.[10]

Other Army chaplains were faced with U.S. racial turmoil in similarly vivid circumstances. Chaplain Chester R. Lindsey, American Baptist, for example, accompanied the 327th Airborne Infantry Battle Group, 101st Airborne Division, into Little Rock, Arkansas, in 1957 during the first confrontation over the integration of public schools. Although it took

---

See footnotes at end of chapter.

nearly 4 weeks, Chaplain Lindsey managed to establish rapport and friendship with local ministers and citizens of the city. More important, Lindsey and the many other chaplains with units quelling the 1950–1960 racial upheavals, became particularly aware of the need to face the moral aspects of the struggle and the needs for equality in the Army as well as the nation. Unfortunately, it was only after those nationally organized civil-rights' protests and violent racial riots of the 1960's that the Army began to make strides toward establishing better race relations.[11]

As late as March 1974, Chief of Chaplains Gerhardt W. Hyatt reminded the Army clerics, many of whom by then had received special training in race relations:

> . . . you and I are vital to the present effort and largely responsible for the days ahead. . . . We must do all that we can to reduce the claim which prejudice and racism have on the lives of the people we serve. . . . All human beings must be freed from those personal and institutional abuses which rob life of meaning and fulfillment. As clergymen, we are privileged to share in the humanization of organizations and in the process of social change that can only be achieved when people more perfectly understand the will of God.[12]

The tragedy is that chaplains had been told the same thing a quarter of a century earlier by the president of Howard University. Addressing a convention of the Military Chaplains' Association in 1950, he identified religion as the potential power to change American attitudes toward minorities. "The only people in America who can give that power," he had told the active duty, Reserve, and retired chaplains present, "are represented in this hall . . ."[13]

In an 1892 report to Congress the Secretary of War encouraged the establishment of a separate corps for chaplains. In rather odd sentence construction, he began: "The soul of an army is organization. Our chaplains have none."[14] From nearly a century's perspective, those strangely-combined sentences sound like a parody of the chaplaincy's later response to the racial issue.

Although Army chaplains became deeply involved in the struggle for better race relations beginning in the late 1960's, their influence might have been more effective had they recognized the problem of discrimination as a "strategic opportunity" for their ministry decades earlier. Fortunately, they were beginning to see the potential of consolidated efforts in other areas and gave added emphasis to the value of a unified approach to other aspects of their ministry.

See footnotes at end of chapter.

REVITALIZING CHAPEL ORGANIZATIONS

Religious denominations in the United States have historically provided some means of periodic fellowship and community service for their membership. Virtually every church body has at least one lay organization for that purpose. Translating that concept into a military community was not particularly difficult for Roman Catholic and Jewish chaplains who, for the most part, simply adopted civilian organizational guidelines for their military laity. The Roman Catholic "Holy Name Society," as an example, was well established on Army installations by the beginning of World War II.

But Protestant chaplains found the matter of organizing lay groups far more difficult. Organizations that were specifically denominational met with limited appeal or were, by their very nature, restrictive in their membership requirements. The civilian, interdenominational "Society of Christian Endeavor" was one of the few that had been introduced on military posts with broader appeal. Similarly, the "Young Men's Christian Association" (YMCA) had been sponsoring social programs for soldiers since the Civil War. For the most part, however, these organizations were outside groups offering services for the soldier. They provided little or no means whereby he could do things for himself or his military community.

The "Service Men's Christian League" (SMCL) of the 1940's was a first attempt to create an official Protestant lay organization comprised solely for the members of the U.S. military. Despite difficulties in drafting membership requirements that satisfied the vast range of Protestant convictions, the SMCL became an active and successful organization during World War II. Largely through the combined efforts of that organization and the General Commission on Army and Navy Chaplains, the popular military-oriented periodicals, *The Link* and *The Chaplain,* came into existence.[16]

Throughout the history of the U.S. Armed Forces, independent religious lay organizations have also sprouted in various areas. In some cases these groups have continued to this day. The originally British "Officers' Christian Union" (OCU), for example, organized its first group in the U.S. Army in 1943. By the end of World War II, OCU groups were established at the two U.S. military academies and shortly thereafter spread to other U.S. installations. The OCU was organized primarily to

See footnotes at end of chapter.

provide opportunities for informal Bible study and generally emphasized lay support of chaplains wherever possible. In recent years the OCU was reorganized and titled the "Officers' Christian Fellowship." Similar organizations, like the "Christian Servicemen's Fellowship," the "Navigators," the "Protestant Religious Education Services, Inc.," and the "Overseas Christian Servicemen's Centers" have contributed immeasurably to the spiritual growth of lay people in the military.[16]

Enthusiasm for the chaplain-sponsored SMCL began to wane with its decrease in membership following World War II. A 1949 editorial in *The Chaplain* attempted to renew interest in the group by reporting that some chaplains were using its programs to combat delinquency and vandalism among teenage dependents.[17] It was obvious, however, that a revitalization was needed to make the organization appealing to the young men and women just entering the Army. Consequently, 3 months before the outbreak of the Korean War, the General Commission, together with representative Army, Navy, and Air Force chaplains, began revamping the SMCL. The end result, which was to concentrate on the aspect of fellowship and a Christian use of leisure time, was called the "United Fellowship of Protestants in the Armed Forces." [18] Despite the supposed revamping, however, it is hard to recognize any significant difference between the United Fellowship and the former SMCL. Undoubtedly because the Korean War diverted the attention of the military from garrison life to the battlefield again, little impetus could be given to something designed for the occupation of the soldier's "leisure time."

Following the Korean War, a new attempt at Protestant lay organizations developed among servicemen and their dependents with the U.S. Army, Europe (USAREUR). Originally the movement had no connection with any pre-established group nor was it influenced by civilian organizations trying to be supportive to military communities. Rather, it was a simple case of military congregations forming their own local lay groups for social gatherings, Bible study, or chapel projects. In January 1952, for example, wives of servicemen assigned to the 16th Field Hospital in Germany formed a group called "The Women's Guild." It could be likened to any civilian "ladies aid" group so common in the United States. In the fall of that same year, the American women in Nuremberg organized a similar group and chose the name, "Protestant Women of the Chapel." [19] In a few cases, groups were formed through the combined efforts of members of different faiths. In Ansbach, for instance, Protestant

See footnotes at end of chapter.

and Jewish dependents joined together in an "Association of Church Women." [20] In much the same way, the men and youth formed similar groups that were totally autonomous and had little or no connection with the United Fellowship of Protestants, any civilian church group, or, for that matter, with any neighboring chapel groups.

Chaplain John I. Rhea, Presbyterian U.S., serving as a division chaplain in USAREUR, and Colonel Powell Fraser, a protestant layman assigned to Headquarters, USAREUR, seemed to be the first to recognize the potential for uniting these groups in a European-wide organization.[21] By 1954 the USAREUR Staff Chaplain, Edwin L. Kirtley, Disciples of Christ, agreed that such a strategic opportunity was available. Consequently, he gave official direction for the unification plans. Members of Kirtley's staff set out to establish guidelines for garrison and family-oriented groups by gleaning suggestions from the goals and purposes of those already in existence. Kirtley further encouraged all Protestant chaplains in Europe to establish similar groups but asked them to adopt unified goals to provide inter-chapel fellowship under common names: "Protestant Men of the Chapel" (PMOC), "Protestant Women of the Chapel" (PWOC), and "Protestant Youth of the Chapel" (PYOC). Chaplain Kirtley arranged conferences for representatives of the local groups and through them European councils and local area councils, following the lines of Army-area commands, were elected. Within a short time, a complete network of these common organizations tied together Army chapel congregations throughout the entire European command.[22]

The Protestant Personnel of the Chapel movement influenced the initiation of similar, although less-organized, lay groups among the USAREUR Catholic and Jewish personnel. Within a matter of a few years, it spread to Protestant chapels in the continental U.S. By 1959 the movement began to receive guidance and encouragement from the OCCH and during the next 4 years coordinated efforts with similar groups in the Navy and the Air Force.[23] During the following decade, the lay-initiated movement matured into three vitally active and effective lay organizations, providing men, women, and youth with religious fellowship and social activities, as well as opportunities for meaningful service projects. Perhaps more important, they built a unity within the religious congregations on U.S. military posts and provided a common bond among the laity throughout the United States Armed Forces.

See footnotes at end of chapter.

ATTEMPTING TO UNIFY RELIGIOUS EDUCATION

Following World War II, the increase of families on military installations also brought attention to the field of religious education. Dependent children of servicemen flocked to Sunday and Sabbath schools wherever they were organized, usually outnumbering adult attendance at worship services. By 1954 an estimated 85,000 Army, Navy, and Air Force children were enrolled in chaplain-organized Protestant Sunday schools alone. Like the original lay organizations in Europe, however, the schools were completely independent using curriculum materials chosen at the discretion of the particular chaplain assigned and purchased through the local, non-appropriated chaplains' fund. Since the children of servicemen moved so often, there was no continuity to their religious training. In some cases they heard the same lesson over and over again. "I haven't anything against Moses," commented the young son of a sergeant, "but there must be someone else in the Bible for me to learn about." [24]

Several chaplains had suggested the need for some kind of unified curriculum in the religious schools, but the Chief of Air Force Chaplains, Charles I. Carpenter, was the first to foster the idea as a strategic opportunity. Early in 1952, Carpenter discussed the idea with representatives of the National Council of Churches and the Protestant Church-Owned Publishers' Association. They decided that if such a program were adopted it should include the Army and the Navy as well. Consequently, Protestant chaplain representatives of the three services held an exploratory conference on the subject at Buck Hill Falls, Pennsylvania, in March 1952. They agreed that a unified curriculum was the answer to providing a continuing program of religious instruction for the mobile military dependent and that the courses could be established around three common and basic themes—the Bible, the Church, and the life of Christ.

Chaplain Carpenter carried the suggestion to the Armed Forces Chaplains Board. The Board "bought" the plan and appointed a Religious Education Committee—representative chaplains from the three services and a spokesman from the Protestant Church-Owned Publishers—to work out the details. Chaplain Wayne L. Hunter, Presbyterian U.S., former Deputy Commandant at the Chaplain School, was the first Army representative on the committee. The committee agreed on a basic curriculum by the fall of 1953. Although the materials were to come

---

See footnotes at end of chapter.

from various denominations, the Publishers' Association agreed to underwrite the project and to provide a central office for ordering in Nashville, Tennessee. The "Unified Protestant Sunday School Curriculum for Armed Forces" was announced in the field by the end of that year. The following spring the Navy produced and distributed a training film for all the services to teach chaplains and Sunday school teachers how to use the material.[25]

Meanwhile, attempts to establish unified curricula for Catholic and Jewish dependents were also being made. Chaplain Clarence D. White, Roman Catholic, was directed to develop a coordinated program for Catholic dependents in the USAREUR area. White conducted an experimental program of his first development in late 1952 and revamped the curriculum with the suggestions that resulted. His final product was a 3-year series called "The Way, The Truth, The Life." In April 1953 he secured the approval and blessing of Pope Pius XII for his course and by the following year the Armed Forces Chaplains Board obtained the Roman Catholic Military Ordinariate's approval to introduce a similar series throughout the U.S. military. Further revisions resulted in the "Catholic Family Program of Religious Instruction." [26]

While the Armed Forces Chaplains Board was working on the Protestant curriculum, it sent a request to the National Jewish Welfare Board to devise a similar system for Jewish education. The "Religious School Curriculum for Jews in the Armed Forces" was eventually produced to serve the needs of Orthodox, Reformed, and Conservative members of the military forces and their dependents.[27] Jewish guidelines point out, as do the programs for the other faiths, that "periodic revisions are made to keep the curriculum current and updated." [28]

Religious education in the Army received another boost with the approval for the employment of full-time civilian Directors of Religious Education (DRE's). In 1948 the chaplains' section at Fort Bragg, North Carolina, employed Miss Bryan Johnson, a graduate of the Assembly Training School in Richmond with a degree in religious education. The subsequent employment of DRE's at many stateside and overseas installations freed many chaplains from the administrative details of religious schools and added further quality to both on-post and inter-post religious activities.[29]

The enrollment figures from Sunday and Sabbath schools on Army posts throughout the world gave a picture of the tremendous

See footnotes at end of chapter.

opportunities for religious education within the military. In 1955 Chaplain Matthew D. Blair, Methodist, reported that the combined attendance of children and adults in the religious schools at the Grant Heights Chapel in Tokyo was 1,250. By 1960 the OCCH knew of at least eight Sunday schools in the continental United States with enrollments of over 1,000. Fort Benning, Georgia, reported 2,090 in attendance.[30] In some cases, the special circumstances on Army posts offered challenges beyond the imagination of most civilian clergymen. The yearly rotation of officers and their families at the Command and General Staff College, Fort Leavenworth, Kansas, for example, required the repeated, annual recruitment of 100 to 150 new volunteer Sunday school teachers. Despite this taxing transition, Chaplain Theodore V. Koepke, Missouri Synod Lutheran, serving on the post from 1959 to 1964, reported that the weekly attendance in the Sunday school averaged 1,400. Divided into two sessions and held at three different locations, the school often involved the simultaneous work of four colonels serving as voluntary superintendents.[31]

Although the unified-curriculum approach, which has continued in the Armed Forces to the present day, did help to eliminate the problems caused by the lack of continuity, it also generated some controversy. Protestant chaplains and volunteer teachers associated with theologically fundamental or conservative denominations began to charge that materials in the Unified Curriculum were insufficiently based on Scripture and contained liberal interpretations of the Bible. As a consequence, Sunday schools under their leadership continued to use specially ordered materials either in place of or supplemental to the Curriculum literature. The OCCH saw this as detrimental to the theory of the unified approach and strongly encouraged all Protestant chaplains to use only the Curriculum materials. It further directed that written explanations had to be submitted whenever previous orders for the Unified Curriculum were cancelled. Although it explained that such reports would be used as suggestions for making the literature more acceptable, many chaplains in the field interpreted the directive as having made the Unified Curriculum mandatory.[32]

"The volume of criticism of the Unified Curriculum increased markedly over previous fiscal years," noted the OCCH's *Summary of Major Events and Problems* for the 1960 fiscal year. "This is probably accounted for, at least in large part, by the increasing number of using Sunday schools, the aggressive promotion of the Unified Curriculum by

See footnotes at end of chapter.

chaplains at every level, and the explicit solicitation of criticism by the Chief of Chaplains." [33]

Attempting to assuage the criticism from many chaplains that the Curriculum materials were too expensive for local non-appropriated chaplains' funds, the OCCH assumed the financing of the program. The theological problems, however, continued to arise. By 1963 the Chief of Chaplains received a complaint from Lieutenant General William K. Harrison, USA retired, in his capacity as President of the Officers' Christian Union. He questioned "what appears to be the effort of the chiefs of military chaplains to exercise ecclesiastical authority over all chaplains of the different Protestant denominations in matters essentially theological" and referred to "regulations making mandatory" the use of Sunday school material chosen by the chiefs. The Chief of Chaplains quickly replied that no Army regulations or directives enforced the use of the Curriculum and that no chaplain or teacher risked punishment, coercion, or intimidation for refusing to do so. While the Chief pointed out the theory behind the unified approach, he also emphasized that dependents voluntarily attended Protestant "general-type" Sunday schools and that nothing prohibited the establishment of denominational schools wherever the need existed.[34]

By mid-1964 the National Association of Evangelicals, an organization of conservative Protestants, charged that chaplains were being requested to use Sunday school literature that contained "heresy." Registering their complaint with the Secretary of Defense, they objected to certain Unified Curriculum materials which distinguished between "legendary" and "historical" accounts in the Bible. Again the OCCH defended its position by maintaining that no chaplain was compelled to use the material and that no serviceman or dependent was forced to attend the schools.[35]

Occasionally the indiscreet enthusiasm of an individual chaplain for the Protestant Unified Curriculum added fuel to the controversy. One chaplain stationed in Germany in 1965, for instance, insisted on using the material even though two-thirds of his volunteer teaching staff opposed it. The dissenting teachers resigned and one complained directly to the President of the United States. That single incident resulted in the OCCH having to prepare a lengthy report on the history of the Curriculum and to emphasize once more the lack of any official mandate to use the material.[36]

See footnotes at end of chapter.

Despite these difficulties, the unified approach to religious education in the Army survived and has continued to this day. Further support of the program was made through the establishment of religious education libraries and the regular publication of the *Religious Education and Audio Visual Journal* to provide resource materials. While the two decades of work in the area emphasized the difficulty in uniting the efforts of Army chaplains, they also helped to build a mutual understanding and appreciation of their different views and produce an ecumenicity generally unparalleled in civilian communities. Over the years the boards and committees responsible for securing Protestant materials have labored to incorporate suggestions from the complaints and constructive criticisms of those in the field in order to provide a curriculum acceptable to more than 30 major religious denominations.[37]

ESTABLISHING PROGRAMS FOR RELIGIOUS RETREATS

To members of a military organization the word "retreat" bears the unsavory connotation of fleeing the enemy. At best, it refers to an evening ceremony for lowering the national colors. Because of the influence of Army chaplains, however, U.S. soldiers came to know and regularly use the term according to an alternate definition: "a period of group withdrawal for prayer, meditation, study, and instruction under a director." [38]

The value of religious retreats for chaplains was well established by the end of World War II. Within 2 months of the German surrender, 1-day conference retreats for the battle-weary clergymen were held in Italy, France, and England.[39] Former Chief of Chaplains William R. Arnold convinced the War Department to allow as many European-based chaplains as possible to visit Palestine before returning home. On 24 July 1945 the first party of 20 arrived in the Holy Land for the rare privilege of visiting the biblically historical sites.[40] By 1949 arrangements had been made for groups of civilian clergymen to conduct conferences and devotional exercises for U.S. Armed Forces' chaplains in both the Far East and European Commands. The retreats were arranged to acquaint the military clergy with the latest theological books and ecclesiastical trends in the United States.[41]

But the concept of a period of "withdrawal for prayer, meditation, study, and instruction" was not restricted to chaplains. For some time they had individually planned locally sponsored religious-emphasis days for the personnel in their own units. In the early 1950's so-called "preaching missions," utilizing notable civilian speakers, became popular on military posts. Usually organized to offer an entire week of religious meetings and worship services for troops on scores of installations, they were often inaugurated with great fanfare and publicity. At the initiation of one of these missions, planned for 82 Army and Navy centers in 1951, President Truman sent a special message of encouragement:

> As we build up our military strength to secure the free world
> from aggression, we must be equally diligent to strengthen the moral
> and spiritual life of our armed forces.[42]

Since the very concept of a religious retreat involves the aspect of withdrawal, the ideal situation requires a special place set apart from familiar surroundings. USAREUR Staff Chaplain Edwin L. Kirtley, who had directed the birth of the Protestant Personnel of the Chapel movement, recognized another strategic opportunity—the provision for a special retreat facility for American soldiers in Europe. He was aware of programs sponsored by the British and Dutch forces in Germany and especially admired the British soldiers' retreat house near Hannover. When Chief of Chaplains Ivan Bennett visited the European Command in 1953, Kirtley took him to visit the British facility. Shortly thereafter the USAREUR Chaplain received command approval to establish a similar center for U.S. troops. After surveying the available hotels under American control, Chaplain Kirtley chose the facilities in the magnificent Bavarian Alps near the picturesque village of Berchtesgaden.[43]

Interestingly, Berchtesgaden had been chosen hundreds of years earlier as the development site for a priory of the Augustinian monks. For Americans and Europeans, however, the name evoked memories of the infamous "Third Reich" because of its specially-constructed sanctuaries for its leader, Adolf Hitler. Uniquely, the first American flag to fly over the former Nazi refuge belonged to a U.S. Army chaplain. Chaplain William J. Reiss, Missouri Synod Lutheran, had used the flag in war-time burial ceremonies for U.S. soldiers. It was the only one available when the 101st Airborne Division rushed to the village at the end of the War in hopes of capturing Hitler. Although the "Fuhrer" was not to be found in his sanctuary, two of his leading commanders, Goering and von Keitel, were. Chaplain Reiss, in fact, served as the interpreter as General Maxwell Taylor received Herman Goering's

See footnotes at end of chapter.

surrender at Berchtesgaden. Today Chaplain Reiss' flag holds a place of honor in the 101st Airborne Division's Museum at Fort Campbell, Kentucky.[44]

General Orders No. 66, Headquarters, USAREUR, dated 17 March 1954, established the American Religious Retreat Center in Berchtesgaden effective 1 June 1954. At 1100 hours on 6 July the retreat facilities were officially dedicated on the site of a former rest hotel for the Nazi Air Force. Chaplains of the three major faiths participated in the ceremony which marked the first time such a project had been officially sponsored by the U.S. Army. By December of the same year a Retreat House Chapel, constructed in accordance with the prevailing Bavarian architecture, was also dedicated. Symbolically, a large cross stands on a 6,000-foot summit overlooking the entire scene. It was erected triumphantly beside the famous "Eagle's Nest"—Adolph Hitler's former Tea House.[45]

The Berchtesgaden Rereat Center was eventually equipped to accommodate several hundred participants at a single retreat and quickly became the popular gathering spot for virtually every major military religious gathering in Europe. PWOC, PMOC, and PYOC groups made it their convention center, Sunday school teachers gathered there for training and inspiration, and denominational leaders used it for their special convocations. But most important, Army chaplains scheduled year-round retreats for Protestant, Catholic, and Jewish servicemen. Within 10 years of its dedication, the Center had been used by 100,000 U.S. Armed Forces' personnel and their dependents.[46] In its continued existence for over 2 decades it has undoubtedly proven to be one of the most valuable and popular developments by the Army Chaplaincy. Chaplains who have had the opportunity to serve at the Center often reflect on that assignment with such phrases as, "my key ministry," and "the most satisfying and rewarding [period] in my entire ministry." [47]

When John A. Dunn, Roman Catholic, Staff Chaplain of the U.S. Army Forces Far East, visited Germany in 1954, he was so impressed by the new retreat center at Berchtesgaden that he sought approval from the Chief of Chaplains to establish a similar center in Japan. With the "blessing" of the Chief, command approval was obtained near the end of the year. A former Japanese resort, the Sorakaku Hotel on Sagami Bay in Oiso, was chosen for the Far East facility. It was appropriately named "The Kapaun Religious Retreat House" after the Korean War hero, Emil J. Kapaun. Its unofficial name, however, was *"Chokumahan Chonkuk"* ("Little Heaven"). Chaplain Loren T. Jenks, Disciples of Christ, commented: "Only those who have lived in the conditions of Korea can fully appreciate why it seems like 'Little Heaven' . . ." [48]

The Japan retreat center was established by General Orders No. 456, Headquarters, Army Forces Far East, on 22 November 1954, and the first group of servicemen entered the facility the following month. Shortly after its dedication, the Eighth Army Religious Retreat Center was opened on Nam San Mountain in Seoul, Korea, and has continued in operation to this day. Although smaller than the center at Berchtesgaden, both the Kapaun Retreat House and the Eighth Army Retreat House remained as active in drawing religious gatherings as the European center. Because of the reduction of U.S. forces in Japan, the Japanese facility was closed in November 1957. [49]

The concept of setting aside times for religious meditation and study has remained in the U.S. Army to the present day. Thousands of soldiers on U.S. installations and abroad have voluntarily participated in a variety of such programs under the individual or combined guidance of hundreds of Army chaplains. Ranging from a simple "Duty Day With God," to which only the men of a company-sized unit might be invited, to a massive, post-wide "Moral and Religious Training Day," the retreats have been praised as invaluable assets to the religious lives of American soldiers. Similarly, special retreat facilities, either officially established by the Army or temporarily used through the generosity of a loaning civilian organization, are regularly occupied whenever offered. As late as 1971, a religious reatreat center was briefly established in the battle-torn Republic of Vietnam at Cam Ranh Bay to allow American servicemen a place for rest and religious reflection even in the midst of war. Nearly every venture in the area of religious retreats has proven to be beneficial and, in a way, provided a *Chokumahan Chonkuk*, "Little Heaven," to many of the participants. [50]

ENHANCING CHAPLAIN TRAINING

The reestablishment of the Army War College at the outbreak of the Korean War resulted in another move for the Chaplain School. Since Carlisle Barracks was chosen for the home of the War College, the Army and Air Force Chaplain School was forced to relocate. While under the supervision of Chaplain Joseph R. Koch, Roman Catholic, who had succeeded Arthur C. Piepkorn as Commandant in October 1950, the Chaplain School moved to its twelfth new home, Fort Slocum, New York,

See footnotes at end of chapter.

in April 1951. Koch referred to the move as "the first step toward making Fort Slocum the West Point of the Chaplain Corps." [51]

The history of Fort Slocum, located on an island off New Rochelle, dated back to the Civil War. During World War II it had been used as a prison, but in October 1949 it was placed in "moth balls." Once again the historic post was to become vibrant with the heavy Korean War-time training schedule of the Chaplain School and its co-inhabitant, the Armed Forces Information School.[52] A 1951 editorial in the *New York Times* welcomed the announcement of the planned move with special praise:

> When a need arises a chaplain doesn't ask what a man's belief is; he asks what help he can give him. It is this common duty that draws them together and it is the resulting spirit of brotherhood that makes the Army and the Air Force chaplain school . . . an inspiring place. . . .
> It is pleasant to know that the school will be moved to Fort Slocum a few weeks hence—a good and not-so-far-away neighbor.[53]

Chaplain Koch was convinced that Fort Slocum offered the best facilities the School had had in its 33 years of existence. "We like to think of the Chaplain School as a reservoir of spiritual and moral values for the Army and for the Air Force," he said.[54] Concurrent with the anti-Communist mood of the day, the initial Slocum curriculum included lectures on the religious development, philosophy, and literature of the Soviet Union.[55]

Within a year of the Air Force's departure from the School in 1953, the first volunteers under the seminarian training program—originally developed to meet the demands of the Korean War—began to arrive at Fort Slocum. Donald E. Ausland, a student at Luther Theological Seminary, St. Paul, Minnesota, was the first to become a Reserve second lieutenant assigned to the Chaplains' Branch, "Staff Specialist." He was commissioned on 13 August 1953 under the special regulation allowing such appointments which went into effect in April of that year.[56]

Chaplain Luther W. Evans, United Lutheran, succeeded Chaplain Koch as Commandant in April 1954. Evans, in turn, was followed by Chaplain Edward T. Donahue, Baptist, in August 1955, and Chaplain James T. Wilson, Methodist, in March 1957. During this period the Chaplain School faculty produced the first fully integrated program of instruction. meshing many of the smaller subject areas into departments with coordinated teaching plans. Courses on subjects like Military Intelligence, Transportation, Medical Service, Command and Staff Organization, Functions and Procedures, etc., were dovetailed with courses on the staff duties of chaplains. As a consqeuence, students were not only introduced to the intricacies of the service but also taught the relationship of their future duties to the sometimes-baffling maze of military organization.[57]

It was during the 1950's that the Chaplain School also gave its first concerted attention to the history of the Army Chaplaincy. The official U.S. Army Chaplain Museum was established at Fort Slocum on 14 August 1957 and formally dedicated by the Chief of Chaplains on 10 February 1958. Since that time, the Museum's directors have attempted to develop it into a display area for chaplain memorabilia dating back to the American Revolution as well as a repository of chaplain related historical documents for the benefit of researchers. Chaplain Parker C. Thompson, Southern Baptist, who served as the Museum's director while also heading the School's Non-resident Department in the late 1960's, contributed much of his personal time and resources to make the Museum an interesting and useful facility. He was followed in 1972 by Chaplain Wayne C. King, Southern Baptist, the Museum's first full-time director.[58]

During the mid-1950's there were three levels of training offered at the School—the Basic Course, the Company Grade Course, and the Advanced Course. Students on each of the levels attended the courses on a temporary-duty basis since none of the courses exceeded a 3-month period. But the Department of the Army's Education and Training Review Board issued a study in 1958, known as the "Williams Board Report," which recommended the establishment of a "career course" at all service schools, including the Chaplain School. The career-course idea called for a detailed program of study for advanced students offered over a 9-month period.

The Williams Board Report resulted in several years of extensive planning by the Chaplains' Branch. The general mood in the leadership of the Chaplaincy favored the idea and it was recognized, for the most part, as another strategic opportunity—enhancing the training of Army chaplains. Since such an extended course would require a permanent change of station (PCS) for each of the students involved, it necessitated complicated planning in personnel management. The most practical

_____
See footnotes at end of chapter.

deterrent to the plan was the lack of adequate quarters on or near Fort Slocum to accommodate PCS students and their families.[59]

Chaplain Wayne L. Hunter, Presbyterian U.S., who followed Chaplain Wilson as Commandant in June 1959, was involved in much of the struggle with that problem. Tentative plans for a career course to replace the Advanced Course were approved and the Company Grade Course was eliminated. While much of this work was going on, Chaplain Hunter tragically died of a heart attack in September 1960. He was eventually replaced by Chaplain Charles E. Brown, Jr., Methodist, in December of that year. Shortly after Brown's succession as Commandant, a decision by the Department of the Army eliminated the biggest barrier to the establishment of the chaplain career course—the School would be moved again, but to a larger post with available housing. Fort Hamilton in Brooklyn, on the southwestern tip of Long Island, was to become the thirteenth home for the U.S. Army Chaplain School.[60]

Just as preparations for the move from Slocum to Hamilton were being made, President Kennedy announced his nomination of Chaplain Brown as the next Chief of Army Chaplains. Brown, who had also organized and served as the first President of the Army Chaplain Board and been the first chaplain to graduate from the Army War College, assumed the position as Chief of Chaplains on 1 November 1962. Only a few days before, the Chaplain School had completed its move to Fort Hamilton under the direction of Brown's successor as Commandant, Chaplain Gregory R. Kennedy, Roman Catholic.[61]

The move to Fort Hamilton was termed "a wondrously appropriate one" by a Brooklyn official who pointed out that the city was known as "the borough of churches." [62] The General Commission on Chaplains and Armed Forces Personnel agreed and added that "the School has a magnificent location with excellent facilities."[63] Fort Hamilton did allow the Chaplain School to expand its activities. Not only did the Career Course become a reality with the first PCS class graduating in 1963, but nonresident training through correspondence courses also expanded to give Reserve and National Guard chaplains more current instruction. Successive Commandants following Chaplain Kennedy were: Ralph H. Pugh, American Baptist (February–July 1965); William J. Reiss, Missouri Synod Lutheran (July 1965–January 1967); Edward J. Saunders, Roman Catholic (February–October 1967); Theodore V. Koepke, Missouri Synod Lutheran (October 1967–January 1971); William V. O'Connor, Roman Catholic (February–July 1971); Chester R. Lindsey,

See footnotes at end of chapter.

American Baptist (August 1971–March 1975); and John J. Murphy, Roman Catholic (since March 1975).[64]

Throughout the last 10 years, the Chaplain School continued to modernize its facilities and update its curriculum for the 9-week Basic and 9-month Career Courses. It also initiated a new resident training program for National Guardsmen and Reservists, greatly expanded its training for chaplain enlisted assistants, and opened a 2-week course for senior chaplains called the "Chaplain Field Grade Officer Refresher Course." While Chaplains O'Connor and Lindsey served as Commandants, a modified "Indiana Plan," using a small-group method of instruction, was planned and first used in 1971. The Career Class which entered the School that year was also the first to receive concurrent instruction from Long Island University for master's degrees in either guidance and counseling or sociology. By then the School had grown to include a staff and faculty of 45 chaplains, 8 officers from other branches, and scores of civilian and enlisted instructors and administrative-support personnel.[65]

Within 3 years of the School's move to Fort Hamilton, staff personnel at Continental Army Command were recommending that the institution move again. They suggested that, rather than spending money trying to revamp old facilities into classrooms, a permanent installation be built at some other site. But the Chief of Chaplains in 1967 declared himself "firmly committed" to the continued location of the School at Hamilton because of its central location in an area with many educational opportunities. After 12 years at Fort Hamilton, however—the longest time it had remained at one place since 1918—the School took on further responsibilities, was renamed the "United States Army Chaplain Center and School," and moved again (September 1974) to Fort Wadsworth on Staten Island, New York.[66]

Over the years the Chaplain School has been referred to informally as "The Home of the Chaplaincy." Because of its constant movement, some chaplains have jested that their "home" ought to be equipped with wheels. Despite its mobility, however, the Chaplain School continued to expand and improve its training program with every change in physical scenery.

DEVELOPING SPECIALIZED SKILLS

Since World War II, training for chaplains has not been restricted to the courses offered at the Chaplain School. Especially in the years

---

See footnotes at end of chapter.

following the Korean War, the OCCH arranged for specialized education for many chaplains in a diversity of subjects including, among others,
religious education, journalism, communication skills, the use of mass
media, and financial management. Similarly, as administrative demands
increased, more chaplains attended various military schools to build the
branch's efficiency in a technological army.

It is impossible to list the variety of educational opportunities given
to select chaplains over the past 20 years, but examples can be found to
demonstrate both the diversity and the extent of that training. Chaplain
William V. O'Connor, Roman Catholic, a scholar in his own right
through the private pursuit of education, not only became an expert
mountain climber and Master Parachutist through Army training, but
also a scholar in Russian language and area studies through an Army-
sponsored program at Fordham University. An example of the most
prodigious training in a single field for one chaplain, however, is found
in the career of Chaplain Clifford E. Keys, Nazarene. A *cum laude* and
magna cum laude graduate from junior college and seminary, Keys attended the Command and General Staff School, the Army Finance
School, the Army Management School, the Army Signal School, the
Army Management Engineering and Training Agency, the U.S. Navy
Post-graduate School, and the Industrial College of the Armed Forces.
In addition he received a Master of Science degree in Business Administration through George Washington University and attended the graduate schools in Business Administration of the University of Michigan
and the University of California in Los Angeles.[67]

Specialized training for Army chaplains, however, has received more
attention during the past decade in the area of counseling than in any
other field. "Every experienced chaplain knows," wrote Roy Honeywell
in his brief history of the chaplaincy, "that some of his most important
duties are not religious or but incidentally so. These may relate to virtually any matter of importance to a soldier or his family and may range
from considerations of life or death to those which are ridiculously
trivial." [68]

The role of the chaplain as a counselor was readily accepted by the
end of World War II. A 1947 article in the *American Journal for Sociology* praised chaplains for having "contributed markedly to the mental
health of their troops" and referred to them as "safety valves to many

---

See footnotes at end of chapter.

soldiers." [69] A training film for recruits in 1949—"From Whence Cometh My Help"—virtually advertized the chaplains' availability as counselors. [70]

Undoubtedly the strategic opportunity for chaplains to increase their skills for ministry through counseling was first recognized by those assigned to medical commands. As early as 1947 hospital chaplains were meeting in regular conferences with doctors, nurses, and welfare officers to learn better techniques in their dealings with patients. [71] Many of them pursued a continuing education at their own expense and used that knowledge, combined with their daily work, to become particularly proficient in dealing with psychological and emotional problems. As they moved on to new assignments, their enthusiasm for better counseling spread to other chaplains who followed their example in enhancing their skills.

When asked to note the most significant events of his military ministry, Chaplain John W. Betzold, Orthodox Presbyterian, listed: "The value of human feelings of warmth, understanding and patience in dealing with a serviceman and his problem(s)." He continued by explaining:

> I often felt positive results were achieved by the serviceman when he had a sympathetic ear to pour his troubles into—for the ear was often a throughway to two hearts. My training and theological stance were not compatible with the sort of non-judgmental approach I have described. However, this rationale—of hearing a person out and then assisting him in the healing process—works for the good of both parties and is basic to the application of the healing balm of the Gospel. Over the years, this method of separating the man from his problem, or loving the·man and not his problem ("sin?") and making him see the value of becoming responsible for himself and his acts—really works. I have seen its value in family as well as individual situations. How else does the love of God go from my heart and mind to another? [72]

While serving on the staff of the Surgeon General from 1963 to 1970, Chaplain Betzold was instrumental in the introduction and establishment of Clinical Pastoral Education (CPE) for Army chaplains. Started first as a 1-year course at Walter Reed Army Medical Center, CPE training spread to other Army hospitals and eventually was offered through civilian institutions and agencies. More important, the development of counseling skills moved beyond the hospital setting to virtually every aspect of the chaplain's ministry. During most recent years, scores of chaplains have been trained to deal more effectively with emotional distress, marriage and family problems, human relations, and drug and alcohol abuse. [73]

See footnotes at end of chapter.

ACCEPTING THE CHALLENGES WITH THE GUIDON

Chief of Chaplains Ivan L. Bennett retired from the Army on 30 April 1954 to become a field secretary for the American Bible Society and the Executive Secretary for the Washington City Bible Society. It was an appropriate post for a man with over 30 years of experience in ministering to soldiers. Within 1 year of its founding in 1817, the American Bible Society has continued to this day in offering free Scriptures to servicemen via chaplains. Its old record for distribution of nearly 3 million Bibles, Testaments, and Scripture-portions during World War II was surmounted during the war in Vietnam. In 1970 alone, chaplains asked for and freely received an incredible 4,272,596 copies. Much of that latter distribution was supervised by another retired Army chaplain, Steve P. Gaskins, Jr., United Methodist.[74]

President Eisenhower nominated Patrick J. Ryan, Roman Catholic, to be Chief of Chaplains as Bennett's successor. The nomination was approved by Congress and Ryan assumed the two-star post on 1 May 1954. Ryan had been an Army chaplain since 1928 and served as the 3rd Infantry Division Chaplain in North Africa and the Fifth Army Chaplain in Italy during World War II. He was the first Roman Catholic to serve as Chief of Chaplains since William Arnold's retirement in 1945 and only the second Catholic-appointee since the establishment of the office in 1920. Even more unique, Ryan was the only man in history who served as Deputy Chief of Chaplains on two separate tours (April 1946–July 1948; August 1952–April 1954).[75]

Patrick Ryan inherited the leadership of the Army chaplaincy at a time of change, both in the military ministry and the military itself. During his service as Chief of Chaplains, chapel organizations, unified curricula for religious schools, and the retreat house programs matured into established practices for the chaplaincy. Serving under Secretaries of the Army Robert Stevens and Wilbur Brucker, and Chiefs of Staff Matthew Ridgway and Maxwell Taylor, Ryan led the chaplains in a steady pace to keep current with an organization that changed its trends along with its uniform. Passed into history with the "brown-shoe Army" was the old chaplains' tendency toward an isolated ministry. One chaplain of the day maintained that Ryan had achieved "the best approach to an all-around religious program we've ever had in the Army." [76] Even Ryan believed that "the Army's religious program today is in a stronger position

---

See footnotes at end of chapter.

than at any time I can remember in my twenty-eight years of service." [77]
Much of that had come about because of his singular philosophy:

> The chaplain is not some effete busybody or do-gooder; nor is he
> a religious recluse who lives in an ivory tower. He is a virile, fully
> trained specialist who has a vital mission to perform and who, given
> the opportunity to perform his work with command support, will be
> a valuable member of the military team.[78]

Chaplain Ryan, who was appointed a Prothonotary Apostolic by
Pope Pius XII, retired from active duty on 31 October 1958 and became
Executive Vice President of the *Catholic Digest*. He was succeeded as
Chief of Chaplains by Frank A. Tobey, American Baptist. Chaplain
Tobey exemplified the careers of many chaplains whose background
included assignments as enlisted men and line officers in the Army before
entering the ministry. Tobey's military experience began as a private in
the Massachusetts National Guard in 1922. After advancing to an NCO,
he was commissioned a second lieutenant, but his desire to serve as a
Christian minister as well as a soldier led to his seminary training and
eventual appointment as a chaplain in 1940. In 1941 he was called to
active duty with the National Guard's 43rd Infantry Division, later transferred, and served throughout the rest of the War in the Southwest
Pacific. After his assignments as X Corps and Eighth Army Chaplains
during the Korean War, he held several other leadership roles, including
Deputy Chief of Chaplains from July 1954 to October 1958.[79]

Tobey was a chaplain who made little pretense about his position
regardless of his rank. When first informed by the Secretary of the Army
of his nomination as Chief of Chaplains and asked, "Do you feel that you
can do the job?" he swallowed deeply and replied, "I shall do my best." [80]
He later wrote: "To me it was an unexpected honor and privilege especially as I had served in the Regular Army for only eleven years." [81]

Chaplain Tobey held a passionate concern for the religious faith of
the American soldier. During the Korean War, he insisted on setting up
an altar in an apple orchard at Panmunjom one Sunday despite being
told that few soldiers were in the area because of the resumption of the
peace talks. As he welcomed the roughly 10 men who came to worship,
he was surprised to see among them General Matthew Ridgway, then Far
East Commander. While chatting with the chaplain after the service,
Ridgway told Tobey that his Scripture reading had been studied by the
general and his wife in Tokyo that very morning. "The thing that impressed me," commented Tobey, "was that Ridgway, hard-bitten fighting

See footnotes at end of chapter.

soldier that he was, had daily devotions with his wife at home." [82] Tobey's decision to hold the service in the first place was probably influenced by memories of World War II. His most cherished recollection was of a nighttime Communion service in a malaria-infested area of Milne Bay, New Guinea, in 1943:

> At least two hundred men came forward out of the jungle night, knelt down on the damp ground, within that small circle of light to receive the elements of Communion—black men, white men, enlisted men, non-coms, and officers. Many were deeply moved as was I—their eyes glistened with tears. It mattered not that the ground was wet, that the bread was leavened, and that the juice was from stewed prunes—for they communed with their Saviour, they experienced the cleansing power of His cross and prepared to meet their God. This experience I will never forget nor did many of them for whom it was "the *last* supper." [83]

Continuing many of the programs established before him, Chief of Chaplains Frank Tobey saw the completion and publication of the new *Armed Forces Hymnal* in March 1959—a revision project of *The Hymnal: Army and Navy* which had taken 7 years to complete.[84] It was also during his tenure that the special Seal of the Army Chaplaincy was adopted and produced through the guidance of the Army's Heraldic Division. The blue disc with a white dove, open book, and Christian and Jewish chaplains' insignia, bears the birth year of the chaplaincy, 1775, and its motto: *"Pro Deo et Patria."* [85] But a more lasting tribute to Chaplain Tobey's service is found in his own reflections more than 10 years after his retirement:

> Because of my civilian ministry totaling more than fifteen years I desired and tried to regard all chaplains as my peers, fellow priests of God.
> . . . I endeavored to the best of my ability to be a spiritual leader as well as a good administrator and to meet the challenge of my day in the best possible manner.
> At the time of this writing I have been retired from the Army for twelve years, ordained for forty-five years and I am seventy-one years of age.
> In retrospect, I am grateful that I had the opportunity to serve thus my God, my country and my fellowmen.[86]

When Chaplain Tobey retired from the Army, accepting a pastorate at the Balboa Union Church in the Canal Zone, the Chief of Chaplains' position was passed to Charles E. Brown, Jr. There were some natural

---

See footnotes at end of chapter.

evolutions in Brown's life; his father had also been a Methodist minister and had served as a National Guard chaplain in the 1920's. The new Chief originally applied for a National Guard chaplain's commission while serving a church in Denver, Colorado, in 1940. Before his assignment to a Guard unit, however, he was offered and accepted a Reserve commission. Called to active duty with the 30th Infantry Division in early 1941, he served in North Africa and Italy during most of World War II. Besides serving as president of the Army Chaplain Board and Commandant of the Army Chaplain School, he had also held the Seventh Army Chaplain's position in Europe and graduated from the Army's War College, Command and General Staff School, and Command Management School. Interestingly, Brown had been something of a protege under Chaplain Patrick Ryan, with whom he had served throughout much of his career.[87]

Brown's term as Chief of Chaplains (1 November 1962–31 July 1967) could be described as the beginning of the controversial period for the Army Chaplaincy. Criticism of the military ministry, both in regard to its organization and the over-all policy which allowed for the employment of chaplains by the U.S. Government, was virtually nonexistent following World War II. There was a pacifist movement among some American churches prior to the Korean War which called for the replacement of the traditional chaplaincy with a "supra-national ministry to all men, friend and foe alike." [88] Similarly, in 1955, a professed atheist attempted, through court action, to force the government's discontinuance of the employment of chaplains.[89] Such isolated attacks, however, had gone by largely without notice or appreciable support. When columnist Drew Pearson renewed some of the criticism in 1957, however, he brought national attention to some of the questions about the chaplaincy never fully considered by many Americans.[90] By 1962 Rabbi Martin Siegel, a former Navy chaplain, called for a revamping and civilianization of the military ministry. Editors of the *Christian Century*, which had published Siegel's controversial work, commented later: "Few articles in recent years have elicited a heavier or more critical mail . . . Volleys of protest were shot in this direction by military chaplains of high rank and low from almost every branch and subdivision of the armed forces. . . ." [91] Although executives of chaplains' endorsing agencies announced plans to study the chaplaincy, the same periodical suggested that their in-house review could hardly be free or thorough.[92] By the latter part of 1963, a New Jersey chapter of the American Civil Liberties Union challenged the con-

---

See footnotes at end of chapter.

stitutionality of the chaplaincy in a letter to the Secretary of Defense, Robert S. McNamara.[93] During the following 3 years, a book titled *The Military Establishment* gave further critical views of the chaplaincy and a whole barrage of articles and letters in clergy-oriented periodicals began discussing the legality and philosophy of the special ministry from seemingly every angle.[94]

The criticism of the chaplaincy actually had little connection with Brown's administration or the specific chaplains of that day. Rather, it grew in direct ratio with the increasing unpopularity of the American military involvement in Vietnam. During Brown's nearly 5 years in the chaplain-leadership role, U.S. troops in Vietnam soared from a few hundred advisers to 450,000 combat and combat-support personnel. U.S. losses in the war had leaped, roughly, from 30 to 16,000.[95] Even though some chaplains bristled at Brown's hard-charging policies, which stressed the number of services they conducted as well as the amount of time they spent in soldiers' work areas, many of them joined him in outspoken defense of the chaplaincy and whole-hearted support of America's Indo-China policy. Brown's personal opinion—"Once this nation has committed itself to a struggle, we are committed to it"—was labeled by one editorialist as "fatalistic stupidity."[96]

The rumblings over the military and the chaplaincy continued long after Chaplain Brown's retirement in July 1967. Despite those disputes, however, he remained firmly committed to the conviction that "there is no greater opportunity for a young minister to reach young men" than in the military chaplaincy. "You wear the same clothing, eat the same food, serve together, live together and in some instances," he added, "you have the privilege of dying together for freedom."[97]

The appointment of Francis L. Sampson, Roman Catholic, as Chaplain Brown's successor, may have appeared to some as a public-relations' attempt to rescue the image of the chaplaincy. Sampson was, after all, a highly-decorated airborne hero of both World War II and the Korean conflict. He wore the Distinguished Service Cross for his bravery in Europe and his exploits had been featured in three national television programs. Besides that, he had authored two books, numerous articles for periodicals, and was an outstanding athlete who had won seven Army regional tennis championships during his career.[98]

But the 55-year-old major general with 25 years of Army experience did not rely on his past prowess to impress the critics of the chaplaincy and the military. His service as Chief of Chaplains from 18 August

1967 to 31 July 1971 was characterized by a genuinely personal esteem for
the chaplain's calling and a deep respect for the soldier's profession. An
excerpt from one of his speeches, delivered a few months before his retirement, captures much of the philosophy under which he operated:

> In civilian life many people misunderstand the military mission.
> I have spoken at various universities and have been challenged
> by this misunderstanding. I have been asked how I can wear the
> uniform which symbolizes war and also wear the cross upon it sym-
> bolizing peace. One would think they should find the answer to
> the very question they proposed—for such questioners are of lofty
> academic standards, positions and responsibilities.
>
> It is very easy for me to tell them that, by law and by statute, the
> mission of the military of the United States is, first, to preserve
> peace. Second, to provide for the security of our country, its borders
> and internal security. And third, to implement national policy as it
> pertains to peace treaties with friendly nations which of themselves
> cannot repel the aggression of avaricious neighbors.
>
> I see nothing in this mission that does not appeal to the highest
> ideals of any man—regardless of his religion. Indeed, it was Cardinal
> O'Neal, the great Churchman, who once said if he had not been a
> priest he most certainly would have had to be a soldier, because they
> are both called to the identical things—that is—the preservation
> of peace, the establishment of justice when it has been lost, and the
> providing of security with protection for the weak and the inno-
> cent.[99]

But neither the logic nor the distinguished career of Chaplain Sampson could quell the storm. The anti-military, anti-chaplain spirit grew
more vocal as U.S. casualties and expenditures in Vietnam reached their
peak in the late 1960's. A former Jewish chaplain-veteran of World War
II charged that a rabbi "is unable to question the premise on which wars
are fought, once he dons the uniform." [100] The American Jewish Congress,
an advocate of church-state separation, called for the end of the military
chaplaincy and a former Jewish Air Force chaplain, teaching at Columbia
University, maintained that consecrated and pious men in the military
ministry were hampered by the "ambiguity" of being "servants of the military." [101] An organization called "Clergy and Laymen Concerned About
the War in Vietnam" sponsored Army stockade visits by an anti-chaplain
Roman Catholic bishop from Puerto Rico to counter Cardinal Cooke's
annual Christmas visit to American military installations.[102] The *Christian
Century* claimed that the anti-war spirit was hurting chaplain recruitment
and, at the same time, published an article that labeled the chaplain as a

"front man for the Army" giving "military indoctrination to the religious" rather than "religious indoctrination to the military." [103] "Despite widespread church opposition to the Vietnam War," said the *New York Times,* "support for the United States war effort remains strong among many military chaplains. The chaplaincy, largely as a result, is under renewed fire by critics seeking an end to the institution of clergymen in uniform." [104] Meanwhile some clergymen, like the president of the Southern Baptist Convention, strongly criticized the participants in the Vietnam Moratorium Day (15 October 1969) and declared their actions "an insult" while "our men are bathing the soil of Vietnam in their own blood." [105]

It is interesting to note that among those who had participated in Sampson's promotion to Chief of Chaplains were Generals Ralph E. Haines and Harold K. Johnson.[106] Both Haines and Johnson were outspoken men of religious conviction and principle. Ironically, Johnson's convictions seemed generally ignored by the public and Haines' religious experience was sometimes ridiculed.[107] It is undoubtedly too early to accurately evaluate the era, but it appears as if the image of the chaplaincy suffered considerably as a result of the emotional turmoil of the time. It was a troubling period in which critics called for a prophetic ministry by chaplains on the one hand, and scoffed at the religious convictions of a military leader on the other.

Although few people probably read it, Representative Floyd Spence of South Carolina submitted for the *Congressional Record* of 30 June 1971 an article by Chaplain Norman C. Miller, Methodist, a member of the Army Reserve. Miller had responded to critics of the day, who labeled him a "warmonger," in words expressive of the opinions of many of his fellow chaplains:

> . . . why are you so selective as to whom you will help and save? . . .
> You are saying a man drafted by his country to serve in the Army Forces is not worthy to receive the word of God. You told me you had no words of comfort, no compassion for the wounded and maimed, no benediction for the dying. You tell me, in your action, that you have no consolation for the heartbroken parents, for a shattered dream of a wife and children. . . .
> War is horrible and tragic. It is a shame so many are called to die to protect freedom. Yet in the last year America lost over 58,000 in automobile deaths. More than the total lost in the Vietnam war. However, you do not find young men burning their drivers license in protest, or dismantling their autos. Have you ever seen a well-meaning clergyman, solemnly intoning the names of 58,000 auto-

mobile deaths from the steps of the national or state capitol? . . .

I hate war . . . Yet I will not join the peace moratorium . . . For my Bible tells me there is something worse than war, it is human slavery, human bondage, in which man is no longer man, either in spirit or body.

I shall work for peace, and pray for peace within the framework of my government and I shall hope in God.[108]

But a 1969 article in the *Washington Post,* based primarily on interviews with chaplains at Fort Jackson, South Carolina, was typical of those which had received far more national attention. Unfortunately the underlying debate over the relationship between a chaplain's military allegiance and his religious conscience was lost, in some instances, by the overzealous and blatant militarism of chaplains themselves.[109]

Chaplain Sampson passed the "guidon" of the Chaplains' Branch to Gerhardt W. Hyatt, Missouri Synod Lutheran, on 1 August 1971. There was no way, however, in which the former Chief could avoid passing the criticism of the chaplaincy along with its leadership. The publication of a book, *Military Chaplains: From a Religious Military to a Military Religion*, and a later, 66-page statement of the American Civil Liberties Union, "The Abuse of the Military Chaplaincy," continued the attack against an institution nearing its bicentennial. While much of the furor in the campaign against the chaplaincy quieted with the cessation of American combat-involvement in Vietnam in 1973, many of the rumblings have continued to this day.[110]

Hyatt, a soft-spoken, skilled administrator, appeared to weather the severity of the storm with quiet resolution. As a native of Canada, he was the first foreign-born Chief of Chaplains in any of the U.S. military services Having served in two civilian parishes during most of World War II, he entered the chaplaincy in June 1945. But his ability to handle the complicated intricacies of Army paper work resulted in repeated assignments to the OCCH and, in 1960, to the Office of the Deputy Chief of Staff for Personnel. In 1968 he was the Staff Chaplain, Military Assistance Command, Vietnam (MACV), and in January 1970 became the Deputy Chief of Chaplains.[111]

Whenever Hyatt found himself in an administrative or student role he usually accepted opportunities to assist at local civilian churches. He was instrumental, in fact, in the establishment of two Lutheran churches in Virginia during his Washington-based assignments.[112] That personal attention to his own ministerial calling appeared to flavor much of his philosophy of leadership. Repeatedly, as Chief of Chaplains, he stressed the pastoral role of military clergy and attempted to foster a spirit of frank discussion and openness between chaplains of varying ranks and experience. After the OCCH had given considerable support to training sessions and pastoral conferences in order to sharpen the chaplains' parish skills, Hyatt emphasized: "The sole purpose for his investment has been to enable chaplains *to be more effective in their basic role as pastors to the Army family*. There is no other legitimate reason for our existence . . ." [113] "Rather than lead you by the hand," he once wrote his fellow chaplains, "I have tried to lead by climbing with you . . . I insist that when you write or talk to me and members of my staff, that you tell it like it is whether you think I will like it or not! There is too much at stake to do otherwise." [114]

During Chaplain Hyatt's assignment as Chief of Chaplains, the U.S. Army went through another one of its sweeping reorganizations. Continental Army Command, Combat Developments Command, and Third U.S. Army were eliminated as a Forces Command (FORSCOM) and a Training and Doctrine Command (TRADOC) came into existence. The object was decentralization and elimination of unnecessary levels of management. Hyatt welcomed the same goal for the chaplaincy; his many years in administrative positions had not dimmed his vision of the value for open communication and direct access to fellow workers regardless of rank or title. [115]

BUILDING NEW HOUSES OF WORSHIP

Actually, it was through much of the earlier work of Chaplain Gerhardt Hyatt that the Army's first major chapel construction program since the beginning of World War II went into effect. He was assigned to the OCCH in 1952 to work in the area of supply. Shortly after his arrival and the succession of Ivan Bennett as Chief of Chaplains, a complaint was received about the extremely inadequate chapel facilities at Camp Kilmer, New Jersey. Not only was the entire building in a poor state of repair, but the chancel ceiling, reported the chaplain, was so low it was difficult to stand beneath it—not to mention the disquieting echoes from an adjacent latrine that were hardly conducive to worship.

Chaplain Bennett sent Hyatt to inspect the chapel, joined by the First Army Engineer and the Staff Chaplain from First Army, Edward ("Big Ed") R. Martin, Roman Catholic. The latter couldn't have been a better choice to accentuate the chaplain's complaint. Martin stood over 6½ feet tall and couldn't even get into the chancel without stooping over. As a result, the Engineer directed a remodeling program to give the post a respectable house of worship.

When Hyatt returned to Washington, Chaplain Bennett told him that he had heard of some work being done on a large program for military construction and thought that the chaplains should have some input to it. Actually the program had been going on for several years with virtually no attention either to or from the Chaplains' Branch. Hyatt objected to the suggestion that he was the man for the job, pointing out that construction was not his responsibility and that a civilian in the OCCH was in charge of such matters. "Well, from now on," retorted Bennett, "he isn't—you are!"

Chaplain Hyatt set out through the caverns of the Pentagon to receive a crash program of on-the-job-training in military construction. He met regularly with military and civilian experts in logistics and the Corps of Engineers. Through them Hyatt became educated on the procedures and learned how to incorporate requests for new chapels. More important, he established long-standing friendships that would benefit the Chaplains' Branch for many years to come.

After the submission of a model design, a sample chapel was constructed at Dugway Proving Ground in Utah as a guide for future planning. Studies were made and new drawings submitted for 300 and 600-seat chapels that included adequate facilities for religious education. Sixty-five of these new buildings were planned and authorized during 1953–1954. Fort Ord, California, received the first of the large, modern chapel centers in what had developed into a $20,000,000 construction program throughout the Army. Chaplain Hyatt had traveled to countless installations, making plans for future positions and layouts of the new chapel centers. On posts not scheduled to receive a new chapel, he helped to convince many commanders to set aside appropriated or welfare funds for the remodeling and beautification of older, contonment chapels.[116]

Throughout the history of the United States, chaplains have conducted religious services for the men and women of the Army in virtually every conceivable structure known to man. While the shape, size, or history of the buildings were never as important as the faiths that were shared within, the permanent construction of modern chapel facilities beginning in the late 1950's added evidence to America's commitment to support the ministry of chaplains whenever possible.

See footnotes at end of chapter.

But hardly had that construction program been initiated before the rumors of war began to plague the country and the Army once more. Called again to the far corners of the world, chaplains would leave the beauty and solemnity of their new chapels and return to the battlefield. There, amidst man's greatest tragedy, they would call on God for forgiveness, comfort, and eternal peace under the common canopy of heaven.

FOOTNOTES

CHAPTER IV

[1] *New York Times,* 6 September 1951, p. 3.

[2] "Statement of Special Conference of Theological Seminary Professors Meeting in Washington, D.C., August 17–21, August 1953," Records of the Army Chief of Chaplains, Record Group 247 (hereafter referred to as RG 247), file 000.8, National Archives, Washington, D.C. (hereafter referred to as NA).

[3] Jacob W. Beck, "The Christian and Race Prejudice," *The Chaplain,* October 1945, p. 37.

[4] Charles E. Byrd, "The World's Biggest Problem," *The Chaplain,* March 1946, p. 21.

[5] Ira Freeman, "I am Intolerant Toward Intolerance," *The Chaplain,* July 1947, pp. 14–16.

[6] Melvin J. Friesen to Chief of Staff, United States Army, 11 January 1947; BG J. W. Anderson to Commanding General, Philippine Ground Force Command, 20 January 1947, RG 247, file 201.2, NA.

[7] Minutes of the Army and Navy Chaplains' Organization, Tokyo-Yokohama Area, 11 December 1945, p. 2, U.S. Army Chaplain Center and School Archives, Ft. Wadsworth, NY (hereafter referred to as USACHCS).

[8] Richard M. Dalfiume, *Desegregation of the U.S. Armed Forces* (Columbia, MO: University of Missouri Press, 1969), p. 155; Philip T. Drotning, *Black Heroes in Our Nation's History* (New York: Cowles Book Co., 1969), p. 193.

[9] Walter G. Hermes, *Truce Tent and Fighting Front* (Washington, D.C.: Office of the Chief of Military History, 1966), pp. 104–105.

[10] John C. Britcher, "The Chaplain and Integration" (USACHCS C–22 Research Paper, December 1973), pp. 5–8.

[11] Walter S. Baker, "Ministry in Civil Disturbance" (USACHCS C–22 Research Paper, 30 November 1973), pp. 2–12.

[12] Gerhardt W. Hyatt, DA Chief of Chaplains Newsletter, 1 March 1974, p. 1.

[13] Mordecai W. Johnson, "America's Religion and its Negro History" (Address delivered at Military Chaplains' Association Convention, Washington, D.C., 9–11 May 1950), *Military Chaplain,* July 1950, pp. 21–22.

[14] *Report of the Secretary of War; Being part of the Message and Documents communicated to the two Houses of Congress at the beginning of the First Session of the Fifty-Second Congress* (Washington, D.C.: Government Printing Office, 1892) 5:18.

[15] Roy J. Honeywell, *Chaplains of the United States Army* (Washington, D.C.: DA Office of the Chief of Chaplains, 1958), pp. 238–242.

[16] See *Military Chaplain,* April–May 1949, p. 27; Various entries on specific organizations, USACHCS.

[17] *The Chaplain,* May 1949, p. 37.

[18] *Ibid.,* July–August 1950, pp. 9–10, 22; May–June 1951, p. 1; September–October 1951, pp. 7–9; May–June 1967, p. 25; *Army, Navy and Air Force Journal,* 24 February 1951, p. 703.

[19] *A Brief History of the Protestant Women of the Chapel* (anon., n.d., [USAREUR?], [revised 1962]), USACHCS.

[20] *The Chaplain,* pp. 46–47.

[21] Albert C. Wildman to Rodger R. Venzke, 29 November 1973, USACHCS.

[22] *Ibid.;* Edwin L. Kirtley, Historical Questionnaire, 18 January 1974, USACHCS; *The Chaplain,* p. 26; *Brief History of PWOC,* USACHCS.

[23] *OCCH Summary of Major Events and Problems, 1 July 1959–30 June 1960,* pp. 124–127; "PMOC in USAREUR," *The Christian Century,* 1 April 1959, pp. 393–394; *Development of Religious Retreat Programs in the U.S. Army* (anon., n.d., [USAREUR?]), pp. 62–63, USACHCS.

[24] Daniel B. Jorgensen, *Air Force Chaplains 1947–1960* (Washington, D.C.: Government Printing Office, [1961?]), p. 233.

[25] *Ibid.,* pp. 231–233.

[26] *Ibid.,* 234–235.

[27] *Ibid.,* pp. 235–236.

[28] *Ministering to Jewish Personnel in the Absence of a Jewish Chaplain: A Manual for Jewish Lay Leaders* (Washington, D.C.: Government Printing Office, 1970), p. 18.

[29] Albert C. Wildman, Historical Questionnaire, 22 October 1973, USACHCS; Albert C. Wildman to Rodger R. Venzke, 29 November 1973, USACHCS; See also Ruth McKelvie, "A Military DRE: Joys and Frustration of," *The Chaplain,* September–October 1966, pp. 30–34.

[30] "Army's Largest Sunday School," *The Chaplain,* April 1955, p. 26; *OCCH Summary of Major Events and Problems, 1 July 1960 to 30 June 1961,* p. 75.

[31] Theodore K. Koepke, Historical Questionnaire, 20 February 1974, USACHCS; See also *The Chaplain,* August 1960, p. 39.

[32] See *OCCH Summary of Major Events and Problems, 1July 1959–30 June 1960,* pp. 74–76; *1 July 1960 to 30 June 1961,* pp. 75–76.

[33] *OCCH Summary of Major Events and Problems, 1 July 1960 to 30 June 1961,* p. 77.

[34] *OCCH Historical Review, 1 July 1962 to 30 June 1963,* pp. 81–82.

[35] *New York Times,* 16 June 1964, p. 47.

[36] *OCCH Historical Review, 1 July 1965 to 31 December 1966,* pp. 159–160.

[37] See *Ibid.; OCCH Historical Review, 1 July 1962 to 30 June 1963,* p. 92; *1 July 1968 to 30 June 1969,* p. 99.

[38] *Webster's Seventh New Collegiate Dictionary,* 1971 ed., s.v. "retreat."

[39] *New York Times,* 21 July 1945, p. 9.

[40] *Ibid.,* 25 July 1945, p. 2.

[41] *Army and Navy Journal,* 25 June 1949, p. 1251.

[42] *New York Times,* 11 December 1951, p. 7; See also "The Armed Forces Preaching Missions," *The Chaplain,* May–June 1952, pp. 12–13.

[43] *Development of Retreat Programs in US Army,* pp. 35–37, USACHCS.

[44] William J. Reiss, Recorded Interview, 27 October 1973, USACHCS.

[45] *Development of Retreat Programs in US Army,* pp. 35 & 45, USACHCS; See also Julia Lacy, "Berchtesgaden Then and Now," *The Chaplain,* February 1956, pp. 25–28.

[46] *The Chaplain,* April 1964, p. 54.

[47] Oris E. Kelly, Historical Questionnaire, 5 October 1973; Donald F. Carter, Historical Questionnaire, 28 December 1973, USACHCS.

[48] *Development of Retreat Programs in US Army,* pp. 73, 65–66, USACHCS; *The Chaplain,* December 1956, pp. 25–29.

[49] *A Digest of Information: Kapaun Religious Retreat House, Oiso, Japan* ([US Army Forces Far East Chaplains' Section?], n.d.) and related materials from files of Osborne E. Scott, New York (copies, USACHCS); Jorgensen, *Air Force Chaplains 1947–1960,* p. 248; "Religious Retreat Center at Seoul," *The Chaplain,* August 1964, pp. 35–39.

[50] After Action Report file, Chaplain Section, Hq, USARV/MACV, Appendix XX and XXI, USACHCS; *The Chaplain,* December 1963, p. 51; Leonard F. Stegman, Historical Questionnaire and inclosures, 23 October 1973, USACHCS; Emil F. Kapusta, Historical Questionnaire and inclosures, 11 October 1973, USACHCS.

[51] *New York Times,* 12 February 1951, p. 25.

[52] *Ibid.,* 6 May 1951, p. 65.

[53] *Ibid.,* 13 February 1951, p. 30.

[54] *Army, Navy and Air Force Journal,* 22 September 1951, p. 97.

[55] OCCH Report to the Secretary of the Army, 25 October 1951, RG 247, file 319.1, NA.

[56] *Military Chaplain,* January 1954, p. 24; *Army, Navy and Air Force Journal,* 10 April 1954, p. 960; 19 June 1954, p. 1284.

[57] Duncan N. Taylor, Historical Questionnaire, 26 October 1973, USACHCS.

[58] *OCCH Summary of Major Events and Problems, 1 July 1957–30 June 1958*, p. 52; *New York Times*, 18 August 1957, p. 87; Information Office files, USACHCS.

[59] See *OCCH Summary of Major Events and Problems, 1 July 1959–30 June 1960*, pp. 66–68.

[60] See *Ibid.; The Chaplain*, December 1960, p. 40; *Frontlines*, August 1959, p. 1; *New York Times*, 13 March 1962, p. 24.

[61] *New York Times*, 28 July 1962, p. 8; 12 September 1962, p. 11; Charles E. Brown, Jr., General Officers' Biographical Information File, Army War College Library, Carlisle Barracks, PA.

[62] *New York Times*, 26 September 1962, p. 28.

[63] *The Chaplain*, December 1962, p. 36.

[64] *Ibid.*, April 1964; Information Office files, USACHCS.

[65] Education Advisor and Information Office files, USACHCS.

[66] See *OCCH Historical Review, 1 July 1965 to 30 June 1966*, p. 186; *1 July 1967 to 30 June 1968*, p. 109; Information Office files, USACHCS.

[67] William V. O'Connor, Recorded Interview, 29 October 1973, USACHCS; William V. O'Connor, Biographical Sketch, Information Office, USACHCS; *The Chaplain*, July–August 1968, p. 48.

[68] Honeywell, *Chaplains of the US Army*, p. 295.

[69] Edgar Gregory, "The Chaplain and Mental Hygiene," *American Journal for Sociology*, March 1947, pp. 420–423.

[70] *Army and Navy Journal*, 9 July 1949, p. 1307.

[71] See *Ibid.*, 25 October 1947, p. 205.

[72] John W. Betzold, Historical Questionnaire, 4 December 1973, USACHCS.

[73] See *Ibid.; OCCH Historical Review, 1 July 1968 to 30 June 1969*, pp. 17, 23–24, 106; *The Chaplain*, October 1962, p. 48; August 1963, p. 54; January–February 1969, pp. 15–20.

[74] *The Chaplain*, June 1954, p. 46; Steve P. Gaskins to Rodger R. Venzke and inclosures, 2 July 1974, USACHCS.

[75] Patrick J. Ryan, General Officers' Biographical File, Army War College Library, Carlisle Barracks, PA; *Army, Navy and Air Force Journal*, 20 March 1954, p. 855, "Lace-Curtain Chaplain," *Newsweek*, 29 March 1954, pp. 80–81.

[76] *Catholic Digest*, April 1957 (reprint) as included in Patrick J. Ryan, Historical Questionnaire and inclosures, 20 Febraury 1974, USACHCS.

[77] *New York Times*, 7 October 1956. p. 75.

[78] *Catholic Digest*, April 1957 (reprint), Ryan, Questionnaire and inclosures, 20 February 1974, USACHCS.

[79] Frank A. Tobey, General Officers' Biographical File, Army War College Library, Carlisle Barracks, PA.

[80] Casper Nannes, "A Visit With Frank A. Tobey," *The Chaplain* July–August 1970, p. 21.

[81] Frank A. Tobey, Historical Questionnaire, 4 October 1973, USACHCS.

[82] Nannes, "A Visit With Tobey," *The Chaplain*, July–August 1970, p. 21.

[83] Tobey, Questionnaire, 4 October 1973, USACHCS.

[84] *OCCH Summary of Major Events and Problems, 1 July 1958–30 June 1959*, pp. 63–64.

[85] *Ibid.*, pp. 15–17.

[86] Tobey, Questionnaire, 4 October 1973, USACHCS.

[87] Charles E. Brown, General Officers' Biographical File, Army War College Library, Carlisle Barracks, PA; Casper Nannes, "A Visit With Chaplain Charles E. Brown, Jr.," *The Chaplain*, May–June 1971, pp. 12–15; *New York Times*, 3 November 1962, p. 15.

[88] *New York Times*, 12 May 1950, p. 25.

[89] *Ibid.*, 21 December 1955, p. 24.

[90] Drew Pearson, "One Church for Protestant GIs?" *Washington D.C., Post and Times Herald*, 14 July 1957, p. E5; *OCCH Summary of Major Events and Problems, 1 July 1957–30 June 1958*, p. 54.

[91] Martin Siegel, "Revamping the Military Chaplaincy," *Christian Century*, 8 August 1962, pp. 959–960; See also 19 September 1962, pp. 1119–1120; 7 November 1962, p. 1359.

[92] *Christian Century*, 6 March 1963, pp. 292–293.

[92] *New York Times,* 15 September 1963, p. 46; "In Dubious Battle," *Newsweek,* 1 June 1964, p. 82.

[93] John M. Swomley, Jr., *The Military Establishment* (Boston: Beacon Press, 1964), p. 199; "Peale Pulls Out All the Stops," *Christian Century,* 27 May 1964, p. 692; Arthur E. Sutherland, "The U.S. Constitution and the Military Chaplaincy," *Military Chaplain,* May–June 1965, pp. 21, 28–29, 31; Theodore J. Wilson, "The Chaplaincy and Free Exercise of Religion," *The Chaplain,* May–June 1966, pp. 3–6; Albert F. Ledebuhr, "Military Chaplaincy: An Apologia" and William R. Miller, "Chaplaincy vs. Mission in a Secular Age" and Norman MacFarlene, "Navy Chaplaincy: Muzzled Ministry," *Christian Century,* 2 November 1966, pp. 1332–1337; resultant letters to editor, 30 November 1966, pp. 1476–1478, and 4 January 1967, p. 18.

[95] For chronologies and statistics see R. Ernest Dupuy and Trevor N. Dupuy, *The Encyclopedia of Military History* (New York: Harper & Row, 1970), pp. 1249–1252; *New York Times,* 28 January 1973, p. 25; "Chronology: Generation of Conflict," *Time,* 6 November 1972, pp. 22–29.

[96] James H. Laird, "Policy in Vietnam Compounds Error," *Detroit Free Press,* 18 March 1967, p. 10; See Also Nannes, "Visit With Brown," *The Chaplain,* May–June 1971, p. 13.

[97] Nannes, "Visit With Brown," *The Chaplain,* May–June 1971, p. 15.

[98] Francis L. Sampson, General Officers' Biographical File, Army War College Library, Carlisle Barracks, PA; Francis L. Sampson, Biographical Sketch, OCCH.

[99] Francis L. Sampson, Dedication Address at the Medical Memorial Chapel, U.S. Army, Ryukyu Islands, *Army News Features,* 8 March 1971, U.S. Army Command Information Unit, Washington, D.C.

[100] *New York Times,* 27 March 1968, p. 59.

[101] *Ibid.,* 18 May 1968, p. 10; 4 June 1970, p. 8.

[102] *Ibid.,* 14 January 1970, p. 10.

[103] Robert E. Klitgaard, "Onward Christian Soldiers: Dehumanization and the Military Chaplain," *Christian Century,* 18 November 1970, pp. 1377–1380.

[104] *New York Times,* 22 June 1971, pp. 37, 70.

[105] *Southern Baptist Chaplain,* January–March 1970, p. 8.

[106] *The Chaplain,* November–December 1967, p. 44.

[107] See Harold K. Johnson, Chief of Staff, to Army Personnel, Subj: "Image of the Army," 2 March 1965, USACHCS; "The Four-Star General Who Calls Men to the Lord," *Moody Monthly,* November 1972, p. 22; Margaret Eastman, "Did the General Love Jesus Unwisely and Too Well" (including references to "The General Fights for Jesus," *Washington, D.C., Star-News,* 6 August 1972), *Army Times Family,* 21 February 1975, pp. 4, 10.

[108] Hon. Floyd Spence, South Carolina, "He is Called Warmonger by Ministerial Friend," *Congressional Record, House,* Tuesday, 29 June 1971.

[109] *Washington Post,* 2 September 1969, pp. 2, 6.

[110] *Military Chaplains: From a Religious Military to a Miiltary Religion,* ed. Harvey G. Cox (New York: American Report Press, [1971?]); "ACLU Holds the Chaplaincy 'Compromised'," *The Chaplain,* Fall Quarter 1973, pp. 20–21.

[111] Gerhardt W. Hyatt, Biographical Sketch, OCCH.

[112] *Ibid.*

[113] Gerhardt W. Hyatt, DA Chief of Chaplains Newsletter, 1 June 1972 (emphasis in original).

[114] *Ibid.,* 1 October 1972.

[115] *Ibid.,* 1 June 1973.

[116] Gerhardt W. Hyatt, Telephone Interview, 23 January 1975, USACHCS.

CHAPTER V

Vietnam:
The Longest War With Prolonged
Effects

GLIDING SLOWLY INTO FURY

Two announcements from the Far East on 2 September 1945 resounded with international effect and left their mark on American history. One was the formal surrender of the Japanese, bringing an end to World War II. The other was a little-noticed declaration of independence by a nationalist leader in a small French colony. Ho Chi Minh, an American ally during the War, and his League of Independence for Vietnam—the "Viet Minh"—were determined to prevent the reestablishment of French colonial rule in Indochina. The French were equally determined to repossess their former holdings. Military conflict resulted, but the average American considered the problem foreign and of no particular consequence to his nation. By the time the 7-year battle between the French and Viet Minh concluded, however, new developments in the matter had drawn the United States into the beginning of the longest war in American history.

U.S. attention focused on Vietnam with the advent of the Cold War and awareness of the Communist leanings of the Viet Minh. In 1949 a journalist noted:

> The question arises as to what, if any, action we will take if the Reds, after conquering all China should spill over into neighboring Asiatic countries, including French Indo-China. . . . The Secretary of State strongly intimates that we will not permit such territory to be brought under the Communist regime. However, he is not explicit as to what action we should take to prevent it.[1]

See footnotes at end of chapter.

Actually, U.S. economic and military advisory support were sent to aid the French in Indochina as early as 1950, but the eruption of war in Korea diverted the attention of most Americans. In fact, when General Pierre Janson, director of Catholic chaplains in the French Far Eastern forces, and fellow Chaplain Georges Boulard were stabbed to death by Viet Minh troops in June 1951, most U.S. chaplains were not even aware of the incident.[2]

By mid-1952 France had lost 18,000 soldiers trying to hold on to Indochina. "She would like to let go," wrote one reporter, "but the pressures on Paris to continue the war are strong." He continued with the prophetic insight of an unidentified American observer in Paris who said that a single catastrophe would force the French to "either pull out of Indo-China or go over to full wartime mobilization. If they pull out," he added pointedly, "the question is put to us." [3]

That catastrophe came in 1954. Desperately trying to regain a stronghold in the Communist-dominated north, a French garrison of 15,000 men had fortified their position at a village 220 miles west of Hanoi—Dien Bien Phu. Viet Minh forces stormed the area continually for nearly 6 months and finally cut off every attempt at French resupply. On 6 May 1954 a final assault overcame the starving defenders and a terse radio message echoed around the world: "C'est fini!" Nearly 5,000 French troops had lost their lives and 10,000 were taken prisoner. Only 73 men escaped.

The disaster essentially spelled the end of French involvement in Vietnam. A 19-nation Conference on Far Eastern Affairs met at Geneva, established a cease fire, and recognized two independent nations in Vietnam, divided by the 17th Parallel. Although the U.S. refused to sign the agreements, they accepted the basic principles; they also reserved the right to intervene in the case of a violation. French forces were withdrawn, except for those directing and training the South Vietnamese Army, and the United States assumed a heavier role in economic aid and military supply.

Ngo Dinh Diem replaced Emperor Bao Dai as the head of government in Saigon and in October 1955 the Republic of Vietnam (RVN) was formed in the south with Diem as President. Nearly 4 years later, in 1959, two U.S. military advisors were killed in a terrorist attack on the military base at Bien Hoa—the first Americans to die in the Vietnam fighting.

See footnotes at end of chapter.

By 1960 Communists in the south organized the National Liberation Front and their military arm, the Viet Cong (VC), became the primary enemy. Subsequent to a report from President Kennedy's special envoy to Vietnam, General Maxwell Taylor, the first U.S. combat-support troops were sent to the country in December 1961. American military personnel in Vietnam had increased over the 6-year period from a few hundred to more than 3,000. Two months later, on 8 February 1962, the U.S. Military Assistance Command, Vietnam (MACV), was established. MACV was more than a military headquarters for the administrative control of the increased number of U.S. troops. Psychologically, it was a demonstration of American determination against a Communist take-over in South Vietnam.[4]

The United States glided into the fury with little fanfare. For the American soldier it had been a quiet and unfamiliar way to go to war. No bands announced "The Yanks Are Coming," no headlines called him the savior of democracy and freedom. In fact, there were no beachheads to storm, no conventional invasions to repell, no discernible front lines of combat, and no easily-identified enemy. Silently, slowly at first, through the complicated course of international politics, American soldiers found themselves in a strange land and a bitter conflict. Simply because they were there, they were joined by Army chaplains.

ESTABLISHING A MINISTRY IN AN EMBRYO WAR

Chaplain John A. Lindvall, Assemblies of God, was the first Army chaplain to arrive in Vietnam. He was originally on his way to Okinawa, but when he arrived in Hawaii his orders were changed assigning him to the new MACV Headquarters in Saigon. Two days after his arrival on 26 February 1962, he was joined by Chaplains William S. Staudt, Roman Catholic, and Elmore W. Lester, Episcopalian.[5]

Apparently those assignments had been made so rapidly that there was no immediate arrangement for channels of supply. Informed in Hawaii that his contact for equipment would be the U.S. Army Head-quarters in the Ryukyu Islands, Lindvall wrote the senior chaplain there in early March. He indicated he would send a requisition list soon but added, "We are here without much of anything and it looks like it will take some time to obtain these things. I was wondering if you would be able to help supply us on an emergency basis." He asked for such things as hymnals, Communion elements, and chaplain field kits. "One of our

---

See footnotes at end of chapter.

chaplains," he noted, "having been in the Army only five months hadn't even been issued a field kit." [6]

Chaplain Edward M. Mize, Episcopalian, the Staff Chaplain in the Ryukyu Islands Headquarters replied:

> . . . Your letter was the first word that I had that this command would have supply responsibility for your support. . . . No one though is inclined to quible and we will do everything within our capability to support you. . . .[7]

Although Mize directed the immediate delivery of 17 different items to Vietnam, apparently he had no chaplain field kits to spare since none were included in the shipment.

Meanwhile, three more Army chaplains arrived in Vietnam—Thomas F. Grodavent, Roman Catholic, and Robert B. Howerton, Jr., Methodist, on 2 March; Joel E. Andrews, Methodist, on 23 March. Chaplain Lindvall informed Chaplain Mize in April that a Protestant Air Force chaplain was also there and that, with the anticipated arrival of a Catholic Air Force chaplain, their total would be eight. "Frankly we could use twice that many," he added, "because we have people in scores of places scattered throughout the 600 mile length of this country. . . . This certainly is a challenge and after reading that Ft. Hood, Texas will have 50 chaplains, my only desire is that a number of these new chaplains could serve in this country where many of our people may only see a chaplain a couple times during their entire tour here." [8]

Chaplain Andrews had arrived with the 39th Signal Battalion from Fort Gordon, Georgia. He was among the few key staff officers of the unit who were informed of their classified destination before their departure. With many of those men, Andrews studied a world map trying to find the location of the unfamiliar country. It was not until their plane had finished refueling in the Philippines that the battalion commander officially informed the rest of the soldiers they were headed for Vietnam.

Arriving on a typically scorching day, Andrews and the signalmen were directed to their "hotel"—a large tent-city on Tan Son Nhut Air Base. He conducted his first Sunday worship service in the mess tent, the only available shaded place with chairs. Within a short time, however, his unit was deployed throughout the country setting up a communications' network to assist South Vietnamese military operations. The chaplain was constantly on the move trying to cover roughly 15 different areas, including places as far away as Pleiku, Da Nang, Qui Nhon, and Nha Trang.

See footnotes at end of chapter.

Traveling and life-style were relatively secure and serene at first. Chaplain Andrews visited his units by sedan and aircraft, staying a few days at each place. His time in an area was consumed with worship services, counseling, circulating among the men for informal chats, and occasionally joining in a softball or volleyball game. But an inevitable, traumatic experience stunned the members of the battalion a short time after their arrival. Two soldiers had gone to a little village to set up a small transmitter so the area chief could call for help in case of a VC attack. They were on their way back to their unit in a boat when a group of Viet Cong fired on them, sinking their boat and killing one of the men.[9]

"We had a huge memorial service at the plane site before the body was shipped off," recalled the chaplain, "and it had an unusual, sort of unsettling effect upon everybody. . . . that was the first and it happened within 2 months after we arrived. . . . then we had more, probably from 15 to 25 more during the year that we were there."[10] Unsettling as it undoubtedly was to the men who were there, most Americans were not overly disturbed since the total number of those who were killed throughout the entire conflict was only 42 at the end of 1962.[11]

Chaplain Andrews remembered that some of his men saw the purpose of their work as an aid to stop Communist aggression, but many of them regarded their assignment only as a military job with little consideration of the international situation. Like many chaplains who followed him, Andrews took it upon himself to emphasize the anti-Communist campaign in his Character Guidance lectures. While the official position was an optimistic view that U.S. aid would be limited and the conflict soon ended, Andrews and his men could see the situation grow with the regular arrival of more and more American troops. "As a matter of fact, when I came back," said the chaplain, "I was convinced it was going to be a long and drawn-out struggle."[12]

Chaplain Lindvall, a junior lieutenant colonel at the time, said in several of his letters that a full colonel chaplain was needed in his position. He was not only attempting to coordinate the work of an increasing number of Army, Air Force, Marine, and Navy chaplains arriving in Vietnam but also working in a headquarters that already had eight general officers. He contacted a variety of people for advice and help, including Chaplain Edwin L. Kirtley, the founder of the Protestant Personnel of the Chapel movement—"How I wish we had someone like you here."[13] He asked for guidelines to establish a chaplains' section, lay organizations, and religious retreats. He inaugurated a chaplains' fund, sought out lay leaders

See footnotes at end of chapter.

to conduct worship services in isolated units, secured the help of local missionaries, predominately from the Christian Missionary and Alliance, personally conducted three to four field services per week during his constant travels, and actually did organize two religious retreats in Dalat in November.[14] Nevertheless, he was troubled by further problems, such as the lack of organization and coordination of the scattered chaplain activities in Thailand and the demands for religious coverage for the large number of American dependents in the Saigon area. In his mid-tour report to the OCCH, in which he outlined many of his recommendations, he added: "I feel we shall be in South East Asia for a long time and we must plan for larger numbers of Army chaplains to serve our Army personnel here." [15]

Despite those convictions, neither the chaplains there nor the OCCH could foresee just how extensive the conflict would become. Lindvall's replacement in February 1963 was Chaplain Robert S. McCarty, Southern Baptist, another lieutenant colonel. McCarty's early correspondence before his arrival demonstrated the relatively calm approach to America's initial involvement; he asked about the availability of housing and schooling, in anticipation of bringing his family, and whether or not he should bring his dress blue uniform.[16]

SERVING QUIETLY IN A TIME OF TURMOIL

Secretary of Defense Robert S. McNamara had visited Vietnam in May 1962 and had expressed the opinion that U.S. aid and personnel in the country would probably level off. By the end of the year, U.S. military forces there numbered 11,000. During the early part of 1963, U.S. Army chaplains (increased to 10) and their counterparts from the other Armed Forces were scattered throughout the four corps areas dividing the country, serving under the Support Command, the Military Advisory Assistance Group (MAAG), and MACV. The approach of Army chaplains to their ministry in Vietnam necessarily varied from that in previous combat situations primarily because of the vast dispersion of U.S. personnel. From the very beginning of American involvement in Vietnam, the chaplains' section in MACV fostered the concept of "area coverage" as opposed to the normal unit coverage. U.S. Army, Navy (Marine), and Air Force chaplains were encouraged to coordinate their ministries by serving all U.S. personnel within their geographical areas, regardless of service or unit connection.

See footnotes at end of chapter.

While offering an obvious practical solution to the unique situation in Vietnam, the area coverage concept was not always easily implemented. Identity with a specific unit, and especially with a particular branch of service, has traditionally been as important to the military chaplain as a civilian clergyman's relationship with his own congregation. Obviously, the rapport which a chaplain was able to build over a period of time with the officers and men of his own unit could not be immediately translated to every neighboring element which happened to pass through his geographical area. Similarly, the possessiveness of a few commanders toward the activities of the chaplains assigned under them occasionally hampered the cooperative attitude being encouraged by higher commands. Necessity, however, ordinarily overruled preference. It was not only impractical but often impossible for a chaplain to serve only the men of his specific unit when elements of that organization were scattered over great distances while elements of another chaplain's unit were immediately adjacent to his home base. The chaplain area coverage concept, consequently, grew out of the demands of the Vietnam conflict and has received study and emphasis since then throughout the U.S. Army.[17]

Opinions of officials that the conflict would soon end continued to be heard. In May 1963 a Defense Department spokesman said that the "corner has definitely been turned toward victory" over the Viet Cong. But the political unrest in South Vietnam added complication to the situation. Buddhists objected to the Roman Catholic-dominated government of Diem, led protest riots, and shocked the world with self-immolations by fire. In November a military coup overthrew the government and assassinated Diem.[18]

Meanwhile, American attention was diverted by a stunning blow to their own nation. "I was in my office at Ft. Myer on that fateful Friday, 22 November 1963," recalled Chaplain Peter S. Lent, General Conference Baptist, "when I heard a soldier outside the window call, 'have you heard the news, the President's been shot.' I immediately turned on the radio and heard the initial reports from Dallas." Lent, serving as a chaplain with the Army's ceremonial unit, the Third Infantry, was to participate, 4 days later, as an escort officer for VIP clergy in one of the most historic funerals at Arlington National Cemetery. "I remember the schedule of burials that day because the last one on the list was John F. Kennedy and his rank was listed as Commander in Chief." [19] Earlier that day, a last-minute request for a Roman Catholic chaplain had suddenly placed Chaplain Lawrence K. Brady in the solemn procession leading the casket of the fallen President

---

See footnotes at end of chapter.

through the streets of Washington. Although unplanned and completely unknown to the millions of viewers, it was a uniquely appropriate choice. Chaplain Brady had been the first chaplain to wear the green beret of the Army's Special Forces, a group that received much of the former President's attention and favor.[20]

Lyndon B. Johnson's sudden ascent to the Presidency was burdened with the question of U.S. involvement in Vietnam. While some U.S. citizens began to regard the issue as a foreign civil war of no rightful concern to their nation, others saw it as another blatant attempt at Communist encroachment that had to be curtailed with military force. Army chaplains, especially those serving in Vietnam, tended to agree with the latter view, although they sought little public attention for their opinions. Their attitudes were influenced, undoubtedly, by a desire to honor the memory of the increasing number of their men who were giving their lives in the conflict. Similarly, many of them seemed far more shaken than the average American citizen by the persecutions and atrocities conducted by the VC, especially against missionaries.[21]

By the end of 1963 U.S. troops in Vietnam numbered 16,500 and 78 of them lost their lives there during that year. Yet total chaplain strength in the Army, reflecting the still somewhat mild approach to the war, was actually nearly 100 less in mid-1963 (1,286) than in the previous year (1,373). Actually, it was not until 1966 that this number began to increase substantially toward the peak level for the war period, reached in October 1968 with 1,924 on active duty.[22]

The events of 1964 and early 1965 spelled the beginning of America's deeper involvement in Vietnam. The political turmoil in South Vietnam, often including bitter rivalry between Buddhists and Roman Catholics, continued until June 1965 when Air Vice Marshall Nguyen Cao Ky became Premier of the eighth government for the RVN in 20 months. While American leaders were considering the possibility of bombing attacks on North Vietnam in early 1964, two U.S. Navy destroyers were attacked in August by North Vietnamese torpedo boats in the Gulf of Tonkin. Congress passed the "Tonkin Gulf Resolution" pledging full support for U.S. forces in Vietnam and authorizing the President to take "all necessary measures to repel any armed attack." The number of American personnel, serving in advisory and combat support roles, was continually increased until eventually, in March 1965, a more direct involvement was assumed with the arrival of the first U.S. combat forces (Marines). U.S. Army

See footnotes at end of chapter.

combat units began to arrive in May. By mid-year the total U.S. casualties since 1961 numbered 1,484 killed and 7,337 wounded.[23]

Obviously, Army chaplains were also entering the country in increasing numbers. With the consolidation of MAAG and MACV in May 1964, and the establishment of the United States Army, Vietnam (USARV) in July 1965, their task of administrating and coordinating the religious coverage of U.S. troops mushroomed. Included among those in the feverish pace at the MACV Headquarters in late 1964 was the senior Jewish chaplain for the command, Meir Engel. Engel was a 50-year-old native of Tel Aviv, Israel, who had first served on active duty in the U.S. Army chaplaincy (1943 to 1946) after immigrating to the States and being ordained as a rabbi in 1942. Re-entering active duty during the Korean War, he had served in various assignments prior to his arrival in the RVN in August 1964.[24]

On 9 December 1964 a letter was sent to Chaplain Engel through MACV from the Office of the Adjutant General informing him of his mandatory retirement by 30 November 1967. Less than one month later, a terse, tragic message from MACV was sent in reply: "Chaplain Engel died 16 December 1964 of a heart attack." [25] "This command suffered a great loss today," began a letter from General William C. Westmoreland to MACV personnel on the date of Chaplain Engel's death. "His keen sense of humor, religious tolerance, high intellectual acumen, and his friendly spirit had endeared him to the members of this command . . . " [26] Although not a battle casualty, Chaplain Engel was the first Army chaplain to die in Vietnam.

With the establishment of USARV in 1965, the natural question of supervisory control of Army chaplains arose. MACV, as a joint command, previously served as the supervisory headquarters for all U.S. personnel in Vietnam. But the establishment of an Army headquarters (USARV) suggested that all Army chaplains would naturally be a part of the new organization. A staff study was prepared by the MACV Command Chaplain in November 1965, however, which concluded that any Army chaplains and their assistants who were serving MACV advisory teams should remain assigned to MACV. One of the reasons listed for this decision was the fact that these chaplains performed advisory functions to RVN Armed Forces chaplains in their areas. In early 1967, as MACV Headquarters prepared a revision for their Organization and Functions Manual, the distinction between Army chaplains under

---

USARV and MACV was reiterated. In essence, all Army chaplains in the country came under the supervision of USARV with the exception of those specifically assigned to the MACV headquarters or serving MACV advisory teams.

But on 3 June 1967, a MACV Comptroller staff study asked staff elements to submit a listing of functions which could feasibly be transferred to USARV. Initially, the MACV Command Chaplain submitted a negative reply. A few weeks later, however, the chaplains' section was asked to reconsider its decision and strongly encouraged to identify responsibilities that should more appropriately be under the direction of USARV field operations. The MACV Command Chaplain reversed his desision and, consequently, in October of that year 13 chaplains and 13 chaplain's assistants serving advisory teams in the Corps Tactical Zones were transferred to USARV control. The transfer was made, in part, to help foster the area coverage concept; the "chaplain team" (one chaplain and one chaplain's assistant) could provide religious coverage not only to the advisors but also to Civil Operations and Rural Development Support (CORDS) civilians, as well as to the small isolated Army units within their geographical areas.

The new arrangement remained in effect for 2 years. The only Army chaplains assigned to MACV during that period were those within the headquarters itself. But in February 1969 the MACV Command Chaplain prepared a new staff study which again emphasized the support roles of those chaplains serving advisory teams and recommended their return to MACV control. The staff study maintained that those chaplains provided professional and technical assistance to the RVN Armed Forces chaplains in their areas, kept the senior U.S. advisors informed of the proper courtesies due Vietnamese religious institutions and holidays, and monitored the orientation of newly assigned U.S. advisory personnel to culturally sensitive areas. In light of the emphasis by then on Vietnamization, and since there was no provision for advisory functions under the USARV structure, the recommendation was approved on 15 October 1969. All chaplains and their assistants serving advisory personnel were again placed under MACV control.[27]

In actuality, the transfer of chaplains from MACV to USARV and back again was primarily a paper-work exercise. The work of the chaplains in the field remained essentially the same regardless of their chain of command. While the technical assistance role of chaplains serving MACV was more strongly emphasized, nearly every U.S. chaplain in Vietnam

See footnotes at end of chapter.

provided guidance to unit personnel regarding the important religious aspects of the country in which they were serving.

STRUGGLING TO MINISTER IN THE FACE OF DEBATE

In February 1965 a Viet Cong attack on the U.S. compound at Pleiku resulted in eight Americans killed and 109 wounded. Subsequently, retaliatory U.S. air raids were directed on North Vietnam. President Johnson made several attempts to negotiate a peace settlement during the year, always preluding his offers with cessations of bombing raids. But each offer was rejected by the North Vietnamese and with each rejection the war dragged on.[28]

To add to American troubles, dissident elements in the Army of the Dominican Republic mutinied and attempted to overthrow their government in mid-1965. Communist leaders in the area jumped at this new chance to take advantage of what had originally been a democratic revolution. The 82nd Airborne Division and numerous other U.S. Army units were rushed to the area to restore order. Similar to the situation in Vietnam, many Army chaplains accompanied the troops to the Caribbean country and were constantly on the move trying to provide religious coverage to the units scattered throughout the area. There were times, during the 18-month involvement, when U.S. casualties in the Dominican Republic were actually higher than in Vietnam. Among the numerous chaplains who served there, Chaplain Arthur F. Bell, Southern Baptist, recalled that fellow-Chaplain Roger W. Heinz, Missouri Synod Lutheran, seemed to have a knack for ending up in the hottest spots. Returning to his headquarters from conducting a service at an outlying unit one day, Heinz' jeep was stormed by a stone-throwing mob which slashed the vehicle's tires and wounded the driver. Somehow they managed to escape and Heinz' fellow chaplains included a unique, jesting phrase in the day's incident report: "Chaplain stoned." [29]

By the time U.S. units were withdrawn from the Dominican Republic in late 1966, most Americans had forgotten they had even been there because of the growing debate over U.S. involvement in Vietnam. Mass demonstrations against the U.S. presence in South East Asia had already begun in late 1965 and the military in general became the scapegoat for the anti-war attack. At the same time, other American citizens felt compelled to support their men in combat, wrote thousands of encouraging letters and shipped boxes of gifts addressed to "Any GI in

See footnotes at end of chapter.

Vietnam." Most of those mailings were sent to military chaplains for distribution among their men. Similarly, President Johnson declared 28 November 1965 as a "Day of Dedication and Prayer for Those Risking Their Lives for Peace in Viet-Nam." [30] Meanwhile, General Harold K. Johnson, the Army's Chief of Staff, pointed out that "the Army is not a policy making organization" but rather "an instrument of policy."

> Essentially, we are being employed by our government to restore stability or to provide a climate of order in which government, under law, can function effectively in those instances where the United States has been asked for assistance and it is clearly in our national interest to provide assistance.[31]

Since American involvement was attacked by some U.S. citizens on moral grounds, it was only natural that chaplains became the focus of some of that debate. Newspaper articles either glorified them beyond reality or else sarcastically attacked them as hypocritical warmongers. Occasionally, some chaplains began to take public sides on the issue, either supporting or questioning the war-effort. A Jewish chaplain who admitted that he had been opposed to American involvement in Vietnam before his arrival in the country, related the attitude of many chaplains when he later concluded that while "our present policy of continuing the military struggle is not a pleasant one, the prospect of giving in to a brutal, tyrannical aggressor is much less attractive." [32] Most chaplains seemed resolved to minister to their men wherever they were called and to support an attitude of loyalty to one's conscience and religious convictions in the face of the agonizing questions.

One chaplain made an attempt through humor to awaken some civilian clergymen to the seriousness of the military ministry. Chaplain Frank O. Vavrin, Lutheran Church in America, published a facetious "advertisement" in a denominational paper offering to exchange parsonages with anyone willing. He offered a " 'do-it-yourself' pup tent or poncho strung between trees," very wet weather, a congregation in foxholes, neighboring VC, as well as a guaranteed salary, C-rations, medical care, and a 30-day annual leave—"if you make it." Ironically, some civilian pastors took the ad seriously and offered to help out for a 30-day period; the OCCH replied just as seriously and suggested that they apply for commissions as chaplains.[33]

In actuality, South Vietnam was being swamped with visiting clergymen. Like many of the official and semi-official visitors from the States, some of the clerics came on a "special mission" and unfortunately re-

---

See footnotes at end of chapter.

turned as "experts" on the progress of the conflict. In most cases, each was cordially welcomed and even General Westmoreland expressed his appreciation for their concern and requested their prayers for his soldiers. Nationally-known figures like Francis Cardinal Spellman and Doctor Billy Graham were particularly popular with the troops and many of them anticipated their arrival. But as the war continued, many clergymen, some without any sponsorship at all, poured into the country. The task of escorting these visitors began to hamper the chaplains' own work. Chaplain Theodore V. Koepke, Missouri Synod Lutheran, MACV Staff Chaplain, and Chaplain Daniel O. Wilson, American Baptist, USARV Staff Chaplain, asked the OCCH for help in reducing the deluge of visiting preachers. Koepke reported that 10 such visits had been made during the last month of 1965 alone. In one case, a clergyman on a "fact-finding mission" spent 4 days in the country and returned to start a huge money-collecting campaign to produce "religious literature" for American soldiers. At the same time he claimed that chaplain coverage in Vietnam was sparce and, in one case, so bad that a chaplain read his sermons from an Army manual. Such incidents eventually resulted in a tightening of the policy governing visiting clergymen in the war zone.[34]

Occasionally the overzealousness of an Army chaplain to identify with his men and to not be a burden on them while on combat missions produced added problems. Photographed with a .45 caliber pistol and a fragmentation grenade hanging from his belt, one chaplain received particular attention and publicity in January 1966. "I don't want to be a drag when the going is hot and heavy," he had been quoted as saying. "I ought to be able to earn my keep with these men. But I would only use these things in self defense—my job is to save souls and not to take lives." The Chief of Chaplains quickly sent out a policy statement to senior chaplains and major Army commands. Interestingly, he did not insist that chaplains not carry weapons but reminded them of the "serious repercussions caused by unwarranted actions of chaplains who permit themselves to be photographed while carrying weapons." He also reminded them of the traditional position set forth in the Geneva Convention and Army regulations and suggested that chaplains request the presence of a public information officer during interviews with the press.[35]

GIVING WITH COMPASSION

Through 1966 U.S. forces in Vietnam grew until 389,000 were in the area by the end of the year. Combat deaths by then totaled over 6,000

As could be expected, there were Army chaplains included in both figures.

Chaplain William J. Barragy, Roman Catholic, had entered the chaplaincy in 1953 from the Archdiocese of Dubuque, Iowa. Arriving in Vietnam in July 1965, he was assigned to the 1st Brigade, 101st Airborne Division. Near the end of his 12-month tour, on 4 May 1966, he was a passenger on a CH–47 helicopter carrying ammunition and troops into one of the many combat areas. For unknown reasons—there were no witnesses at the time—the aircraft crashed and burned on impact. The 50-year-old priest became the first Army chaplain to be killed in action in Vietnam. Chaplain Barragy was posthumously awarded the Legion of Merit.[36]

Chaplain William N. Feaster, United Church of Christ, had just been ordained in 1963 and entered the chaplaincy in January 1965. On 19 September 1966, roughly 3 months after his arrival in Vietnam, he was wounded by a short round from friendly artillery while serving with the 196th Light Infantry Brigade. His wife, Lieutenant Judith C. Feaster, an Army nurse stationed in Seoul, Korea, was rushed to his side at an Army hospital in Saigon. Tragically, despite all medical efforts, he died 1 month later on 26 October.[37]

Chaplain Michael J. Quealy, Roman Catholic, had entered the Army in the same month as Chaplain Feaster. He arrived in Vietnam on 13 June 1966 and was assigned to the 3rd Brigade, 1st Infantry Division. On 8 November a U.S. battalion on "Operation Attleboro" violently engaged two Viet Cong regiments near the Cambodian border. Although not assigned to the unit, Chaplain Quealy heard of the battle and caught a helicopter ride into the area. After checking at the battalion command post to learn where the heaviest fighting was, he dashed to the field and began to assist with the wounded and give last rites to the dying. "Chaplain Quealy appeared to be everywhere," noted a later citation. He spotted one seriously wounded man some distance away from the main group and crawled to his side under intense fire from three enemy automatic weapons. By the time he arrived, the man had died—but the chaplain knelt, administered last rites, and then noticed still another wounded soldier. While kneeling by that man's side, Quealy himself was mortally wounded. On 26 January 1967 the Silver Star was posthumously awarded to Chaplain Quealy for his courageous and selfless sacrifice and his inspiration to the men he had served.[38]

"I like to think of this situation in terms of the parable of the Good Samaritan," commented Chaplain Emmitt T. Carroll, Disciple of Christ, in regard to the American presence in Vietnam.[39] With similar philosophies, hundreds of Army chaplains were responsible for guiding and, in some cases, establishing civic action projects by their units throughout Vietnam during the years of U.S. involvement in the country. Even after the appointment of civil affairs officers, chaplains continued to encourage and support innumerable contributions of money and labor for the welfare of the Vietnamese people. Engineers built roads and dug wells, medical personnel provided health care, and thousands of soldiers gave of their own time and money to assist local schools, orphanages, and leprosariums. Many chaplains contacted home-town civic and church organizations in the States and initiated charitable donations of everything from soap to clothing. "Our troops have made a solid contribution toward winning the minds and hearts of the villagers through their civic action programs," commented Lieutenant General John L. Throckmorton, then Chief of the Army's Office of Reserve Components. "While this type of activity is not as dramatic or newsworthy as a military operation, it is nonetheless necessary if the government of South Vietnam is to gain the support of the people."[40] To most chaplains, however, the strategic value of their civic action to the war effort was secondary. They were moved rather by a common compassion for humans in need. Said a Vietnamese Roman Catholic priest to Chaplain Donald R. Dawson, Presbyterian USA: "Chaplain, the people of my refugee village told me that the Protestant minister has much love for them."[41]

Even more intense was the chaplains' love for the men they served. "Ever since Bunker Hill, the man behind the man behind the gun has carried a Bible, comforted the wounded and prayed for the dead," noted *Time* magazine.[42] Actually, so many Army chaplains were volunteering for duty in Vietnam that the OCCH had to disapprove some of the applications. As of 30 August 1966 there were 219 Army chaplains in the country.[43] Following Chaplain Thomas J. Confroy, Roman Catholic, on his dangerous rounds with the 1st Infantry Division, *Look* magazine's senior editor for the Far East, Sam Castan, wrote:

> . . . He never pressures anyone into coming to this church [a clearing in the jungle], he never asks why the buddy who came last time has not returned. His sermons are brief and often mention the value of suffering as a means to understanding what Christ Himself endured. He never speaks of the nearness of death—everyone here knows it full well. The hardest part of Father Confroy's work comes after Mass, as he waits at the aid station for those who have received

Holy Communion, struck into the jungle, and will be soon returning for Extreme Unction, the last rites of his Church.[44]

Castan also reported how the men laughed one day. as an incoming mortar round interrupted one of Confroy's services. He jumped in a foxhole atop three other men. As the smoke cleared and the men crawled out, the chaplain remarked, "One good thing about Vietnam is that nobody sleeps during Mass." But the writer was particularly moved by an expression of the chaplain's deep love for his troops: "The men I attend are each day faced with the ultimate reality, the final physical reality of death. I know now what every priest must know: the full meaning of compassion." With tragic irony, the correspondent himself was killed only a few weeks after filing the chaplain's story.[45]

"Usually I move right with the battalion and dig foxholes along with the men," reported Chaplain John H. Herrlinger, Lutheran Church in America. "Our altar is the front of a jeep, our pews Vietnamese soil and our roof the burning Oriental sky. Men grow up in a minute over here." [46] The feeling between the chaplains and their men was often mutual. "While most of the troops in Vietnam may be indifferent to churchgoing," wrote one reporter, "they nonetheless have a high regard for the churchmen who share the dangers of war with quiet heroism that wins affection and awe rather than medals." [47] When asked about his chaplain, James M. Hutchens, National Fellowship of Brethren Churches, one soldier replied: "I can't talk about him. You just wouldn't understand. You haven't been with us." [48]

During 1967 U.S. forces and casualties in Vietnam increased sharply. In August President Johnson announced a new ceiling on U.S. troops for the war zone as 525,000. In June they had already reached 463,000. At the end of 1967 U.S. casualty figures (from January 1961) totalled 15,812 killed and 99,305 wounded. Bombing raids on the north were intensified while U.S. and South Vietnamese forces entered the demilitarized zone (DMZ) for the first time. Repeated offers for peace negotiations from the United States were regularly turned down by the North Vietnamese and American demonstrations against the war became even more prevalent.[49]

It would be ludicrous to assert that soldiers were unaffected by the constant debates over the war. It would be equally absurd to say that they all responded positively to the ministry of chaplains. "As long as I've got to kill, I'm not going to church," said one trooper to Chaplain LaVern W. Gardai, American Lutheran. "I'll listen to 'Thou Shalt not

See footnotes at end of chapter.

Kill' when I get home." Others told him to "go over and preach that stuff to the Viet Cong. Maybe we'll win the war." Injured in a helicopter crash while helping to evacuate a wounded soldier, the chaplain still maintained that "we can't let evil rise up and take what it wants anywhere in the world." [50] "Perhaps not every soldier, bothered by the controversy at home over the war would want to speak to him [a chaplain]," said Chaplain Edward J. Saunders, Roman Catholic, Commandant at the Chaplain School. "That is not the important thing. Just that he's there, available at all times for any help and guidance they may seek, means a great deal to our fighting men. . . . You must remember that a chaplain is not in the army to justify war or to be a cheerleader for hostilities." [51]

The more than 300 Army chaplains in Vietnam continued to be scattered throughout the country. Those serving in more "secure" areas set out to build chapels—some so elaborate that they contained electronic organs and stained glass windows, and others nothing more than a specified tent with rough wooden benches. Although the USARV construction program labeled "Chapel/Theater" as number 38 in a list of 46 priorities, most chaplains constructed their churches with voluntary labor and contributions, and frequently named them in honor of members of the unit who had been killed in action. [52] Chapel construction in Vietnam increased until it reached its peak in November 1970 with 203 permanent or semi-permanent U.S. military chapels in use throughout the country. That number then began to decrease so that by November 1971 there were 150. By the end of the U.S. combat involvement in Vietnam, there were only 16 U.S. military chapels still in use in the country. In most cases, wherever it was feasible, the structures were turned over to the Chaplain Directorates of the RVN Armed Forces. [53]

Because of the extensive use of the helicopter in Vietnam, most chaplains were not restricted to a specified area. Often using a base camp as "home," they regularly traveled to outlying elements of their units. Even the far-flung, small contingents of advisors, who lived and worked in isolated villages, were able to have some regular contact with a visiting chaplain who flew in with the supplies and mail. [54] But no matter where they were assigned, chaplains were no more secure than the men they served. In many cases, the streets of Saigon were as dangerous as the jungles far to the north or the Delta region below.

Chaplain James J. L. Johnson, National Baptist, was a 34-year-old native of Marlin, Texas, who entered the Army in 1965 and joined the

4th Infantry Division in Vietnam 1 year later. He attended a religious retreat at Cam Ranh Bay in early 1967 and boarded a C–47 aircraft on 10 March to return to his unit. For unknown reasons, the plane crashed and burned. The crew and all the passengers, including Chaplain Johnson, were killed.[55]

HONORING THE COMMON FOR UNCOMMON DEEDS

Chaplain Ambrosio Salazar Grandea, Methodist, had moved with his parents from his home in the Philippine Islands to the United States at the age of 18. During postgraduate work at Boston University, he had served a church in New Hampshire before entering the Army in 1960. Arriving in Vietnam in November 1966, he was conducting a worship service for men of the 4th Infantry Division on 25 May 1967 when he was wounded by an enemy mortar round. After treatment in Vietnam, he was evacuated to a hospital at Clark Air Force Base in the Philippines. There, near his birthplace, Chaplain Grandea died only a few days later on 13 June 1967.

The chaplain's wife, Mrs. Jacinta Grandea, working as a nurse in Baltimore, Maryland, had first been informed that his wounds were slight, but each new message carried reports of the growing seriousness of his condition. At her own expense, she left for the Philippines to be with him, but was stopped while changing planes in San Francisco by an officer who informed her of her husband's death. Six months later, 2 days before Christmas, Mrs. Grandea participated in a dual ceremony at Fort Meade, Maryland—after receiving the posthumous awards of her husband's Silver Star and Purple Heart, she was sworn in as an Army nurse. Mrs. Grandea volunteered with the stipulation that she be sent to Vietnam. "We are engaged in a tough war in Vietnam," she said. "All of us have to do our little bit to end the task with success and honor." [56]

On the uniforms of only a handful of soldiers in the United States Army can be seen a distinctive ribbon attached above all the others. That tiny piece of cloth with white stars against a bright blue background indicates that the wearer is a recipient of the nation's highest award— the Medal of Honor. Throughout American history, only three Army chaplains—all serving in the Civil War—had ever received that distinguished tribute to gallantry.[57] But for their services rendered during the last 2 months of 1967, the Medal of Honor was to be awarded to two Roman Catholic Chaplains: Charles J. Watters and Angelo J. Liteky.

See footnotes at end of chapter.

Chaplain Watters was a 40-year-old native of Jersey City, New Jersey. After his ordination in 1953, he had served parishes in his home town as well as in Rutherford, Paramus, and Cranford, New Jersey. In 1962 he became a chaplain in the Air National Guard and 2 years later entered active duty as an Army chaplain. In July 1967 he had already completed his 12-month tour in Vietnam but had voluntarily extended his service there by 6 months. On 19 November 1967, while assigned to the 173rd Support Battalion, 173rd Airborne Brigade, he was moving with the men of one company on an assault near Dak To. An intense battle broke out and Watters dashed to the front to aid with the wounded and administer last rites to the dying. Spotting a wounded paratrooper standing in shock in the field of fire, Chaplain Watters ran forward, picked up the man on his shoulders, and carried him to safety. As the American unit rushed forward, Watters was again seen in front, caring for another wounded man; when they were pushed back, the chaplain was between the lines recovering two more fallen comrades. The battalion was forced to pull back and form a new perimeter. Despite efforts to restrain him, Watters dashed out three more times to recover wounded men. Finally, while distributing food and water to those still fighting and helping medics bandage the wounded, Chaplain Watters was also killed. For his "conspicuous gallantry . . . unyielding perserverance and selfless devotion to his comrades," the chaplain was posthumously awarded the Medal of Honor by Vice President Spiro Agnew on 4 November 1969.[58]

Chaplain Liteky, born in Washington, D.C., in 1931, and educated at colleges and seminaries in Florida, Alabama, Pennsylvania, and Virginia, entered the Army chaplaincy in July 1966. On 6 December 1967, 9 months after his arrival in Vietnam, he found himself in a fierce battle along with the men of Company A, 4th Battalion, 12th Infantry, 199th Light Infantry Brigade. They had engaged the enemy near Phuoc-Lac in the Bien Hoa Province. Initially the men of Liteky's unit were momentarily stunned and hugged the ground under intense enemy fire. But the chaplain noticed two wounded men ahead of them and crawled within 15 meters of an enemy machine gun, placing himself between the men and the hostile fire. During a brief lull, he quickly removed the men from the field to a helicopter landing area for evacuation. His action inspired the others to rally and direct heavy fire against the enemy positions. Liteky, meanwhile, began to move upright through the area, stopping to aid wounded and administer last rites. Since one wounded man was too heavy for him to carry, the chaplain laid down on his back, pulled the soldier onto his chest, and forced his way to the landing zone with his elbows and legs. Returning to the battle, he calmly extracted another fallen trooper entangled in dense, thorny underbrush. Again and again he returned to evacuate the wounded from the battle area. By the time the unit was relieved the following morning, it was obvious that Chaplain Liteky, who was also wounded, had personally carried more than 20 men to the evacuation site. On 19 November 1968, Chaplain Liteky stood in the White House with four other soldiers to receive the Medal of Honor from President Johnson.[59]

The political turmoil in South Vietnam eventually led to another change of governments with General Nguyen Van Thieu elected as President in September 1967. Despite the skepticism of some Americans, military leaders were beginning to express optimism about the progress of the war. General Westmoreland said that he had "never been more encouraged in my four years in Vietnam." [60] Chief of Staff Harold K. Johnson maintained, "We are definitely winning in Vietnam . . . If my observations are borne out—I recently returned from my eighth visit to Vietnam—then I believe we will see some real evidence of progress in the next few months." [61] Chaplain John K. Durham, American Baptist, although he had been wounded twice in 4 months, said, "I believe we belong in Vietnam. It would be unthinkable, at this late date, to pull out. . . . There are significant indications that we are winning the war." [62] President Johnson, meanwhile, had declared that he would stop the bombing "when this will lead promptly to productive discussions." [63]

But the events of early 1968 did not seem as promising as the optimism expressed. Communist forces struck heavily against major cities in the south during the Tet (Lunar New Year) offensive. Viet Cong troops raided the U.S. embassy in Saigon, overran the Chinese quarter of Cholon, and seized the city of Hue.[64] In Hue at the time was an Army chaplain who, said one reporter, "really had no business being there. But the infantrymen he loved were being killed before the battlements of Hue's imperial Citadel and the Rev. Aloysius P. McGonigal wanted to go. . . . He practically fought his way to the battlefield." [65]

Chaplain McGonigal was a Roman Catholic Jesuit who held a graduate degree in physics and was working on his Ph.D when he entered the chaplaincy for the second time in 1966. He arrived in Vietnam in October 1967 and was actually assigned to Advisory Team No. 1, MACV, 1st Aviation Brigade. Apparently, however, in thorough harmony with the area coverage approach, he made a habit of wandering throughout

See footnotes at end of chapter.

the I Corps area to visit the men in the field. He was determined to be with those most in need rather than to be restricted to one unit. Precisely because of his dedication to that philosophy, he was killed at Hue on 17 February 1968 "with a unit that was not his own in a battle he could have missed." [66]

RESPONDING TO ATROCITY

The *News Sheet* of the American Division in Vietnam was a mimeo-graphed, in-house "newspaper" that regularly carried items about the weather, an occasional cartoon, and reports of the latest combat assaults by elements of the division. The Sunday, 17 March 1968 edition included the following notes about the previous day's activities:

> . . . For the third time in recent weeks 11th Brigade infantry-men in Task Force Barker raided a Viet Cong stronghold known as "Pinkville" six miles northeast of Quang Ngai.
>
> "Jungle Warriors," together with artillery and helicopter support, hit the village of My Lai early yesterday morning. Contacts through-out the morning and early afternoon resulted in 128 enemy killed, 13 suspects detained and three weapons captured. . . .[67]

While some of the men who may have read that account were apparently aware of the more sordid details of what actually happened, it was 13 months later before a former enlisted man, Ronald L. Riden-hour, brought public attention to the matter. Based on information con-tained in his letter to government officials, the Department of the Army launched an investigation which not only stunned the American people but resulted in 13 officers and elisted men being charged with various court-martial offenses, including murder and assault to commit murder. The most well-known of the trials concluded with the conviction of First Lieutenant William L. Calley, Jr., on charges of premeditated murder of more than 100 Vietnamese non-combatant men, women, and children. The first witness called by Calley's defense attorneys was a former Army chaplain, Carl E. Creswell, Episcopalian.[68]

Creswell's testimony was considered important because of a brief exchange of words he claimed to have had with Calley's superior officers during a briefing preceding the My Lai incident.

> The officers were discussing recent Vietcong outrages, he said, and he heard one officer remark that if American troops received any fire during the impending assault "they'd level the village."

See footnotes at end of chapter.

Father Creswell said he reproached the officer: "I didn't think we made war that way."

He said the officer merely replied: "It's a tough war." [69]

Although no Army chaplains accompanied the men when they entered My Lai that day, ironically Chaplain Creswell was apparently the only chaplain to have received a first-hand report of the incident shortly after it happened. Serving as the American Division's Artillery Chaplain, Creswell also covered the unit's aviation battalion. A helicopter pilot, who was flying support for the mission, reported to Chaplain Creswell his conviction that civilians had been unnecessarily and purposefully killed during the operation. Creswell verbally passed the report to the American's Division Chaplain, Francis R. Lewis, United Methodist.

The precise sequence of events, let alone the specific conversations, were difficult to reconstruct. A special investigation directed by the Secretary of the Army under Lieutenant General William R. Peers uncovered conflicting reports. Chaplain Lewis, pointing out the difficulty in recalling details of occurances $1\frac{1}{2}$ years after they had happened, maintained that he had passed Chaplain Creswell's report to at least four of the division's key staff officers. He said that some of them seemed to be aware of the matter and told him that they were looking into it. During later testimony, however, only two staff officers remembered Chaplain Lewis making such a report and one of them said that he thought the chaplain was talking about some other matter.

Lewis said that he was satisfied that the incident had been properly investigated after conversing with the task force commander, Lieutenant Colonel Frank Barker, who had been in charge of the operation. The chaplain remembered that the lieutenant colonel told him he had concluded that civilians had been killed, but that they had died as a result of artillery and aircraft fire and cross fire between U.S. and VC forces. Since Barker was himself killed in subsequent action and no records could be found of such an inquiry, it was impossible to verify this report.

Chaplain Lewis had also concluded that the matter was not as serious as Chaplain Creswell's report had sounded when no similar reports came from the chaplains more closely connected with the unit. Although Task Force Barker was an organization comprised of segments of various units, the specific men involved at My Lai came from a battalion originally covered by Chaplain Harry P. Kissinger, Associated Gospel Churches. Neither Kissinger nor the two brigade chaplains, Ray-

See footnotes at end of chapter.

mond P. Hoffman, Episcopalian, and John C. Carey, Roman Catholic, received reports of any atrocity.[70]

Although Chaplains Lewis, Creswell, Hoffman, and Kissinger were called to testify in various subsequent investigations, nothing more could be determined than what Creswell himself had concluded: "In hindsight, I feel I should have done more." [71] Nearly 5 years after the incident, he further commented:

> I felt, at the time of the trials, very much betrayed by the Chaplains [to] whom I had entrusted my knowledge of the My Lai event. If a history of a fumble enables future Chaplains to hang on to the ball, this exercise will be worth . . . our troubles. As Santana [sic] said: "Those who do not study history, are condemned to repeat it." God forbid that in a similar situation, any Chaplain should ever be content with the actions I took.[72]

"Such incidents, along with general frustration about the conduct of the war," commented the *New York Times*, "have served to revive the old 'two masters' problem concerning chaplains in the armed forces." [73] The Executive Secretary for Chaplains of the United Church of Christ insited that chaplains be instructed to support officers and enlisted men who refuse to carry out orders they consider immoral or illegal.[74] While subsequent classes at the Chaplain School did, in fact, deal with the matter of legal orders and the means of properly reporting alleged atrocities, the highly-publicized My Lai tragedy certainly did not enhance the image of the chaplaincy. Among the reams of material written on the subject, at least one author strongly insinuated that the chaplains' ministry was virtually ineffectual.[75]

While the terrible circumstances at My Lai received more publicity, another situation of a similar, though less complex incident involved the kidnap, rape, and murder of a Vietnamese girl by a small group of U.S. soldiers. Though little credit was given to him for it, Chaplain Claude D. Newby, Latter Day Saints, was the first to properly respond to the report when a troubled soldier related the incident as he had heard it. Newby, a former military and civilian policeman, took the report to the Army's Criminal Investigation Division (CID) and the responsible individuals were eventually arrested and tried.[76]

ACCEPTING NEW CHALLENGES IN COUNSELING

The unpopularity of the Vietnam conflict added further responsibilities to the ministry of chaplains. In 1965 an Army Message revised the

See footnotes at end of chapter.

Army Regulation that provided guidance for the disposition of conscientious objectors. It directed that individuals applying for separation under the provisions of that regulation should attend a counseling interview by a chaplain. The directive, published as a superseding revision of the regulation in 1966, required chaplains to submit a report of such interviews including an opinion of the sincerity of the applicant and whether or not the objection was based on religious convictions. A similar regulation was published for the guidance of Reserve components.[77]

The revisions were apparently not burdensome to many chaplains who already had been giving such counseling without submitting a written report. But the OCCH believed some difficulties would arise if chaplains were not aware of a 1964 Supreme Court decision which defined a religious belief as "a sincere and meaningful belief which occupies in the life of its possessor a place parallel to that filled by the God of those admittedly qualifying for the exemption." In other words, this implied that a sincere philosophy, not necessarily compatible with orthodox religious doctrines but based on a power, being, or faith to which everything else was subordinate, was also a valid basis for conscientious objection. Consequently, the OCCH directed the Chaplain School to clarify this distinction to students during courses in subject areas dealing with such matters.[78]

By 1967 a request from the Director of Enlisted Personnel, DA Office of Personnel Operations, resulted in the establishment of a Conscientious Objector Review Board to render decisions on cases requesting such classification. A member of the OCCH was detailed as one of the members of this board and the Chief of Chaplains suggested that the policy guidance for the group include references to the Supreme Court decision. But The Judge Advocate General did not agree and pointed out that the Public Law governing the Military Selective Service Act of 1967 did not include in its definition of a religious belief convictions that were essentially political, sociological, or philosophical. Consequently, the OCCH passed out new guidance to the field in its monthly newsletter for January 1968.[79]

Undoubtedly because of these changes in guidance and the growing debates over conscientious objection, some chaplains became thoroughly confused as to precisely what they were to determine during the interviews of such applicants. The Director for Government Relations, National Council of the Churches of Christ in the U.S.A., expressed the concern that chaplains might be inclined to influence the decision of applicants rather than to help them articulate their convictions. Similarly, publicity over the contention by a civilian speaker at a chaplains' training conference that chaplains should oppose the nation's draft law, added further perplexity to the matter.[80] It is not surprising, in light of all this guidance and debate, that in 1969 the Conscientious Objector Review Board complained that many chaplain interview reports were "lengthy and meaningless, incomplete or inadequate." Further instruction was sent to the chaplains in the field entitled "Policy Guidance on Interviewing Conscientious Objector Applicants in the Armed Forces" and "Supplementary Policy Guidance on Conscientious Objectors" and apparently the matter was eventually clarified.[81]

During this same period, the infatuation of many American youth with the use of various drugs produced new problems which automatically spilled over into the nation's armed forces. Consequently, added attention had to be given to the counseling of the addict. When Chief of Chaplains Francis Sampson visited the Far East in early 1969, "the major problem brought to his attention was the use of drugs, especially in Korea and Thailand."[82] As a consequence, workshops for chaplains on "Ministering to the Drug User" were conducted on an Army-wide basis.[83] Chaplains also participated in efforts to combat alcoholism and, in some cases, became members of local command councils to devise more efficient means of dealing with the problem in the Army.[84]

Obviously such problems threatened the moral base of the nation and, as an immediate consequence, endangered the combat-effectiveness of U.S. units in Vietnam. A great deal of attention was given to solving these difficulties and in nearly every case, at virtually every level, the opinions and guidance of chaplains were sought. While assigned as a Mobilization Designee in the Medical Command Staff Chaplain's Office, Reserve Chaplain Viggo O. Aronsen, American Lutheran, correlated the results of numerous drug and alcohol abuse clinics held at Medical Command installations. "As a former EM, the one point I put foremost in the document which was bucked up to DA," he noted, "was that no man would turn himself in if he was then going to be court martialed for it!" Whether it was because of his suggestion or not, amnesty for offenders who were seeking help became Army policy and Aronsen added, "to think that a 'week end warrior' had a chance to make a partial contribution is a good feeling."[85]

The struggle to find some effective means of dealing with drug abuse in Vietnam intensified in the late 1960's and early 1970's. Chaplains became integral parts of the "healing teams" at the USARV Drug Treatment Facility (established first at Long Binh and later moved to the U.S. Army Hospital in Saigon) as well as the anti-drug educational programs in individual units. But even the briefest perusal of the drug treatment appendix to the MACV Command Chaplain's After Action Report, prepared at the end of American combat involvement in Vietnam, catches the note of frustration that permeated many of the attempts at rehabilitation. Some chaplains maintained that every program resulted more in paper work and the compilation of statistics than in actual aid to drug users. Others spoke out against what they believed to be a double standard which virtually ignored alcohol abuse by "lifers" (older NCO's) and concentrated on narcotics abuse by younger soldiers. Nevertheless, considerable time was given by chaplains to personal and group counseling, and to their own training sessions and conferences as part of the concerted effort by the Army to overcome the problem. In fact, several significant ecclesiastical leaders who visited Vietnam in 1970 and 1971 praised the efforts being made. Dr. Robert V. Moss, president of the United Church of Christ, maintained that more innovative and significant means of combating drug abuse were being used by the Army in Vietnam than by domestic organizations in the United States. Dr. Robert C. Marshall, president of the Lutheran Church in America, and Dr. Oswald C. J. Hoffman, speaker on the International Lutheran Hour, made similar assessments.[86]

During the same period, the increasing problems related to race relations were receiving equal attention from chaplains in Vietnam. The Army's determination to foster racial harmony and equality resulted in the assignment of Chaplain Benjamin E. Smith, United Presbyterian, to develop a Human Relations Program for USARV. Smith and his successors, Chaplain Roland F. Day. National Baptist, and Chaplain Paul J. Bailey, United Church of Christ, saw to it that Human Relations Councils were established at all levels, down to and including company-sized units. Human Relations personnel were appointed on orders, unit educational programs were developed, and a system of staff visits and instruction was initiated. By November 1972 Chaplain Bailey had developed the USARV Race Relations/Equal Opportunity Affirmative Action Plan. The Plan was essentially an educational system to aid personnel in recognizing and changing discriminatory practices within units. Along with the concentrated attack on drug abuse, however, the Human Relations Program in Vietnam came to an abrupt halt with the notification of the

See footnotes at end of chapter.

cease-fire agreements in 1973 and the eventual withdrawal of U.S. military personnel.[87]

Although much of the work of Army chaplains toward solving the problems of drug abuse and racial discord was to continue in other assignments both in the U.S. and overseas, it is interesting to note the unique existence of such programs in a combat zone. In contrast to those who served in World War II and the Korean Conflict, Army chaplains in Vietnam were involved far more in noncombat-related pastoral duties. Undoubtedly, the vast dispersion of troops, the large number of support units in relatively secure areas, the national turmoil over U.S. involvement in Vietnam, and the popularity of the anti-establishment philosophy among many young soldiers all contributed to the necessity for a ministry far beyond the consoling of men in the emergency situations of the battlefield. Conscientious objection, drug abuse, and race relations were among the major concerns. But chaplains in Vietnam were also heavily involved in the day-to-day counseling of soldiers with a myriad of other decisions and problems ranging from marriage to Vietnamese girls to arrangements for compassionate leaves and reassignments. In a sense, it could be said that the chaplains' ministry in Vietnam was among the most challenging ever faced in the history of the branch. More than a salve to soothe the effects of battle, the chaplains' work had begun to penetrate the very depths of human psychology in an attempt to serve the soldier who faced his own inner conflicts.

STRUGGLING TO HELP WITH BODY AND SPIRIT

It took a month of long and arduous fighting to suppress the 1968 Communist Tet offensive, but limited success was gained and Hue was recaptured by U.S. and Vietnamese forces after 26 days. Nearly a year later, while irrigation canals were being dug near the city, mass graves of hundreds of the city's former inhabitants were found—victims of a huge massacre that had been conducted by the Viet Cong during their occupation of the area. President Johnson, facing the turmoil over the war in the U.S. and determined to bring the fighting to an honorable conclusion without political influence, announced his decision to retire at the end of his term, and, at the same time, stopped the bombing once more in an appeal for truce talks. Finally, in May of that year, discussions between the U.S. and North Vietnam were opened in Paris. Whatever brief optimism may have been generated, however, was quelled with the

See footnotes at end of chapter.

end-of-the-year reports that the U.S. had lost 14,592 servicemen in Vietnam during 1968 alone.[88] Numbered among the final statistics for that year was Jewish Chaplain Morton H. Singer.

Singer had served as a rabbi in New York prior to entering the Army in 1967. After graduating from the Chaplain School, he served at Fort Sill, Oklahoma, for 1 year before being transferred to Vietnam in November 1968. Six weeks later, on 17 December 1968, Chaplain Singer boarded an aircraft at Chu Lai Airfield after visiting units in the northern I Corps area. The plane crashed and burned shortly after take off and the rabbi became the ninth chaplain to lose his life in Vietnam. "Rabbi Singer was an outstanding Chaplain intensely dedicated to his work," wrote Lieutenant General Richard G. Stilwell, Commanding General of the XXIV Corps. "He spared no effort in ministering to the Jewish personnel throughout the entire I Corps Tactical Zone. His death was a great shock to the officers and men of this headquarters and saddened all of us who knew him." At Mrs. Singer's request, the chaplain was buried on the Mountain of Rest, a hilltop that borders Jerusalem in Israel.[89]

Richard M. Nixon, newly elected President of the United States, appointed Henry Cabot Lodge as the chief U.S. negotiator in Paris and warned the North Vietnamese that America would not tolerate continued attacks in the south. In March 1969 the Defense Department announced that U.S. forces in Vietnam numbered 541,500—the peak level during all of their years of involvement there.[90] Those forces were comprised of a generation of young people who were beginning to be more socially, politically, and philosophically conscious than any group of American youth that had preceded them. There were those who struggled with the spirit to understand and do that which was right and those who struggled in a physical way to serve a nation they believed had to be right. The challenge for chaplains was to relate and minister to them by joining in the same struggles.

Chaplain Orris E. Kelly, United Methodist, who had both enlisted and commissioned service in the Army prior to becoming a chaplain, was the 4th Infantry Division Chaplain from July 1969 to July 1970. When asked later to relate the most significant events of his ministry in a combat situation, Kelly cited his efforts to help men deal with problems of conscience, such as, "How can I kill in a war I don't believe in, to destroy a person I do not have any understanding of?"[91]

See footnotes at end of chapter.

I do not believe that the chaplain's position is to uphold or disprove the administration['s] position on war or politics. I considered myself a spiritual advisor to the soldier to help him with questions of conscience. The soldier must make up his own mind as a free agent. Chaplains cannot assist growth and maturation to responsible adulthood by imposing their own viewpoints. The chaplain becomes a facilitator of growth by helping the soldier clarify the issues and make his own decisions.[92]

Chaplain Thomas J. McInnes, American Baptist, surveyed a typical group gathered for one of his services and wrote:

There they sit tired, bone-tired, dirty, sweaty, and grimed. There they squat, often unshaven, always armed and disarmingly alert. . . .

What an awful responsibility to represent the prince of rebels among young rebels!

Their language may be profane, their habits gross, their stories ribald, their thoughts shocking, their gestures obscene, their motives suspect, their hatreds just at parade rest.

But there they are having come to hear of him who came not to call the righteous but sinners to repentance.

May they hear and hear well before they meet the horseman death.

God help them—and me—in this brief span![93]

Hundreds of Army chaplains were decorated for acts which were essentially motivated by love and a desire to be of some aid to such men as those. "I think that the most significant part of my ministry was the year spent in Viet Nam," recalled Chaplain Joseph E. Galle, III, Southern Baptist. "It was a year of frustrations, anxieties, and fears. However, being able to share my feelings as well as my faith with fellow chaplains and other Christians, made the year not only memorable but meaningful."[94] For his brave determination to assist and comfort the wounded during a June 1969 attack on elements of the 25th Infantry Division, Galle was awarded the Silver Star.[95] For similar service under nearly identical circumstances, and virtually at the same time, Chaplain Ernest B. Peck, United Methodist, with the 101st Airborne Division, received the same award.[96] Some chaplains, like Gene M. Little, Southern Baptist, were decorated for courage in unique situations. In September 1969 Chaplain Little calmly entered a building in which a troubled and armed American soldier had isolated himself, threatening to kill anyone who approached. Little remained with him, quietly persuaded him to turn over his weapon, and encouraged him to accept medical help. For his bravery and devotion to his men, Chaplain Little

See footnotes at end of chapter.

received the Soldier's Medal.[97] By the war's end, Army chaplain awards included not only the two Medals of Honor, but also 719 Bronze Stars, 586 Army Commendation Medals, 318 Air Medals, 82 Purple Hearts, 66 Legions of Merit, 26 Silver Stars, and numerous other decorations.[98]

Chaplain Don L. Bartley, Presbyterian U.S., was one man who received several of those awards. Bartley had studied at Union Theological Seminary in Virginia during the 1950's. One of his professors was Ben L. Rose, Presbyterian U.S., who had served as a chaplain in World War II and considered it a privilege, as a Reserve chaplain, "to open the eyes of many young theologians to the opportunities of ministry as a military chaplain." [99] After serving a civilian church in Virginia for a few years, Bartley entered the chaplaincy in 1961. Seven years later he arrived in Vietnam to serve with the 196th Infantry Brigade of the Americal Division. During his assignment with the unit, his courageous ministry had earned for him the Silver Star, the Purple Heart, and the Air Medal. Tragically, on 8 June 1969—near the end of his tour in the country—Chaplain Bartley was killed while on a special assignment with MACV when a jeep in which he was riding struck a land mine. Adding to his previous decorations, Chaplain Bartley was posthumously awarded the Legion of Merit, the Joint Service Commendation Medal, and a second Purple Heart.[100]

Chaplain Roger W. Heinz, Missouri Synod Lutheran, who had survived the action in the Dominican Republic only a few years before, was also killed in Vietnam in 1969. He had served in a civilian parish in Connecticut for 3 years, entered the Army in 1964, and arrived in Vietnam in August 1969 to serve with the 5th Special Forces Group. On 9 December, after conducting a worship service for a Special Forces' team southwest of Da Nang, Heinz was killed when the helicopter in which he was leaving the area crashed into the side of a mountain and burned. Chaplain Heinz' widow was among the many who received special letters from the White House that year. The President's message said in part:

> I pray for the day when this war can be ended, and peace restored. I wish that your husband could have lived to see that day. His courage, his devotion and his sacrifice have brought it closer. When it comes, there will be a special place in the thoughts of his countrymen for him, and for you, and for the others who have borne the burdens of loss.
>
> Mrs. Nixon joins me in extending our deepest sympathy . . . You will be in our prayers, and in our hearts.[101]

See footnotes at end of chapter.

WEEPING WITH THOSE WHO MOURN

In June 1969 President Nixon began a slow withdrawal of some of the U.S. forces from Vietnam. He insisted that in the future the U.S. would avoid similar involvements and would limit their support to economic and military aid without committing combat personnel. Although by the end of the year over 50,000 troops had been withdrawn and news was broadcast of the death of Ho Chi Minh, the Paris talks had reached a stalemate, Lodge had resigned as the chief U.S. negotiator, and a large moratorium against the war was held in Washington.

1970 was a year of continued tragedy and turmoil. While more U.S. troops were being withdrawn and efforts were made to support a "Vietnamization" program, Prince Norodom Sihanouk of Cambodia was overthrown by a coup. U.S. forces were sent briefly into the country, against heavy American protest, to destroy Viet Cong sanctuaries; Congress repealed the Tonkin Gulf Resolution and approved the Cooper-Church amendment barring future operations in Cambodia without specific legislative approval.[102]

The tragedies of the year struck on both sides of the Pacific. One of them was endured by the chaplains of the Republic of Vietnam. The Vietnamese Chaplaincy dated back to 1951 when indigenous Roman Catholic priests were assigned on an informal basis to work with their forces under the French. By 1954 the branch was integrated with the RVN Armed Forces and 4 years later a Protestant element was formed. By 1964 Buddhist chaplains came into the services and the branch was administered by three directorates representing the separate faiths. MACV chaplains had established liaison with the Vietnamese chaplains, guiding and supporting their work wherever possible. In the spring of 1970, 85 RVN chaplains were studying at a training school in Dalat, nearing their graduation from a basic course. A sudden enemy attack was launched against the school. Sixteen of the unarmed chaplains were killed and 13 were wounded in a single, stunning blow. The deaths resulting from that one attack outnumbered the losses of U.S. Army chaplains during the entire course of their 11-year service in the war.[103]

One month later, and thousands of miles away, Ohio National Guardsmen were called to restore order during an anti-war rally at Kent State University. Chaplain William B. Reinhardt, Missouri Synod Lutheran, was called from his parish in Cleveland to join his fellow citizen-soldiers who had just participated in quelling disturbances over a truckers' strike. Students at the university had burned the Army Reserve Officers Training Corps (ROTC) building and taunted the guardsmen facing them. "When you have troops with gas masks on, and they disperse their gas, and they have their weapons, with a few thousand students surrounding them and throwing things," said Reinhardt, "—well, it was a very rough situation." [104]

Suddenly some of the guardsmen opened fire on the students, killing four and wounding ten. "Stunned. Shocked. I cried," recalled the chaplain. "I talked to many of the men, and they were horror-stricken. Many men cried." Moments later Reinhardt circulated among his men and the students, trying to restore reason. He held a brief devotion for the guardsmen: ". . . we're not as perfect as we would like others to believe we are . . . Father, forgive them." He spent nearly 2 hours among students, sometimes enduring shouted obscenities, trying to remind them that they were a common people attempting to find the best course for their nation. "We have to remember," he insisted, "that the National Guard is made up of citizen soldiers. The guardsman is a student, a father, brother, barber, butcher, dentist, minister, businessman, public relations representative, salesman. He's your neighbor. He's not a monster in a green uniform." At the same time he agonized, "There must be some way in our modern society that we can find better methods as Christians, as Americans, to solve our differences other than inhumane, animalistic behavior." [105]

Easter Sunday of 1970 welcomed few crowds as impressive as the more than 8,600 soldiers of the 101st Airborne Division who gathered at one of their camps for a single service. "There were 33 chaplains who participated in the joint service following which nine Catholic chaplains concelebrated Mass and 19 Protestant chaplains conducted a communion service," wrote Chaplain Clifford E. Keys, Nazarene.[106] But as impressive as such gatherings were, few chaplains were unaware of the struggles their ministry was facing in the prolonged effects of the Vietnam war. Chaplain Leonard F. Stegman, Roman Catholic, USARV Staff Chaplain, reminded the military clerics in one of his newsletters:

> These are difficult and trying days in Vietnam. The survival of the Army here, and also of our nation as a whole, is becoming more and more dependent on highly viable and morally motivated leaders. The problems faced by our commanders in Vietnam now and in the months to come, will test their patience, ingenuity, and ability to the limit. Deeply involved in these problems are the activities,

See footnotes at end of chapter.

aspirations, and desperations of the men under their care, engendered by the character of todays youth.

From conversation with countless commanders, I know that they are desperately seeking help to fulfill their responsibilities. I also know they are looking to you their chaplains as never before to be their support in the difficult area of human relations and for spiritual and moral leadership. In this crisis we as chaplains can be real "performers" or "duds." We can gain all or lose all for the image of the Chaplaincy for the next generation.[107]

One of the "performers" was Chaplain Phillip A. Nichols, Assemblies of God, serving with the American Division. Leaving a civilian church in Bonners Ferry, Idaho, to join the Army Chaplaincy in June 1969, his total military career lasted only 16 months. Arriving in Vietnam in March 1970, he was killed on the evening of 13 October while accompanying men of the 198th Infantry Brigade when a concealed enemy explosive device detonated near him. One of those leaders who had to face the challenges referred to by Chaplain Stegman was Nichols' brigade commander. "Phil's absence will be keenly felt by all in the Brigade," wrote Colonel William R. Richardson to Mrs. Nichols. "I admired him for his continuous efforts to go to the field, in spite of inherent dangers, in order to be with the men of his battalion and to provide them spiritual assistance. . . . his compassion for his men endeared him to every soldier, making his death a shocking experience for all of us." [108]

ENDING WITH HONOR WHERE HONOR IS DUE

American involvement in Vietnam had continued so long that many soldiers and their chaplains returned for repeated tours in the country. The Chaplain School curriculum included a variety of subject areas and special classes to acquaint incoming chaplains with the country and the types of ministry they would anticipate there.[109] The Chaplain Agency of the Combat Developments Command at Fort Lee, Virginia, had been constantly busy developing and testing new equipment for chaplains in the field—especially for those in Vietnam. The portable altar and worship kits, formerly 25-pound units in metal cases, were replaced with compact, 6-pound kits in easily-carried, waterproof fabric bags. The former portable pump organ gave way to an electric model and finally to a cassette tape recorder with pre-recorded hymns.[110]

Meanwhile, the chaplains' ministries in Vietnam had become as varied and intricate as in any other theater of operation. They ranged

---

See footnotes at end of chapter.

from brief devotions in the jungles for isolated combat patrols to elaborate services in beautiful chapels at stabilized camps; from counseling a soldier about his "Dear John" letter between rocket attacks to participating in drug rehabilitation programs; from informal chats with men while they ate "C" rations in the field to well-planned devotional programs at the new religious retreat center at Cam Ranh Bay. It was a coordinated ministry not only involving chaplains from all the branches of the U.S. Armed Forces, but also those in the forces of the Republic of Vietnam and the variety of other nations represented, such as Australia and Korea. While the drawdown continued, morale of the soldiers became one of the chaplains' primary concerns. "One of the most important problems they have to meet today," reported the President of the United Church of Christ on his return from a visit in the war-ravaged land, "is the fear that each man cannot help experience, that he will be 'the last man killed in Vietnam.' " [111]

Among the Army clerics, Chaplain Merle D. Brown, American Lutheran, was the last. The 31-year-old native of Pennsylvania had entered the Army in 1969 and went to Vietnam in August 1970. Having served first with the 11th Brigade of the Americal Division, he was later assigned to the 198th Infantry Brigade of the 23rd Infantry Division. On Easter Sunday, 11 April 1971, Chaplain Brown died in a helicopter crash.[112]

The statistics of Army-chaplain losses in America's longest war reflected a variety as broad as the duties they performed. Seven were Protestant, four were Roman Catholic, and two were Jewish. Their skins were white, black, and brown. They came from places as distant as Israel and the Philippines, and served in one nation from New York to Idaho. Yet there was a unity in their devotion, a commonness in their sacrifice, and a oneness in their purpose—to minister to the American soldier wherever he was called.

As the withdrawal of American troops continued, chaplain strength in Vietnam dropped rapidly. In November 1970 USARV had 308 chaplains on their roles; one year later they numbered 152.[113] By then President Nixon had cut the level of U.S. forces in the country to 139,000.[114]

But de-escalation proved far more difficult than had escalation. The return of prisoners of war became a primary concern of many Americans while Henry A. Kissinger, representing the U.S., conducted secret negotiations with the North Vietnamese in Paris. Not unlike the situation in Korea 20 years earlier, the talks in 1972 were on-again, off-again, interrupted regularly with military attacks and counter-attacks. In desperation, President Nixon directed the mining of North Vietnamese ports and the blockade of supply deliveries to the country. On the other hand, by June 1972, U.S. forces had been reduced below 60,000, and their roles reverted back to advisory and combat support positions.

The situation seemed bleak at the end of 1972 when Mr. Kissinger's attempts toward a settlement seemed constantly frustrated and heavy, round-the-clock raids were directed on the north with U.S. B-52 bombers. But the bombing, mining, and shelling of North Vietnam was halted in January 1973 as renewed progress was made in Paris.[115] Only 19 Army, 11 Air Force, and 2 Navy chaplains remained in Vietnam in the combined USARV-MACV Headquarters under the supervision of Chaplain Emil F. Kapusta, Roman Catholic, as the final cease-fire document was signed in Paris on the evening of 27 January 1973. Two months later, on 28 March, Chaplain Kapusta took part in the deactivation ceremonies of his headquarters in Saigon and minutes later boarded a plane as the last U.S. chaplain to leave Vietnam.[116]

"Looking back on all these years—all of the blood and agony—I have to wonder what we accomplished," reminisced retired General Paul D. Harkins who had served as the U.S. commander in Vietnam from 1962 to 1964.[117] "Vietnam will haunt this country in a hundred ways for decades to come," wrote an American author.[118] Future historians will dissect the war, the nation, the Army and the Chaplaincy during those decades. They will evaluate and re-evaluate the causes, the effects, the blunders, and successes. Hopefully they will not reduce that period of history to statistics and policies, ignoring the sacrifices of the common people who were necessarily involved.

Few recollections from that time captured the emotions of the period as well as those of a civilian minister in Lexington, Kentucky, attending the funeral of a 19-year-old soldier—one of the nearly 46,000 American servicemen who were killed in Vietnam. "This whole business of war disturbs me," he wrote. "I have never felt compelled to enlist as a chaplain. The truth is, I am not eager to see war firsthand." He didn't know the soldier, his family, or anyone at the funeral. In fact, he only attended the service on an impulse.

Surveying the grief-torn family, he could tell they were poor and common people—faceless people who "put gas in your car, or sell you shoes, or fix your gutters, or deliver your mail. . . . nobody to me. Or . . . more to me than I ever could realize." He followed them in his car to a

---

country cemetery. "I was going to see the boy buried because I felt indebted to him. He died for me and my kids. He deserved some respect."

As the procession passed people busy at their daily routines, he thought: "Heroes die so kids can play ball on vacant lots, and women can mow their grass, and students can learn or demonstrate, and disc jockeys can sell soft drinks." When the quiet and simple service concluded, he walked over to the mother and father and took them by the hand. "I wasn't acting the preacher," he wrote. "I was just a man with two youngsters of his own." "I came because I'm grateful," he told them. "I didn't know your boy, nor do I know you, but thanks. Thanks a lot." [119]

Thousands of miles away, at virtually the same time, Army Chaplain Wendell E. Danielson, Evangelical Covenant, was standing in the center of a semicircle of dirty and wet soldiers sitting on Vietnamese sand:

> In a few moments we would close our services with the hymn, "God Bless America." This, for us, is difficult to sing. The words are simple enough but they compel a response. I knew the Doc wouldn't make it past the fourth line. He never finished, "From the mountains, to the prairies." Tears come to his eyes and he stops singing. Nobody, however, notices. Others would begin looking at the ground, or their hands, or at the sky. "God bless America, my home sweet home." ...
>
> During the coming months I will continue to work here. There is much that must be done—instruction to give, an example to set. Who will do this? For my men this is my responsibility. They must be shown faith and love and courage. If my example in living these virtues is not louder than my words I become the tinkling cymbal.
>
> So the responsibility remains the same ... The opportunity is always here to bring men to God and God to men. This is and will always be the high calling. To do less is to do nothing.
>
> *The Lord of hosts is with us; The God of Jacob is our refuge.*[120]

FOOTNOTES

CHAPTER V

[1] *Army and Navy Journal,* 13 August 1949, p. 1436.

[2] *New York Times,* 14 June 1951, p. 8.

[3] *New York Times Magazine,* 8 June 1952, p. 9.

[4] For chronologies of the Vietnam conflict see R. Ernest Dupuy and Trevor N. Dupuy, *The Encyclopedia of Military History* (New York: Harper & Row, 1970), pp. 1249–1252; *New York Times,* 28 January 1973, p. 25; "Chronology: Generation of Conflict," *Time,* 6 November 1972, pp. 28–29.

[5] John A. Lindvall to OCCH, 9 August 1962, U.S. Army Chaplain Center and School Archives, Ft. Wadsworth, NY (hereafter referred to as USACHCS).

[6] John A. Lindvall to Edward M. Mize, 14 March 1962, USACHCS.

[7] Edward M. Mize to John A. Lindvall, 23 March 1962, USACHCS.

[8] John A. Lindvall to Edward M. Mize, 12 April 1962, USACHCS.

[9] Joel E. Andrews, Recorded Inteview, 1 December 1972, USACHCS.

[10] *Ibid.*

[11] "War Casualties: 1961-72," *Time,* 6 November 1972, p. 22.

[12] Andrews, Recorded Interview, 1 December 1972, USACHCS.

[13] John A. Lindvall to Office of the Chaplain, Hq, 4th U.S. Army, 28 May 1962, USACHCS.

[14] John A. Lindvall to Robert B. Howerton, 21 June 1962; John A. Lindvall to Cleo Buxton, O.C.U., 23 June 1962; John A. Lindvall to Warren MacPherson, Assemblies of God Servicemen's Department, 26 June 1962; John A. Lindvall to Robert S. McCarty, 24 October 1962, USACHCS.

[15] John A. Lindvall to OCCH, ATTN: Ch (Col) Bernard Fenton, 9 August 1962, USACHCS.

[16] Robert S. McCarty to John A. Lindvall, 12 October 1962, USACHCS.

[17] See chronology *New York Times,* 28 January 1973, p. 25; Historical Report for CY 1972, Appendix XII, MACV Chaplains' Section, USACHCS.

[18] See chronology *New York Times,* 28 January 1973, p. 25.

[19] Peter S. Lent, Historical Questionnaire, 29 November 1973, USACHCS.

[20] Lawrence K. Brady, Biographical Sketch, accompanying orders, and interview notes, USACHCS.

[21] *Lutheran Chaplains Newsletter,* Second Quarter 1963, p. 6.

[22] *OCCH Historical Review, 1 July 1962, to 30 June 1963,* p. 114; *1 July 1968 to 30 June 1969,* p. 121, and intervening issues, s.v. "Personnel Strength."

[23] Dupuy and Dupuy, *Encyclopedia of Military History,* pp. 1251–1252.

[24] *In Memorium: Chaplain (Lt. Col.) Meir Engel* (New York: National Jewish Welfare Board, 1965) ; *The Chaplain,* Summer Quarter 1973, p. 7.

[25] Personnel Records of Meir Engel, U.S. Army Reserve Components Personnel and Administration Center, St. Louis, MO (hereafter referred to as USARCPAC).

[26] William C. Westmoreland to MACV personnel, 16 December 1964, as quoted in *In Memoriam: Chaplain Engel.*

[27] MACV Command Chaplain Staff Study, Subj: "Review of HQ MACV Organization and Functions," 21 February 1969, USACHCS; "Chaplain Activities," *MACV Command History 1970,* pp. XII 18—XII 21; *1972–1973,* pp. F5—F6, DA Center of Military History, Washington, D.C.

[28] See chronology *New York Times,* 28 January 1973, p. 25.

[29] Arthur F. Bell, Personal Interview, 21 January 1975, USACHCS.

[30] *Army News Features,* Hq, U.S. Army Command Information Unit, Washington, D.C., Release No. 12, 19 November 1965; See also various news clippings regarding letters and gifts, Vietnam file-1965, USACHCS.

[31] Harold K. Johnson, address to National Security Industrial Association's Annual Luncheon, Washington, D.C., 7 October 1965 (War Office *Speech File Service,* No. 10–2–65), USACHCS.

[32] See *OCCH Historical Review, 1 July 1965 to 31 December 1966,* p. 82.

[33] *Ibid.,* pp. 81–82.

[34] *Ibid.,* pp. 71–75; See also Theodore V. Koepke, Historical Questionnaire, 20 February 1974, USACHCS.

[35] *OCCH Historical Review, 1 July 1965 to 31 December 1966,* pp. 64–66; See also various news clippings on story of Chaplain Curtis Bowers, Vietnam file-1966, USACHCS.

[36] Personnel Records of William J. Barragy, USARCPAC; *The Chaplain,* Summer Quarter, 1973, p. 7.

[37] Personnel Records of William N. Feaster, USARCPAC; *The Chaplain,* Summer Quarter 1973, p. 8.

[38] Personnel Records of Michael J. Quealy, USARCPAC; General Orders No. 554, Hq, 1st Infantry Division, 26 January 1967; *The Chaplain,* Summer Quarter 1973, p. 8; January–February 1967, p. 46; "Chaplain's Death," *Time,* 18 November 1966, p. 82; "God's Warriors," *This Week,* 26 March 1967, p. 2.

[39] "Ministers Comment on the War: 12 Disciples are Chaplains in Vietnam," Disciples of Christ *The Christian,* 22 May 1966. p. 4.

[40] John L. Throckmorton, address to National Commission of the American Legion, Washington, D.C., 2 March 1966 (War Office *Speech File Service,* No. 4-2-66), USACHCS.

[41] *Frontlines,* November 1966, p. 8.

[42] "The Chopper Chaplains," *Time,* 11 February 1966, p. 68.

[43] *OCCH Historical Review, 1 July 1965 to 30 June 1966,* p. 234.

[44] Sam Castan, "Father Tom Confroy: Church is in His Combat Pack," *Look,* 12 July 1966, pp. 75–76.

[45] *Ibid.,* p. 76; "Sam Castan, 1935–1966, *Look,* Senior Editor," *Look,* 12 July 1966, pp. 77–78.

[46] *Pacific Stars & Stripes,* 9 March 1966, p. 9.

[47] "The Chopper Chaplains," *Time,* 11 February 1966, p. 68.

[48] *Ibid.;* See also James M. Hutchens, *Beyond Combat* (Chicago: Moody Press, 1968).

[49] Chronologies *New York Times,* 28 January 1973, p. 25; *Time,* 6 November 1972, pp. 22 & 29.

[50] "Wounded Chaplain Tells of Ministry in Vietnam War," *A Mighty Fortress,* January 1967, p. 1.

[51] Gus Engelman, "Army Padre Aids Morale in Viet Nam," *New York World Tribune,* 12 February 1967, p. 20.

[52] Hq, USARV, Subj: USARV Construction Priority System, 18 November 1967, USACHCS; See also various entries on Vietnam construction, Vietnam file—1965–1973, USACHCS.

[53] Chaplains' Section, Hq, MACV, to OCCH, Subj: "After Action Report—The U.S. Army Chaplaincy in Vietnam at the time of Cessation of Hostilities," 21 February 1973, p. 4, USACHCS.

[54] See Riggin B. Luetscher, "Helicopter Circuit Rider," *The Chaplain,* July–August 1967, pp. 14–17.

[55] Personnel Records of James J. L. Johnson, USARCPAC; *The Chaplain,* Summer Quarter 1973, p. 8; November–December 1967, p. 43.

[56] *Baltimore News American,* 20 December 1967, pp. 1 & 3; *The Chaplain,* May–June 1968, p. 53; September–October 1967, p. 50; Summer Quarter 1973, p. 10; Personnel Records of Ambrosio S. Grandea, USARCPAC.

[57] See Volume II entries on Chaplains Milton L. Haney, John M. Whitehead, and Francis B. Hall; Roy J. Honeywell, *Chaplains of the United States Army* (Washington, D.C.: DA Office of the Chief of Chaplains, 1958), p. 124.

[58] Personnel Records of Charles J. Watters, USARCPAC; General Orders No. 71, Hq, Department of the Army, 20 November 1969; News Release No. 949–69, Department of Defense, 4 November 1969; *The Chaplain,* March–April 1968, p. 48; Summer Quarter 1973, p. 11.

[59] *OCCH Historical Review, 1 July 1968 to 30 June 1969,* pp. 23 & 44; Copies of citation and biographical data on Angelo J. Liteky furnished by DA Office of Information, USACHCS; *The Chaplain,* September–October 1968, p. 48.

[60] *New York Times,* 28 January 1973, p. 25.

[61] "End of Vietnam War in Sight," *U.S. News & World Report,* 11 September 1967, pp. 44–45.

[62] "Vietnam Casualty," *American Baptist Chaplain,* October 1967, pp. 1–3.

[63] *New York Times,* 28 January 1973, p. 25.

[64] "Chronology: Generation of Conflict," *Time,* 6 November 1972, p. 29.

[65] *Washington Post,* 21 February 1968, p. C22.

[66] *Ibid.;* Personnel Records of Aloysius P. McGonigal, USARCPAC; *The Chaplain,* May–June 1968, p. 49; Summer Quarter 1973, p. 11.

[67] *Americal News Sheet,* 17 March 1968, p. 1 (copy at USACHCS made from original in personal files of Francis R. Lewis, Aberdeen Proving Ground, MD).

[68] *U.S. Army Command Information Fact Sheet,* No. 180 (DA Office of the Chief of Information), 2 April 1971; *New York Times,* 11 December 1970, p. 9.

[69] *New York Times,* 11 December 1970, p. 9.

[70] Francis R. Lewis, Recorded Interview, 11 April 1973, USACHCS; Harry P. Kissinger, Recorded Interview, 1 November 1973, USACHCS.

[71] *New York Times,* 30 January 1972, p. 6.

[72] C. Edward Creswell to Rodger R. Venzke, n.d. (received 12 November 1973), USACHCS.

[73] *New York Times,* 30 January 1972, p. 6.

[74] *New York Times,* 3 January 1970, p. 17.

[75] See Martin Gershen, *Destroy or Die: The True Story of My Lai* (New Rochelle, NY: Arlington House, 1971), pp. 210, 276–277, 280, 287.

[76] The story of this incident, although using pseudo names, was published in Daniel Lang, *Casualties of War* (New York: McGraw Hill, 1969). Chaplain Newby, referred to as "Chaplain Gerald Kirk" in that book, detailed his involvement in letters to Rodger R. Venzke, 20 February 1973 and 6 March 1973 (USACHCS).

[77] Message, Department of the Army, No. 742770, 4 December 1965; Changes to para 4c and 4d, AR 635–20, 5 January 1966; AR 135–25, para 7a (3) (a) and b-d; See also *OCCH Historical Review, 1 July 1965 to 31 December 1966,* pp. 43–44.

[78] See discussion of the implications of "United States versus Seegar" in *OCCH Historical Review, 1 January 1967 to 30 June 1968,* pp. 34–35.

[79] *OCCH Historical Review, 1 January 1967 to 30 June 1968,* pp. 36–37.

[80] *Ibid.,* pp. 38–39.

[81] *OCCH Historical Review, 1 July 1968 to 30 June 1969,* pp. 38–39.

[82] *Ibid.,* p. 17.

[83] *Ibid.,* pp. 23–24.

[84] See William R. Hett, "Dust Off," *The Chaplain,* January–February 1969, pp. 15–20.

[85] Viggo O. Aronsen, Historical Questionnaire, 12 October 1973, USACHCS.

[86] Chaplains' Section, Hq, MACV, to OCCH, Subj; "After Action Report—The U.S. Army Chaplaincy in Vietnam at the time of Cessation of Hostilities," 21 February 1973, Appendix XXIX, USACHCS.

[87] *Ibid.,* Appendix XXVIII.

[88] *Testimony of a City* (Washington, D.C.: Embassy of Viet Nam, 1969); *New York Times,* 28 January 1973, p. 25; Time, 6 November 1972, pp. 22 & 29.

[89] Personnel Records of Morton H. Singer, including Richard G. Stilwell to Mrs. Eva Singer, 4 January 1969, USARCPAC; *The Chaplain,* May–June 1969, p. 47; Summer Quarter 1973, p. 12.

[90] *New York Times,* 28 January 1973, p. 25.

[91] Orris E. Kelly, Historical Questionnaire, 5 October 1973, USACHCS.

[92] Orris E. Kelly to Rodger R. Venzke, 23 November 1973.

[93] Thomas J. McInnes, "Thoughts Before a Field Service," *The Chaplain,* January–February 1969, p. 10.

[94] Joseph E. Galle, III, to Parker C. Thompson, 11 October 1973, USACHCS.

[95] General Orders No. 9071, Hq, 25th Infantry Division, 12 July 1969.

[96] General Orders No. 9993, Hq, 101st Airborne Division, 31 July 1969.

[97] General Orders No. 12668, Hq, 25th Infantry Division, 10 October 1969.

[98] Clifford E. Keys, OCCH, to Chester R. Lindsey, USACHCS, and inclosure, 5 April 1973, USACHCS.

[99] Ben L. Rose, Historical Questionnaire, 15 October 1973, USACHCS.

[100] Personnel Records of Don L. Bartley, USARCPAC.

[101] Personnel Records of Roger W. Heinz, including Richard M. Nixon to Mrs. Roger W. Heinz, 20 December 1969, USARCPAC.

[102] *New York Times,* 28 January 1973, p. 25.

[103] See "Fact Sheet, Military Chaplaincy, Republic of Vietnam Armed Forces," and "The Republic of Vietnam Armed Forces Chaplaincy," Chaplains' Section, Hq, MACV, n.d., USACHCS; *In Memory of Our Fellow Chaplains of the Vietnamese Armed Forces, Dalat, April 1970* (RVN: Hq, MACV, 21 April 1970), USACHCS; Harold B. Lawson, "Liaison with Vietnamese Chaplaincy," *Frontlines,* March 1967, pp. 1 & 5; *The Chaplain,* January–February 1971, pp. 2–8.

[104] *Lutheran Witness Reporter,* 17 May 1970, p. 3.

[105] *Ibid.*

[106] *The Chaplain,* September–October 1970, p. 46; See also *The Screaming Eagle* (101st Airborne Division), 13 April 1970, p. 1, USACHCS.

[107] *Newsletter,* Office of the Staff Chaplain, Hq, USARV, November 1970, p. 1.

[108] Personnel Records of Philip A. Nichols, including William R. Richardson to Mrs. JoAnn B. Nichols, 25 October 1970, USARCPAC.

[109] For examples see *Chaplain Orientation RVN* (USACHCS: December 1968); Marilyn W. Hoskins, "Building Rapport With the Vietnamese," Student Handout 2225/12-1, February 1971, USACHCS.

[110] See "Chaplains Go Mobile," *Soldiers,* June 1971, p. 35; *Pacific Stars & Stripes,* 15 April 1966, p. 9.

[111] Statement of Robert V. Moss, Press Release, Office of Communication, United Church of Christ, NY, 2 February 1971.

[112] News Release, No. 445, Department of the Army, 22 April 1971; *The Chaplain,* Summer Quarter 1973, p. 14.

[113] Chaplains' Section, Hq, MACV, to OCCH, Subj: "After Action Report—The U.S. Army Chaplaincy in Vietnam at the time of Cessation of Hostilities," 21 February 1973, p. 3.

[114] *New York Times,* 28 January 1973, p. 25.

[115] *Ibid.*

[116] Chaplains' Section Hq, MACV, to OCCH, Subj: "After Action Report—The U.S. Army Chaplaincy in Vietnam at the time of Cessation of Hostilities," 21 February 1973; Emil F. Kapusta, Historical Questionnaire, and inclosures, 11 October 1973, USACHCS.

[117] "Among the Famous and the Forgotten," *Time,* 6 November 1972, p. 29.

[118] *When Can I Come Home? A Debate on Amnesty for Exiles, Antiwar Prisoners and Others,* ed. Murray Polner (Garden City, NY: Anchor Books, Doubleday and Co., 1972), p. 12.

[119] Bob W. Brown, "Thanks a Lot!," *The Chaplain,* August 1967, pp. 30–33 (as reprinted from *Together,* March 1967).

[120] Wendell E. Danielson, "A Chaplain in Vietnam," *The Chaplain,* August 1967, pp. 3–6 (final line: emphasis in orignal, Psalm 46:11).

EPILOGUE

For a few months following World War II, many Americans still tuned in their radios on Sunday mornings to hear the familiar strains of "There's a Long, Long Trail Awinding" and an announcer repeat:

> Once again the Blue Network presents "Chaplain Jim— U.S.A.," the story of the problems—spiritual, moral, and emotional—of your men in the Army....

Carried over nearly 50 stations in the United States, "Chaplain Jim" was a weekly, half-hour radio drama loosely based on actual experiences of Army chaplains. Although he was listened to with admiration for more than 300 consecutive weeks, "Chaplain Jim" faded into anonymity along with "Lorenzo Jones," "Front Page Farrell," "Just Plain Bill," and other radio favorites.

So it has been with much of the history of the United States Army Chaplaincy. This brief volume, covering the past 30 years of the 200-year story of that Branch, has only touched on some of the highlights of the ministry to the military. As in any organization, the roles of the chaplaincy have contained the names of individuals whose personal stories alone could fill as many pages as this composite set of volumes.

Since World War II there have been, for example, the normal "firsts" as well as the unusual. The Reverend Alice M. Henderson, African Methodist Episcopal, broke a 2-century tradition when she accepted her commission in July 1974 and became the first woman to enter the Army chaplaincy. More than 20 years earlier, it was just as unusual when Presbyterian minister Percy Ipalook donned the uniform; Chaplain Ipalook, assigned to the First Alaskan Scout Battalion, was an Eskimo.

There were also the career rarities of John J. Allen, who served simultaneously as an Army chaplain and the Chief of Staff of the Salvation Army, and Delbert E. Gremmels, Missouri Synod Lutheran, who entered the chaplaincy while living in Taiwan as a missionary. Or one could turn to the distinguished and confusing careers of the Roman Catholic twin brothers, Chaplains Gerard Joseph Gefell and Joseph Gerard Gefell, and the father-and-son combinations like Methodist Chaplains James A. Connett and Reynold B. Connett. Even Chaplain John T. Axton, Jr., Congregational, son of the Army's first Chief of Chaplains, probably merited a single book—he served on active duty for nearly 35 years. Then there was Colin P. Kelly, III, son of one of America's first World War II heroes. When Kelly was only 19 months old, President Franklin Roosevelt addressed a letter to whomever would be President in 1956 asking that the former bomber pilot's son be given an automatic appointment to West Point. But Kelly opted to enter the academy through competitive examination, served 4 years as an armor officer after graduation, left active duty to study for the Episcopal ministry, and returned as a chaplain in 1973.

The ancient Apostle John ended his Gospel with a single, captivating sentence:

> But there are also many other things which Jesus did; were every one of them to be written, I suppose that the world itself could not contain the books that would be written.

For 2,000 years that sentence has aroused the imaginations of common readers, theologians, and historians alike. Hopefully, if nothing else, these volumes will have done the same regarding the chaplaincy and will result in more extensive research of this unique ministry.

Understandably, some critics may argue that the history of the Army chaplaincy is more than a composite of individual tales. It is true that, as in any institution, there have been significant developments in organization, programs, regulations, and general philosophy. Yet, as some officers from other branches have jested, chaplains have never marched very well. Figuratively, that characteristic brings to mind the words of Henry David Thoreau:

> If a man does not keep pace with his companions, perhaps it is because he hears a different drummer. Let him step to the music which he hears, however measured or far away.

More than any other military group, the chaplaincy has always been composed of individuals with a tremendous diversity of backgrounds and beliefs. They represent in one small organization the vast conglomerate of American religious convictions. Perhaps because of that phenomenon, the Army chaplaincy has never been easy to evaluate. Some authors have erroneously painted them as a group of super heroes. While a few of them have indeed been heroic, it has hardly been a characteristic inherent in the entire organization. Others have criticized them as militarists and self-seeking opportunists. But it is equally ludicrous to so label the entire institution. Perhaps the most unfair portrayal has been to show them as bungling comedians, oblivious to human suffering, who piously bless the machines of war before military conflict.

If there has ever been anything truly common in their goals, it has been their compassion for human beings and their simple desire to bring the home-town church or synagogue to the men and women serving in the United States Army. The wondrous thing is that a country preacher from Kentucky, a learned rabbi from New York, and an ethnically-oriented priest from Boston have been able to work together at all, let alone serve in a single organization striving toward common goals. Whatever glory is to be given them must be for their struggle to bring compassion into the military and to enrich the lives of American soldiers, even under circumstances where love has been a rare commodity. Whatever criticism has been leveled against them must be for those times when they lost interest in that struggle, forsook their high callings, and failed to boldly speak of a divine will in what may be termed "ungodly" situations.

The name "chaplain," as many know, came from a legend of a Fourth Century soldier named Martin of Tours, which related how he severed his own cloak with a sword to provide a shivering beggar with the only gift he was able to give. That night, so the story was told, Martin had a vision in which he saw Christ wearing the half-cloak he had given to the beggar. The experience resulted in Martin's conversion and the devoting of his life to the service of the Church. In later years Martin became the patron saint of France and his cloak was considered a sacred relic, carried into battle by French kings. The officer in charge of the *cappa* or *capella,* as the cloak was called in Latin, was given the French title "chapelain"—from which was derived the English "chaplain."

While the story of Martin's cloak may be legendary, the fact of his compassion was not. Hopefully, in years to come, that same virtue may be regularly attributed to those who assume the title: "Chaplain, United States Army."

BIBLIOGRAPHY

BOOKS

Andrus, Burton C. *I Was the Nuremberg Jailer*. New York: Coward-McCann, 1969.

Appelquist, A. Ray, ed. *Church State and Chaplaincy*. Washington, D.C.: General Commission on Chaplains and Armed Forces Personnel, 1969.

Appleman, Roy E. *South to the Naktong, North to the Yalu*. Washington, D.C.: DA Office of the Chief of Military History, 1961.

Barish, Louis, ed. *Rabbis in Uniform: The Story of the American Jewish Military Chaplain*. New York: Jonathan David Publishers, 1962.

Bewley, Charles. *Hermann Göring and the Third Reich*. Toronto: Devin-Adair Co., 1962.

Cecil, Robert. *The Myth of the Master Race: Alfred Rosenberg and Nazi Ideology*. New York: Dodd Mead & Co., 1972.

Clark, Mark W. *From The Danube to the Yalu*. New York: Harper & Brothers, 1954.

Cox, Harvey G., ed. *Military Chaplains: From a Religious Military to a Military Religion*. New York: American Report Press, [1971?].

Dalfiume, Richard M. *Desegregation of the U.S. Armed Forces*. Columbia, Mo: University of Missouri Press, 1969.

Dehoney, Wayne. *Disciples in Uniform*. Nashville, TN: Broadman Press, 1967.

Drotning, Philip T. *Black Heroes in Our Nation's History*. New York: Cowles Book Co., 1969.

Dupuy, R. Ernest and Dupuy, Trevor N. *The Encyclopedia of Military History*. New York: Harper & Row, 1970.

Gershen, Martin. *Destroy or Die: The True Story of My Lai*. New Rochelle, NY: Arlington House, 1971.

Gilbert, G.M. *Nuremberg Diary*. New York: A Signet Book by the New American Library, 1947.

Greenhaw, Wayne. *The Making of a Hero: The Story of Lieutenant William Calley, Jr.* Louisville, KY: Touchstone Publishing Co., 1971.

Ham, Ernest A.; Hobgood, Clarence E.; and Moore, Harmon D., eds. *And Our Defense is Sure: Sermons and Addresses from the Pentagon Pulpit.* New York: Abingdon Press, 1964.

Hammer, Richard. *The Court-Martial of Lt. Calley.* New York: Coward, McCann & Geoghegan, 1971.

Hanayama, Shinsho. *The Way of Deliverance: Three Years With the Condemned Japanese War Criminals.* Translated by Harrison Collins. New York: Charles Scribner's Sons, 1950.

Herbert, Anthony B. with Wooten, James T. *Soldier.* New York: Holt, Rinehart & Winston, 1973.

Hermes, Walter G. *Truce Tent and Fighting Front.* Washington, D.C.: DA Office of the Chief of Military History, 1966.

Hersh, Seymour M. *My Lai 4: A Report on the Massacre and its Aftermath.* New York: Random House, 1970.

Honeywell, Roy J. *Chaplains of the United States Army.* Washington D.C.: DA Office of the Chief of Chaplains, 1958.

Hutchens, James M. *Beyond Combat.* Chicago: Moody Press, 1968.

Jorgensen, Daniel B. *Air Force Chaplains 1947–1960.* Washington, D.C.: Government Printing Office. [1961?].

Keith, Billy. *Days of Anguish, Days of Hope.* Garden City, NY: Doubleday & Co., 1972.

King, Edward L. *The Death of the Army: A Pre-Mortem.* New York: Saturday Review Press, 1972.

Kinkead, Eugene. *In Every War But One.* New York: W. W. Norton Co., 1959.

Knoll, Erwin and McFadden, Judith Nies, eds. *War Crimes and the American Conscience.* New York: Holt, Rinehart, and Winston, 1970.

Lang, Daniel. *Casualties of War.* New York: McGraw Hill, 1969.

Matloff, Maurice, ed. *American Military History.* Washington, D.C.: DA Office of the Chief of Military History, 1969.

Middleton, Harry J. *The Compact History of the Korean War.* New York: Hawthorne Books, 1965.

Mossman, B.C. and Stark, M.W. *The Last Salute: Civil and Military Funerals, 1921–1969.* Washington, D.C.: Government Printing Office, 1971.

Mulvey, Timothy J. *These Are Your Sons.* New York: McGraw Hill, 1952.

Polner, Murray, ed. *When Can I Come Home?: A Debate on Amnesty for Exiles, Antiwar Prisoners and Others.* Garden City, NY: Anchor Books, Doubleday and Co., 1972.

Porter, John B. *If I Make My Bed in Hell.* Waco, TX: Word Books, 1969.

Reed, David. *Up Front in Vietnam.* New York: Funk & Wagnalls, 1967.

Sampson, Francis L. *Look Out Below.* Washington, D.C.: The Catholic University Press, 1958.

Shin, Roger Lincoln. *Wars and Rumors of Wars.* New York: Abingdon Press, 1972.

Staudacher, Rosemarian V. *Chaplains in Action.* New York: Vision Books, Farrar, Straus & Cudahy, 1962.

Swomley, John M., Jr. *The Military Establishment.* Boston: Beacon Press, 1964.

Tonne, Arthur. *The Story of Chaplain Kapaun: Patriot Priest of the Korean Conflict.* Emporia, KA: Didde Publishers, 1954.

Vance, Samuel. *The Courageous and the Proud.* New York: W. W. Norton & Co., 1970.

Vida, George. *From Doom to Dawn: A Jewish Chaplain's Story of Displaced Persons.* New York: Jonathan David Publishers, 1967.

Voelkel, Harold. *Behind Barbed Wire in Korea.* Grand Rapids, MI: Zondervan Publishing House, 1953.

Voorhees, Melvin B. *Korean Tales.* New York: Simon & Schuster, 1952.

Watson, Tom, Jr. *T. J. Bach, A Voice for Missions.* Chicago: Moody Press, 1965.

Weigley, Russell F. *History of the United States Army.* New York: MacMillan Co., 1967.

White, W. L. *Back Down the Ridge.* New York: Harcourt, Brace & Co., 1953.

PERIODICALS

In addition to the specific articles listed, other items, as indicated in the footnotes, were taken from the following: *Army-Navy-Air Force Register; Baltimore News American; Journal of the Armed Forces* (previously *Army, Navy and Air Force Journal* and *Army and Navy Journal*); *New York Times; Pacific Stars & Stripes; Paterson, New Jersey, News; St. Louis Globe Democrat; Washington, D.C., Post;* and *Washington, D.C., Star.*

For the benefit of the reader, the following periodicals' publishing organizations are indicated in parentheses:

The Alliance Witness (Christian Missionary and Alliance)
The Chaplain (General Commission on Chaplains and Armed Forces Personnel)
The Christian (Disciples of Christ)
Crusader (American Baptist Convention)
Doubletime (Lutheran Church-Missouri Synod)
Frontlines (Presbyterian Church in the U.S.A.)
In Step [previously *A Mighty Fortress*] (Lutheran Council in the U.S.A.)
Lutheran Chaplains' Newsletter (National Lutheran Council)
The Lutheran Witness Reporter (The Lutheran Church-Missouri Synod)
Military Chaplain [previously *Army and Navy Chaplain*] (Military Chaplains' Association)
The Southern Baptist Chaplain (Southern Baptist Convention)

"ACLU Holds the Chaplaincy 'Compromised,' " *The Chaplain,* Fall Quarter, 1973, pp. 20–21.

"Among the Famous and the Forgotten," *Time,* 6 November 1972, p. 29.

"Are the Churches Failing Our GI's?," *Military Chaplain,* April 1953, pp. 4–6.

"The Armed Forces Preaching Mission," *The Chaplain,* May–June 1952, pp. 12–13.

"Army Sermon Service," *Newsweek,* 22 March 1948, p. 84.

"Army's Largest Sunday School," *The Chaplain,* April 1955, p. 26.

Bare, Paul W. "Front Line Chaplain," *Military Chaplain,* October 1952, pp. 14–15.

Barnett, Ike C. "The United States Air Force Chaplain School," *The Chaplain,* February 1963, pp. 2–6.

Beck, Jacob W. "The Christian and Race Prejudice," *The Chaplain,* October 1945, p. 37.

Brown, Bob W. "Thanks a Lot!," *The Chaplain,* August 1967, pp. 30–33.

Byrd, Charles E. "The World's Biggest Problem," *The Chaplain,* March 1946, p. 21.

Castan, Sam. "Father Tom Confroy: Church is in His Combat Pack," *Look,* 12 July 1966, pp. 75–76.

"Chaplain's Death," *Time,* 18 November 1966, p. 82.

"Chaplain Heroes," *Newsweek,* 30 October 1950, p. 75.

"Chaplains in Korea," *The Chaplain,* November–December 1950, pp. 35–37.

"Chaplains for the ROKs," *Time,* 1 June 1953, p. 60.

"Chopper Chaplains, The," *Time,* 11 February 1966, p. 68.

"Christianity and Communism: An Analysis by Members of the Faculty of Garrett Biblical Institute," *The Chaplain,* January–February 1950, pp. 9–12.

"Chronology: Generation of Conflict," *Time,* 6 November 1972, pp. 22–29.

"Church in Uniform, The," *Time,* 4 August 1950, p. 68.

Danielson, Wendell E. "A Chaplain in Vietnam," *The Chaplain,* August 1967, pp. 3–6.

Dicker, Herman. "The U.S. Army and Jewish Displaced Persons," *The Chicago Jewish Forum,* Summer 1961, pp. 290–298.

Eastman, Margaret. "Did the General Love Jesus Unwisely and Too Well," *Army Times Family,* 21 February 1975, pp. 4, 10.

"End of Vietnam War in Sight?," *U.S. News and World Report,* 11 September 1967, pp. 44–45.

Engleman, Gus. "Army Padre Aids Morale in Viet Nam," *New York World Tribune,* 12 February 1967, p. 10.

Fleming, Thomas J. "God's Warriors," *This Week,* 26 March 1967, p. 23.

"Four-Star General Who Calls Men to the Lord, The," *Moody Monthly,* November 1972, p. 22.

Freeman, Ira. "I Am Intolerant Toward Intolerance," *The Chaplain,* July 1947, pp. 14–16.

Gates, Sherwood. "The Strength of America," *The Chaplain,* July–August 1950, pp. 27–28.

Gerecke, Henry F. "Assignment With the International Tribunal as Spiritual Advisor," *Army and Navy Chaplain,* July–August 1947, pp. 2–5.

Gigliotti, Frank B. "Christian, Soldier, Friend," *The Chaplain,* May–June 1950, pp. 22–33.

"God's Warriors," *This Week,* 26 March 1967, pp. 2–23.

Gregory, Edgar. "The Chaplain and Mental Hygiene," *American Journal for Sociology,* March 1947, pp. 420–423.

Hale, Wallace M. "U.S. Chaplains Revive Religion Among German PW's," *Army and Navy Chaplain,* January–February 1946, pp. 10–11.

Hett, William R. "Dust Off," *The Chaplain,* January–February 1969, pp. 15–20.

Imrie, Matthew H. "The Fort Knox Experiment," *Army and Navy Chaplain,* April–May 1947, pp. 2–6, 32.

"In Dubious Battle," *Newsweek,* 1 June 1964, p. 82.

Jaeger, Vernon P. "Experiences in Korea," *Military Chaplain,* October 1950, pp. 1–2.

Johnson, Mordecai W. "America's Religion and its Negro History," *Military Chaplain,* July 1950, pp. 21–22.

Klitgaard, Robert E. "Onward Christian Soldiers: Dehumanization and the Military Chaplain," *Christian Century,* 18 November 1970, pp. 1377–1380.

"Lace-Curtain Chaplain," *Newsweek,* 29 March 1954, pp. 80–81.

Lacy, Julia. "Berchtesgaden Then and Now," *The Chaplain,* February 1956, pp. 25–28.

Laird, James H. "Policy in Vietnam Compounds Error," *Detroit Free Press,* 18 March 1967, p. 10.

Lawson, Harold B. "Liaison with Vietnamese Chaplaincy," *Frontlines,* March 1967, pp. 1 & 5.

Ledebuhr, Albert F. "Military Chaplaincy: An Apologia," *Christian Century,* 2 November 1966, p. 1332.

Luetscher, Riggin B. "Helicopter Circuit Rider," *The Chaplain,* July–August 1967, pp. 14–17.

MacFarlene, Norman. "Navy Chaplaincy: Muzzled Ministry," *Christian Century,* 2 November 1966, pp. 1336–1337.

McBride, James L. "The Chaplain's Handicaps," *The Chaplain,* October 1945, p. 31.

McInnes, Thomas. "Thoughts Before a Field Service," *The Chaplain,* January–February 1969, p. 10.

McKelvie, Ruth. "A Military DRE: Joys and Frustrations of," *The Chaplain,* September–October 1966, pp. 30–34.

Miller, Luther D. "Moral Effect of Military Service," *Army and Navy Chaplain,* July–August 1945, p. 11.

Miller, Luther D. "The Chaplains in the Army," *Army and Navy Journal,* 20 September 1947, pp. 49 & 74.

Miller, William R. "Chaplaincy vs. Mission in a Secular Age," *Christian Century,* 2 November 1966, pp. 1333–1334.

"Ministers Comment on the War: 12 Disciples are Chaplains in Vietnam," *The Christian,* 22 May 1966, p. 1.

"More From Behind the Barbed Wire," *Army and Navy Chaplain,* July–August 1946, pp. 27–28.

Nance, Ellwood C. "What War Service is Doing to Ministers in Uniform," *Army and Navy Chaplain,* October–November 1945, p. 34.

Nannes, Casper. "A Visit With Chaplain Luther D. Miller," *The Chaplain,* March–April 1969, pp. 9–12.

Nannes, Casper. "A Visit With Chaplain Frank A. Tobey," *The Chaplain,* July–August 1970, p. 21.

Nannes, Casper. "A Visit With Chaplain Charles E. Brown, Jr.," *The Chaplain,* May–June 1971, pp. 12–15.

"Our Servicemen Need Chaplains," *Christian Century,* 8 April 1953, p. 405.

Parker, Roy H. "Religion at Work," *The Chaplain,* January–February 1952, p. 10.

Payton, Jacob S. "Toward a Lasting Peace," *The Chaplain,* September 1945, p. 26.

"Peale Pulls Out All The Stops," *Christian Century,* 27 May 1964, p. 692.

Pearson, Drew. "One Church for Protestant GIs?" *Washington, D.C., Post and Times Herald,* 14 July 1957, p. E5.

"PMOC in USAREUR," *Christian Century,* 1 April 1959, pp. 393–394.

Randolph, Jennings. "Time for a Department of Peace," *The Chaplain,* March 1946, pp. 14–15.

"Refresher Course," *Time,* 14 January 1946, p. 52.

"Religious Retreat Center at Seoul," *The Chaplain,* August 1964, pp. 35–39.

"Sam Castan, 1935–1966, *Look* Senior Editor," *Look,* 12 July 1966, pp. 77–78.

Siegel, Martin. "Revamping the Military Chaplaincy," *Christian Century,* 8 August 1962, pp. 959–960.

"69th Advanced Conference Course," *Military Chaplain,* October–November 1948, p. 14.

Sutherland, Arthur E. "The U.S. Constitution and the Military Chaplaincy," *Military Chaplain,* May–June 1965, pp. 21, 28–29, 31.

"Testimony of a City," *Vietnam Bulletin* (Embassy of Vietnam), 1969, pp. 1–33.

"Uncensored Dope," *Time,* 10 September 1945, p. 20.

"Vietnam Casualty," *American Baptist Chaplain,* October 1967, pp. 1–3.

"War Casualties: 1961–72," *Time,* 6 November 1972, p. 22.

Wildman, Albert C. "Christianity in Korea," *Military Chaplain,* October 1950, pp. 6–8.

Wildman, Albert C. "The Work of Chaplains in Korea," *The Chaplain,* March–April 1952, pp. 28–29.

Wilson, Theodore J. "The Chaplaincy and Free Exercise of Religion," *The Chaplain,* May–June 1966, pp. 3–6.

"Wounded Chaplain Tells of Ministry in Vietnam War," *A Mighty Fortress,* January 1967, p. 1.

U.S. MILITARY AND GOVERNMENT PUBLICATIONS AND DOCUMENTS

All of the following are on file at the U.S. Army Chaplain Center and School Archives, Fort Monmouth, NJ, unless otherwise indicated.

After Action Report, Appendices I through XXXVII, Hq, U.S. Army Vietnam and Military Assistance Command Vietnam, Chaplains' Section.

"After Action Report—the U.S. Army Chaplaincy in Vietnam at the Time of Cessation of Hostilities," Hq, U.S. Army Vietnam and Military Assistance Command, Chaplains' Section, 21 February 1973.

"Americal Division News," *Americal News Sheet* (mimeographed), 17 March 1968, p. 1.

Army Regulations 635–20 and 135–25 (with specific reference to changes published in 1966).

Brief History of the Protestant Women of the Chapel, A, (mimeographed), anon, n.d., [USAREUR?], revised 1962.

"Chaplain Dies on Easter Day," *News Release,* DA Office of the Chief of Chaplains, No. 445, 22 April 1971.

"Chaplains Go Mobile," *Soldiers,* June 1971, p. 35.

Chaplain's Hour, The, Lectures 1 through 52, DA Office of the Chief of Chaplains.

Chaplain Orientation RVN, U.S. Army Chaplain School, Fort Hamilton, NY, December 1968.

Christensen, Robert E.; Pullen, Richard T.; and Totten, James C., eds. *The Tropic Lightening in Korea: 25th Infantry Division.* Atlanta, GA: Albert Love Enterprises, n.d., U.S. Army Military History Research Collection, Carlisle Barracks, PA.

Circular Letter, DA Office of the Chief of Chaplains (previously under Hq, Army Service Forces, and War Department), No. 300 through 344, 1 September 1945 through 1 May 1949.

David, Allen A., ed. *Battleground Korea: The Story of the 25th Infantry Division.* 25th Infantry Division Public Information Office, Division History Council, 1951, U.S. Army Military History Research Collection, Carlisle Barracks, PA.

"Day of Dedication and Prayer for Those Risking Their Lives in Viet-Nam," *Army News Features,* U.S. Army Command Information Unit, Washington, D.C., No. 12, 19 November 1965.

Department of Defense *News Release,* No. 949–69, 4 November 1969.

Development of Religious Retreat Programs in the U.S. Army, (mimeographed), anon., n.d., [USAREUR?].

Digest of Information: Kapaun Religious Retreat House, Oiso, Japan, (mimeographed), anon., n.d., [U.S. Army Forces Far East Chaplains' Section?], on loan from files of Osborne E. Scott, NY.

"8600 Attend Easter Service," *The Screaming Eagle* (101st Airborne Division), 13 April 1970, p. 1.

Fact Sheet, Military Chaplaincy, Republic of Vietnam, (mimeographed), anon, n.d., Hq, U.S. Military Assistance Command Vietnam.

Frederikson, Oliver J. *The American Military Occupation of Germany 1945–1953.* Hq, U.S. Army Europe: Historical Division, 1953, U.S. Military History Research Collection, Carlisle Barracks, PA.

General Orders,

No. 9993, Hq, 101st Airborne Division, 31 July 1969.

No. 9071, Hq, 25th Infantry Division, 12 July 1969.

No. 12668, Hq, 25th Infantry Division, 10 October 1969.

Hoskins, Marilyn W. "Building Rapport With the Vietnamese," *Student Handout,* 2225/12–1, U.S. Army Chaplain School, Fort Hamilton, New York, February 1971.

"Incident at Son My," *U.S. Army Command Information Fact Sheet,* No. 180, 2 April 1971.

In Memory of Our Fellow Chaplains of the Vietnamese Armed Forces, Dalat, April 1970, Hq, U.S. Military Assistance Command Vietnam Chaplains' Section, 21 April 1970.

Johnson, Harold K. Address to the National Security Industrial Association's Annual Luncheon, Washington, D.C., 7 October 1965, War Office *Speech File Service,* No. 10–2–65.

Jones, Joseph W. "The Republic of Vietnam Armed Forces Chaplaincy," Hq, U.S. Military Assistance Command Vietnam Chaplains' Section, n.d.

Maddox, Paul J., ed. *The Contribution of Chaplains to the Occupation European Command,* (mimeographed), U.S. European Command Chaplains' Section, 1 March 1948.

Ministering to Jewish Personnel in the Absence of a Jewish Chaplain: A Manual for Jewish Lay Leaders, Washington, D.C.: Government Printing Office, 1970.

Military Chaplaincy, The, A Report to the President by the President's Committee on Religion and Welfare in the Armed Forces, 1 October 1950.

Minutes of the Army and Navy Chaplains' Meetings, Tokyo-Yokohama Area, 27 November 1945 through 13 May 1946.

Monthly Newsletter, DA Office of the Chief of Chaplains, January 1963 through January 1975.

Office of the Chief of Chaplains Summary of Major Events and Problems, 25 June 1950–8 September 1951; 9 September 1951–31 December 1952; 1 July 1957–30 June 1958; 12–16 January 1959; 1 July 1958–30 June 1959; 1 July 1959–30 June 1960; and Office of The Chief of Chaplains Historical Review, 1 July 1960 to 30 June 1961; 1 July 1962 to 30 June 1963; 1 July 1963 to 30 June 1964; 1 July 1964 to 30 June 1965; 1 July 1965 to 31 December 1966; 1 January 1967 to 30 June 1968; 1 July 1968 to 30 June 1969; 1 July 1969 to 30 June 1970; 1 July 1970 to 30 June 1971.

Piercy, Geri Sias, ed. *PWOC Heart and Hand* ("Approved by USAFE and USAREUR for use by military chaplains and leaders"). [Hq, U.S. Army Europe Chaplains' Section?], 1971–1972.

Religious Support Manual: ST 16–159, U.S. Army Chaplain School, Fort Hamilton, NY.

Report of the Secretary of War; Being part of the Message and Documents communicated to the two Houses of Congress at the beginning of the First Session of the Fifty-Second Congress, Washington, D.C.: Government Printing Office, 1892.

Rogers, Martha. *History of the Post Chapel, United States Military Academy.* Revised by William Blewett. West Point, NY: United States Military Academy, 1967.

Spence, Floyd. "He is Called Warmonger by Ministerial Friend," *Congressional Record, House,* Tuesday, 29 June 1971.

Stadtmauer, Saul A., ed. *24th Forward: The Pictorial History of the Victory Division in Korea.* 24th Infantry Division, n.d., U.S. Army Military History Research Collection, Carlisle Barracks, PA.

Storaasli, Gynther. "Farewell Remarks of Commandant to Graduating Class," 29 August 1946, U.S. Army and Air Force Chaplain School, Carlisle Barracks. "Historical Events" file. 370.7.

Throckmorton, John L. Address to the National Security Commission of The American Legion, 2 March 1966, War Office *Speech File Service,* No. 4–2–66.

"U.S. Army Chaplains on Active Duty on 31 December for 1941 through 1952," DA Office of the Chief of Chaplains, file M–9.

"USARV Construction Priority System," Hq. U.S. Army Vietnam, 18 November 1967.

MANUSCRIPTS AND UNPUBLISHED DOCUMENTS

Carlisle, PA. U.S. Army War College Library. General Officers' Biographical Information File: Ivan L. Bennett; Charles E. Brown, Jr.; Luther D. Miller; Roy H. Parker; Patrick J. Ryan; Francis L. Sampson; Frank A. Tobey.

Fort Monmouth, NJ, U.S. Army Chaplain Center and School Archives. Walter S. Baker, "Ministry in Civil Disturbance," C–22 Research Paper, December 1973; Lawrence K. Brady, Biographical Sketch; John C. Britcher, "The Chaplain and Integration," C–22 Research Paper, December 1973; Arthur C. Piepkorn, "Statement of the Legality and Constitutionality of the Chaplaincy," (address delivered to Chaplains' Conference, Fort Leonard Wood, MO, distributed by Walter McLeod, 11 December 1963); Albert C. Wildman, Diary, 18 February 1941 to 11 June 1945, and 12 November 1950 to 18 November 1950.

New York. United Church of Christ, Office of Communication. Robert V. Moss, Statement, 2 February 1971.

Princeton, NJ. Princeton Theological Seminary. Edward A. Simon, "The Influence of the American Protestant Churches on the Development of the Structure and Duties of the Army Chaplaincy, 1914–1962," STM diss., 1963.

St. Louis, MO. U.S. Army Reserve Components and Administration Center. Personnel Records: William J. Barragy; Don L. Bartley; Wendell F. Byrd; Robert M. Crane; Meir Engel; William N. Feaster; Herman G. Felhoelter; Ambrosio S. Grandea; Kenneth C. Hyslop; Roger W. Heinz; James J.L. Johnson; Emil J. Kapaun; Byron D. Lee; Aloysius P. McGonigal; Philip A. Nichols; Michael J. Quealy; Morton H. Singer; Charles J. Watters.

St. Paul, MN. Bethel Theological Seminary. Ronald Wiley and Robert McNeil, "A History of the Baptist General Conference Chaplaincy Program," Historical Research Project. [1968?].

Washington, D.C. DA Office of the Chief of Chaplains. Biographical Sketches: Francis L. Sampson, and Gerhardt W. Hyatt; Personnel Records: Kenneth C. Wilson; James W. Conner; Francis X. Coppens; Leo P. Craig.

Washington, D.C. National Archives. Record Group 247. Office of the Army Chief of Chaplains, 1946 through 1953, decimal files (1946–48): 000.3 to 000.76; 000.76 to 006; 123 to 200.6; 200.6 to 201.39; 201.5 to 210.1; 211 to Chaplain General File; 380.01 to 400.38; Chaplain Equipment; 631 to 730; decimal files (1949–50): 210.8 to 230; 414.1 to 474; 619.3 to Debit Vouchers; 000.77 to 031.1; 123 to 210.1; 210.455 to 231.2; 461 to 631; 414.1 tq 461; decimal file (1947–53): 319.1 Vol. I to 319.1 Vol. VII; decimal file (1946–48): 319.1 to General File Vol. V.

QUESTIONNAIRES, INTERVIEWS, AND LETTERS

All entries are on file at the U.S. Army Chaplain Center and School Archives, Fort Monmouth, NJ. Historical questionnaries are indicated with "HQ"; interviews with "PI" for personal interviews, "RI" for recorded interviews, and "TI" for telephone interviews. A short line indicates the author's name in letters addressed to him (e.g., "John Doe to ____, January 1974").

Andrews, Joel E. RI, 1 December 1972.
Appelquist, A. Ray to ____, 18 June 1973.
Aronsen, Viggo O. HQ, 12 October 1973.
Audick, Albert E. to ____, 3 January 1974.
Bell, Arthur F. PI, 21 January 1975.
Betzold, John W. HQ, 4 December 1973.
Bloxham, Earl S. HQ, 10 October 1973.
Bone, Lawrence H. to ____, 30 July 1974.
Brooks, William. TI, 27 September 1974.
Burgreen, Charles L. to ____, 9 October 1974.
Carroll, James C. HQ, 25 October 1973.
Carter, Donald F. to ____, 21 September 1973; HQ, 28 December 1973.
Carter, James A. to Parker C. Thompson, 13 November 1973.
Clemens, Dorothy S. to ____, 30 April 1974; 15 May 1974.
Creswell, C. Edward to ____, [received 12 November 1973].
Eggers, Carl R. to ____, 12 February 1973.
Elson, Edward L. R. to ____, 1 May 1974.
Fenton, Bernard J. to John A Linvall, 16 August 1962.

Fleischer, Edward J. HQ, 22 March 1974.

Galle, Joseph E., III, to Parker C. Thompson, 11 October 1973.

Gaskins, Steve P. to ___, 2 July 1974.

Gefell, Gerard J. HQ, 11 October 1973.

Gefell, Joseph G. HQ, 15 October 1973.

George, Richard A. to ___, 10 October 1973.

Halperin, Martin to ___, 14 January 1974.

Handy, John W. HQ, 24 October 1973.

Handy, Robert T. HQ, 17 November 1973.

Heindl, Elmer W. HQ, 3 May 1974.

Hope, Holland HQ, 16 January 1974.

Hundley, Maury to ___, 2 September 1973; RI, 8 November 1973.

Hudson, Carl R. to Patrick H. Hyde, 10 May 1970; TI, 10 October 1974; to ___, 4 December 1974.

Hyatt, Gerhardt W. TI, 10 October 1974; 23 January 1975.

Irby, Richard L. TI, 8 November 1974.

John, Harry W. to ___, 12 December 1973.

Jungfer, Richard W., Jr. HQ, 4 October 1973.

Kapusta, Emil F. HQ, 10 October 1973.

Kelly, Orris E. HQ, 5 October 1973.

Kertzer, Morris N. HQ, 10 October 1973.

Keys, Clifford E. to Chester R. Lindsey, 5 April 1973; HQ, 19 October 1973.

Kinney, Harrison B. to ___, 13 February 1973.

Kirtley, Edwin L. to William T. Carter, 7 December 1973; HQ, 18 January 1974.

Kissinger, Harry P. to ___, 16 March 1973; RI, 1 November 1973.

Koepke, Theodore V. HQ, 20 February 1974.

Lent, Peter S. HQ, 29 November 1973.

Lewis, Arnold M. HQ, 29 October 1973.

Lewis, Francis R. RI, 11 April 1973.

Lindvall, John A. to Edward Mize, 14 March 1962; 12 April 1962; William J. Moran, 23 May 1962; HQ, Fourth U.S. Army, Office of the Chaplain, 28 May 1962; Robert B. Howerton, 21 June 1962; Cleo Buxton, 23 June 1962; Warren MacPherson, 26 June 1962; 19 July 1962; Bernard Fenton, 9 August 1962; Robert S. McCarty, 24 October 1962; 21 November 1962.

Loy, Leland L. HQ, 12 October 1973.

McCarty, Robert S. to John A. Lindvall, 21 November 1962.

Mize, Edward M. to John A. Lindvall, 23 March 1962; 26 March 1962.

Moran, William J. to John A. Lindvall, 16 April 1962; 16 November 1962; William S. Staudt, 8 May 1962.

Murphy, John J. PI, 31 October 1974.

Naylor, Duncan N. HQ, 26 October 1973.

Newby, Claude D. to _____, 20 February 1973; 6 March 1973.

Oberleiter, Carl P. TI, 1 November 1974.

O'Connor, William V. RI, 29 October 1973.

Oostenink, Dick J. PI, 18 October 1974.

Opfinger, A. to _____, 30 November 1973.

Paddock, William S. to _____, 15 October 1974.

Paul, William E., Jr. HQ, 6 April 1974.

Poch, Martin C. HQ, 3 December 1973.

Pomeroy, Dudley T. HQ, 13 October 1973.

Prudell, Harold O. HQ, 30 October 1973.

Reinhardt, William B. to _____, 3 October 1973.

Reiss, William J. RI, 27 October 1973.

Rose, Ben. L. HQ, 15 October 1973.

Ryan, Garry D. to _____, 29 November 1973.

Ryan, Patrick J. HQ, 20 February 1974.

Shalowitz, Morton to _____, 29 May 1973.

Scharlemann, Martin H. HQ, 4 October 1973.

Schoech, Oscar W. to _____, 17 April 1973; 30 April 1973.

Schroeder, Philip J. to _____, 17 April 1973.

Smart, James R. to _____, 21 January 1974.

Snowden, Roscoe to _____, 10 October 1974.

Staudt, William S. to William J. Moran, 26 April 1962.

Stegman, Leonard F. HQ, 1 November 1973.

Suelflow, August R. to _____, 17 May 1973.

Taylor, George O. HQ, [October 1973?].

Terry, Roy M. HQ, 30 October 1973.

Thomas, Jack L. Commandant, U.S. Army Chaplain School, 25 September 1972; to _____, 8 May 1973.

Thompson, Parker C. PI, 29 October 1974.

Tobey, Frank A. HQ, 4 October 1973.

Urey, John H. to _____, 19 June 1973.

Voelkel, Harold to _____, 14 April 1973.

Wagner, Harold M. to _____, 15 November 1973.

Wildman, Albert C. HQ, 22 October 1973; to _____, 29 November 1973.

INDEX

'Those who cannot remember the past are condemned to repeat it.'

George Santayana, *The Life of Reason*, 1905

In Ancient Greek mythology, the Moirai are the three daughters of Nyx, the goddess of the night. You may know these sisters better as the Fates.

1

EDEN VALLEY, CUMBRIA
September 2023, 8:07 p.m.

And now they are completely screwed. They just don't know it yet.

Nina had left the motorway earlier, just before it became impassable, a slick pool of rainwater spilling out across four carriageways where workers had already downed tools to flee the sudden storm. Taking the exit had seemed the right thing to do. So much so that Nina hadn't discussed it with her two sisters, just indicated and swung the car. A unilateral eldest child decision, the latest in a series of many.

Then Nina had nudged her snub-nosed Mini Clubman onto an almost equally busy A-road. But then, buoyed by familiarity, she had escaped that traffic by slipping away, onto the lanes that had criss-crossed their childhood. Burrowing through smaller and smaller roads that began to curl around each other like the inner workings of a shell.

Lizzie, the middle child, watched uneasily as they surged further into the darkness, leaving behind the reassuring twinkle of hundreds of headlamps. For a while, she could still see them in the mirrors, strung along the horizon like fairy lights, growing fainter.

They're long gone now.

Now the sisters are well and truly corkscrewed into the remote Eden Valley. The black, spiky trees on either side of the lane seeming to draw together like a zip behind them. As if the rest of the world was never really there.

When the sisters started this journey from their dad's house in Cheshire several hours ago, at least the rain had a perkiness to it. A sense of occasion as it teamed up with the late afternoon sunshine to become a rainbow.

But the energetic rain was followed by a sudden blackening of the evening sky that snuffed out the stars, one, two, three, like the cheap candles their father blew out on his birthday cake. The cake he'd bought for himself and presented to his guilty daughters over lunch.

Now the sky is black and the water sprays chaotically all over the car as if someone is standing above it with their thumb over the end of a hose. The thunder booms erratically and lightning cracks through the now starless sky like the whip of a madman. The thick trees on either side of the winding road sway, loose and dangerous. On this dark night, they are just shadows and suggestions, nothing is solid here.

Condensation runs down the inside of the windows as if the car itself is sweating. The overworked heater smells of burnt dust and headaches. There is no reception; the maps on their phones are empty spaces with spinning wheels. Nina taps her phone, snug in its dashboard cradle. Nothing. She tries to ignore the tiny shiver that runs down her arms. Flexing her hands on the wheel to expel it.

The car radio splutters in and out again, bringing only snatches of bad news. High winds, flooded roads, grounded planes, bad people. Overhead, a lattice of lightning cracks through the sky

and thunder rolls lazily behind it. Now there is only static. Nina snaps the radio off and rubs her forehead.

Neither Lizzie nor Aisa seem to have noticed how low the petrol gauge is, and Nina is chewing over how best to tell them. It's been red for a while and if she's not quick, it'll start beeping.

'Are you sure you know where we are?' Lizzie asks gently. She knows they needed to come north from Cheshire, through Cumbria where they once lived, but the map is hazy. She knows too, that whenever she questions Nina, her older sister grows defensive, as if the worst accusation in the world is to not be fully in charge of a situation. Lizzie shrinks pre-emptively.

'Don't you recognise it?' Nina says. 'We actually used to live just down the road, this is—'

'Moirthwaite?' Lizzie says, peering nervously into the gloom. 'Gosh, is it really?'

'Yes, well, near to it anyway. The village is just a bit further along, but I'm low on petrol, so I need to go to the old garage. It'll be fun, reliving our childhood and—'

'What old garage?' Lizzie asks.

Nina swallows. She was sure there was a petrol station around here somewhere. She used to go there with Dad to fill up the car sometimes. She'd push the hose in for him and he'd get her a secret pack of Smarties from the little shop. Though perhaps that was the other side of the village. Or somewhere else entirely. *Shit.* 'You know,' Nina says. '*The* old garage.'

'How low is the petrol?' Lizzie asks.

'We'll be fine,' Nina says, trying to ignore the pounding in her head.

'It's been thirty years since we lived here,' Lizzie says nervously. 'Are you sure you know the way?'

'I absolutely know the way,' Nina lies. 'And we get a bonus trip down memory lane, to boot.'

'It's just that, Aisa's flight is—'

'Aisa's flight is what?' a voice says from the back seat. Aisa sits up and squints out of the window. Her chin-length dark hair is tousled, her Stevie Nicks T-shirt crumpled, as if she's just woken up on the set of a music video. Two white AirPods hang like speech marks on either side of her face. She tugs them out. 'Where the hell are we?'

'We just need some petrol,' Nina says.

'Can you get me some sparkling water?' Aisa mumbles, sliding back down in her seat. 'I feel a bit car sick.'

'Maybe you shouldn't have had so much wine at lunch,' Nina says.

'I had, like, one glass.'

'Sure you did,' Nina says. 'If by glass you mean one of those giant Toby jugs.'

'Oh, piss off.'

Aisa rolls her eyes and puts her headphones back in. She's anxious about making the flight, but that plays second fiddle to the other thing. The thing she struggles to name. The way her family makes her feel. Small, sad and difficult. A more acute alienation since their mother died.

A wave of nausea radiates from Aisa's stomach. She did drink too much wine, but she's damned if she's going to admit that to her know-it-all eldest sister. Instead, she closes her eyes, turns up her music and tries to tune everything out.

They shouldn't be here together like this. They're out of practice. And it really was a long, awkward day. Was their dad always such hard work? Or has he got worse since their mother, Rosemary, died in spring? It's not a topic they broach often. It's too raw, even now.

4

But still, they did their duty today, cake and cards for his sixty-eighth birthday and lunch in a place of his choosing – a Harvester, much to Aisa's distaste. 'You used to love Harvester,' he said, looking hurt. 'I used to love Little Chef too, but it's hardly…' She'd withered under Nina's gaze. After lunch, they spent the requisite amount of hours stifled in the too-warm house. Then they fled.

Lizzie was looking forward to catching the TransPennine Express from Manchester Piccadilly to Carlisle. A single window seat from which she would watch the viaducts and city bric-a-brac rush past, gradually replaced by little towns and bright green Lancashire countryside. And she had her book ready in her bag for when the sun slipped out of view around Morecambe Bay, leaving her with nothing to look at. A thin tea from the trolley, a pack of toffees. Or a chocolate bar. Maybe both. No finer way to spend some time.

Aisa was supposed to be getting a flight back to Paris from Manchester Airport tonight, but the plane was cancelled due to extreme weather. She is looking after an artist's cat. She put a few extra handfuls of dry food in its bowl when she left before dawn this morning, but she was supposed to be with it the whole time she stayed. ''E 'as a stress problem,' the artist had explained when she first arrived last week, with perfect Parisian pomposity. 'Poisson needs company.'

'I won't leave his side,' she said, before leaving to hook up with someone she'd met at the airport almost as soon as the artist left the apartment.

'Doesn't *poisson* mean fish?' Nina had asked last week, when Aisa called, trying to get out of Dad's birthday on grounds of feline mental health.

'Yeah. It's a cat called Fish,' Aisa replied. It's the kind of wry joke you're not supposed to laugh at. But Nina laughed anyway.

And then said bollocks to Aisa missing the celebration. The compromise was flying here and back in one day. Which worked out terribly.

Still, Aisa had managed to find a seat on the first plane out of Newcastle first thing tomorrow, preferring to sleep at the airport than spend the night in suspended animation at her dad's house, the missing shape of her mother looming too large for her to handle.

They should have kept the change of flight plans to themselves, because the whole incident set their dad off on one of his almighty flaps and before they knew it, he'd railroaded them into a complicated and unnecessary plan.

So now, instead of having three peaceful journeys home, they're jammed together in Nina's Mini in the middle of nowhere, swinging up and down hills, sliding around severe bends and skimming black lakes that draw poets by day and, by night, ghosts. It's just like when they were small and Nina was de facto babysitter, her little sisters like ducklings, waddling behind her everywhere she went. Tonight, Nina is supposed to be dropping Lizzie home on the Solway Coast and then cutting across the top of the Pennines to drop Aisa at Newcastle Airport, before driving herself back to Edinburgh. Which would be straightforward if her car wasn't on the brink of wheezing to a stop, and if she'd admitted, just a little sooner, that she couldn't remember exactly where the—

'Garage!' Lizzie says, pointing at the horizon.

'I know,' Nina says, biting back her relief. 'Right where I said—'

'But it's closed.' Aisa slumps back in her seat.

It's not just closed. The garage shop is boarded up and the pumps have been vandalised. Nina switches off the engine to save fuel, feeling at once exhausted, guilty and annoyed.

'We need to find another garage,' she says, hoping that a take-charge attitude will pre-emptively nix any criticism. 'Do either of you have reception?'

'Nope,' Aisa says tersely, her phone still glued to her hand. Lizzie fumbles around in her big fabric handbag, pushing books, gloves and dog treats out of the way.

Nina grits her teeth. 'Come on, Lizard.'

When Lizzie finally pulls out her phone, it's switched off.

'Sorry,' Lizzie says, turning on her phone and wondering why any of this is her fault. When the screen eventually lights up, the five-year-old phone can't find a network. 'Do you have a road map in the car?' she asks Nina, who shakes her head.

'A paper map? To go with her monocle and penny farthing?' Aisa says, rubbing her eyes and switching off her music. 'The signal will be back soon, Nina, just keep driving until it comes on.'

'I don't have enough petrol to just keep driving.'

'Well, you know you've not passed a garage yet, so there's no point going back that way, and as we can either go backwards or forwards, let's just go forwards. Jesus.'

'Thanks, Aisa, remind me how long you've been driving?' Nina says.

'I don't need to know clutch control to work out that if we've not passed a garage the way we came, there's no point going back that way.'

Nina is breathing heavily through her nose now, which Lizzie knows very well is a precursor to a shouting match. 'Please,' she says, 'fighting isn't going to help anything.'

'You sort it out then,' Aisa says, pressing play on her music again and closing her eyes.

So far, it's as if they have skimmed along the edge of the storm, but stopping here has allowed the weather to catch up

with them. A frantic shard of lightning appears right above the garage, then the thunder claps so loud it could split the sky.

The Mini sits useless on the potholed forecourt, like a toy in comparison to the hugeness of the electrified sky. In the back, Aisa keeps her eyes shut, fully checked out again, but Lizzie and Nina stare at the boarded-up little shop.

'I think there's a house behind, I should see if there's someone there,' Nina says. 'Or at least a payphone.'

'Draw straws?' Lizzie says, but Nina shakes her head. She reaches into the back and pulls at a raincoat that's been caught under Aisa, who lifts her leg with a grunt to release it.

And then Nina is out of the car, using her phone as a flashlight while Lizzie marvels at her bravery.

Nina approaches the little shop with rising panic. Could there really be someone out here to help them? She looks back just briefly at her sisters, sitting vulnerable in the car she's stupidly allowed to nearly run out of fuel. Two grown women, but not to her. To her, they will always be her soft middle sister, frightened of her own reflection. And little Aisa, so determined to be fierce that she'd run headlong at danger just to prove something. Nina takes a deep breath and walks on.

The shop is so much smaller than she remembers and the bulk behind it is just an old outbuilding, not a house at all. But maybe there's a phone on the forecourt somewhere. As the rain thumps on her hood and rushes down her face, she runs the light along the wooden boards that cover the windows, then turns the corner and sees a payphone attached to the wall. She dashes to it, lifts the handset and hears nothing. It's dead. Of course it's dead. She can't see the Mini from around this corner and allows herself to shed a couple of frustrated tears, cuffing them quickly on her jacket. As she turns to walk back to the car, something grabs her shoulder.

8

2

8:25 p.m.

Nina screams, and then freezes, eyes screwed shut.

'Oh my God, are you OK?'

Nina opens her eyes, lifts her phone cautiously and illuminates Lizzie standing in front of her, holding her own phone as a flashlight.

'I thought I heard you scream. Oh, you're tangled.'

Nina turns carefully, finally daring to breathe again, and sees that it is just a mess of overgrown brambles snagging her, not a person. The ends drape over her shoulder like fingers.

'Yeah,' she manages to say, allowing the breath back into her lungs.

Lizzie carefully teases away the brambles and Nina notices that her sister has rushed out without stopping to get her coat. She is soaked, and Nina's chest rolls with an emotion she can't fully articulate. Gratitude, irritation, care and guilt, stirred unpalatably together.

Back in the car, Lizzie shivers in her baggy T-shirt as she pulls off her jumper and lays it along the parcel shelf to dry.

'That smells like a wet dog,' Aisa sniffs.

'Hey,' Lizzie says, pointing at Aisa's phone. 'Don't you need 3G to listen to music?'

Aisa looks at her as if she's mad. 'Um, no. I'm listening to my downloaded songs?' Her inflection rises in a way that reminds Lizzie how much younger Aisa is than her. 'And it's 5G now, Lizard.'

Just as she starts to feel stung, Lizzie catches a slight smile from Aisa as she turns away. Aisa has always made Lizzie feel old, even when she was a teenager. It's only been in her thirties that Lizzie realised she rather likes being 'old'.

Nina stares out at the empty road ahead. This was once the main road between a string of tiny villages and sparse towns, but then the bypass came and sucked all the cars away like a big magnet. No wonder the garage closed, it was probably struggling for business when they lived here. Nina closes her eyes, brings up a patchy mental image of a map, then gently starts the engine.

They crawl along. The sky is the blackest Nina has seen for years, stars chased away by the storm, tucked into some secret pocket of the sky like precious coins. Even in the car, they can feel the temperature drop as they drive near the river, as if the water is draining something from them.

A tiny junction appears, bolstering Nina's developing plan. Yes, she knows where she is. And she knows where to go for help. She swings for the junction without indicating and ignores Lizzie's questioning look.

The ornate old white signpost catches the headlights as she turns: 'Moirthwaite – 5.'

Five miles? *Christ.*

It's much further from here than Nina thought. She looks at the petrol gauge, beeping occasionally but softly, like it knows it's pointless. Can she make it another five miles? Nina looks in the rear-view mirror at Aisa, either asleep again or pretending

to be. She looks back at Lizzie, clearly trying to hide her worry behind a thin-lipped smile. 'This'll be fun,' Nina says brightly.

At first, the lane slopes gently upwards, but it quickly drops down again. Nina slips out of gear into neutral and lets the car coast, picking up speed. OK, this could work. As they roll along, the headlights pick out a slight rising slope ahead, which she thinks is then followed by another downhill slope. The narrow road is marked by a tough little stone wall on each side. Yes, that's the hill where she used to put it in third gear for Dad.

Momentum carries the car upwards and Nina sighs in relief, perhaps they can make it after all. The car skips over the brow and then free-falls.

It all happens so quickly. The lightning, the thunder. The puddle of water so black it's like antimatter. She brakes, jamming the car into gear to try to get more control. But it's too late. The Mini plunges into the water at the bottom of the hill. The engine cuts out but the wheels keep moving, the silent car like a headless chicken, completely out of control.

They glide through the water and settle against a thick, curved tree, which has broken through the drystone wall and now leans into the road like a pregnant belly.

Nina scrabbles to free herself from her seatbelt and pushes her door open. The air is freezing out here, the wind and rain so wild that her hair is plastered to her face before she can even get out.

Her legs are swallowed up to calf-height and in the shock of the cold gritty water, she slips awkwardly.

'Shit!'

Lizzie's door is trapped by the tree, so she shuffles across to the driver's seat to follow Nina out, while Aisa pops the back door cautiously open.

'Oh my God, Nina, are you all right?' she calls to Nina, who

is now sitting in the road, near the edge of the puddle, face twisted into a grimace. Her hands are clutching her right ankle.

'Obviously not.'

Back in the car, Nina is now claiming to be fine. But the pain is written across her face as she sits in the driver's seat, door open, twisting the key. The engine clicks drily, like a tutting tongue.

'We can't stay here,' Lizzie says gently to Aisa, as they stand in the dark behind the puddle, lashed by rain and staring at the stranded Mini.

'I know,' Aisa says. 'But she can't exactly walk far.'

'I heard you and I can!' Nina calls out, but when she tries to step out and put her weight on the damaged ankle, she buckles backwards onto the seat.

The others rush into the water to help prise her out of the car.

They flank her, their arms around her shoulders, as she hobbles from the Mini, locking it pointlessly. Who could steal it? Car thieves don't tend to carry spare fuel.

They pause a moment, letting the layers of silence peel back until they can just make out the sound of the wind and the rustle of animals hiding from the storm.

'Why don't we try Jane's house?' Lizzie says suddenly. 'Moirthwaite Manor, it's just a bit further along from here, I'm sure it is.'

'Good idea,' Nina says.

'Isn't there anywhere else?' Aisa says quickly. 'I hate it there.'

'How do you even remember it? You were, what, four when we moved away?' Nina winces, hopping slightly on her good leg.

Aisa opens her mouth, ready to keep it going, but Lizzie gives her a pleading look to stop before this descends into another row about semantics and memory. Always the peacekeeper. And besides, if anyone remembers Moirthwaite Manor, it's Lizzie.

*

Their mother, Rosemary, had worked at the big house for years as a housekeeper, often taking Lizzie with her to play with Jane, the little girl who lived there. Sometimes Nina and Aisa came too, when their dad, Bob, was in the pub or working odd jobs. But it was usually just Lizzie, and that's when she liked it best.

Memories gather. Of whispering secrets, hide-and-seek, playing in the woods. Of kindred spirits, unspoken understandings. Of, probably, her last proper platonic friendship. Something she's not really missed, but still.

'Yeah,' says Nina. 'Good idea. We can use their landline and call a breakdown service.'

'And an ambulance,' Lizzie says.

'Over my dead body am I calling an ambulance for a sprained ankle. Paramedics are busy enough, trust me.'

'You're a midwife, not an expert on every medical situation,' Aisa says, then her voice softens. 'And we're just worried about you.'

'They might even have some petrol there,' Lizzie says, changing the subject. 'For their ride-on mowers. Remember how big the grounds were?'

Aisa stares up at the sky as if hoping for some god-hand to scoop her up. She shakes her head just slightly, but the others don't notice.

'Yeah, I remember the grounds,' Nina says, a strange look passing briefly over her face. 'Hopefully the water's not borked the engine and we just need a bit of fuel.'

'We should just walk back to the motorway and hitchhike,' Aisa says.

'Nina can't walk that far, Aisa,' Lizzie says.

'And it doesn't matter how far I can walk, hitchhiking is mental.'

Aisa scowls, her fingers gripping the fabric of her sister's jacket. 'I don't want to go to that house.'

'Why not?' Lizzie asks gently, but Aisa just stares down at her wet feet.

'I don't ... I don't know, but I just—'

'Oh, enough of this,' Nina says. Then she adds softly, 'Please, I'm in a lot of pain.'

3

8:59 p.m.

There is water in their ears and the seams of their wet jeans have savaged their inner thighs and behind their knees. Lizzie's jumper is still wet, and it's true, it does smell like a damp dog. So *she* now smells like a damp dog.

Nina winces with almost every step, and the others' shoulders ache under her weight.

Conversation had stilled first to grumbling, and now to nothing at all. It's bleak and dark, they are three lone women in the middle of nowhere. None of them want to let on to the others that they're scared, so each nurses their private fear in silence. They slowly follow the narrow lane up over the brow of a little hill and then down again until they reach a driveway, framed by two huge pillars, carved from the same red stone as everything else around them. On top of each pillar sits a stone fox, their tails and noses chipped away. A sign clatters in the wind. As it briefly settles, they can make out the name with their phone lights. So many letters have worn away that it now reads MOIR AI.

'This is it,' Lizzie says, but they knew that already.

In the far distance, a few lights now sketch the outline of a village. A couple of hours' walk in normal circumstances. They

turn into an unlit driveway, scattered with gravel and rife with potholes. Nina cries out when her bad leg slips sideways into a dip.

'Are you OK?' Lizzie asks softly.

Nina nods and Aisa squeezes her arm.

Either side of the drive, the trees are layered like spools of lace. Lizzie and Aisa use their phones in their free hands to cast enough dim light to see a little way in front of them.

'I wonder if Jane will be there,' Lizzie says, knowing it's unlikely. She's the same age as Lizzie – thirty-eight – and even she has left her parental home.

The long driveway winds upwards, then down, following the contours of the land, and they shiver even in their coats. Summer has not long ended, but they'd forgotten that the seasons do what they like up here.

'I think I've got trench foot,' Aisa says.

'Hopefully they'll let us dry our socks and shoes on a radiator,' Lizzie says, trying to remember if there even were radiators. There were fireplaces, she knows that. But then, it's decades since she's been inside and it's probably changed beyond all recognition.

The storm is still behind them, but every so often the sky lights up, and on this most recent flash, they finally see it. Moirthwaite Manor.

The unlit building is about a hundred metres away, matte black as if someone has cut a square out of the navy sky.

'Maybe they've had a power cut,' Lizzie says. 'With the storm and everything.'

Aisa looks behind her from where they've come. Just more layers of dark things. Trees, a squirming black sky, the driveway, the roads behind it. Like some kind of gothic papier mâché. She

feels a tingle in her feet, fight or flight activated. She hasn't felt such a visceral fear since … well, since she was last here. *Where did that thought come from?*

'I don't like this,' she hears her voice saying, childish and high.

'Yeah, there aren't any other house lights around here, so all the power must be out,' Nina says, ignoring Aisa.

'There are no other houses,' Lizzie says. 'Don't you remember?'

'There must be some,' Nina says. 'Between here and the village.'

'No,' Aisa says, looking behind her just briefly. 'They were completely alone out here, and so are we.'

They look up, eyes adjusting slightly, but find little reassurance. Moirthwaite Manor is the shape and – in this light – the colour of an ink pot. Solid, unwelcoming.

'I thought it was bigger,' Aisa says.

'Yeah,' Lizzie says. 'I remembered it being more like … Downton Abbey or something.'

Moirthwaite Manor is big compared to normal houses but dwarfed by its surroundings. Trees so tall they must have seen dinosaurs. Or at least, Lizzie thinks with a shiver, the Black Death. She doesn't remember them being so massive. But then, in her memory, this place was a living, breathing monster, needing constant tending. Now, it lies still as a corpse. Where is everyone?

Nina starts to shuffle forward, jostling her sisters. 'Come on,' she says as Aisa and Lizzie get pulled along with her.

As they edge closer, more of the house becomes clear. A large front door is set deep into the stone frontage, with big picture windows on either side. The next floor up, three large windows are spaced equally along. Lizzie has a sudden memory of looking up at that right-hand one, where Jane would sit watching, waiting for her to arrive.

17

A crack of lightning fizzes through the whole sky and everything is suddenly, grotesquely, lit. The stone of the walls, a palette of blood and rust. The smashed fountain, green with slime. The circular gravel end of the drive with space for several cars, now empty, save for tufts of long grass and tangles of thorns. A slab of wood has been tacked on to the roof, like a dog with a patch of lighter fur. Graffiti snakes around the corners of the building, the competing designs and clashing colours like tattoo sleeves.

The moon has peeped out from behind a black cloud, bleeding light into the sky. Against that milky backdrop, it is clear that the house has been long abandoned.

'Gosh,' says Lizzie. 'I wonder what happened.'

'Does it matter?' Nina says, her voice hoarse and face slick with rain. 'The point is—'

'There's not going to be any petrol or a landline,' Aisa says. 'So there's no point going any further.'

'We have nowhere else to go though,' Nina says, her voice almost lost to the wind.

An ornate arched lintel over the doorway has crumbled away at one end, like a droopy eyebrow. The windows are thick with dust and grime and there's a security sign stapled to one of the window frames with a silhouette of a German Shepherd.

Nina leans against the front wall and reaches for the door handle, but Aisa knocks her hand away. 'What the fuck are you doing?'

'Going inside, at least it'll be dry.'

'You can't go in, it'll be locked and—' As Aisa protests, Nina twists the handle and pushes the door open.

The first thing they notice is the cold. Somehow, it feels colder inside than out. A frozen silence, years in the making, is embedded in every crevice. This place is a stranger to sunlight.

They run their phone flashlights along the floor cautiously, the terracotta tiles now a uniform dust-grey.

They shuffle further inside cautiously, waiting for an alarm to sound or a German Shepherd to come barrelling towards them, but nothing happens. They try to ignore the scurry of things hidden by the darkness.

Although seemingly intact, the building smells earthy as they walk deeper into it. As if the ground has reclaimed it and is just biding its time before swallowing it whole.

A staircase rises up out of the darkness, slivers of its ornate balustrade lit briefly in the light.

Lizzie remembers her mum cleaning that staircase. Eschewing the vacuum cleaner and rubbing at the carpeted runner with a thick wet rag, dragging out every speck of dirt carelessly crushed there by Jane and her father. And others? Were there others? She tries to picture this place as it was, but reality gets in the way.

Some of the treads now have holes in them and the demarcation of paint along the edges is the only hint that a carpet was once in situ. How lightly Jane would skip down these steps to greet Lizzie, who had to stand in her socks so she wouldn't leave a trace of herself and her ordinariness in this extraordinary space.

All that work keeping this place polished and shiny, and now look at it.

Lizzie flicks a light switch near her shoulder, but nothing happens, of course. She sweeps her phone light around the hall and finds another switch, an old-fashioned chunky nobble of a thing. She tries that too. For a moment, she imagines hearing a whirr of something, a crackle, but it's wishful thinking; they remain in the dark.

Still using phone flashlights, they check the first room on their right – the library – but aside from the dusty bookshelves

and an armchair, there's not much else. Just a few old books, rotting to mulch.

Lizzie feels a pain in her chest at the waste, but doesn't risk ridicule by saying so. She had borrowed so many books from here. Jane's mother had once collected them and they'd been untouched since she died. 'No one will care if you don't bring them back,' Jane would say, but Lizzie always did. With one exception, *The Secret Garden*, still a favourite, sitting on her own double-stacked shelves back home.

'This is like a bad film,' Aisa says behind them. 'Siri, show me a stereotypical horror-film setting.' No one laughs.

They back awkwardly out of the library and then check the room on the left. It's in better condition, dusty but fairly neat. Two giant Chesterfield sofas are pushed together into a V surrounding the fireplace, which still has a pile of wood next to it. Their phone lights pick out matches and candles on the mantelpiece, even a couple of woollen blankets on one of the sofas.

'The door was unlocked,' Nina says. 'How was all this not ransacked? There's not even any graffiti inside, it's crazy.'

'Maybe no one knows it's all here,' Lizzie says, helping lower Nina onto one of the sofas.

'Maybe it's usually locked,' says Aisa, quietly, before lighting the candles. A fizz of burning dust making her jump.

The room is at once huge but cramped. The sofas are at such a strange angle, it's as if they've dropped from the sky. Near the window, in front of thick velvet curtains, a table lies on its side and a bureau is askew towards the back of the room, empty drawer open like a lolling tongue.

'Shall we close the curtains to keep the cold out?' Lizzie says, but Nina shakes her head.

'Any moonlight is more useful.'

Lizzie squats down in front of the fireplace and shines her phone light cautiously up the chimney.

'Looking for Father Christmas?' Aisa says.

'No, birds' nests. But it's OK, it's clear. Somehow.'

The sisters' socks dangle like Christmas stockings in front of the now glowing fireplace. Their shoes steam slightly on the hearth. As they sit exhausted on the sofa, Aisa's heart rate is rising. 'I have to catch that flight, Lizzie,' she says.

Lizzie isn't paying attention. She's looking around at the extra slivers of the room now illuminated by the fire's glow, snatches of memories dancing in the light. There's a certain pride that she built that fire, but a greater unease that they shouldn't be sitting here in front of it. They are intruding, no question, but there's no one to ask for permission.

'Nina,' Aisa says sharply, turning to her other sister instead and pushing the dusty blanket back off her jeans. 'We can't stay here.'

'We should at least see out the bad weather,' Nina says. 'Even if you get a later flight, the cat'll be fine.'

Lizzie stirs then, her heart always prone to animals in need. 'How much food did you leave him, Aisa?'

'Enough for the time I was away. I just didn't think I'd still be stuck here.'

'He'll be OK for another day,' Lizzie says. 'He'll be a bit hungry and need a lot of cuddles but—'

'But what if he shits everywhere? Or rips the place to shreds looking for food?'

'He'll probably just sleep,' Lizzie says. 'He'll be OK, try not to worry.'

'I'm not worried about the cat, Lizard. I'll lose my star rating

on the pet-sitting site if his owner complains and then I'll only get rubbish jobs in future. Looking after pet rats in some sinkhole of a town.'

'Maybe you should just stay in one place for a bit then, how about that?' Nina says.

'Maybe you should just mind your own business, Nina, how about that?' Aisa stands angrily and pulls her damp socks back on. 'I've had enough of this bullshit. You two can sit here in the dark if you like, but I'm not waiting around for Dr Frank N. Furter to appear.' If the others get the *Rocky Horror* reference, they don't react, which winds Aisa up even more. Mum would have liked it.

'Hey,' Lizzie says quickly. 'Don't be silly. Let's talk about this.'

'What's to talk about?' Aisa says. 'I need to get to the airport and are you planning to just leave your car floating around in the lane, Nina, or what?'

Nina frowns. 'We'll go and move it tomorrow, we can—'

'What will be different tomorrow?'

'It'll be daylight.'

'And? You still need to get a breakdown service out and—'

'OK, fine,' Nina says, trying to free herself from the blanket to stand, but then sitting back down in pain. 'Look, why don't we walk to the village and find a phone somewhere, call a breakdown service.'

'You can't walk that far,' Lizzie says. 'You know you can't. Me and Aisa will go.'

'And leave her here alone?' Aisa says, pointing to Nina, who glares back. 'No offence, Neen, but whether you admit it or not, you're pretty vulnerable here all alone with a smashed-up ankle. No, you two stay here and I'll go,' Aisa says. 'I'll call the AA and then I'll walk on to the main road and hitch to—'

'Are you mental?' Nina says.

'That's the second time you've used that word today, it's really fucking problematic—'

'I'll go,' Lizzie interrupts. 'I'll go to the village, call the AA and then come back.'

Aisa looks at her older sisters. Imagines being stuck here with old bossyboots while clueless Lizzie wanders around out there, getting lost. 'Just let me go,' she says.

Lizzie looks at her little sister. So small, so feisty. Always taking unnecessary risks and spur-of-the-moment decisions. 'I'll go,' Lizzie says.

'I said *I'll* go,' Aisa says, tugging her damp jacket on.

'No, I—' Lizzie starts to say softly, but Nina eases herself to standing with a wince and hobbles to the fireplace. The others watch as Nina lifts the found box of matches Lizzie used to light the fire. She doesn't need to explain. Ever since they were little, this was a way to settle arguments. The only way.

'Fine,' sighs Aisa.

'OK,' says Lizzie, uneasily. 'I guess.'

Nina teases two matches out of the box, snaps the end from one and tosses it into the fire. Turning awkwardly away so her hands are out of view, she arranges them to appear the same length between her fingers.

She thrusts out her hand.

'Whoever gets the short straw goes for help.'

4

NINA – 9:35 p.m.

Nina stands at a diagonal, leaning most of the weight on her good leg. A wave of nausea sweeps over her. She always feels sick when she's hurt, but she hardens her face to not show it. The last thing the others need is her falling apart. A leader needs to be decisive, make decisions. She stands by that, even after everything.

She thrusts the matches towards her younger sisters. 'Go on, take one then,' she says, more snappily than intended. Lizzie's eyes grow watery in the flickering light of the dismal fire. Hopefully Lizzie will get the short straw and then Nina can fix it when she's gone and won't be offended – the logs are stacked up all wrong and it'll peter out in no time. But then ... the thought of being stuck with Aisa in this mood ...

Lizzie pinches one of the matches with her fingertips. Aisa snatches the other one.

Nina sits back down heavily, a little plume of dust dancing up around her. 'Let's see who got what then.'

Lizzie and Aisa have their matches in their palms, held out like offerings. In Lizzie's palm, a full-length match. In Aisa's, a ragged short straw.

'I don't think this is a good idea, Nina,' Lizzie starts, coming forward as if approaching a judge's bench.

'Fair's fair,' Aisa says, already pulling her shoes on.

It's funny, thinks Nina, how fairness isn't a concept that makes a regular appearance in her adult life, unless she's with her sisters. Then fairness – or the lack thereof – is a guiding principle and constant source of acrimony.

'I don't think you should go alone,' Lizzie says, turning to appeal directly to Aisa.

Aisa scowls. 'Don't you trust me?'

'It's not you,' Lizzie says.

In the dim light, Nina can see lines on her sister's face that weren't there before. Thirty-eight, but she always seemed so young. So immature. As a child, Lizzie would grind to a halt in almost all situations, overwhelmed and in need of rescue by their parents or Nina. Even by Aisa, despite her being so much younger.

It boggles Nina's mind that Lizzie is a living, breathing, autonomous person. That when she is under her own steam in her own house, she makes adult decisions and does things for herself. Lizzie, who used to cry under the pressure of choosing something to spy in I-Spy, somehow pays bills and cooks dinner and has a job. God, and has sex. Has she ever had sex? She must have … but, how? With whom?

Nina wouldn't have been surprised to learn Lizzie just powered down and went to sleep when she was out of view, like a Furby. Although Furbies don't shout and lash out in their sleep, and Nina distinctly remembers that side of Lizzie.

'I just don't like you being out there by yourself,' Lizzie says, and Aisa laughs then. An actual belly laugh, not the sardonic gunfire she normally peppers them with. A laugh that splits her face in two, revealing her beautiful sharp teeth.

'If you could see the places I've been by myself,' Aisa says.

And so they wave her off from the front door, her narrow shoulders and angry stomp soon swallowed by the darkness.

'Are you sure we should let her do this?' Nina says to Lizzie.

'No. But you try stopping her.'

Nina makes her way back to the living room, leaning on the wall for support. Lizzie trails behind her.

'I hope she's OK,' Lizzie says. 'Do you think she knows how to call the AA?'

The things that Lizzie worries about ... Nina shakes her head.

'No?' Lizzie says, her voice higher and shakier than before.

'No, I wasn't ... Oh God.' How long will they be stuck here like this? 'Yeah, I think she'll be fine, Lizard. It's one phone call.'

'But she doesn't drive, do you think she'll understand their questions? Maybe I should go after her.'

'You don't drive either,' Nina says, sitting back down with a sigh. 'I really think she'll be fine.'

Not that she'd admit this to Lizzie, but Nina is worried about her car as well as her sister. About the hassle, the paperwork, the cost. About what happens if water has got in the engine and wrecked it. Will the insurance cover it? Will she get a courtesy car? She can't remember what her insurance policy says, but she can't do her patient visits on a bloody bicycle like she's in *Call the Midwife* ... In the middle of the night, in Edinburgh, chaining her chopper to the fence. That's if they let her have access to patients again. *Don't think about that.*

'Everything will be fine,' she says firmly.

'I hope you're right,' says Lizzie. 'How's the ankle?'

'Better, I think. I managed to put more weight on it just then. Hopefully by the time Aisa gets back, I'll be up and dancing.'

Lizzie clearly isn't listening. She's staring around the room, squinting into the corners.

26

'Weird being back,' Nina says.

It was meant as a statement. But Lizzie answers as if it was a question just for her. She was always proprietorial about this place. And about their mum. 'It is a bit, yeah. I'd like to have a look around actually, do you fancy it?'

Nina nods, and gestures for Lizzie to help her move. 'Why not.'

They're in the hallway again, pointing their phones into the next room along, in the middle of the house. It's smaller than the front rooms.

'His office,' Lizzie says, without elaborating.

Nina sniffs the air from the doorway and instantly regrets it. Something has died in here, a rat or a rabbit maybe. The sweet cloying taste of rot hangs heavy in the air, waiting God knows how long for someone to come along and smell it.

This house is surprisingly cluttered considering it's been completely abandoned. She'd have expected it to be picked clean by now. From the doorway to the office, they can see an old metal filing cabinet and some tattered cardboard boxes that they dare not disturb.

Still in the hall – ducking under the lazy twirl of a spider's legs, much to Lizzie's distress – they shuffle into the dining room. There was once a huge antique table in here, with paintings on the wall and a big glass chandelier. Now there's a couple of dining chairs with their seats missing and not much else.

They move on to the kitchen at the back of the house. The floor is more ragged in here, a few floorboards at angles like pulled teeth. There's a huge stove, which used to steam and clank and fill the whole place with noise. The inside of the old fridge, with its Bejam's logo hanging by a thread, is coated with black mould and dusted with rodent droppings. An image of

her mother on her knees checking the cupboards springs to Lizzie's mind. What would she have been doing? Writing a list, a shopping list, that's right. She did all the family's shopping for them.

'It's bigger than I remember,' Lizzie says.

The kitchen *is* huge. Lined with great wooden worktops leading to a vast larder in the corner. How many people lived here? Nina only remembers it being Jane and her dad, though they did have other staff. From here, she can see a few tins in the larder and her stomach growls, though they'd presumably be decades out of date.

'I can't believe this place is empty,' Lizzie says. 'Looks like it's been this way for a long time too.'

'Maybe they couldn't afford to run it,' Nina says. 'What did Jane's dad do?'

'I have no idea,' Lizzie says. 'I can't even picture his face, it's really weird.'

They head towards the stairs, testing the first tread in case it gives way.

'Do you really think Aisa'll be OK?' Lizzie says.

'Of course, I told you that already,' Nina replies, hoping her voice doesn't give away her own worries. Aisa has always been a mouse who acts like a lion, it's amazing she's not been in more scrapes. Or maybe, Nina thinks with a pang, Aisa just tends her scrapes in secret. She's always been like that, ever since she was little. 'Ow, God.' Nina catches her bad ankle awkwardly on the next step. 'I need to sit down.' She perches on the second step and looks up at the ceiling, checking there's nothing ominous about to drop on her head from the darkness. As she looks around, a tiny light catches her eye in the corner of the hallway. 'Maybe there is electricity after all,' she says, pointing to it.

'What?' Lizzie says, hovering in front of her with her back to the door. She turns round quickly, confused.

'There was a ...' But there's no light in the corner. Nina blinks and rubs her eyes. It's not the first time she's seen floaters, usually at the end of a very long shift. And this has been a very, very long family shift. 'Don't worry, it's nothing.'

5

ROSEMARY – 1973

No matter how wide I open them, my eyes can't take in the whole house. I feel like an ant.

I'm sweaty from cycling here, my uniform soured up, and the mascara I sneaked on is probably halfway down my face. I'm half an hour early because Mum was so sure I'd be late, and I have no idea where I should put my bike. Its rusted body and wheezy old wheels feel obscene here and I flush guiltily like I've been caught smoking or I'm wearing frilly knickers on my head. Everything here is so… grand. So… proper.

And then I feel guilty all over again for thinking bad thoughts about the bike. Dad's bike. The seat lowered as far down as it'll go to accommodate me when I stop, I can only press one foot to the ground at a time, like a see-saw. My sole, treasured inheritance. This bike and the wristwatch I'm wearing, even though I can't fully trust its timekeeping.

As I stand, staring gormlessly up at the windows and fanning my sticky face with one hand, I remember my mum's words. Her prophetic, philosophic, wise guidance. 'Don't cock this up, it's your last chance.'

My other chances, of course, are left behind to gather dust

along with my 'bloody expensive' uniform that Dad had to do overtime to afford. Poor Dad.

I could try to come up with a decent excuse, or blame friends, or boys or … I don't know, Edward Heath. But the simple truth is that everything was going OK. I wasn't a straight-A fifth-former, but I was clinging on. And then Dad died just before my mock exams, I went bananas, and everything else slammed into a wall.

My mum could barely look at me when I was expelled. 'First of the family to go to grammar school,' she kept saying.

'First of the family to get booted too,' I'd said, and she walloped my legs.

So now I'm staring up at my last chance, hands slick on the handlebars, half-hoping they made a mistake and don't have a job for me here, and I can go home and back to bed. Lick my wounds and work out what to do with my life. Then the front door opens, a woman in a black uniform comes out. She's shaped like a Scotch egg and her grey hair, whipped up in a neat bun, frames her face, which is as red as a postbox.

'Whut yer djarn standing there like that?' she says, bustling over, and then looks behind her quickly and tugs my arm. 'Rosemary?' she asks and I nod. 'Stash your push iron there, lass, and then we'll get t'work.'

6

LIZZIE – 9:55 p.m.

Lizzie has helped Nina back into the living room – an ironic name given it feels like a mausoleum – where her sister now lies on one of the sofas, near the fire. Lizzie has packed her in with both the blankets, shaken again for dust (and spiders), which Nina grumbled about but allowed to happen. It's the best place for her. Not just for Nina's sake, but for all of them. If Aisa gets the AA to come and fix the car, Nina needs to be able to drive it.

Lizzie has had driving lessons. A lot of them. More than she'd admit. But she always felt like she was being asked to ride a bucking metal bronco through streets surrounded by soft, vulnerable humans. It just felt like a bad idea, something that should never be allowed. In the end, she realised that driving wasn't the problem, she was. It was a relief to let her provisional licence expire.

Aisa, on the other hand, has not had any lessons as far as Lizzie knows. Yet she would almost certainly seize the keys and attempt to drive the car if Nina was out of commission. So yes, Nina recuperating in front of the fire is by far the best plan.

Lizzie has made her way carefully up the stairs, testing each tread in turn. They used to run up and down these steps, Jane

and her. 'I'm not allowed to run up the stairs at home,' she remembers saying giddily, a rule and a conversation long ago archived. And that feeling, God yes, she'd forgotten that feeling. That when she was here, she was in Jane's jurisdiction. That Lizzie's mother, Rosemary, 'the help', had to adhere to those rules too.

At home, their mum tucked kitchen roll into their necklines when they ate their tea so that they wouldn't spoil their clothes after just one day's wear. When Lizzie had first eaten in the kitchen here, she'd asked her mum for the kitchen roll out of habit and been passed a fancy-looking napkin instead. Jane just shook her head when Rosemary held one out to her as well, and food had dripped from her chin onto her dress. Lizzie remembers looking nervously at her mum, but her face remained neutral. Later, she realised that Rosemary couldn't tell Jane what to do, she just had to clean up after her.

How must that have felt for their mum? But she never complained. Perhaps that's why she was kept here so long, way beyond Jane's dad really needing a housekeeper three days a week.

The light on Lizzie's phone illuminates a space in front of her that's about the size of a small dog, nothing more. She has to sweep it constantly to get a sense of where she is and where to tread. The floor seems intact, but who knows. It creaks and sighs as she steps along, back in her damp shoes and coat.

A crack of lightning and boom of thunder startle her, rattling the roof and windows. She can't remember a storm ever being this close, it's like it's chased them here. She hopes Aisa is all right out there, but at least if the storm is dancing around them here, her little sister is walking away from it.

The house settles again and Lizzie realises she'd been frozen still, breath held and jaw locked as the sky crackled over her.

Gosh this is strange, she thinks, trying to come back into her body and move normally. *Take a breath, take a step. Come on, Lizzie, it's just Jane's house.*

That one summer holiday she was here more than she was at home, and then never again. Her friendship with Jane switched off like a tap. Did she even say goodbye before they all moved down to Cheshire?

She stops suddenly, winded by a memory. Dad driving a van up ahead, Mum grinding her teeth with tension in the Mini as they followed. They were moving house, that's right. Moving from Cumbria to Cheshire, completely out of the blue as far as Lizzie remembered. At first, they'd stayed with a great-aunt who looked like Miss Marple, then moved to a rented place that she can barely picture anymore, and a few years later bought the house in Northwich that her dad still lives in now. Nina and Aisa were sulking about not seeing their school friends again, and Lizzie had asked quietly if they could stop in to say goodbye to Jane. 'She'll be home, she's always home.'

Lizzie hadn't let it drop. Unusually for her, she'd carried on pleading, moaning, until her mother turned slowly from the front seat, eyes red raw from crying. A look that Lizzie couldn't read. 'I'm afraid you won't be seeing her again,' she said. 'But I'm sure she'll be OK.'

Lizzie steps into a back bedroom. She'd often played hide-and-seek in this very room. Jane loved that game, almost as much as Aisa did when she was younger. Lizzie found it very high stress. The pressure of someone else counting down, trying to stuff herself into nooks and crannies that Jane – who, of course, knew the house best of all – would rumble almost immediately.

What's left here today is a skeletal version of the scene from that memory. A bare metal bed frame still set up in the middle

of the room, an empty picture frame on the wall, a dusty bulb that doesn't work. A cold feeling runs through her and she rushes back out onto the landing to try to shake it off.

Even though it's unnerving to be alone up here, it's nice to finally have some thinking time. It's been tough, spending a whole day with her family. Her dad trying to take an interest in her job, asking about career progression and whether she'd thought about opening her own 'doggy daycare'.

'They seem to do a roaring trade around here,' he'd said, sitting in the same old recliner he'd had since he retired. 'People who work, leaving their pets and all that.'

'I work in an animal sanctuary, Dad, not a kennels.'

'Come on, Lizard. Don't you want some of those doggy day-care big bucks?' Nina had joked, sitting in their mother's chair.

'Don't you want to be the top dog?' added Aisa. That glint in her eye, the pleasure she got from winding people up. Adorable cheekiness when she was little, it was much more annoying in adulthood.

And it *had* lightened the mood, but did her life and choices really have to be fodder for them like that?

She wonders what Jane went on to do. Jane had loved animals as well, although … An image flutters just out of reach. Something about animals. Something weird. No, the memory is gone.

The next door opens onto a large bathroom, and she teases it open cautiously, suspecting it to have been taken over by hideous spiders. 'Attercops', that's what her mum called them. Nan too. Lizzie still chuffing hates them, whatever their name.

The clawfoot bath is in surprisingly good shape. Heavy brass taps peer over one end, a black plug sits squat near the plughole, making her jump.

This must have been where Jane had baths. Unlike the Kelsey sisters, who only had a bath and hair wash on Sundays back then, Jane probably soaked in here daily. Her dad had enough money not to worry about the immersion heater.

Lizzie thinks of her own little tub at home on the Solway Coast, the Radox she still uses, just like her mum. Washing away the mess of the animals. She has to use strong, squeaky shampoo that strips the dog smell from her hair but also the lustre, so she just wears it pulled back. She reaches a hand up to smooth it. Maybe it's lucky Jane isn't here to see who she's become.

The only person who ever seemed pleased with who Lizzie had become was her mum. Eventually. 'Reach into that drawer there,' her mum had said in one of their final hospice conversations.

'Which one?' Lizzie asked, scanning the two bedside drawers and dreading what might be in there. Her mum's fingers were too thin for her rings by then and she pointed her bare fingers at the top one.

'Read it when I'm gone,' she added, the exertion wrinkling the paper-thin skin of her forehead as Lizzie pulled out the envelope.

And Lizzie had just dried to a crisp in that moment. Unable to cry. Unable to swallow. Her mouth sealed shut. *When I'm gone.* She'd not said that before.

And, weeks later, she had finally opened it. Steaming the envelope as if she was in a mystery novel, not wanting to tear through the seal her mum's dry lips had managed to make. The card inside had a picture of a dog on it, and was filled with a shakier version of the handwriting she'd grown up with, and tried to adopt for her own.

The last lines were the ones that meant the most.

*Every choice you've made has been your own, even
when the others took the mickey. So, you're exactly
who you chose to be, and exactly where you belong.
And I'm proud of you.*

I'm quite proud of me too, Lizzie had thought. Still thinks.
Something she wouldn't dare utter to her sisters, living – in
their various ways – bigger lives. But Lizzie loves her job and
her little house. She likes the time she gets to herself, without
having to apologise for reading on the sofa and not wanting to
go out. The people she works with respect her, maybe even like
her. And her secret, the cherry on the cake. She finally has that,
after all these years of believing it was out of reach to her.

Lizzie wonders where Jane is now, whether she has lots of
friends, a big life, a family of her own. Where might she live?
She wasn't born here, was she? Her mum and dad had moved
here when she was tiny, but Jane never had the accent. Her dad,
still faceless in Lizzie's memory, didn't have it either. How does
she know that? She can't picture him, can't conjure up his voice,
but somehow she knows that.

Wherever they came from, perhaps they had returned there.
She feels strangely more alone at the thought.

7

AISA – 9:45 p.m.

They would deny it, but her older sisters definitely shared one of their looks when Aisa drew the short straw. It's not the look itself that boils her piss the most, although it *does* boil her piss, it's the fact that they think she doesn't notice. That she can't read the little message that fizzes between the older two. Nina making her judgements and Lizzie absorbing them, never speaking up for her little sister.

Aisa is too young to understand, Aisa is being a brat, Aisa needs protecting, Aisa is making up stories.

Well anyway, bye.

She'd assured her sisters that she had enough phone battery to call the AA if she found reception before she reached the village. In reality, she's barely got 30 per cent, but she wasn't about to tell them that. She snaps the flashlight off to save power and takes a sharp breath.

God, it's dark. She feels swallowed up by it. A shiver runs up her legs and across her shoulders, even colder in her damp clothes after the brief respite by the fire.

She pictures a warm airport lounge, curling sandwiches and a coffee machine. Not long now. Aisa has no intention of going

back to that house. And why did they have to stop there of all places? After all this time?

She'll call a breakdown service when she gets to the village, as promised, but then she'll get a taxi to Carlisle railway station, where she can get a train to Newcastle Airport. She knows the northern train networks backwards, ingrained during her younger years. Every step, she tells herself, is a step towards escape. Hopefully the smelly old phone box is still there, but if not... God, whatever. She'll bang on doors if she has to. She's not going back to that house.

Something flickers in her memory. A sliver of the red of the phone box they could see from their old shared bedroom. Pulling the fairy-patterned curtains to one side. Dark skies lit by village lamp posts. The squeak of the phone box door. Mum.

Why would her mum have been using the phone box? They had a landline; it wasn't Victorian times. Maybe they'd not paid the bill. Yes, that's probably it. When Dad lost his job. The recession, the great unmentionables.

She just worked and worked, their mum. Every uniform pressed, every meal cooked from scratch. God, exhausting. Never her, never Aisa. She laughs a moment, actually audibly laughs into the cold, dark air. She doesn't even have her own place, just a suitcase. It's probably not possible to find a more polar opposite lifestyle.

'I envy you so much, my little Ace,' her mum had said. It was one of their last conversations in the hospice, Rosemary talking painfully slowly, while Aisa scrabbled to try to escape. 'You're the biggest person I know, you make the whole world seem small.'

'I don't feel big,' she'd managed to say, before pulling her hand away and almost running out of the room. When she finally went back, buoyed by two rancid coffees from the machine, someone else was visiting. Not a back of the head she recognised.

Dark, slightly curly. Her mum knew so many people. Behind the stranger, the indignity of her mother's bald head, peeking from her headband, crushed Aisa to pieces. What a waste. She'd left without saying goodbye, feeling a coward.

On the next visit, the final visit, her mum told her to pull an envelope from the top drawer of her bedside table. 'Read it when I'm gone,' her mum said, avoiding her eye.

'I don't want you to go,' Aisa had managed to say, before burying her head on what was left of her mother's narrow lap, and crying like a child.

Aisa left the funeral barely a week later, before either of her sisters. She handed in her notice on her flat, quit her job and fled. Head down, running straight into the house-sitting, freelance-working, credit-card-stretching life she lives now. But the more she travels, the smaller the world still seems without Mum in it. The only scrap of her she has left is the still unopened envelope tucked in the passport holder, its corners grey and softened.

Above, the air feels swollen with threat, the gods of thunder sucking in air and preparing to bellow. The moon is barely visible and the whole sky squirms with dark clouds, only a few stars able to peep out from behind the velvet curtain. She focuses on the brightest one. God knows what it's called, or which constellation, but it's the one she always sees as brighter than the others. The one she pictures her mum peeking through. She doesn't believe in God, ghosts, fucking horoscopes, none of it. But she desperately wants to believe her mum is watching, keeping her safe.

She will never admit this to anyone.

She has reached the end of the long driveway and turned towards the village. Her phone battery has dropped to 29 per cent, but she puts the flashlight on anyway and points it back along

the lane they had driven down to get here. The car is still there. She heads towards it. Water pools around the Mini's tyres, rain bouncing off its roof. Maybe the engine has dried out though? Aisa doesn't have a clue how cars work, but she's always felt she'd be a natural driver. She trudges up towards it, but as she gets closer, she realises she doesn't have the keys. Oh well, fuck it, it probably wouldn't have started anyway.

As she turns to go, her phone light catches the mud around the bank they'd scrambled up. Their footprints almost washed away. Jesus, Nina has big hooves, she thinks. Then she looks again. Counts. Swallows. There are four sets of footprints here, aren't there? One bigger than the rest.

She turns round suddenly, but of course she's alone. It's a sign of life, isn't it? Someone has been around here, someone must have squeezed past in their own car and then stopped. Come back and investigated the car, peered inside to see if anyone needed help. Maybe they've taken note of the registration plate and gone off to call for help themselves? Maybe help is already on its way, and Aisa can concentrate on getting to Carlisle station, getting to the airport and getting back to Paris and that ridiculously needy cat. Oh God and the bath, the clawfoot tub sitting in the window looking out over Montmartre like a perfume advert. The thought of opening a Burgundy and pouring it straight down her throat as she soaks, it's enough to make her run.

But would someone really call for help like that? Would they bollocks. She sighs and looks again. Her imagination is playing with her. It's so muddy, it's hard to make anything out. And those bigger prints could be from their trainers slipping and sliding earlier.

Aisa turns round, but she's still completely alone. And when she lifts her head to the sky, even her mother's star has disappeared.

8

ROSEMARY – 1974

'Don't you fall for one of those borstal boys,' my mum warned when I first took the job here.

'It's not a borstal,' I argued. 'That's just a nickname.'

'If the nickname fits...' my mum said, turning away before I could argue.

I don't know what you'd call it here. Depends who you ask. A tight ship, the Brigadier might say – not that he'd ever talk to me. He's in charge of the boys and has nothing to do with household staff. That's the lady of the house's domain, Mrs Proctor. This place is a second chance for poor unfortunates, Mrs Proctor would probably say. Though she's like one of the horses when they're out on her runs – blinkered.

I don't speak much to the boys themselves, so I don't know what they'd call it here. I imagine, at first, it must seem like Shangri-La. A bed and food, no questions asked. I take them glasses of water when they're working outside, I wrap their sandwiches in paper in the mornings and wash their bedding – which is even worse than cleaning the toilets – and sometimes, I find a stray boy loosened from the pack. He'll be thinking – I can always see them thinking – about running. 'He won't come after you,' I always tell them, but they don't always believe me.

And I've heard whispers, things the other staff say when they think I'm not listening. About punishments, equipment, 'the Brigadier's funny ideas'. Things they think I'm too young or squeamish to hear about. And maybe they're right.

Well, anyway, I haven't fallen for a borstal boy, I've fallen for a Brigadier's son. (Who, for what it's worth, would call what the Proctors do here 'a misguided social experiment'.)

William has just finished university, spending the summer here before starting a job in London. When I heard from the staff that he was coming, I assumed he would treat me with the same quiet contempt that his mother did, adopting a begrudgingly patient, patronising tone that I imagined they called 'dealing with the natives'. But he didn't. From the day he arrived, he got involved with the 'boys', joining them for their manual work and even eating with them in the kitchen while his parents ate later in the silent dining room. And he was kind to me. Praising my work as if it mattered. And I swelled with pride.

He arrived with floppy dark hair and a CND badge, which the Brigadier ripped clean out of his T-shirt and crushed under his riding boots. Now he has a haircut like the rest of the boys – 'a man's haircut', according to his father. One of the house rules: women's hair is long and tied back, men's is a regulation short back and sides.

It's a rotten job, mine, but it's been enormously enriched by the time William carves out to see me. It was, I'm more than happy to admit, an infatuation. At first. But it wasn't entirely unrequited. He wasn't *infatuated*, and it took a while for him to stop talking to me in a kindly older brother kind of way and take longer looks, flirt a little, but it did happen.

When I admitted I'd been expelled from grammar school, he said he envied me for going in the first place – he was home-schooled by the Brigadier and would have loved to have been

expelled from that. For the last three years, he's been studying in London. He laughed when I asked if he'd seen the Queen, I think he thought I was being ironic. 'You'd love the galleries,' he said, 'and the discos.'

'I'd love to see *Grease* in the West End,' I said. 'Or *Joseph and the Amazing Technicolour Dreamcoat*.'

He gave me another look like he did about the Queen, but I think he could tell I was being serious. 'There's something for everyone,' he smiled.

Then he suggested I sign up to that new Open University. I won't, I'm not old enough and, to be honest, other than doing the village panto and listening to music, I have no idea what I want from my life. But I'm flattered he thinks I could.

We sneak away on my break most days now. At first, we'd just walk around the grounds. Then we'd sometimes sit on the soft grass up near the stream where the garden becomes a fairy-tale wood. Now we just run straight to the wood, no time to waste, to lean up against a big fat oak that shelters us from eyes and ears. The whiff of escape is as powerful as any pheromone. Because I know he's moving to London, I know boys like him don't stay around here, but maybe... maybe a girl like me could also leave.

9

NINA – 10:05 p.m.

Where will Aisa be now? Nina tries to picture the journey she'll have taken. Back out of the house, down the potholed drive and then onto the lane. Will Aisa pause to get her bearings? Has she ever paused?

I hope she's OK.

Overhead, the thunder taunts her. A sudden stalactite of lightning appears like a distress flare, colouring the dirty glass window bright white. Shit, Aisa is surrounded by trees. Does she know not to touch them when there's lightning? Does she know not to lean wearily on their bark, not to shelter from the electric rain, her size four feet standing on the roots. The same way she used to stand on Nina's bigger feet when they were kids, Nina walking around and Aisa screaming with laughter. Nina should have warned her about the trees. Nina and all her Duke of Edinburgh treks and survival weekends, and she didn't think to check if her sister knew the basics.

Is anyone safe being outside in a storm? At least no one else will be out in this, no one … bad. It's funny, of course, that when Aisa is off living her own life usually, Nina doesn't worry like this. She doesn't even know where her sister is most of the time, her transient life leaving metaphorical snail trails all over the

world, while Nina has stayed firmly put, roosting. Or helping other people to roost.

For all Nina knows, Aisa could spend her time running around bad neighbourhoods in the early hours of the morning, wearing a 'rob me' sign and throwing bundles of cash around. She didn't even know Aisa was in Paris until her little sister tried to use it as an excuse to get out of seeing Dad. But now that Nina knows precisely where Aisa is, knows the big swampy nothing she's navigating on her own, she can't put it out of her mind.

With a grunt, she eases her sore ankle off the sofa and wrestles the dusty blanket off herself. The fire wasn't great to begin with, now it's dwindling to nothing. Has Lizzie ever built a fire before? Nina camps so often that it's second nature. As a Girl Guide, she was a natural at learning these skills. Signing her up was one of the first things her mum did when they moved to Cheshire. They were all signed up for a bunch of stuff, thinking about it. In Cumbria, the Kelseys had never been ones for extracurricular clubs and costly hobbies, but in Cheshire they were hurtled into a programme of swimming, trampolining and art club. Maybe, looking back, it was an attempt to ensconce them in a new life, with new friends, as quickly as possible.

Lizzie soon dropped out and retreated to her books, and Aisa just wanted to play with the kids who lived on their new road and then, as a teenager, smoke and listen to music. But Nina carried on with the active stuff. Girl Guides became Rangers and Duke of Edinburgh. Then there was orienteering and mountain climbing and long blistered treks through the Highlands throughout university and right up to the present day. Relishing being the one to hold the ropes, to administer first aid, to build a life-saving fire. If only she still had her camping stuff in the car, but she'd cleaned everything out last week, anticipating having to hand the work car back if things don't go her way.

*Don't think about that. The investigation, the angry family...
not now.*

The soft thud of a door closing somewhere in the house
makes her spin awkwardly around, but there's no one there.
It must be Lizzie exploring. Or the wind, maybe. Though this
house is surprisingly sure and true, even as a storm buffets it.

Nina inches painfully towards the hearth. God, Lizzie has
made a pig's ear of this.

Nina uses one of the logs to pat what's left of the burning
logs into a base and then starts again.

She pulls a nearby book towards her, checks again to see if
Lizzie is watching, and then tears out the brittle pages. It's some
old children's book, *The Coral Island*, and there sure as hell aren't
any kids around here, but seeing it still makes her feel creeped
out. The illustrations don't make her feel any better as she balls
up the pages. Wild weather and shipwrecks, is that so different
to tonight? And then three lads, young men maybe, clinging
together. She bundles them all briskly onto the embers, where
they fizz and spit as they catch alight. On top, she places the
thinnest of the logs, wincing a little as she has to crab around
on the floor, leaning on the fireplace for balance.

She used to read books to Aisa. A regular occurrence filed
away in her memories, catching light as she twists more of these
old pages for burning. She used to read to her all the time.
Curling up to her sister's little body on her half-sized bed, kissing the top of her head and reading page after page until she
fell asleep. She would have done anything to protect her. A little
pinball that ricocheted into Nina's life. But now, she sighs, now
she's letting Aisa traipse around in the back of beyond, during
a storm, miles from anyone she knows. How could she explain
that to Dad, if... She doesn't finish the thought.

This is ridiculous, she tells herself, struggling back to the sofa

and sitting down heavily. They're all grown women, even Lizzie with her deer in the headlights approach to modern life. But Nina will always be an older sister, always be the one blamed for not looking after the little ones. And, she allows just briefly, tonight's fiasco was her fault. If she'd just stayed on the M6, she'd be through the roadworks by now, have swung into a service station for petrol and probably be dropping Lizzie at home. And then it would have been her and Aisa for the last leg. She's learned nothing.

'You have to let other people help sometimes, love,' her mum had written in a card, a picture of a rock climber on the cover, given sealed to Nina on the instruction to read it after Rosemary had died. Nina had opened it that same day, sitting in the car park of the hospice, unable to stop herself. 'And you deserve to be as happy as anyone else. But you're always so busy worrying about others, you're missing out on living your own life.'

Nina had wanted to go back inside and argue. To demand that Rosemary explain exactly how Nina was supposed to do any of this. To undo these hardwired habits. It wasn't fair. Had her mum forgotten that she was expected to look after her sisters, expected to be the eldest?

And besides, she was in this now. Her life, her career, it was all based around worrying about others. She can't even remember having a passion for midwifery, it was more pragmatic than that. She was unflappable, good at biology and couldn't wait six years to qualify as a doctor.

'Do you even like this job you're choosing over me?' Tessa, her last girlfriend and a disillusioned paramedic, had asked once. She'd not said anything because she didn't want to lie, but she didn't have a good answer to the obvious follow-up: then why do you do it?

Her mum was right, that was the worst part, and she realised

too late to tell her. Too late to ask, what the hell should I do then? How do I let other people in?

She wondered if the others had been given deathbed advice like this. They didn't talk about it. She didn't dare ask in case they did, and it was kinder. She regretted opening that envelope more than anything. It had left her cross, and she still felt indignant even when it got to the funeral. Digging her heels in, becoming even more isolated, even more bossy.

You don't have to fix everything and you're not responsible for everyone.

Her manager had said something similar, multiple times. It was the reason she'd not progressed higher, an inability to delegate. Which was ironic, or maybe just irritating, because her ability to 'work under her own steam' was seen as a strength when she first qualified. Whatever people say they like best about you will always end up being the thing they end up hating. She said exactly this to Tessa's back as she was leaving. She had paused, as if to argue, but then just shrugged. 'I'm not coming after you,' Nina had muttered, then prayed Tessa would come back. She didn't.

Another memory starts to form. Here, right here in this house. She and Aisa. Aisa's skinny little shoulders, those tatty denim shorts she always wore. Her little fingers curled around Nina's. That little hand slipping away...

But why would they have... Mum, of course. She'd brought them to work and, as usual, left Nina in charge. Lizzie and weird Jane had wandered off and Aisa had immediately run amok. Where had she gone? Was it hide-and-seek? Oh God, Aisa loved hide-and-seek. How could something so fundamental about her have been forgotten?

But she'd hidden too well, and Nina had started to panic.

Nina must have looked for her in this very room, but that

part of the memory is missing. Just the feeling remains. Fear. The knowledge that Nina had to find her, that she couldn't admit what had happened to Mum. Nina feels her chest grow tight, and throws the blankets back off her legs, breathing deeply.

She wonders if Lizzie or Aisa remember that day too, though she has no idea what day it even was. It was summer, she knows that. Warm enough for Aisa's shorts, warm enough for... Yes! That striped Tammy Girl dress Nina loved, picked up from the church jumble sale.

If you'd asked Nina this morning about playing hide-and-seek in Moirthwaite Manor, she'd probably have drawn a blank. If you'd asked her to describe her favourite childhood dress, she'd have told you she never wore them. A tomboy, through and through. But oh, she loved that dress. And she loved Aisa. And she was absolutely terrified about what had happened to her.

Has she made the same mistake?

10

LIZZIE – 10:15 p.m.

There are nine doors up here, all branching off from the long galleried landing. The central nervous system of the house. Lizzie leans against the wooden balustrade for just a moment before pulling herself back. It could have been riddled with woodworm, ready to crumble like a Victoria sponge, but it feels as rigid as a spine.

Alongside the bare-bones bedroom she'd once hidden in are two mirror versions along the back wall, plus one on the corner at the back of the house, which she doesn't remember going in. She steps inside now. The identical metal bed still has a thin, old-fashioned mattress on it. Striped, impressed with buttons, like a child's seaside dress. An old towel folded at its foot.

She remembers now why she wouldn't have gone in here before, it belonged to the groundsman. What was his name? Lizzie can picture him now, tending the tomatoes in the greenhouse or pulling up weeds. He had his work cut out, the surrounding woodland belonged to the house too and there was once a beautiful lawn, plenty of bushes and flower beds. But he was devoted to it, she remembers now. Devoted to the grounds and to Jane's dad. Her parents used to talk about that in hushed, sometimes sardonic, voices.

He can't have been that old, maybe younger than she is now, but he seemed ancient to them. He'd shout at Jane and Lizzie for trampling through his fresh beds, then chase after them and apologise. Lizzie would glow hot with shame and pity, but Jane seemed to enjoy this moment of awkwardness.

'He knows I'm in charge,' Jane said once. 'I just click my fingers and he does what I say. He's like a dog.'

And Lizzie's dad had said similar, that's right. Called him an oddball with nowhere else to go, like some kind of stray. But it was affectionate too, like he worried about him. And it's not like Dad had many places to go either – he seemed to exist almost solely in the pub back then. Though she had a vague sense of Dad and the groundsman being friends. What was his name? A... Al... A-something, anyway.

A door clicking shut somewhere downstairs snaps her back to the present. Nina just cannot rest, can she? Lizzie just hopes she's not making her ankle worse.

She looks around. This is a tiny room for a whole grown man, she thinks, looking at it now. Room for a single bed, a narrow wardrobe and not much else. Why did he put up with it?

Between the four back bedrooms is the bathroom – which she doesn't dare visit again in case of spiders – and another separate toilet which sits by itself in a room little bigger than a cupboard. Although she can feel a prickle in her bladder and hasn't used the loo since Dad's, there's no way she's going to squat over that. God only knows what's living in it.

She walks along the landing, elbow grazing balustrades that look down over the stairs. Along the wall, there's a thin door that gives her a sudden rush of déjà vu as she teases it open. It's an airing cupboard, still containing a few greying towels in surprisingly good condition and a boiler that is stone cold and

long dead. Classic spider territory, so she kicks it closed with her foot.

The landing coils round to the front of the house, where there are two more rooms. She knows one of them intimately; the other is a complete mystery. It always was. She reaches for its handle now, feeling guilty and on the brink of huge trouble. Jane's dad's room, access as strictly forbidden to her as his office. Did she ever make eye contact with him, or did she have to stare at her shoes like a subordinate?

She remembers only his shadow. A solemn man with sloping hunched shoulders, walking slowly but emphatically so you simply moved out of the way without thinking. But when she tries to picture his head, all she can picture is the back of it. Dark, messy, grey-flecked hair. For his face, nothing. A migraine aura, a glowing absence.

And she cannot picture him existing anywhere but right here. As if he and the house were part of the same organism, he the house's lungs. And now the house is dying without those organs, just a skeleton of its old form. Did he ever leave here back then? Did he go into the village to collect newspapers and milk? What about the school?

Their own dad only ever came to their village primary school if their mother was laid up ill, which was – back then – incredibly rare. Their dad did come to get them while their mum was in hospital once, though. But he was smiling, it was not a sad thing. A warm waft of celebratory beer circling him. Yes, Aisa had just been born. Lizzie would have been four, but she's staggered by the detail she can remember. The little wall along the front playground that the children lined up against at home time. A tiny school building, kids in ragtag uniform that the Kelseys barely stuck to. An intake so small that there were only two classes: infant and junior.

Yesterday, she couldn't have answered questions about that school if her life depended on it. Now she could draw a blueprint to where the overhead projector was kept and remembers the very precise smell of the school dinners cooked on site in the tiny kitchen.

But while she can picture her dad's occasional, chaotic hometime collections, she can't ever picture Jane's dad there. In fact, she can't picture Jane there. *Because, of course, she didn't go to our school.*

She takes a deep breath, flashes her phone light behind her, to check for goodness knows what, and then shoves the master bedroom door open. She steps inside, sweeps the light over the room and gasps. Of everything she's seen in this house, this is the most unsettling.

There are no pieces of furniture, no carpet or curtains. No boxes or books, no rubbish. There is no wallpaper, every scrap of it peeled off, leaving bare plaster, pocked with age. There is not even any dirt, just the faintest tides of dust at the edge of the walls. It is as empty as Lizzie's memory of its one-time occupant's face.

Did someone come in and steal everything? Strip every scrap like a colony of termites? But why would someone clean it too? Out of respect? By way of apology? Lizzie wishes she'd never seen it; it throws up questions she can't really make sense of, let alone answer. She pulls the door shut again, heart thumping.

Outside the big landing window, the wind shrieks and Lizzie shivers, wrapping her coat tightly around her body. Her jumper is still slightly damp, and she can smell the musty wool mixing with her own sweat.

It's a relief to push open Jane's old bedroom door and find the room almost intact.

As Lizzie steps inside and moves the phone light through

the room, she pictures young Jane in here. As if watching a memory from a new angle, her one-time friend waiting at the window with her knees on the seat and her elbows on the sill. There are shelves on either side of the chimney breast which at one point were filled with dolls. Collector's items from Jane's dad that they weren't allowed to play with, inherited from his family. None of them are here – she wonders if Jane still has them. Perhaps she has passed them down to her own little girl. A ripple of jealousy catches her breath. *Am I jealous of Jane for being a mother, or her imaginary daughter for having one?* She thinks it's probably the latter.

There's the little desk that Jane sat at to do her work. Homework? Did she go to private school? There are some posh ones around here, their exact details missing from Lizzie's mind because those were worlds to which she and her sisters would never have belonged. But … Lizzie stops and closes her eyes for a moment, feeling the room and its memories crowding around her.

No, Jane didn't go to any school. She was home-schooled by her dad. Lizzie shudders at the thought but can't work out exactly why.

Home-schooling isn't wacky these days, is it? Especially since the pandemic. It sounds pretty nice to Lizzie now, who never fully relaxed around all those other kids. But back then in the early nineties, it was the preserve of crackpots, hippies and the ultra-religious. Was Jane's family religious? It doesn't ring any bells, but maybe they followed one of those discreet faiths …

No wonder her mum brought Lizzie here so often. She must have seen Jane as an ideal friend for Lizzie, someone who had no other options. How lonely Jane's life must have been outside of her visits. Everything about the room makes the girl in her memory seem even smaller, even more alone. The double bed,

something that to Lizzie was the preserve of adults, seems somehow monstrous. It's made from brass, dulled by age but obviously expensive. It's high off the floor, and she remembers her and Jane jumping from the rug onto the mattress and down again.

She realises she's almost doing it now, bouncing on her toes on the dusty rug and springing backwards to sit on the bed. The bed springs groan as she lands. Its mattress is covered with a sheet, but she can feel the buttons through it, hard as spinal vertebrae. In the corner of the room, an eiderdown is slumped like a body, but she can make out a familiar floral pattern. How can any of this still be here? Aren't abandoned buildings normally smashed to bits, at the mercy of the weather and looted down to their pipes?

Lizzie perches on the edge, glad of the softness, but alert, ready to run. She sweeps the light around the room from this new angle and something in the corner makes her jump off the bed in recognition. A doll's house sized replica of this house. She remembers it now. Remembers with a shudder what Jane kept in it. Surely *they* are not there anymore? She creeps closer and as she does, she hears a footstep behind her.

11

AISA – 9:58 p.m.

Her phone is now at 26 per cent, but she can't bear to part with the light again. The sooner she can get off this lane, through the village and away towards civilisation, the better. As she tramps along, the very distant hum of the M6 calls her. She's doing sums. Trying to work out the latest time she can get to Newcastle Airport and still get her flight to Paris. What time is it now? Coming up for ten o'clock. Even if she walked at top speed, she couldn't possibly reach the motorway on foot and thumb a lift in time. And though she'd deny it to her clucky sisters, she's too scared to do that anyway now.

No, the best plan is still to get to the village, find a phone and call a taxi. Even if she has to wait a while for it, so long as she gets to Carlisle by the time the last train leaves, she'll be fine.

She says it out loud to herself, 'I'll be fine,' and tries to believe it.

Aisa will cycle drunk through Berlin late at night and think nothing of it, jog in Central Park with headphones in and go home with whomever she chooses in any city, but it's here she feels scared. It's too empty, too black. If a tree falls in a forest and all that.

She knows she'll be in trouble with her sisters for ditching

them, but when isn't she in Nina's bad books for some bullshit or other? Or treated to Lizzie's sad old teddy bear eyes? Besides, she has to get back to that bloody cat, who has probably long eaten through the extra food she put down and is clawing the furniture in retribution. She should have stayed there instead of coming to a birthday celebration to be pawed at and worried over and patronised.

'You can always stay here,' her dad had said at lunch, apropos of nothing. 'You don't need to stay with strangers.'

'I don't stay with strangers, Dad,' she said, necking another glass of wine, at which Nina frowned.

'Just strange animals,' Lizzie said, nervous of her own joke until Nina joined in laughing.

'I don't like you having to rely on people you don't know,' Dad had carried on, somehow managing to eat a soft potato so loudly, so annoyingly, it rattled right through her. 'Not when you've got a family.'

'I've not been taken in like an old stray,' she'd snapped. 'I'm a professional house sitter. This is my fucking job.'

'Aisa!'

'What, Nina?'

They'd stared each other down until Lizzie had practically squeaked in distress. 'I'd love to have you to stay sometime, Aisa. If you ever have a gap in bookings, I mean.'

'Thanks,' she'd managed. *Over my dead body*.

While she fumes, churning over a greatest hits of Kelsey jokes at her expense, she hears a twig break behind her. Aisa freezes.

She stands still now, imagining someone rushing up on her, seizing her neck. But nothing happens. No more twigs break, no more footsteps. She swallows, breathes again and turns around slowly. Her phone lights up a useless little pool in front of her

and she lifts it higher, hand shaking. All she sees is black on black. Black trees, black road, black rain, black sky.

It has been a while since she heard thunder. She turns back around and walks shakily on. As if summoned, the sky suddenly cracks open, purple and blue, a sonic boom. She spins around to make use of the light, just in time to see something tuck into the hedge a little way behind her. Jesus Christ. Jesus fucking Christ. She walks faster, swallowing, not sure what else she can do.

Maybe one of her sisters decided to come after her. Maybe they don't trust her. She'll be blind with fury if they have, and so relieved she could throw up. But right now, her neck and back are sweating, her pulse is loud in her ears and her vision is blurring with fear.

Because if it's not one of her sisters, who is it?

12

ROSEMARY – 1974

He leaves tomorrow. William. London, a train ride that may as well be a rocket to the moon. I asked to go with him. This afternoon. My stomach rolls at the memory as I pedal home, remembering his shock.

'I can't,' he spluttered. 'I mean, I'd love to bring you but…' and he talked about shared houses and single rooms and work and my family here and our lives and … and … and … I hadn't cried, but he stroked my face and pulled me in as if I had. Afterwards, it struck me that he'd said 'bring' not 'take'. That, in his mind, he was already there.

'I mean it,' he said. 'I'd love to, it just needs a little planning.'

'OK,' I said.

'No.' He lifted my chin up and forced me to face his sincerity. 'I mean it, Rosemary. I've never felt like this about anybody, I was dreading leaving you, but I can't stay here, not with … them. I didn't dare hope that you'd leave your whole life to come with me. Just give me some time and I'll be back for you.'

I said nothing, but he saw my silent question.

'I promise,' he nodded.

13

NINA – 10:27 p.m.

'Gosh, you made me jump,' Lizzie says, turning around.

'Sorry, Lizzie.' Nina hadn't been thinking. She should have called out as she came up, she knows how skittish Lizzie can be. She's standing like a frightened rabbit in the middle of the room, unfashionable jeans spread slightly apart, arms with their thick grannyish coat sleeves too long over the hands, holding her phone out in front of her like a gun. Or maybe more like a white flag.

Nina leans on the door frame for support, her phone light pooling with Lizzie's so she can see a fair bit of the room. Like the lounge downstairs, it's strangely intact. A big brass bed with a mattress on it, the kind of bed she's helped many rich women in Morningside deliver home-birthed babies on. The loose sheet has no obvious holes or even marks. The thick velvet curtains hang either side of the big window, whose window seat still has a cushion in place. Empty shelves sit either side of the chimney breast and in one corner sits a small desk.

Nina was never invited into this room when they were children. The three of them would be brought over in the back of their mum's car, but once they arrived, they split into two: Jane and Lizzie, Aisa and Nina. Rosemary was gone, busy until

lunchtime, and it was Nina's job, as ever, to keep Aisa out of trouble. Whether she succeeded on those days is neither here nor there, but no one succeeded overall. And her little sister is still trouble. Still sails too close to the wind, has no plan, no security.

Any given day – not that their contact is anything like daily – Aisa could be in Ireland, Indonesia or Italy. She wasn't always nomadic, she went to university for three years and lasted the course, she rented a flat in Manchester and took a job. What was it? Something in marketing, something... Nina shakes her head, it didn't matter how many times Aisa explained it, it meant nothing to her. Something about influencers? Social media... something. It sounded like selling snake oil to her.

Anyway, that's a thing of the past. Not long after their mother's funeral in November, Aisa quit her job, left her flat and started house sitting and doing weird online freelance work. The first she heard of it was when Nina texted the family WhatsApp to say she'd be in Manchester for a work course and did Aisa want to meet up.

'Can't,' she'd replied. 'I'm in Barcelona for a month.'

Aisa continues to live a life that makes no sense to Nina. She's flummoxed on an emotional level, like how does Aisa cope with having no space of her own? Nowhere to retreat? But the logistics also blow Nina's brain. Like, where is all Aisa's stuff? Where does she get her post sent? To Dad's? And does her bank know that she's basically homeless? Where is she registered on the electoral roll? But when Nina tried to ask exactly that, Aisa laughed her head off at such limited thinking. 'Who votes anymore? I'm post-political.'

Until last week, everyone knew where Nina was on almost any given day. Delivering babies or checking blood pressure or listening to tiny, rapid heartbeats. And when she's not at work,

she's most likely at home in her flat or walking on Arthur's Seat, overlooking the city. Occasionally out in the country, camping with friends from work who know almost nothing about her. *Will they stop inviting me if... Stop it. Stay in the present,* she tells herself.

And when she is out there, lying under the stars next to a campfire, listening to medics share their war stories, Nina feels big and brave. A lioness stalking on the plain as the great sky rolls over her. But really, she's a house cat, with a finite territory. Aisa reminds her of that. Seems to delight in reminding her, mouth twisted sardonically as, yet again, Nina walks into a trap and proves herself old and uncool. Despite that, that old imperative is throbbing ever harder: keep Aisa out of trouble.

She looks back at Lizzie, who seems to be away with the fairies, her forehead crinkled in thought. 'Maybe we should go after her,' Nina says, nodding towards the window. Lizzie doesn't answer, doesn't seem to be listening.

'Is your ankle better?' Lizzie asks, eventually, flashing her phone light at Nina's foot and then looking up with those guileless eyes.

'I got up the stairs OK,' Nina shrugs.

'Oh good.' She pauses, sweeping the light towards something on the floor. 'That's Jane's.'

Nina shuffles closer, trying not to wince as she drags bad ankle with good.

'The doll's house?'

'Yeah. Well, it's kind of a doll's house and kind of a ...'

Nina waits, but Lizzie doesn't explain what she means, she just stands there. Lizzie is a complete enigma to Nina, always has been. So still and quiet.

Eventually, Lizzie steps towards the doll's house again and Nina moves closer too, unsure what's going on.

Lizzie stands still for another moment, staring down at the miniature house as if building up the nerve to act. Then she takes a big breath, stoops down suddenly and shines the flashlight of her phone inside.

14

LIZZIE – 10:29 p.m.

Lizzie stumbles backwards so fast that she clatters into Nina, who was hovering just behind her.

'Ow! God!' Nina scoots backwards awkwardly until she can sit on the edge of the bed and gingerly rub her ankle.

'I'm sorry,' Lizzie starts, holding her hands up in surrender, the light of her phone swinging as she moves. 'I just...'

But Nina isn't listening, she's carefully prodding her ankle and turning her foot one way, then another. Her own phone is next to her on the bed, flashlight beam pointing up towards the ceiling so one strange column of space is lit, dust motes twirling.

Lizzie stares in silence for as long as she can and then squats down, knees clicking, in front of Nina. 'Are you OK?'

'Yeah, I'll live. What were you looking at anyway?'

Lizzie sits on the bed next to Nina and shines her flashlight towards the doll's house. 'It's a replica of this house,' she says quietly.

Nina squints briefly, disinterestedly. 'Oh yeah,' she says, and then returns to her foot.

But Lizzie uses her light to study it again, glad of the distance. It's made from wood, about two-foot square, the same ink-pot shape as Moirthwaite Manor. The roof has been painted grey,

and the walls have been washed with a sort of rusty red colour to match the local stone, each individual brick picked out with a delicate brown line. The windows have proper wooden frames, but no glass, so little hands can easily open them. Just as Jane's once did.

From here, Lizzie can see the top floor easily, both the front and the side windows. She can make out that the grounds-man's bedroom and Jane's bedroom (this very bedroom) are wallpapered and filled with tiny miniature furniture. A little desk and chair. A tiny wire bed to replicate that on which they now sit.

But when Lizzie lights up Jane's dad's miniature bedroom, it's not empty like its real-life counterpart. Instead, the room has been used for a very different purpose.

Lizzie wasn't expecting them to still be there. She'd rather hoped she'd imagined the whole thing, but no. *Crumbs, Jane.*

Lizzie moves closer, steeling her nerve. The shock has worn off, but it's been replaced by something deeper, something that turns her guts to liquid. Before she realises it, she's making a strange noise, a low frightened moan that's seeping out like air from a punctured tyre.

'What are you doing??' Nina says, easing herself up and shuf-fling closer, flashlight bouncing all around.

Lizzie opens her mouth to explain, but she can't find the words so instead she keeps shining her light back through the top right window of the house. 'She used it as a display case,' she says, but Nina clearly doesn't understand. 'Look closer.'

Nina grabs Lizzie's arm for support and leans closer to the doll's house, then snaps her head away. 'Jesus Christ. Nina backs away. 'That girl was always weird.'

She was, probably, but something about this sad little col-lection of animal skulls makes Lizzie want to cry. Each one

carefully – lovingly – skinned, cleaned and polished. 'She just liked collecting them,' Lizzie says quietly.

Nina doesn't answer, and when Lizzie turns around, she sees her sister shuffling out of the room, shaking her head.

The skulls are loosely stacked in size order: rabbits at the bottom, their bulging eye surrounds and two thick front teeth looking almost comical. They fill the width of the room and support the next row of squirrel skulls. Lizzie recognises the curious 'pincer' shape of their jaws. Like little ivory lobster claws. Stuffed between a row of squirrels' heads and the wooden ceiling are the odds and sods. Little mice, with cartoon eye holes. Birds with beaks like knives. Other little bones, lying carefully across like rafters. Teeth dotted here and there. Everything is yellow with age but was once carefully preserved. A layer of dust sits over them and Lizzie is tempted to blow it away, but stops at the thought of causing an avalanche of skulls.

Jane only had four of these in her collection the first time she showed them to Lizzie. A rabbit, a mouse, a bird and a squirrel. She'd given each of them one of the bedrooms, tucking the cleaned skulls in the miniature beds, under the hand-knitted blankets. Who knitted those blankets? It can't have been Jane's mum, she'd left when Jane was still a toddler, though Jane didn't like to talk about it often. But the knitting is too rough and the sizes too specific to be shop-bought. Was it... maybe... Yes. She has a dim memory of her own mum knitting little things sometimes. Could she have made them for Jane? Lizzie knew her mum felt sorry for Jane. An uneasy jealousy ripples through her again.

On the miniature version of Jane's bed, the little blanket has flowers just like the eiderdown over there. But Jane didn't put a skull in her own tiny bed in the doll's house, that's right. Gosh, it's all coming back now. Jane's miniature bed was reserved for

a doll version of Jane herself. Lizzie looks in the doll's house again, letting the light fill the toy version of the very room she's standing in. And yes, there it is, lying under the bed. Jane. What if…

Lizzie whips around suddenly and drops down until she can shine her own light under the real-life bed. From her awkward squatted position, she can see that there's nothing there. No mannequin, no human being lying in wait. No body.

Why would there be a body?

You've read too many manor house mysteries, she tells herself, dusting her aching knees as she turns back to the little house and plucks out the wooden Jane. It's dressed like she always was. A pinafore dress, a blouse, long socks. Dark hair bunched. Her head is not wooden like the rest of her, it's knitted, the wool rough with age and grey with dust. Lizzie blows it away, gently cleans her old friend and places her back in her bed. *Where are you now, Jane?*

15

AISA – 10:39 p.m.

Every step out here feels fraught, as her city trainers slap the ground, damp and ill-equipped. I'm here, I'm here, I'm here, yells the rhythm of her footsteps, ringing out across the grey countryside. Still no one emerges, but she was so sure she saw someone behind her. The fear builds up like steam in a kettle so she has to stop herself crying out. That would hardly help, but this is unbearable.

The narrow road is made narrower still by the stubby stone wall running along each side, twisting and coiling with the bumpy land like a snake. Lactic acid shoots up her calves and her damp shoes pinch her feet. Her hands, peeking out from her jacket, are bitten by the brutal wind. It feels personal. And there's a lot more of it to come before she reaches civilisation. Did she imagine seeing something hide? Maybe it was a bit of sheeting tied to a gate or something? Maybe.

Aisa looks behind her, squinting into acres of nothing, and then carries on. In the distance, in several directions, lone houses dot the distant landscape. Their dim lights flicker like dying stars, too far to reach on foot. Maybe even cut off by flooding if the earlier part of tonight's journey is anything to go by. Oh crap, could the village be cut off? *No, don't think about that.*

God, who would choose to live here like this? Sitting ducks, alone and vulnerable. She kind of understands why her parents lived nearby; they were born around here and simply lacked imagination. Her dad was from a beer family, several generations working at the stinking brewery on the road to Penrith; her mum was the daughter of factory workers. They were schooled here, met here, married here, had kids here. The real surprise is that they left here.

But some people, they actively chose this place. Some of these houses will be filled with people who have seen other ways of life and yet chose this one. Psychopaths.

The lactic acid has climbed to her thighs, her jeans are rubbing her legs and her coat is wet through. She wonders just briefly if she should ditch it, if its dampness is just making her colder. But she can't bear to peel it off and have fewer layers of protection between her body and this weather.

Her phone now has 23 per cent battery. She'll have to conserve it more carefully soon. She'll have to switch the light off, but the thought of being alone out here in the darkness...

She swallows, her throat dry and stomach aching with hunger. When did she last drink something? There was the wine at lunch. Then a few cups of tea in the afternoon. Was that it? God. And she barely ate her lunch too, just nudged all those carbs around her plate with her fork. She looks at her Apple Watch, itself on the last wisps of battery, and sees that she's blasted through her Move goal on this walk at least. When she gets to the village, if there's any shop still open, she's going to buy a whole loaf of white bread and just bore a hole in it with her teeth, climb inside.

A small stone skims across the road behind her, stopping against her heel. Kicked by a foot? She stops dead, a wave of panic running the length of her body, coating her in a sudden

sweat. So there *is* someone following. Oh God. She hears the slightest rustle. Nina? No, her ankle. Lizzie. Please be Lizzie, sent by Nina to bring her back and too nervous to know what to say. Please fucking hell in heaven be Lizzie.

Aisa stays still, listening keenly to every sound which blends into a whoosh of wind and a crackle of leaves and branches. And... and... Shit. And what sounds like a footstep. And another. Treading ever so lightly with painful, cautious care. If it was Lizzie, she would have spoken up. Surely?

Aisa closes her eyes, building up the nerve. She has her light on like a beacon, there's no point pretending she's not here, so she turns suddenly and sweeps the flashlight of her phone around, expecting something terrible.

There's nothing there but the hideous skeletons of the trees, layer upon layer of wooden shadows. Neither of her sisters is here. The footsteps have stopped. Whoever was following is pretending otherwise. This isn't good. This isn't bloody good. Shit.

Aisa always believed she would put up a good fight. She lives out there, unapologetically taking up space and fearlessly throwing herself at life; she always knew she'd be handed a bill for it eventually because that's how it goes. But she never thought it would be here, in the arse end of nowhere, where her worst memories reside.

She runs into the woods on her left, bag clutched tight to her, ducks behind a tree and then turns her flashlight off. She can't hear any footsteps, but she doesn't wait around, plunging deeper among the trees, zigzagging in the dark. If someone is following her, they'll have to track her by sound alone now she's switched off her light. She treads as quietly and quickly as she can, grabbing the thick wet tree trunks to swing herself around, glad of the soft forest floor, robbing her steps of their noise.

A sudden memory. Running through trees, away from something. But what? She shakes it away and focuses on the present. She still has no reception, there's no reception at the house, and she's damned if she'd call her sisters anyway. There's no one she would call. No one she could call.

She slows and clings to one of the trees, trying to keep her breathing steady and inaudible. She curls herself into the smallest shape possible in case whoever is there turns their own flashlight on. Then she inches forward carefully, peering behind the tree and staring the way she just came. She sees absolutely nothing. The stars and thin moon can't reach her through the canopy of trees. She listens hard, but hears nothing useful over the wind.

She's a sitting duck and needs to keep going, so Aisa grips her bag close to her body with her elbow so nothing inside rattles and gives her away. As she has on so many other nights, she teases her keys out of her pocket, a jumble of metal for the apartment building in Paris, a million miles away from here, and positions each key between the fingers of her right hand. Then she brushes her fingers against her passport holder and its precious cargo for good luck. She needs to survive this dreadful night so she can finally read that card. *Yes, Aisa, that's how it works.*

She weaves across the woodland for another minute, aware that a straight line makes her very easy to follow. Then she ducks in behind another thick tree and peers out, trying to let her eyes adjust. She still feels like prey, just waiting to be caught, but she can't just keep running and getting lost in the woods. Especially as whoever is following her must know this countryside far better than she could.

The lightning flashes then. Followed almost immediately by thunder, a short bombastic burst like mighty hands clapping. It's close by, another episode will follow soon. She almost hides

from it, burying her head into the bark of this ancient tree. But she forces her lids to stay open, forces herself to keep looking, waiting for the sky to light up and show her what – who – she's dealing with …

When the lightning comes again, she scans as far as she can, scouring the woodland as the sky pulses bright yellow and blue. Just before it fades again, she sees it. Him. Them. The silhouetted figure crouching low to the ground, heading her way.

16

ROSEMARY – 1975

'A flying visit,' she says. There's something in the look that accompanies her words. Or maybe it's in the way she smooths an invisible crease from her corduroy skirt, that makes me think she knows. More than knows. Owns. That she owns William, owns his time, owns his affection. Controls how it is all parcelled up, metered out. She gave me Friday off, which I'd been so chuffed about at the time, and that's when he arrived. Gone by Sunday. She didn't need to mention it, I wouldn't have known, but she did.

'Anything else, Rosemary?'

'No, ma'am.'

I place the tea things on the low table in front of her and scuttle away like the dormouse I am. Gritty-eyed, sweating from my temples, biting clumps from my cheeks, I slam straight into one of the boys standing shirtless in the hallway.

'What on earth?' I say, my voice haughty as if becoming an immediate representative for the household. I can smell him. Ammonia and sweat.

He just stands there, shaking, and I catch up with myself and realise what I'm seeing.

'Kitchen,' I say, knowing it's empty.

He thunders in there, with me following behind, skirt hitched. I point to the larder, grab the mop and bucket I'd filled ready to use and slop the water haphazardly everywhere, slicking the terracotta.

I stand in the doorway, working my mop while the boy is pressed against the tins in the larder, quivering. His pale skin shines like a flare, but when the Brigadier comes marching down the hallway, I look up as placidly as I can.

'Wet floor?' he says.

Well obviously, I don't say. 'I can fetch you anything you need, sir,' I say, hoping the fear-rattle is not as obvious to him as it is to me. 'I wouldn't want you to slip.'

He puts his hands on his hips. He's wearing those awful jodhpurs he insists on, and I see his hawk eyes scanning the floor for footprints. There are none, of course, I wetted it only after the boy's bare feet were safely across, but I find myself following his gaze anyway.

'Very good,' he booms, turning to leave and then looking back, just quickly, directly at my chest. 'Very good.'

I hear the front door and the crunch of gravel, then moments later the engine of his big old car as he goes off to see if the boy has made a break for it on tarmac. I wait until I'm sure the Brigadier has gone and then I call out, 'It's OK, you can come out.'

The boy doesn't move. He's pinned close to the wall, as if the tins of luncheon meat and jars of pickle are his brothers-in-arms and he won't give them up.

'It's OK,' I say, moving closer. As I do, I notice the marks on his wrists. Livid red bracelets, weeping blood in places.

He looks at them now too, as if noticing for the first time. 'Insubordination,' he whispers. 'So I had to do "Reflection".'

He's not the first trembling boy to escape from Reflection, but

this one is different. He doesn't live here, he comes by day and gets food and a bit of cash in hand. The Brigadier has probably forgotten that, has seen him as just another head in his cattle drive. But this one has a family, the cook told me.

'Go home, Bob,' I say.

17

NINA – 10:37 p.m.

Nina is sitting on the floor in front of the hearth, fixing the sloppy job Lizzie did with the fire and trying to warm up. Her shoes are steaming slightly to the side of the grate, socks draped over them. It hadn't been nice putting them back on to go upstairs, but they were a form of armour at least. Now she wriggles her naked toes on the dusty rug, one of the old blankets lying over her shoulders.

If she closes her eyes and lets the smell of burning wood flood her head, she could almost believe she was out camping. Somewhere with a crystal sky, surrounded by gently swaying, scented trees, with rain pattering on the roof of her trusty old tent. Nothing fancy, just a classic lightweight two-man, long and narrow with a little porch that makes her feel like she's the hungry caterpillar, all swaddled and fat. She'd give anything to be tucked up in her tent now. Especially with Tessa, exploring the open spaces of the world together, though she'd have never admitted that. Never wanted to be dependent, only depended upon ... She stops for a moment and sits up. *A tent.* There was always a tent in the woodland out the back, who did it belong to?

That's right, Alan. Alan the groundsman. A quiet man,

dedicated to the land and the garden, shy around the girls. He would make them little hedgehogs out of teasels, little corn dollies. He must have had a room in the house, all the staff did except their mum, but he preferred the tent. She wonders what happened to him. How devastated he would be to see the ruin that surrounds this place.

Either her ankle is much better or adrenaline has deadened her nerves, but either way, she's glad to be out of that haze of pain. Able to think more clearly. It could almost be cosy now that a proper fire is burning, if it wasn't so dusty and creepy. Even lying down with a blanket, her shoulders are rigid and her nerves are fizzing.

The door opens behind her and she turns awkwardly, but it's just Lizzie.

'Hey,' she says as Lizzie walks over, arms full of the old eiderdown from upstairs. 'Finished in the pet cemetery?'

Lizzie visibly bristles but says nothing. Instead, she walks cautiously over to the sofa and lays the eiderdown gently over it. 'Thought this would be warmer than those old blankets,' she says. 'I've checked it for creepy-crawlies.'

'Oh Lizzie, you didn't have to. I could have checked it myself.'

By the time she started secondary school, Nina had removed so many spiders for her sister that she was immune from fear and would frequently be called upon by other kids to perform this skill. On camping trips, it was she who could clasp any wriggling beast between two hands, no longer needing a cup and a piece of paper. Even now, she's designated bug catcher, taking enormous pride in scooping up insects that make other adults quake. 'You're my Bear Grylls,' Tessa used to joke when Nina removed a hefty moth or shooed a spider outside. God, why is she thinking about Tessa so much tonight? *Move on, Nina. That would never have worked out.*

78

'It's OK, I just gave it a good shake,' Lizzie says, but Nina notices her peering nervously into its folds anyway. 'Want to share it with me?'

Nina shakes her head but moves a little so she's not absorbing all the heat herself. 'Don't worry, you curl up.'

Lizzie nods gratefully. 'I'm pretty tired,' she says, 'so it'll be nice to just rest a minute. Don't let me fall asleep though.'

'I won't,' Nina says, smiling to herself. 'I just want to keep an eye on the fire so it's still going when Aisa comes back.'

Outside, the storm still ruffles the trees but it's not as violent as it was earlier. She hopes Aisa has escaped the worst of it. Maybe she's somewhere warm and dry in the village now. Even if it's just that little phone box that was outside their old house.

Nina looks over at Lizzie, bundled in her eiderdown like a satisfied house cat. Now she just needs Aisa back, and then she can rest knowing they're both safe and warm. Always the eldest.

She sees it in the families she visits as a midwife, firstborns still in pull-ups themselves being prepared for their new role as big sister or brother. A role that comes with very few perks, but that they generally seem excited for. Had she been excited? She was two when Lizzie was born, no chance of remembering that. But she remembers Aisa. Remembers her growing in their mum's tummy, worrying about the skin stretching too thin so the baby could poke its fingers out. Worried about their mum dying in childbirth like all the women seemed to in old books and films. And then Aisa appeared. Fully formed from day one, a ball of energy and spirit. Nothing like the others, immediately just herself. But always wanting to be in the mix with Nina and Lizzie. Always following them around, glued to Nina in particular. A loyal little puppy, who would snarl and bite if you ever called her cute. Which she was, that much is clear from all

the old photos, but at the time she was too much of a pain in the arse for Nina to realise it.

Aisa was a fibber too, gosh she told whoppers. And she was never one for dolls. She was like a little doll herself but hated dresses, choosing to clothe herself in ridiculous ensembles even then. 'Let her choose,' their mum would say. The same mum who years earlier had rigorously reviewed Nina and Lizzie's outfits, liking them to match as if they were from a catalogue, and scouring the charity shops for similar stuff.

And Aisa loved playing hide-and-seek. She's a bit like that now. You never know where she'll be. Never calling for help, never seeming to be without money. Always hustling, a heat-seeking missile for an opportunity.

Maybe everyone would have plenty of money if they didn't have rent or mortgages to pay, or council tax and bills. But the very idea of that life makes Nina cringe. She loves her own space too much. She never breathes as easily as she does at home, with its high ceilings and open-plan main room. The fact that she bought it brand new, and that no one else has ever slept there or washed up in the sink, was well worth chaining herself to a mortgage. A mortgage that will have to be met, come what may.

But Aisa's life is perfect for her, Nina concedes. She was never going to play a straight bat. And good for her, Nina thinks, and wishes they were the kind of family to say that out loud.

A noise from outside brings her back to the moment. A sudden, indescribable noise. Over before she could analyse it. Something falling? A breaking branch? A car door? She didn't grab hold of it in time, but she definitely heard *something*.

Maybe Aisa is back? Perhaps she ran to the village and back, or found a house along the way, used their phone and begged a lift.

Nina hoists herself carefully to standing and heads to the

window. Lizzie watches her lazily, seemingly unaware of the sound or Nina's sense of urgency.

She presses her nose and eyes to the window. A figure is standing on the driveway, fifty feet or so away, motionless. Could it be Aisa? But why isn't she moving?

She squints and tries to make it out, but the dim light of the fire makes the darkness outside even blacker, less penetrable. She blinks, wishing she'd worn her glasses, but they're in the car. It takes a moment for her eyesight to settle, but when it does, all she can see are the black trees standing like sentries, closing them in. There was no one there.

18

LIZZIE – 10:45 p.m.

Lizzie's eyes keep drooping to a close. But Nina seems to have renewed energy now, pacing around like a guard dog despite her duff ankle. It's making Lizzie feel even more exhausted. Before she came down by train to her dad's house this morning, she'd been at the sanctuary all night watching over a stray dog found with a damaged leg.

The poor thing was so frightened that even with a cast and a cone collar, he was hurling himself into things and making it worse. She'd checked in on him as she was about to leave. She'd been so ready for her bath, a Manhattan in a vintage glass and some lovely, secret company. Instead, seeing how sad the dog looked, she had opened up his crate and let him climb onto her lap as she sat against the wall.

He was some kind of curious mixture of breeds. A smiling husky face, squat little body and solid legs. Thick hair that came off in her hands and coated them like fingerless gloves. He finally fell asleep while she stroked him, his pulse slowing and his limbs gradually losing their tremble. She resolved to stay like that as long as he needed, and ended up staying the night, calling to move her plans to the next day – tonight – just in the nick of time. Not that that's worked out well.

She finally nodded off in the early hours and woke up a few hours later, curled up to the dog's warmth. Her shift should have ended at 6 p.m., and it was closer to 6 a.m. when she left, but it was worth it. Or rather, it felt worth it at the time. Now she feels nauseous with lack of sleep, and even sadder than she expected at missing out on plans. Until recently, Lizzie's favourite type of plan was to have no plan.

When she was still upstairs, she could hear the rain drumming on the black slate roof, but in this front room, you could almost forget the weather. Until the occasional crack of thunder and lightning, at least. But out there, poor Aisa can't possibly forget the weather. She must be soaked. She pictures her little sister, rain running down her perfect nose, hair plastered to her face, and feels sick with worry. Lizzie should have gone. But it would have been futile trying to argue with Aisa. If she'd pushed too hard, Aisa would probably have peeled off her coat and gone out bare-armed just to make a point.

'You'd cut your nose off to spite your face,' as their mum used to say to her, but with affection. Almost as if she was impressed by Aisa's total commitment to being a contrarian, while she – Mum – always did the right thing.

They say each subsequent sibling that arrives has to find a role for themselves, a niche. Like, we already have a Nina, we can't have two people good at building fires and staying calm in a crisis and climbing mountains or whatever it is she does. So Lizzie came along and chose ... what? She's not really sure. A small, quiet life. And then Aisa took what was left. A loud, ludicrous life.

Aisa is the coolest person I know, she thinks, closing her eyes and nestling further under the thick eiderdown. *Wonder what she'd say about me?*

*

The fire is roaring now, and Nina has taken root again in front of it, jabbing at it a little with the rusty poker and laying another two logs carefully on top. The eiderdown is surprisingly unmusty. A light layer of dust came loose when she shook it, but that's all. God knows when it was last washed, but beggars can't be choosers.

She thinks of Jane lying under it all those years ago. Her dark hair in bunches, her serious eyes. The way she would smile when Lizzie arrived, but then cover her mouth as if her pleasure was a secret. 'I've got something to show you,' she'd often say, holding out her hand for Lizzie to take it, to pull her into whatever adventure Jane had planned. She always had something to show her, and sometimes it wasn't a nice thing so Lizzie's stomach would clench in anticipation. There were often weeks between visits, and she thinks now how lonely Jane must have been in that time. Lying in that giant bed at night, with just her dad and the hired help for company by day. No wonder she was a bit different. What was Lizzie's excuse?

'You should have been born a century ago,' her mum said once. 'You'd have been happier in the past.' And hadn't she shrunk at that? Yet when something so similar was said to her again recently – 'You're like a gift from a bygone time' – hadn't she just swelled with pride? Tonight, after hours with her family, she feels ever so small again.

As her eyes start to close, she imagines herself shrinking down even more, dissolving away until she is the size of that little Jane doll, climbing into her miniature bed next to a mausoleum of animal skulls. Until finally, she thinks nothing at all.

19

AISA – 11:03 p.m.

Aisa slumps against the tree and tries to picture what she just saw, and how far away he was. It was a split-second silhouette, but he wasn't there before and it wasn't her imagination.

She's not going to run; she refuses to be prey. She looks at her phone, still no reception, of course. And 22 per cent battery. She's all on her own, several miles from her sisters now. If she called out to them, if she allowed herself to admit she needs them and just screamed for them, it would still do no good. Instead, she turns on the flashlight, covering it with her hand for a moment, and then stands and shines it where she saw him, hoping to dazzle his eyes and then run at him with her keys. She bounces on her toes, looking, looking. Where is he?

And then she sees a figure even closer to her. Still low to the ground. This time on all fours. Terrified. A fox. Skinny nose, mangy body. She shudders with relief, a low moan leaving her body before she can stop it.

Oh thank Christ.

'Filthy nasty thing,' she says to the back of him as he scurries away and she picks her way back towards the road. Bring on the hunt, she thinks, and imagines the savaging from the social media dogs if she ever voiced that.

She doesn't really mean it, just that old instinct to be contrary kicking in. She's delirious with relief, her blood spiced with it. She treads harder, with a renewed desire to get to the village and get the hell away from here.

It's far quicker to get through the trees when she's got the light on. It turns out she'd barely even grazed the woods, even though it felt like an entire life had passed in there. In under a minute, she's back on the road.

A fox! Just a fox. And not some crazy killer. And not her sisters either, coming to check up on her. A small part of her is disappointed, but the larger part is relieved. To be self-reliant is a credo she's proud of, and she's managed to slip out of a terrifying situation with it intact.

How much further is the village anyway? The lights still twinkle up ahead, but no closer than before, even after walking for ages. It's like a mirage or something. She plods on, feet rubbing against the thin trainer soles, but so glad to be alive, she could almost start running. Almost.

She tries to remember what the village has to offer but all she can really remember is the phone box, which is hopefully still there, plus snatches of the tiny school and their house. Her bedroom. No, *their* bedroom, all three girls shared a room until they moved to Cheshire. Then everything changed. They stayed with an old relative for a few weeks, a great-aunt who looked like Skeletor, then they moved to a house in Northwich with a bedroom each. Their mum stopped working and took up amateur dramatics, even doing Theatre Studies and Textiles A levels at the local college. Their dad embarked on the job track he would stay on until he retired. Eventually becoming Robert Kelsey, Station Master, Northwich Station.

He would bring home route maps for them to use for

artwork, and she'd study them instead, plotting her eventual escape. She can still reel off the exact route of every branch of the old GWR and LNWR network, should anyone ever require it. Now it's Northern Trains, but it's the same old lines, the same tendrils spilling out across the Pennines, near where she now walks.

Her feet thump along the tarmac, but the village lights stay as far as ever in the distance. One of them is her old house. Number 2, Teapot Lane. A storybook address. She wonders who lives there now, if they're happy. If they have little girls. If one of them is dreaming of escape.

She's still thinking of this when she realises her wrist is vibrating. Her Apple Watch, warning of low battery or... She pushes up her damp jacket sleeve and sees them in all their glory. Notifications. Notifications!

She stops dead, terrified that she'll chase the reception away as she checks her phone, still being used as a flashlight. Only 19 per cent charge, but good old-fashioned 3G and one little bar of reception. She watches the charge tick down to 18 per cent as everything floods in. Social alerts. Emails. WhatsApp messages. She doesn't know what to check first, and stands for a moment, smiling with relief.

The text message is from the airline. Her flight has been delayed by an hour. It's nearly half-eleven now. She needs to be at Newcastle Airport by 4 a.m. at the absolute latest and she could still make it. Shit. She had all but given up, but she could make it yet. On a mad whim, she opens her Uber app, but obviously there are no cars available.

But there is a car just sitting idle back at the house... and there's still one bar of reception. She only really has one option. The option she had promised to take all along. As much as it

kills her to leave her notifications unread, she saves her battery power to google the number for a breakdown service. It comes up painfully slowly, but she finally calls it, and then presses the phone to her ear and waits.

20

ROSEMARY – 1980

I can feel Bob shaking next to me as the vicar prompts him. 'I do solemnly swear…' Our relatives, in the main, laugh. Maybe thinking of their own last-minute wedding nerves. The mean-spirited among them, especially Bob's parents who we were in two minds about inviting at all, might think he's having second thoughts, that he wants to bolt. But there's no chance. My favourite relative, my dad's Aunt Winnie, clutches my mum's hand in the front pew, but my mum pats her arm reassuringly.

I squeeze Bob's hand and look up. His grey suit shimmers slightly under the dramatic light pouring through the stained glass, and his thin moustache trembles a little as he returns my smile. He has what my mum calls an interesting face. I think he's handsome, but he's not pretty like some men. He's not neat and smooth. He's more… carved from molten rock. His face formed by life, the way a pebble is shaped by the sea. A scar through his eyebrow, a dent on his chin. A slight shake in his hands sometimes. I love him. And I feel sorry for him. But mostly I just love him.

This is not wedding jitters. He was full of nothing but excitement last night when he banged on my mum's door at gone midnight, having necked a happy skinful from his stag do in

The Fox. She'd chased him away up the road, waving a tea towel at him. But she didn't mind really. She loves Bob, was glad to see me settling down. I'm twenty-three, an old maid in the eyes of a woman who married Dad when they were both nineteen.

No, it's not nerves. I cast an eye to the back of the church just quickly, a glimpse of the scrawny blanketed knees and thinning grey hair of the Brigadier in his wheelchair. I'd thought it was a safe bet, inviting them. Never imagined that they'd actually come, not with his condition. I'd hoped they might stump up a good wedding present and, if I'm honest, that was my driving motivation. In the last few years, bemoaning how difficult it is to get good workers 'these days', Mrs Proctor has dropped heavy hints about there being provisions in their wills for loyal staff. It's the main reason I'm still there. Money maintains my proximity to people that cast long shadows over people I love.

But no wedding gift could ever make up for the Darth Vader shadow the Brigadier has thrown over my happiest day.

Alan is here too, wearing a suit that I can only imagine once belonged to the Brigadier when he was still in his prime. Even so, I can see slabs of Alan's scarred wrists, flashes of his ankles. Reflection never worked on him, or maybe it's still working now. He's the only boy left. And certainly not a boy anymore. He's here to push the chair, while Mrs Proctor drifts dreamily alongside. A proprietorial serenity on her face. Her member of staff, her village church, the stained glass paid for, the family crypt in pride of place.

They won't come to the reception, they say, after the ceremony. Relieved, I thank them as they leave. Bob talks in a quiet, urgent voice to Alan, avoiding looking over as the Brigadier grasps my hands. I'm propelled towards him, receiving a kiss on both cheeks. He has an underground river of strength undiminished

by age or illness, and I'm carried along it. As I scrabble to free myself, I nearly trip over the train me and my mum spent so long embroidering.

'A lovely ceremony, Rosemary,' Mrs Proctor says, offering me a powdered cheek to graze with my own. In contrast to her husband, she has no strength, no physicality at all. Her hand brushes my arm, and I think that she might think that constitutes affection. For a moment, I'm struck with pity for their only – and long gone – son. 'A little something,' she says, and offers me an envelope. 'Don't open it now,' she cautions, as if people like me aren't used to getting gifts and might not know the decorum.

'Thank you,' I say.

As soon as they're installed in the big car, Alan at the wheel although I'd be amazed if he had a licence, I tear into it. It's a card. *Congratulations on your wedding. Warm Regards, Brigadier and Mrs Proctor.* One crisp five-pound note flutters out.

21

NINA – 11:20 p.m.

Lizzie is snoring on the sofa, one arm dangling free, legs splayed, mouth open. As buttoned up as she is by day, by night she is the opposite. Unfurling and taking up space. Making noise. *So that's all there inside you then*, Nina thinks. *You could be* more. Lizzie claims she's happy with her lot. A tiny, terraced house in a small seaside town, a job looking after waifs and strays, piles and piles of second-hand books and a belly rounded by hot chocolate and doorstep sandwiches. Nina has more than this and she's not particularly satisfied, so surely Lizzie's contentment can't be real.

Tessa once said that Nina deliberately picked other shift workers so she always had a reason to let things fizzle out. *We're too busy... our schedules clash...* 'That won't happen to us,' Nina said, knowing full well it would. Not wanting it to, but too scared to jump in with both feet.

Nina hears another noise outside, close to the house. Was she wrong to mistrust her eyes before? Maybe there is someone there. She tries to tune out Lizzie's snoring and the crackle of the fire. Is it Aisa? If it is Aisa, she'll come inside any moment. But if it isn't... Nina waits, silently, listening hard.

She's still trying to get her bearings, to work out the direction, when another noise reaches her, closer and louder this time.

She gets back up slowly and walks as quietly as she can to the window. Balancing on her better leg and casting a quick protective look at Lizzie, she hides most of herself behind the curtain and squints out. If it was Aisa out there, she'd have her phone flashlight on, but there's nothing there, no light.

Nina squints, trying to make out individual shapes, but it's just one big, dark nothing. No Aisa. No one? Or is someone out there, hiding from her? Overhead, she can hear the trees moving, can hear the static in the sky. The grumble of thunder threatened, but she heard two noises that were distinct from this, she knows she did.

And again now. A third noise. Inside the house this time. Footsteps? The direction confuses her, scrambling as it reaches her ears, so when she tries to place the source of the sound within the house, her mental image of the house spins and fractures like an Escher drawing.

Nina is always level-headed; she has always had to be. Births can spiral out of control and as a midwife she is there to wrestle them back, without ever letting on that she's worried. Pressing emergency buttons to call in crash teams while keeping neutral eyes on the birth partner, whisking blue newborns to get oxygen while the mothers lie panting, endorphins curtaining them from reality. And even when the worst happens, the absolute worst, she is calm. She is the strong oak tree that grieving mothers weep against. Just as she is the one who fixes the ropes on climbing trips. The one who solves colleagues' problems. The captain of the work netball team, rallying and unflappable. She clenches her teeth and tells herself this is still true, despite what happened last week.

There is only one scenario that sends her spine to jelly, and that's enclosed spaces. Sometimes, even getting a hoodie stuck on her head can send her heartbeat rushing up like a rocket.

Traffic tightly wound around a narrow lane makes her breath quicken. Embarrassingly, she would rather lie down and die than get stuck in a tunnel or be shut into a lift. But life is adaptable, and she simply runs up the stairs at the infirmary and everything is fine.

None of that is a problem here anyway. The house is huge, this room is enormous, plenty of slightly dusty, smoky air to breathe. She takes a gulp of it now. She will not let panic grip her. This is a creaky old house and they've already looked through it while searching for blankets, Lizzie more than once. No one is here. No one is here.

It is probably full of rats though. Or mice. Never the twain together, Lizzie told her that. As if they've carved up the world like the Sharks and the Jets. Where did that come from? She hasn't thought about that since... since Mum.

West Side Story was their mum's favourite, although Rosemary liked absolutely any musical she could get her hands on. The sisters were raised on the kind of content you'd never dream of showing little kids now. *The Rocky Horror Picture Show*, *Little Shop of Horrors*, even *Hair*, for God's sake.

The happiest she'd ever seen her mum was when her amateur dramatics group put on *Oliver!* and she got to play Nancy. Belting out 'I'd Do Anything' and 'Oom-Pah-Pah' to a revolving selection of Kelseys in the audience each performance, to help her nerves.

Nina had forgotten that by the end though. God, she should have played Mum her favourite songs in the hospice. Why did none of them think to bring in her CDs? Make her a Spotify playlist? Why didn't Dad?

Focus, Nina!

Yes, this place is probably full of vermin of various stripes who all hid when the sisters came barging in earlier and have now

ventured back out. Maybe even attracted by the heat of the fire, or the smell of human bodies. Nina sniffs one of her armpits. Ripe from the walk, dank from the rain. Maybe some creatures find that heady mix delicious. Either way, it can't be a person. Who would come all the way out here in a storm and not just knock on the door or announce themselves? But still.

She tugs on her coat, still a little damp. Then she teases on her stinking socks and trainers, wincing a little.

Let Lizzie sleep, she thinks, watching her for a moment and then testing her weight fully on her ankle. Much better. Definitely good enough to go and do another recce through the house, just in case. She won't be able to rest if she doesn't check, even though she's probably overreacting.

But, even without acknowledging to herself that she's worried, Nina plucks one of the heavy candlesticks from the mantelpiece with one hand, weighs it in her other palm like a baseball bat. Just in case. Didn't they have some like this, growing up? A pair of them that came out at Christmas... Probably cheap copies.

With one final glance at Lizzie, scratching her stomach in her sleep and muttering nonsense, Nina creeps out into the hall.

22

LIZZIE – 11:35 p.m.

Lizzie drifts in and out of sleep. Her eyes open for a while, taking in the flames of the fireplace, the grey corners of the room, and then she slides back to the nineties, when she and Jane were eight years old.

She is thinking about the first lunch she had here, a picnic packed for them in the Moirthwaite Manor kitchen by Rosemary, but nothing like they'd ever have had at home. Scotch eggs, ginger beer in glass bottles, paper-wrapped doorstep sandwiches with thick-cut ham instead of Billy Bear sausage. And that Labrador and the smugglers' tunnels... She opens her eyes. That was *Famous Five on Kirrin Island*, not a memory of her and Jane's time together.

She sighs, stares at the ceiling and tries to picture reality. Did they ever even have a picnic? Yes, yes they did. They'd sat in the woodland out the back on a crochet blanket that left little Os all over their legs.

Her eyes close as she focuses on the details. A heavy wicker basket from the cupboard under the stairs, that Mum had dusted off with a proper feather duster. A flask of lurid Kia-Ora, which they weren't allowed at home because it sent Aisa loopy with the E-number colourings. They did have doorstep ham sandwiches,

that was true. And a bag of crisps each, and a thick slice of cherry cake. Jane let Lizzie have hers and she ate both slices and felt sick.

She'd lain on that picnic blanket clutching her stomach while Jane tried to wind her up with scary stories and bad ideas. That's right, she'd forgotten that about Jane. How she would sometimes try to take their games in directions that Lizzie didn't like. How she'd have talked you into something before you realised what was happening. And how Jane could lie, spilling tall tales that even Lizzie recognised as the imagination of a desperately lonely child. How Jane could be cruel.

Most of the time, Lizzie let it wash over her. She herself was the middle child of a bossy older sister and a fibbing younger sister, so nothing Jane did could rile her up too much. Unless she invoked the Rosemary Clause.

Your mum likes me best.

Your mum has to do what I say.

Your mum would prefer to be at my house than yours.

Lizzie feels heat prickle her neck at the memory. She realises she's pressing her nails into her palms now, just as she did then, counting all the kinds of animals she could think of, anything to distract her and stop her reacting. To react was risky. Mum needed the job, more so after Dad lost his, and the Kelsey girls could never risk rocking that boat.

'She's probably a bit jealous because her own mum's gone,' Lizzie's mum would say on the way home, as Lizzie glumly pressed her forehead to the window and let it bash her as the potholes bounced the car. 'You've got to let it wash over you.'

'She was saying mean things about you though.'

'There'll always be someone saying something, and you can't stop that,' her mum shrugged. 'But you can choose whether you let it bother you.'

*

The exact details of Jane's mother leaving were hazy even then. And no matter what Jane did, no matter how much she goaded, Lizzie never, ever mentioned it in retaliation. It was tempting, and sometimes the words would line up in her throat like bullets, but she just had to swallow them down.

The talk in the village was that Jane's mother had run off with a gardener who'd been working there for the summer, although that seems a little cliched now she thinks about it. Maybe she's mangling the memories with something out of a book. Besides, village talk is a cheap commodity, rarely useful in the world outside that bubble. They used to say things about Jane's dad too. *I heard he once killed a man.* She shakes her head, eyes still closed. *You idiot. That's from* The Great Gatsby.

The village did gossip about him, but that was probably because he ignored them. Alan used to pop up there from time to time though. She remembers him walking past and giving her a wave. Maybe he drank with their dad in the pub.

To think of Dad then is to think of another man entirely, and so Lizzie rolls onto her side to avoid doing that. Instead, she teases at the edges of Jane's dad, the cut-out shape of him in her mind. The empty room. Perhaps someone bought this place and started to clear it all out. Maybe you would start there as it's the biggest room? They gave up pretty soon, whoever it was. Or perhaps they'll be back. She shivers, although they're hardly going to show up tonight in this weather.

He always wore dark clothes. Sometimes a black hat too, she remembers that, like something out of a storybook. He seemed older than Lizzie's parents. Slower, a little stooped, very set in his ways. It's hard to picture him as a dad. A father, yes, in the abstract sense, but not a dad like Bob is a dad. She can't picture

him ever playing the spoons to make kids laugh, or chasing them around the garden.

Rosemary used to say Lizzie was nurturing too. 'You'll be a lovely mum one day.' She'd stopped saying that eventually. Not because Lizzie wasn't caring, she was frequently laughed at by her family for being *too* caring – the rescued bee, the fostered hedgehog – but probably because everyone thought Lizzie would be alone forever.

As she falls back asleep, Lizzie dreams of overhearing Jane and her mum in the kitchen down the hall. Rosemary using the same soothing voice on Jane that should, by rights, have been reserved just for Lizzie and her sisters. And Jane's voice rising, becoming upset. Tantrumming and stamping her foot. Lizzie having to bite her cheeks so hard that she tasted blood, but never retaliating. As the memory morphs into another dream, the thumping of her foot grows louder and louder, her complaints mutate into screams.

Lizzie wakes again with a start, the voices overlapping her sudden rush of consciousness. But there's no one here and the noise has stopped.

23

ROSEMARY – 1986

'I think we should go to the funeral,' I say, as Bob flinches. 'Well, I should go anyway. As a member of the household staff. But I thought maybe you—'

'If I go, it'll only be to make sure he's definitely in that grave,' Bob says. 'Then I'd like to take a piss on it.'

It takes me and the cook days to organise and prepare all the food. Mrs Proctor has convinced herself that all the 'old boys' are likely to turn up to pay their respects, an idea that is so laughable I can barely repeat it to Bob. 'The grave'll be flooded if they do,' he says.

The manor is filled with flowers, though it's unclear who sent them or if Mrs Proctor called for them to be delivered from the florist she likes in Penrith. They were here when I arrived to work, the day after the Brigadier finally wheezed to a stop. Mrs Proctor had glided down the stairs dressed head to toe in black, a veil over her thin face. It was not just for show, I'm certain of that. She looked genuinely lost without him. 'I'm so sorry for your loss, ma'am,' I said, bowing my head a little.

'It's all of our loss,' she said, her voice barely above a whisper. 'The world's loss, really. He changed so many lives.'

*

On the day of the funeral, I leave Nina and Lizzie with the childminder and dress in the closest thing I have to mourning clothes. My black work skirt and shoes, plus a black satin shirt I found at the church jumble sale. I put my make-up on in the bathroom, going heavy on the mascara in full confidence that I won't shed a tear, and then go to see if Bob's made up his mind. He's sitting on our bed wearing his wedding suit, which strains a little at the waist and is totally the wrong colour.

'Are you sure?'

He nods, unconvincingly. 'Want to check he's actually dead and this isn't one of his lessons.'

The church is patchily filled. Far fewer people than when my own dad passed away, and considerably drier eyes. Aside from Bob and Alan, I see no former boys and I'm glad of it. At the front, Mrs Proctor is flanked by a man and a curly-haired brunette, the woman is wrestling with a dark-haired toddler about Lizzie's age. The man is clearly William. I haven't seen him in over ten years, but I recognise his posture. It's the opposite to his father's, a deliberate stoop, an apologetic rounding of the shoulders. And I recognise his head, the hair that I once wound my fingers through, a million years ago. He's grown it longer again so it scuffs the nape of his neck, and a little thrill goes through me that he's not cut it military style for the funeral. It's his equivalent of pissing on the grave.

I feel briefly strange and warm and I look at Bob, guiltily, but he is staring at his shoes. His six-year-old wedding shoes.

The funeral is, as funerals are, full of descriptions of someone no one in the congregation would recognise. Except, perhaps, Mrs Proctor with her dreamland view of her late husband. I watch William and his wife intently. If it were Bob and me, we would

pass the fractious child between us to try to distract her, but that would certainly not work with Mrs Proctor sitting between them. I'm tempted to go over and offer to take the poor little thing for a walk around outside, show her some flowers and let her have a run out, but I can't do that to Bob.

Afterwards, Mrs Proctor and William stand in the church doorway as the rest of us file out, mumbling our condolences. 'Thank you,' they each say in turn. But then William seems to wake up and realise who I am, and I see him smile, just briefly.

'Rosemary,' he says, his voice barely audible. I nod. And then get jostled from behind by the sub-postmaster from the village, clearly keen to get to the food he knows is laid on at the manor.

'We'll talk later,' I say lightly.

Outside, I see William's wife and daughter walking around the graveyard. She's pointing to the flowers, and then squats to blow a raspberry on the little girl's neck so she dissolves into giggles.

Back at the manor, I swing between being staff and guest, funnelling empty plates into the kitchen, topping up glasses, but making small talk too. Bob swings between drinks, growing pinker and louder, talking boisterously to anyone who'll listen about absolutely nothing.

I don't get to speak to William again, but I introduce myself to his wife and am surprised when an American accent replies. 'I'm Selina,' she says. 'And that little rugrat you saw earlier was Jane, but she's having a nap now.'

A ripple of excitement runs through me. Foreign accents always have that effect on the rare occasion that I hear them in real life.

'Is it your first time at the manor?' I ask.

'Sure is,' she says. 'Not for want of asking.'

'Mrs Proctor can be like that,' I whisper, feeling reckless for saying so.

'Not her,' Selina says, a little louder than I would like. 'She's been begging my husband to bring us up here. Was appalled we didn't want to marry here, even. Can you imagine?'

'Yes, I can,' I say, my expression grim. We both laugh and are shot an angry look from the lady of the house, her arm firmly wrapped through her son's, her pale face anguished.

'No, it was all William,' Selina says quietly. 'He would never have come back here if he could help it. Like, never ever. I thought he might do a moonlight flit last night.'

He's good at that, I want to say, but that's hardly fair. And not exactly current.

'Hopefully we can put in our time today and then get out of Dodge tomorrow,' she says.

I'm about to say something back when I hear a little squeak from Mrs Proctor across the room. We both turn again and Selina gasps as her mother-in-law folds over on herself, one arm still clutching her son, the other her heart. William, grey with shock, helps lower her into a seat.

Within five minutes, she's dead.

24

AISA – 11:36 p.m.

Aisa has been on hold for five minutes when a real human finally answers. After hours by herself, save for that horrendous fox incident, her mouth feels dry and unwieldy, as if it has forgotten how to form words.

'I need help, our car broke down, well, it ran out of petrol—'

'So you need fuel?' the woman cuts in with alarming good cheer.

'Yes, but we also hit a tree. So that needs dealing with.'

A pause. 'Are you OK, madam? Do you or does anyone with you need medical attention?'

'No, we're all fine,' she says, surprised by the wobble to her voice. 'But I'm running out of battery and I really need you to send someone to help. Please.'

In the background, a clatter of keyboards and the hum of voices speak of call centres with strip lighting, a vending machine, a smoking room. Having never made it past a week of working in such places while at uni, Aisa suddenly feels a roaring nostalgia. She shakes her head to get rid of it.

'OK, so your car hit a tree and is it damaged externally or internally?'

'Externally? No, I don't think so. And internally, you mean like

the engine? Yeah, I think…who knows? If I was a mechanic, I wouldn't be calling you.'

'Madam, please—'

'Sorry, sorry, I'm just really cold and really hungry and I need this car fixed.'

'Can I take your membership number?'

'I'm not a member and I don't know if my sister is—'

'Your sister?'

'The driver. But I'll just pay whatever, I need this sorted. Unless…How much is it likely to be?'

'I really couldn't say, the towing costs will be a fixed amount, but the actual repairs—'

Aisa sighs and closes her eyes. What difference does it make, they still needed rescuing.

'Can I take your name?'

'Aisa Kelsey. A-I-S-A, not Asia.'

She's standing as still as she can as the wind buffets her and her knees knock into one another. She daren't move, as a millimetre either way could nix the reception. She doesn't know if she'd have enough battery for another five minutes on hold if this whole circus started again.

The woman continues to pepper her with questions that she can barely answer.

'Yes. No. Yes. Mini of some kind,' she says, her jaw juddering in the cold, making her voice sound strange, like her jaw is wired. It *feels* like it's been wired, aching from the bitter chill and from gritting her teeth through the awful muzak. 'Please help, I'm freezing my tits off here.'

The woman at the end of the line laughs, as if in surprise, and then collects herself with a cough. 'And what's the location of the car?'

'Moirthwaite Manor,' Aisa says, flattening her vowels as she always does when she deals with sunshine southerners.

'Moirthwaite Manor? Wow, that's a little bit hard to say, isn't it? Like a tongue twister.'

'Sure,' Aisa pinches her nose with her free hand.

'And what's the postcode there?'

'I have no idea.'

There's a pause long enough for Aisa to do a full body shiver.

'No matter,' says the woman at the other end, her accent one of those vaguely south-eastern ones that could be from anywhere outside of London. But not London itself, which is only full of other accents in Aisa's experience. 'Could you give me the rest of the address? The street name, maybe?'

As she speaks, Aisa imagines her micro-bladed eyebrows, the sheen of her skin, her neat high-street clothes and sighs. *Why am I like this? This woman's not done anything wrong.*

'I don't know that either. Look, I really don't mean to be shitty, and I know you're just doing your job, but I'm running out of time, so can you just google it or something?'

The pause is as good as a sigh, then the voice comes back even higher, exasperation masked with squeaky practised professionalism. 'OK! No worries! Can you give me any more information so I can make sure I send the van to the right place?'

'It's in the Eden Valley, in Cumbria. Not far from Penrith, but I don't remember any more than that and I've got hardly any battery left.' Without thinking, she pulls the phone from her ear just briefly and winces. 'Seven per cent actually.' She snaps the phone back, glad to hear that the call hasn't cut off.

'Oh fiddlesticks. OK, I'll be quick.'

Aisa looks down the empty lane, grit glistening from the rain. She feels no closer to the lights of the village than she was earlier, but at least she can go back to the house and pretend this

was her plan all along. No need to mention she was intending to ditch her sisters and find a taxi. She only hopes the mechanic will come quickly enough that Nina can get her to the airport.

Aisa can hear the tapping of a keyboard and drums her own foot impatiently. 'Will they bring petrol with them then? Actually, I don't know if the car's petrol or diesel.'

'Can you ask the driver?'

'She's not with me at the moment.'

'Oh yeah. Well, they'll bring a bit of both, enough to get you going again. Oh, I think I've found the address, but, Miss Kelsey, are you *sure* you're at Moirthwaite Manor?'

'Yeah, I mean I will be by the time—'

'Moirthwaite Manor on Black Tree Lane?'

'Black Tree Lane, that's it.'

'And you said it's an abandoned house, is that right? It's not your property?'

'Yes, but I'm sure no one will mind if—'

'Miss Kelsey, are you and your sister by yourselves? It sounds a bit … weird.'

'What?' *How would she know that?*

'When I was googling it for the address, there were some funny results. Some reports from urban explorers—'

'That doesn't surprise me, but can we just—'

'Should you really be in there, I mean, it sounds—'

Aisa's pulse starts to beat through her scalp. 'Sounds what?'

'It's just that they say—'

The phone dies in Aisa's hand.

25

NINA – 11:35 p.m.

Even with her ankle still sore, it's easier to scan the house properly by herself, without Lizzie and Aisa. When they first looked around this place, newly arrived and wet through, it was a cursory glance for firewood, for signs of something helpful. A quick check for danger, from holes in the roof or tilting walls and not … whatever she's looking for now. Now she can take the time to check this place properly, find the source of that noise and make sure there isn't someone here with them.

It was almost certainly the wind, but it sounded too much like footsteps to rest easy. And if Nina doesn't take care of this stuff, who will?

There are rows of books still in the library, an old armchair whose fabric has split, the meat of it springing out. A book lies open on its arm, was that there before? She doesn't remember it, but it must have been.

Heavy velvet curtains cover the library window and she holds her breath as she pulls them open, but no one is there.

Too many horror films as kids, she thinks. What were her parents thinking? She was often allowed to take a quid and a note from her mum to the post office and select from its ten or so rental videos. She'd grab the scariest one she could find, thrust

the money and the note over the counter and then she and her sisters would watch it on the TV that had been lumped upstairs by their dad. She recognises now that this was to keep the kids out of the way so their parents could either argue or 'have an early night'. The sisters wouldn't sleep properly for weeks after watching the 'video nasties'.

Out in the hall again, Nina pokes her head round the front room door and sees the reassuring, quilted mound of Lizzie on the sofa, still fast asleep. They shared a room for the whole of Nina's childhood, but she'd forgotten what a noisy sleeper Lizzie was, her nose snuffling into the pillow like a truffle pig. She'd forgotten the sleepwalking too. Waking up to find her banging around in the wardrobe, or trying to get down the stairs. Getting clobbered for trying to help her without waking her. 'You shouldn't disturb a sleepwalker, it could give them a heart attack.' A myth she believed until A-level Biology.

Nina treads carefully down the hall, her ankle clicking a little but the pain reduced to a dull throb now. As she shuffles, a draught bites at her feet and she shivers. Where did that come from?

She moves away and hovers in the doorway of the old office, muscle memory preventing her from going inside. She – well, everyone – was banned from that room. She remembers the arch of Jane's dad's back sitting in the chair that was slightly too small for him, bent over his desk. Remembers the fear that ran up her legs when she thought he might see her and question what she was doing. Just to hear his voice was enough to turn her to jelly.

She steps inside, one foot, then the other. Pauses, heavy candlestick dangling from one hand, phone in the other. Nervously waiting. As if the ceiling might collapse in outrage, or Jane's dad might appear suddenly and boom at her.

The desk is still here, pushed to the back of the room behind some boxes. The old metal filing cabinet is on the floor, its drawers hanging out like someone's emptied its pockets. She steps closer, the air unpleasantly sweet, and dreads finding the source of the rot. A dead rabbit or rat probably. She thinks of the little skulls upstairs and shivers despite herself. *Freak.* Then she sees them. A row of hooks, and three straggly birds' bodies hanging from them. Pheasants, or maybe grouse. Christ, how long have they been there? They look ragged, but not mouldy. Has the cold preserved them?

The dining room next, where, in the centre of the ceiling, an ornate rose swells and intricate cornicing skirts along the edge of the room like fancy icing on a wedding cake. Nina pictures her mum, tiptoed on a chair, dusting along the edge. Rosemary was strong and lean. A wiry kind of strength that came from constantly moving. Here, in this house, it's easier to remember her at her fullest. By the end of her life, she was a carcass, greying in front of them. But here, God, she must have been younger than Nina was now.

Rosemary wore a black dress with a white trim to work, with a black cardigan and flat black shoes. A bizarre monochrome uniform, but it seemed normal to them back then. At home, she'd scrape her fair hair into a bun and pull on the softest, comfiest clothes she could find. T-shirts of Dad's that draped over her lean frame, tracksuit bottoms and shorts in summer. Nina is the same and can think of nothing worse than hoicking herself into uncomfortable pinched waists and rigid underwires. Out of work, she'll also pull her fair hair into a bun and slip into a pair of joggers and a hoodie. 'You should just cut some arm holes in a sleeping bag,' Tessa said once. It wasn't a bad idea.

She feels a pull in her chest. For Mum. For Tessa. The tugging sensation fades, and Nina rushes back out of the room before it returns.

The kitchen has no blinds or curtains, so the great sheet of glass urgently reflects the flashlight from her phone, stinging her eyes and making her jump. The wooden worktops are still in good nick; she's seen reclaimed worktops like these in fancy apartments when she does home visits. People would spend a fortune to get their hands on what has just been left for dead in here.

Once, this room would have been filled with activity. Cake baking and big suppers being cooked for Jane's dad and whoever might have been visiting him. Who would have visited that man? She doesn't remember any visitors when she was here. But anyway, every crumb has been long picked clean. Now only a line of dust marks where the worktops meet the tiled walls.

Nina's stomach rumbles. Thinking of big suppers, when did she last eat? Lunch at the Harvester with Dad and then a slice of that too-sweet birthday cake.

She's ravenous, but she hadn't realised until now because her thirst was – is – so overpowering.

She steps closer to the big Butler sink that was once kept so clean by her mum's gloved hands, puts the candlestick down and twists the brass cold tap. The pipes chug and whistle a bit, but nothing comes out.

As she stands back up, feeling even thirstier now, a face stares back at her and she jumps in alarm, but it's just her reflection. Still, it reminds her about the footsteps and pushes her to keep checking. Lizzie is lying vulnerable in the other room after all, sleeping soundly because she knows she can rely on her big sister. Everyone can.

*

Nina is upstairs now, walking slowly and carefully around the upper rooms, shining her flashlight into every space. She had plugged her phone in while she was driving and still has an almost full battery now. How much did Aisa have? She should have given Aisa her phone to take. She looks at the time. Aisa has been gone hours. The village was less than five miles from here, although it's awful weather. But she should be back soon, surely?

Nina holds her phone in her left hand, which feels a bit unnatural but means her stronger right arm can hold the heavy candlestick. She feels faintly ridiculous but faintly (yes, she has to admit it, much more than faintly) freaked out.

As her heartbeat races, she reminds herself that she is the trespasser here. She's walking around like she owns the place. But if someone else is here and thinks she's out of line, why haven't they confronted her?

She grips the candlestick tighter and steps into the bathroom. It's three times the size of Nina's shower room at home. A big metal bath with frou-frou decorative feet swims in the middle of it. She peers quickly in it, no one there, then grabs the door and looks behind that. There's something swinging on the back of the door, an old towel or dressing gown, and it touches her as it sways, making her suck in her breath.

Turning back to face the room, it's clear no one is in here. It's surprisingly clear of anything, not really dusty and not as dirty as she'd expect. Even the sink is clean of limescale. These old ceramic sinks seem to stay in good condition though, far better than the basin that came with her new-build apartment, already stained. But it doesn't sit right. Nothing here sits right.

She leans against the basin stand to take the weight off her sore ankle, closes her eyes for a moment. This place doesn't feel like shelter, it feels like a held breath. Her throat tightens.

The water in these taps is probably switched off like downstairs, but she turns the cold one on the off-chance and nearly laughs in delight as the water flows, no chugging and burping. She puts the candlestick and phone down carefully and, with her hands cupped, slurps the water. It's icy cold but tastes normal. Better than normal, it tastes like heaven itself after all these hours. She feels it cooling her throat, her chest shivering as it rushes downwards.

The flashlight beams from the sink to the ceiling, a great column of light. As she dips back down to scoop more water, she hears a creak. It's an almost imperceptible sound that she wouldn't have heard if she wasn't on high alert. A floorboard maybe... or a door. It's pitch black behind her. She freezes, replays the sound in her head. It was a door, somewhere down the corridor. No question.

Nina tries to think, tries to plan her next move, but she's still frozen with fear, the water rushing relentlessly, noisily, on.

She feels the air change behind her. Someone has come into the room.

She swallows, her hand reaches for the candlestick, but she knocks it onto the floor and hears it roll away. Fuck. She wills herself to turn round. It must be Lizzie. Or maybe Aisa has come back. But why aren't they saying anything?

Sweat runs down her back, she is still at the sink, water still gushing, the phone still blasting its light unhelpfully into the air. She reaches for it carefully and flips it over to snuff out the light and turn the window next to the sink into a black mirror.

Then she sees it. A face. Just a sliver of eyes in the soupy darkness. Just for a second before fear overtakes her.

Then everything goes black.

26

ROSEMARY – 1987

I got eight hundred pounds in the will and the promise of a job for as long as Moirthwaite Manor remained in the possession of the Proctor family. Neither inheritance thrilled me. The money went on a new Mini. By which I mean a seven-year-old Mini, but new to us.

I had assumed that the 'job for life' would be a moot point, but the manor was under something called a 'fee tail' that meant William was forbidden from selling the house. Apparently, the Proctors' wills specified that it must be held by the living male descendant of the Proctor family. 'If only my husband had been a woman, hey,' Selina said.

At first, William avoids my eye. Then, he simply avoids me. Leaving Selina to handle the household staff, the way his mother once had. She hates it here. Unequivocally detests it. The Californian sunshine she once leaked everywhere has disappeared behind a permanent rain cloud and her sense of humour has become more and more acerbic. When they first moved in, a couple of months after the shock of both deaths, she already had a haunted, drawn look. 'It's like a crypt,' I heard her say, as she surveyed it through the eyes of the afflicted, rather than a novelty visitor. I'd spent days scrubbing and polishing,

directing Alan to make the outside as pretty and neat as possible, and felt a shiver of disappointment that it went unnoticed. Or worse, that all my polishing had just made the horror of the house shine that bit brighter.

Although she hates the house, the grounds, the isolation, the village, the mud, the … everything, Selina seems glad to have me to talk to. Our girls are a similar age, and one time I even brought Lizzie over on my day off while Nina was at school. We sat in the garden on an old blanket and ate a picnic I'd prepared the day before and left in the fridge. The girls sat in shy lumps at first, before eventually cautiously bonding over a game of pulling out clumps of grass and sticking their fingers in soil.

'I ran away to London to get the real English experience,' she told me. 'And didn't I just get that in spades.'

William has taken to shutting himself in his office all day, though sometimes when I take him coffee in the afternoon, I can feel him appraise me. I'm embarrassed that I'm still here to be appraised but glad that I don't look too flabby or shabby, then feel guilty for thinking such things.

Selina and Jane spend their days in the living room or the library. I vacuum and polish around them, stopping for a tea while Selina has coffee ('I still don't know how you drink that stuff') and trying to rally her spirits. The more I try, the more irritated she gets and eventually I stop and just let her unload her frustrations.

'I feel homesick for everywhere else I've ever lived,' she says one day, the rain steadily beating on the windows like it wants to be let in. 'I didn't feel homesick for California in London, because I had *London*. Here, I feel homesick for California *and* London.'

'I feel the opposite of homesick,' I tell her. 'Well, I guess I am

sick of my home. I've never lived anywhere else and I'm bored to death.'

'Why don't you leave?'

'People like me don't leave.'

'People like me didn't leave, until I just did,' she says. 'Sometimes, you just gotta.'

'If I lived in Hollywood, I wouldn't leave,' I say, and she laughs.

'I lived in a town called Cedarville in Modoc County,' she says, which means nothing to me. 'It was further to Hollywood from there than London is from here. It's beautiful and it's isolated. A huge forest, a couple of lakes ... everyone hunts and fishes, and not much else. It's so fricking boring.'

'Sounds like here,' I say, and she nods, watching the rain out of the window, one hand on Jane, who has curled up next to her on the sofa.

'Yeah,' she says. 'And like I said, sometimes you just gotta leave.'

27

LIZZIE – 12:20 a.m.

Lizzie wakes up with a jolt.

'Oh.'

She's lying facing the other way on the sofa; she must have spun herself round as she slept.

Sometimes she finds herself in the kitchen at home, sometimes on the bedroom floor. And, of course, those other times when she's woken up in the nick of time, pyjamas around her ankles, perched on a dining chair just about to pee.

They all laughed about it when she was little, although she always burned with mortification, how her parents would wake up in alarm as she wandered around the house.

Occasionally she worries: what if one night she just pops her front door open and keeps walking until she hits the sea? She bought a big bolt for the front door, just in case.

She grapples to sit up and pats the eiderdown for her phone, finally curling her fingers around it. The fire is now a lazy orange glow slunk down low behind the grate, the light and heat barely reaching her.

She taps the screen on her phone. It's past midnight. She slept for over an hour and just feels dizzy rather than refreshed. Outside of her, there is nothing. No more thunder, no more

anything. She feels a curious sense of loss. That swirling storm had been a reassuring soundtrack, in a way. A reminder of things bigger than her and bigger than the immediate problems to be solved. Now, there is just a distant wind, and inside here there is silence. The kind of silence that begs for sound. A pin dropping, that's the cliché. Or a scratch at the door. A knock from an unknown hand. A breath in her ear. *Gosh, stop it.*

She's never known quietness like this, even in her seaside town that all but shuts down for winter. The crackle of the fire rings out as loud as fireworks in this void. She feels absolutely tiny, like she and Nina are something out of a fairy tale, the two sisters fast asleep in this terrifying house in the middle of the woods. She's amazed, really, that she was able to fall asleep given the gothic surroundings. And even more amazed that Nina must have given in too.

Lizzie's throat is dry, rough with dehydration and probably from snoring. She'd bobbed around through feverish, chaotic dreams, maybe she was sleep-talking as well as moving around on the sofa. Her sisters used to complain about that when they shared a room a million moons ago. Telling her she'd mumbled the names of boys from school, or pop stars, delighting in watching her cheeks glow red. When she got really into *The Lion, the Witch and the Wardrobe*, the television version of one of her favourite books, they told her that she'd been mumbling rude things about Aslan the lion.

Her shoes and socks are still by the hearth, the socks looking decidedly crispy in the flickering light. She wills herself to flip back the covers. She should heave herself up to go and put her socks and shoes on, but it's so cold and she's the closest to cosy she'll get before she's finally in her own home.

Lizzie thinks about her little house; she would be there by now if she'd caught the train like she wanted. Why does she

never stand up for herself? She really would have preferred to get the train. A nice cosy window seat, reading her Agatha Christie, buying a warm drink and a Flake from the trolley.

'Neen?' Lizzie rubs her eyes and looks around the room. The receding light of the fire has returned the corners to a chalky darkness. On the other sofa, a mound of blankets hides Nina's sleeping body. At least her poor injured sister is finally getting some rest.

Lizzie reaches for her phone again and puts the flashlight on, sweeps it around the room. She frowns and sweeps it back again, slower this time. Something isn't right. She scans again, trying to work out what's missing.

The shoes.

She points the light back towards the hearth, where it illuminates a single pair of shoes, her own. She flicks it back to the mound of blankets and finally heaves herself up, the chill of the room coiling around her. She shuffles to the other sofa and pushes down softly on the blanket. 'Nina?'

Her hand meets no resistance, sinking onto the sofa cushion beneath the pile of fabric. When she peels back the layers, no one is there.

Maybe Nina's gone to the toilet. Or she's patrolling around again. She'd need her shoes to wander around in this cold, dark place.

Lizzie climbs back under the eiderdown and listens, but the house is silent. Even the thunder seems to have stopped, the pattering of the rain is taking a rest. How long has Aisa been gone? Lizzie does the maths on her fingers, but doesn't know exactly how far past the five-mile sign they drove, so the equation dies in her hands.

Maybe Aisa already came back and she and Nina are both waiting outside for the breakdown people. Better them than

her, it's so cold. And yet, those old green bubbles of sibling envy start to rise in her gut. If they are together, they were probably glad she was asleep. Probably out there taking the mickey out of her. Out of boring old Lizard. *Stop it, that's not what's happened.*

She thinks about calling out, but stops herself. Regardless of where the others are, Lizzie is still sitting in the middle of an abandoned lounge in the heart of a derelict house in the middle of nowhere. Crowing like a big hen and drawing attention to herself is not the smartest move.

For a whole minute, Lizzie just sits still on the old sofa and listens. It's exactly how she handles a new animal in the sanctuary. Sit back, give them space, watch what they do. Listen to their sounds, look into their eyes. Animals will tell you who they are in sixty seconds; people aren't much different. Houses... well, let's see.

She tries to ignore her nagging worries and closes her eyes, shutting out anything but the noises that might tell her whereabouts in the house Nina is moving. She counts in her head, but by fifty-eight, fifty-nine, sixty, there's been no sound. Just a void.

With a deep breath, she swings her legs out from under the covers again and paces quickly to the fireplace. She tugs on her now scratchy socks, stuffs her feet into her still-damp trainers and then dumps a couple of extra logs on the fire. Oops. A great cloud of ash jumps up and scatters the floor. The already limp fire now looks suspiciously flattened.

She looks around, expecting to see Nina rolling her eyes, but Lizzie is still alone. She kneels down and blows a little to get the dying orange glow to spark and catch into flames again. It doesn't play ball.

Using her phone flashlight, she picks carefully through the stack of logs for a few smaller, drier pieces to stuff into the grate, bracing herself for an onslaught of spiders. OK, that's the best

she can do, that should keep things warm while she goes to look for Nina.

Feeling slightly braver after surviving the logs, Lizzie walks to the window and peers outside to look for either of her sisters. But there's nothing but squirming darkness.

There's no way around it, she's going to have to go and look around the house for Nina. Oh blimey, why couldn't she just be on the train home?

28

AISA – 11:44 p.m.

Aisa stares at her phone, now just a useless glossy pebble. She blinks a couple of times as if this will somehow activate night vision, but then she sags in defeat. She can't see shit. It's pitch black, the moon is still being strangled behind layers of clouds, while the village is still twinkling like a mirage, a million miles away.

And what the hell was all that about anyway? There are urban explorer reports about Moirthwaite Manor. Well, so what? It's an abandoned building, it's bound to have been found and photographed.

When Aisa is in Amsterdam, she often hooks up with an urban explorer called Torbjørn. A gentle guy with a very nice beard and the biggest feet she's ever seen. He's from Norway. No, Finland. No, Norway. Somewhere like that. He and his little online group are obsessed with breaking into abandoned places to photograph and film them. When she first met him, he was fresh from climbing out of an old bunker under the Vondelpark, his breath still warm with celebratory beer and strong weed. Anyway, perhaps to someone like the breakdown company woman, those kinds of pictures look spooky. They *are* spooky. Yes, she tries to convince herself, it's just something like that.

'Who are you, Aisa?' he'd asked that first night, over bottles of craft beer (what else?). Not *what do you do*, not *where are you from*, but *who*. She'd faltered. No one had ever asked her that question, and she didn't have an answer. No sarcastic rejoinder ready to shoot from the hip, no borrowed song lyric. She'd kissed him instead of answering, but the question had lain heavily around her neck even when she woke up in his room the next morning.

Torbjørn would have been in that house like a rat up a drainpipe if he was here. Maybe that AA woman was just a bit unadventurous and didn't have any experience of the kind of circles Aisa moves in. *The circles I orbit*. She's not truly part of any circles, not really.

Who are you, Aisa?

She stares at the village ahead, trying again to work out which of those lights might belong to their old house. Maybe their old shared bedroom. If it even faced this way. As her sisters have constantly reminded her tonight, she was only four when she left, she must barely remember it. So why does so much of it feel deadly clear?

Enough of that. The woman said she was sending someone. Didn't she? Aisa runs back over the bizarre conversation again. Yes, she definitely said she was sending someone. Aisa thinks so anyway. Maybe. Did she? Well, Aisa chooses to believe.

OK. She looks at her Apple Watch, itself in desperate need of recharging. It's nearly midnight. *If* she goes back to the house and *if* the mechanic comes and fixes it by 3:30 a.m., and *if* Nina can take her straight to the airport and the roads are clear... she could still make her flight. Just. Aisa could be back in Paris before that absurd cat opens its lazy eyes and all this could be a weird memory.

That's an awful lot of ifs. But it's her best hope. Walking to the village could take another hour or more, and then there's no

guarantee there'll be a taxi nearby. Or that the phone box will still be there and still working, and not turned into a sodding defibrillator. But at least if she walks on to the village, she doesn't have to go back to the manor house. She wouldn't ever have to go back. Why would she choose to head towards a place that had turned her blood cold at its very mention? *Because my sisters are there.*

She stands motionless, legs aching from all the wet, cold miles. *Who are you, Aisa? What matters to you?*

They do have a fire at the manor at least. And she would be doing the right thing, a good thing. She sighs, knowing she has no real choice. She couldn't really leave her sisters like that, not knowing where she'd gone. Whatever they already think of her, however reckless they might think she is, she couldn't do that.

By the time she's finished the thought, she's already turned to face the darkness that she's just spent ages walking through.

Aisa *should* be welcomed as a conquering hero, but no doubt there'll be something for them to gripe about. Something to dispute. How long it took, or the great crime of not having enough battery. *Well, at least I went out and sorted it while you roasted yourselves like a pair of pigs.*

That's the lot of the littlest, always having to prove herself, perennially looked down on. Never mind that Lizzie's never even left the country – probably doesn't even have a passport – she still looks at Aisa like a naif.

Aisa who has travelled to more countries than she's kept count of … And OK, she's not had any long-term relationships, but that's a choice. That's a good choice. And relationships or not, she's had a lot of sex. Way more than them, she's certain. Lizzie is probably still a virgin. But Aisa's still the baby? Fuck off.

Getting all riled up helps to distract her from how cold it is. How cold and how scary. *Jesus, this is so fucking scary, it's*

almost funny. Middle of nowhere, check. Thunder and lightning, check. Abandoned manor house, check. All that's missing is the escaped maniac from a nearby asylum.

Almost funny, but she's not laughing. She pictures herself from above, seen at a remove. A vague notion she's had since she was a child, imagining herself being watched. Performing to that witness. In her teens, she would imagine her friends or the boy she liked watching her. She would cover her body with her hands when she changed, alone. Or, feeling bold, dance around her room to songs the coolest people at school would approve of, weighed down with affectation and awkwardness. When Rosemary died, if Aisa didn't stop herself in time, her mother would be the imagined witness. Aisa's face wet with tears that she'd try to hide from her. Now, she wants to shrink from view again, imagining that somewhere in this great openness there's a malevolent presence watching her. A dark, unblinking thing. What does it see? *Who are you, Aisa?*

'Oh my God!'

Aisa recoils from something's touch, gasping for air, but when she taps her Apple Watch for its pathetic glimmer of light, she sees it was just a huddle of brambles. She'd veered too close to the hedge.

This is going to take so long. It was bad enough walking along here in a small pool of phone light, but now she's trudging back blind, legs so heavy she can't imagine running away even if danger did strike.

She puts her head down, forces her legs to move faster, and hurries back. She will never tell anyone about this thought, but right now, she just wants her sisters.

29

LIZZIE – 12:38 a.m.

The air in front of the fire is warm, but the rest of the room is so cold that Lizzie wraps herself tightly in her coat and layers one of the old blankets on top, swaddling herself so just her head is poking out, childlike. She looks like she's playing Mary in a school nativity play. Although Lizzie only ever played one of the animals in the manger.

As she scouts around for anything else to ward off the cold, she notices that Nina's coat is no longer drying on the back of a chair. She grips her phone and, using its flashlight, steps out into the empty hall.

'Neen?' she whispers uselessly, too scared to raise her voice.

She creeps through the rest of the downstairs, looking for any sign of her older sister. It's so dark outside of the phone light that she could miss her while being in the same room. But it's not like Nina might be hiding behind a door. Why would she be? And, of course, she isn't.

But Lizzie is thorough, at first for her own peace of mind and then out of astonishment. Surely Nina hasn't just picked up and gone? There is no sign of her in the bathroom, although the tap is now dripping a military drum tattoo that seems to urge Lizzie along. The back bedrooms offer nothing. She won't

be in the spider cupboard. Nina probably thinks no one knows about her claustrophobia, but you don't get to keep secrets like that for long in a five-person family in a two-bedroom house. Still, to be thorough, Lizzie pulls the cupboard door open just briefly, peers in and then clicks it shut.

She even goes back into the eerily empty master bedroom, heart thumping as if she'll get in trouble. It's still empty, and even weirder on second viewing. The way it has been picked clean, like one of those little skulls.

If Nina was here, she'd certainly have heard Lizzie clattering around on her search and come to her. Perhaps Lizzie was snoring and Nina had sought peace and quiet somewhere else. Maybe even taken some strong painkillers from her bag – it has been known – and crashed out on Jane's bed. Lizzie lets this hope swell for a moment, but when she twists the handle and pushes open the door to Jane's room, there is no one there.

Of course there isn't.

Nina must have gone out looking for Aisa, it's the only explanation. Not trusting her little sister, worrying about her. Forgetting, as Nina always has, that she has another little sister who might like to feature in her concerns once or twice.

Lizzie paces to Jane's window, kneels up on the window seat as Jane herself used to, cups her hands like a visor and looks out. There is a creaminess to the sky now, a suggestion of moonlight that helps her make out the tall trees and the once-gravelled circle at the top of the driveway. She sees no human movement and no glow of phone flashlights. She looks in vain at her own phone, but, of course, there's still no reception. She can't just call her sisters and ask where they are. She can't call anyone.

She climbs off the window seat and heads back downstairs, legs feeling heavy with the weight of what they're going to be asked to do. She has made the decision before she can talk

herself out of it, now she just needs to keep going. She doesn't want to stay here alone and she needs to check Nina hasn't fallen over somewhere out there, overestimated how much her ankle could take, perhaps. But if Aisa comes back and finds them both gone... Lizzie thinks for a moment.

Back in the lounge, she tears a piece of paper from the notepad she keeps in her bag and digs out a biro, dusted with unidentifiable crumbs.

Stay here, I'm coming back. Lizzie x

She sheds the blanket she's been wearing, it's not right to take someone's belongings, and forces herself out of the door.

It's so much colder outside than Lizzie realised. While she slept in front of the fire, a steely bitterness replaced the wildness of the storm out here. Now, the chill whips her face as she steps further outside and pulls the door closed behind her.

The flashlight on her phone seems absurdly dim. The moon has come out a little more, but its light is strangled by trees before it can reach the ground. She stumbles a few times as she makes her way back down the driveway while half-memories flit through her mind. Car journeys from the village, her mum working, Jane and Lizzie running around here, welly boots, tired legs, hedgehogs, puddles.

She reaches the bottom of the driveway and is surprised by the wave of relief she feels to be out of that place and on public ground. It's a little less dark away from those trees, the sky over her a little lighter. Out here offers the hope of other people, of rescue, and of finding Aisa and Nina. Stepping onto the lane, she looks to the right in the direction of the car, and then to the left, towards the village.

The village is still miles away. *What to do? Which way to go? Come on, Lizard, think.*

The car is only a few minutes' walk up the other way, and the breakdown people might have told Aisa to meet them there. Perhaps Aisa came and got Nina to wait there with her and the car keys while Lizzie slept. Perhaps they're both curled up in the car? She feels tears prickle at the thought of it. Her sisters snuggled up together like puppies in a basket while she flails around uselessly out here. *Calm down, breathe.*

It makes sense to check the car first, she tells herself, and feels relieved not to have to trek all the way to the village just yet.

Lazy girl.

It's not laziness, she says to herself, to her mum, to her sisters, it's conserving energy.

She heads up the slight slope and down into the dip, the phone only illuminating her own hands and the empty air she's walking through. After a few careful minutes, she sees the Mini. It's sitting forlorn in a puddle, but it doesn't seem to have drifted further into the road, so at least any other vehicles won't smash into it. Not that there's likely to be any.

She shines her pale light over its front, the little bug eyes and the grille like a mouth, locked in a grimace. 'Oops,' it seems to say. She always loved her family's old Mini, felt terribly guilty when they replaced it with a bigger Ford in Cheshire. She wonders if that's why Nina chose this one, even though she pretends not to be sentimental. *Don't worry,* Lizzie thinks, as she places a hand on its bonnet, *help will be here soon.*

But help isn't here yet and neither are Nina and Aisa, so she'll have to do the long walk after all. Unless she goes back to the house.

Her legs pump a little harder; she sucks in a gulp of cold air

as she walks straight past the turning for Moirthwaite Manor. She really doesn't want to go back to the house by herself.

Her shoes are still damp and she can feel blisters swelling on her heels and little toes. Her body is rebelling against her decision to leave, trying to get her to down tools as it so often does. It's not like she doesn't walk anywhere normally, she walks every day. And in these very shoes! Miles and miles, in all weather. Sometimes she takes the better-behaved dogs from the village she lives and works in all the way down to the roaring sea, along the flinty beaches, by the smugglers' coves whose romance she moved for in the first place.

'God, it's grim,' Aisa said, the one time she and Nina came to visit. But it's not grim, it's breathtaking. Just because there are no nightclubs like the European beaches Aisa heads to doesn't make it grim. Although Aisa would probably laugh at that, nightclubs are probably passé now. It's probably all pop-up sex jamborees now or something.

As she walks, Lizzie keeps checking her phone for reception, but it's as dead as a dodo. This old phone struggles to find reception at the best of times, so it's unlikely to burst into full 3G out here, but still. But still.

It's 1:22 a.m. now. She feels like she's been walking for hours, but it's only been minutes. The rain is still drizzling and the lights of the village are as far away as they ever were. She stops for a moment and thinks. *Is this really the right thing to do?*

As she stands motionless, the air grows quiet without the sound of her footsteps, but then other steps fill the silence for just a moment. Then they stop too.

Other footsteps. Oh gosh, *other footsteps*. She's suddenly blind with panic, brought back to the moment with a jolt. She is trapped in the terrible now with no idea what to do. *God, Lizzie, think.*

The footsteps have stopped now and Lizzie looks around, but she still can't see anyone. Despite its weakness, her phone flashlight just seems very good at making everything outside of it look blacker. She slowly flips her phone round and presses it to her body, muffling the light. Her eyes adjust to the thin moonlight, but she still sees nothing, just empty fields, violent brambles and a drenched, potholed lane.

She closes her eyes for a full minute, heart thumping like a mad monkey the whole time, and listens, sniffing the air. She cannot hear anything now and she can't smell anyone. No wellington boot smell, no wax jacket or leather. No other sweat. Just her own.

She takes a cautious step, and then another. Nothing happens. She must have imagined it, she tells herself, as she walks on with trembling legs.

30

ROSEMARY – 1987

They've been arguing again. Selina is snappy and I can smell that William is smoking in his office, something that only happens when he's really unhappy. More than unhappy, actually, terse. Borderline cruel.

'We used to be a team,' I hear Selina cry.

I'm in the kitchen and she's in the hallway outside the office door. Jane is having her nap. I stay deathly still, I don't want her to know I'm here and I feel embarrassed.

'Bill,' she says, a name I've only ever heard her call him. He's not a Bill. 'Bill, please, we can't just not talk about this.'

The door flies open suddenly and she stumbles into the room.

'All you ever do is talk about this,' he growls. 'Can't you understand, I have no bloody choice.'

'There's always a choice,' she says. 'And you're choosing this fucking house over your wife.'

For a moment, neither says anything. In the kitchen, I stand in the middle of the larder, hoping the cook will come bustling back in from the garden and break the spell. Instead, Jane begins to cry from upstairs. 'Mama, mama.' She never cries for her dad, I notice, and for all Bob's faults, the girls love him and he loves

them. They cry for me first, but they'll switch to calling Dad if I take my time. That's how it should be.

'Jane wants you,' William says softly, conciliatorily.

'At least someone does,' Selina says as she heads for the stairs.

When I go up later to put the fresh sheets on their bed, I see her suitcase lying open on the floor. I leave the bed as it is and creep back out.

Sometimes, you just gotta leave.

31

AISA – 1:18 a.m.

As she walks, a song keeps running through her head, a remixed, chopped-up version of 'Alone at a Drive-In' from *Grease*. She never liked it, always preferred the others. 'Summer Nights', 'You're the One That I Want'. Silly songs that sounded like nonsense when she was little until she realised – in her teens – that they were all about shagging.

'Alone at a Drive-In' was moany drivel, as was 'Hopelessly Devoted to You'. But the latter was the one that made her mother cry. Said it reminded her of Dad. The former was the one that always got Rosemary riled up, as if it was the first time she'd seen it. 'Danny bleating on about being abandoned when he was the one acting like a knob.'

Am I the one acting like a knob? she thinks, wondering if her sisters were glad to be shot of her. Has she left them back at the house through devotion, or does she abandon people? She abandoned Dad after Mum died. She knows she did. Knows it from the watery look he gives her when she can bear to see him.

The wind is shunting her and the rain starts to spit again. An aftershock of the storm, a final insult. Her bones ache from these miles. *I could have been walking around Paris.* Through the Jardin du Luxembourg where she always feels like an interesting

134

person. Or the Marais, past the Church of Saint-Paul Saint-Louis. Or over the Pont au Change. At that spot, she always thinks of her mother. Of how she would have loved to see the settings of *Les Misérables* in real life, and how such a concept would have seemed absurd to Rosemary. Out of bounds. But it turns out, Aisa knows now, that you *can* just choose to do things. To go places. If only she'd told her mum before it was too late.

The week before last, Aisa was in Amsterdam. And before that, New York. Well, New York *adjacent*, but she'd gone into the city every day. The whole damn place like a monument to her mother's favourite musicals. *Hello, Dolly! Rent, Hair, West Side Story.* She'd practically finger-clicked and jazz-stepped through the Upper West Side battleground of the Sharks and Jets, even after her long journey from the apartment in Westchester County.

If you could see me now, Mum, she'd thought, and then, *Scratch that. If you could see* this *now, Mum. You should have seen this.*

If she gets back to the house fast enough, she could still be back in Paris this time tomorrow, overfeeding Poisson and taking ironic pictures of the Eiffel Tower for Instagram. Caption: Where?

And then on to Marrakesh, where she'll be able to squeeze in a round trip by train to Casablanca, so long as the house rabbit doesn't throw a fit. *Casablanca* is not a musical, of course, but still a Sunday afternoon favourite. Rosemary mouthing along with every line, while Aisa sat on the arm of the sofa playing on her Game Boy, one foot dangling over her mum, who would stroke it absentmindedly.

And after that, she's heading to London. *Mary Poppins. Oliver!* She might even go to see *Wicked* again, which she and her mum watched for Rosemary's sixtieth birthday.

But she's not there yet. Nowhere near Paris or Casablanca or London. She's here, in the rain, in the one place she never wanted to return. Not that she'd thought of this place for a long

time. She barely remembered it until tonight. But she doesn't like what she does remember. She wishes she could shove her AirPods back in and listen to music, block all these bad things out. She'd pretend to be listening to something new and interesting, but, as usual, she'd actually be playing the musicals playlist she made for her mum, when she was dying.

'How will they stay in my lugholes?' her mum had laughed weakly, as Aisa held out her own AirPods in her palm, just as she used to hand over crap bits of art brought home from school.

'They just will, Mum,' she'd said, trying to keep the tears out of her voice. Tears that threatened to burst and wash every word away. Tears that made Aisa come to see Rosemary alone, unable to bear the reflected sadness in her sisters' eyes, or their dad's moronic attempts to look on the bright side. There is no bright side of terminal cancer, you fool.

Her mum had smiled so broadly as she'd listened to the tracks that Aisa had spent hours selecting, and Aisa had simply sat watching her, stroking her arm, until she fell asleep. There is no one else on earth she would hand her phone over to like that, just happy to make them happy. Correction, there *was* no one else on earth.

That's enough of that. She chases the sadness with a quick, barking cough and pays attention to her present instead, just like her mindfulness app always tells her while she argues with it.

Aisa's walked the same route back towards the manor. A reluctant boomerang. The journey seems quicker on the return leg, as if she's being winched along by invisible thread. A little moonlight has been swirled into the sky and she can see the surroundings for what they are. Bleak and empty, but benign. No foxes. No people. Nobody is watching her. She's safe. And she's nearly back with her family, some of them anyway.

But then, the big footsteps in the mud near the car. Did she

imagine them? Were they just from the sisters' own feet sliding around?

She hurries on, not wanting to be in that house, but secretly wanting to be with her sisters, pretending not to care but desperately wanting the safety of numbers.

Her feet slap the wet tarmac and the steps ring out across the empty fields and up and down the lane. It sounds for a moment as if they're echoing. She stops to check her theory, but the echo has stopped too. After a minute or two, she carries on.

Finally, she reaches the sign – MOIR AI – which swings gently, the metal hooks whistling with the motion. The driveway looks darker than the lane, the tall trees bending over it like a canopy, closing off the moonlight. Sanctuary with her sisters, but at what cost? She doesn't want to be in that house any longer than she has to be.

She walks slowly, treading carefully and quietly up the driveway. When she reaches the house, Aisa stands for a moment looking up at its monstrous facade. When she arrived here earlier with her sisters, her adrenaline was clogging up her vision. But now she is too exhausted for flight or fight, too exhausted for anything. She stares at each of the front-facing windows in turn, a memory popping up for each, like opening an advent calendar. She even dares to look up at the window that somehow she knows was Jane's dad's room even though she doesn't remember ever actually meeting him, just seeing his legs and feet from some hiding place or other.

Who was that other man they used to see here? The one who shot all the rabbits? Some kind of gardener or something? He gave Aisa a rabbit's foot once. The weirdo. Shyly handing it over when he found her once, hiding and scared. Or was it… she found him? She frowns, but the memory is gone.

She steps closer to the front door, takes a final lungful of outside air and then reaches for the handle.

32

LIZZIE – 1:30 a.m.

To her right, big empty fields roll away from her, occasionally filled with enormous bales of hay, wrapped tightly in a shiny black coating just catching the moonlight, looking like alien eggs that have dropped from the sky.

To her left, the woodland is dense and layered. Leaves, branches and trunks create a monochrome collage that looks too thick to move through, but she knows – the memory seizes her chest for a moment – she knows that you can weave through all of that, running as hard as your lungs will allow.

An animal.

Something about an animal.

A hurt animal.

She and Jane running after it. Lizzie wanting to help, to look after it. Jane saying she wanted that too, but...

Lizzie shivers in her coat and plunges on. She didn't dress for this, she dressed for a birthday lunch. A pretty jumper and smart jeans, neither of which have enough give for all this walking. It's easily been a mile now, probably more. She looks at her phone to see the time and notices the bar of reception. How long has it been there? A tiny bar of hope. She stops dead, scared that she might chase this away if she takes another step.

For a moment, she just stands still at the side of the road, surrounded by woodland and empty fields that might swallow the reception up again. Using the flashlight function has zapped some of her battery too. Unlike Aisa, who is always on social media, or Nina who is always on WhatsApp groups sharing jokes and memes with work friends, Lizzie hardly uses her phone. A few texts from friends at work, the odd emergency call when an animal she particularly connected to finds itself back at the shelter. Occasional exchanges in the sisters' WhatsApp group, Made in Kelsey, a name picked by Aisa that makes no sense to Lizzie.

The one person she would love to send a message to, would love to receive a message from, only has a landline.

What should she do? Maybe she should call a breakdown service, but Aisa should have already done that. Aisa might be calling right now from the village, her own phone not finding this tiny hotspot, and if Lizzie calls too, won't that just confuse everything? She doesn't know the number either, and has no 3G to look it up. But mostly, the thought of calling up a busy call centre – as a non-driver with no money – and answering questions about cars and how she'll pay for the call-out simply overwhelms her.

First, she tries to call Nina. If she's out here too, she might also have reception. It doesn't even ring, just goes straight to voicemail. She knows this voicemail well, or used to, but it's changed. She's sure it used to list alternative numbers for reaching the hospital, the maternity unit, the health visitors. It still has Nina's same brisk, bossy tone, but now it says that she's on temporary leave and is not allowed to speak with patients, to call the main maternity unit instead. Temporary leave? Does that mean she's booked holiday time? Nina told them she couldn't

stay over at Dad's because she had a shift the next day, but it sounds like she was fibbing.

Lizzie doesn't have time to ponder this now, but sticks a mental pin in it until later. She tries Aisa next, and the voicemail instantly clicks in. A recorded voice – Aisa is too cool to lower herself to record her own message – offering no alternatives.

For a moment, Lizzie wants to let out the tears that are swelling in the corners of her eyes. A desperate pang of helplessness, of worrying she'll do the wrong thing and everyone will be cross with her. Worrying, as she so often does, that she's already done the wrong thing, without even realising it. Of wishing her mum was here to take over, to make things right. The way she always did.

There is one other person to try.

'I'm not a damsel in distress,' she told Rafferty, the first time they met. He'd come to volunteer at the shelter and had rushed over to help her with some big bags of dry food.

'I can tell that.' He'd appraised her from under his long dark curls. There was a glimmer of… she almost couldn't bear to believe it, but he'd seemed rather *impressed*. So much so that she'd decided to cultivate this stance of independence, to wear it a little higher like a brooch. When she allowed him to hold the door to the dogs' units open, he'd rewarded the perceived concession with a gallant nod.

And when she passed him, brushing his shoulders with hers and noticing that he wasn't wearing a coat as she'd first thought, but a cape like Sherlock Holmes might wear, her stomach pulsed. A feeling she'd only ever had vicariously, through romantic storylines in books. *Oh dear,* she'd thought, *I'm in trouble here.*

They were supposed to get together last night, but the stubby little dog had put paid to that. Rafferty was expecting to have seen her tonight instead, but he will have understood, guessed,

she'd been delayed. She calls his number, heart beating faster as it begins to ring.

She'd taken Rafferty back to her house after work on the same day they met, four months ago. She'd never felt so safe with another person, so why not? She'd opened up the front door and saw her house as he was first seeing it. The rows and rows of bookshelves, almost every wall covered. The cosy furniture, piles of throws and cushions. Mismatched but loved. The tea things laid out on the little dining table because it always felt to her like a treat, walking in and seeing it taken care of, the leaves already in the pot ready for hot water.

'I'll get another cup,' she'd said.

Four rings, five. It's well past midnight, he will be asleep. But she hopes…

'I love your house,' he'd said, as they lay in her bed afterwards, him naked and her in her nightie. 'It's perfectly you.'

'You don't even know me,' she'd said.

He'd reached for her hand and kissed it. 'Yes I do, Elizabeth.'

And he does. He understands her every bump and scrape, the life she's carefully created. Two odd socks becoming a pair. Her sisters would certainly call him odd, if they were to meet him. And even though he'd like to meet them, he never pushes. Never pressures her for more time than she can give. She needs some nights alone, spent reading. And nights with him laughing and kissing, those too. It just works. She's so dangerously, intoxicatingly content that she dare not admit it, lest she lose it.

The phone rings out and stops. And for the first time since they met, she feels a grumble of frustration. She'd found it charming when he first explained his stance. He likes writing and receiving letters. He likes handshake agreements. He does not like to feel connected every day, every moment, but sees

things like telephones as tools that have become overlords to people. 'So you're off the grid?' she'd asked, smiling.

'No,' he said. 'I begrudgingly have a landline. A lovely old Bakelite that I found in that charity shop and tea rooms near the park, do you know the one?' Of course she knew the one. How she'd not seen him in there was the real mystery. 'So I can't use a mobile phone to shift arrangements all the time and feel like I've fulfilled my friendly obligations with a "like" or something ... If I say I'll be somewhere, I have to be there.'

She thinks back to when she called yesterday to move their date to tonight, they'd arranged for him to go to her house. He has a key and maybe ... Yes, there's still reception. She calls her own number. It rings, three, four, five times. And then her own voice picks up.

'This is Lizzie, please leave a message and I'll call you back.' Beep.

'Rafferty?' She waits, hoping she might have woken him, that he will snatch up the receiver. But no. 'Rafferty, it's me. I hope you hear this. My sisters and I ran out of petrol and we're stuck in Cumbria at a place called Moirthwaite Manor. I know it's a lot to ask, but if there's any way you could come here and—' Something doesn't feel right, she pulls her phone from her ear and looks at it. The call has dropped. The reception has disappeared.

She has no idea if any of her message was recorded.

33

ROSEMARY – March 1992

I twist the heavy shafts of the candlesticks so they line up perfectly. I could probably chuck them on the floor or throw one through the window for all the notice that'd be shown. But I can't help myself. A job done well, that's pretty much the only thing I have in my control.

I see it in Nina too. It can seem like fussiness, or maybe bossiness, the way she'll take over a job I've given one of her sisters. Straightening their beds or washing out the milk bottles. She'll wind people up with it, I can't imagine a future husband enjoying her briskly taking over whatever he's doing, but it'll see her true.

Capability, more than anything else, is the key to... not success, God, I'm not that deluded, but... survival. Drop me in any town anywhere and I'm sure I'd find a bit of work, a place to wash my clothes, a butcher that'll do me a cheap offcut. Nina is the same, even at ten. Whereas Lizzie... it doesn't bear thinking about. Drop her in any random town and she'd land on her bum and stay there, stuck like a beetle on its back. Aisa is too little to be tested, but already I can imagine her doing fine. Maybe with her it's less capability and more... ballsyness?

It's bloody boring being capable. No one would choose it as

their top attribute in a lover or, I don't know, a Hollywood star! But it keeps the kids clean and fed and has kept me in work all these years.

William relies on my capability, I know that, but it's an unseen foundation in his life. *I* am an unseen foundation in his life. He will never open a cupboard and not find what he needs. Or ask where his good suit is – not that he's asked that in a long time – and not be told where to find it, slippery in its cover from the dry-cleaner's in Penrith. My capability allows him to drift through life, and in return, I take home £90 a week.

Occasionally, he'll notice extra evidence of effort, or he'll lean on me more than is strictly acceptable and then slip an extra tenner or two into my envelope on the Friday. I've put more sweat into polishing that monstrous mirror on the landing today and put in some additional hours with poor Jane, so I hope that he'll top me up this week. Then I can get the phone switched back on.

I sit for a moment on the sofa, its cushions freshly scrubbed but smelling a little of mildew. I run my hand over the fabric. Checking for lint, smoothing out creases. It's second nature now, so I even do it at home, even though our sofa is 90 per cent lint and 10 per cent crease.

I close my eyes as the blood pools in my legs and the throb in my feet feels almost audible. I've not stopped since I got here and I just need a moment. As pins and needles start to climb up my calves, I stroke the mahogany wood, upholstered horsehair seats and velvet cushions. This sofa was once incredibly fancy. Now it's a museum piece.

William has finally agreed to buy leather sofas. Chesterfields, something befitting a room of this scale. Something easier to keep clean. I wasn't sure he'd heard me, but then the other day he said they were on order. I'm not sure why I care really, it's

not my house. But then, spending two decades doing basically the same thing is tragic if you don't even care. I choose to care.

I have the house to myself now. William is out on patrol pretending that he isn't. We're all on invisible tracks, aren't we, repeating the same endless patterns, giving them meaning to justify the waste of time. Alan is doing God knows what in his shed, and Cook has gone into town, mumbling something about catching the butcher. I'm pretty certain she's catching the four o'clock at Newmarket, probably losing the beef money so William will have to have ham hock instead. Unless Alan's caught something edible in the woods.

When I sit up again, an hour has passed. I must have slid into sleep and the afternoon has dissolved behind my back. The girls have long finished school and will be home with Bob by now. Or, more likely, the younger two will be home in the charge of Nina while Bob sinks one (one standing in for any number under the sun) at The Fox and Hounds. 'Networking,' he calls it now, amused with himself as he sways a little in his old work boots. He heard that word on the radio.

I'm lucky to have girls, everyone says, as that way I have ready-made babysitters. I smile and nod, but feel a little sick at this. Not a chance in hell that I'm going to see my girls skivvying the way I do. I'm not exactly sure how, but if I achieve nothing else, I'll make sure they can choose the course of their own lives and not have it handed to them by circumstance. So far, it's not exactly going to plan and Nina seems determined to take on a quasi-parental role despite my best efforts. Trying to cook the dinner or bathe Aisa. Every day, I walk back into the opening credits of *999*. I keep expecting Michael Buerk to pop out with a withering remark.

I do a final scan of the house, straightening things, breathing onto brass and silver, wiping away flecks of human evidence with

my sleeve. The dining table has been set up, but William will eat much later when the cook is back, too distracted to notice he's not getting what he's paying for. A cold supper has been set out for Jane in the kitchen: cheese and bread, the last of this year's tomatoes and a boiled egg. This is my favourite part of the day. Seeing it all set right, all correct. Like a theatrical stage before the audience arrives.

William should be back by now though. When I go, Jane's all alone. Aside from Alan, who doesn't count. My own children are probably alone too, but three is a different kind of alone to one. A bubble of guilt slides up my throat, but I swallow it back down.

There is another set of candlesticks here – there are sixteen in all, dotted around various mantlepieces and in cupboards. Almost all of them never used. They've been here longer than me, probably worth more than me too, if you added it up. I wonder, as I walk a little closer to the cupboard where the silverware is kept, how much a pair might fetch. I wonder too, if anyone other than me has looked in this cupboard since William's parents died and the estate was priced up by solicitors before being handed over.

I have a carrier bag of Jane's old clothes hanging on my arm, my jacket draped over my shoulders even though it's still warm, and am heading to my car. Now that work is shut away behind that front door, my mind turns – as it often does – to concern for Lizzie. I worry about her meekness. The others have picked on her so much that she keeps it quiet, but I'm sure she's still got that imaginary friend who has bobbed in and out of her life for as long as I can remember.

The gulf between her and Nina is growing ever more

pronounced, despite only a two-year gap. Nina is like a little adult, Lizzie a big bairn. Far more so than little Aisa.

I look up and catch Jane's curtain falling back into place. Another lonely girl I'm failing. If only William would let her go to school rather than teaching her himself. I think he's too terrified that Selina will come back and take her if Jane's ever out of the house without him.

'What you got there?'

I swear Alan is on wheels, I didn't hear his big feet approach. I turn to face him, craning my neck to look him dead in the eye. He's hovering next to the burbling fountain, looking as if he regrets speaking. Poor Alan, never has a big man been less at ease with himself. 'Nosy parker,' I say, but I smile to reassure him. 'It's just some of Jane's old clothes for Save the Children,' I say, lowering my hands gently and making a mental note not to dress Aisa in any of these cast-offs if I ever bring her here.

'And how are your children?' Alan asks, in his soft, stilted voice.

'Waiting for me,' I say, still smiling, but he looks hurt. 'Oh I'm only clarten, Al, they're doing well,' I add. 'Thanks for asking.'

I load the bag into the boot of the Mini, closing it carefully because the handle has a tendency to fall off.

'What time have you got?' I call to Alan, as he heads for the side of the house towards his shed. My dad's wristwatch is for comfort only now, the hands no longer move.

'Five after five,' Alan calls back.

I look up again at Jane's window. I should have left five minutes ago, but she's alone, and she's only a kid. Maybe I should go back inside, read to her while we wait for William. Maybe I should take that time, it's not much to give her. Not after everything she's been through.

The distant rumble of an engine grows closer and I sigh in relief.

'Sorry,' William says as he climbs out of the big old Mercedes, speaking to the top of my head rather than my face. 'Time got, you know…'

'Away from you,' I add. 'I know.'

'I'll put a little extra in your pay this week,' he says, finally meeting my gaze until I look away.

34

AISA – 1:38 a.m.

The doorknob is still slick with rain when she turns it, half-expecting it to be locked, her sisters shutting her out for taking too long. But it opens silently again, no creaking wood, no squeaking hinges. Last time she came in here, she was mob-handed and they all had lights on their phones, but now she is stepping into total darkness. Alone.

The moonlight of the pale grey sky doesn't cross the threshold and it takes a moment for her eyes to adjust as she steps inside and listens. She can hear the gentle crackle of the fire from the front room but no voices. They're probably asleep.

Even standing in the hall in this swirling darkness makes her lungs feel tight and her heart race. A draught bites her ankles, as if the cold night is trying to swallow her whole. But what alternative is there? If she wanted to wait in the car, she'd have to get the keys from Nina anyway, waking her up in the process.

There's a smell in here that she didn't notice when they first arrived. An iron smell: soil, rusty nails or ... blood? *Stop being dramatic.* But Aisa stays rooted to the spot anyway. The whole house feels like a trap. She tries to tell herself that she's just rattled from the weird reaction of the woman on the phone who was spooked by the very concept of urban explorers, but it's not

really that. She felt like this before too. Like she was returning to somewhere she'd successfully escaped.

'Will you walk into my parlour?' said the spider to the fly.

Aisa swallows. It's not like her to dither. Normally, she's made a decision before she even knows there's one to make. Buying a plane ticket. Applying for a ludicrous house-sitting gig on the other side of the world. Saying yes to a date, walking out on a date. Whatever.

In that front room are the two people she should feel closest to in the world. Shared DNA, shared history. But they have never felt like that. It was always Nina and Lizzie – the older, sensible ones – and Aisa, the agent of chaos. The only person who she ever truly felt close to was her mum. A shared look, a quick touch of the hand. They just understood each other. Every adventure, every risk she takes now, she's taking for two. Living the life her mum couldn't. But her sisters would never understand that.

Even now, she's preparing for the criticism from Nina. Never mind that she's called for help, she won't have called for it quick enough. Or she'll have called the wrong person. It should have been Green Flag or whoever. Or she'll be too wet from the rain. Or too ... just too something. Always too something.

She reaches, as she often does, into her bag. Touches the passport holder containing her mum's envelope. *Breathe, stay calm.*

She steps further into the dark and then gently pushes the door of the living room open. It's still pretty dark inside, but the fire is just about hanging on and a yellow glow pulses around it. She steps inside properly and walks towards the sofas, where her sisters lie completely hidden by blankets. For a moment, her stomach flips as she realises just how vulnerable they are,

sleeping like this. It was Aisa stepping through that unlocked door just now, but it could have been anyone.

Aisa walks to the fire, tucks her bag safely to the side and then kneels to assess it, on trembling, aching knees. She's rubbish at stuff like this, never one for camping, but even she can tell this fire needs a bit more wood. She teases a few thin logs from the pile and places them carefully onto the glowing embers. She leans back on her haunches and watches. They're not catching. She blows a little, but nothing much happens, just a scattering of twinkling sparks landing on the hearth.

'Neen,' she says, too tired for ego. 'This fire is shit. What shall I do?' She hates the whine in her voice, but Nina hasn't answered anyway. 'I'm back by the way,' she says, louder now. 'Thanks for the red carpet.' Neither pile of blankets stirs.

She blows haphazardly on the fire again and then sighs and gives up, walking over to one of the sofas, which has a big fat eiderdown on it. She pats it, but the mound of fabric just sinks, a puff of dust rising up.

'What the f—?' She pulls it back, but there's no one there, just the sunken old cushions of the Chesterfield.

She rushes over to the other sofa, but she already knows, even before she peels back the blankets, that there's no one there.

'Where are you two?'

She looks at the fireplace again, realises what's missing: their shoes and socks. The coats are no longer drying on the back of the old chairs either. She stands in front of the fire feeling furious. What the hell are they playing at? Did they go after her? But she'd have passed them, surely?

Aisa looks around for any other trace of them, but there's nothing here except old blankets and a dying fire. Weren't there two candlesticks on the mantelpiece before too? She's sure she lit two when they first arrived. There's only one now. Why have

they taken a candlestick with them? Perhaps their phones ran out too so they lit a candle for light. And then what? Went exploring like Wee Willie Winkie?

She goes back out into the hall and calls their names. No reply comes, the strange iron smell fills her head.

Maybe they've gone to sleep upstairs, in more comfortable beds. Maybe there's a fireplace up there too. Maybe … Well, she needs light to go upstairs and look for them, so she goes back into the living room and picks up the other candlestick with its stub of old wax. As she does, a piece of lined paper flutters to the floor, luminous in the firelight.

A note. Lizzie's looping handwriting, not a million miles from the writing on her envelope, but less shaky.

Stay here, I'm coming back. Lizzie x

35

LIZZIE – 1:47 a.m.

Lizzie waves her phone around and tries to find reception again. She walks a little further towards the village, hunting for a pool of connection, but the phone remains steadfastly useless. Oh well, Aisa will have already called someone, there's no real need for Rafferty to trek all the way here in the middle of the night. However much she might have liked him to, however much she might be ready to be a damsel for him.

Lizzie looks up at the mottled sky. After the flamboyance of the storm earlier, it seems to sag with fatigue. A few dogged stars manage to shine through and she's glad of that. It's meaningless, but she can't stop attributing meaning to things since Mum died. Like one of those stars is Mum herself, watching over Lizzie, even though that star has been up there for so many hundreds of years that it's actually already dead. But still, she can't help herself. She doesn't tell her sisters this. She's already a laughing stock to them.

What would Mum have said, if Lizzie had been able to call her tonight? She'd have kept Lizzie on the landline, while calling the breakdown service on the mobile and somehow making up the spare beds at the same time. 'We'll get you back here and then see what's what,' she'd have said. She was so flipping

capable, all of the time. Nina has decided to pick up that baton, whether anyone else wanted to make a play for it or not.

Lizzie walks slowly back towards the house, phone held in front of her for light. There is no sign of any more reception, that brief patch seems to have been an anomaly. She shouldn't stay out too long in case the others are back at the house. She wonders if Nina and Aisa are nearby, or perhaps there's another route back. Maybe they've been emboldened by each other's company to go through the woods. Or perhaps Nina didn't even come to look for Aisa and went off to do something else. Or perhaps... She stops herself. Not that. Nothing could have happened to Nina. Could it?

No, this is just the usual run of play and Lizzie is always the last to know. From the epic to the inconsequential. Because, *of course,* Nina just went off tonight without bothering to wake Lizzie up to tell her. Nina has form for this. She'd not even told Lizzie about Mum's illness for almost a week after the diagnosis. She didn't tell Aisa either. Nina and Dad kept it to themselves, hoarding all that extra time with her. Minutes mattered then, let alone days.

Now isn't the time.

It's never the time, that's the problem. By the time Lizzie has built up the nerve to say something, everyone else has moved on. Like when they got back from Moirthwaite Primary School one day, to that little terraced house down there in the village behind her, to find a borrowed van packed with their stuff, their dad at the wheel. Their mum sat in the Mini behind it, popping the door for them to climb in. Aisa and Nina griped the whole way down the M6, rejecting every point being made – 'We'll find somewhere that you can all have your own rooms and the school has more children to be friends with' – while Lizzie barely said anything. A week later, still struggling to make friends in

this new town in Cheshire, at the school with a strict uniform and even stricter teachers, Lizzie finally asked why she didn't get to say goodbye to anyone. Especially to Jane. Her mum had opened her mouth, frowned and said, 'I can't deal with this now, Lizzie.' And that was that. For thirty years.

36

AISA – 1:47 a.m.

Aisa stands in front of the fireplace, Lizzie's note in her hands. Her knees are still trembling, her jeans stuck to her skin with rain and sweat. She thrusts her legs closer to what's left of the fire, chasing the warmth.

Stay here, the note says. But why? And where has Lizzie gone? Where's Nina for that matter?

God, her feet ache. She puts the note back down on the mantelpiece, then leans down and starts to prise off her damp shoes.

She keeps her socks on and kneels down in front of the fire. It's not going to last much longer, but help should be here soon anyway. She puts on a couple more logs, but they just seem to flatten it further. She looks around and finds a mirror wrapped in a few sheets of old crinkled newspaper. She pulls it off the dusty mirror, scrunches it into a few balls and pokes them into the gaps between the logs, blowing until it catches. She spots another newspaper in the corner, but she'll save that for later.

Then she sits down heavily on the sofa, Lizzie's note in her hand, wrapping an old eiderdown around her for warmth. Was this quilt here earlier? She doesn't think so, but she's glad to

have it now. Her knees knock together – something she'd always thought was a linguistic myth – and she tucks them under her, folding herself smaller and smaller as the flames finally pick up in the grate.

She's so tired. She can feel her eyes closing, but she shakes herself awake. No way is she lying in this creepy house passed out like some babysitter in an old horror film. Fuck. That.

She tries to replay the conversation with the woman on the phone, but it's all chopped up like a bad poem. Did she say help was coming? Would she have gone ahead and arranged the call-out even after the line dropped? She hopes so.

She's trying not to prod at the other parts of the phone conversation. The strange turn it took. But she can't help it. The fact that there have been urban explorers (hardly urban, seeing as this is in the arse end of nowhere, but whatever) should reassure her. It's not uncharted territory.

But she remembers some of the things that Torbjørn told her, when she asked to go exploring with him sometime. That the minute there's a crack anywhere, a damaged roof or a broken window, the weather will get inside and so will people. People will strip a place down to its pipes and the weather will destroy it. The floors get spongy, staircases collapse and all the paint peels. She'd insisted that didn't put her off, anything for an experience, but then he told her about the shit. If the weather can get in, so can the animals and birds. Pigeon poo everywhere, mice or rats and definitely spiders. Maybe some rabbits, a few animal corpses. Fine, she'd said, I'm not that bothered about coming with.

Moirthwaite Manor isn't exactly squeaky clean, but it's not as bad as Torbjørn made out. Maybe that security sign with the dog on it wasn't total bollocks and there's a firm looking after it, keeping the elements out?

Something else puzzles her too, something from the here and now. She looks again at the note.

Stay here, I'm coming back. Lizzie x

I'm coming back. But what about Nina? If Nina was still here when Lizzie left, she wouldn't have had to leave a note. She would have just told Nina where she was going and that she'd be back. And if Nina went with Lizzie, the note would say 'we're coming back'.

Nina must have left first, it's the only explanation. Maybe she left and told Lizzie to say here, but Lizzie shat herself and ran off after her?

Aisa won't give in to this creeping fear. No. She looks around her, taking stock. No, she'll sit here in this room and front it out. Imagine herself to be an urban explorer, try to see this as an adventure despite it feeling like anything but. *Take nothing but photographs, leave nothing but footprints*, that's the 'urbex' motto apparently. She looks at her dead phone. She won't be taking any photos. The floor is dusty, but she can't see any individual footprints either, just general 'scuff' marks where they've all been moving around since they arrived.

Why would Nina have left in the first place though? Maybe her ankle was better and she decided to head off in a different direction to find reception. Cover all bases. That would make sense, staying still is not really Nina's speciality, even with a busted ankle. Or maybe she came after Aisa. That's even more likely.

There's only one road to the village though. So if Nina was walking along that, Aisa would have passed her on the way back.

Aisa thinks about the figure she thought she saw ... The crouching figure that turned into the fox. But what if that

first glimpse was not a fox but a person, as she had originally thought? She didn't stick around to find out, just assumed it was the fox she later saw.

What if… Oh shit. And Nina is still out there, walking miles to the village unnecessarily on her damaged leg. Not knowing that she can turn back now, that help is on its way. And now Lizzie is out there too. Does she know the way to go? She thinks of clueless Lizzie, at the mercy of the night and whoever else is out in it. Lizzie is not equipped for that. And Nina should be resting. She pictures her mum, finding out her daughters are all scattered around in the darkness.

'At least you've all got each other,' she'd said once, in the hospice. Rosemary knew they weren't close, but the lie had given her comfort, so Aisa had smiled.

'Yeah, there is that.'

Where are my sisters?

37

ROSEMARY – April 1992

It's getting a bit close, this weather. A warm spell. I can feel my skin growing tacky under my clothes, can smell a richness from my body that I woke up with from the warm night. It sets Bob off. He was trying it on this morning before I left. He'd brought me a tea in bed, which he only ever does when he wants to get his leg over. 'Why are you grinning like a chimp?' I said, and watched him wither in front of me. The tea slopped on the bedside table as he set it down and left the room.

He doesn't deserve that. And it's not bad when it does happen. It's better than not bad, and he tries very hard. But it just feels like a chore sometimes. Another thing on the to-do list, and one of the many I'm not paid for. And I hate that. I hate that I feel like this. Bob is the kindest man I've ever met. The most devoted. No one has ever looked at me the way he does, a gaze that seems to whitewash anything I might have ever said or done wrong. Like a priest or something, exonerating me. I can't complain that he'd never go anywhere without me, that he adores me to a fault, when that was exactly why I chose him in the first place. And will always choose him.

I've washed down the terracotta in the hallway, it gets filthy every day, and now I'm watching each tile change colour as they

dry like autumn leaves. How many seasons have I watched the trees outside turn from green to red? How many times have I washed these floors?

All these years have slipped past me and I'm still here. Still scrubbing down the terracotta and polishing the silver, only now I slip some of it into my pocket. How is that for personal growth?

There is a sound from the floor above, a door opening – I must get Alan to oil those hinges – and the sound of Jane's light footsteps scurrying onto the landing.

'Rosemary?'

'Coming up, love.'

I have been here for hours now, watching her play with her contraband dolls, listening to her practise French, even though the only French words I remember from school are *piscine* and *boulangerie*.

Only once has Jane seen me looking at my watch, but I felt terrible about it. It's nearly six. Bob will be itching to get to the pub, the girls will be hungry and I want to take this sticky uniform off, get in the bath and drown myself.

'It's a week today,' she says as she rearranges her books, her prim voice without a hint of local dialect.

'Sorry, love?'

'My birthday, silly.'

'Oh yes,' I say. 'I know that very well.'

'I think Mummy might bring me something this year.'

I freeze. The air in my lungs crystallises like ice and my mind jams up. I never know what to say, even after all this time. Jane doesn't seem to notice, carefully reordering her books by height order as she prattles.

'I think eight is quite a big birthday, don't you?'

I nod.

'I think she might have been waiting for a big birthday. I know she thinks about me every day, because you said.'

'She does, I'm sure of it.'

I have painted myself into a corner, but how could I tell her any different? No kid deserves to think their mother doesn't care. Or that she's not coming back.

'Will you be here on my birthday?'

I think, *Will I?* I work here Monday, Wednesday and Friday, so … and then realise I'm being stupid. It's a week today, so of course I'll be here.

'I wouldn't miss it,' I say. 'And I'll bring you a little something.'

I cannot afford to buy a little something, but Nina is bound to have something she doesn't want anymore.

'I'm sorry, love, I really should go. My girls are waiting for me.' I realise immediately this was the wrong thing to say because her shoulders slump and her voice quivers a little.

'Will you tell me about them again?'

I'm never getting home.

'Well, as you know, there's Nina, my eldest. She's ten now and almost as tall as me. She's a bit bossy, but she's a good girl. And Aisa is my youngest, as you know' – *because you know all of this and could recite it in your sleep and you're just playing for time, but how can I be cross* – 'and she's very funny and bolshy and can climb like a monkey.'

'Is she your favourite?'

'Mothers don't have favourites,' I say quickly. 'And then piggy in the middle is Lizzie. She's your age and she loves books and animals.'

'I love books and animals.'

'Yes, you're quite similar really.'

'Is *she* your favourite?'

I smile. 'I've told you a million times, mothers don't have favourites. Unless they only have one child.'

'So I was my mother's favourite?'

'Of course.'

'You were friends, weren't you?'

I hesitate. 'We were. I liked her very much.'

'I think she's going to come this year,' she says firmly. 'And I think she's going to bring me a really big present. I didn't get one from her for—' She counts on her fingers. 'Five years, so five years' worth of presents adds up to a big one.'

I feel uneasy. This is snowballing and when the day comes, and her mum is a no-show, Jane'll feel all the worse for it.

'I hope I get a doll's house,' she says. 'One with little tables and chairs, a bed like mine, sofas and a kitchen, everything this house has. Daddy always buys me books and thinking things, but I'd like something to play with as I'm not supposed to play with these.' She looks down at the antique dolls on the bed next to her. 'Maybe Mummy could bring me a doll's house, what do you think?'

'Would you like me to bring Lizzie to play here sometime?' I say, desperate for all this talk about her mother to end. Lizzie could do with a playmate, one that actually exists.

Jane spins around then, a smile on her face. 'Yes, please,' she says. 'I'd love that. We can talk about books and animals.' I breathe out slowly, glad to have found a diversion. But she continues. 'And if Mummy buys me a doll's house, we can play with that.'

I rush down the stairs, now over an hour late leaving. I hear William finishing up a phone call in his office and wait.

'Yup, yup,' he barks. 'And you.'

The phone lets out a little bleat of a ring as he puts it down, hard. I hover closer, thinking, and then I knock softly.

'A doll's house,' I say, and he raises his eyebrows. 'For Jane's birthday next week, she'd really like one. Maybe Alan could...' I trail off and head for home.

38

LIZZIE – 1:57 a.m.

The lane seems to twist and dip far more on the way back to the house and Lizzie can feel every individual stone through her thin trainer soles. These are the same shoes she uses for everything, and they're normally up to any task. In the summer, she switches to a fresh pair of flip-flops that she gradually destroys throughout May to September, dropping them in the bin just as the weather turns. She smiles for a moment, thinking about the summer just gone. Her first with Rafferty, taking a stroll together with ice creams. Walking up to Silloth Lighthouse. A life together that could skim each season, bouncing from year to year. What a pleasant thought.

This particular pair of trainers are fraying at the eyelets, but they've done her well for several years now. Walking the dogs, cleaning the kennels, doing home visits to check prospective 'pet parents' out. A part of her job that terrifies and fascinates her. She never knows if the paperwork will match reality as she knocks on those doors, standing alone gripping her clipboard. People pretend to have no children because they've fallen in love with a dog unsuited to families, and then Lizzie in turn has to pretend she's not spotted the little shoes, or the last toy they've forgotten to hide. People can turn nasty when you say

no in person, so she waits to get back to work and then emails the rejection.

She has to look out for telltale signs of dog fighters and has to check against the registry of people banned from looking after pets. She has sat in a living room as neat as an army barracks, with a trembling woman who insisted she wasn't trying to adopt a pet for her banned husband. In fact, that she was no longer with him. And please, please would Lizzie just say yes. *Please.*

But, most of the time, she gets to place sweet pets with forever families where they'll be loved, walked and cuddled for the rest of their lives. Those are the placements that make the job worthwhile. But those too are the jobs that used to leave Lizzie sad in ways she couldn't find the words for. The nights after those dogs left for their bright futures used to be the ones spent in the bath until the water got cold. Now they're spent with Rafferty, and that sadness no longer descends.

The empty fields are now on her left as she walks her boomerang route. A scarecrow makes her jump. She glares at it, at its middle-of-the-field audacity and sinister hat. She hadn't seen him when she first walked past and imagines that he grew up out of the earth after the downpour. She doesn't look at him any longer than she has to, her imagination making him move, talk, walk towards her. She rushes on.

Her phone battery is at 50 per cent. She knows she should probably turn the flashlight off to conserve energy, but she can't bring herself to do that. It's dark and scary enough without navigating this journey blind.

The woodland is now to the right as she walks back. The trees here have grown so high that the pale moon is lacerated by them, appearing only in lines like a barcode.

The wind is still wild and unpredictable, but the storm seems to have passed. It's raining lethargically, there's no real gusto, but

her hair is still wet from earlier, hanging in a limp ponytail that drips down her back. Wrapping her coat tighter around her, she tries to start running but stumbles within seconds, immediately out of breath. Gosh, she's so unfit. She used to run through these woods for hours. Whipping in and out of the trees, hand in hand with Jane. What she wouldn't give for little-kid fitness.

Legs pounding.

Mouth twisted in horror.

Fingers tangled, pulling each other along.

They were chasing a rabbit that had been badly hurt by a bullet. By Alan's bullet. He was obsessed with the rabbits trying to eat the fruit and vegetables he grew. Obsessed with catching them and 'teaching them a lesson'. His voice so soft, she'd had to lean in to hear it, but the meaning as sharp as a blade.

They'd been trying to catch the rabbit before he could. Trying to mend its mangled paw, to bandage it so Lizzie could take it home with her, planning to ambush her mum when she finished work.

They'd followed it all through the woods, adrenaline letting it run and run despite its leg being barely more than a stump. They'd kept up with it as it flew through the undergrowth, right by Alan's tent like it was marking it with its scent. Alan's tent, that's right. He had a bedroom in the house but often chose to sleep out in the woods instead. 'He means no harm,' said her dad. 'But best not go in that tent, he's very protective of things.'

They'd followed the rabbit past the greenhouse and then into the potting shed, where they thought they had it cornered. The memory makes Lizzie feel colder, more vulnerable. She doesn't keep prodding at it, just doggedly walks on. But there's no way on earth she's turning off this flashlight.

Almost there now. The thin grey road winding back towards

her sisters. She can tell them that help might be on the way. Maybe. How will she explain Rafferty to them?

She finally reaches the driveway and looks past it up the road towards the car. It seems like a joke that there's a car right there but they just can't use it. This whole night seems like a prank. Some kind of elaborate hoax being set up by an unseen puppet master. Come on – a storm, then a closed garage, then a car running out of petrol and then a spooky old house ... it's almost too perfect. She seeks comfort in this as she pushes herself up the drive and finally reaches the front door. She is just in a story. A nice cosy mystery.

As she steps inside, the door to the front room opens and Aisa steps out. 'Thank fuck you're back,' she says. 'Where's Nina?'

39

AISA – 2:28 a.m.

'I thought Nina went to find you,' Lizzie says, stepping back in surprise. Her voice is so quiet and slow, so apologetic, that Aisa's usual irritation thaws. It's not Lizzie's fault she's a dial-up connection in a 5G world. 'Didn't you see her out there then, Aisa?'

'Well, no, because … I mean …' Did she? It was too dark. But that figure … the footsteps …

'Did you follow the road?' Lizzie asks softly.

'Yeah, of course I followed the road, Lizard.'

Lizzie looks down at her feet, which spill out of the kind of knock-off trainers that make Aisa almost nauseous with melancholy.

'Sorry,' Aisa says, 'I didn't mean to snap.' Her sister is too gentle for any kind of confrontation and Aisa can't handle someone else's tears. 'It's a relief to see you,' she adds and Lizzie smiles. 'Look, come into the living room and we'll work out what to do,' Aisa says. 'I've got the fire going again.'

Lizzie trails silently after her, like she's nursing a wound. The front door closes behind them and they shuffle down the dusty hall and back into the living room. The fire has picked up and Lizzie flops onto the floor in front of it, unbuttoning her

coat and peeling her fake Converse off her feet. She holds out her palms and rubs them together in the heat and then heaves herself back up to sit on the sofa that Aisa was just sitting on. By the proprietorial way Lizzie is wrapping herself in the eiderdown, it must have been her who found it.

Aisa perches on the other sofa and wraps herself in one of the nasty thin blankets, unsure what to say. Aisa is closer in age to Lizzie than Nina, but they have never paired off, never found any middle ground to occupy. Although 'middle ground' is exactly how Aisa would describe Lizzie, were she feeling snide. A middle of the road, middle sister. Aisa looks at her now, at her pale skin and frizzy hair, her badly fitting charity shop clothes, and wonders, where is the rest of her?

Lizzie was always an oddball, more content with animals' company than people. Except for weird Jane, and that probably wasn't a good thing.

They stare at the fire in silence, exhausted. It feels like hours since they were all here together. Two isn't enough.

It's like one of those stocking-filler puzzles where you had to move the pieces around one by one until the numbers were in the right order. Or, in Aisa's case, you pulled the pieces out in a rage and got told off. Lizzie would get her puzzle close enough and sit back satisfied. It was only Nina who would work and work at it until she'd solved it. She was never going to sit here and wait, was she?

Lizzie looks across at Aisa, her mouth opening just a bit, but she snaps it closed again, her eyes filling with tears in the flickering firelight. It's like dealing with a paper doll, Aisa thinks. Lizzie is too fragile for this world, like a skittish animal.

'Oh!' remembers Aisa. 'I saw a fox out there.'

Lizzie brightens then. 'Oh wow, aren't they gorgeous?'

'Yeah, I guess,' Aisa says. 'It freaked me out a bit.'

'Whereabouts was it?'

'On the way to the village.'

'I wonder if Nina saw it too,' Lizzie says, with that exhausted, dreamy voice. 'Although I don't know which way she went.'

Aisa frowns. 'You don't know? Didn't she say where she was going?'

Lizzie looks startled. 'No, she left while I was asleep. I assumed she was going after you.'

Aisa flinches. Leaving without waking Lizzie, that doesn't sound right.

'But Nina was still here when you fell asleep?'

'Yeah,' Lizzie says, rearranging the eiderdown around her as she lies down on the sofa, her face sagging like a loose mask. She looks like she could fall asleep again. 'We were both in here, waiting for you to come back.'

'Did Nina go to sleep too?' Aisa asks, sticking her own feet closer to the fire but still aching with the cold.

'No,' Lizzie says, yawning until her eyes run. Or maybe she's crying again as her voice is trembling now. 'She said she'd stay awake to tend the fire but—'

'But she was gone when you woke up?'

'Yeah.' Lizzie sounds uneasy now, guilty even. 'And the fire was nearly out by then.'

'Does that make sense to you?' Aisa snaps and Lizzie looks down, every move like a timid animal.

'No,' she says eventually. 'No, it doesn't.'

40

ROSEMARY – April 1992

'Lizzie!' I shout up. 'We need to go if you're coming!'

I hear a thud as she gets down off her bed. This is an old house, wedged between other old houses, and it tells tales. She's been sneaky-eating again, her footsteps are heavier than ever. I know it's boredom, I know it's loneliness and I sympathise. But we also can't afford double helpings at the moment.

She plods down the stairs and into the living room, a nervous look on her face. She's wearing her good blouse, which strains a little, and Nina's old jeans.

'Lovely,' I say, and her tense shoulders drop a little. I look around the room. 'Where's Aisa?'

'Dunno,' says Nina.

'Have you seen her, Lizzie?'

'She wasn't in our room,' Lizzie says, in her soft, slow voice.

I look around again. 'Aisa, where are you?'

There's silence but for the prattle of Australian kids' TV from the corner.

'Aisa?'

I hear a giggle. Her distinctive little laugh, like delicate rain, the top notes on a piano ... it melts my heart to soup.

'Where are you?' I smile and listen again, then follow the

172

noise to the window, where I find her curled up on the sill, hidden by one of the curtains. I scruffle her hair – which needs a good brush – and kiss her on the nose. 'You'll be the death of me, you little monkey. Be good for your sister.' I cringe at how easy it's become to say this. I hear Bob's slow steps as he lumbers out of bed, followed by a pause as he scratches his arse, and then a few more plods as he makes his way downstairs for a wee. 'And be good for your dad,' I add.

It's tipping it down, but yesterday it was sunny. So bright you couldn't see straight. You never know what the weather will do in this valley. The only time there's a guarantee is winter, when it's just plain freezing. The little Mini is sitting in a big puddle like a rubber duck in a bath, and I unlock my door and slide in, popping open the passenger door from the inside. Lizzie climbs into the front, vibrating with excitement. I don't send her to the back seats, let her have this moment

'Are you feeling all right?' I ask. She's never been invited to a friend's house before and never asked to have anyone over at ours. Unless you count the friends in her head. She's eight years old and I suddenly wonder, *Does she know how to do it? Does she know how to play?*

'Looking forward to meeting Jane,' she says, softly, oblivious that they met as tots. Of course she knows how to play, she has two sisters and goes to school every day. If there was something wrong ... something missing ... the school would have said. They're quick enough to tell me that Aisa plays tricks on boys who aren't nice to the others. I smile, I can't help myself. She's my sunshine. My naughty little sunshine.

We drive through the village, dodging puddles, and out into the countryside. Some days, most days, I don't really see it. I don't see its scale, its drama, its beauty. I grew up here, next village along, I know it like I know my own body in the bath.

I'm as bored of it too. I certainly didn't think I'd still be here, but then ... where else could I go? But sometimes, I recognise it for the marvel it is. Sometimes, like when my body produced these whole human beings, I recognise its power. And today, the sun shining through the rain, the slick roads like veins of silver through these epic hills and ancient woods, I recognise its beauty.

'Isn't it beautiful,' I say to Lizzie and she nods.

'Breathtaking.'

It's such an adult word for such a little girl and I'm tempted to laugh, but I don't. Poor old Lizzie, she's got an old brain in a young body, that's all it is. Same as Jane. Sort of.

We climb the last hill and see Moirthwaite Manor on the right.

'Foxes,' Lizzie says happily, pointing to the pillars of the arch and two statues I've never paused to look properly at before.

I swing the Mini onto the drive and as we bump our way up to the house, I gently go through the rules. Shoes off. Please and thank you. Quiet voice. Knock before you go anywhere – actually, best not to go anywhere, just stay with Jane or me. And don't disturb Jane's dad while he's working.

'What does he do?'

He was going to be a writer, he said. That summer when I followed him around like a little duckling and he let me eat from his hand when no one was looking. His parents didn't approve, his father in particular, so he'd been strong-armed into studying for a career in finance, but back then, he still had hope.

'He ... I don't know. He just moves money around and has a lot of phone calls about it, so you need to be quiet near his office.'

As we pull up, I tuck the Mini to the side of the drive where it's not such an eyesore and yank on the handbrake. It screams

and sighs – I need to get it seen to – but it holds. Sometimes, that's all you can hope for.

We climb out and I watch Lizzie take the place in. Her jaw drops slightly and she steps back a little as if unable to consume it all with her eyes this close up. It is impressive. Made from the same red stone that everything around here is, looming tall and wide. Each of these windows is almost the width of our whole house and I'm used to that, but I'd forgotten that Lizzie didn't know. That she'd not experienced this scale of anything before, that she's not had much to compare our lives to. This is the first time that she's seen how small our family's world really is. How it slots so easily into the corners of other lives.

I swallow. Is this a mistake?

'Is that Jane?' she says, pointing up at Jane's window.

'No pointing, love.'

We step inside and I see it as if for the first time again. I was twice her age, but it had whipped my legs from under me, the way it's doing to her. The scale of the staircase, the high ceilings, the chandelier over our heads, tinkling with threat as the wind from outside snakes through the hallway. Its grandeur always seems on the cusp of ruin, despite mine and Alan's efforts.

I close the door and whisper, 'Shoes off before anyone sees you,' but Jane is already running down the stairs. Lizzie tugs her shoes off in the least gainly way I've ever seen anyone do it. Jane stops and waits a few steps up – dressed in a velvet dress with a lace trim collar – and stares down at Lizzie. I have a sudden compulsion to bundle her up in my arms and leg it out of the house, but instead I smile. 'Jane, this is my daughter, Lizzie. Lizzie, this is my . . . this is Jane.'

They stare at each other, Lizzie like a rabbit in headlights, blinking in a panic. Jane smiles but says nothing for so long, I cough out of embarrassment.

'What do you like?' Jane says.

'Animals, biscuits, books,' Lizzie reels off like she's addressing a drill sergeant.

'Animals? Oh good.' Jane smiles. 'Put your shoes back on, we're going to look for rabbits.'

'Is that OK, Mum?' Lizzie asks and before I can answer, Jane nods.

'Of course it is, it's up to me.'

41

LIZZIE – 2:33 a.m.

Stupid, stupid Lizard. *Of course* Nina didn't go off without saying anything. Even if she was worried about Aisa, she would have said something. She would have woken Lizzie up and told her what was happening. Given her specific instructions for keeping the fire going. For all Nina's bossiness, she wasn't sneaky. She wouldn't just slope off. Gosh, if Lizzie had thought a little longer, hadn't been so addled from waking up suddenly like that...

And if Nina had gone after Aisa, then Lizzie would have seen her out there. She'd have caught her up, as Nina would have been so much slower, and they'd have been walking towards the same spot of reception. Who would she have called? A thought blooms like a headache and she calls out, 'Aisa?'

Aisa is pinching the bridge of her nose, walking up and down in front of the fire with the blanket trailing like a cape. She whips her head round and barks, 'What?'

'There's something else. I... I meant to say as soon as I got back bu—'

'What now?'

Aisa is always so acerbic. Always has been, even when she was little. Or maybe... maybe that was just her way of being heard.

'What is it, Lizard?' Aisa repeats, no effort to hide her annoyance.

She wants to tell her sister that help is coming. But is it? She left a message on her own voicemail, after all. She doesn't even know that Rafferty is there, let alone if he will hear it. He could have been asleep in his own bed. It's a whole lot of nothing, and she can't bear to talk about Rafferty when Aisa is in such a dismissive mood.

'Nothing,' she says.

'What was it?'

'Don't worry. I just wanted to say that...' She gropes for something plausible. 'I just keep thinking how spooky it is here. I hope we're safe.'

Aisa sits down next to her, curling in on herself and looking nervously at the fireplace.

'You're not the only one to say that about this place,' Aisa says, quietly, looking behind her suddenly as if she'd heard something, then slowly turning back.

'What do you mean?'

'The woman I spoke to at the breakdown company, she asked if I was safe here. I don't mean like the usual solo female traveller questions or something. But, like, she had to google the house name to find it 'cos I didn't know the address and some urban explorers' reports came up.' Lizzie must have frowned in confusion without realising it because Aisa tuts. 'They're people who break into abandoned places and explore them. They write site reports for other urban explorers to follow and, anyway, the reports about this place worried her and she said it sounded weird.'

'Did you ask her why?'

'Yeah, but the call cut out,' Aisa says. 'And I just... I just came back and you and Nina were gone and I didn't know where and

then you came back and that ... that took over my thoughts. I just figured she was a numpty who hadn't heard of ...' Aisa trails off and Lizzie feels her cheeks colour.

Lizzie tries to imagine what urban explorers might write. Are they the types to be easily spooked? They sounded pretty brave to her. 'Maybe there is something here we should be scared about.'

Aisa looks up.

42

AISA – 2:36 a.m.

'Something here like what?' Aisa says, dredging as much attitude as she can muster. 'Like a... like a ghost or something?' She forces a smirk as she says it, tries to break into a laugh, but scrunches up her eyes instead.

I don't believe in ghosts.

I don't believe in ghosts.

I don't believe in ghosts.

'You're mocking me,' Lizzie says. 'But I think you're scared too.'

Scared? I'm absolutely terrified. I haven't felt this level of fear since I was a child and I just want Mum. I just really want my mum. 'I'm not scared, Lizzie. I'm freezing cold and I'm pissed off, but I'm not scared. I just want to work out what's happened to Nina, make sure she's OK and then wait for the mechanic.'

'Me too.'

Oh, where the hell is Nina? Without her, Aisa has had to assume the role of group leader when she's only ever comfortable as a lone wolf. And if she had to put together a team, she would have picked almost anyone else she'd ever met before she'd choose Lizzie. Poisson the cat would show more gumption. But Lizzie is made from cardboard, and the slightest hint of

people being fed up with her will crumple her to pieces, so Aisa needs to be nice. Nice-adjacent, anyway.

Aisa pinches the bridge of her nose, trying to make sense of this. She instinctively slides her phone from her pocket, ready to search for these urbex reports herself. Grasp the nettle, see what has been said. Of course, her phone is dead.

But whether they can read them right now or not, there clearly are some out there about this place.

She tries to weigh up the options, picture all the moving parts. A rescue truck could technically arrive any minute, so they can't just go off to the village. And Nina is missing out there, and hurt. Aisa looks out of the window as if she'll see her sister marching up to the house, but no one is there.

'Maybe we should wait in the car?' Aisa says, trying to sound casual.

'But Nina has the keys,' Lizzie whispers apologetically.

'Fuck.'

Lizzie flinches, she's never liked swearing. As far as Aisa knows, she still says 'tish' instead of shit.

Aisa casts around for something to say. Something that isn't fear-based and doesn't involve a Rubik's Cube of a decision.

'I'm freezing,' she says eventually, nodding towards the fireplace. 'It's not kicking out much heat now.'

Lizzie nods and starts prodding about in the grate, sparks flying from the embers that are left. She adds some more logs and then looks around.

'There's paper over there.' Aisa walks towards a slightly dishevelled newspaper stuffed in the corner of the room and barely visible in the light from the candles. She stoops to pick it up and passes it to her sister, who takes it gingerly as if it's made from spiderwebs. It's not as crumpled as she thought when Lizzie

holds it up. 'Hang on,' Aisa says, as the masthead glows briefly in the reflection of the fire. 'What's the date on there?'

Lizzie squints and holds the paper up to one of the candles. 'Oh,' she looks up at Aisa, her face flushing. 'Gosh. It's yesterday's date.'

'Yesterday, as in yesterday? As in this year, not an anniversary of yesterday?'

Lizzie nods and drops the paper as if it's contaminated, dangerous. 'Literally yesterday,' she says, and shuffles closer to Aisa, who grips her sister's arm.

'Shit,' she says. 'Someone has been in here recently. Very recently. What if—' Aisa doesn't want to say it and she doubts Lizzie wants to hear it, but it's too late, she has to. They have to face up to this. 'What if they found Nina?'

43

ROSEMARY – May 1992

It feels like these kids are never at school. They go back after February half term and then it's Easter. They go back after Easter and it's May half term. It won't be long until it's the summer holiday and then the whole thing starts again. *I should have been a teacher,* I think, as I scrub the big range with a Brillo pad, trying to move the immovable. What the hell has Cook been doing, grilling the food directly on the flame, like she's living out in the woods with Alan?

I imagine what it's like to look forward to the holidays. To be able to plan a schedule of events, to bundle the girls into the car and take them to Windermere or to play on the beach in Barrow. I smile and imagine packing a picnic in a cool box. And a big stripey bag containing a ball, a windcheater, a bottle of sun lotion. I can almost smell it on their warm skin. To just let each day unfurl in front of us, chips for lunch if they want, ice cream. Me reading on a sandy towel while they splash around. It's not much. Small dreams, but still out of reach. More than anything, I would love to be able to give them my time.

It's getting lighter in the evenings, there's more of the day waiting for me when I get home, and every day, I tell myself I'll keep some energy back. I'll hug them all when I get in and

I won't just immediately start on straightening the house and cooking the tea. I'll just *be* with them. But it never pans out that way. The house is fuller than ever as the girls grow, their stuff scattering. Scrunchies everywhere, Aisa's toys underfoot. And there's a lot more of Bob too. Money is getting thinner and thinner and he's had his wings clipped, having to make do with a couple of skems at home instead of the pub. He plods around like a big dog, getting in my way and then looking chastened.

I've started locking myself in the loo, just to have five minutes, even though I've worked more or less by myself all day. The guilt roaring in my ears. *But it's not the same though*, I think, as I finally manage to move a lump of something black and molten. *It's just not the same.*

Sometimes, when I'm here working away, it's like a portal opens up. A latch slips off the gate and I'm not here but back *there*, in the past. I'm sixteen. Skinny and excited. A new perm on my head and an unbroken heart. The whole world is there and I just have to step into it. Only, the closer I get, the more I realise it's more like a cinema screen. You'll just bang your head if you try to climb through.

I realise I'm being watched at the same time I realise I've stopped scrubbing. I turn, though I know who it is already. No one else treads so lightly, like a little forest fawn.

'Y'all right there, love?' I say.

'Rosemary?' Jane says and I wonder if her vowels will ever flatten, if she'll ever sound like she lives here. That she's been here since before she could talk properly. 'Do you think…'

'What is it, Jane? Don't be shy,' I say, with more patience than I know I'll have left for my girls when I get back.

'Well, I was hoping you might bring Elizabeth back to play with me again soon.'

Elizabeth? For a moment I don't know who she means and then the penny drops. 'Lizzie?'

'Yes, I had such fun with her before.'

'I'm not sure, Jane, I don't want to irritate your dad, bringing people here.'

'I'm sure Daddy won't mind. He knows how lonely I get here, without a brother or sister or ...' She lowers her eyes and a cruel thought takes flight before I can stop it. *Is this for show?* 'Or a mummy,' she says.

I think about her birthday. About how disappointed she was when – of course – her mother didn't turn up again. Of how many doll's-house blankets I guiltily produced for her, knitting on my days off. I even got Alan to help me make a little doll version of her, which was a right faff. I'll never attempt to knit a tiny human head again. But she's only eight. It's not for show, she's lonely as anything.

'Of course I'll bring her,' I say. *If you promise to stop pining for your mum*, I want to add. The *idea* of her mother, anyway, as Jane can't possibly remember Selina. Her energy, her wit, her hatred of this house.

Then I think about Lizzie's ravenous hunger and the scrapings of the food budget. Two birds ... 'Why don't I bring her over and make you two lasses a picnic?'

44

LIZZIE – 2:40 a.m.

They. They. An unknown 'they' was in this house, coaxing Nina away. *Snatching* Nina away. All while Lizzie slept. Just a great lump, snoring on the sofa, while her injured sister was taken against her will. Stupid, stupid Lizzie. She thumps herself hard on the side of the head. Once, twice and again.

'Hey,' Aisa says, alarmed. 'Don't do that!'

'But someone has taken Nina and it's my fault!'

'No,' says Aisa, shaking her head and frowning. 'No one has taken Nina, don't be silly. I was getting carried away... It's all a bit weird, but she's obviously just gone off looking for something. You'd have woken up if something bad had happened, wouldn't you? There's no way you'd have slept through it. Even you.'

'Even me?'

'Even you.'

'But the newspaper,' Lizzie says. 'It's proof someone was here.'

'Yesterday,' Aisa says quietly. 'That's all.'

Oh gosh, why did she have to lie down earlier? She'd felt safe with Nina here, so safe she could just fall asleep. It didn't cross her mind that Nina was vulnerable. Even with her bad ankle, Nina is just... Nina. She's always OK. But how well did Lizzie actually check if she was here before dashing off? She only had

a quick look in each room, assuming Nina would make herself known if she was in one of them. But maybe she was here and in trouble somehow, or hurt, and Lizzie just swanned off and left her.

'I just feel so bad,' Lizzie says, quietly.

Aisa takes a deep breath and then grabs Lizzie's hands. 'Honestly, I'm sure Nina's fine,' she says, unconvincingly. 'I'm sure she'll be back any minute to tell us off for something. But I think we should have a proper look through the house while we wait, just in case ... you know, in case she did just fall asleep somewhere upstairs or ...' Aisa doesn't finish the sentence and Lizzie is grateful.

Lizzie shoves the eiderdown away, embarrassed by the way she'd been gripping it. She does her coat back up, stuffs her aching feet back into her trainers and checks her phone for battery. Enough to use the light for a good while, thankfully.

Aisa says her own phone is long dead, so she grabs a candlestick, cupping one hand around it to shroud the small flickering flame. Even though Lizzie's light is stronger, Aisa leads the way. They walk slowly, to keep the flame safe and to scour every inch of the house this time. Neither has said it, but Lizzie knows they're not just looking for Nina, but for signs of what might have happened to her too.

They check out the kitchen first. There's nothing much in here: a disused fridge, a giant cold Rayburn. They look in all the corners, and venture into the larder this time. Tucked on the gnarly old floor just inside the door, there's a bulky blue cool box, the kind the Kelseys used to take on trips to the beach in North Wales after they moved to Cheshire. It's an incongruous shock of colour, almost cartoon-like. Aisa starts to squat down, but the flame flickers wildly as she moves, so Lizzie takes over.

Bending over it, she opens the lid cautiously and is surprised to see long life milk, margarine and a pack of open biscuits, twisted at the neck. The sisters look at each other. Next to the cool box is a small camping stove with a chipped old-fashioned red kettle balanced on it. In the flashlight glow, its bottom is visibly blackened.

'I think someone might have been staying here after all,' Lizzie says.

Aisa gives her the kind of look that means 'no shit' but instead she draws her face into an almost smile and says, 'It doesn't mean anything bad though. You get squatters all over the place, they're usually harmless. The urban explorer I hook up with says people get in these places to strip them and do graffiti, and there was graffiti on the outside, wasn't there?'

'Yes,' says Lizzie. Relieved also that maybe the only reason Aisa has heard of urban explorers was because she's romantically involved with one.

'And graffiti artists are harmless, OK?'

'OK,' Lizzie says, and then she realises she'd been rude not acknowledging the nugget of personal information out loud. 'So, is he your boyfriend, the urban explorer?'

Aisa pauses. 'Sure,' she says.

Lizzie opens her mouth to add that she's not the only one with a beau, but Aisa turns away and the moment is lost.

They check the rest of the downstairs rooms and then climb the stairs. Aisa opens the bathroom with a bang and Lizzie cringes.

'There's a loo roll under there,' Aisa says, pointing to the U-bend behind the old toilet. 'And some bleach. God, this is almost civilised.'

The discoveries seem to be awakening something in Aisa, some sense of adventure or some kind of compulsion to explore.

For Lizzie, every tiny sign of life unpicks a nerve, one by one. Do graffiti artists and thieves bring newspapers to read? No, someone has been staying here, she thinks. This is someone's territory, and they've barged into it. Did Nina pay the price?

They look in the back corner bedroom. 'Alan's room,' Lizzie says, and Aisa stops moving.

'Alan,' she says. 'Yeah, that was his name, wasn't it.'

Lizzie looks at her. 'You remember him?'

'Yeah,' Aisa says. 'A little. Strange bloke.'

Lizzie nods and then shakes her head. 'I always thought he was more sad than strange.'

They walk out quickly and check the other back bedrooms. Aisa calmly moves out of the way when a huge spider comes barrelling towards them like tumbleweed. Lizzie scrambles back onto the landing, brushing herself as if covered in them.

Aisa looks at her but has the kindness not to comment.

They open the master bedroom. It's absolutely pointless, Lizzie knows it's horrifyingly empty, but they must look, if only to be doing something.

'One room left,' Aisa says, as they close the master bedroom door. 'Let's hope she's in there, curled up.'

'I checked it thoroughly,' Lizzie starts, but does she hope she checked it properly or that she missed her sister? 'But yeah, you're right. She could be in there.'

They look at each other and then push the door. Aside from the lounge, this is the most cluttered room. The one with the most hiding places and corners.

'Nina?' Lizzie says and they stay deadly still to listen for a reply.

Nothing.

'Nina, stop dicking about,' Aisa calls. She's trying to smile, but her eyes look wild with fear.

They check under the bed, then Lizzie pulls up each sheet and blanket.

'She's not Flat Stanley,' Aisa says.

The thick curtains still hang either side of the window seat and they tug them at the same time, fanning them like a mother's dress, like the black skirt their own mother used to wear here.

She is not here. Not one trace of her is here. There is no sign of ... anything. Nothing to suggest a struggle. *No blood.* Nothing. But Lizzie runs her light along every wall and surface anyway, because to stop looking is to admit something she's not ready to admit.

Lastly, she runs her light over the doll's house.

Aisa bends down, accidentally snuffing her candle, so Lizzie walks closer with her light to compensate. 'Bloody candles. Hey, are those ...?' She snaps back and crawls backwards on her hands.

'Bones,' Lizzie says apologetically. 'Yeah.'

'Jesus fucking Christ,' Aisa says, standing. 'God, Lizzie. I can't ... I can't put a brave face on this. This is really, really creepy. This isn't ... this isn't right.'

'I know,' Lizzie whispers. 'I thought they were Jane's from when she was a kid, but maybe someone ... someone else is ...' she trails off. The light has settled on the lower part of the doll's house and she spots something she didn't notice before. Or forgot. The floor of the miniature lounge is visible through the window, and it's set a few inches higher than the bottom of the doll's house. Lizzie gets onto her knees to look closer, pressing the lower part of the wooden wall carefully, tenderly.

Aisa shoots her eyebrows up in question, but Lizzie can't say, not yet. She needs to check. Her fingertips work their way gently around, as if feeling for a tender spot on a dog in pain, until eventually, at the back of the house, she finds it. A gentle push reveals a barely visible hinge, and a small panel flips open.

'Another level,' Lizzie says, turning to look at Aisa. 'Underneath.'

'I know,' Aisa says, her voice distorted as if her teeth were chattering. 'I know.'

Lizzie sits back, awash with memory now. All the missing pieces tumbling at her so fast she can't focus on any one of them. The day they followed the injured rabbit into the shed. The place Jane wanted to show her. *Oh tish*, she should have remembered. She really should have remembered. The extra rooms, windowless, under the main house.

Aisa runs out of the room, navigating the dark, her dead candle swinging in her hand as Lizzie follows behind with the phone, its light bouncing erratically. As they start to climb down the stairs, Lizzie stops. 'Aisa,' she says, 'look.'

Aisa turns from a few steps below and sees what Lizzie is pointing at. From this angle, they can both see that the tides of dust on the stairs carpet have been disturbed, as if something has been dragged through them. Or someone.

45

ROSEMARY – June 1992

My feet are killing me before I even start work. Five miles, walk, fuelled only by tea. I'd woken up early to drive out to the garage and fill the car with the last of my wages, which I'd left on my bedside table the evening before. But when I reached for them first thing, I found an empty brown envelope.

I'd gone to sleep while Bob was at the pub last night, spending the fiver I'd pulled out for him. He must have come back, grabbed the rest and snuck back out. When I saw what he'd done, I had to run downstairs to the loo. A sudden rush of nausea swept over me from toes to gut and I only just made it to the back door and threw up outside in the yard instead. Then I had to boil a kettle and wash it all away. All the while, Bob slept on up there, snoring like a drain, sweat on his temples and beer breath filling the room.

'How could you?' I said to him as I rushed up to chuck my clothes on, no time for breakfast, no time for anything. I am never late, I hate to be late. I am capable, dependable, I have to be. 'There's no bus, Bob, how could you?'

He sat up, groaned in pain and lay back down. Without answering me, he fell back asleep, mouth open like a fish.

'I hope you choke,' I said to him, but then silently took it back.

'He's not well,' that's what my mum says. 'It breaks a man, losing his job. His way of life. It's an illness.' She doesn't know the half of what's troubling Bob, but my dad lost his job in the biscuit factory just before he was diagnosed, and my mother has long conflated the two. I'm not convinced it had anything to do with Dad's cancer, I think it just shakes down that way sometimes, but we've never had the same outlook.

It preys on my mind as I approach the age he was and wonder. Some nights, I lie awake and run through all the things I've not done with my girls, and the experiences I've not given them while I tread water to earn money that doesn't even stretch. If cancer took me now, like it took my dad, what would they remember of me? My back as I left each morning? All the things I had to say no to. Holidays and sports clubs and days out. But what good is that way of thinking? There's no other option, I'm unqualified and Bob is out of work. When those worries well up inside me, I have to tell myself that one day there will be a way out of this, a way to give them everything they deserve. I just don't know how yet.

I kissed the girls goodbye this morning, whispered to Nina to make sure they had their breakfast before school, and then dashed off. Maybe I could have called in sick – our line is cut off, but the phone box is right by our house – but William keeps me on because I'm dependable. It's certainly not out of any residual feelings or even loyalty. If I cease to be dependable, what am I? And besides, I'd lose the wages from today, or have to make up the time tomorrow, and I've got envelope stuffing to do.

*

When I get to the front door, there's a moth lying dead on the doorstep. I pretend I haven't seen it and rush round to the back door instead. Round here in Cumbria, moths are a sign of death or letters. But dead moths... that can't be good, can it? I think again of my dad and blink rapidly to wipe the image. It helps no one to think like that.

I struggle through the day, dodging questions from Jane about when Lizzie can come back. I had to go and get her from school on Wednesday and bring her back here to 'play' for my last few hours. Using up precious fuel and not even giving Lizzie a say in it. She'd come out of Jane's room pale-faced when it was time to go, unable, or unwilling, to tell me why.

My feet hurt, my back aches, I still feel sick, as if I absorbed Bob's hangover while I slept next to him. I even told William about the car not being available, hoping he might give me a lift home, but he turned his attention back to the papers on his desk before I'd even finished.

While William was teaching Jane this afternoon, I managed to sneak a bit of rest on one of the new sofas that finally arrived this week. They're not as soft as the old one, but I was too tired to care. I managed a kind of one-eye-open dog nap in case I was caught, but luckily I wasn't disturbed. I can't make it a habit, but I feel like every day takes a little more toll than the last and the thought of carrying on like this for another twenty years crushes me. I need a way out. We all do.

I open the front door of Moirthwaite Manor ready to leave, relieved that the moth is gone, when I hear Jane behind me. I muster every bit of energy left not to sag my shoulders in despair. I don't want to bring Lizzie back here, I don't want to feed her to the lions, to assuage guilt, to prop up another kid. But I know I'll have to. I wait for the inevitable questions, but instead, she says, 'Rosemary, can I show you my artwork?'

'Of course you can, love.' I turn around with a smile that fades as I look down. She holds up a piece of wood that she must have found. Pinned to it, with needles from the sewing basket, is the moth from earlier. It's splayed, as if in flight, its furry little body with a needle through the middle, its wings intact and beautiful. My breath catches in my throat and I lose control of my smile for just a moment.

'You don't like it?'

'No, no, I do. It's very … scientific.'

'I did it for Lizzie. She says she likes moths and butterflies. Everything except spiders, she said.' She thrusts it towards me eagerly. I take it – what else can I do? I take it and carry it straight out in front of me, like a tea tray. 'Make sure you give it to her,' she says.

I've just finished stuffing the horrible gift into the hedge down the driveway when Alan catches up to me. I just want to get home, but I've been too brusque with him recently and Bob always reminds me to be kind to him, they used to be close and I know Bob worries about him, so I manage to dredge a smile up.

'Bob not picking you up?'

'Not today, Al.'

'That's a shame,' he says, his voice so soft I have to step closer to him to hear. He smells … sour. 'I wanted to ask him about doing some work. A lot of the bushes need taming and it's a two-man job really.'

God, we need the money. But I shake my head. Bob hates coming back to the house, the cost is just too high. 'Sorry, Al, he's tied up at the minute. Doing some stuff up in Penrith.'

He frowns, and I feel awful because I know he's trying to help.

'Sorry, Al, I really need to go, but thanks for the offer.'

I walk away as fast as my aching arches will let me, and

when I look back, he's walking slowly back to the house in his lolloping way.

Bob needs a purpose and we need the money. Something to get him out of the house. He wants to work on the trains, he always has, but he hasn't gone to ask at the station. Too worried they'll say no. I'll talk to him later, encourage him again. He'll be full of apologies about the petrol money, and I'll have to forgive him, because if I don't, he'll feel guilty. And when he feels guilty, when he feels anything, when he remembers... he drinks. And when he drinks, clearly, he runs his mouth. This time, he's obviously told Alan, or someone who knows Alan, that we're skint. Next time...

46

AISA – 2:57 a.m.

Lizzie stays swaying on the landing, her mouth open in horror, but Aisa's not messing around. She rushes down the stairs to the hallway, getting swallowed by the darkness now that her candle has gone out. As she reaches the bottom step, she can't even see her hand in front of her. She swallows, waiting for Lizzie to catch up, looking wildly around into nothing. She steps down into the foyer and looks up towards Lizzie, still aglow at the top of the stairs, gripping her phone.

'Come on,' she hisses.

Then she sees it. A thin ribbon of light just underneath the bottom step in front of her. Confirmation.

As soon as she saw that miniature house, the extra rooms, it all came back to her. The space beneath the house. She and Nina had been playing hide and seek, and Aisa had found that little door under the stairs. It must still be there now, a few feet away from where she stands.

Back then, she'd climbed into the cupboard, found the trapdoor and climbed down a few steps. All she was thinking about then was hiding.

Lizzie lumbers down the steps as Aisa feels her way to the cupboard under the stairs. 'Over here, Lizzie,' she calls, pulling

the door open. Back then, it was filled with bric-a-brac, picnic baskets and wellies, ideal for a little body to weave through and hide. But as Lizzie shines her phone's flashlight inside, they can see that the cupboard is now empty.

It's wallpapered with roses – a pattern Aisa suddenly remembers but couldn't have described if you'd asked her. It's not as dusty in this cupboard as it is in the rest of the house, but it's still grubby. Footprints are visible on the bare stone floor and there's a section in the middle where the dust has been mostly rubbed away.

With Lizzie hovering behind her gripping her phone and pointing its light at the floor, Aisa stoops into the cupboard. She could almost touch the furthest wall just by reaching up a hand, there's nothing in here blocking the way.

But when she squats down, she can see that the slabs of stone are not all the same. Most are sealed together with concrete and dirt, but one has a clear gap around it. She remembers this, remembers finding the trapdoor, and feels around.

The ring is still set in the stone floor slab, just like it was back then. It had been partly open when she found it as a little girl, just a chink of light visible in the black of the cupboard. She'd expected it to be difficult to move, but when she wrapped her little fingers around the metal ring and pulled, it slipped up easily. And now, as she does it as an adult, she can see why. It's hinged with some kind of spring mechanism to make it quiet and quick. And the light is on down there now too, just like it was then.

'If that leads where I think it does,' Lizzie says, 'there's another way in too.'

'What?' Aisa looks around at her sister. 'You knew all along?'

'I'd forgotten,' she says. 'But I was there too. Remember?'

'I—' *Jane* was there, Aisa remembered that. But Lizzie too? If Lizzie was there, why did she let Jane ...

Lizzie looks at her, as if waiting for a reaction.

'I'd forgotten,' Aisa manages to say, as her memories shuffle like a pack of cards yet again.

'It's amazing what you can forget, isn't it?' Lizzie says, her eyes seeking Aisa's. 'It's even more amazing what you can convince yourself of, even when the evidence is right in front of you.'

Aisa stares at her sister's back as she turns away again. *What evidence is right in front of me?*

47

LIZZIE – 3:00 a.m.

They both peer down at the wooden steps, which are lit by bare bulbs hanging from a long wire which seems to run along the wall and along the passage. So there *is* some electricity here then... What else is still here? *Who else?*

She'd known this all along, but she'd forgotten. And it seems Aisa had too. What else have they pushed out of their memories?

'You go first,' Aisa says and Lizzie blinks in surprise. Aisa is usually the first to barrel into any situation, to heck with the consequences. Lizzie looks at her, so much smaller still, even though they're both adults. Her shoulders have hard little knots on them, her elbows as sharp as knives. Lizzie looks at her little sister's face and sees a brief hint of confusion and fear, which washes in and out again like a tide.

If Aisa is scared, things must be really bad. And yet, Aisa's reticence stirs something in Lizzie. If her little sister needs her to step up for once, then she'll do it. She'll flipping well do it.

'Of course I'll go first,' she says, as boldly as she can manage.

Each light bulb flickers as they brush past. Lizzie heads down carefully, her knackered grey trainers testing every step, gingerly at first and then with something approaching confidence.

The stairs curl in a dog-leg and then land in a dark recess, the light not quite reaching here. She rushes through a brick archway and comes out in a kind of foyer. Behind her, she hears Aisa take a sharp breath.

In her memory, sketchy as it is, this underground foyer was huge. It's actually barely bigger than her dad's little living room. There are several closed doors to the left of them and only one to the right, which is open and leads to a long passage.

'That's the way that leads to the shed,' she says.

Aisa stares up along it and then back at Lizzie, a strange look on her face. She was so little, of course she can't remember any of this. But Lizzie and Jane had come down that passageway all those years ago. It was horrible, filled with spiderwebs that Jane had destroyed one by one with her fingers.

'Oh,' Lizzie says, bending a little at the knees.

'What?'

'I just . . . I just remembered something, it's OK.'

The spider. The spider that Jane caught in her hand and chased Lizzie with, when they first came down here.

Why did she do that? It was so mean. Lizzie remembers the surge of anger that she'd had to swallow back down.

'You remembered something about down here?' Aisa's eyes are wide, the whites of them looking almost orange in this weird light. She looks terrified, something Lizzie can't remember seeing for a long time.

Get it together, Aisa needs you.

'No, nothing like that.'

Aisa had needed her then too. She was here, alone, a little four-year-old crouching in the dark by herself. Where was Nina? She was above them still, clattering around in the hallway cupboard they'd just been in tonight. That's right, the Kelsey sisters had split up when they first arrived. Aisa and Nina had

been playing hide-and-seek while Jane and Lizzie went off on their own. Then they'd eventually made their way under here and found Aisa hiding. Jane had spoken to Aisa and calmed her down while Lizzie had called up to Nina in the cupboard. 'If you're looking for Aisa, she's down here.'

But why did she and Jane make their way into this place before that? Lizzie closes her eyes and tries to remember, but the mental film just spools back to the beginning. Running through the woods, wild, exhilarated and terrified.

They both look up the long passageway now, which is also strung with the same kind of bulbs, each illuminating a little patch. As far as she can see, it looks surprisingly clean now, no spiderwebs nor mouse droppings. Someone has cleaned it recently, Lizzie can see tides of dust along the edge, as if the middle has been brushed.

The end of the tunnel is too far and too dark, despite the light. The whole thing must be a hundred metres long and change, the floor is flagstone and the walls are brick. However old Moirthwaite Manor is, this section looks like it's been here the whole time, so it must predate the electricity. Maybe little candles once lit the way for the servants who lived down here. Lizzie imagines a gust of wind blowing them all out, and shudders at the idea of being plunged into darkness. What if the lights go out suddenly now?

The thought makes the back of her neck tingle and she turns quickly, but no one is there, and Aisa is still in front of her.

She reaches into her pocket for her phone, grips it like a gun in a holster, ready to pull it out and switch the flashlight on again.

She glances one more time up the passageway that she'd come down all those years ago, with Jane, and then back up it with her sisters afterwards, Nina and then Aisa. Jane hadn't been with

them. Jane had stayed here. It was the last time Lizzie saw her. They moved so soon afterwards that she never even said goodbye to Jane, let alone had another glimpse at her house.

What happened to Jane?

48

ROSEMARY – June 1992

'Nan brought a book round for you,' Nina shouts from the kitchen as I walk into the house. 'It's on top of the telly.' The telly that is blaring, with Aisa sitting right up in front of the screen. Lizzie is lying on the sofa with her head in a book. I think it's one borrowed from Jane; it looks prehistoric. Most worrying, I can smell burning.

'A book for me?' I say. That's my mother in a nutshell, even managing to use inanimate objects to judge me. When do I have time to read a book? 'And have you been cooking, Nina?'

'Just toast,' Nina says, sliding some plates into the bubble-filled sink as I walk into the kitchen.

'How much washing up liquid did you use? That's expensive, Nina.'

'Not much,' she says quietly, plunging her hands into the sink so the bubbles slop over onto the floor.

I close my eyes and pinch my nose to stay calm when a thought strikes me. 'Did Nan come in?'

'Just to drop off the book,' Nina says. 'She said she didn't have time to stop.'

I look around at what my mum would have seen – and judged – on arrival. The floor is covered in bits. The vacuum broke last

year and we've been using a carpet roller, but it's a losing battle and the carpet is visibly waving a white flag. Or a dirty grey one. I keep the house relatively tidy, but there's not always time for a full scrub and polish.

There's a full laundry basket next to the washing machine, which is itself full of clean washing that should have been hung out today. A basket of ironing sits in the middle of the living room like a marooned shipwreck and all the boxes from my envelope-stuffing job are stacked against the wall.

'Lizzie!' I shout, before I can stop myself. 'What are you doing just lying there like a lump?'

Lizzie looks up from the sofa, stung.

'How can you just sit there reading while I'm working and Nina is looking after Aisa and Dad is …' I waver. *Doing some cash in hand that it's best not to know about.* 'And Dad is out. You're a big girl now, you need to pull your weight.'

She looks down at her tummy.

'No,' I say, kicking myself. 'Not weight, like … just *helping*, Lizzie. Without being asked.'

'What shall I—' she starts and then runs aground. 'Can I ask just this time?' she says quietly.

'Just, look. There's that washing in the machine, that could go out on the whirligig.'

'OK.'

'Did I do something wrong letting Nan in?' Nina asks, rinsing the last of the plates and stuffing them on the draining rack as Lizzie plods into the kitchen and starts yanking the washing out of the machine and into a basket.

'No, no, none of you have done anything wrong, I just … I'm embarrassed that she saw—'

'Us?' Aisa says, jutting her chin out at me and glaring.

'No, God no, not you, sweetheart. Not you three.' I sag against

the wall. I've not even got my shoes and tights off and I've fudged it all. 'This house is a mess, that's all. And I spent all day polishing someone else's house and I just … I'm tired. I need a bath.'

Nina cringes.

'What is it?'

'That was the last of the hot water.'

I say nothing. I sit on the dip of the sofa that Lizzie has vacated and close my eyes tight for several minutes. When I open them, the girls have all tiptoed upstairs and the whirligig in the yard is tipping sideways with the clothes Lizzie has hung up.

After the girls are fed, again, I'm looking forward to a cup of tea in the bath now that the water has finally heated up again. Bob will put the girls to bed, a gesture he's made a few times recently as part of his ongoing apology tour for taking the petrol money. Then I remember what day it is. Friday. He gets his pay packet today. As a reward for his efforts this week, he's going to the pub after work, as per our new arrangement.

'Girls,' I call. 'Brush teeth and bed!'

'All of us?' Nina calls back. 'Or just Aisa?'

'All of you need to get ready for bed, but you big ones can read for a bit.'

I kiss them all goodnight and head back downstairs, flopping on the sofa. And then begins the review of the day – the mistakes, the regrets, the to-do list that has grown like the magic porridge pot. My mum, dropping off a book she seems to have bought from the library clear-out called *The Seven Habits of Highly Effective People*. It has a sticky note on it in her large writing, all capitals.

I THOUGHT THIS MIGHT BE HELPFUL TO YOU.

For a long time, she acted like I was nothing but a disappointment – the once golden girl who could have gone on to A levels, maybe even university, and instead became a 'scullery maid'– so it's nice that I've been promoted to a disappointment who may yet have the potential to become highly effective.

I toss the book onto the pile of paperwork and bills I'm yet to deal with (even in a minimally effective way) and think of Lizzie. I was unfair to her earlier, cruel even. I know she'll still be awake up there, reading. I should go up to see her, give her a cuddle and apologise. She's eight, why would she think to put the washing out? Do I even want an eight-year-old – or any of the girls – to feel obliged to hang out washing? No. If I achieve nothing else as a mum, I want them to have higher hopes and expectations than me.

'Mummy?'

Aisa has crept back downstairs, her long-loved, straggly teddy under her arm and her nightie dragging on the floor, a hand-me-down from Jane that makes her look like a Victorian ghost.

'Are you OK, Ace?'

She shakes her head and then takes a running jump, landing on top of me. She wraps herself around me and I kiss the top of her head.

'I'm scared,' she says. 'But don't tell them.'

'Them?'

'Nina and Lizzie, they'll laugh at me.'

'Is it because of that film again?'

'If I say yes, you'll say we can't watch those films again and they'll blame me.'

I sigh, because she's right, I already don't want them watching those films again as this is the third time Aisa's got back up this week, and last week was no better. But I don't want this little weight off my lap. I don't want to lose these little arms around

my neck. I know it won't be long before Aisa is as hands-off as the other two – or, even worse, I'm as hands-off with her as I am with the other two.

'Let's watch *Grease* together and then you can sleep in our bed just this once,' I whisper to her. 'But don't tell the others.'

49

AISA – 3:06 a.m.

Aisa looks at Lizzie's back. She's taller than Aisa, but hunched over a little, her body forming a question mark. Her hair is pulled back into a ponytail, a mousey brown that might have bits of blonde in, but it could just as easily be grey. Aisa wants to ask, 'Don't you care?' but she fears the question says more about herself than Lizzie.

But just look at her. She wouldn't hurt a fly. And yet, Lizzie was the last person seen with Nina earlier today, and the last person seen with Jane all those years ago. And let's not beat around the bush, Aisa thinks. Let's not bother to pretty up the thought, because it's not for external consumption anyway: she is weird. Lizzie is objectively different. And sometimes, that's enough.

Lizzie takes a step forward, and Aisa follows. This atrium area is a kind of L shape. The passageway running behind them, and then four doors in front. One of them is barely visible around a slight corner.

It's almost a mirror of the top floor of the house, but without the bathroom, loo and airing cupboard. They approach the first door.

'Open it,' she says, and Lizzie spins round to look at her.

'Me? OK, yes, OK.' She reaches out for the doorknob, twists it

and pushes the door cautiously open. It's black inside, but when Lizzie sweeps the phone flashlight around, it's just a disused cupboard. Same as it was all those years ago.

Aisa exhales.

They stand in front of the next door. Aisa looks up at her sister for signs of . . . what? She's not really sure. Maybe signs that Lizzie has done something terrible, or that she plans to do something terrible.

Lizzie scrunches up her eyes, reaches forward to turn the knob, but Aisa stops her.

'Did you check down here when you woke up earlier and Nina was gone?' she says.

Lizzie frowns. 'No, you know I didn't.'

'So you just suddenly remembered that this whole layer existed?'

'You know I did. Same as you.'

'You never actually said that, you just ran off and then pointed to the light.'

'Don't you trust me?' Lizzie says quietly.

'I don't trust anyone.'

She wants to ask if Lizzie really left the grounds earlier. If she even went to look for Nina or just hid somewhere and watched Aisa return. But to do so crosses a line. It would either break Lizzie's heart or crack her veneer. And what might be behind that surface? What might have been behind there all this time, hidden just below but reliant on no one being interested enough to look?

Because what happened to Jane back then? And what happened to Nina tonight? And does anyone else know about this secret layer? If the mechanic knocks on the door, there's no chance the sisters will hear it down here. Rescue could have been and gone already, if it's even coming at all.

Lizzie seems to be waiting for her to say more, but instead Aisa reaches suddenly for the next doorknob and shoves it open. It's dark again and Lizzie switches her phone flashlight back on. She seems to know what she's looking for, has an air of ownership, as if this is her domain now.

It's a bigger room this time, more like the back bedrooms on the upper level. An old brass bed lies on its side without a mattress, a dry old water jug sits on a dusty side table and there's a tall wooden wardrobe shoved against the wall. A servant's room from long ago, perhaps.

'What was that?' Lizzie whispers, looking around.

'What?'

'A noise,' Lizzie says, pointing towards the wardrobe. 'I think it came from in there.'

'Open it then,' Aisa says, backing away slightly. She didn't hear anything. Nothing at all over the rush of her own blood through her ears.

In her hand, the candlestick feels heavy and slick with sweat, despite the cold. She lifts it slightly, holding its end in her other palm, readying herself. Is all of this a trick?

Lizzie approaches the wardrobe like she's walking to the gallows. A small brass key sticks out of one of the doors and she turns it, looking back at Aisa just once before pulling it open. Then the other door. Nothing. An empty wardrobe, no hangers, no clothes, nothing. Aisa breathes out in relief.

For a moment, nothing happens and then a small black shape flies out from underneath the wardrobe, zigzagging through the room. Aisa recoils, but Lizzie stands stock-still. 'It's a mouse,' she says, the corner of her lips twitching in a half smile.

The little body bashes into the bed frame and then slips behind it, out of view.

50

LIZZIE – 3:10 a.m.

'Oh my gosh,' Lizzie says with relief, her hand on her heart. 'Reepicheep the Mouse,' she says, 'from Narnia.' She smiles but Aisa doesn't return the sentiment. Chastened, Lizzie leads the way back out into the foyer.

'Come on,' Aisa says. 'Open the next door. Please?'

Impatience and fear are radiating off Aisa. Lizzie can hear her sister's breath, can tell from the way she's shuffling her feet on the stone floor that she's fed up. The glow that Lizzie warmed herself with earlier is fading. *Come on, get yourself together.*

Lizzie closes her eyes to collect herself, takes a deep breath and then opens the third door briskly. At first, she can't make anything out. It's just a squirming pile of darkness. But then her eyes adjust, and her flashlight catches them and she slams the door shut.

Spiders. So many spiders, crawling over a pile of charred logs and charcoal. Lizzie loves every single living creature, except them. She hates them in fact; she hates them so much and she can feel them on her. She pats herself down and shakes her hair, tears at her coat to pull it from her.

'There's nothing on you,' Aisa says crossly and louder than Lizzie would like. But she can still feel them on her skin, under

her skin, in her ears. She can feel their webs around her throat, feel their evil lightness, barely there but there nonetheless as they move around inside her sleeves.

She throws her coat on the floor and then starts to pull at her jumper.

'Lizzie, get a grip! Jesus Christ!' Aisa grabs Lizzie's arms and pins them to her side. 'There's nothing on you,' she shouts, pushing Lizzie away in defeat and then picking up her coat. Aisa shakes it firmly, turns it inside out and shakes it again. 'Put this back on and pack this crap in.'

It takes all of Lizzie's effort to squeeze out the images, to accept what Aisa is saying and to keep her clothes on. She tentatively pushes her arms back into her coat sleeves and ignores the itching on her scalp.

'Sorry, Aisa, you know how I get.'

'Yeah,' Aisa says. 'I know. You wouldn't hurt a living thing, would you.' It feels more like a statement than a question, and a strange one at that.

And now they are standing outside the last door that Nina could be behind. This is the last chance before they accept that Nina really isn't here.

51

AISA – 3:12 a.m.

The final door. A black hole in her memory for all these years is suddenly filled in, rich with garish detail and alive with fear. She feels it like electricity across her back, her scalp. She has woken from nightmares on the cusp of pushing this door open, yet all the time she'd forgotten it was real. Can there be anything more frightening than realising that a bad dream was actually a memory, and then finding yourself back in it?

She and Nina had been together, playing hide-and-seek in the house. Lizzie and Jane had been somewhere else, they'd paired off as soon as Mum had brought them here. But they'd met back down here, by accident or design, she doesn't remember. And then the four of them had faced this door.

Aisa draws a deep breath, puffs her chest up and juts her jaw like she did thirty years ago, on this spot. When Jane asked who was brave enough to go through the door with her.

'What's in there?' eight-year-old Lizzie had asked, backing away slightly.

Jane had smiled, but not a nice smile. Not a menacing smile though, it was more... sad. Nina hadn't wanted to go in. She was already sweating in the enclosed foyer, already uneasy and making noises about leaving.

'One of you has to go in, fair's fair,' Jane said. It was classic kid logic. Because no one *had* to go in, why should they? But none of them said that.

They decided to draw straws. Where did they even get straws from? Nina had them, that's right. They used some candy cigarettes, warm from her pocket, the little card with a footballer on still inside the box. They each had great stacks of those little men back home, fought over them even though none of them followed football.

They fought over everything, Aisa and Nina loudly, but Lizzie through watery eyes and pleading to their mum. Which sister would go first on a swing or sit in the front seat of the car or choose the first Quality Street at Christmas. It drove their parents bonkers. So their dad had taught them about drawing straws. And they'd taken to it with such gusto, refusing to do anything without drawing straws, that *that* had driven their parents bonkers too. But that day, down here, it was still a novelty. One Jane had adopted as her own too.

Nina had passed the pack over and Jane had teased three candy cigarettes out. Three, not including herself, because Jane was going in regardless. Aisa had puffed up with pride. She, Aisa, was to draw a straw alongside her much older sisters and their friend, to do older girl stuff. Brave girl stuff.

Jane had snapped one of the candy cigarettes, the sudden violence of sound cracking through the dusty passageway, then turned her back to arrange them.

The sisters lined up as if preparing to take medicine, and then each pulled a candy cigarette straw.

Why didn't Aisa remember this earlier? Why didn't her memory plunge her back here as she'd pulled the broken match to go out on that wretched journey to the village. The outcome was the same: Aisa's small hand holding the short straw and

her sisters immediately panicking and petitioning for a redo. And the fury, the outrage of that. 'No,' she'd said, her little voice ricocheting off the stones, 'I'm going in.'

'Why won't you ever back down?' her mum used to say, but a thread of affection ran through the complaint and always seemed to Aisa like tacit encouragement. So she wore it with pride, her bravery, her boneheadedness. She may be smaller, she may be younger, but she's braver than the other two put together. Brave to the point of recklessness, but there's a cost to everything.

And that day, nearly thirty years ago, she was damned if she was backing out. Even as her knees quivered beneath her shorts, as her heart banged so loudly she thought the others might hear, she still stood stiff next to Jane as the bigger girl put her hand on the doorknob. The same doorknob that juts vulgarly out at them in the dim light now.

Jane had paused for effect, and Aisa had watched her intently. But the pause had grown, and Jane had sagged a little, the moment trickling out of Aisa's grasp. 'Are you sure you want to go in, Aisa?' Jane had whispered. 'It's OK if you don't.'

But Aisa had protested. Of course she had. 'I want to go in.'

Behind her, Nina and Lizzie had been whispering about something and when Jane opened the door and Aisa followed her in, the older sisters had run off laughing. But Aisa stood her ground and stayed. She had stepped in, matching Jane's stride, ignoring the retreating footsteps behind her, the wild laughs.

Footsteps... Lizzie *had* run off. She wasn't lying about that. Aisa closes her eyes with relief. Lizzie wasn't lying, and she couldn't have done anything to Jane – she had fled and left Aisa with Jane. And she surely didn't do anything to Nina earlier tonight either. Of course she didn't.

Aisa turns to Lizzie now, haunted and pale in the light from

her phone. She is limp, weak, watered down. She is good. She is kind. She is Lizzie.

'Lizzie,' Aisa says, nursing the return of that peculiar but reassuringly familiar mix of pity, irritation and affection that Lizzie always generated. 'Let me go in first, OK?'

Lizzie could never hide her reactions, and right now relief washes through her face. 'Are you sure?'

'I'm one hundred per cent sure.'

52

ROSEMARY – July 1992

The girls are with me at the manor again today and my nerves are on fire. I have spent nearly twenty years calmly keeping the cogs turning without so much as a squeak. Now, every sound I hear, I imagine it's them smashing something ancient or bursting into William's office. They've paired up and run off, Nina with Aisa and Lizzie trailing around after Jane. It was so much easier when we could still afford a childminder.

At least I can feed them a big lunch here. Since Cook had her win on the horses and quit, it's fallen to me to prepare meals when I'm here, and I know there's always more than will be consumed. Then I can just do buns for dinner. I wonder what it's like to not measure out your life in meals and money.

I'm hanging out the sheets, usually my favourite task. There's something incredibly satisfying about pushing dirty, smelly linen into a washing machine and pulling it out a few hours later with all human traces washed away. Hanging the washing out on a warm day, the air scented with the lashings of fabric conditioner I'd never use so liberally at home, the fabric fluttering gently in the breeze. But today, I'm distracted, watching as at least some of the girls leg it around the garden chaotically, voices a bit louder than I'd like. Then I hear the shot.

It's like in a film. The sound cracks through the sky, the birds flap up like they're on fire and in the corner of my eye, something thumps to the floor. I drop a sheet in the basket and scan the garden for a clue to what has just happened, reassurance that the girls are OK. My pulse beats in my ears and my eyes take nothing in.

'Nina!' I call, my voice sounding outside of myself in the panic. 'Aisa! Lizzie!' I see the blue of Lizzie's T-shirt first, then her legs sticking up from the ground like two chipolatas. I gasp and then I'm running, and Nina is running from somewhere else, and Aisa is running from behind a tree and I get there just as Jane, who was God knows where, is yanking Lizzie up by her arm, laughing.

'I panicked and fell over,' Lizzie says, blushing the colour of a phone box.

For a moment, I can't speak.

'Lunch in ten minutes, Jane,' I say, unable to look my own girls in the eye for reasons I genuinely don't understand. As I turn towards the house to start preparing tea, I slam into Alan's chest; two pheasants hang limp in his hand.

'What the f—'

'Rosemary, you can't keep bringing your girls here like this,' he says, looking to the side of me, struggling to make eye contact, even when we were teenagers.

'Excuse me?'

'It's not safe, Ro. I'm shooting rabbits and birds, and I'm not looking for little girls running about.'

'It's only occasional,' I say firmly, although the thought of what might have been is still stirring my guts with a spoon. 'So why don't you tell me when you're planning to go on a shooting spree and I'll keep them home.'

'It's not like that,' he says, his gentle voice more urgent than usual. 'I'm reacting, the shooting's not planned.'

'Don't react then,' I say, and I can see him suck in air to reply when the doorbell rings out from the house. I'm glad of a reason to storm off.

The man at the door is a bit older than me, as narrow and bent as a banana. He's wearing stiff clothes that must be boiling him, and giant sunglasses. He clears his throat but waits for me to talk, squinting behind his brown lenses.

'Can I help you?'

He's carrying a battered briefcase and I expect he's trying to sell something, but he might be here for William, who does occasionally get visitors, so I need to be polite. I look him up and down and my heart sinks as I realise that this strange creature could be yet another private detective. They're all shifty and they never find Selina, nor give William reassurance that she won't sneak back and swipe Jane.

'I'm, um, well, I was hoping . . .' he dries up and looks at me desperately. His face looks familiar, but I can't place him.

'Are you here to see someone?' I prompt, peering round him to see if there's a company name on his car, but I don't see any vehicles. I am using what Bob refers to as my Hyacinth Bucket voice, something learned from the long-gone housekeeper whose footsteps I now walk in.

'Well, not a person, I'm here to see the house. If I may?'

'The house?' I look behind me, heart cantering suddenly. Is William selling the house? But no, I remember, he's not allowed.

He wipes his forehead with a very bright white handkerchief, stuffs it back in his pocket and scrunches up his eyes. 'I'm sorry,' he says, 'I'm not explaining myself well.'

'Would you like to come inside and have a glass of water?'

'Thank you, I've had a long walk.'

'You walked here?'

The man nods, looking embarrassed, but I can hardly judge him, I was on foot twice last week and have the blisters to show for it.

William was absolutely adamant he wasn't to be disturbed today, so I quietly encourage the man into the library, where no one goes anymore. When William first moved back, he and Selina stocked these shelves together. Removing most of the traces of the Brigadier's collection and filling it with their own. It was the happiest I ever saw them, even though they must have been filled with dread about their new lives. I think they used the books as a kind of language to each other, choosing titles and holding them up and laughing, or smiling while I slid a tray of tea and coffee in and asked a few inane questions. I've never been much of a reader.

William had long stopped claiming to be a writer by then, but he still made noises about being a reader. As far as I know, he hasn't picked up a single book since the separation. I could probably get away with not dusting them at all, but I will. I always will.

Once through the door, the man swallows so hard that I hear it through his throat, and grinds to a halt in the centre of the room.

'Take a seat, I'll get you that drink.'

In the kitchen, I peer through the windows as I run the tap, but I can't see the girls now. I tiptoe past the office, but the door is open, the room empty. At the foot of the stairs, I can hear William moving around upstairs. As I slip back into the library, the man shoves a book back onto the shelves and gratefully takes the glass.

I wait for him to drain it and then he hands it back, his

sunglasses now pushed up through his hair and his darting eyes more visible.

'Thank you,' he says, 'that was very kind. I was flustered and ... it's taken a lot to come here.'

'Are you here to see the master of the house?' I ask.

'The Brigadier?' He stands up straight and looks around as if expecting him to walk in.

'The Brigadier died, I'm afraid, a few years ago now.'

'He did? And his wife?'

'Her too.'

He smiles, then immediately covers his mouth. 'I'm sorry. I'm very sorry.'

I look at him closely. 'Don't be,' I say. 'You stayed here didn't you? I thought I recognised you.'

'Rosie?'

'Close,' I say. 'Rosemary.'

He looks at me with pity now. At least he got out.

'You haven't changed,' he says and we both smile awkwardly, because he has changed beyond recognition and I should have. I should have moved on long ago. 'I've come to make peace with it,' he says, then takes a long gulp of water. 'It's bigger, in my memories. It's ...' He grapples for the word, his sad face suddenly screwing in on itself and turning red. 'It's worse,' he says, 'in my head.'

'I'm sorry, I don't remember your name, I think you were here when I was really new.'

He starts to pace, one finger tracing the titles, frowning as he clatters into the edge of the shelves like a daddy-long-legs.

'It's Daniel. Daniel Pettyweather.'

Daniel. Those eyes. I see them now, see him, as he once was. A timid boy who struggled to keep up with the physical demands of the work. I remember seeing two others helping him, and

them getting in trouble too. *He won't learn. He won't grow strong.* And I remember the three of them going for Reflection. Slipping in each other's wake like minnows.

It was worse, Bob told me, for the last one in line. He'd have to watch it twice before it was his turn. But I don't want to think about that. I never want to think about that.

'Is this a … normal house now?'

I nod. 'No boys,' I say gently. I know the memories are painful and these men need handling softly. 'Those days are long gone.'

The door opens and Alan comes in, looking at the man as if I'm not here. 'I think you need to go,' he says, and then they face each other and flinch. Were they here at the same time? It's too hazy to remember the specifics, and William had all the records burned when he first moved in.

Alan is a foot taller than Daniel, who shrinks away and looks at me for help.

'It took a lot to come here,' he says to me. 'I just wanted to see it. I don't want any trouble.'

'You'll get no trouble,' Alan says softly. 'But it's time to go.'

❖

53

LIZZIE – 3:14 a.m.

Nothing happens.

The door doesn't budge.

Aisa's arm falls back to her side.

Lizzie can hear her own heartbeat roaring in her ears and exhales more breath than she thought possible. 'She can't have gone in there if it's locked,' she says, only briefly relieved. Because if Nina's not down here, where is she?

Aisa says nothing. Not even the F-word. Then she grabs the door handle again, as if sneaking up on her prey, and twists it urgently, shoving the door with her shoulder.

Nothing.

She sags then, but starts feeling around the door, growing more frenzied as she moves. 'Lizzie, light,' she snaps, and for a moment, Lizzie doesn't understand, but then she holds her phone up, following Aisa's movements with the beam. 'Look,' Aisa says, nudging Lizzie's hand up higher so the phone light picks up the detail of a heavy metal bolt across the top of the thick door. A detail the dim bulb lights did not reach.

'Shouldn't we—' Lizzie starts, but it's too late. Aisa has drawn it back and twisted the doorknob again and this time it opens with a creak.

Aisa pushes the door and makes to step in, but stops suddenly and takes a big gulp of air. 'It looks the same,' she whispers.

Lizzie puts a hand on Aisa's shoulder, but she shakes it off and steps inside. Lizzie follows, cautiously, with the phone held aloft, but it's not totally dark in here. A few more of the bulbs are strung along the wall and she can see and hear how they're powered now – a generator buzzes softly in the gloom.

This is not an empty room, it's filled with bric-a-brac, as if someone had scraped all the left-behind mess from over the years and chucked it here to be dealt with later. A couple of wooden chairs that she remembers belonging to a full set in the dining room. Old gardening equipment, a big watering can, a length of hose. There's a sickly sweetness in the air. Rot?

The door closes behind them and Lizzie rushes to it, props it open with an old paint can. The bolt... If that fell across, they'd be screwed. Why would there be a bolt on the outside, anyway?

'It doesn't look like anyone is here,' Lizzie whispers.

Where on earth is Nina?

They stand still in the centre of the room as their eyes adjust, and the shadows take shape. There is another source of grey light, which makes Lizzie jump. It's a boxy old TV on a trolley, with a video player underneath, the kind they'd wheel in at school to show an old Disney film on the last day of term. A cord runs from it to the generator and the screen is on, flickering but soundless. Who was watching it? Aisa looks at her, but she has no answers, and she returns her eyes to the walls.

When Lizzie looks closer, she realises with a jolt that there is a pale picture on the screen, it's not just a grey blur. She's looking at the very passageway they just walked down. Then the screen jumps, changes, and now it's the foyer they were just in, with the doors they just tried.

'Aisa, look.' Lizzie points at the screen. 'Just watch.'

Aisa squats down in front of the TV and her mouth drops open. She looks up at Lizzie, who nods frantically, and then back to the screen again.

They watch, transfixed, as it jumps from one scene to the next. Living room. Library. Dining room. Office. Kitchen. The outside of the house now, the untidy once-lawn and the scrubby drive. Now the back, the old shed and the old door to the kitchen.

Someone was watching them? A security guard? Why wouldn't they come and speak to them? Help them?

She hears something behind her and turns to look, startled. There is still no one there. But by the back wall, there are more signs of someone. The someone who must have set this monitor up. The someone who must have watched them come in. The someone who ... who hurt Nina?

There's an old-fashioned camp bed on the floor, a blanket on it. They both stare at the same time, squinting to make out the shape. Because it's not just a blanket, it's not limp, it's bulging. It's ...

Aisa is running over and tearing back the fabric before Lizzie can stop her.

'There's someone there!'

54

ROSEMARY – July 1992

I rush to open the front door, dumbstruck by Alan's never-before-seen strictness. A gentle giant, I've always called him. 'A woolly woofter,' says Bob, though I know he cares for him deeply and would do anything for him. But I wouldn't cross Alan right now. His eyes fix on the man, his spine straightened to its full height so he fills up the hallway like a T. rex.

'OK,' Daniel says, looking between Alan and the open door. 'I just wanted to—'

'Daniel?'

We all turn and stare up the stairs, where William stands at the top, gripping the banister tightly.

'William?' Daniel says finally. '*You're* here?'

'I am,' William says, 'for my sins.' He takes a few steps down. 'Are you leaving already?'

Daniel looks at Alan, and then back at William, who nods.

'I see.'

Alan's cheeks flush and he stoops again, reduced back to his usual shape. 'I thought it was best...' He grinds to a halt.

'No matter,' William says, taking the rest of the stairs slowly. He pats Alan on the arm, who then scurries away without

another word. 'He is very protective,' William says, 'don't mind him.'

William and Daniel stare at one another for a moment, their eyes glassy and wide.

'Rosemary,' William says, without breaking Daniel's gaze. 'We'll take tea in the front room, please. Or coffee?'

Daniel swallows again, a noisy, ragged journey up and down his neck. 'Tea,' he croaks. 'Please.'

The tray clatters as I carry it through to the living room. William is sitting on one sofa and Daniel on the other. He has taken his suit jacket off and folded it next to him, but his face still looks like boiled ham.

I was due to polish this afternoon, so I'm conscious of the fine dust beginning to tide at the edges of the room. I don't know if William ever notices such things, or if he ever comes in here. He just seems to bob between his office, the kitchen and his and Jane's bedrooms. It's not like at our house, where there's always some or all of us jammed on the sofa, arguing over what to watch and who has to get up to change the channel. Our front door opens directly onto the living room, the stairs run up the wall and it's the only route through to the kitchen. 'It's like Piccadilly Circus in here,' Bob says at least once a week, even though he's never been to London in his life.

'Can I help with that, Rosemary?' William says sharply and I realise I'm just standing in the doorway like a lemon.

I snap to and shake my head, carrying the tray to the coffee table and placing it carefully.

'Shall I pour?' I ask, but William waves me away.

I pull the door closed behind me but stay where I am, ear to the wood, trying to shut out all the other noises in the world. I don't know what I'm expecting. There are no voices coming

through the door and I'm about to walk away, assuming the wood is too thick, when I hear Daniel speak.

'I heard your parents are dead,' he says, and my eyebrows shoot up to my hairline. As opening gambits go, this one is bold.

'Thankfully so,' William answers.

I walk away, my nerves failing me.

Half an hour later, William and Daniel appear in the kitchen, where I'm sorting through the larder and making a list. Daniel pokes his head into the room and mutters something about having bread and milk in here. 'Sometimes that was all,' he added. 'All day, I mean.'

'I know,' William says.

'Until you came back, anyway.'

They go out into the hall and hesitate. I watch from the doorway of the larder as William soothes Daniel in a low, quiet voice. After a minute or so, William asks, 'Would you like to see …' but I can't make out what he says and Daniel is shaking his head emphatically.

'Everywhere else,' he says.

I hear them mount the stairs, a stilted pattern of sounds as if they're stopping to catch a breath every few steps.

When Daniel finally leaves a little later, William marches into his office and I hear the bolt slide across. I make a strong coffee, put a biscuit on a plate and knock on the office door.

'Yes?'

'It's me,' I say, uneasily. 'Can I come in?'

I wait, about to give up when I finally hear the squeak of the chair, his footsteps and the bolt.

The door opens suddenly inward.

'Coffee,' I say, and push past him before he can protest. He

needs it, I know he does. I put it carefully on the desk, not touching any of the paperwork – bills and something about stocks and shares, as far as I can see. I don't see anything about Selina, but I know it's there somewhere. The latest pointless report.

He's been crying, there's no mistaking it. His eyes are fringed in purple and his nose is runny.

'And a biscuit,' I say, placing a hand on his arm just briefly as I put the little plate down. The touch feels unnatural and I look away, a sudden rush of guilt and embarrassment. It's been so many years.

'He was one of the boys then,' I say, although I know. 'I vaguely remember him.'

'You would have been very young,' he says.

'So were you,' I say. And for a moment, I wonder if we're still talking about Daniel. 'He'd come back to—'

'Make peace with his memories,' he says, his voice thick. 'No one believed him, he said, so he started to think he'd imagined it.'

'That would drive me mad,' I say. 'Knowing things had happened and no one believing me or not being able to tell anyone.'

'Well, yes,' he says, and I regret crossing that line. I don't hold it against him for ending a summer fling all those years ago. If anything, I'm cross with myself for giving it so much credence.

'Do you think it helped him?'

'What?' he says, throwing back some coffee as if it was a shot of whisky.

'Coming here—'

'No, God no,' he says. 'That didn't help any of them, did it.'

I shrink at his expression. 'Sorry,' I say quietly. 'I meant, coming back here now. Proving to himself it all existed.'

'I don't know; it looks different now, and my parents are

long gone. The worst of it, the Reflection stuff, that's not there anymore is it.' It wasn't a question, but I shake my head anyway, the back of my neck prickling at the thought. 'At least I could tell him he didn't imagine it, though,' William says. 'But he seemed quite surprised that I'd come back here.'

He wasn't the only one, I think, but I say nothing.

'Rosemary,' he says quietly, putting his coffee cup back down. 'I really did try to help them.'

How? How exactly did running away to London help them?

'I should crack on,' I say, stepping away and closing the door behind me.

Back in the hall, I press myself flat to the wall, eyes closed, and catch my breath. I don't want to hear it. It's not my job to absolve him and his family.

I think about Daniel. About how old he must have been when he arrived. They were supposed to be sixteen, but some of them lied, hearing there was a place that would take them in no questions – or very few questions – asked. I was sixteen when I first arrived; it's easy to spot the gradients of your own age. A few of them would definitely not have been sold fags.

It must have felt like a sanctuary at first. Free food and lodging. Just a bit of labour to pay their way. Tops off in summer, roasting themselves golden as they trimmed hedges and picked fruit. Huddled in winter, sharing a jar, boys in a barracks. The mandatory lessons from the Brigadier might have sounded curi-ous, but just something to roll their eyes through. Same for the benign-sounding consequences when expectations of behaviour weren't met. Thinking about what you've done. Growth through reflection. God knows where he picked this stuff up, as he was certainly not a certified psychiatrist.

These were boys with nowhere else to go, boys who clung to

one another and tried to make it work, this last resort. But one by one, they all cracked. All except Alan, who outlasted everyone.

I am suddenly acutely aware of my girls. Of their soft little bodies. Their trusting brains, their open hearts. Of them here, in this house, swallowed up by what looks, at first, like a benevolent beast but can turn itself into a malicious monster. I want them with me. I think again of school holidays spent with them rather than *coping* with them, of paddling in the sea and sitting at the table helping them do art, or taking Lizzie to the zoo. One day, I tell myself, for what must be the thousandth time.

One day I'll give them everything they deserve. But right now, I want them in our little car, driving away. I don't want them treading on the same stones that poor Daniel trod. The same stones that my Bob once trod. Briefly, but enough to create ripples that we all still live with. God, I want to get away from here. Where the hell are the girls?

55

NINA – 3:10 a.m.

Nina wakes up with a start. Is that a voice? Maybe even voices? They sound far away, maybe even imagined.

And where am I? Why am I in pain?

Nina blinks, sits up a little more and waits for the dizziness to settle again. It's gloomy in here, wherever she is, but not pitch black. Bulbs dot the walls, casting a thin yellow light. There's no one else in here, that's clear. *Wherever here is.*

Gingerly, she tests her arms, her hands, tensing and turning them until they click. She's very sore, but nothing is broken there. Her back feels unbearably tender, as if she's been punched and kicked all over it, but her spine allows her to sit up, to twist around. She swallows, readying herself. She leans over, at the cost of her aching spine, and feels all the way down her left leg. It feels bruised in spots, but nothing is sticking out or broken. And now the other. Even before she reaches her ankle, it's screaming in pain. It hurt before she passed out, or fell asleep, or whatever, she remembers that, but not the how or the why.

It's dark here, no light, no windows, no fire. She's alone, she can tell. Alone, with a busted ankle and bruises all over her and a brain that feels like a battered pea rolling around her skull.

Nausea sweeps over her and she lies back down, then rolls onto her side and throws up over the side of her... whatever this is. A camping bed. Wet chunks of birthday cake land on the floor. When she's done, she feels better but more scared.

She has no idea how much time has passed or what happened. Her thoughts are scrambled and her memory is fuzzy. The car broke down... and she was looking around a house. A cold and empty place. Is she still in it? Did she hit her head? But she's on a bed, she didn't hit her head on a bed and then cover herself with a blanket, which she can feel slipping around as she moves.

Someone.

Someone else did it.

Someone else did all of it.

A shiver runs up her bruised body and chatters her teeth. It's dark in here, dimly lit by a few old-fashioned bulbs and the distant grey glow of some kind of screen in a far corner. No windows. The camp bed she's on is the old type, a metal frame, an austere piece of stretched canvas held in place with serious looking hooks. Her eyes adjust, and despite the distracting pain, she can see more now. No windows, one door. Her chest tightens. A tall ceiling, with old hooks hanging from it.

She eases herself to sitting and tries to remember what happened. Her sisters were with her. Did they put her to bed? Did they... did they leave her? Did she leave them? Something stirs. She left... one of them. They were in a room, weren't they, she and Lizzie in front of a fire. Lizzie was sleeping and Aisa had gone for help. That's right, and Nina came up to look for... She remembers that bathroom. A hood. Eyes. Oh fuck!

Nina doesn't know what to do. Nina always knows what to do, but not now. Her sisters are in danger, maybe already hurt

by the person who hurt her. She's the oldest sister, *in loco parentis*, the buck stops with her. Just like it did in the delivery suite, when she made a catastrophic error with her last delivery. And now she's out of ideas again. And she's scared. And she's in a ton of pain.

For the briefest of moments, she wants her mum and dad. She'd wanted them back then too, hadn't she, when she was far younger? That day. That last day, when they came here while their mum worked and she was in charge of Aisa. And of course Aisa wanted to play hide-and-seek, she always did. But she'd hidden too well, for too long, and it hadn't felt like a game.

And where are her sisters now? Aisa was out in the storm, traipsing around in the dark, did she come back? And Lizzie was asleep in front of the fire. Asleep and vulnerable. Oh God, what the hell has happened?

She hears a noise. Footsteps outside. Whoever put her here, whoever scraped her off the floor of the bathroom, is back. Fuck. She lies back down and pulls the blanket over her head and tries to stay still.

The door opens with a crack. Two people come inside. She can tell from the footsteps, and the whispering. The whispers sound female, but she has her arms over her ears, her head muffled by a blanket. And female doesn't necessarily mean safe. She knows that, though she hates to admit it.

If these are the people that put her here, they know full well where she is anyway. But they might believe that she's still sleeping. Still knocked out. Maybe they think she's dead?

More whispering. She strains to hear, catching only wisps. It sounds like someone said, 'It doesn't look like anyone is here.'

But I am here. You put me here. Unless . . . ?

Still she stays quiet, motionless. It could be a trap.

More whispering, almost audible but not enough. She swallows, hears footsteps coming closer.

'There's someone there!'

Is that Aisa?

Before she can react, the blanket is pulled back from over her and she scrunches her eyes up in fear and balls up her fists protectively.

'Nina!'

'Oh, thank God it's you,' Nina says, sitting up and immediately reaching for her aching head, eyes filling with a sudden shock of tears. Aisa sits down next to her, rocking the camping bed and then wrapping her skinny arms around her. Nina's bruises hurt so much under the pressure that she feels on the brink of vomiting again, but she doesn't want to stop her little sister. 'Aisa,' she manages.

Lizzie rushes over. 'Thank goodness, Nina,' she says.

'What the hell happened to you?' Aisa says as she kisses Nina's face, just like she did as a little girl. 'You smell of vom.'

'I think someone hit me,' Nina says slowly, the words feeling misshapen in her mouth. 'And then I woke up here. And I was sick, be careful where you tread.'

'We need to get out of here,' Aisa says. 'Can you walk?'

'I don't know.'

Her own voice sounds odd, as if she's speaking through water, or she's drunk. Seeing her sisters has rooted her to the spot, a wave of exhaustion following in the slipstream of relief. They need to get out, they have to get away, but she really wants to fall back asleep.

'Come on,' Aisa's voice is insistent now as she and Lizzie help Nina to stand. There is a searing pain in her ankle, not to mention her back and head.

They start to shuffle through the room towards the door, pain

pulsing with every step. As they pass a damaged section of wall, Aisa flinches and stops for a moment. 'I was looking in the wrong place,' she mumbles.

'What are you looking at?' Nina mumbles, but then she catches sight of the boxy old television screen in front of her. 'Oh God, look.'

56

ROSEMARY – July 1992

As I comb the house for the children, I whisper the prayer my mother used to say with me when she was putting me to bed. It probably doesn't sound that comforting, what with the clanger dropped in line four, and I don't think it's even a proper prayer, but a bastardisation of something she heard on TV. But it's comforting to me. She even said it the night my dad died, her voice catching in a way she's not allowed it to since.

Watch over us, watch over us.
Tuck us safe to bed.
Watch over us, watch over us.
'Til we're all long dead.

Although if there is someone watching over us, he or she has really dropped the ball. I don't lie safely in bed at night, I lie there listening out for signs that the landlord has come good on his threats and is going to turf us out. Or that our car is being towed away. Or I lie there and imagine how things could be. I walk myself through a day in my perfect imagined life, from the moment of waking until falling asleep. The breakfast we would eat, the house we would have – a room for each of the girls – the way I would fill my time and theirs if it was up to me. Sometimes, this is a comfort. Other times, more often, it feels so

far removed from my real life that it becomes a self-flagellating whip in my hand. I don't want much, that's the saddest part of it. I don't want much and it's mostly for them, but it's still out of reach.

I check the front room, leaving the tea tray at first, but then think better of it and gather it all sloppily. The still-full pot weaves around and knocks over the milk jug and the drips beat onto the floor as I rush into the kitchen. I slide it all onto the sideboard, making even more of a mess. This is not like me. Bob jokingly calls me Cool Hand Luke because I can hold a hundred things in my hands at once, and often have Aisa climbing up me at the same time. Although I don't think Bob has seen *Cool Hand Luke*.

I check the larder in case the kids are on some kind of food raid, but they're not here. I pause and breathe, in and out as slow as I can manage. There is no need to worry, they're just playing and having fun.

They're not in the library either, where Selina's books lie accusingly on shelves, no longer read. I rush upstairs, listening for signs of life but hearing none. Aisa is obsessed with hide-and-seek at the moment and the disused bedrooms at the back are full of ideal crawl spaces, but she's not here. None of them are. Nor in the bathroom.

Alan's room on the corner is next and I wince as I open it – expecting to find a dead raven in his bed or something – but there's nothing here. No sign of the kids. Nothing weird either, and no real sign that he ever sleeps here. Bob told me that he still sleeps in his clothes, in case he has to leave in a hurry. He's been here for years, longer than me, and he is absolutely, almost frighteningly dedicated to William and this place, but he's still expecting to run. I can believe it, there's nothing here

239

that couldn't be scooped into a rucksack in less than a minute. Poor Alan.

They're not in the linen cupboard, so I rush on to Jane's room, which is the obvious place really. It was once William's room, from childhood through to his early twenties. He had the same bed that Jane has now, the same bookshelves were then loaded with hardbacks and poetry books, which were eventually absorbed into the library. Even in my panic, my mind conjures up a memory of William and me walking around the woodland behind the house, him quoting Wordsworth as I swooned. Idiot.

The girls aren't here, but I can see the detritus of their earlier games, which reassures me a little. Jane and Lizzie ran straight up here when we first arrived, and the doll's house has been pulled out into the middle of the room, so they must have played with that for a while. Alan did a good job on it, the delicate attention to detail brings a lump to my throat. It is a perfect replica of the place he loves, despite no evidence it has ever loved him back.

The curtains in each window are the correct colours, made from scraps of fabric we scratched together that were pinned up carefully by his giant fingers. I tease the windows open to look closer and gasp as a tiny skull rolls out. What the bloody hell?

'Lizzie!' I shout, standing up and running back out of the room. 'Nina! Aisa!' William must be able to hear me. For years, I have perfected the silent creep-around, but now I don't care. I rush down the stairs and out the front door, listening for their voices as I stand in the middle of the gravel turning circle, fighting nausea. I should have found them by now.

'What's wrong?' Alan says, appearing from the side of the house.

'Have you seen the girls?'

'Your girls?'

'Yes, my girls, not that little weirdo, Jane,' I say, before I can stop myself, the image of the skull rolling around my mind.

Alan flinches as if I'd slapped him. 'Don't say that,' he says quietly. 'She's not had it easy. Neither of them have.'

'No, I know, I'm sorry. You know I love Jane to bits, but have you seen the kids or not?' I say and he shakes his head.

As I rush off, he calls after me, 'I'll look too.'

57

AISA – 3:17 a.m.

'What?' Aisa asks, punch-drunk from relief that Nina is alive but nauseous with fear knowing someone really did attack her and drag her here.

And this room ... it *is* the one she saw all those years ago. Those were not nightmares, they were memories.

It was just her and Jane then. Jane was Lizzie's best and only friend. Aisa knew her too, but they had never been alone together. Yet she followed Jane into this room. She trusted her.

In her memory, the wall was dead ahead when she first entered the room, which would make it the back wall that Nina's camp bed was pushed up to, but now she knows why she had it twisted. Thirty odd years ago, she'd actually walked in sideways, crab-like, with one ear to the door, listening as her sisters legged it and left her. So she was facing the side wall, Jane to her left, tugging her in further.

'I was the one who found them,' Jane had said proudly, the excitement rattling her breath a little. She'd grabbed Aisa's hand then, her palm unfamiliar after holding her sisters' hands, like wearing someone else's shoes. 'No one else knows,' Jane had whispered.

The room was full of junk then too, Aisa thinks, and there

were some tools on the floor near the gap. A tiny little shovel, and a blunt knife like you'd use to ice a cake. A small pile of stones had been stacked neatly.

'I've been coming down here while Daddy works upstairs,' Jane said. 'On the days your mum isn't working.'

Aisa hadn't known what to say. She had stared and stared at the gap in the stones, trying to understand what she was looking at.

'I have to be really careful,' Jane continued, her hand growing damper against Aisa's own. 'I can't let it just … fall out.'

'Let what fall out?'

'Look closer,' Jane said.

And Aisa had. Pulling her hand from Jane's and stepping closer to the wall, pressing her nose to the cool black gap between the stones and squinting.

'Fucking look!' Nina's voice cuts through Aisa's memory, snapping her back to the present so fast she feels sick.

Nina is leaning on both of them for support, pointing at the boxy old TV.

'Oh shit, it's gone.'

The screen shows the empty living room where they'd set up camp hours ago. It's barely visible, more snow than detail, but they can make out the sofas where they'd spent their time earlier.

'Was someone watching me sleep earlier?' Lizzie says.

Nina shrugs, her voice slurs with exhaustion. 'Probably. Keep looking.' Lizzie and Aisa stare at the screen.

'What are we looking for?' Aisa asks.

'I thought I saw someone.'

'The one who hit you?' Lizzie whispers.

'I don't know,' says Nina, her voice smaller than usual. 'I need to know. We need to know so we can work out what to do.'

They stand in silence, Nina's weight dragging the side of

Aisa's body down, all their faces glowing like black-and-white photos in the silvery-grey light of the screen. The screen seems to change more slowly now they're watching intently. Showing the empty hallway for an age and now the library, lounge, office and dining room. Now the kitchen, the big disused fridge looming uselessly in shot. Time ticks, but still they stay. Watching the screen change to show a bedroom. The big empty one, scraped clean of any traces of the past.

Still they wait, Lizzie clearly itching to get out, fidgeting on the other side of Nina. 'We're not safe here. We really should—' But as the shot changes again, Aisa sees what Nina must have seen. In the middle of the screen, now showing Jane's bedroom, a figure sits on the bed. A small doll in their hands, the doll's house on the floor and something on the bed by their leg. Their face obscured by a hood. They stare, each trying to recognise, trying to make out the details.

'Is that a fucking gun?'

The camera cuts away.

58

ROSEMARY – July 1992

I've checked the whole house through. Well, everywhere except William's office, but he's sealed in there like an iron lung, there's no one getting in or out. My head swims, when did I last see them? Lunchtime, or... Yes, Aisa snuck up on me when I was stretching to reach something in the larder. I snapped at her. My baby.

Nina can't have been far behind because Aisa said she was going back to her. But maybe... I told them not to roam too far, but it's all relative. At home, 'not too far' is the patch of green opposite the house that all the neighbourhood kids play on. Not too far here is... the horizon?

I go out the front first, check they're not waiting by the car. Wishful thinking, there's no one there. I check the old fountain – Aisa is small and silly enough to have climbed into it – but it's just full of rainwater and a faint trace of green slime.

The trees mask the driveway, so I pace down it a little way, but I don't think they would have come here, there's nothing but miles of fields this way, it would take them hours to walk home.

These trees must be centuries old. They've barely grown in the twenty years since I first gaped up at them, yet they're hundreds of feet high. I wonder, just briefly, if Daniel paused to look up

at them. I wonder how far he's walked since he left. If he ran as fast as he could to get away, or collapsed against the pillars of the gate, catching his breath or vomiting. Did he see the girls?

A thought punches me in the stomach, but I talk myself down almost immediately. He couldn't fight his way out of a wet paper bag and my girls aren't stupid, they'd not go off with someone like that. He doesn't even have a car to bundle them into. Still, I can't shake this ominous feeling.

I wonder if Bob would remember Daniel. Maybe there's more to him than his frailty suggests.

I peer around the right-hand side of the house, fringed by blackberry bushes that would take the whole place over if they were allowed. Alan hacks them down every autumn, and they climb back more aggressively than ever, thriving on their own destruction.

No one is there.

I cross in front of the house again, peering in the windows just in case, but it's dead inside. I skirt the left-hand edge of the building, brushing against its cool red stone as I go. I stop still and scan the grounds, squinting as if that will help me see through the trees that pepper the garden and then take over the land behind. I don't see anyone.

At the back of the house, the greenhouse is empty of people, full of tomato plants and bags of iron-rich soil that smell like blood.

I stop and listen, hoping that Aisa's loud laugh will ring out, but there's nothing, a void. Even the wind is still.

'Nina?' I call, gently at first. 'Aisa? Lizzie?'

Nothing.

'Nina!' I shout now, a Plimsoll line of panic reached, a point of no return. 'Nina! Where are you?'

I feel sick. How can all three of them – no, all four of them

246

– be gone. I imagine telling William that Jane has gone too. The thing he's spent years panicking about, building a bunker around her and refusing to let her live out in the world. Only for her to leave him just like Selina did.

I rush towards Alan's tent, the flaps still staked open like a smiling mouth. I can see already that there's no one there, but I have to check. I know Alan, I care for Alan, but sometimes it's the quiet ones. And he's troubled – the gods can strike me down for saying this, but all those boys were troubled. You never really know how trouble will re-emerge later on.

I poke my head inside. It smells of his sweat. There's an earthiness in my mouth, like I'm tasting him. He's been sleeping out here, a jug of water and a flannel sits in the corner, a pile of clothes neatly folded next to it. That old book he carries around, the one he used to read for comfort when I first met him. *The Coral Island.* I'm looking for ... I don't know what I'm looking for. I don't want to admit it to myself. Evidence of something bad. But there is nothing here that is not his. No clothes, no shoes, no signs of – as they say in the paper – a struggle.

I crawl back out and collide with something hot and warm. As I cry out in surprise, it says, 'What are you doing in my tent?'

I stand up with a start. 'I'm still looking for the girls,' I say, 'have you seen them?'

'No, I looked everywhere but ...' he stops. 'Why would they be in here?'

'Hide-and-seek,' I say, aware that I'm blushing.

'This isn't a good place for children,' Alan says, his voice almost lost to the warm air.

'That doesn't help,' I say. 'And you were a child when you first came. As good as.'

He says nothing.

It was a cruel thing to say, and it doesn't undo his point. It

wasn't a good place for him either. I've pieced together scraps from what he, William and Bob have variously said. Alan *was* a child – fifteen – running from home and pretending to be much older. He'd been in trouble with the police, I never knew what for, but Bob does. He was supposed to go to a borstal – a real one – only he got away. And he's been hiding ever since.

His big size was misleading, but as soon as he opened his mouth it must have been obvious he was underage. Still, they invited him in. He worked harder than anyone, but he still messed up. Got in trouble, was punished, but begged to be allowed to stay.

He was made to sleep outside, but he liked it so much that it wasn't a punishment and was moved to isolation somewhere else. Somewhere dark and frightening. When William came back after university, only twenty-one himself, he begged his father not to do that to Alan. Not to do it to any of the boys. Several times, he rescued him and brought him back out to his tent. But then William left, and the others did too. But still Alan stayed.

'I'm sorry,' I say, as he snatches up the book and hugs it like a baby. 'I just need to find them.'

59

LIZZIE – 3:21 a.m.

'We need to go,' Aisa says, tugging Lizzie's coat.

The paint can is still propped in the doorway and a small breeze slips in from the passageway and nips at Lizzie's skin. She pokes her head out, just quickly, but no one is there. Whoever was sitting on the bed is still there. Or at least, not down here. Yet.

'Will you be able to walk with our help?' Lizzie asks Nina, who nods, no longer arguing.

It's disorientating to see Nina like this. She's always been so strong and capable. Always the older sister who Lizzie was happy to hide behind. And even though Nina clashed with their mother so much as a teenager, rolled her eyes behind her back, tried to rally the sisters to gang up on her, Nina looks so like her that perhaps Lizzie was happy to let her act like a surrogate parent when Rosemary wasn't around. Same fair hair, same strength, same sharp nose and full-lipped smile. Nina was *almost*. Almost Mum. Almost enough. Until there was no Mum and no one could take that place.

'We shouldn't just rush out there though,' Lizzie says, finding that she has more of a voice now Nina is so quiet. 'They could

be on their way down here, we should let the camera do a sweep again and check.'

'Fuck that,' Aisa says, casting a look behind her at the wall. 'We just need to go.'

'Lizzie's right,' Nina says, her voice wavy and depleted. 'I'm not in any fit state to leg it if we cross paths.'

'Fine,' Aisa says, and Lizzie tries to hide the pride flushing through her despite everything.

Even though there is an armed gunman upstairs, sitting in wait on the old brass bed. Even though they're stuck here in a deadly situation. Even though someone clobbered her sister and dragged her into, effectively, a dungeon, Lizzie is still *thinking*. She is still breathing. Still putting one trembling foot in front of the other. Still speaking up and being *right*.

You can keep being you through anything, she realises. *You can stay awake through any nightmare.* It's a thought she files away for the future.

'Let's watch it through one more time,' Lizzie says, 'and check they're not on their way to us. Then we can go.'

60

NINA – 3:26 a.m.

They stare at the screen, huddling together like they used to when they watched horror films as kids. Only this time Lizzie and Aisa are flanking Nina, where it used to be Aisa in the middle, pretending she wasn't scared.

'I don't even know how you two found me,' Nina says, keeping her eyes on the screen. 'Or how I got in here.'

Aisa pulls away slightly and looks at her, head cocked to one side in a way that is so reminiscent of their mum. 'We found you 'cos we both remembered ... stuff. Remembered that this was down here and we'd looked everywhere else.'

'You searched the whole house and ... and it was empty?'

'Yes,' says Lizzie. 'We looked everywhere.'

'And then we came down here,' says Aisa. 'And this room was the last place we tried.'

'So that person up there—'

'Was either hiding or had gone away and come back, yeah.'

She thinks of the hood and the eyes. Who is it? Why are they still here?

'Maybe they wanted to pick us off one by one,' Nina says.

'We have to stay together,' Lizzie says.

Their eyes fix on the screen again. The image flicks to the empty kitchen.

'Was this door locked?' Nina asks.

Aisa nods. 'Bolt,' she says. 'On the outside, obviously.'

'Jesus, we need to get out of here,' Nina pants.

'We still need to check where the gunman is,' Lizzie says.

'It won't be long, Neen,' Aisa says.

Aisa is talking, but the words are receding, breaking across the surface as Nina sinks away from them. She can feel her sisters' arms around her aching shoulders. In the space between the bulbs, darkness squirms and sucks up air. The more conscious Nina becomes, the more she grows accustomed to the pain, the less she is able to cope with this enclosed space.

Not now. Please, not now.

But it's too late.

It begins to swallow her. She can't breathe, she can't see properly. She wants to claw her way out, wants to run, but her legs feel like stone and she's stuck to the ground through pain . . . and panic.

'The door,' she manages to say.

She can feel her sisters' warmth against her, can feel the tension in their bodies as they watch the screen, waiting for it to flip from the empty rooms to the bedroom. But Nina can't stay focused on the screen. The weight of the house smothers her. She scrunches her eyes shut. She feels trapped, the passageway no longer an escape but a snake, winding itself around this room, around her neck. She slaps her cheeks, one side, then the other. But it just makes tears spring from her eyes and that won't help.

'Open it. Open the door more.'

Nina leans on Lizzie, who keeps watching the screen, while Aisa pulls the door open more, carrying an old dining chair across to quietly prop it wide open.

Nina begins to breathe easier, counting her breaths, the way she was shown. Not by colleagues with expertise, but by a YouTube video sought in shame.

'One … two … three …'

'What are you doing?' Aisa asks, aghast.

'Focusing,' Nina manages to say, her voice calmer. Aisa opens her mouth but says nothing and looks back at the screen with Lizzie.

Nina is rarely scared as an adult. Not by heights when she climbs, not by the life-and-death decisions she makes at work. Not by meeting new people or leading training sessions with graduates. Not living alone and scooping spiders out of the bath, nor driving at night. Almost nothing scares her, except closed spaces.

And she was terrified down here in the passageway all those years ago. On that final day when they were still kids. She burns with the shame of it even now, but she'd wet herself. Just a tiny bit. But enough.

It was the fear of losing Aisa, the nightmare places her panic had led her to. Imagining her little sister bent out of shape somewhere, drowning in a pond or run over by a car. Or suffocating. She gasps for air now, the memory operating her body.

Then she'd finally found her down here. This creepy underground layer, the sense of being trapped down here, where no one knew to rescue them. The pressure of being the oldest.

That day thirty years ago, as Jane snapped the candy cigarettes Nina had been saving as a treat for Aisa, the desire to leave had quickly become a drumbeat in her head, then a cacophony in her chest and finally a physical pressure that took over her whole body. Not that she would have admitted it. Not that she ever would admit it.

And as they reached the final door that time, decades ago, the four of them burrowed as far underground as it was possible to be, Nina had felt her heart race even faster, a sickening rush that bubbled down to her guts. Then after Aisa had plucked the short straw, Nina's bladder started to go. She told Lizzie to tell the others they needed to leave and then just legged it. And the further she ran up that passage and out into the woods, the more she laughed. At herself, and then simply in wild relief. Lizzie was in hot pursuit, which for Lizzie was a chaotic stumble, and she may have been laughing too. Laughter is contagious, especially at that age.

Once they'd escaped, Nina had happily peed the rest out behind a tree. That's right, that's what they all did when they played in the woods. Alan had been walking towards his shed when they came bursting out and she remembers being conscious of hiding her bottom as she relieved herself. A new thing, a new way of having to think. And then pulling off her damp knickers and stuffing them in a knotty old hole in the bark, worrying what he would think if he found them.

'Feeling better?' Aisa asks, slipping her hand into Nina's.

'Yeah,' she says. 'A bit.'

Aisa isn't watching the screen properly, Nina realises. She keeps looking at the wall to the side of the TV, squinting in the thin grey light. She feels Aisa's weight shift a little, she's moving.

'What are you—'

'I just need to see, need to check I'm not going mad. Just keep leaning on Lizzie, OK?'

Aisa has split away from them and is walking nervously over to the wall. Nina and Lizzie keep watching the screen as it flips through the scenes.

'Can one of you shine a light over here?' Aisa says, her voice small.

Keeping her eyes on the screen as it shows the empty hallway, Nina turns her phone flashlight on and holds it up so it highlights the wall.

Aisa moves closer to the damaged section and peers in, then stumbles back so quickly she nearly falls over. 'Oh fuck.'

The camera is showing the upstairs landing now, but Lizzie and Nina have shuffled over to see what Aisa is reacting to. Nina peers through the gap in the stones, propped up by Lizzie, unsure what she's looking for until, like the moon emerging from behind a cloud, she sees it.

61

AISA – 3.35 a.m.

Jesus fucking Christ. I knew it. I knew it. I fucking knew—

62

LIZZIE – 3:35 a.m.

Oh my God, it's—

63

NINA – 3:35 a.m.

Shit.

She stares, uncomprehending.

No, she stares with *too much* comprehension. Nina knows exactly what she's seeing – exactly what Aisa must have seen when she was still tiny.

She looks at Aisa, still that same little girl, deep down. That same little girl that was telling the truth all those years ago. Who was laughed at and dismissed, who was told to stop making up stories. Called a drama queen, a fibber, an attention seeker. Their mum even taking Nina and Lizzie to one side and telling them to just ignore it. Not to engage. That Aisa would only get worse if she was encouraged, and they needed to be big girls and help their sister.

But Aisa was telling the truth all along. Sitting at the kitchen table with the Crayolas in the old biscuit tin, tongue peeping out of the corner of her mouth as she concentrated, carefully drawing what she'd experienced. Where did that picture go? That was at their great-aunt's house, of course it was, because they'd left their old home, the one in Moirthwaite. But she clearly didn't forget it.

When did she stop talking about it? Did she carry it all this time or absorb it so deeply even she didn't know it was there?

'Why didn't you say anything?' Nina manages to say. Images of what her little sister must have carried are still clouding her thoughts. *Poor Aisa*.

Aisa's eyebrows shoot up. 'Are you kidding right now?'

'What?'

'Why didn't I *say* something? I said something over and over! You all called me a liar.'

'No, I know, I'm sorry. I know you told us back then, I know that Mum... that we all—'

'Right then,' Aisa says.

'But that was *then* and we were just kids and... I mean, why didn't you say anything *now*? As an adult? Did you remember it this whole time?'

Aisa's eyes blaze and her fists curl, but then she sags and shakes her head. 'Not the whole time, no. It comes and goes, I think. I've had a few dreams about... And then tonight it all, y'know. It's like little bits and pieces were always there, but the whole thing, the whole *memory*, was just out of view. And I never wanted to see it anyway.'

'Oh, Aisa.' Nina reaches to pull her sister into a hug, but Aisa shakes her off. The fire is back in her eyes.

'Anyway, you can talk. Or rather *not talk*. Exactly how and when would I have told you any of this? Either of you?'

They both look over at Lizzie, who stands awkwardly in front of the screen, her palms up in surrender.

'What do you mean?' Lizzie says quietly, her wet eyes flicking between the screen, the wall and her sisters.

'We don't fucking talk!' Aisa shouts. 'We don't know anything about each other!'

Nina stumbles back in surprise and Aisa reaches to stop her falling, alarm on her face.

'Sorry, I'm sorry, Neen, it's not the time, I'm just…' She looks behind her at the damaged wall. 'It's a lot. Tonight. *That. This*. All of it. But it's not the time.'

'You're right though,' Nina says as she allows herself to be helped to a more stable stance. 'We don't talk, and I'm sorry. I get it. We should talk. I just… I need to sit down.'

Lizzie grabs another old dining chair and pushes it behind Nina. She sits heavily, nausea hitting again.

'Are you OK, Nina?' Aisa says, softly now.

'I'm bruised all over, we've just seen a… I mean, no. No, I'm not. And neither is she,' Nina points at Lizzie. 'And neither are you, Aisa. We're not OK tonight and I'm not OK, actually, in general.' Her sisters look at each other and then stare back at her. 'I made a mistake at work,' Nina says. It's the first time she's admitted it out loud and it surprises her. 'I screwed up, actually. Badly. And the baby nearly…'

'Jesus,' Aisa says.

'Yeah. The baby survived, but it could have gone differently. And if I'd got a second opinion, if I'd double-checked my assumption, it never would have got that far. Anyway, I lied about it and now I've been suspended, and I don't know what's going to happen and I don't know if I'll get to do my job ever again and—'

'You will,' Aisa says, squeezing her hand.

Lizzie nods, 'Yeah, you will. Everyone makes mistakes, you're only human.'

'Yeah, but the thing is…' Nina sucks in a lungful of the stale air. *Is she really going to say this?* 'The thing is that I don't even know if I want to do that job anymore. I don't know what I want to do and I think…'

God, where is this coming from?

'I think maybe I've not been honest about what I want from my life ... avoiding taking risks and, y'know, daring to love people ... and I've been using my job, you know, like an excuse.' She puffs out the breath she's been holding.

'Well,' Aisa says. 'Shit.' She looks behind her at the damaged wall and then raises her eyebrows at Nina. 'Tonight is full of surprises.'

'Um,' Lizzie says, apologetically. 'I'm really sorry to change the subject but ... the camera is going to show the bedroom any second and we need to know if they're still there.'

They stare at the screen. A shiver runs across Nina's shoulders and her vision clouds for a moment. She reaches for Aisa's hand, gripping it in hers like she always used to. She's so grateful when Aisa lets her, that she feels tears on her cheeks.

The screen finally reaches Jane's bedroom. The figure still sits on the bed, but as they watch, the figure slowly stands up.

'Oh shit,' Lizzie says and the others look at her in surprise. 'He could be on his way down here, we have to go. Now.'

64

ROSEMARY – July 1992

I've been outside too long. The girls could easily have made their way back into the house looking for me. The air is sticky and pressurised and I'm acutely aware of the sweat running down the inside of my legs.

'Can you keep looking out here?' I say and Alan nods. 'Thanks, Al.'

I push the back door open and step into the kitchen, shaded and cool, just the gentle buzz of the old fridge in the corner. There's no one in here, but I still call out for the girls, then for Jane.

My voice is quieter now, exhausted by the search. It doesn't make sense. We're in the middle of nowhere and there's four of them, they can't just disappear.

I step into the hall and then look inside the dining room. Nothing. They're not tangled in the curtains or wedged under the huge and largely redundant table.

When I first came, one of my jobs was to set it up for dinner each night. Two places, opposite ends, for the Brigadier and his wife. When William came back with Selina in tow, I did the same. Selina took one look at it and said, 'There's no fricking way I'm going to eat my dinner sitting there like Mr Peanut.' I

laughed despite myself and liked her even more. She was never going to last up here, I should have known it then. I should have warned her. Should have warned him. This place will eat your marriage and spit out the bones.

Back out in the hall, I see that William's office door is ajar. I can hear rustling inside and step closer, looking through the gap. He's sitting in his chair, papers strewn in front of him.

The normally untouched whisky decanter that I diligently dust every week is open on the desk, almost drained. An ashtray I've not seen in years sits on the desk, a couple of butts squashed in it. 'It's not enough,' he says. At first, I think he's talking to himself, but then I realise he's aware of me. He's looking straight into my eye as I press it to the space between door and frame.

I straighten up and step inside. 'What isn't enough?' I say, softly, as if approaching an injured animal.

'Everything I've done with their money.' His voice gurgles with the spirit that he must have swallowed far too fast. 'It's not made up for it.' He looks up at me, his eyes wet and red. 'And it's not brought her back.'

Her. I don't react. I can't react.

I walk closer, my palms held up. 'I know Daniel's visit upset you, but it's not your fault.'

'She was right,' he says, to himself more than me. 'I chose this place, I chose their ... bloody legacy and I let her go.'

'You didn't do anything wrong and you tried to ... Look, I'm sorry, William, I want to talk about this with you, but I need to find the girls first. Have you seen them?'

He shakes his head. The one thing he's feared more than Selina never coming back is Selina coming back and taking Jane. But he doesn't seem to realise that I mean Jane too. That she's missing.

'All this money,' he says. 'It pours in, it pours out and it doesn't help.'

I don't know, to this day, how his parents got their money. I'm sure brigadiers aren't paid millions, but there was a title somewhere in the family history, a lordship once removed or something. William's family inherited this house, and money with it. Shares, maybe. I don't know, it's not my world. I don't understand how rich people get their money, or how they keep it. Especially as they never seem to work. William was an accountant in London for a time, but not now... Maybe having money is work in itself.

And now his parents are long dead, William spends his time – and their money – trying to assuage his own guilt. I know he gives a lot to charity. He pays his staff fairly. I mean, it's still meagre, but I earn more per day here than Bob used to in the factory. It's still not enough without Bob's wage, but it's better than I'd get anywhere else around here. William can't possibly imagine, I'm sure, even if he thinks he can.

'I think it helps,' I say. 'I think it helps the charities that you give to, I think it helps the village, 'cos I know you always give generously, church fundraising and all that.'

That long summer that I was sixteen and he twenty-one, we could talk for hours. Anything I said seemed to fascinate him, hearing details of my life that I now recognise as a kind of poverty tourism. A glimpse behind the curtain. And I was fascinated by him. He knew so many facts, could quote so many poems. Now we struggle to say a sentence or two to each other. He's still so raw since Selina left, so bitter and lonely, that I'm scared to make things worse. This is the longest conversation we've had in years.

'And your money helps me,' I say, and he looks up. 'My wages,'

I add, looking down and wishing I hadn't started. 'Me and mine would be even more stuffed without them.'

'I envy you and yours,' he says and I laugh, despite everything. 'It's true,' he says, his cheeks growing red. 'Your lives must be so simple.'

'Right,' I say. Only a rich man could say something so bloody stupid. 'Have you seen the girls?' I say again.

'Which girls?'

'My girls and Jane.'

He frowns and tries to stand up, knocking the desk so that the glass lid of the decanter slides off and smashes on the floor. 'Jane?'

'Don't worry,' I say quickly, bending to pick up the pieces and chucking them in the waste paper bin. 'They're playing hide-and-seek but... I need to be getting home now and I need to find them.'

'Oh, OK,' he says, sitting back down. 'Does Jane play OK? Does she know the rules?'

'The rules?'

'Of hide-and-seek? She's never... I didn't think to...'

'Everyone knows the rules of hide-and-seek,' I say and realise too late that he's not really talking about Jane now. He's talking about himself.

William was his parents' prototype. The success story that buoyed them on to try to model other young men in his image. When he left for university, and his parents inherited this house, they seemed to truly believe that they could turn waifs and strays – as they were known in the village – into young men just like William. If they were taught discipline and self-reflection. If they were educated and exercised. It was, of course, total bollocks. William turned out good and kind and bright despite their coldness, their rules. And William's parents

didn't have any of the skills needed to help. The young men and boys coming through these doors were knackered and bent out of shape. Runaways, addicts, drinkers. In need of a bed and a little cash. They were not looking to become an experiment, a Frankenstein's monster.

William is looking up at me now, with wet, worried eyes.

'Don't worry,' I say. I think of the skulls in the doll's house, Lizzie's reticence to come here sometimes. 'Jane plays really nicely with Lizzie. You've done a good job with her.'

For a moment, there's the glimmer of the old William I remember, of the old danger, the dormant attraction. 'Rosemary,' he says softly. 'I'm sorry I just left like that, back then. I was young and—'

'Rosemary?'

We both turn to the noise, outside in the hall. It's Alan.

'She's in here,' William calls, breaking the spell.

'I just saw the girls,' Alan says, appearing in the doorway.

65

AISA – 3:37 a.m.

They shuffle out into the hall, Aisa and Lizzie gripping Nina, half dragging her. None of them are speaking. Flashes of what they've just seen in that room, of what she saw thirty years ago, rush through Aisa's head like a mad zoetrope. By the grey skin and bulging eyes of her sisters, it looks like they're battling similar monsters, especially Nina.

'Are you OK, Neen?'

Nina nods, but Aisa can see the erratic rise and fall of her chest, even underneath the layers of clothing. Her eyes are wide and clumps of sweaty hair are sticking to her temple. She's never known her sister to be vulnerable. To talk like she did back there.

They stagger out into the foyer and towards the passageway, the walls feeling closer than ever. Nina grows heavier in their arms until she stops in the mouth of the passageway, its darkness filing away from them like an optical illusion. Like it goes on forever.

Aisa had come to think she'd imagined it all. That she must have. Because it was so unlikely. If it really happened how she thought it happened, someone else would have known about it. The police. The adults. Teachers. Someone. People always found stuff out in the end, didn't they? She'd allowed them to call her

a liar, colluded with them backing down. But now she's here, it feels as real as ever.

Nina stumbles and then stops, sagging.

'Just need to get up the passageway,' Lizzie says, 'and then we're out.'

'Hold my hand, it's OK.' Aisa curls her fingers tighter around Nina's. They're soft, thin and childlike still.

'Come on,' Lizzie says. 'You can do it.'

'I can't,' Nina says. 'I can't go along there.'

'I know you think that,' Aisa says. 'But you can.'

'It's not that simple.'

'But it is.'

'You don't understand.'

'I understand very well, Neen,' Aisa says. She softens her voice. 'It's OK,' she says, squeezing Nina's hand.

Not many people know about Nina's claustrophobia, but Aisa does. Aisa knows so many things about her sisters, about her family, things that they all think they've kept under wraps. The little spy, her mum called her. A little sneak, hiding in tight spots and listening. And always watching. She first saw Nina's claustrophobia years before she knew the name for it. Saw the way Nina would claw at her tight seatbelt in the car, the way she held her breath in narrow alleyways and avoided the water chutes on the rare family holidays to Pontins after they moved to Cheshire.

'You're one of the bravest people I know,' Lizzie says to Nina now. 'We can do this together. We'll be outside in no time.'

They start to move again, Nina wincing with each step, the smell of her sweat, her fear, curdling in Aisa's throat.

When Aisa ran along this passageway back then, thirty years ago, she was alone and – yeah, fuck it, it's not too big a word – *traumatised*. The bigger backs of her older sisters had already

made their way up the long passageway to freedom and by the time she had come out of that room, they were nowhere in sight. Had she stood a moment, and got her bearings, or just run hell for leather? She doesn't remember. She pictures herself then. A stripey T-shirt and those denim shorts she loved to wear, both of which she threw away afterwards, stuffing them in the kitchen bin as if traces of the badness had soaked into them.

A gasp of sadness leaks out of her, lost under the thunder of footsteps. Four years old. Running for her life through this horrible pit, out of this dungeon.

Her mum seemed to believe her, but only when they were alone. That night, she'd got back out of bed after the other two were asleep and crept downstairs. Rosemary stroked her head and told her that sometimes we experience things that other people won't believe. And that Aisa just had to keep those thoughts to herself and trust that they were real, but that telling other people wouldn't give her what she wanted. She would never be believed. But that she could always tell Mum. Mum and no one else.

'Not even Dad?' she'd asked and Rosemary's hand had paused on Aisa's forehead just a moment.

'Let me handle Dad,' she'd said eventually.

Aisa looks across at Lizzie, who is gripping Nina with one hand, her handbag under the other arm. It reminds her, 'Nina, I called for a breakdown truck and they could be here any minute, do you still have your car keys?'

They stop and Nina pats her pocket carefully. 'Yeah,' she nods.

'Phew,' Lizzie says. 'Now hurry up. Please.'

They start to move again when Aisa realises. Her legs grow cold, a sudden shiver running down the backs of them. 'Oh no,' she says.

'No, I said I do have them,' Nina says, taking another awkward step, but Aisa is frozen.

'It's not that,' she says. 'I just realised that I left my bag up there in the living room, I have to go and get it, it has everything in it.'

'There's a man with a gun up there,' Lizzie says, more sharply than Aisa has ever heard Lizzie speak. 'There's nothing in your bag worth taking that risk.'

'My passport,' Aisa says.

'You can get an emergency one tomorrow,' Nina says. 'Please, we can't stay here talking, I can feel the walls... I can't breathe properly, we need to get out.'

'It's not that,' Aisa says. 'Mum gave me a card, before she died. It's in my passport holder.'

'Mum wouldn't want you to risk your life,' Lizzie says. 'All our lives.'

'I'm sure you remember every word,' Nina says, an edge to her voice. 'I know I do.'

'You got one too?' Aisa asks.

'We both did,' Lizzie says quietly. 'And mine means so much to me too, but you can't risk—'

'But you don't understand,' Aisa says, a sudden stream of tears sliding down her cheeks. Her sisters stare back at her as she whispers, 'I've not read it yet.'

66

LIZZIE – 3:40 a.m.

'Then we'll all go and get it,' Lizzie says. 'Safety in numbers.'

'No,' Aisa says. 'We can't do that. It's too risky and we'll make too much noise getting Nina up the stairs.'

'You're right,' Nina says. 'I don't want you to go up by yourself, but I'd make everything worse. You should go with Aisa though, Lizzie, I can do this alone. I'm OK, I promise, I—'

'No,' Aisa says, cuffing her surprising tears away with her sleeve. 'You're not fucking listening to me. *I* need to go up, just me. I'll get my bag and then I'll just get out the front door. You two carry on up the passageway and meet me at the side of the house. There are no cameras there, we never saw it on the screen.'

Lizzie looks at Nina, expecting her to take over with a different plan. To pull rank. Instead, she just nods. 'OK, yeah.'

'OK?' Aisa says.

'Yeah, but go quickly,' Nina hisses. 'And be careful.'

'I love you, Aisa,' Lizzie blurts out as her younger sister makes for the steps. There's a pause, and then the sound of quiet laughter.

'Love you too, Lizard,' she replies. And then she's swallowed up.

They watch and listen as her careful footsteps rise up the

stairs. There's a pause, presumably as she opens the hatch into the cupboard, and a few more footsteps. Then nothing.

'God, I hope she's OK,' Nina says. Her voice is still diminished and raspy.

'Well, she has to be,' says Lizzie firmly. 'And we have to be out there to meet her. Ready to start again?'

'Ready,' Nina says, leaning her weight on Lizzie, who tries not to groan under the strain. She heaves dogs around all the time, she can do this.

'I can do this.'

'What?' Nina says, but Lizzie doesn't reply. They start to half walk, half shuffle up the passageway. Hand in hand, fingers threaded together. The light from the bulbs is dim but steady, no flickering, and she can look out for spiders without letting on.

'Watch over us, watch over us,' Lizzie starts.

'Tuck us safe to bed,' Nina joins in.

'Watch over us, watch over us. 'Til we're all long…'

'Christ, that was a dark prayer,' Nina says with a sharp laugh. 'Where the hell did Mum get that from?'

'Nan,' Lizzie says.

'Figures.'

By the time they reach the end of the passageway, they've undone their coats and are fanning their faces. The steps rise up eight or nine feet, cruder and more rickety than the ones leading to the cupboard. Just simple metal rungs set into the stone, more like a ladder than a staircase.

'Are you going to be able to—' Before she can finish, Nina has grabbed the highest rung she can reach and is pulling herself up using just one of her legs, the other dangling.

'I'm used to rock climbing,' she calls down to Lizzie. 'This is the easiest bit.'

As Nina climbs, Lizzie can see bruises blooming on her neck,

just underneath her ponytail. What on earth happened to her? Since finding her, they've had one thing after another to deal with and discover, and she still doesn't know how Nina ended up down here.

'I think someone hit me,' she'd said. That was all.

'Nina,' she says, as she climbs onto the lowest rung.

'Yeah?' Nina asks, panting, and not slowing.

Lizzie wants to say that she's scared. That she wants her mum. That she's never seen anything like *that* back there. That she's worried about Aisa. That she's sorry about Nina's job. That she hopes Nina can find the contentment she herself has found. That she loves them both very much but doesn't know, hasn't ever known, if they love her back.

'Nothing,' she says, as Nina pushes the trapdoor up into the shed.

67

AISA – 3:41 a.m.

She shouldn't have laughed when Lizzie said she loved her. It's a Kelsey affliction, laughing at inopportune moments. Their dad was the worst for it, back when he still laughed a lot. Before Mum died. One time, her parents were called into her secondary school after Aisa got in trouble for swearing at a teacher. While the headmaster was droning on about his disappointment, and that calling Mr Bobbins 'Mr Bollocks' was a suspendable offence, her dad had burst out laughing. Seconds later, their mum and Aisa were doing the same. God, she'd forgotten all about that.

But she shouldn't have laughed tonight. It was a surprise, that was all. No one has said those words to her since her mum died, though her dad has tried in his own way. 'Take care of yourself, love,' meaning approximately the same thing. More or less.

She quietly climbs the steps as far as she can before the ceiling gets in the way. The lights flicker once, and she gasps, then covers her mouth. Did anyone hear that? Overhead, the trapdoor they'd come through earlier is back in position and she holds her breath, worried about the noise, but when she pushes up with her fingertips, the square hatch moves upwards silently.

A black hole opens above her head. She stops to listen, then climbs up carefully.

A little of the light from below illuminates the cramped space she's crawled back into, the faded rose wallpaper and the sloping wall and, in front of her, a door. She closes the trapdoor behind her carefully to keep her sisters safe, holding it the whole time to keep it quiet. A shadow of the Aisa she once was is in here with her, scrunched tight. That little girl was determined to do everything by herself. To be big. *I've not changed*, she thinks, with less pride in her stubbornness than usual. She was scared then and she's scared now. But there's no option, she can't leave that envelope up there, unread. The last fragment of Mum.

That figure on screen could have made it down here by now. Could be standing just the other side of the door, in the hallway. Gun cocked. *Oh well*, she thinks, reaching for the cupboard door, *only one way to find out.*

68

ROSEMARY – July 1992

William tips the dregs of the whisky into his tumbler as I follow Alan out, trying not to shove him into a run. When we're finally in the kitchen out of earshot, I grab his arm and say, 'Where are the girls?'

He frees his arm and steps back. 'In the woods. I was heading to check my shed again and I saw them running hell for leather.'

'All of them?'

'No, just your biggest two, I think.'

I rush to the window to look out but can't see them.

'What about Jane and Aisa?'

'I don't know,' Alan says. 'I came to tell you as soon as I saw the first lot.'

I pinch the bridge of my nose and close my eyes. I wish he'd stayed to see if the other two came out, but it's better than nothing. 'Thanks, Alan, I'm sure the others aren't far behind.'

Alan is heading back to his shed as I trudge up through the garden towards the trees. It's cooler here, under this canopy of leaves, and I finally allow myself to feel a little relieved. I can see Nina and Lizzie in the distance. Nina is squatting behind a tree and Lizzie is keeping watch. My mother would call them feral for peeing in the open air, but I see a sister looking out

for another sister. That's important. I hope they never lose that closeness.

I can't see Aisa or Jane at first, but as I get closer to the older two, I hear a commotion behind me and turn. Aisa bursts out of the shed and starts running towards her sisters, who then run towards her. I hike up my skirt and run too, desperate to grab them, hug them.

We all reach each other at the same time and I scoop Aisa up in one fluid movement and scrunch her into me.

'Mum,' Nina says, her voice as small as I've ever heard it, but I cling to the littlest one and say nothing, just feel her heart hammering through her thin T-shirt. Aisa is crying – which she rarely lets herself do in front of her sisters.

'Where were you?' I say softly to her, and then more sharply to Nina and Lizzie. 'Where the bloody hell were you?'

Aisa snivels something into my neck that I can't make out.

'Hide-and-seek,' Nina says, her voice cracking just a little. 'Just around the house.'

'I looked everywhere,' I say. 'I was so worried.'

'We were underneath,' Aisa says, pulling back and looking at me. I think of all the blankets I pulled up, the bedclothes dangling down, how did I miss them?

'Where's Jane?'

'She's still inside,' Lizzie says.

I look back at the house, then at my girls. 'Does she know you're not playing hide-and-seek anymore?'

'Yeah,' Nina says, 'she saw us leave.'

Moments later, I see Jane heading to the back door of the house. She doesn't turn to wave.

It's gone five and I've paid more than my dues today. We head to the car, swinging in to see Alan in his shed on the way. The girls stand outside as I open the door and step in,

apologising. 'Sorry I was a bit snappy, I was just worried, but I really appreciate your help today.'

He's sitting on the stool, staring at the floor. 'Rosemary,' he says. 'Aisa came out of the passageway. It's not safe down there.'

We were underneath.

69

NINA – 3:46 a.m.

Nina sweeps her phone light around the old shed, looking for the door. It's surprisingly tidy in here, far tidier than the house. Alan's stool is still here, on its back like a dead bug with its legs in the air. But there's a richness to the air. It smells alive, despite the decay. Several sacks of soil are stacked up. The top one has been slashed down the middle, a trowel sticking out of it like a dagger.

Along the length of the wooden shed, an old door is propped across two barrels as a makeshift worktop. Several little plastic pots sit under a plastic lid, presumably to protect them from the weather. They look freshly tended.

They push the shed door outwards, which shrieks in the night air. 'Gosh, that's loud,' Lizzie says.

Nina bites her lip and braces for pain as she steps outside. Her ankles are both clicking and aching, and the damaged one has swollen up like a grapefruit and she's had to loosen her laces so much that the shoe is at risk of slipping off.

The air tastes sweet out here after the stuffy cellar. They pick their way through the trees, the light of their nearly drained phones helping them to avoid raised roots and heavy stones, but making the area surrounding them appear blacker, denser.

'Do you think it's Alan that's still here?' Lizzie whispers. 'Did you see him?'

'I didn't see who hit me, just their eyes ... but they did look a bit familiar. Mum always said he'd never leave this place,' Nina says.

'We were so young,' Lizzie says, as if that explains everything.

Thirty years ago, Alan had been in these woods, walking his slow, loping stomp. He'd had a rabbit slung over his shoulder, twine wrapped around its leg, its ears flopping down his back. Nina hadn't cared about that so much as about hiding herself as she peed. She remembers that Lizzie had flinched at the sight though.

Had Alan seen them that day? She doesn't know. He always seemed to be in his own world, but always there, too. Always, somehow, just round the corner. He can't have been that old. Younger than they are now, but older than them and therefore on the other team. The adults.

He'd headed for his shed, and then ... she doesn't remember. A few minutes later, Aisa had appeared. And the relief overtook everything.

It's rough going, the uneven ground that was once a vast garden has been reclaimed by nature. Clumps of grass and mud, stones and dips. Nina nearly slips and Lizzie catches her with a grunt.

'This is really difficult,' Nina says suddenly, the words coming out before she has a chance to stop them.

'Oh,' Lizzie says, threading her arm through hers. 'But you can do it, you're Nina.'

And of course she can do it, she's Nina.

They carry on carefully until the house looms in front of them. The dark stones bouncing the chilled air back to them, like a slap in the face.

'We should turn this off,' Nina says, snuffing out her light before Lizzie can reply. She does the same. They press themselves to the wall, Nina using it for support as well as hiding. 'Aisa?' she whispers, as they inch their way awkwardly around to the side of the house.

There's no reply.

They lean against the cold wet stone and Nina looks at her phone.

'It's been over twenty minutes since she left us, it can't take that long to get one bag… not unless…'

'This doesn't feel right, does it,' Lizzie says, straightening up. 'You stay here, I'm going to go in the back and make sure she's OK.'

'But—'

'But nothing, we know the man who hit you is inside, whether it's Alan or not. That means you're safe out here, you can rest your leg and I'll go in and make sure Aisa is OK.'

'But, Lizzie—'

'It's not up to you, Nina. It'll be two versus one when I'm in there, right now it's one on one and that's not OK.'

Nina thinks about the card from her mum. *You have to let other people help sometimes, love.* Wherever this new courage has come from in her sister, Nina shouldn't crush it. 'OK,' she says. 'If you're going in through the kitchen, I'll go round the front in case she comes out that way.'

Lizzie starts to move away, but Nina catches her hand.

'Good luck, Lizzie, you're being really brave.'

Lizzie pauses. 'Thank you,' she says, and then rushes off towards the back of the house.

Nina shuffles along the wall, zipping her coat back up, the heat she built up earlier long gone. Either adrenaline or the cold is making her whole body shake, but she keeps going until she

reaches the corner of the house and then squats down painfully to creep under the first window. She can't hear anything and lifts her head, but the dusty velvet curtains are blocking most of her view and the dirty glass doesn't help. She can make out the fireplace, part of a sofa and the eiderdown still on it.

Was it really only tonight that they first went in there and lit a fire? Just a few hours ago, but a different dimension. An alternate reality where Alan was a distant memory, and their biggest problem was a lack of petrol and a twisted ankle.

But, of course, that's not entirely true. Aisa clearly has stuff going on, it's not normal to dismantle your whole life and Littlest Hobo it across the world. And Lizzie ... poor Lizzie, always so insular, so alone.

And me, she thinks. *Would the others have ever guessed about my problems if I hadn't blurted them out?* That every night when she should be asleep, she's replaying the birth that went wrong. The decisions. The dropping heart rate. The confusion of her colleagues when she stopped them coming closer, stopped them helping. The tiny cry, the relief that her bad decisions hadn't ... but who knows.

And the biggest secret of all. The one that wakes her up with a start every time she starts to slip under, the one she doesn't let take full form. The relief at not having to do it anymore. The kernel of hope that they'll say she can't return. And yes, the absolute fear over meeting the mortgage, the shame of telling people, the ostracism that always happens when a colleague falls and the world they've left closes up around the exit wound. But the relief, the dizzying relief, of being able to choose a new path.

The bruises on Nina's back and neck throb and her head fogs for a moment. She slaps her face and the sound rings out like a whipcrack in the dead air. Now is not the time for life decisions. All her decisions were made long ago, it's too

late for reinvention. It's the time for gritting her teeth and holding on.

She shuffles gingerly to the impenetrable oak front door, pressing her cold ears pointlessly against it. She can hear nothing.

Nina takes a big gulp of air and then, leaning on the facade of the house, starts to shuffle towards the other window to see if Aisa is in the library.

Her progress is slow, but she's nearly at the window now. She turns back, just quickly, to check the front door hasn't opened. No. OK. Another deep breath and then Nina takes a big, painful stride into the dark. Colliding silently with something. Someone. The dim moonlight picks out the hood, the eyes. The same eyes she saw earlier. As she opens her mouth, a gloved hand is slapped across it.

70

ROSEMARY – July 1992

Aisa is asleep in my lap, TV off, big two in bed. On the tape deck, a mixtape of my favourites from the musicals plays softly. But they're not really comforting me tonight.

My tea is long cold and my throat feels like dry straw, but I don't get up to make a fresh cup. I don't want to disturb my little girl and I don't want to break this spell. Her life is going to change so much soon, in fact it already has. Let her have this last little bit of the old one.

Will she ever understand? Will the penny drop when she's older and realises what happened? The thought makes my eyes fill and I pepper her crown with kisses. She smells like baked bread. I can't bear this alone much longer.

It's Friday, so Bob is spending some of his wages in the pub. He's held it together well these last weeks, it's felt like progress. But what's that Bible story about houses built on sand? We've been treading water for a long time, now I need him to swim. Arguably more than I ever have before. Even more than I did five years ago.

The pub is three doors down and I hear the ringing bell, the yells of last orders. Not long now. A few minutes later, the sound of the bar spills onto the streets. It's a male sound, a primeval

pack thing, and I can't stand it. I don't imagine William has ever been inside The Fox, or any other proper pub for that matter. I imagine him and Selina went to their fair share of bistros and wine bars when they lived down in London though.

I think then of Jane. I promised Selina I would look out for Jane. I imagine what she would say if she knew I'd just left her today, without checking she was OK. No matter what other people think, Selina adored that child, and that child had been down there, *underneath*.

I make a vow silently. To Selina, to Jane. And then I scoop Aisa up and shuffle awkwardly upstairs as I hear Bob's footsteps outside. I lay her down and take a look at all three of the girls sleeping here, in the only bedroom they've ever known. I've wanted more for them for so long, but this house, for all its faults, had always given them stability and security.

The front door opens and I close the girls' door and head downstairs to survey the damage. Bob is inside and still upright, which is a start. Swaying a little on the mat, but in reasonable condition.

'How do?' he says, looking up as I descend.

'Let me make you a coffee.'

While the kettle boils, I run through it in my head, trying to find the words.

He's slumped on the sofa now and I watch through the doorway as his eyes close and his head snaps back, waking himself up and zonking out, over and over again.

I call out, 'I need you awake.'

He raises his eyebrows in hope and struggles to a stand.

'Come in here,' I say.

He plods through, hands outstretched towards me, but I point to the table. He pulls out one of the dining chairs, its

seat covered with socks that I've been meaning to pair up and ball, but he sweeps them onto the floor enthusiastically and I don't say anything.

'You've got plans for me, Ro?' he says, eyes sparkling through their semi-drunken sheen as I pour water onto the milky Nescafé and stir vigorously. He's looking older. Drink and worry have frayed his edges, greyed his hair. But he's still my Bob.

'Drink that,' I say, sliding the mug in front of him and standing back quickly before he can grab my bum.

He blows on it a bit and then gulps it down like medicine, wiping his mouth with the back of his big hand.

Oh, Bob. Always so keen, always so devoted, long before I even noticed him. It's a life sentence, but he doesn't seem to mind. Or hasn't, until now. Even when he must have suspected that—

'What is it, Ro?'

'It's the girls,' I say, and he frowns. 'They found the Brigadier's cellar.'

71

AISA – 3:46 a.m.

The door from the cupboard opens quietly and she hovers for a moment, squatting on her haunches like an animal, ears pricked. It's hard to hear over the hammer of blood in her ears, but she can't waste time. She steps out carefully.

Aisa is alone in the hallway – at least she thinks she's alone. She should have taken one of her sisters' phones for light, but it's too late now, she's wading into blackness, all her other senses heightened.

She can still smell that rich iron tang, tinged with the smell of the kind of wax jacket that her dad used to wear to walk their dog Ralph when they were much younger. Sometimes, she'd go with him to Marbury Park near their house. Happy to have a little time just them, talking about what he'd seen on the trains, spotting squirrels or brainstorming how they would build the perfect tree house, if any of those big park trees were able to fit in their garden. Then she turned thirteen and didn't want anything to do with him. So completely that she'd forgotten that she ever had. Poor Dad.

She crosses the hall and listens at the door of the living room, but there's no sound from inside, so she pushes it open carefully.

The fire is still glowing, just a tiny sliver of orange under the dust and ash. It's a reminder that they really were here earlier. The three of them first, and then in various batches of two. She pinches herself hard on the arm to really underline it. This place she's avoided for so long in her mind, and now she's standing in the belly of the beast.

She just needs to grab her bag and go. But where is it? The light is still navy and grey and the sun not yet up outside. She squints but can't see it and can't remember where she'd slung it when she first came in, looking for Nina and Lizzie. She checks under the eiderdown on the sofa, and then the blankets on the other one. No dice.

It's not on the old dining chair, or near the window. She finally spots it, tucked to the side of the fireplace where she'd put it to dry out. As she goes over, she sees that Lizzie's note is still on the mantelpiece, so she grabs it and drops it on the glowing wood. No need to leave clues that they'd been here. It fizzes and is swallowed into black soot.

Aisa scoops up her bag, breathing heavily with relief, and opens it. She rifles through her tat and reaches the zipped compartment, feeling from the outline that the passport holder is still inside. Still, she has to check. She has no intention of ever coming back here and she's not leaving without that envelope.

But it's there. The edges of the passport slightly wavy from the damp, but the envelope unscathed, as soft and precious as before. She leaves it there, now is certainly not the time to read it, zips the bag back up and hoists it over her shoulder, snatching it to her side to silence its rattle.

Shit, did anyone hear that?

Aisa listens but hears nothing. She just needs to get out the

front door now and run round the side to her sisters. Escape is so close she can feel it, pushing her on. She pulls the lounge door handle and it opens wide. Revealing a gun. Held at chest height. In shaking hands. Blocking the exit.

72

LIZZIE – 3:46 a.m.

Lizzie makes her way along the side of the house towards the back, whispering to herself.

Watch over us, watch over us.

Tuck us ...

Tonight, the words circle around her mind, but she can't catch hold of them. Bats, flapping in the corners of her mind. Out of control and scared. She starts again.

Watch over us, watch over us.

Tuck us safe to bed.

Watch over us, watch over us.

'Til we're all long dead.

It's no bloody good. Mum *is* long dead. And maybe they are too, they just don't know it.

She reaches the back of the house and turns her phone light off. The darkness is a shock, but Lizzie shakes it off and peers through the window into the kitchen. It's hard to make anything out, it's just dusty shapes and darkness, but nothing seems to be moving. No one appears to be there.

What on earth would Mum make of this? Her old domain, abandoned and thick with dust when once it shined like a new pin. And inside and all around it, her girls, scattered and

vulnerable. And poor Dad, left at home by himself, oblivious in that empty house. What will he do if anything happens to them?

You hardly ever see him anyway, what difference would it make?

She winces. It's true. Before her mum got ill, Lizzie visited a couple of times a month, and stayed the night whenever she could. Sometimes Dad would be away, riding the trains with his retiree's railcard. Mum would cook Chimney Pot Pie or bangers and mash and Lizzie would tell herself that next time she'd admit to being a vegetarian. She's not eaten meat in years, except when Mum cooked it. She never owned up.

Who cooks for Dad now? Every time she visits, they get sandwiches at the local pub and she flees before dinner. He's thinner, she realises. Is he eating? Mum would never let him go hungry.

'I'm sorry,' she whispers to herself. *Tell him yourself, when you're all away from here.*

Lizzie presses her ear to the door, but she hears nothing else. No words, no footsteps, no gunshots.

Gunshots?! What has happened to us?

Anything could be happening in there, but all she can hear is the wind and the distant swaying of trees. If she hadn't seen that gunman on the bed with her own eyes, she'd think she had imagined it. It wouldn't be the first time she'd imagined things.

Lizzie reaches for the back-door handle. Did they check this earlier? She can't remember, but when she takes a deep breath and starts to turn it, she meets no resistance. When it's wide enough to slip through, she listens again, but there's nothing. No one.

She steps carefully into the dark kitchen, the sound of her scuffed old trainers ringing out through the silence. She waits, but no one comes, so she steps further into the room until she feels her way to the internal door that leads to the hallway and

stairs. Her eyes are still adjusting, the darkness just a block, but then they begin to pick out shapes. A person, standing in the doorway of the lounge, gun cocked.

73

ROSEMARY – July 1992

Bob has had three more coffees and a huge glass of water while we talked. Or, rather, I talked, he mostly absorbed. He's fully upright now, completely engaged. You'd never know he'd had a drink in his life, let alone six pints a few hours ago.

Whatever anyone may say about Bob, when it really matters, there's no one more reliable, no one braver. It takes me back to that day, five years ago, when the pin was first pulled out of the grenade. He held me together. And I don't deserve him. That is a granite-hard fact. No matter what he drinks, what he messes up, however much he might wind me up in the normal run of family life, I cannot fault him. The man is a hero.

'I should just get it done,' he says, taking the car keys off the hook, but I draw the line there, coffee or no coffee. I can't have him getting pulled over, fingerprinted, shoved in a drunk tank somewhere in Penrith.

'I'll drive you,' I say.

I leave a note taped to the TV just in case one of the girls wakes up and can't find us. I say that we had to pop out to help a friend and to go back to bed. To help themselves to breakfast if we're not back by morning, hoping to God that we will be.

And not to call Nan. The last thing I need is my mother getting a call. The last thing I need is my mother. Full stop.

I drive in silence. It's a journey I have done so many thousands of times, on my bicycle as a teenager, then by car and occasionally on foot. I have done it happy and sad, pregnant and excited, grieving my father, fuming at my mother, worrying about my future, and in relief. I have done it recklessly, feeling I had no choice. And now, this last time, it seems brand new.

I'm glad I'm not here alone, plunging around these tight bends and weaving through giant monstrous trees that sway dangerously even in summer. I wish I was in bed. I wish more than anything that I was back home in bed, the girls in the next room, safe. No, that's not true. I wish that me, Bob and the girls were miles away from here, cuddled together. My family is all that counts now. They're the home, not the house. My auntie said just the same thing when I called her, earlier this evening, asking to stay.

I pull onto the drive but stop about halfway up to the house. We don't want to be seen. The familiarity grabs me by the throat. When I look across at Bob, he seems frozen. I cannot keep doing this to him.

'You OK?' I say as we climb out and he nods, reaching for his little toolbox. But he's not.

He never is when he comes back here.

You'd not know it was July. We huddle closer together for warmth and I reach for Bob's hand. 'We don't hold hands enough,' I tell him and feel him plant kisses on the crown of my head. 'I love you so much,' I say. 'You know that don't you?'

'I do,' he says, his voice muffled by my hair.

'I hope the girls are OK back home,' I whisper, as the big house looms into view.

'Of course they're OK,' he says. 'Because they're together.'

The downstairs lights are all switched off, but I look up and spot that Jane's light is on. I didn't know that she still slept with it on, and feel a sudden stab of sympathy and guilt.

'Wonder if Alan's here,' Bob says and I nod.

'He's always here, isn't he,' I say, more to myself than Bob. 'He's probably in his tent though, so we should be extra quiet around there.'

'Yeah, probably,' Bob says softly. 'Poor bugger.'

We've brought torches, but we don't switch them on – drawing attention to ourselves will blow everything. 'Make sure you're quiet with those tools,' I whisper and he holds the toolbox to his body as we approach the shed. 'I'll wait here and keep watch,' I whisper. 'Not that I can see a bloody thing.' I hug him good luck and then watch as he carefully opens the door to the shed and steps inside. He stands still for a moment and I wonder if he can really handle this. But a moment later, he's disappeared.

74

NINA – 3:51 a.m.

Nina can't breathe properly. She can taste soil and dirt on the thick fabric covering her mouth. She tries to get away, tries to shout out, but it's useless, she's trapped. The pain rising up from her ankle is so intense that for a moment her vision goes. A white heat, radiating from her toes all the way up to her scalp.

Someone huge is behind her, dwarfing her, his arms wrapped around her. She can hear the squeak of a wax jacket against her own puffa coat. She has never felt claustrophobia while standing outside, but she does now. The panic wraps itself around her even tighter than this man's arms.

'Stop struggling and I'll let you go,' the voice says, and the familiarity of it hits her in her bones.

She goes limp. Moments later, she can breathe again. The man is holding her arms, but her face is open to the wind and she sucks in the air as fast as she can.

'Please don't shout for help,' he says, his warm mouth close to her cold ear. She shudders but manages not to make a noise. 'I don't want to hurt you,' he adds. His voice is soft, low, a rumble that passes through her right to the pit of her stomach. He slackens his hold so she can pull away, turning to face him.

That face. The same one that she saw in the mirror moments

before everything went black. There was only one person it could have been.

Alan is massive. Even bigger than she remembers, back when everyone was bigger than her. Now it's more of a novelty. He is twice as wide as her, he looks more like a building than a person. The hood of his wax coat is up over his forehead, but she can see his eyes and that's enough.

'You did hurt me,' she says, quietly.

'I didn't mean to, Rosemary,' he says, one heavy hand landing on her shoulder like a kettlebell.

'I'm not Rosemary!' she cries.

75

AISA – 3:47 a.m.

Aisa's first thought is, *So that's what a gun looks like*. Dark wood, polished metal, a leather handle, it resembles something that might sit on the wall of a naff old pub. Some kind of deadly horse brass.

Her second thought is, *How the hell am I still alive?*

'Don't move,' the voice says quietly.

And Aisa doesn't. She doesn't move her head, or her eyes. She keeps them fixed on the barrel, on the hole where a bullet could come flying out. All it would take is one finger twitch.

The gun is everything, the only thing.

The light is so dim in here, just the disappearing glow of the fire. Yet she can make out the gun's precise lines. Maybe her eyes are just filling in the gaps, drawn from years of ingesting Hollywood films. But everything around the gun is a blur. The person, the door.

Aisa hears their voice as if she's reading it on a subtitled film, fractured and delayed between ears and understanding.

'Aisa,' it says, and then she looks up. *How do they know my name?*

It's a woman. She'd have known that from the voice, if she'd not been too scared to process the information.

A light suddenly comes on, Aisa flinches and for a moment sees nothing. But the woman has lowered the gun so it hangs by her side and has pulled a torch from somewhere. Aisa's eyes ache with the shock of it and she covers them with her hands and bends at the knee, her whole body reacting to the flood of light after hours in a void.

'What are you doing here?' There's a new something in the woman's voice – surprise, but… if Aisa trusted herself and her instincts right now, she'd also say the woman sounded happy. But Aisa is clearly losing the plot in the face of a firearm.

'We ran out of petrol,' she says. 'We just needed to take shelter.'

'Here?'

'Well…' *Obviously.* She fights the urge to be sarcastic to someone holding a gun. 'Yeah,' she says. 'Here.'

'Just randomly here?' the woman says.

'It was a shortcut gone wrong. I'm sorry, but how do you know my name?'

The woman pulls her hood down awkwardly with her torch hand, the light bouncing around the walls and ceiling. A crop of dark wavy hair and a thin face stare back.

'Jane?'

'Your mum—'

My mum?

'She showed me your photo, I recognised you from that.'

'What?'

'Aisa,' Jane says, 'I didn't want to do it like this, but…' She fumbles to get something out of her pocket. As she places the gun down to free up both hands, Lizzie comes pelting down the hallway.

'Lizzie!' Aisa shouts. 'Don't!'

But it's too late. Lizzie is lying on top of Jane, the gun knocked out of reach.

'Lizzie's here as well?' Jane says, muffled by Lizzie's body. Then a shout comes from outside, the fear in it so acute that Aisa feels her blood grow cold in her veins.

'I'm not Rosemary!'

76

ROSEMARY – July 1992

Bob has been down there for ages now. If he doesn't come out soon, the sun will come up and then God knows what we'll do. Alan strikes me as an early riser, and his tent is only fifty yards away, and he has the ears of a hunter.

I don't dare put the torch on, I think its glow would probably be visible through the thin tent fabric. I have nothing to do but worry and seize up, so I walk in small, slow circles to stay awake, keep my legs moving. I'm wearing an old Miller Lite T-shirt, tracksuit bottoms and an anorak, which rustles when I move. I get too hot, so I take it off, and then I get too cold. I won't feel just right until we're well away from here. Away from this house, away from this village. Away from these memories. How I ever thought I could ... we could ... live with them. I really could slap myself.

I wonder how many circles I've done now. A hundred. Three thousand. I have no idea. But I almost wish I could make this harder for myself, leg weights or something, anything to bring it closer in line with what Bob is going through. He hasn't complained. He's just down there, yet again, working away to fix the wall that allowed Aisa to see the—

'Shit!'

I'm on the floor before I realise what's happened, landing with a bump and a grunt. Shit, shit, shit. Did Alan hear?

I sit perfectly still, my legs at awkward angles from the fall, listening hard and trying to control my breathing. Just as I think I've got away with it, I hear the sound of a zip fifty yards away.

My bright blue anorak will act like a beacon if Alan shines a torch around, but taking it off will create a cacophony of swishes. As I hear him bustle out from the tent, his heavy footsteps treading onto the sun-hardened ground, I lie down as quietly as I can, willing myself smaller. There are no leaves to cover myself with, nothing to hide behind. I'm lying on the side of the shed nearest his tent.

He stands still and says nothing. I know he's listening, but I also know there's no reason for him to think I'm here. He's not looking for me. I stay still, scrunching my eyes shut as if that makes me less visible, and I hear him take another step. *Please, Alan,* I think, *just go back inside.*

Finally I hear the jangle of the tent zip as he brushes against it, climbing back in, but I also hear a noise from inside the shed. The rattle of Bob's toolbox as he pushes it up from the passageway onto the floor of the shed. 'Stop,' I hiss. 'Stay there.'

Thank God he must have heard me because the noise stops. We both stay still and silent. The hatch must still be open on the shed floor, but Bob doesn't come up. I barely breathe.

It feels like hours, it's probably seconds, but I eventually hear the steady sound of the zip as Alan seals himself back into his cocoon. I crawl to the door of the shed as quietly as I can and whisper the all-clear to Bob. He climbs up in silence, closes the hatch as if he's handling a sleeping newborn, and then clutches the toolbox to his chest again to stop it rattling.

We don't say a word until we reach the car, halfway down the drive. I unlock the driver's side, slide in and pop his door open.

When he climbs in under the dim glow of the interior lights, I see that he's covered in dust, pale as the moon and trembling. As I lift the handbrake, he stares ahead. I roll the car down towards the road without turning the ignition or putting the lights on, using muscle memory from driving this way ten million times before. As we reach the gates, I turn the key, stare ahead and grope for his hand. All the way home, I only drop it for gear changes, then snatch it back up. It sits in mine, shaking like a little mouse plucked from the wet mouth of a cat, just in time.

77

NINA – 3:53 a.m.

The front door flies open, and Nina can make out the frenetic movements of Aisa, holding a torch that she's got from God knows where. Then she sees the shape and shuffle of Lizzie, holding her lit-up phone in front of her like a taser and someone else, a woman in a hood. The woman stalks towards them, and—

Shit, is that a real gun?

'Get away from her,' the woman says to Alan, lifting the gun to her shoulder.

'That's mine,' Alan says. 'And it's not loaded.'

'This gun belonged to my grandfather, the Brigadier,' the woman says, and Nina feels Alan's heavy hand shake on her shoulder.

'Jane?' Alan says.

Jane? Jane is here?

'It's not really yours, my dad just let you use it. And I found the bullets,' Jane says, jutting her chin up. 'Oxo tin, second shelf down in the shed. Right?'

Alan slowly backs away. Letting Nina slump, he cowers into himself as Jane keeps the gun trained on him. 'Is he ...' he says. 'Is he here?'

'Who?' Jane says, staring at Alan.

Nina couldn't have described Jane in any detail before tonight. Vaguely dark, vaguely skinny. Eight years old. But seeing her up close, Nina recognises her as clearly as if she was a member of her own family. It's not just that she's still skinny, still dark, it's the essence of her. The sharpness, the grit. The bravery.

'Who?' Jane says again, jabbing the gun slightly forward.

'The Brigadier.'

'He's been dead for fifty years!' Jane says.

'I get confused,' Alan cries. 'I have a note, in my pocket.'

'A note?' Jane says, and then looks round at the sisters. 'What note?'

Alan starts fumbling in his pocket and Jane presses the gun closer to him.

'No tricks,' she says, but he's pulling out a piece of folded paper and offering it to her. She is holding the gun with both hands, so she lets go with one, grabs the note and tosses it towards Lizzie and Aisa. Then she grabs the gun tightly again.

Lizzie catches the folded letter, but Aisa snatches it, holding it awkwardly in the torch light. 'This looks just like Dad's writing,' she says.

'My friend Bob wrote it,' Alan mutters.

'What the actual...' Aisa starts.

'Just read it,' Jane says, the gun shaking just slightly, almost imperceptibly. 'Please.'

'All right,' says Aisa. 'It says, "This is Alan. He means no harm. He gets confused sometimes about what year it is and who people are. He has permission to look after the house. Please leave him alone, he is happy here."'

'I told him to put the last bit,' Alan says.

'Do you mean Dad's been here, like, recently?' Aisa says, looking at her sisters and Jane as if they'd know, then back to Alan.

'He comes every month,' Alan says, looking down at his feet. 'He helps me.'

'He helps you?' Nina says, sounding sceptical.

'Here?' says Lizzie. 'Dad comes back here?'

'Every month,' Alan says again. 'No matter what.'

With their mum gone, and Dad retired from the railways, all he seemed to care about was his girls. And, in response, they try hard not to spend any time with him. If you asked Nina why, she couldn't really tell you, except that being in that house, with all those reminders of Mum, it's too much. It's just too much.

They've tried to get him to join the social club in the town, but he says it's for old people, and besides, he has a friend that he helps out, tidying up the garden and stuff.

'That's enough for me,' he said earlier, or rather yesterday, when they tried again. 'I have my friend.'

'Bullshit,' Aisa had coughed, and they'd all laughed, the three sisters, hiding their hysteria in the kitchen.

'Isn't he a bit old for imaginary friends?' Nina had said, remembering too late that Lizzie also used to make up imaginary friends to stave off loneliness.

But Dad wasn't lying, was he? The truth is standing in front of them. The truth bashed her over the head earlier tonight. Her body still throbs with the pain of it.

Nina can't take all this in. She should be pleased to see her sisters. And pleased to see that 'the gunman' was Jane, who is actually defending her, rather than wanting to hurt them. But she's just so confused. And hurt.

'Why did you call me Rosemary?' she says, looking up at Alan.

'You really do look like her,' Jane says, still holding the gun rigidly towards Alan, but casting a look over her shoulder at Nina. 'The way she used to look.'

'This really isn't Rosemary?' Alan says. 'But she looks just the same, I saw her working here … the other day, it was—'

'That was thirty years ago! And Mum is dead,' Nina shouts.

'I'm sorry, I forget things these days …' Alan says, tears clouding his rheumy eyes. 'Rosemary died?'

'Enough of this soap-opera dementia act! You hit Nina over the head and you could have killed her,' Aisa says, moving her own body in front of Nina's. 'Then you dragged her downstairs like a bag of spuds. Look at her!'

Alan is shaking his head. 'No,' he says. 'No, you're wrong. She was looking in the mirror and she saw me and fainted. I think I scared her and I thought it was … I thought she was Rosemary and then she just—'

'She fainted, so you, what, dragged her all the way down into a dungeon?'

'I'm sorry, I'm sorry,' he cries. 'I panicked. I just wanted to keep her safe until she woke up, it's not safe in the house if those explorer men come in, and they could find my tent. I carried her down as best I could and then I went to the river to get white willow bark.' He holds out something in his hand, but Nina recoils. 'It'll help the bruises,' he says, sounding hurt.

'My dad told me that Alan was looking after the place when we left,' Jane says. 'But I had no idea he'd still be here, or that he was suffering from dementia now and—' The noise of a car engine interrupts her. They all turn to stare down the drive at the bouncing lights, heading their way.

Alan flinches. 'No one should come here,' he says. 'Your dad told me that, Jane.'

78

LIZZIE – 4:02 a.m.

They watch as an old car bobs cheerfully, obliviously, towards them. Lights on full. It bounces over potholes, sloshes through puddles. In this new light, the true horror of the building is lit up like a cathedral. Or maybe it's more like a dilapidated haunted house ride at the fair. Ivy has crept up the sides, poking its green fingers into every hole and gap. The lintels of the window frames are riddled with holes, great chunks missing like someone has taken a bite out of a Cadbury's Flake. The glass is all intact, but it's tinged green, shining like cats' eyes in the glare. The building looks bigger in this light. A great crumbling mountain of a building, floodlit for full dramatic effect.

The Morris Minor pulls up at the small crowd, the handbrake ringing out like a yelp. For a moment, the lights stay at full beam, keeping the windscreen black, the insides unknowable to everyone except Lizzie, who rushes forward.

'It's Rafferty,' she cries out, the silhouette of a man finally becoming visible as the lights dim.

'Who?' Aisa says, looking at Nina, who shrugs.

'My boyfriend.'

'Boyfriend?' Nina says, but Lizzie rushes forward and opens the driver's door.

'You came!'

'The one time you're a damsel in distress?' he says, climbing out carefully. 'Of course I came, it's probably my only chance to ever rescue you.'

For a moment, Lizzie forgets about her sisters. About the fact she is bedraggled and probably smelly. About Jane. About that cellar and its secrets. About Alan and the gun. About all of it. She's just so happy to see him. A relief that she's never experienced before. The purity of the feeling staggers her.

'How long did it take you to get here?' she says, kissing him on the lips and wrapping her arms inside his smoking jacket, limpetting onto his warm body. 'When did you hear the message?'

He hugs her back, their hearts mashed together. 'I heard it while you were leaving it,' he laughs, looking around. 'Wow, look at this place. But, er, problem was I was half asleep, and in my delirium, I thought you'd come home and were talking to me. When I woke up again to use the toilet and saw you weren't actually there, I realised what must have happened and I came downstairs and saw the light on your answering machine.'

'You left *yourself* a message?' Nina asks from behind her. 'When did you do that?'

'When I went out looking for you,' she says, then realises that Nina doesn't know any of what happened while she was missing.

'I called 100 to ask the operator to call you back,' Rafferty says.

'It doesn't work that way,' Lizzie laughs and he smiles rakishly. Oh God, he's just so lovely.

'Well, it didn't, no. So I listened to the message again and got on your computer and looked up the name you'd said. Moirthwaite Manor. Luckily, there's only one.'

'Very lucky,' Aisa says behind them.

'I didn't even pause to get dressed, for shame. And then the

old girl got me here.' He pats the bonnet of the Morris Minor, the headlights still shining in a thick pool that they've all gravitated towards. 'Top speed of sixty-five and I did it all the way.'

'Rafferty restored this himself,' Lizzie gushes, turning to her sisters and Jane before she can stop herself. They at least have the good grace to fake interest.

'You know about cars?' Nina says and Rafferty tilts his head modestly.

'A little.'

'Do you happen to have any spare petrol?' she asks and Rafferty nods.

'Elizabeth said in her message that you'd run out, so I brought some with me.'

He walks around to the boot, twists the handle and pulls out a jerry can. She sees that her sisters are thrilled, they're not mocking, even though he's wearing vintage striped pyjamas, a smoking jacket and his old-fashioned boots, such was his hurry. She squeezes him to her again, the fuel sloshing in the can.

Nina, Lizzie and Rafferty climb into the old car to drive down to the Mini, Nina in the front with her seat pushed back and her bad leg – her worst leg – stretched out.

'Hang on,' calls Lizzie through the window as they're about to drive off. 'Where did Alan go?'

'He can't have gone far,' Jane says, speaking for the first time since she held the gun to him.

'I guess he never has.'

79

AISA – 4:21 a.m.

Jane showed her the bullets as soon as they walked back inside, rummaging in her pocket and then furtively opening her hand, that same smile she always had when she did something sneaky. A smile Aisa had forgotten for thirty years.

'I didn't know how to put them in,' she said, her voice quiet and intense as it ever was. A voice Aisa couldn't have described yesterday. 'I was so out of my depth.'

'I don't think any of us knew what we were doing tonight,' Aisa says, a sliver of the old awkwardness, the old excitement she'd felt when talking to one of her older sisters' friends as equals. 'Except maybe Lizzie.'

'Good old Lizzie,' Jane says. 'God, I forgot what she was like. I've missed her, I think.'

Now Aisa sits on the sofa and Jane fusses with the fire before turning to her and throwing her sooty hands up. 'I don't know what the bloody hell I'm doing,' she laughs.

'An absolute mood,' Aisa laughs, surprised to be able to.

'I can't believe you're here. All of you,' Jane says, getting a small flame going and then sitting on the same sofa as Aisa. Her voice has a faint Midlands twang now she's more relaxed. 'And

I'm so sorry I ...' She screws up her face. 'I mean, what the hell am I saying, but I'm so sorry I *held you at gunpoint*.'

'You were outnumbered,' Aisa says. 'But I mean, yeah, it wasn't my favourite part of the night. I can't believe I didn't wet myself.'

'This is the most I've laughed in some time, which is messed up,' Jane says.

Aisa doesn't know what to say, so she just waits.

'My dad died last week,' Jane says. 'So, you know, not a barrel of laughs in Casa Proctor.'

'I'm so sorry,' Aisa says, trying to picture Jane's dad but drawing a blank. Legs. Shoes. Adult male. That's about it.

'That's why I'm here,' she says. 'I have his phone now. His old brick.' She smiles. 'And I'd been putting off coming up here, but I got an alert earlier this evening. Someone had triggered the cameras. They hadn't been on for years, but someone had switched them on and ... Well, I was worried, to be honest.'

She stretches her hands towards the fire and Aisa notices they're shaking. She wants to reach out and hold them, but she doesn't.

'I was still coming to terms with things, not just Dad but ... other things. Things I knew I'd have to deal with, things your mum told me. And then it seemed like someone might get to those things first and force my hand, so I ... I just got a train up to Penrith and got a taxi here and—'

Aisa can't keep up with the story. 'Sorry, hang on. You said earlier that my mum showed you my photograph and you just said she told you things. You went to see her at the hospice, didn't you?'

'Yes, just once.'

'So it was you that I saw that time. I'd gone to get some air and when I came back, she wasn't alone.'

'I didn't realise, I'm sorry, I—'

'I just left when I saw you. It meant she had company and running away is kind of my thing. It … it was hard. At the end. Intense.' Aisa frowns. 'Did you not come to the funeral?'

'I didn't know she'd died,' Jane says. 'I guess no one else knew how to contact me except her. I called the hospice a couple of weeks after I saw her and they told me I was too late. Said she'd left me a card though.'

'You got one too?'

Jane nods. 'I think she meant to give it to me when I saw her, but I … I was too upset that time, I just left. I regret that now. Anyway, they sent it on to me.'

'Don't feel bad, of course you were upset. She looked so ill at the end, it was hard for us all.'

'No, well, I mean yeah, I was upset, seeing her so … diminished … But … no. The reason I was so cut up that last time was because …' Jane sighs and turns to Aisa, their eyes locking. 'She finally told me what happened to my mother.'

80

ROSEMARY – July 1992

Bob gets back with the hired van while the girls are at school and we work on autopilot, silently shoving boxes and bags into the back of it. Lifting the few bits of worn furniture we're going to take, not knowing how long we'll need to stay with my auntie in Cheshire and stash it in her garage. As long as it takes to get new jobs and find a house, I guess.

This house looks filthy as we expose its hidden parts. Layers of dirt that have been covered by daily life suddenly revealed. A rectangle of wall that had been hidden by the TV, the original colour, untouched by sunlight. The girls' heights through the years, grooved into the kitchen door frame. Moment upon moment captured in the wood, left for some other family to paint over. I press my palm to Aisa aged three, remembering how she slowly rose onto her toes, thinking we hadn't noticed. I run a thumb over Lizzie when she had that growth spurt at six and went briefly from a broad bean to a string bean. Nina, at the top of them all, almost too old to want to do this anymore. I have a compulsion to kiss every one of these little marks, but I stop myself. There's no time for maternal madness today.

As we do a final sweep of the upstairs, I realise how many of these things were donated in the early days of our marriage

314

and feel a rush of grief and pity for everything we're going to leave. Our bedroom looks smaller somehow, with all our clothes bagged or binned. This bedroom where we barely slept last night, Bob grunting and twisting, working through his hangover prematurely. And me just lying there, planning what I would say, how I would do what I need to do. And thinking about the girls. How we're about to rip their roots up out of the soil, and we'd better bloody make it count.

'If we're to go when the girls finish school,' Bob says, rubbing his hand through his dust-flecked hair, 'you should—'

'I know,' I cut him off with a squeeze of his rough hand. 'You can do the last bits?'

'Yeah,' he says, looking around at the scraps and shrugging. 'There's not a lot, is there.'

I bump up the drive and park in the usual spot, tucked into the brambles where I first took Jane to pick blackberries. Teaching her to choose the sweetest ones just on the cusp of ruin. My little car settles into the grooves in the gravel that it's gradually made over the years. I have the manor keys in my bag, but it's not my usual work day, so as ridiculous as it feels, I walk to the front door and lift the heavy brass fox knocker.

Jane is watching me from her window as I slam the knocker down. I'm trying to act calmly.

Same as ever. Even though nothing is the same.

It takes a long time for anyone to come to the door. I wonder if William is napping. He pretends not to, but I know he likes a nap. I know his daily patterns as closely as Bob's.

Behind the door, I hear the shuffle of day slippers on the terracotta tiles I'd cleaned just yesterday. Another of these spaces that I know so intimately but that were never really mine. The door handle is fumbled and turned, and the door finally opens.

'Rosemary,' he says. 'Is everything OK?'

William's hair almost reaches his shoulders, the back of it curling around his neck like those brambles. It's normally worn slicked back, a look that was bookish, even raffish, when he was twenty-one. But loose and unkempt, it makes him look derelict now. I'm struck that he always has it neat and tidy when I'm here, and as he reaches a hand up to smooth it, something tiny loosens and slips inside me, a pull to him that I've not felt in years. I reach for his hand, which surprises both of us, and then I ask if I can come in to talk.

'Of course,' he says, turning with a slight sigh.

He's aged prematurely in front of me and I hadn't really noticed. He's wearing dark brown cord trousers, and a navy shirt that I washed and pressed myself. His hair is thinning, a few peeks of scalp visible where his fingers have just urgently combed.

He reminds me of someone and it takes a moment to realise that he looks like the Brigadier. I'd not seen it in him before, but it must haunt him every time he looks in the mirror, before he greases his hair back and shaves the grey off his chin.

We are in the hall, and I can't help but laugh when he offers to make *me* tea. But I let him, following him to the kitchen and watching him fill the kettle, spark the hob.

'I came to let you know—' I start.

'Are you leaving?' he says, his eyes meeting mine. I nod. 'You've given us a lot of years, Rosemary. I can only thank you.'

This is not how I had planned it. Not what I was expecting. As he fills the teapot with leaves and reaches for cups, I carry on with my speech, even though it feels redundant now.

'We've got an opportunity,' I say. 'Bob's been offered a job down in... down south.' The lie feels angular, hard to get out of my mouth, but he doesn't seem to notice.

'Good for him,' he says. 'I know it's been hard.'

'The problem is, we need to go today. It's all happened really quickly.'

'Today?' He rubs a hand over his face. 'Jane will, well… you know. We'll both—'

'Me too,' I say, my voice catching in my throat. It surprises me, but I mean it.

He steps towards me but stops. Now he's closer than he should be, yet he doesn't touch me and I don't touch him.

His breath is heavy, equine. I can feel its warmth, just barely, on my face. My chest feels tight, my heart batting up to its edges like a little boat, edging back and forth on its harbour rope.

'William,' I say. The familiarity of that nose. The narrow shoulders. Inheritance is such a curse. 'William,' I say, softer this time. There are things he still doesn't know, things that cannot be taken back if said out loud. That can only be said once, said now.

He looks back at me, expectant but also… resigned, I think. Like he already knows, and I just have to say it. Not Selina. Not that. He can never know that, or all of this was for nothing. The other thing.

'It's just…' I start.

William stares back, his breath quickens. But I think of Bob. His arms trembling with exhaustion as he loaded the van. The care he took over packing up the girls' things: Lizzie's books, Nina's favourite pens, Aisa's special teddy. William could not tell me which is Aisa's special teddy. It's far too late to teach him now. It's far too late to even think about telling him. I step back from the edge. The time for this confession has long passed.

'It's just that… I still have one more favour to ask,' I say, and the moment, the portal to a different outcome, closes.

'One more?' he says, and smiles in surprise. He pours the

tea into the cups as he says, 'You've never once asked me for a favour.'

'Well, I need to leave with no notice, I think that's a favour.'

'You should have left years ago, Rosemary,' he says, handing over my tea. He hasn't made it how I take it. I say nothing and he smiles again, a sort of sad smile. 'What's the other favour?'

'I hate to ask, but I need to borrow some money. I was hoping...' I swallow. 'I was hoping five hundred pounds, which I know is a lot but... It's expensive to move and to start over and—'

He shakes his head and takes my tea, placing it down next to his. Then he puts both hands on my shoulders and pulls me to him awkwardly. Our chests collide, we're out of practice at any kind of proximity and a gasp slips from my lips.

'I can't lend you money,' he says into my hair and my shoulders sag. 'But I have two thousand in cash, give or take.' I don't understand and open my mouth to ask, but he interrupts. 'It's the least you deserve. Just take it. Start again. Somewhere much better than this.'

Our tea sits cooling on the side, but I know we won't drink it now. A full stop has been reached. I feel ancient and exhausted, millennia old. A moment reached, a secret kept. I sag under its weight.

William goes to the safe in his office and I'm hovering in the doorway when I see a movement in the corner of my eye.

'Are you leaving me too?' Jane says, biting her lip. She's holding a French textbook in one hand and a pencil in the other. I must have interrupted a lesson.

'Sit on the stairs with me a sec, love,' I say.

She sits down daintily and I sit flush to her, our hips touching. I put my arm tentatively around her. She's not a tactile child normally, but she leans in to me.

'I'm leaving this job, Jane, but I'm not leaving you. OK?'

'You are, you're leaving like Mummy left, and you always said you wouldn't.'

'I won't be working here,' I say, but I lift my spare hand to my heart and pat my chest. 'But you will always be in here, and I hope I will always be in there.' I point to her narrow chest. 'Just like your mummy is.'

Her chin wobbles, just briefly, and I can see her fighting tears. She almost never cries, but she lets herself now.

'I will write to you,' I say, as the tears slide silently over her sharp cheekbones. 'I promise.'

'Mummy never writes,' she says. 'And you won't either.'

'One day,' I say, whispering as I hear William's footsteps approach, 'I will tell you what happened to your mummy, but you have to know that she loved you with all her heart.' William is in the hall now. 'And I promise,' I say, using my normal voice again, 'that *I* will write. Cross my heart and hope to die.'

81

ROSEMARY – July 1992

The girls are finally asleep in the back of the Mini, exhausted from hours of complaining and questioning. My mother didn't help matters, asking awkward questions right in front of them as we said goodbye. I knew Aunt Winnie would tell her, gloating probably, as there's always been rivalry between that side of the family and this, but I hoped my mum would at least listen to my reasons. The reasons I'd cobbled together anyway.

'I just don't understand why you have to go so soon?' she'd said, clutching the girls to her even though she barely sees them. It's not like she's always on hand for babysitting.

'We just need to get settled before Bob starts the job,' I say, hoping she doesn't ask for more details on this imaginary job, hoping he actually gets one before she comes to visit. William's money won't last long otherwise, despite being so much more than I expected.

I can't tell her the truth. I can't tell anyone the truth. That Aisa saw something in the cellar of Moirthwaite Manor, and if she goes in there again, if she tells a teacher, if she convinces somebody to look … everything unravels. I have to get her away. If I could get Jane away too, I would. I made a vow to myself, years ago, that I would make sure she was looked after. The best

way for her to be looked after is for William to take her far away from this place and start a new life. I told him as much earlier. Only after he'd handed me the envelope of cash, of course, in case he reacted badly. But he didn't, he seemed to listen.

I said that it wasn't the best thing for Jane to stay, but I couldn't tell him the full reason why and so I just have to pray he took it on board. And that, in the meantime, Bob has fixed the cellar wall well enough to stop her getting through it again. Poor Jane. I have to trust that Jane won't tell anyone. That she has no one to tell. If she was going to tell her father, she would have. *I hope.* I wonder if she'll ever realise what she unearthed, maybe when she's a mother and her mind wanders back to her own childhood. God, I hope not. But then, if she doesn't, if they stay there unloved, unclaimed, is that really right either?

ROSEMARY – 1987

Bob is here, right beneath me, in the Brigadier's cellar. The way my belly is churning and my heart is thumping, you'd think he was wrestling a dragon down there rather than performing some basic handyman functions with his friend. But in some ways, both of those things are true.

I've already mopped the hallway floor, now I'm pretending to be dusting the balustrades. Circling the cupboard door like a dog waiting for its master.

I don't like him being here. Not just because it's my domain, a parallel life I've cultivated to the side of him. But mostly because of the effect it has on him. He insisted he was OK right up until we got here, but he's not. He got blotto last night and on the drive over this morning he was shaking like a little terrier.

William wants every trace gone. Of what, he didn't say. I've

not been down there myself, but Bob knew exactly what he meant as soon as I relayed the message. Cash in hand. Generous amount. Alan can't do it by himself. It needs to be someone William can trust. Someone who understands. And Bob understands all too well.

Selina is in the office with William, arguing again. Ordinarily, I would discreetly retreat to another part of the house, but I'm rooted here. I need to see Bob the second he's out of there, need to hug him and make sure he feels safe. To throw my body on the bomb.

'I don't care what you say or do,' I hear Selina say. 'You will *never* keep my daughter from me. Never.' She starts to emerge, just her thin shoulder, exposed by the loose T-shirt. Suddenly she's yanked back inside and William emerges instead. I have never seen him look like this. But I've seen this expression before, on his father. It punches the air from my lungs and I stumble in my panic to move out of view.

'You're not taking her anywhere,' he shouts. I rush into the library, my duster in hand. William storms up the stairs towards Jane's room and Selina shuffles into the hall, dragging a suitcase. Even from many feet away, I can see her trembling. I watch as she stands by the front door, staring up in the direction of her child. I think she's going to go upstairs to continue the fight until they tire themselves out as usual. Though this is more extreme, far more aggressive than I've seen them before. Instead, still shaking, Selina grabs her handbag from the hook, pulls on some shoes from a pile I've not long straightened and storms out. Seconds later, the front door opens again and she flings her keys onto the floor, then slams her way out.

William is still upstairs, guarding Jane, when Bob comes up into the hall. 'I can't do it anymore,' he says. 'Not today.'

'What about Alan?'

'He's already gone,' Bob says. 'We'd just started on the thing they used for Reflection. We got it down off the wall OK, but it left a big hole and it was... it was hard for us to touch it...' He rubs his wrists automatically, and I reach out and take his hands in mine. 'Alan made up some rubbish about tomatoes and went off to his shed ages ago. It's a right mess down there, but I can't... not today.'

I tell Bob to wait in the car, put the cleaning things away and then rush out. It's my normal time to leave anyway, give or take. As we head down the drive, en route to the childminder, I try to ask more.

He just shakes his head. 'We shouldn't have gone down there,' he says. 'I'd forgotten what it was really like.'

It's heady today, but thick rather than hot. Still, I wouldn't like to be out in it. Not like whoever that is down the lane, struggling with something. As we get closer, I realise it's Selina and her suitcase. I didn't think she'd actually go this far, not with all her stuff. She's threatened so many times, but this looks different. And he had looked different. For the first time, I saw his genes in action. Saw a glimmer of what William might be capable of, when pushed. Selina's crying so hard that her face is puce and she's clattering away from the house, the case banging into her legs so she zigzags around like a dying wasp.

I pull up next to her and Bob jumps out, flipping the passenger seat forward so she can climb in the back.

'Are you sure?' she says, as Bob takes her suitcase and tries to stuff it in the boot.

'Of course,' I say. As she settles herself, I reach back and pat her arm, just quickly. I try not to picture William's face earlier, the way the tendons on his neck had bulged like they were ready to snap. 'You're with friends now.'

I feel like I'm harbouring a fugitive as I let her into our house

while Bob walks to get the girls. If she's shocked by the size and chaos of our two-bed terrace, she doesn't let on. 'We don't have a spare room,' I say, 'but the sofa's quite comfy. If you want to stay.'

'Thank you,' she says. 'You're a real pal.'

Now she's wearing a big Hofmeister 'Follow the Bear' top as a nightie and I'm wearing my Stevie Nicks T-shirt and shorts. We look like we're at an overgrown sleepover. Rizzo and Sandy. The girls are finally in bed, Bob is in the pub and we're on the sofa, drinking the bottle of wine that I won in the school Christmas raffle last year. It's about the only booze Bob doesn't like and I'm not normally a wine drinker either, but Selina is. I can tell that from the way she swallows, trying not to show what she thinks of this cheap plonk.

She has just told me that she's going back for Jane. And I've just misunderstood.

'Yeah, you'll make it work,' I say, and she looks up from the glass she's staring into, twirling it in her palm like a crystal ball.

'No,' she says. 'I mean I'm going back to get her, and then we're *both* leaving.'

'He won't let you,' I say and she looks at me sharply. 'But you know he won't, Selina. He'll fight you, and he has the money and determination to do it.'

'He chose that house over me,' she says. 'He doesn't get to keep Jane too. I've told him that and it scares the crap out of him, he knows I mean it.'

'Where would you go? If you had Jane, I mean?'

'She's on my passport, so—'

'The States?'

She nods. 'Yeah, take her to Cedarville to see where her mom grew up. Show her all the sights – the churches, the lake, my daddy's tackle shop. Not forever, because it's boring as hell and

I'd never do that to Bill, but just for a little bit. To show him … to make him realise, you know?'

She takes a big gulp of drink, grimaces just slightly.

'I just have to get my daughter, Rosemary.'

I have always liked the way she says my name, turning it from three clear syllables into a sloping Roh-s'm'rry. The wine has gone to my head, because I only just stop myself saying this out loud.

'I feel so dumb for throwing the keys back in,' she sighs, stretching her suntanned legs out like a cat about to clean itself. 'But if I show up banging on the door, there's no way he'll let me come in and just take her. He's as determined to stop me as I am to take her. I don't think there's anything he wouldn't do. You've not seen how he gets, not when he's really angry.'

I don't say anything, but I think of earlier. And I think of the Brigadier.

'I can't be apart from her,' Selina says. 'I just can't.'

'No,' I say, 'you can't. No mum can.'

'No,' she says slowly. 'No mom can.'

I look at her – how far is she willing to go? How far is any mother willing to go? All the way. Of course she is. And how well do I know William really? Is she right to be scared?

'Maybe you should try talking to him with someone there to keep you safe, someone neutral? If you knock on the door and—'

She shakes her head. 'There is no one neutral. If you or Bob did it, he'd fire you, Rosemary. And I don't really know anyone else. If I lawyer up, he'll do the same. And he has far deeper pockets. I just need to get her out.'

I stare at my glass and imagine it was one of my girls in that house, behind that locked door.

'I think I know how you can get in without him realising,' I say. 'But you can't ever, ever tell William that I helped you.'

*

We wait for Bob to crash home, stagger up the stairs and fall flat on the bed. I peel his shoes off for him, pop the window open to let the booze fumes out and then check on both the girls one last time, kissing their foreheads. It's a sticky night and their sweaty, pink skin coats my lips with the taste of salt.

No, no mother can be apart from her children.

Selina has changed into some jeans and a long-sleeved T-shirt and tucked her suitcase next to our sofa. I've already told her that she can take some of Lizzie's clothes for Jane, they're a similar age, so she doesn't have to waste time in her room. She can just grab Jane and go. I have to trust that she'll know how to keep her own child quiet on the way out.

I'm still wearing my T-shirt and shorts so I can just slip back into bed afterwards without any faffing, not that Bob's likely to wake up easily. And then, first thing tomorrow, I'll drive them both to the airport.

I switched my wine for tea as soon as we came up with this plan, but I'm glad that my senses are still slightly deadened. If I think about this too clearly, I don't know if I'll be able to go through with it. I only hope that I'm OK driving the car, it's still new. New to us. But when I sit in the driver's seat, window down, the fresh night air brings all my senses to the front. Adrenaline also helps me stay sharp as we rattle along the thin road from the village to the manor.

I have never been out here at night. The fields and hedges seem to be writhing with menace. A huddle of bats flap up towards the moon and the little stone walls that guard the road seem like sharp incisors, ready to swallow us up. 'Are you sure about this?' I say and Selina nods.

'Are you sure, Rosemary?'

Am I? Too late to back out now. 'Of course.'

I've told her everything I know about the passageway, but as I've never actually been in it, she's still going in blind. What I've gathered from Bob and Alan, and some of the boys over the years, is that it leads from the floor of the shed down to under the house, then, somewhere, there is a set of steps that lead up to the hallway cupboard. As long as she finds those steps, and goes up quietly, she'll be able to move around the house without anyone knowing. She just needs to get Jane, slip out of the front door and make it down the drive, where I'll be waiting in the car.

As she climbs out of the Mini, our flaky old torch in her hand, I think of something else. 'Don't put your torch on until you're fully in the passageway,' I whisper. 'And avoid Alan's tent. If he hears you, he'll raise the alarm or ...' I think of the gun he uses for rabbits, but I don't want to scare her. 'Just be really careful, OK?'

'OK,' she says quietly. 'Thank you so much for this, Rosemary.'

'Good luck, Selina.'

I've quietly turned the car around without putting the lights on. Now I'm ready to roll away down the drive as soon as the precious cargo is on board. I'm not thinking about William. I'm resolutely not imagining him finding Jane's bed empty tomorrow. Walking around that monstrous house, desperately looking for the people he loves. I'm not thinking about looking him in the eye knowing I helped squirrel them away. Instead, I'm thinking about how long Selina's been gone. I'm wearing my dad's old watch, the only watch I own, and wondering if it's keeping time correctly because it feels like Selina left the car hours ago, but apparently it was only thirty minutes. How long is this passageway?

An hour later and she's still not out. I've left the car where it is and walked up to the house. The lights are all off, at least at

the front of the building, and I wonder if she ended up reconciling with William and they're curled up asleep while muggins stands out here, shivering. That doesn't feel likely though; I can't imagine her not coming out to tell me to go home. Maybe even William thanking me for bringing her back.

The moon is bright enough for me to see that all the curtains are closed, but Selina took our only torch, so I can't see much else. I pick up a tiny stone and weigh it in my hand... But if I'm wrong, and it's just taking her much longer to extract Jane, chipping William's window won't help her.

Oh God, I wish I knew what to do. It's cold now, my T-shirt and shorts ridiculously flimsy against the night air. I walk around the side of the house and follow the path she would have taken until I reach the shed. Alan's tent is just over there, but there's no light or movement from inside. I take a deep breath and open the shed door, not sure if I imagined the squeak. I can barely see the floor, and squat down, knees clicking from years of scrubbing on them, and gently pat the floor in front of me until I touch the rim of the entrance. As my eyes adjust, I can see that the hatch is still up. It's lucky I didn't fall.

There's nothing else for it, I take a deep breath and climb down.

The passageway itself is lit with dim bulbs and I can just about see all the way along. It's cold and slightly damp, as if the seasons can't reach down here, and I'm shivering as I walk along with my bare legs and tennis shoes. I can see cobwebs and mouse droppings, it smells ripe but somehow dead too. God, I don't want to be here.

I'm reminded of the stupid prayer my mum used to say when she put me to bed and whisper it to myself as I step carefully along the passageway. I can barely see Dad's watch in this dim light, but whatever it says, I feel like I'm running out of time.

I speed up and my urgent footsteps echo back to me, but there's a thin reedy sound too. A voice? A cry? I stop to listen, hoping it's my imagination. Then I hear it again. It could be her, or it could just be the whistle of old pipes, the wind trapped somewhere.

'Selina?'

There's no answer and I rush forward, emerging from the passageway into a kind of open hallway, with some doors off it. I'm punch-drunk, reeling that there is a whole other layer to the house. Bob has only described it in slivers, and in my head, I'd joined them together into some fractured thing that was nothing like this. This is huge. A full shadow version of Moirthwaite Manor was lying under my feet all these years.

There are three doors ahead of me – no, my mistake, there's one more round the L-shaped corner. She could be behind any of them. I look for the stairs, the ones she was supposed to go up, but there's bits of wood piled up and slabs of metal propped all around the walls. I can just make out a kind of dark enclave and I think the staircase might be in there, but there's a lot of detritus in the way. I'm briefly furious with Alan and Bob for leaving it like this, but that's hardly fair.

I think, from the little Bob said, the stairs must be there. One thing's certain, she can't have gone up there. But at least that means William can't come down and find me here, not through all that.

Selina probably couldn't even see the stairs. So she's either come back out the passageway and not told me, or she's still down here, devastated that the plan failed.

I hear the sound again. It must be her. But she can't just stay here crying and I can't stay out all night. I need to find her.

I try the first door, but it's just an old cupboard. A prehistoric mop and bucket, a broom that looks fit for a witch. The next

door opens onto an empty bedroom, coated in dust. By the look of the bed, this hasn't been used since the boys left. I shudder, imagining having to spend the night here.

The next room is an old coal store full of creepy-crawlies. I shut that one quickly.

The sobbing has stopped, and I wonder if I just imagined it as I reach for the last door.

How I wish I'd imagined this.

82

ROSEMARY – 1987

'What did you do to her?' I cry.

Selina is splayed motionless on the floor, her head on Alan's lap. His hands are stroking her hair and he's sobbing quietly. Lying on the floor in front of them is a strange long ladder, with two straps at each end, tattered as if they've been slashed. Our old kitchen torch is on the floor next to Alan's knees and I reach for it, running the dim light over this … thing. When I do, a blade sticking through the bars near one end bounces the light back to me. It's covered in black blood.

'What the hell is …' I swing the light round to Selina. Her face looks pale and serene, but blood has pooled from her throat, soaking her hair and Alan's lap. There's so much of it that nausea suddenly sweeps through me and I battle not to vomit.

'I didn't do anything,' he sobs. 'I just found her. She was caught up and I tried to help her … I did, Rosemary, I promise.'

'Oh Christ, we need to get her to a hospital.' I slide onto the floor next to her, trying to find a pulse on her tattered red neck. I can see the damaged wall from where Bob and Alan must have pulled this contraption down. 'What the hell is that ladder thing?'

'Reflection,' he whispers. 'I found her caught in it. Her ankles

and hands were in the straps and … he made it so you couldn't get out once you were in, not without—'

'The Brigadier?'

He looks behind him as if the dead man could yet appear, then nods. 'And she kept saying she thought it was the steps. I told her to stay still, but she didn't. She made it worse.'

'Oh Christ, Alan, I can't find a pulse, lay her down, we need to do mouth to mouth.'

He's not listening, he's still rambling as I brush the hair from her face and pull her from his lap onto the floor. My friend, my poor friend.

'We'd got it off the wall yesterday, but we just left it propped up. We didn't want to keep touching it.'

I put my hands on her chest, hoping to feel it moving, but it's not. Alan is still slumped on the floor, his hands in his lap as if she's still there.

'She was facing the wrong way, Rosemary. We had to stay upright on it or the blade would cut our backs, but she's short so the blade was by her neck … and she wouldn't stop panicking and moving and then it fell on the floor with her still caught in it.'

I've never done CPR, I've only ever seen it on *Casualty*, but I have no choice. I put my mouth over hers. She tastes of iron and wine. I close my eyes and blow everything I have into her. Once, twice, five times. I rise up, and Alan is still babbling about finding her. About hearing people in the grounds and going to his shed and hearing a cry.

I lattice my hands together and press onto her chest. She feels so fragile, like I might crack her open. I take a deep breath and then I push down, gently at first and then harder. There's a gurgling sound and more blood appears from her throat. No breath. And I know then that there's nothing I can do. Nothing I could have done. 'Alan,' I say. 'She's dead.'

*

I run up the passageway and down the drive so fast I think my lungs could genuinely rupture. I can't pump my legs fast enough, can't get the key in the ignition, can't work the handbrake with my shaking, sweaty hand. I have to get to Bob, have to get him back here to help. Alan is completely useless by himself. But everything seems insurmountable. My feet slip off the pedals. I can't risk the lights waking William, so I slide along in the dark, rolling without the engine, knocking the car into brambles and God knows what like a pinball.

When I hit the lane, I manage to get the engine started, flip the lights on and rattle back to the village. I slide into the usual parking spot outside our terrace and sit there, for just a moment, staring at the phone box. I could phone the police now, anonymously, and no one would know who I was. As far as anyone knows, I've been asleep in bed next to Bob like I have been every night for seven years and change.

Would they believe Alan if he said I was there? That she was trying to sneak into the house to the kidnap her own child, on my instruction, and got caught in a ... bloody torture device that my own husband had left there? A device that those poor boys had once been strapped into. The fear they must have felt, having to stay rigid, knowing that going slack even once would have pushed their backs onto that blade. Those boys, like Bob and Alan, who both have police records from back along...

I slap my own face. A woman is dead. She's dead because of me, but all the cogs in my head are churning through ways to get *myself* out of this. A woman, a mother, a friend, a wife, a daughter, is dead. I climb out of the car and unlock the house. Inside, our own phone sits waiting. I could call 999 and confess. It was an accident. It wasn't anyone's fault and—

'Mummy?'

I look up at the stairs. Nina is at the top in her nightie, golden hair plastered all over her forehead and her tatty old dog teddy hanging from one hand.

'Are you OK, love?' I whisper, climbing halfway up the stairs and then realising my fingers are red with blood. I put them behind my back, lean forward to kiss Nina on the forehead and then shoo her back to bed. 'I'm just getting a glass of water, do you want one?'

'Yes please, Mummy.'

I go back downstairs and wash my hands until the water runs clear and my cuticles are shredded. Back at the manor right now, Alan is sitting on the floor next to her body, waiting for me and Bob to come back. To tell him what to do, to fix this. As I carry a beaker of water back through the living room, I spot Selina's suitcase. Everyone thinks she left. If no one finds her case ... but could I really ...

I take the beaker of water up to Nina and check on Lizzie. It's OK, they're both all right. They're safe. We're all OK, we're all safe. I repeat it like a prayer as I go in to wake Bob up. Yesterday, he couldn't finish the job. Now he has a far worse task to fulfil.

I put the suitcase back in the boot and we carry the girls to the car. It's too early really, but we can't wait and risk Alan running to wake William, or William coming down to inspect the work, maybe braving the passageway, and finding them like that. It's all too messy, each one of us involved. But it was my idea. I sent her into that tunnel, I gave her the loose, sloppy directions that sent her stumbling into the wrong room looking for steps. Bob and Alan left that contraption lying there, ready to snap its jaws one last time. And Alan, heavy-handed Alan, cutting the straps on her arms and legs with his hunting knife even though it was already too late, her throat had met the blade.

There's no other option.

We pull up to the house and Bob climbs out with his toolbox and waves to William, who is standing in the window of his bedroom, staring out. Bob walks as naturally as he can around the side of the house as William slides his window open and calls down to me, combing his fingers through his hair. He looks so benign now, but what would he do if he knew the truth?

'Bit early isn't it, Rosemary?'

I swallow and try to sound normal. 'Sorry, William, there's a lot more to do than they realised, so Bob wanted to get an early start on it.'

'Are you coming in too?'

I shake my head and desperately try to keep my voice level. 'Just dropping Bob off. I'm not in today, remember?'

'Oh,' he says, 'sorry. A lot on my mind. Don't know if I'm, you know…'

'Coming or going,' I say, my voice sounding screechy and frantic in my head.

He raises one hand in goodbye and closes the window with a bump. I lean on the car and wait for my heart to stop hammering.

The girls have already conked out again by the time I pull into the lay-by by Ullswater, alert for early hikers.

It's clear though, no one is watching as I pull the suitcase from the boot, pop it open and stuff it with extra stones from the side of the road on top of the carefully folded clothes.

My children and the mountains sleep, as I stagger down to the jetty, look around one more time, then let go.

83

JANE – 4:41 a.m.

'The skeleton,' Aisa says. 'Fuck.'

I stare at the fire, imagining how frightened my mother must have been, alone, injured, just trying to reach me. And then falling…

'Oh God, Jane, I'm so sorry about your mum.'

'Yeah, me too,' I say. 'Thirty years of wondering about her, but I never made the link. I thought I'd actually imagined them… those bones.'

'Me too,' Aisa says. 'After a while.'

'And honestly, we left this house soon after you moved and I didn't think about them much at all.'

I feel Aisa shift next to me. Have I lifted thirty years of weight from her, or given her a greater burden than ever? She didn't imagine it, but the reality was worse than she could have ever guessed.

'There's something else,' I say. Because I've learned it's better to know everything, however unpalatable. And I feel a frenzied need to unburden.

'Something other than my dad burying your mum in the wall of your childhood home?' Aisa says. 'Something besides that?'

I smile, I can't help myself. Then I start to laugh, and so does

she. And I notice just how sharp her teeth are. I run my tongue along my own upper set, pointed, dangerous. Wolf teeth, my dad always called them. The two of us, the wolf pack.

I reach into my pocket, pull out the envelope and offer it to her. She fumbles and it drops to the floor, the scrawled name staring up at us.

As Aisa reaches down, she says, 'This is my mum's writing.'

I just nod. I know this hand so well, after thirty years of letters and cards, birthdays always remembered. First to Moirthwaite Manor and then to the new-build we moved to, not that long after the Kelseys left.

'What does it say?'

'You can read it, I don't mind.'

She swallows and carefully pulls out the card. A picture of a doll's house on the front, and a shaky version of Rosemary's looping writing on the inside. I watch as she reads. There are only a few paragraphs.

A confession. An apology. Finally, a suggestion.

I'm sorry I waited so long to tell you. I was a coward, yes, but I wanted to protect everyone. Once the truth is out, there's no going back. And I was so scared you would tell your dad, and he would come for her. So now you know you probably have a little sister out there, and I think you would be good for each other.

'Rosemary knew it was hitting me hard that I'd have no family left when Dad died,' I say, finding myself explaining, guilty at knowing about this for longer than her. Guilty that I'd not sought her out yet. 'He got ill around the time that she ... when she realised she wasn't going to get better.'

'So my mum cheated on Dad.' It's not a question. Aisa's voice is flat. Disgusted.

'Just once, according to the card. I wasn't sure whether to believe it, but I asked my dad if he'd had an affair with Rosemary when I was little. I just blurted it out last week and I could tell, just from the look on his face. He said it was just after my mum left. He was lonely and angry, and I guess your mum felt guilty. And I think Bob... I don't think he was coping at the time, that's me reading between the lines though.'

'But your dad—'

'He didn't know about you, no. And I didn't tell him, it was too late to do that to him.'

Aisa doesn't say anything. For a moment, I think she's angry, building up to storming off, but then she unzips her handbag and shoves her hand in, pulling out an identical envelope.

'I've not been able to,' she says. 'I knew there was something, deep down, you know, and I couldn't bring myself to look.'

'How about you do it now?'

She stares at it for a moment and then suddenly slides her thumb under the flap, opens it in one quick move and lets the card fall out. On the front, a picture of Liza Minelli from *Cabaret* stares out. Aisa rubs her thumb over Liza's face, takes a deep breath and flips the card open. 'Who are you, Aisa?' she whispers to herself.

It feels intrusive to watch, so I look at the fire. What's left of it.

I'd read my own card from Rosemary in my staffroom, while my assistant boiled the kettle and fussed around with biscuits, chatting away about nothing. It felt incongruous for life to be happening while I read this message from beyond the grave, but if anyone can handle that kind of dissonance, it's a funeral director.

'I don't know for sure,' Aisa reads from the card as Liza's cartoon kohl eyes bore into me, 'who your biological father is. But there's a very strong possibility that it's William Proctor. To get myself to pick up this pen, I convinced myself this was about health. That you need to know who you are so you can keep yourself safe and well. Things run in families, as you know. But it's not that. Not only that, anyway. Aisa, you are the most alive person I've ever met.'

Her voice cracks, but she doesn't look up and I watch in awe as she manages to keep reading.

'Having you as a daughter has been such a source of joy for me. You've brought me so much happiness, and a few near heart attacks, but mostly happiness. I know every part of you and I love every part of you, but if you don't know this ... then I'm getting in the way of you, Aisa, knowing every part of yourself. I know that now. I'm sorry I didn't realise it before.' She pauses and takes a breath. 'The one person I haven't told is Bob. I understand if you can't keep this from him, but I hope you'll find a way to fit things together. He loves you so much that I couldn't bring myself to take that away when he was already losing me.'

Aisa looks up. She's not crying, she looks more shocked than upset. The dazed look I see on the loved ones' faces when people have died suddenly, like they just can't quite make it feel real. Right up until the service, anyway.

She looks at the card again, and finds her place. 'Whatever you decide, I hope you look up Jane, I think she could do with a sister. Her address is in my book. More than anything, I hope you'll forgive me, my little Ace.' Her voice breaks, but she reads the last line. 'Because I'm so, so sorry. I will love you forever and ever, Mum.'

'You don't have to believe it,' I say. 'No one has done tests; we can't know for sure.'

339

She nods and keeps staring at the card. She brushes her fingertips over the words, brings the envelope to her nose but seems disappointed. 'It just smells like my bag,' she says.

So this is my sister, I think. Do I need a sister, like Rosemary said? I don't know. I needed one when we lived here, when all I had was Dad but he was consumed with – *by* – the house, and all its ghosts. I was always so jealous of Lizzie, of her having two sisters, a mum. I was probably horrible to her because of it. Having someone else to absorb Dad's sadness back then would have been some relief. But that's not a sister, that's a human shield.

At first, it was worse after Rosemary left. He couldn't handle the house without her and none of the local women he got in to help understood what he really needed. None of them were her.

Once we left, moving to the Midlands where there was no memory of any one and it was all brand new – even a new-build house – Dad became a different person. It wasn't immediate, of course. At first, he kept coming back here to check on it, and then arriving home dragging his shadows with him. Then he set up some mad CCTV system that, back then, buzzed a pager if anyone broke in. They never did. And Alan was here anyway. I didn't know he'd ever updated it to his mobile number, right up until his chunk of a phone buzzed earlier tonight. Alan turned the system off years ago, but—

'Did you turn on that big switch by the front door earlier?' I say, and she looks up, blinking.

'What?'

'Don't worry, it doesn't matter.'

It wasn't exactly dark days followed by light, it was more that we slowly emerged through grey. Once we left Cumbria, I had a good childhood. And my dad loved me, I never doubted that.

He became a writer. Not a very good one, but a fulfilled one. I'm not sure he would have wanted anyone to actually read his grand works, he just liked writing them. I laugh, but Aisa doesn't look up from the card. The words must be scored into her retinas by now.

But I guess I'm not totally unaffected. I mean, I played with a skeleton as a child. *I played with my mother's skeleton*. And I stayed obsessed with death. With containing it. I'm a funeral director after all. I did an art degree, but I'm a funeral director. I don't think it would take a psychiatrist to unpick that.

I watch her as Aisa reads it all over again. She has his hair, I think. And his teeth. And the same shoulders as me. It's up to her if she chooses to see this though, so I say nothing.

To have a sister would have meant to share him. I'm not sure if I would have wanted to share my dad when he was alive, but, fuck, I wish I could share this grief.

I hold my hand out to Aisa and she takes it in hers, just briefly, and then lets it fall. 'Are you OK?' I say.

'I don't know,' she says.

'The car's fixed,' Lizzie says, as she barges through the door, brushing herself off.

84

JANE – 5:22 a.m.

Rafferty offers to take Lizzie home with him, but she shakes her head. 'Thank you, my love, but no. I need to sort some stuff out with my sisters,' she says, 'so I'll get the train back later.'

'Are you sure?' he asks.

'Yes, I'm definite. A hot chocolate and a flake,' she says, 'that's what I'm ready for.'

If he's put out, he doesn't show it. Instead, he grabs her by the waist like she's Elizabeth Taylor, not Lizzie Kelsey, dips her slightly and kisses her for so long that we all look away.

'Did Lizzie just *dismiss* that sweet maniac who drove three hours in a *Wacky Races* car to help her?' Aisa says quietly.

'Yeah,' I say. When I pictured what Lizzie might be like as an adult, I just pictured child Lizzie but stretched, not—

'An absolute queen,' Aisa says.

'Good for her,' Nina says. 'Thanks again!' she calls after Rafferty, pointing to the Mini.

'My pleasure,' he says, smoothing his collar and climbing into his car.

'There's something else we need to do,' I say to the Kelseys, although Aisa already knows what I've decided. 'It's not going to be nice but—'

'Jesus Christ, Jane,' Aisa interrupts. 'That's putting it mildly.'

'My mum,' I say. 'She's ... There was an accident when we were little and your parents and Alan were involved and they covered it up and—'

'The bones,' Nina says, rubbing her forehead. 'Is that what you're saying?'

I close my eyes and nod. 'We could go to the police,' I say. 'But I had a different idea.'

'But it's not going to be nice,' Aisa adds, quietly. 'Like she said.'

Nina rebuilds the fire and then lies on the nearest sofa, the shotgun next to her at her request.

'I get that Alan didn't know what he was doing, but he still did it,' she says. 'And he's still out there somewhere.'

She can't go back down with us, she's too hurt and we need her to be able to drive as soon as this is done. This. What a tiny, tiny word.

I open the hallway cupboard door, shine my torch around. I haven't been down here since I was a child. I don't know if I can do this, if I can really—

'Take my hand,' Lizzie says, shoving ahead of me. 'I'll lead you there.'

'And I'll be just behind,' Aisa says. 'We've got you.'

Epilogue

JANE – Six days later

The beautiful black coffin sits backstage, ready for its final performance. It's quite unique, made from black poplar wood. Dad chose it himself, one of the more amusing of our final conversations, me propped on the bed with the brochure I'd brought with me from work, him telling me to just chuck him in an old cardboard box. 'It's more ecological,' he'd said.

'It would definitely be a lot cheaper than the wooden one,' I said, 'but luckily I can get these at trade prices.'

Gallows humour, maybe, but the thought still makes me smile. It was all planned to a T, the poem I would read, the clothes he wanted to be buried in. He even showed me how to do his hair.

Preparing my father's body should have been the hardest thing I'd ever done. But I feel sorry for ordinary mourners, who don't have a hand in these preparations. Alone with their thoughts, treading water, no professional diversions. For me, I was able to use everything I'd learned. I was able to ride pillion on much more of his journey than a daughter normally could.

My assistant, Deb, offered to help, but this was one job I could only do alone. Even before … but especially then. I had worried

I might rush it, my heels snapped at by adrenaline, or fear. But I took as long, maybe longer, than usual. An almost blissful calm. Reunited, at the last moment.

He looked so small on the dressing table. All the time he'd been in hospital, his gown and blankets had hidden the changes. His neck was thinner, his skin looser, I knew that. But underneath, he'd become curled and hollowed, like an autumn leaf. I dressed him carefully, not easy to do alone, and wished I could remember the times that I was small enough to be dressed by him. Though more likely it was my mother and then Rosemary.

The suit he'd chosen was too big for his final body. I cut the jacket slowly along the back with surgical scissors, placed it on him gently and used my hands, and pins, to tailor it. He looked sharper than he had in years. It's always exhausting dressing a body, the dead weight and strange pivot points, but I've been doing this for so long that I was almost on autopilot. Until I placed his shoes. A smell of shoe polish from childhood rushed at me. The way he would buff the toes of my slip-ons, the concentration on his face. Those were easy tears.

And then, when I was sure that I was truly alone, I began the rest of the preparation. Removing the lining of the coffin, the careful latticing, the intricate placement. Hello, goodbye.

I chose my favourite celebrant and my favourite florist, who has filled the funeral chapel with white chrysanthemums for me. A flower that symbolises truth and loyal life. I'm not normally one for symbolism, but it felt right.

I would ordinarily watch this performance from the wings, but I stand at the head of the chapel, gazing at the twenty or so mourners, and clear my throat. 'My father chose a Wordsworth poem for me to read,' I say, my voice quiet and determined. I

do not add that I have replaced it with a different Wordsworth poem, but I think he would approve of my choice. I think they both would.

> A slumber did my spirit seal;
> I had no human fears:
> She seemed a thing that could not feel
> The touch of earthly years.
>
> No motion has she now, no force;
> She neither hears nor sees;
> Rolled round in earth's diurnal course,
> With rocks, and stones, and trees.

It may seem left-field to almost everyone in the chapel, but not the three women on the front bench facing me – Nina, Lizzie and Aisa. And behind them, one man I was expecting and the other I never expected to see again. Alan and Bob.

The wake is held in a nearby village pub that my dad specified, even though I'd never known him visit it. Still, I've changed enough about his service without going against this. The main thing, he emphasised, was that he did not want to be buried in the family crypt in Moirthwaite. No matter what.

I flit between the small groups of people in a daze, not knowing what to say to any of them, not knowing which of Dad's different strands they knew. Only I knew the whole tapestry. I nod and smile at all of their stories, recognising him in almost none of them.

The women from the library are here. And the charity reps, hoping to get some hefty donation from the estate. A few staff from the hospice mill about. And the flotsam and jetsam of

casual friendships from over the years. I recognise very few of them and am glad to have a couple of uni friends, my assistant Deb and, of course, Nina, Lizzie and Aisa.

People are curious to know what I'll do with the money, how much I've inherited. They don't ask that outright of course, they inch around it. Sipping from the edges of curiosity like it's hot soup.

'Will you be moving into the family home?' they ask. They mean, of course, my dad's house in the Midlands; I'm not sure anyone knows about Moirthwaite. Dad barely mentioned it, simply saying that he didn't care what I did with it. 'Burn it, for all I care.'

'Is there much to sort out with the solicitor?' That one skims closer to the bullseye. I smile my dumbest smile and respond only to the actual words they are using – 'Not too much, no' – and not the question they're really asking, then I drift off to do it all over again.

The truth is that I don't want to live in my dad's house and I sure as hell don't want to live in Moirthwaite. I can cancel the fee tail. The law changed when I was a teenager apparently, but we didn't find out until Dad was getting his affairs in order, while he still could. But there's something underwhelming about selling that monster off to be yet another hotel. I'd like to use it to help people, but my family doesn't have a great history of such endeavours. Maybe I really should burn it.

I would have let Alan stay on there, I suppose, but Bob has whisked him and his tent off to live with him in Cheshire, something he's apparently been trying to get him to agree to since Rosemary died. He'd been deteriorating for years, but what happened with Nina was the final straw, and Lizzie called Bob to tell him just that when she finally got reception on the way to my funeral parlour on that bleak, sleepless morning six days ago.

The Kelseys had helped me take everything inside and then, at my insistence, left me there. Nina needed to get her ankle checked over, and they all needed to sleep. I'd watched them leave, Nina in the middle, flanked by a sister on each side. They weren't speaking, we were all shell-shocked, after all. But there was a peace between them, an almost visible understanding.

I spot Nina now, standing next to her girlfriend Tessa at the bar. That was the first call Nina made once she got reception during the drive. Pulling into a lay-by and easing herself out to call in private. An apology, she said, though I don't know for what. And a proposal. They're going travelling, giving up their jobs and camping their way around Europe.

'Working out what we really want,' Nina said. Better them than me.

'I haven't told the others yet,' Aisa says, a plate of untouched sandwiches and cocktail sausages in her hand. I didn't realise she was standing next to me until she started to speak. 'And look,' she says, 'William was your dad, not mine. I'm really, genuinely, sorry for your loss. But the stories in that funeral service meant nothing to me. My dad didn't go to university, he isn't a rich man or a writer. The closest he gets to reading a book is circling the stuff he wants from the *Betterware* catalogue.'

We both look over. Bob is gripping a glass of lemonade so tightly I think it might shatter, Alan is next to him on a bar stool, reading things from a little bit of paper. A middle-aged woman I don't recognise stands awkwardly nearby, undoubtedly trapped by terrible small talk.

'That silly man over there is my dad,' Aisa says. 'That's who my mum chose for me, and I think she was right.'

'I understand,' I say, hoping to hide the disappointment in my voice. But what else could she say, really? She can't even remember Dad's face. 'Just legs,' she always says.

She reaches for my hand. Her nails are dark red, chipped and bitten, but underneath they're just like mine. Even the knuckles. I didn't know you could recognise knuckles.

'I could always do with an extra sister though,' she says. She smiles her pointy smile. 'If you'll have me.'

I flash my mirror teeth back and squeeze her hand, just quickly, as Lizzie and Nina look over and smile sympathetically.

'That's good enough for me,' I say.

I tentatively reach forward, but she hugs me back willingly.

Afterwards, we walk together back to the chapel's garden, wordless. Aisa looks at her wrist. No longer an Apple Watch – 'I was a slave to that thing' – but a bulky man's timepiece, a scuffed face, mottled leather strap, inherited from Rosemary. 'They should be finished, yeah?' I nod. We pass under ornate wrought iron gates, weaving along the little path through all the lives.

We reach the plot just as the men are packing up. Two opposites: fat/thin, old/young. Both look a little uneasy. I feel like they would take off their hats if they were wearing them, but instead they just hover.

'Family?' Old says and I nod.

'My parents,' I say, and feel Aisa's hand suddenly on mine, gripping it. I realise my mistake and my stomach flips right over like a decked fish, but neither man flinches.

'Sorry for your loss,' the younger one says. 'We'll get out of your way.'

The soil is as black and shiny as the coffin itself. The gravestone shines in the fading light. Black granite with perfectly precise white letters that could never say enough. Aisa reads them out, barely loud enough for me to hear, but I know the words off by heart anyway.

'Loving father, William Jonathan Proctor, 1953 to 2023.'

'And loving mother,' I add. 'Selina Mary Proctor, 1955 to 1987. Never forgotten.'

*

Top Google Search results for 'Moirthwaite Manor' in September 2023

Urbex Site Report – Moirthwaite Manor *WARNING*

Visited August 2023

Google Maps location here

Got chased off by gunman. Approach at your own risk.

Urbex Site Report – Moirthwaite Manor

Visited November 2022

Google Maps location here

Visited with Pete G. and Tamsin S. Vast grounds with outbuildings still sound. Furniture visible through windows. Could not get inside as angry man (looked like a vagrant, not a security guard) came running at us from behind the house. Avoid.

Acknowledgements

The dedication at the front nearly read, 'For Ribblestaff Manhattan'. A private joke that precisely one person (my sister) would get. I think that's what having siblings is about. A private universe spun together from jokes, memories and understanding.

My sister (and only my sister) will share the same memories of taking our dog Skipper through a mop-and-chair showjumping course. Of eating lardy cake and watching Saturday wrestling. Of radio shows recorded on my Alba tape recorder and renting *Grease* from the video shop every time we were given a quid. Of colluding against our parents. Of characters invented in the back of the car who are still referenced over thirty years later, like Ribblestaff Manhattan and Mr Delaware Chicken. I don't remember how they started, but that's not the point. I hope *The Short Straw* captures some sense of those private sibling universes.

I started *The Short Straw* in Amsterdam, finished it in Kent and everything in between was written in Hilversum, Henley on Thames, Camber Sands, the Kentish Weald and, most fittingly, Cumbria. It was written while my husband, our ridiculous dogs and youngest two children (making up their own private jokes in the back of the car and being amazingly good sports), picked up and moved five times while we waited for our new home to be

ready. It was written as my beloved eldest two children moved out of the family home and into their shared flat. It was written, in other words, at some of the sharpest points of family life.

A time for considering everything I wished I could do over, those younger years when I was always so frantically busy; wishing I could slip back just for a day and hold hands a little longer, sod whatever deadline was breathing down my neck. Reflecting on the home we'd left behind, not quite as suddenly as the Kelseys, and the home we hoped to make.

It's all in there. It always is.

My amazing husband deserves a top slot in every book's acknowledgements, but he's earned some kind of crown this time. When I was in the final editing stage of *The Short Straw*, I broke my ankle (and came down with Covid the same day). Alongside working, parenting, doing all the dog walking and all the cleaning, he had to butler me food and drink, guide me up and down the stairs, help me sit in a garden chair in the shower, accompany me to X-rays (on one such trip, my name was read out as 'Holly Cheesedog', which almost made the break worthwhile) and turn a blind eye to the bizarre pyjamas I kept ordering for myself when I was high on painkillers. He's just the best.

Special thanks to my wonderful agent, Sophie Lambert, and my trailblazing editor, Sam Eades, who were so kind and understanding when I had to take all our Zoom calls in bed with my leg elevated on a cushion, looking half dead. I am so lucky to have such talented, hardworking and enthusiastic legends in my corner. On that note, I must also thank Francesca Pathak, Zoe Yang, Lucy Brem, Brittany Sankey, Ellen Turner and the whole team at Orion. My heartfelt thanks too to all at C&W, who work so hard for their authors.

Gillian McAllister, as always, has been my sounding board,

confidante and cheerleader. Our friendship is simply one of the greatest joys of my author life.

And final thanks to Richard Shepherd (and Robert Scragg, who introduced us) who gave me such insightful advice on urban exploring and decaying old buildings.

If I've forgotten anyone, I'm sorry. Please blame the pain-killers.

Credits

Holly Seddon and Orion Fiction would like to thank everyone at Orion who worked on the publication of *The Short Straw* in the UK.

Editorial
Sam Eades
Snigdha Koirala

Copyeditor
Francine Brody

Proofreader
Jade Craddock

Audio
Paul Stark
Jake Alderson

Contracts
Dan Herron
Ellie Bowker

Design
Charlotte Abrams-Simpson
Joanna Ridley
Zane Dabinett

Editorial Management
Charlie Panayiotou
Jane Hughes
Bartley Shaw
Tamara Morriss

Finance
Jasdip Nandra
Nick Gibson
Sue Baker

Marketing
Brittany Sankey

Publicity
Ellen Turner

Production
Ameenah Khan

Operations
Jo Jacobs
Sharon Willis

Sales
Jen Wilson
Esther Waters
Victoria Laws
Toluwalope Ayo-Ajala
Rachael Hum
Anna Egelstaff
Sinead White
Georgina Cutler

If you loved *The Short Straw*, don't miss Holly Seddon's electrifying previous novel...

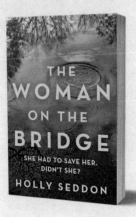

HOW FAR WOULD YOU GO TO SAVE A PERFECT STRANGER?

Maggie is trapped. Dumped on her wedding day, rejected by her family and hounded by a man determined to make her suffer.

Charlotte is desperate. Double-crossed by her only friend and facing total ruin, she will go to any lengths to save what matters.

Two women, one night. A decision that will change *everything*.

AVAILABLE TO BUY NOW

And be hooked from the first page with Holly Seddon's *The Hit List* ...

YOU LIVE AN ORDINARY LIFE. SO WHY DOES SOMEONE WANT YOU DEAD?

On the anniversary of her husband's accidental death, Marianne seeks comfort in everything Greg left behind. She wears his shirt and cologne, reads their love letters and emails. Soon she's following his footsteps across the web, but her desperation to cling to any trace of him leads her to the dark web.

And a hit list with her name on it.

To try to save herself from Sam, the assassin hired to kill her, Marianne must first unpick the wicked web in which Greg became tangled. Was Greg trying to protect her or did he want her dead?

AVAILABLE TO BUY NOW

Reader's Guide

1. What do you think the main themes of *The Short Straw* are?

2. What would you have done if you were the Kelsey sisters running out of petrol near Moirthwaite Manor? Would you have stayed together, split up or something else entirely?

3. Did you recognise the sibling dynamics at play and did they ring true in your experience?

4. Did you relate to one character in particular?

5. Do you think Rosemary did the right thing in telling Jane and Aisa her posthumous secret by letter? Should she have told Bob about Aisa's origins?

6. Which plot twist surprised you the most?

7. Of the surviving characters, who was the biggest present day victim of the events of the past?

8. Did you think Rafferty might be Lizzy's imaginary friend, like the imaginary friend she had as a child?

9. On balance, did Jane and the Kelsey sisters do the right thing in burying Selena with William?

10. Would you ever explore an abandoned building? Has *The Short Straw* changed your mind about this?

For my sister, Cristabel

First published in Great Britain in 2023 by Orion Fiction
This paperback edition published in 2024 by Orion Fiction,
an imprint of The Orion Publishing Group Ltd.,
Carmelite House, 50 Victoria Embankment
London EC4Y 0DZ

An Hachette UK Company

1 3 5 7 9 10 8 6 4 2

A CIP catalogue record for this book
is available from the British Library.

ISBN (Paperback) 978 1 3987 0952 2
ISBN (eBook) 978 1 3987 0953 9

Typeset at The Spartan Press Ltd,
Lymington, Hants

Printed and bound in Great Britain by Clays Ltd,
Elcograf S.p.A.

www.orionbooks.co.uk

THE
SHORT
STRAW

HOLLY SEDDON

ORION

Holly Seddon is an international bestselling author and one half of the popular Honest Authors podcast. After growing up in the English countryside obsessed with music and books, Holly worked in London as a journalist and editor. She now lives in Kent with her family and writes full time.

You can find her on Twitter @hollyseddon, and on Instagram and Facebook @hollyseddonauthor.

Also by Holly Seddon

Try Not to Breathe
Don't Close Your Eyes
Love Will Tear Us Apart
The Hit List
The Woman on the Bridge

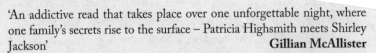

Praise for *Th*

'*The Short Straw* is an intensely re
turns tense, shocking and moving
cut with a knife'

'An addictive read that takes place over one unforgettable night, where one family's secrets rise to the surface – Patricia Highsmith meets Shirley Jackson' **Gillian McAllister**

'Deliciously creepy, and a fascinating study of the complex, often toxic, relationships within families' **Sharon Bolton**

'Utterly gripping and unputdownable' **Jane Fallon**

'Having three sisters, I could relate to the sibling dynamics … It's twisty, gothic, and with a heartbreakingly shocking reveal' **Lisa Hall**

'Holly creates such exquisite tension that you really can't put her books down … I felt the sense of place, the weather, the cold in that house in my bones' **Emma Curtis**

'A spectacularly dark, eerie, and haunting mystery. Should come with a "do not read before bed" warning' **Sophie Flynn**

'Gripping, creepy and drenched in atmosphere'
Catherine Ryan Howard

'*The Short Straw* practically pulses with foreboding and menace. Get ready to stay up all night! Fans of Shirley Jackson and Ruth Ware will love this. No one writes of family dynamics quite like Holly Seddon' **Jack Jordan**

'A highly enjoyable, many-layered mystery with a masterfully handled sense of foreboding … Ending was by turns terrifying, suspenseful, and heart-breaking' **Melanie Golding**

'Three sisters find themselves stranded at the gothic manor house that dominated their troubled childhoods. This irresistible slow-burn thriller is as much a study of family dynamics as it is a creepy & suspense-filled spine-tingler' **Fiona Cummins**

'*The Short Straw* is creepy, twisty and more than a little Gothic'
Sarah Hilary

Preface

This translation is the result of a casual conversation held with the director of a computer center in 1968. In discussing ways and means of making the computer useful to humanistic research our discussion turned to how the computer might assist in the preparation of translations. I confessed my reluctance to undertake a project which I nevertheless felt was essential for a firmer grasp of those two cultural movements marking the beginning of modern times, Humanism and the Renaissance. I had just completed a seminar on Humanism and had found appalling the inability of students to read certain Latin prose works of Petrarch. The obvious worsening of the situation in the study of Latin had convinced me that the only practical solution to the problem was to translate such works as were obviously basic documents in the history of such important cultural movements. Since very few of Petrarch's Latin works had been translated into English in their entirety, the prospect of future scholars undertaking such translations appeared dim indeed considering the excessive length of such works as the collections of letters.

As our discussions continued, it became clear that there was a variety of ways in which the computer could assist in the preparation of such translations. The one that appealed to me most was the use of the computer to prepare a Latin-English word list of Petrarch's letters that would start with the first word of the first letter and end with the last word of the last letter. This would mean that I would have at my disposal a printout that, if carefully prepared, would provide me with the basic and perhaps only tool needed to proceed most rapidly with the translation, that is, by simply dictating it into a dictaphone.

Since I had already started work on a book about Petrarch's Laura in anticipation of the six hundredth anniversary of his death in 1974, I determined to seek funding for the necessary computer assistance that would allow me to initiate the translation of the *Familiari* and by 1974 to carry it at least to the end of the eighth book which, as we shall see, was the original terminal point for Petrarch in the first stages of forming his collection. I was fortunate to win a large grant from the Research Foundation of the State University of New York without which the costs of the project would have been prohibitive. Most of the computer time was kindly donated by our computer center, while all other costs were defrayed by the grant.

The job of keypunching the entire text was begun almost at once, and by the summer of 1969 an alphabetical word list of unique forms was ready and awaited the inclusion of the English meanings. A team of five Latinists and I worked through the summer entering on special printout sheets from one to seven meanings of each word. By the winter of 1969 all entries were completed, and the computer next provided the desired chronological dictionary of all twenty-four books of letters. Circumstances prevented me from starting the translation until the following summer. Between the fall of 1970 and the winter of 1971 I was able to complete the translations of the first eight books. All translations were dictated on belts which were transcribed by a bevy of secretaries and student help.

Meanwhile we found that our computer program could also produce as a kind of by-product, a concordance of the entire collection. This was done almost at once, in the spring of 1970. The concordance ran to 288,000 forms, and should also see publication in 1975. Perhaps even more exciting is the prospect of preparing a dictionary of Petrarch's Latin which might eventually be expanded into a dictionary of Renaissance Latin.

The assumption that the computer's crude list of individual meanings could be transformed into idiomatic English proved to be fallacious, and the original translation was extremely stilted and awkward despite the translator's sense of its correctness. Fortunately my distinguished colleague, Bernard F. Huppé, agreed to polish this rough draft in which he sensed an almost diabolical mechanical touch. My hope had been to render the original Latin turn of expression as precisely as possible, but Professor Huppé convinced me that there were simply too many pitfalls in such an approach. I feel confident, barring some real computer voodoo, that as I proceed with the remaining books and with the *Senili* I shall be able to produce a truly idiomatic translation even in the first draft.

The decision to start this translation series with the *Familiari* was based on the fact that it is the only Latin work completed by Petrarch for which we have a definitive edition.[1] The monumental edition by V. Rossi and U. Bosco was transcribed into the computer verbatim and with its pagination and paragraphing. Original plans called for a facing translation with the exact Latin text of the definitive version. Prohibitive costs made it imperative to exclude the Latin. However, the translation retains the original paragraphing so that despite its rather awkward appearance to an English reader, it does allow him to refer readily to the definitive edition by using the beginnings of paragraphs as flagging devices.

With very few exceptions, the entire translation is my own. I have made minimal use of the outdated and rather impressionistic Italian translation by Fracassetti and only for the purpose of double-checking particularly difficult passages.[2] The recent Italian translation of the first four books by Ugo Dotti came to my attention too late to be of any use.[3] I refrained from using the many Italian fragments contained in the anthology of Petrarch's prose works edited by G. Martellotti.[4] I diligently avoided the English translations by Robinson and Rolfe and by Morris Bishop which are limited to a select group of letters.[5]

In order to avoid burdensome notes, I have identified only the correspondents to whom the letters were addressed. For the identification of specific allusions, whether proper names, events, or other references contained in the text of letters, the reader is referred to the exceptionally detailed, though in some cases outdated, notations appended to Fracassetti's translations. Dotti's notes to the first four books are also helpful.

For identifications of citations from classical and other authors the notes to the Rossi edition are more than ample, as are its subject-matter and name indices. All verse citations are rendered in prose and are incorporated into the text.

Names of authors cited in the text are given in the form in which they appear (Maro, Naso, Publius, etc.). The same holds true of the dates appended to most of the letters. As I shall explain in detail in the Introduction, any attempt to arrive at an exact date overlooks the fact that large numbers of letters, especially in the opening books, are fictitious, and were inserted by Petrarch at the time he organized the collection. The most useful guide to the letters for the identification of dates, correspondents, and of places of writing is Ernest H. Wilkins, *Petrarch's Correspondence* (Padua, 1960).

In addition to Professor Huppé, without whose assistance and advice the present translation would not have been possible, other persons to whom I owe a debt of gratitude include the director of our computer center at State University of New York-Binghamton, Robert Roberson; his assistant for special projects, Alfred Lynn; the Research Foundation of State University of New York whose generous support made it all possible; my secretary, Mrs. Dorothy Huber; my daughter, Adele; and especially my wife whose patience throughout the endless days and nights of hearing the steady pounding of typewriter keys never faltered.

Binghamton, N.Y.
January 1973

1. *Le familiari*, vols. 1–3 ed. V. Rossi, and vol. 4 ed. Rossi and U. Bosco (Firenze, 1933–1942).

2. *Lettere di F. Petrarca*, trans. G. Fracassetti, vols. I–IV (Firenze, 1863–1866).

3. *Francesco Petrarca, Le Familiari, Libri I–IV* (Urbino, 1970). New edition, vol. I, *Libri I–IV*; vol. II, *Libri VI–XI* (Urbino, 1974).

4. *Francesco Petrarca, Prose*, ed. G. Martellotti *et al.* (Milan, 1955).

5. James Harvey Robinson and Henry Winchester Rolfe, *Petrarch, the First Modern Scholar and Man of Letters* (New York, 1914); *Letters from Petrarch*, trans. Morris Bishop (Bloomington and London, 1966).

Introduction

This translation, when completed, will for the first time make available to English readers Petrarch's earliest and perhaps most important collection of prose letters written for the most part between 1325 and 1366, and organized into a collection of 24 Books between 1345 and 1366. The collection represents a portrait of the artist as a young man seen through the eyes of the mature artist. Whether in the writing of poetry, or in being crowned poet laureate, or in confessing his faults, or in writing to Pope or Emperor, Petrarch was always the consummate artist, deeply concerned with creating a desired effect by means of a dignified gracefulness. As early as 1436 Leonardo Bruni wrote in his Life of Petrarch: "Petrarch was the first man to have had a sufficiently fine mind to recognize the gracefulness of the lost ancient style and to bring it back to life." Bruni was confirming a view widely held by humanists of his day that the true father of the new devotion to *humanitas* had been Petrarch. Though greatly influenced by Augustine, Boethius and Ambrose, he was recognized by subsequent generations as the first man of letters to have "approached literature and the *studia humanitatis* in the full knowledge of their significance and of the value which an education of the mind through conversation with the great masters of antiquity was bound to have for the whole of mankind." [1] It was indeed the very style or manner in which Petrarch consciously sought to create this impression that was responsible for the enormous impact he made on subsequent generations.

This first, carefully organized collection of his prose letters mirrors "the most remarkable man of his time; and . . . one of the most remarkable men of all time." As a principal actor in the cultural life of the fourteenth century, and as one of the greatest interpreters of the general political ideas of a very complex period, "he was and is remarkable for his awareness of the entire continent on which the drama of European life was being enacted . . . for his awareness of the reality of times past and times to come." But perhaps what makes him most remarkable is, again in the words of E. H. Wilkins, "the fact that we know far more about his experiences in life than we know about the experiences of any human being who had lived before his time." [2] Or in the words of Morris Bishop: "he gives his correspondents—and posterity, his more remote correspondent—the most complete picture in existence of the inner and outer life of a medieval man." [3] These are the letters of a man of action and of contemplation addressed to a circle of intimate friends who have been called the first *cenacle* of Italian and European intellectuals.

The first eight books of the *Familiari* encompass the most crucial years of Petrarch's life, years that extend from his life and enamorment in Provence, to his crowning in Rome, and finally to the relentless loss of his dearest acquaintances. As we have noted, Book VIII was a natural stopping point in the evolution of the collection, a point that was reached in 1356. From the letters of Book I, which were obviously contrived to project the image of a wise young man dispensing time-honored wisdom to personal friends, to the letters of Book VIII, where he tries unsuccessfully to form a community of scholars from those few who had survived the great plague of 1348, one senses the maturing artist and intellectual. In between we see his growing intimacy with the powerful Colonna family with a stirring assurance to one of its members of Laura's existence (II, 9); his dedication to Rome as *caput mundi* (VI, 2); his adherence to the principle that both the active and contemplative life are equally effective in achieving salvation (III, 12); his ravenous hunger for books (III, 18); his sensitivity to eloquence and music (I, 9; III, 22); his famous comparison of life to a mountain climbing expedition (IV, 1); his dramatic reception of the laurel crown in Rome (IV, 3–8); his consolations and bereavement at the frequent deaths of prominent friends and acquaintances (IV, 12; V, 1); his reaction to conditions in Naples (V, 6); his advice to a Pope on the unreliability of physicians (V, 19); his advice to ruling princes (III, 7, 16; VII, 15); his short-lived enthusiasm for Cola di Rienzo (VII, 5, 7); his view of a proper education of the young (VII, 17); and impressive character sketches (IV, 14; V, 8, 9).

But perhaps the most important letters in these first eight books are I, 1 and I, 9 which provide significant insights into Petrarch's concern for form and style. Many scholars have indeed considered I, 9 a most revealing document because of the evidence it affords of Petrarch's crucial role in the evolution of Humanism. Despite its focus on the importance of eloquence for the thinker and writer, it goes beyond the mere revival of rhetoric and philology to a new vision of nature, of man, and of history.[4] For Petrarch *studia humanitatis* meant the cultivation of the mind through the careful cultivation of speech, *sermo,* which is the ultimate measure of mind's worth. The essential value of human speech, however, lies in its power to disseminate knowledge to others. Internal dialogue is of little value; speech must be outer-directed, it must serve the good of others, of one's neighbors. Even if it employs techniques borrowed from the pagans, it must contribute to the spread of Christian *caritas.*[5]

Human speech is the basic instrument for the process that can be called "authentically humanistic." It is capable of traversing and fusing the most distant epochs and spaces with truths that are eternal. As *Fam.* I, 9 states: "Let thousands of years flow by, and let centuries follow upon centuries, virtue will never be sufficiently praised, and never will teachings for the greater love of God and the hatred of sin suffice; never will the road to the investigation of new ideas be blocked to keen minds. Let us therefore be of good heart; let us not labor uselessly, and those who will be born after many ages and before the end of an aging world will not labor in vain. What is rather to be feared is that men may cease to exist before our pursuit of humanistic studies breaks through the intimate mysteries of truth."

Such then is the mission that Petrarch envisions for human

discourse. In the name of charity its voice echoes antiquity and sounds the future. It teaches the *studia humanitatis* which are intended to nurture the mind through the constant assimilation of the loftiest products of the human spirit from ancient and modern times. The Christian world has perfected the instruments with which to recapture and enrich classical values. The purpose of such studies is truth and not vainglory. If glory does accrue, it must rest with future generations and must serve as incitement for the good.[6]

Fam. I, 1, the dedicatory letter, was in all probability also written in 1350, the same year as I, 9, with the specific purpose of serving as introduction to the collection.[7] It describes the extreme pains taken by Petrarch in trying to give the collection an air of unity by including letters of an appropriate tone and character in order to avoid the deformity of a strict chronological ordering. It touches upon such other details as his search for the best title to give the collection and his careful avoidance of excessively personal matters. Petrarch's concept of stylistic unity reflects a strong, manly style in the opening and closing of the collection, leaving the weakest part for the middle portion. Ultimately the collection was to appear "woven with multi-colored threads."

If we were to combine the spirit of *Fam.* I, 1 and I, 9 with the content of II, 9 in which Laura, St. Augustine and St. Jerome are discussed with equal seriousness; of IV, 1 which describes the famous ascent of Mt. Ventoux; and of IV, 4–8 which describes the poet's critical decision on whether to be crowned poet-Laureate in Paris or Rome, we would see reflected in these first eight books the principal foci of the new humanistic vision.

Turning now to the collection as a whole, the *Rerum familiarium libri XXIV* is one of the three collections of Petrarch's Latin prose letters prepared by Petrarch himself. It contains twenty-four books of letters written to various people presumably between the years 1325 and 1366. The number of letters in the several books varies from eight in Book XIV to twenty-two in Book III. The collection as a whole contains 350 letters.

The great majority of the letters are addressed to definite

persons ranging from obscure priests and monks to the Emperor Charles IV and even to a number of famous writers of antiquity. In many of the letters the name of the correspondent is not indicated. With the exception of the last book, of which ten of the thirteen letters are addressed to illustrious ancients, all the designated correspondents are contemporaries. This last book also contains two letters in verse.

Among the correspondents having ten or more letters addressed to them are Giovanni Boccaccio; Philippe de Cabassoles, Bishop of Cavaillon, a small town in Provence; the Emperor Charles IV; Cardinal Giovanni Colonna; Francesco Nelli, a Florentine prior to whom Petrarch dedicated his second extensive collection of prose letters, the *Senili;* Guido Settimo, whose friendship with Petrarch extended back to their childhood days; and the Flemish Ludwig van Kempen, a learned musician and member of the Colonna circle for whom Petrarch had great respect and admiration, and to whom he dedicated the *Familiari.*

Each letter is introduced by a rubric announcing the subject matter and the addressee if any. The addresses use the form *Ad* with the accusative.

A good number of the letters of the first twenty-three books end with some indication of the date and, less often, place of composition. In these books the date is always indicated in the Latin form and never includes the year. However, eight of the thirteen letters of the last book, most of which are addressed to ancient authors, terminate with a *subscriptio* indicating the place of writing and the complete date, including the year.

As already mentioned, the first letter of the first book is a dedicatory letter to Petrarch's close friend, Ludwig van Kempen, whom, out of respect for his learning and wisdom, he always calls Socrates. The last letter of the last book is also addressed to him.

The individual missives vary in length. In the *Edizione Nazionale* (in octavo) the letters run from less than a page to a maximum of thirteen pages. The form of the letters is generally a running Latin prose except for the two verse letters of the last book, one addressed to Horace and the other to

Vergil. Throughout there are many quotations in prose or verse taken from classical or church writers.

The contents of the collection are extremely heterogeneous. To cite but two extreme examples, Letter IX, 4 deals with a "Revocatio amici a periculosis amoribus," while X, 1 is an exhortation to the Emperor Charles IV to descend into Italy. As Petrarch himself states in the dedicatory letter: "you will find many things in these letters written in a friendly style to a number of friends including yourself. At times they will deal with public and private affairs, at times they will touch upon our griefs . . . or still other matters that happened to come along. In fact I did almost nothing more than speak about my state of mind or any other matter of interest which I thought my friends would like to know."

In his study *Petrarca letterato* (Rome, 1947), Giuseppe Billanovich traces the history of the collection. Since this is considered the latest authoritative view on the matter, I am summarizing it here. The idea of forming a collection of his letters came to Petrarch in Verona in May of 1345 as he feverishly copied Cicero's epistolaries *Ad Atticum* and *Ad Quintum Fratrem,* and the apocryphal letter to Octavian, which he had then discovered. As he then envisioned it, his collection was to comprise letters in both prose and verse. It was not long, however, before he showed a decided preference for the prose form since it meant competing with Cicero, Seneca and the Church Fathers who appealed to him more than did Horace and Ovid. Quite naturally, the series of letters to the ancients, which were to constitute the bulk of Book XXIV, was among his first projects. In fact, he started immediately with a letter to Cicero written at Verona in those very days.

Once the idea of a personal epistolary had taken a firm hold in his mind, it became necessary to return to Provence, where the bulk of his library was located as well as copies of his letters. Having returned there in the summer of 1345, he wrote a second letter to Cicero and began going through the massive correspondence he had on file. The initial stages of the project were slow, what with the necessary listing, selecting, gathering all possible exemplars of classical collections, deliberating on the fundamental canons of epistolary technique (from form of address to date), fixing the number of books and the average size of each and arriving at a possible title. The collection, following the example of the *Aeneid* and the *Thebaid*, was originally to be in twelve books. The first book was to contain twelve letters. The last book was to be reserved for the letters to the ancients and introduced by the two letters to Cicero. The work was to be dedicated to his close friend Socrates. But the constant interruptions caused by other works which he was then in the process of writing (*Bucolicum Carmen, De vita solitari, De otio religioso*), as well as a trip to Italy, slowed the work considerably.

While at Parma in the summer of 1348, Petrarch composed another letter to another great ancient—Seneca. This was inevitable since, next to Cicero, the author of the *Letters to Lucilius* represents an influential model.

It was during Petrarch's first residence in Padua between 1349 and 1351 that the collection really began taking shape. A letter to Varro was added to those to Cicero and Seneca. The dedication and the first letter of the *Epystolarum ad diversos liber*, as the work was first called, were also written during this period and were sent to Socrates in Provence with the date January, 1350. A few weeks before Petrarch's departure from Padua at least six of the ten letters to the ancients (XXIV, 3–6, 8, 10) had been finished, and Boccaccio, who had been sent to Petrarch by Florence to recall its long lost favorite son, was permitted to copy them. Upon leaving Padua, Petrarch took the manuscript with him, and on the first stop at Vicenza en route through Venetia and Lombardy to Provence he read the two letters to Cicero to his traveling companions who discussed them at length as dusk settled. A few days later, he sent *ex itinere* copies of the two letters—introduced by what was to become XXIV, 2—to the poet Enrico Pulice da Costozza.

On his return to Provence in the summer of 1351, Petrarch was able to show to his beloved Socrates only a very incomplete piece of work—the two letters that Socrates had already received, a few other opening ones, plus those to the ancients that Boccaccio had copied. But between the summer of 1351 and August of 1353, he did a great deal of work on the collection. By the spring of 1353, he was able to send a friend (presumably Socrates) as a gift the transcription of the first three books and a fragment of the fourth with the letters arranged in an order that was to be kept intact in subsequent transcriptions and in a form which was to undergo but few substantial changes.

From the summer of 1353, when we find Petrarch taking residence in Lombardy, the progress of the collection continued unabated for many years. In May of 1353, he promised the Venetian Chancellor, Benintendi Ravignani, a copy of the collection and even permitted him to transcribe some of the letters to the ancients, but we find Ravignani still asking for his prize on January 27, 1356. It was not until late that year that the promise was kept and the Chancellor received a copy extending to Book VIII, 9.

Even before this, however, Petrarch had decided that he could not limit himself to a collection of twelve books, and he resolved to increase the number of books to twenty—after the model of Seneca's twenty books of letters to Lucilius and Cicero's total of twenty to Atticus, to his brother Quintus and to Marcus Brutus (a fact discovered by Petrarch at Verona). By September of 1356, he decided that it would be best to compile a separate collection of the letters of his later years: this was to be the *Rerum senilium libri*.

This expansion to twenty books would admit correspondence from the years of the composition of the *Secretum* (1341–42). Petrarch had been enlarging and polishing these letters all the while and then placed them into the second part of Book V and the beginning of Book VI without regard to chronological ordering.

After the embassy to Charles IV in 1356, Petrarch was able to develop the collection much more rapidly, for he was entering those letters which were written after the year 1349 with an eye to inclusion in the collection. In fact, some of the most notable and best constructed letters of the work, found in Book X and Book XI, were composed between 1349 and 1351. Between the early autumn of 1356 and the beginning of 1357 the transcription of letters into the manuscript had gone from Book VIII to at least Book X.

In 1358, Petrarch secured the services of a competent scribe and the collection proceeded rapidly and smoothly. At about the same time, together with Boccaccio and others, he had been introduced to the works of Homer through the translation of Leonzio Pilato. So by 1359 he had decided to increase once again the number of books of the collection, this time to twenty-four, following the example of Homer. During the few following years, Petrarch continued selecting suitable items from his correspondence. Finally, with the completion of the letters to the ancients, another scribe, Gasparo Scuaro dei Broaspini, was charged with the transcription of Books XX–XXIII shortly after March 1363. But this was intended only as a draft to evaluate literary and structural merits. It was not until the years between 1363 and 1366 that Petrarch's favorite scribe, Giovanni Malpaghini, was able to transcribe the definitive form of the last five books.

A vexing problem regarding the nature of the collection is that of identifying the fictitious letters that doubtless are scattered throughout. Vittorio Rossi, the editor of the definitive edition, was among the first to detect the presence of such letters. He believed that Petrarch had to amplify and revise his personal moral, political, and literary views in the letters. Furthermore, artistic exigencies required "fill-ins" if, as is stated in the dedicatory letter, the collection as a whole was to reflect a distinctive tone. Using evidence that emerged as he prepared the definitive version of the *Familiari*, Rossi identifies five letters as fictitious. These are: IV, 1; VII, 11; and XII, 14–16.

It was, however, Giuseppe Billanovich in *Petrarca Letterato*, pages 3–55, who first indicated the extensiveness of the fictitious letters. In his opinion, all those in the first book, with the exception of I, 1, were invented by Petrarch between 1340 and 1351. After indicating how, as a mature artist, Petrarch destroyed many works written in his youth because they no longer satisfied his higher standards, Billanovich maintains that among these must have been his early letters which, as a novice, he had written following closely the rules set by the *dictamina* and with the cadences of the *cursus*. Billanovich marshals persuasive evidence to support his view that Petrarch invented his early letters in the course of a few months.

Turning first to the dates that Petrarch appended to the letters Billanovich indicates how the twelve letters of Book I may be divided into two parts, with the months represented in each part perhaps inadvertently repeating a yearly cycle. Thus the month sequence of the first six letters is January, April, May, June, August; while that for the last six is March, April, May and December.

Billanovich next points out that throughout the Book may be found borrowings from classical writers with whom Petrarch is known not to have come in contact until the period 1350–51, especially Plautus, Quintilian and Horace. We thus find Letters 7, 8 and 9 representing a scholastic trilogy apparently derived from Quintilian's *Institutiones Oratoriae.* All three letters are addressed to Tommaso da Messina and form, as it were, a short tractate introduced by a polemic preface: "contra senes dyaleticos, de inventione et ingenio, de studio eloquentie." Since it is known that Petrarch received a copy of Quintilian's work as a gift in 1350, Billanovich imagines that Petrarch must have written this group of letters shortly after his return from his Jubilee pilgrimage to Rome. Other details singled out by Billanovich on this point are: (1) that Petrarch must have read right through the *Institutiones* and somewhat hurriedly since the citations derived therefrom are taken from a variety of books of the classic work and from well-advanced ones; (2) that in his copy of the *Institutiones* Petrarch made frequent favorable notations in the margins of that portion of the work dealing with Quintilian's invectives against dialecticians; and (3) that no borrowing from Quintilian can be found in the first six letters of Book I nor in the initial five letters to classical authors which represent the beginning of the collection.

Fam. I, 10, which follows upon these three letters, is nothing more than an elaboration of a long citation taken from the *Aulularia.* It, too, introduces an obvious trilogy (I, 10–12) addressed to Tommaso di Messina, except that this time the citations and the styles are derived from Plautus and Horace.

The subjects of these three letters are: *descriptio avari senis*, *descriptio famelici parasiti*, and . . . *ex reliquiis concertationes sopra posite cum dyaletico sene garrulo.*

Of the twelve letters of this first book, seven are addressed to Tommaso da Messina. Having identified the anachronistic nature of the last six, Billanovich tries to do the same with I, 2. He shows that Petrarch had carefully selected the argument in order to win praise of maturity in an age of immaturity, and that every paragraph contains evidence of its having been written later than Petrarch would like us to believe (the too harmonious eulogy of King Robert; the *quadrato canone* of Church fathers—Augustine, Jerome, Gregory and Ambrose; constant citations from works read or encountered later than the residence at Bologna, which the *subscriptio* presents as the presumable place of origin). Billanovich, therefore, concludes that these seven letters to Tommaso as well as the two others addressed to him in the collection (III, 1, 2) are nothing more than "gentili offerte di fama a quel rimpianto compagno di studi e della prima clientela presso i Colonna," and "si rivelano manifeste esercitazioni su lati e spesso usuali temi retorici." The single letter to Raimondo Subirani might also be similarly classified, according to Billanovich.

Proceeding with his argument, Billanovich then presents his conviction that it is precisely because the letters of Book I are fictitious missives (except, of course, for the very first one) that they are addressed exclusively to friends who had died before 1350. This plus the fact that subsequent descriptions of trips were to be addressed to Cardinal Colonna, prompted Petrarch to address the fictitious letters I, 4 and 5 to the Cardinal. Billanovich presents the following points in support of his thesis:

1. It could not have been mere chance that no Gamma (original or closest to the original) form has been found for any of the eleven letters in question (I, 2–12), especially since there is one for the very first letter of Book II. (He admits, however, the possibility that *Fam.* I, 6 to Bishop Giacomo Colonna is a re-working of a real missive since an echo of it is to be found in the late *Sen.* II, 5.)

2. Other letters beyond Book I, which are rhetorical exercises similar to those in Book I, seem more genuine because of the "accenni pratici e precisi che le costellano, particolarmente nell'aperture e nel commiato." In the second part of Book II the *consolatoria* and *hortatoria* after the manner of Seneca and Cicero show "vivace varietà," and in Books III and IV may be found "una serie quasi integra di reale corrispondenza."

3. A comparison with the opening portions of Petrarch's other collection of prose letters, the *Rerum senilium*, will show that the two were compiled by different methods: the latter systematically files real epistles. In the *Familiari*, "le convenzionalità di scuola minacciavano di sormontare," but in the *Senili*, "i casi e i doveri quotidiani stringono troppo."

Billanovich also disputes the authenticity of *Fam*. IV, 1 and 3 by exploring the relations between Petrarch and Boccaccio. He establishes the fact that the Augustinian Father Dionigi da Borgo San Sepolcro had started Boccaccio on the road to becoming "il più grande discepolo" of Petrarch. In Naples in 1338–39 he permitted Boccaccio to copy a verse letter (*Metr*. I, 4) and a prose letter (*Fam*. IV, 2) that had been sent to Dionigi by Petrarch. Billanovich asks why Dionigi did not also show Boccaccio the famous *Fam*. IV, 1 which had presumably also been addressed to him and which Boccaccio would certainly not have failed to include in his collection of Petrarch's writings. In like manner, he wonders why *Fam*. IV, 3 to King Robert never reached Boccaccio, who would certainly have received a copy of it from court friends of Petrarch. Indeed why did not Petrarch himself offer Boccaccio a copy of *Fam*. IV, 1 when the two met in 1351, since the letter was addressed to their closest common friend? Never does Boccaccio allude to the two letters, not even in those works in which one would certainly expect such allusions, the *De vita et moribus domini Francisci Petracchi* and Letters X, 3 and 4 in which affectionate mention is made of Petrarch's *fratello monaco* Gherardo, who figures so heavily in *Fam*. IV, 1. There is little doubt that Boccaccio also would have considered the letter the epistolary masterpiece of his master. It is natural, therefore, for Billanovich to conclude that these two letters are also fictitious and were

composed in 1352 or early 1353 when Petrarch was ordering
the first part of Book IV:

> . . . accorgiamoci finalmente che anche queste due lettere
> sono fittizie: secondo un costume abituale nella parte piu
> antica dei *Rerum familiarium*, formate dopo la morte del re
> e di quel confidente spirituale; non scritto nel '36 e nel '40;
> neppure pronte nel '51: composte nel '52 o all'inizio del
> '53, quando il Petrarca, verso la conclusione dell'ultima
> dimora in Provenza, ordinava la prima parte del quarto
> libro dei *Rerum familiarium* (p. 194).

He then shows how *Fam.* IV, 1 in particular points to late
composition. Like Rossi, Billanovich doubts that the letter
could have been written before Gherardo's unexpected conversion and entrance into a monastery in 1343. In the alle-
gorical interpretation of the letter it is the devout Gherardo
who has little trouble reaching the summit of the mountain,
whereas Petrarch encounters innumerable difficulties. It is
Billanovich's opinion that the idea for the letter came to Petrarch "da due entusiasmi di lettore appassionato" (p. 195):
first from the image of King Philip standing atop Mt. Emo
to gaze upon the two seas in Livy's *Ab urbe condita;* and
then from contemplation of the vanity of man who probes
into the mysteries of nature and the universe without scru-
tinizing his own soul, an idea derived from Saint Augustine's
Confessions.

As for the date of the letter, it was prompted by an "ob-
bedienza a ingegnose convenzioni." In the letter, Petrarch relates that in his thirty-second year Saint Augustine was converted by a sentence from Saint Paul's letters which he had
read by chance in the shade of a "fico salutare." (Petrarch
also alludes to a similar incident in the life of Saint Anthony.)
The ostensible date of the letter, which is 1336, and the reference to the *Confessions* create the analogy between the
humanist and the Church father. The first part of the date,
which gives the month and the day, was simply a happy expedient that enabled Petrarch to establish in well-rounded
figures another milestone in his life: for that day marked
exactly the tenth anniversary of his departure from the University of Bologna.

Billanovich brings further evidence of the fictitious nature of IV, 1. A glance at the biography of Dionigi shows that in 1336 he was in Avignon. Therefore Petrarch did not need to communicate with him by letter. And, if he did, there was no reason for trying to make it appear as though Dionigi were in Italy at the time Petrarch wrote: "inextimabilis me ardor invasit et amicum et patriam revidendi."

Billanovich collated posterior texts of the beginning portions of the collection with those presented to the friend from Avignon (presumably Socrates) to transcribe between 1352 and 1353. Such a collection, involving the first three books and the first three letters of Book IV, shows the majority of variants occurring in these three letters. The most natural explanation for this, in the opinion of Billanovich (pp. 194–197), is that these were the letters that had been either written at the time of transcription (IV, 1 and 3) or extensively retouched (IV, 2).

After devising the structure of Book III, Petrarch had to extract from his papers the letter that he had sent to Dionigi shortly after the latter's transfer to Naples (*Fam.* IV, 2). Nostalgic recollection of and sincere respect for the Augustinian father, who had nourished his spiritual life and introduced him to King Robert's circle, prompted Petrarch to build around this missive a small nucleus of letters which would represent for the reader of the *Familiari* the battles and anguishes of his soul, followed closely (as though to preserve the pattern of eternal oscillation found in his *Secretum*) by a dramatic account of his coronation. *Fam.* IV, 2 falls between the description of the ascent of Mount Ventoux and a supposed answer to an imaginary letter whereby King Robert of Naples was presumably to have offered Petrarch the laurel crown.

Billanovich believes that careful examination of *Fam.* IV, 2 reveals how it too underwent definite, though minor, modifications in order to fit within the new framework. The very last sentences are anachronistic if written in 1339. Since the ideas of these closing sentences are echoed in the subsequent letter to King Robert (IV, 3), it then follows that this one must have been fictitious as well. There are also indications that IV, 2 was modified to fit in with IV, 1: a Vergilian quotation that had been part of IV, 2 in its original form was transferred to IV, 1 and a paraphrase substituted.

Billanovich also casts a doubting glance at letter III, 1. We have already seen him labeling all the letters of the first book addressed to Tommaso da Messina "manifeste esercitazioni su lati e spesso usuali temi retorici." He now includes in this same category the "lontana peregrina dissertazione 'de Thule insula famosissima sed incerta', ostentamente offerta in testa al terzo libro con accademica esultanza per l'erudizione costipatavi." He bases his argument on a misspelling in the definitive as well as earlier versions of the letter which he maintains resulted from Petrarch's consulting a manuscript of Pliny's *Naturalis historia* in the Papal Library at Avignon in 1352 when he presumably began work on Book III of the *Familiari*.

In my unpublished Harvard dissertation I also adduce evidence to cast doubt on the authenticity of III, 8, 19; IV, 17–19; V, 9, 13, 15; and IX, 3.[8] In a chapter later published in *Speculum* XXXIII (1958), I show how Petrarch's practice of splitting excessively long letters into two or more separate epistles (for example, *Fam.* VIII, 7–9) belies the authenticity of some letters in the *Familiari*.

It is, therefore, essential that the reader of this translation bear in mind that a good portion of the collection, especially in the first eight books presented here, is composed of fictitious letters that were added to the collection to produce a desired effect—that of a learned man desirous of providing his friends and contemporaries with wise lessons derived from the best minds of all times and passed on by a devotee of letters who wished to revive in his correspondence the spirit of Cicero, Seneca and Augustine.

1. Eugenio Garin, *Italian Humanism*, trans. Peter Munz (New York, 1965), pp. 18, 19. Page 18 gives a full bibliography in support of the contention.

2. All 3 quotes from Ernest H. Wilkins, *Life of Petrarch* (Chicago, 1961), p. v.

3. *Letters from Petrarch* (Indiana, 1966), p. v.

4. Hans Baron, *La crisi del primo rinascimento italiano* (Firenze, 1970), p. xvi.

5. See *Fam.* II, 9 in which Petrarch explains that the reason he had

abandoned Jerome in favor of Augustine was because of Jerome's reluctance to turn to the pagans, and especially to Cicero.

6. E. Garin, *Italian Humanism*, pp. 19–20; U. Dotti, *Le Familiari*, pp. 5–14.

7. E. H. Wilkins, *Petrarch's Correspondence* (Padua, 1960), pp. 49–50.

8. A. S. Bernardo, *Artistic Procedures Followed by Petrarch in Making the Collection of the "Familiares"* (Cambridge, Mass., 1949).

Rerum familiarium libri I–VIII

To his Socrates.[1]

What are we to do now, dear brother? Alas, we have already tried almost everything and no rest is in sight. When can we expect it? Where shall we seek it? Time, as they say, has slipped through our fingers; our former hopes are buried with our friends. The year of 1348 left us alone and helpless; it did not deprive us of things that can be restored by the Indian or Caspian or Carpathian Sea. It subjected us to irreparable losses. Whatever death wrought is now an incurable wound. There is only one consolation in all this: we too shall follow those who preceded us. How long our wait will be I do not know; but this I do know, that it cannot be long. And however short the wait may be, it cannot avoid being burdensome.

But we must desist from complaining, at least for now. I do not know what your preoccupations or what your thinking may be. For me, I am arranging my belongings in little bundles, as wanderers are wont to do. I am considering what to bring with me, what to share with friends, and what to burn. I have nothing to be put up for sale. Indeed I am richer, or perhaps I should say more hampered than I thought, because of the great number of writings of different kinds that lie scattered and neglected throughout my house. I search in squalid containers lying in hidden places and pulled out dusty writings half destroyed by decay. I was attacked by a bothersome mouse and by a multitude of highly voracious worms; and the spider, enemy of Pallas, attacked me for doing the work of Pallas. But there is nothing that unyielding and constant labor cannot overcome. Therefore, beset and encircled by confused heaps of letters and formless piles of paper, I began a first attack by determining to throw everything into the fire, thereby avoiding a thankless kind of labor. Later, as thought followed upon thought, I found myself saying, "What stops you from looking behind

1. The Flemish Ludwig van Kempen, chanter in the chapel of Cardinal Giovanni Colonna, whom Petrarch first met in France in 1330.

like a tired traveler from a vantage point after a long journey
and slowly recalling the memories and cares of your youth?"
This thought finally dominated, and while the work involved
did not appeal as a grand undertaking, neither did trying to
recall the thoughts and memories of times past seem too unpleasant. But when I began turning over the papers piled at
random in no particular order, I was astonished to notice
how varied and how disordered their general aspect appeared.
I could hardly recognize certain ones, not so much because
of their form but because of the changed nature of my own
understanding. Other things, however, did come back to
mind with considerable delight. Part of the writing was free
of literary niceties, part showed the influence of Homeric
control since I rarely made use of the rules of Isocrates; but
another part intended for charming the ears of the multitude
relied on its own particular rules. This last kind of writing,
which is said to have been revived among the Sicilians not
many centuries ago, had soon spread throughout Italy and
beyond, and was once even popular among the most ancient
of the Greeks and the Latins, if it is indeed true that the
Attic and Roman people used to employ only the rhythmic
type of poetry. Thus, this sizeable and varying collection of
writings kept me busy for several days and made me concentrate with delight and attachment on my own creations,
and especially on those major works that had been interrupted for a considerable time despite the expectation and anticipation they had created in many. But the recollection of
the brevity of life overcame me. I feared indeed an ambush,
for what is more fleeting, I ask, than life, and what more determined than death? I reflected on the foundation that I had
established, on what remained of my labors and on my few
lingering years. It seemed rashness, indeed madness, to have
undertaken so many long and demanding works in such a
brief and indefinite period of time, and to have directed my
talents which would hardly suffice for limited undertakings
to so great a variety of writings, especially since, as you
know, another project awaits me which is the more striking
because actions are more praiseworthy than words. What
more need I say? You will now hear a thing perhaps incred-

ible but true. I committed to Vulcan's hands for his correction at least a thousand and more of all kinds and variety of poems and friendly letters, not because nothing in them pleased me but because to sort them would have required more work than pleasure. I am not ashamed to admit that I did this with a certain tenderness and with many sighs; just as an overweighted boat in deep waters can be lifted above the billows by discharging overboard even its most precious cargo so it was necessary to render assistance, no matter how drastic, to my preoccupied mind. In any event, while these were burning I noticed lying in a corner, a few others which had been saved, not consciously but by mere chance, or perhaps indeed because they had been transcribed earlier by scribes. All of these had somehow resisted the ravages of time. I say they were a few, but I fear that they may appear too many to the reader and too long to the scribe. To these I was more indulgent than the others and permitted them to live not because of their merit but as a consolation to my labor. Actually they seemed not to require much revision. So, weighing carefully the nature of my two dearest friends, it appeared best to divide the writings in such a way that the prose works would be dedicated to you and the poetic ones to our Barbato.[2] This I remembered that you had both once wished for and I had promised. Thus while all these things were being destroyed as I came across them, and—in the mood I was in—being disinclined to spare even these, the two of you appeared to me, one on the left, the other on the right, and grasping my hand, affectionately urged me not to destroy my promise and your expectation in a single fire as I had determined to do. This above all is what saved all those writings; otherwise, believe me, they would have burned with the rest.

Therefore these that are coming to you from among the manly portions of the remains, of whatever sort they may be, I am certain you will be reading with understanding and even with eagerness. I dare not refer to what Apuleius of

2. Barbato da Sulmona, member of the court of King Robert of Naples, whom Petrarch first met in 1341, and to whom he was to dedicate his collection of *Epistolae metricae*.

Madaura once said: "Oh reader, pay attention, you will enjoy yourself"; for where can I find so much confidence that I could promise my reader both amusement and pleasure? But nonetheless read these things, my dear Socrates, and since you are very kind to your friends, perhaps you will enjoy them, for if you approve of the writer's mind you will enjoy his style. What does an attractive figure avail if it is to be subject to the judgment of a lover? It is useless for a woman to beautify herself if she is already pleasing. If any of these pieces are appealing to you I must say that they are so not because of me but because of you. They are all testimonials of your friendship rather than samples of my talent. Indeed nothing among them required great power of speech; this I do not possess and if I did, to speak honestly, I would not use it with this style. Cicero himself did not use such a style in his letters although he was most distinguished in it, nor in those books that required an "equable" style, as he called it, and "a temperate type of speech." And so in his orations we find him using that unique kind of power and a lucid, rapid, and almost torrential kind of eloquence. Such style did Cicero use an infinite number of times on behalf of his friends, often against his enemies and those of the Republic; as did Cato often in behalf of others and forty-four times for himself. I myself am untried in this style, for to begin with I am free from all cares of state, and furthermore my fame, though perhaps provoked at times by the blandishments and threats of critics (with their soft murmurings or hidden hissings), has thus far not had to avail itself of vengeance or evasion, and thus avoided the wounds inflicted by legal actions. Nor indeed has it been our profession to use the power of the word to the detriment of others. Nor, endowed as I am with a deeply resisting and reluctant nature that made me a lover of silence and of solitude, and being an enemy of the forum, and a disdainer of wealth, have I striven for courtroom, judicial or political power or to lease my tongue. It was fortunate indeed that I did not feel the need for such things since perhaps my nature would have deprived me of them had I felt such need. Therefore, you will enjoy, as you have my other writings, this plain, domestic and friendly style, forgetting that rhetorical power of speech which I neither lack nor abound in and which if I did abound in I would not know where to exercise. And as a faithful follower you will find words that we use in ordinary speech proper and suitable for expressing my ideas. But surely all my judges will not be like you. Nor will they all feel or love in the same manner. But in what manner can I please everyone when I have always striven to please a few? Indeed there are three poisonous obstacles to genuine judgment: love, hate and envy. Be careful lest by loving me excessively you may be publicizing something that would best be hidden, for just as love would impede your judgment thus might something else impede the judgment of others. Between the blindness produced by love and that produced by envy there may be a great difference in point of cause, but there is no difference in effect. As for hatred which I had listed as second, I neither deserve it nor indeed fear it. It may happen that you could receive these trifles, read them and then call to mind nothing more than past events in our lives and those of our friends. This would make me very happy since your request will not seem neglected and my fame will be safe. I will not fool myself into thinking any differently. How can we believe that a friend, unless he is another me, could read all these things without aversion or boredom since so many of them conflict and are contradictory because of their uneven style and uncertain goal? Indeed, according to the variety of subject matter, I was often inspired to seek effects that rarely led to a joyful tone and often to a sad one.

Epicurus, a philosopher unpopular with the multitude but considered great by wise men, wrote letters to three of his friends: Idomeneus, Polienus and Metrodorus. Cicero did likewise with Brutus, Atticus and other Ciceros, namely, his brother and his son. Seneca wrote very few except to Lucilius. To know the mind and heart of one's interlocutor is not a difficult art and assures greatest success. To be accustomed to the personality of only one person, to know what he likes to hear, and what you should say, is a good quality in a writer. My fate unfortunately has been completely different. I have spent all my life, to this moment, in almost constant travel. Compare my wanderings to those of Ulysses. If the reputation of our name and of our achievements were the same, he indeed traveled neither more nor farther than I. He went beyond the borders of his fatherland when already old. Though it may be true that nothing at any age is long-lasting, all things are very brief in old age. I, begotten in exile, was born in exile, with so much labor undergone by my mother, and with so much danger, that she was considered dead for a long time not only by the mid-wives but by the doctors. Thus I experienced danger even before being born and I approached the very threshold of life under the auspices of death. Arezzo, not an ignoble city of Italy, recalls all this. It was there that my father, expelled from his native city, fled with a large number of good men. From there, in my seventh month I was taken and carried throughout Tuscany on the arm of a strong young man. Since I enjoy recalling for you these first labors and dangers of mine I might add that he carried me hanging at the end of a rod after having wrapped me in a linen cloth so as not to hurt my tender body just as Metabus had done with Camilla. While crossing the Arno, having fallen as a result of his horse slipping, while trying to save the bundle that had been entrusted to him, he almost perished in the violent current. Our Tuscan wanderings ended in Pisa whence I was once again snatched, this time at the age of seven, and transported by sea into France. We were almost shipwrecked by winter winds not far from Marseilles and once again I was not very far from being denied a new life on its very threshold. But where am I being led, forgetful of my purpose? Since that time to the present I have had either no opportunity or a very rare one to abide anywhere or to catch my breath. As for how many kinds of dangers and fears I have encountered on my trips no one knows better than you except myself. I have enjoyed recalling some of this for you so that you might remember that I was born in danger and have grown old under the same conditions, provided I have now grown old and that even more painful things are not reserved for me in my old age. Such misfortunes, although common to all who enter upon life (for man's life on earth is not only like military service but like actual warfare), vary with each individual as do the battles; and while particular burdens may weigh upon each person, the fact is that the actual burdens differ considerably from one man to another. Therefore in these storms of life, to return to the point, not throwing my anchor for any length of time in any port, and making a number of ordinary friends but unsure of how many true ones (being uncertain of their status and not really having very many), I struck an acquaintance with countless famous ones. I thus had to correspond a great deal with many of them who differed considerably in character and station. As a result, the letters were so different that in rereading them I seemed to be in constant contradiction. Whoever has had a similar experience must confess that to be contradictory was my only expedient. Indeed, the primary concern of a writer is to consider the identity of the person to whom he is writing. Only in this way can he know what and how to write, as well as other pertinent circumstances. The strong man must be addressed in one way, the spiritless one in another, the young and inexperienced one in still another, the old man who has discharged his life's duties in another, and in still another manner the person puffed up with good fortune, the victim of adversity in another, and finally in yet another manner must be addressed the man of letters renowned for his talents, and the ignoramus who would not understand anything you said if you spoke in even a slightly polished fashion. Infinite are the differences between men nor are their minds any more alike than the shapes of their foreheads. And as one particular sort of food not only does not appeal to different stomachs but does not even appeal always to a single one, so it is impossible to nourish a single mind at all times with the same style. Thus, writing entails a double labor: first to consider to whom you have undertaken to write, and then what his state of mind will be at the time he undertakes to read what you propose to write. These difficulties compelled me to be very inconsistent, but I have in part escaped the censure of hostile critics by availing myself of the benefits of fire, and in part by turning to you in the hope that you would accept these letters in secret and without revealing the name of the writer. If you cannot hide them from the few friends that remain (since friendship has the eye of a lynx and nothing can be kept from the sight of friends), urge those who may still have copies of these letters to destroy them forthwith, lest they become upset at the changes I have made in the content or in the style. For I never suspected that you would request, or that I would consent, to gather these things into a single collection; and so, avoiding hard work, what I had said in one letter I would often repeat in another to avail myself of what was mine, to quote Terence. When recently they all were collected together at one time and in one place, after having been written over many years and sent to various regions of the world, the deformity of the collection could be easily discerned though it was hidden in individual letters. Thus a word that had been happily used once in a particular letter being repeated too often throughout the collection began being troublesome. Therefore, I had to see to it that while it was retained in one letter it was eliminated from the rest. Similarly many things having to do with personal matters while perhaps considered a worthy insertion when first written now appear unwarranted, notwithstanding the anxious reader's interest. Seneca chided Cicero for this very thing although I must confess that I shall for the most part follow the example of Cicero more than that of Seneca in these letters. As you know, Seneca collected in his letters all the morality that he had interspersed in almost all his books; Cicero restricted his philosophical concerns to his books and included in his letters accounts of the highly personal, unusual and varied goings-on of his time. What Seneca might feel about Cicero's letters is a personal matter. As for me, I must confess, I find them delightful reading; for such reading is a change from having to deal with difficult matters, and is a source of delight if done intermittently but a source of unpleasantness if done continuously.

Therefore you will find many things in these letters written in a friendly style to a number of friends including yourself. At times they will deal with public and private affairs, at times they will touch upon our griefs which supply plenty of subject matter, or still other matters that happened to come

along. In fact I did almost nothing more than to speak a
my state of mind or any other matter of interest which
thought my friends would like to know. In this I agreed with
what Cicero says in his first letter to his brother, that the true
characteristic of an epistle is to make the recipient more informed about those things that he does not know. This I might
add was also the source of my title. After some thought on
the matter, I initially concluded that the name "Epistles"
would be suitable to them. But because many ancients had
used that title, and because I myself had done so (for various
metrical pieces that I had directed to my friends, as I said
previously), I did not want to use the same title twice, and
liking the idea of a new one, I decided to call the collection
Familiarium rerum liber. In it you will find very few letters
that can be called masterpieces, and many others written on a
variety of personal matters in a rather simple and unstudied
manner, though sometimes, when the subject matter so requires, seasoned with interspersed moral considerations, an
approach observed by Cicero himself. I must confess that
writing so much about so little was prompted by my fear of
caustic critics who, while writing nothing noteworthy themselves, make themselves judges of the talents of others. One can
avoid such impudent rashness only through silence. It is indeed
an easy matter to applaud from the shore in trying to determine
the skill of a helmsman. Against such impudence defend these
unpolished and improvidently released pieces at least by hiding them. That other work I have been polishing with great
care, though not a Phidian Minerva, as Cicero asserts, but a
true portrait and likeness such as it is of my talent if ever
I shall be able to give it the last touches, that work, I say,
when it reaches you, you may set up without concern at the
summit of whatever stronghold you please. But enough of that.
   Another matter which I would gladly remain silent about
must be mentioned. A serious disease is not easily hidden
since it breaks out and becomes visible through its own peculiar features. I am ashamed of a life fallen into excessive
softness. The very order of my letters will testify to this.
My style was strong and sober in the early years, an indicator of a truly strong mind, of the type which was a source

not only to myself but often to others. With the
time it became weaker and more humble and
ck strength of character. It is that style especially
ou to try to conceal. What can one expect others
n I myself blush at rereading those portions?
that I was a man in my youth and a youth in my
old age? Unfortunate and cursed perversity! My intention
was either to change the order or to make entirely unavailable
to you those letters which I now condemn! Neither expedient could have deceived you since you possess copies of the
more doleful ones and the exact date of all of them. I, therefore, take refuge in the power of excuses. Fortune exhausted
me with long and serious battles. As long as my spirit and
courage lasted, I resisted it and urged others to do the same.
When the enemy with her strength and attacks began to
make my spirit and resistance waver, the grand style perished
and I found myself descending to these lamentations which
now displease me. Perhaps the devotion of my friends will
excuse me. Just knowing of their safety was sufficient to prevent me from groaning at the wounds of fate. All these
friends, however, in no time at all were destroyed in almost
one stroke, and when the whole world seemed to be dying
it appeared inhuman rather than manly not to be moved by
it. Before this time whoever heard me complain about exile
or disease or litigation, about elections, or about any of the
public upheavals? Whoever heard me complain about my
place of birth, about ill fortune, about diminished glory,
about wasted money, or about the absence of friends? In such
adversities Cicero revealed himself so weak that while I take
pleasure in his style I often feel offended by his attitude. I
feel the same about his contentious letters and the many quarrels and abuses that he directs against famous men upon
whom he had not long before lavished praise. And I feel the
same about the casualness with which he does all this. When
I read his letters I feel as offended as I feel enticed. Indeed,
beside myself, in a fit of anger I wrote to him as if he were a
friend living in my time with an intimacy that I consider
proper because of my deep and immediate acquaintance with
his thought. I thus reminded him of those things he had

written that had offended me, forgetting, as it were, the gap of time. This idea became the beginning of something that made me do the same thing with Seneca after rereading after many years his tragedy entitled *Octavia*. Him also I reproached and thereafter, as occasion arose, I similarly wrote to Varro, Virgil and others. Some of these letters I have placed in the last portion of this work. I say this here so that the reader will not be filled with undue wonder when he comes upon them. Many of them I also threw in that bonfire of which I spoke. Just as Cicero played the role of a man in his sorrows, so did I, Today, however, so that you may know my present state of mind (nor can it be called envy if I should appropriate for myself what Seneca often says about the unskilled), I have become stronger out of that very state of despair. After all, what can frighten someone who has struggled with death so many times? "The only salvation for the vanquished is not to hope for any salvation." You will see my actions daily become more fearless and my words more bold. And should any worthy cause require a stronger style you will see style itself become more vigorous. Without question a great number of subjects will present themselves but I welcome this because for me writing and living are the same thing and I hope will be so to the very end. But although all things must have their boundaries or are expected to, the affection of friends will allow no end to this work which was begun haphazardly in my earliest years and which now I gather together again in a more advanced age and reduce to the form of a book. For I feel impelled to answer and to correspond with them constantly, nor does the fact that I am so terribly busy serve as an excuse for avoiding this responsibility. Only then will I no longer feel this obligation and will have to consider this work ended when you hear that I am dead and that I am freed from all the labors of life. In the meantime I shall continue along the path I have been following, and shall avoid any exits so long as there is light. And the sweet labor will serve for me almost as a place of rest. Furthermore as the rhetoricians and military leaders are wont to place their weakest parts in the middle, so I shall give to the work both a beginning and an end consisting of the most manly kinds of advice, all the more because as I grow older I seem to become stronger against the blows and injustices of fortune. Finally how I fare in the trials of life remains to be seen, for I dare not try to make any promises. This much is true, however, that right now my spirit is such that I shall never succumb to anything further. "If the world slips into destruction, the crumbling ruins will find me fearless." I want you to know that it is thus that I proceed armed with the advice of Maro and Horace, advice I formerly read about and often applauded but now, at last, in the final days of my life, I have learned to make mine because of the necessities of unavoidable fate.

This discourse with you has been most pleasant for me and I have drawn it out eagerly and as though by design. It has kept your face constantly before me throughout a great number of lands and seas, as if in my presence until dusk, though it was with the early morning light that I had taken up my pen. But the end of the day and of this letter is now in sight. These letters, therefore, woven with multi-colored threads, if I may say so, are for you. However, if I were ever to enjoy a steady abode and the leisure time that has always escaped me, something that begins to appear possible, I would weave in your behalf a much more noble and certainly a unified web or tapestry. I should like to be numbered among those few who can promise and furnish fame; but you shall step forth into the light through your own merits. You shall be borne on the wings of your genius and shall need none of my assistance. If indeed, among so many difficulties I should manage to enjoy a measure of success, I shall make you my Idomeneus, my Atticus and my Lucilius. Farewell.

To Tommaso da Messina,[1] *on untimely appetite for glory.*

No wise man advertises his complaints. There are enough, indeed too many, personal complaints to worry about at home. But do you believe that no one does this? You are wrong; there are very few who do not. The writings or deeds of anyone who is still alive are hardly ever pleasing; death lays the foundations for the praises of men. Do you know why? Because with the body dies envy, just as it lives with the body. You may say "but the writings of many are praised, which if one may boast. . . ." You do not proceed further, but instead as is the custom with angry men, you omit the sermonizing and leave the mind of your listener in suspense. Indeed in my own mind I follow the fleeting truth; I know what you mean; "the writings of many are praised, writings when compared to yours deserve no praises or even readers; while in the meantime none seem to be turning to yours." Recognize in my words your own indignation which would be justified except that you have appropriated for yourself something belonging to the common crowd, and especially to those who are victims or will fall under the spell either of the love or the disease of wanting to write. You must first of all consider whose writings are being praised. Search for the authors: you will certainly find that they have been dead many years. Do you want yours to be praised also? Then you must die. Human favor begins with the death of a man; thus the end of life is the beginning of glory. Should it begin earlier, it would be a most unusual and untimely phenomenon. I shall tell you even more: while any of your contemporaries survive, you will not fully enjoy what recognition you seek; when a grave encloses all of them, there will come those who judge you without hatred and without envy. Therefore let the present age judge us as it will; if the judgment is just, let us accept it with equanimity; if it is unjust, since we cannot turn to

1. Tommaso Caloiro da Messina whom Petrarch knew since his student days at Bologna. Little is known about his life beyond the fact that he too wrote love poetry in the vernacular as can be seen in Petrarch's specific reference to him in the *Triumph of Love* IV, 59–60.

others, let us appeal to the more equitable judges of posterity. Perpetual conversation is a most delicate activity: it is offended at the smallest provocation; and one's presence is always an enemy of glory. Familiarity detracts a great deal from the admiration of fellow men as does repeated intimacy. Have you not observed pedants, that species of men who have become slovenly through wakefulness and fast? Believe me, there is nothing that outdoes them in hard labor and nothing that is more flexible in rendering judgment. While they may read many things most industriously, they really ponder nothing; and whatever substance may be in anything, they disdain to seek it out when they feel they know the writer personally. Therefore there is a single law that applies generally: all the writings of those authors whom these men have seen even once are boring to them. You may say, "such things happen to small minds; the truly great and powerful ones make their way through whatever obstacles." Return Pythagoras to me and I shall deliver to you the despisers of his talent. Let Plato return to Greece, let Homer be reborn, let Aristotle live again, let Varro return to Italy, let Livy appear again, let Cicero flourish again, and we will find a few sluggish praisers of them but also biting and even spiteful detractors, for all of them met with them in their own day. Who greater than Virgil does the Latin language have? Yet you would discover those who said that he was not a poet, but a plagiarizer and translator of the inventions of others. And yet he himself, relying on the faith and judgment that Augustus had for his talent, disdained in a manly fashion the words of his detractors. I am aware that you also are highly conscious of your talent; but where will you find an Augustus as a judge, who we know protected the talents of his day most strenuously and in every possible way? Our kings are able to judge tasty dishes and the flights of birds, but not men's talents. Should they presume to do so, their puffed pride would not allow their eyes to open or to turn and contemplate the truth. And in order not to appear interested in their own age, they admire the ancients whom they disdain to become acquainted with, so that the praise of the dead is not entirely free from insult to the living. It is our lot to live and die among such judges, and, what is even harder, to be silent. For as I said, where do we look for a judge like Augustus?

Italy does have one, indeed the entire world has only one, Robert, the King of Sicily. Oh fortunate Naples whose good fortune has given you the incomparable happiness of having the only ornament of our age. I say fortunate and enviable Naples, most venerable home of letters, which if you appeared to Maro attractive in his day, how much more attractive would you seem now being the place where the foremost judge of talent and learning lives. Let whoever honors talent take refuge in you; and let him not postpone doing so, for all delay is harmful. He is well advanced in age and the world can lose him very quickly. He is worthy of superior kingdoms, and I worry lest I am preparing for myself cause for late repentance by too much delay. Deferring admirable things is shameful and similarly any prolonged deliberation in accomplishing the good becomes dishonest. The occasion must be seized, and one must quickly accomplish what could not be accomplished earlier. Insofar as I am concerned I intend to hasten and to act quickly, "so that," as Cicero says about Julius Caesar, "I am directing all my energies to that. In fact I shall do so most enthusiastically, and perhaps I shall accomplish what often happens to wayfarers when they hasten. If they happened to get started later than they wished, by hurrying they accomplish what they set out to do more rapidly than if they stayed up nights. The same holds with me since I have so sluggishly cultivated this man that I am trying to compensate for my tardiness by hastening." Thus did Cicero write. You however must act through the intercession of friends inasmuch as you are kept from approaching that king not so much because of the intervening straits but because of war. Your country, which none loves more than yourself, lies in the hands of a hostile king. I would say "tyrant" but for my not wanting to offend you. But these matters are very complicated and cannot be determined by our pens but by swords. Therefore I return to the beginning.

If these examples taken from the most famous men do not suffice, I can point to others of a different type and of more recent times and famous for their sanctity. How many rivals did Augustine, Jerome or Gregory have until such time as their respected virtue and their divine and astonishing abundance of writings overcame envy. Hardly any one of these enjoyed any public fame until the day of his death. I find written that only one was fortunate enough to have no rivals and detractors, only one was honored by rich and deserved praise. This was Ambrose, whose fame could not be affected by bitter envy during the course of his life. But perhaps this may be ascribed to the pure simplicity of his doctrine which avoids all ambiguity. The fact remains that in the works of Paulinus who wrote the *Life of Ambrose* we read both the names of his detractors and of the vengeance inflicted upon them by divine judgment. Therefore, bear without lament what you see befalling to the greatest men of talent.

However, you seem to complain in a certain part of your letter about the fact that many men achieved renown during their lifetime. This too, if you would listen to me, you would disregard with confidence. Surely you know to whom this happens; exclusively to those who defend their fame through clamor since they certainly know not how to write. Consider those who like to dress in purple and who with loud outcries draw to themselves the attention of the people. They wish to be known as wise men and are called such by the multitude which assigns swarms of wise men to each city. Compare this to that once flourishing mother of studies, Greece, that gloried in having not more than seven such wise men, a reputation that seemed even to posterity a sign of arrogance. But those who try to justify them say that the reputation fell to them not because of their personal judgment, but through the judgment of the people. Throughout the centuries Epicurus dared to declare himself a wise man, an intolerable arrogance indeed or rather a ridiculous madness to which Cicero refers in the second book of his *De finibus bonorum et malorum*. Today that madness has become common amidst the swarms of our courtiers. Just consider those who spend every minutes of their life in debates and dialectical scoffing and who are constantly stirred up by inane trifling questions. Observe them well and believe my prediction about all of them: the fame of all of them will disappear with their deaths and a single grave will suffice for their bones and their names. When death compels their cold tongues to remain still, not only must they be silent, but there will also be silence about themselves. I could produce examples in abundance and make you yourself a witness to many more—how many garrulous magpies do we know who take delight in squawking before the eyes of the mad multitude and whose voices have suddenly become silent. I refrain from doing so because my enumeration would be superfluous and perhaps even odious to some people. But we spoke about these and many others often in the past and now we must turn to the matter at hand. The purpose of my discussion was not to speak against them but to reply to you satisfactorily, your situation being completely different from theirs. Your reputation will resound when you will no longer be able to speak. Moreover, to be disturbed by a brief period of waiting is a sign of much too impatient a mind. Wait a little while; your wishes will be answered when you cease being an obstacle to yourself. Perhaps a long absence may answer your wishes in part, but death alone will really answer them for you. Recall the famous men of all times; Romans, Greeks, barbarians whose fame was not hurt by their own presence. Perhaps more historical examples will come to your mind since your memory is fresher. Only of Africanus, I recall, could it be said that he was extraordinary through reputation but even more through his presence. The same tribute was paid to Solomon in sacred scripture. Think of another, but I doubt that you will. Virgil, through his excessive zeal to embellish his Aeneas, tried to endow him with this kind of glory, but the truth is unshakable; and too many excuse him by maintaining that he was describing not Aeneas but under his name the strong and perfect man. In the same way that orator who could more truthfully have usurped the reputation for himself attributed it to only one other. I speak of course of that most illustrious prince of orators, Marcus Tullius, who did the same with only one poet, namely Aulus Licinius Archias. But I am afraid that he paid such a compliment to his teacher, a man of mediocre talent, because his love distorted his judgment, for he did not do the same with Homer nor would he have with Virgil.

Returning to you, there is nothing in all that I have said that could cause you to become upset. The only one who cannot bear to be surpassed by one or by a few is that person who stubbornly abrogates for himself preeminence and fame. Let fortune dispose of the destiny of your talent and of your name as it does with all other things. Did you think that her power extended only over wealth? She is the mistress of all human affairs except virtue; and often she even attacks virtue but never does she succeed in overcoming it. Fame, than which there is nothing less stable, she easily overthrows and causes to revolve with shifting favors, transferring it from those who are worthy to those who are not. For this reason nothing is more inconstant and unjust than the judgment of the people on whom fame rests. That such judgment is constantly shaky is not surprising, therefore, since it is supported on such weak foundations. Thus, fortune has power only over the living; death frees man from her. As a consequence such nonsense ceases and, whether fortune likes it or not, fame follows virtue like a shadow follows a solid body. Therefore, dear friend, unless I am mistaken, you have more cause for celebration than for anger if indeed your fate is similar to almost all the outstanding and famous men of the past. And that you may be even more reassured, I shall restore to his proper place the very Africanus whom I had seemed to separate from this company. As I said, although very unusual, his presence did not harm his reputation, yet like other men, envy, despite his many virtues, he could not avoid. In fact his very virtues enflamed and fanned envy. It angers me when I recall that he was harmed by excessive socializing and by contempt bred from excessive familiarity. You will ask where I get such information. I do not want you to suspect that I am transforming the truth. I shall cite the very words of Titus Livy, a very famous writer who, describing a disagreement between Scipio Africanus and Titus Flaminius concerning merit and esteem, reports that Scipio yielded and says, "the glory of Scipio was greater but for that very reason more subject to envy." And immediately afterward he adds, "Moreover, Scipio Africanus had been in public view constantly for almost ten years, something which makes great men less venerable because of excess." This too does Livy say. Therefore you, to bring this letter to a close, should consider yourself fortunate to be a member of such company and you will mark time more calmly recalling the old saying found in Horace that time improves poetry just as it does wine. And somewhat before him Plautus said, "I consider wise men those who use old wine as well as those who enjoy old stories with pleasure." I suspect Horace like you became angered at the thought that so much reverence was shown to the past that he had to defend himself in a long sermon of the "crime" of having criticized Lucilius. In conclusion, think of why we seem to torment ourselves so much. The fame we seek is but a breeze, smoke, a shadow: it is nothing. Therefore it can very easily be scorned by a clear and fearless judgment. But if by chance—since this pestilence usually pursues noble minds more relentlessly—you cannot eradicate this appetite because it is too deeply rooted, at least hold it in check through the power of reason. One must yield to the times and to circumstances. Finally, to summarize my thought most briefly, cultivate virtue while you are alive and you will find fame after your death. Farewell.

Bologna, 18 April.

Fam. I, 3.

To the venerable elder Raimondo Subirani, Attorney at Law,[1] on the fleetingness of life.

You fear, and perhaps rightfully, that, as happens to almost all young people, I have been beguiled by the flowering of my age. I do not promise you, O father, a firm and stable mind free from all vanity, which in this age of ours I consider very difficult to attain and to result from divine grace rather than human power. But I do pledge a mind by no means ignorant of its condition. I feel myself, believe me, while I seem to be in the very flowering of my life, beginning to wither. But why use slow words when referring to a very rapid occurrence? Indeed, I feel myself hastening, running, and to speak most clearly, flying. As Cicero says, "life does indeed fly." He then adds that "the time of this life is really nothing more than a race toward death." And according to Augustine, "no one is permitted to remain a short while or to delay in his progress while on earth, but all are driven equally in different ways. Nor indeed were days any faster for him whose life was shorter than for him whose life was longer. But rather an unequal number of moments were snatched from both. One travelled nearer and another further, but with equal speed. For to travel over a road further is one thing and yet another to travel more slowly. Thus the one who travels to his death over a longer expanse of time does not advance more slowly; rather he covers more of the road." That is what two such famous men have to say concerning the rapidity of mortal life, one asserting that it flies and the other that it runs. Indeed how often did Virgil say that time flies? And even if all were silent on the matter or even tried to deny it, would it fly or hasten more slowly? Please do not think that I speak of such matters somewhat blithely, or, as is the custom among my contemporaries, that I go about plucking gems from the gardens of authors. This habit Seneca called ugly in older people but is considered permissible for us younger ones. In fact nothing seems more becoming to youth. I do not deny that

1. A highly respected resident of Avignon and close friend of Petrarch.

I often read the *sentences* of great writers. I do so to use them among older people should the occasion arise; but just as I hope to arrive at welcomed old age with deserved praise, I consider such things much more important for the sake of leading the good life than for the sake of eloquence. And although I do delight in the study of eloquence, according to my custom, my talent, my bent and my age; nevertheless whenever I consider the wise sayings of others and whenever I produce something of particular eloquence, I view both experiences as useful to life and helpful against the evils of youth rather than as a temptation towards the fancy language of my juvenile discourse. One must indeed be mad to attempt excellence in something which one will probably never achieve and which comes to a few only, and which, were one even to achieve it, would be of limited benefit, and perhaps even harmful—at the same time neglecting what is intended for everyone, useful to everyone, and can never be harmful. However, we know, through the authority of great men and through experience, that eloquence is reserved for the few, while a good life is possible for all. Nevertheless more people seek the former and flee the latter. Such is the nature of men to seek what is difficult and pursue with great desire those things requiring greater toil. As for me, though my age may diminish my credibility, nevertheless I can assert in good confidence that I read not that I may become more eloquent or more witty but a better man, and I apply to all things what Aristotle said about moral philosophy. Yet, if both benefits do accrue, I would not deny that my attempts would indeed be fortunate. I do thank you, however, dear father, for warning me in such a fatherly manner, and I pray that you continue to do so. But rest assured that from this moment I have begun to understand my proper course and to recognize the perils that beset me. I also know a number of very old men who adhere to things of this earth more deeply, more fixedly, and more tenaciously than I. I was deeply touched by what the emperor Domitian said when already grown old: "there is nothing more pleasing than elegance but nothing more ephemeral"; and by what Tullius has Cato the Elder say: "Who is so foolish, though he be young, as to believe that he will live until evening?" Similarly by what Virgil said most seriously and maturely though still very young: "Oh maiden, gather roses while the buds are new and you are still fresh and young, and be mindful that your life hastens as quickly." I am mindful of these things, and although I cannot weigh them fully, yet I do as best I can, and strive harder each day. I do not consider what I seem to others but what I am, and I am aware that this age of mine, my bodily endowments, and whatever else belongs to me—the envy perhaps of others—were given to me as a venture, as a trial, as toil. In sum, I know that I ascend to descend, blossom to wither, grow up to grow old, live to die. Farewell.

Avignon, the calends of May.

Fam. I, 4.

To Giovanni Colonna,[1] *Cardinal of the Roman Church, description of a journey.*

Recently I traveled through France for no particular purpose, as you know, except for the youthful desire of seeing as much as possible. At one point I reached Germany and the shores of the Rhine River carefully viewing the customs of the people and delighting in the sights of an unknown country, comparing each thing to ours. And though I saw many magnificent things on both shores, I nevertheless did not repent being an Italian. Indeed to tell the truth the further I travel the greater is my appreciation of my native soil. And if Plato expressed his gratitude to what he called his immortal gods, among other things, for having been raised in Greece and not in another foreign land, what prevents us from expressing the same gratitude and recognizing our God as the author of our birthright? Unless, of course, it is more noble to be born a Greek than Italian; but whoever says this would also say that a slave is more noble than a master. But no ordinary Greek would dare say this, however great, impudent and imprudent he might be, when he recalls that long before the founding of Rome and before the birth of the empire on its foundations of valour, in short before "the Romans who were masters of the world and toga-wearing people," a certain portion of our country, which at that time was forsaken and deserted, was occupied by Greeks and called Magna Grecia. If it was considered great at that time how huge, how much greater would it have seemed after the overthrow of Corinth, after the devastation of Aetolia, and after the overthrow of Argos, Mycenae, and the other cities, and after the capture of the Macedonian rulers, and the subduing of Pyrrhus and after Thermopylae had been steeped in Asiatic blood a second time! I believe that no one would deny that it is considerably more noble to be Italian than Greek. But I shall speak of these things perhaps at another time. Let us now return to France. I entered Paris, the capital of the kingdom which claims Julius

1. An elder of the powerful Colonna family to which Petrarch was indebted for many benefits.

Caesar as its founder, with the same kind of attitude shown by Apuleius while visiting Ipatea, a city of Thessaly. Similarly, in suspense and in thoughtful anticipation, viewing everything carefully, desiring to see and to discover whether what I had heard about that city was truth or fiction, I spent considerable time in it. When the light of day was spent I devoted my nights to the visit. At last, ambling around and gaping, I observed enough of it to discern the truth about it and the fiction. But since this would be a long story which cannot be satisfactorily told here, I must postpone it until you can hear me recount everything personally. Not to mention the cities in between, I also saw Ghent which is proud of having the same founder as Paris, a magnificent and opulent city. I also saw the wool spinners and weavers of Flanders and of Brabant. I saw Liège, famous for its clergy; I saw the abode of Charles, Aix, as well as his tomb in a marble shrine, frightening to the barbarians. There from the clergy appointed to the shrine I heard a rather amusing story which they showed me as it had been written and which afterward I read in a more discreet form as recounted by modern writers. I should now like to tell it to you also provided, however, that you do not seek verification of it from me but, as they say, from those authors to whom it belongs.

They recount that King Charles, whom they dare equate to Pompey and Alexander by giving him the surname of "the Great," loved a certain ordinary woman desperately and immoderately. Overcome by her flattery and forgetful of his reputation which he was accustomed to cultivate carefully, and neglecting also the responsibilities of his position, and forgetful of all other cares and even of himself, for a long time he devoted himself exclusively to the caresses of this woman despite the indignation and sorrow of his people. When finally there seemed to be no hope since his mad love had closed his royal ears to all advice, an unforeseen death struck the woman who had been the cause of so much evil. As a result a wide-spread joy at first spread throughout the kingdom. This however was followed by an even more serious concern than the former one when the people saw their king overcome by a frightening illness, for his madness was not mitigated by death but instead became transferred to the foul and bloodless cadaver which had been treated with balsam and perfumes, weighed down by jewelry and covered with a purple shroud. Charles began strangely fondling it night and day in an attitude of sadness and longing. It is unnecessary to explain how unbecoming and unpropitious it is for a king to be a lover, for opposites can never be joined without serious consequences. What is a kingdom if not a just and glorious reality? By the same token what is love but foul and unjust slavery? Therefore when embassies, governors and other officials came to the lover or rather to the insane king to discuss very important affairs of the kingdom, he, wretched in his small bed, and with his doors shut and bolted, clung to the loved body, addressing his mistress repeatedly as if she were breathing and able to answer. He would relate to her his cares and labors, whisper blandishments, suffer nocturnal sighs and shed upon her constantly his tears of love. So this king who otherwise, as they say, was most wise, chose this dreadful consolation for his distress. The story adds something which I neither believe could have happened nor really think I should recount. It says that at that time there was in that court a bishop from Cologne, a man outstanding for his sanctity and wisdom, and indeed a primary counselor to the king. Having seen the pitiful state of his lord, and having noted that there was nothing that could be done by human means he turned to God and began praying constantly. He placed his trust in Him, and tearfully sought from Him an end of misfortune. When he had done this for some time and seemed ready to continue indefinitely, one day he found relief through a miracle which became widely known. As he was offering his usual mass and after his very devout prayers and tears which fell copiously on his breast and on the altar, a voice was heard echoing from heaven saying that the cause of the king's madness lay under the tongue of the dead woman. Joyful at this news and following the completion of the sacrificial offering he hurried to the place where the body was. He gained admission through a right granted him through his friendship with the king, and secretly with his finger he felt inside the dead woman's mouth and found a jewel encased in a very small ring under the cold stiff tongue. He then hastened away. Shortly thereafter when Charles hurried according to his custom to the dead woman, he was shaken by the sight of the withered cadaver. He appeared chilled and horrified at the contact with it and ordered it to be removed as quickly as possible and buried. Then turning to the bishop he began to love him, honor him, to embrace him daily more and more, and finally to do nothing unless it was approved by him. He also refused to be separated from him either night or day. When the good and wise man sensed what was happening, he determined to abandon a situation which, while perhaps desirable to most men, seemed burdensome to him. Being worried lest it fall into the hands of others or that it be destroyed by fire, or that it bring to his master any danger, he threw the ring into the deep ravine of a nearby marsh. At that time the king by chance happened to be living at Aix with his chief men, and from that moment that seat of government became preferred above all other cities. And no marshland became more pleasing to him than those waters beside which he sat and which he viewed with pleasure. Even the smell of the place came to please him very much. Finally he transferred his abode there, and in the middle of the marsh at an immense cost he built a palace and a church so that nothing, either human or divine, could draw him away from there. There he spent the remainder of his life, and there he was buried after having carefully ordered that there his successors be crowned and there they begin to rule. This tradition still continues and will continue as long as the reins of the Roman empire are in Teutonic hands.

I have taken more time in telling the story than I intended. But my extensive journey depriving me of the consolation of books, and my constant moving about making it easier to contemplate many things rather than great things, and being unable to fill my letter properly with serious things, I have crammed it as you can see with whatever was ready at hand. Farewell.

Aix, 21 June.

Fam. I, 5.

To the same correspondent, on the same subject.

Having left Aix, but not without first having been wet by
the luke-warm waters reminiscent of Baia—whence it is believed that the city gets its name—I arrived at Cologne which
is located on the left bank of the Rhine and which is famous
for its location, its river, and its people. I was astonished to
find so much civility in a barbarous land. I was equally surprised by the appearance of the city, the seriousness of its
men, the cleanliness of its women. I arrived, as it happened,
on the eve of the feast of St. John the Baptist when the
sun was about to set. Without delay and on the advice of
friends—for I had won friends there through my fame rather
than merit—I was taken from the inn to the river to see a
remarkable spectacle. Nor was I disappointed. The entire
shore was covered with a huge and remarkable crowd of
women. I stood there astounded. Good God, what beauty,
what costumes! Anyone could have fallen in love were his
heart free. I stood on a somewhat higher location in order to
understand what was going on. There was a remarkably controlled crowd. The women were cheerful, part of them girt
with fragrant flowers, with their sleeves folded back above
the elbows as they washed their white hands and arms in the
water and conversed in attractive though foreign whispers. I
never understood more clearly what Cicero liked about the
ancient proverb that "among the known languages everyone is
to some degree deaf and dumb," but I did have the comfort of
very gracious interpreters. You will be astonished to hear that
those heavens rear poetic spirits, so that while Juvenal was
astonished that "eloquent Gaul taught British orators," he
would have been equally astonished that "learned Germany
rears lively prophets." However, lest you misunderstood me,
keep in mind that there is no Virgil here but many Ovids.
(You might say that there was truth in the prediction made
at the end of the *Metamorphoses* where he maintained that,
depending on the good graces of posterity or on his own
talent, wherever the power of Rome or indeed wherever the
Roman name became established after conquering the world,

he would be read with applause by a favorable public.) I made use of these writers and friends as though they were my tongue and my ears whenever it was necessary to answer or understand. As I admired what I saw without knowing what it was, I inquired of one of the persons near me by means of that short verse of Virgil, "what is the meaning of the rush to the river? What do those souls seek?" I was told that it was a very old ritual of the people, widely accepted, especially by the women. They believed that any calamity that might befall throughout the year could be avoided by their washing in the river on that day and that therefrom more joyful things would happen. Thus the ritual had become an annual affair, cherished and cultivated with great enthusiasm. Smiling at this I cried, "Oh happy inhabitants of the Rhine whose afflictions are cleansed by it! Our miseries neither the Po nor the Tiber were able to cleanse. You send your ills across to the Britons by means of the Rhine; we would gladly send ours to the Africans and Illyrians. But we realize that our rivers are more lazy." After a good laugh, we departed rather late.

On the following several days I went about the city from morning to night with the same guides. It was a pleasant enough experience, not so much because of what I witnessed, as from the recollection of our more renowned leaders who had left such illustrious monuments of Roman virtue so far from the fatherland. Among the first that came to mind was Marcus Agrippa, the founder of Cologne, who, although he had built outstanding things at home and abroad, considered that city the most worthy of all to bear his name. He was a builder and distinguished warrior, worthy of having Augustus choose him as a son-in-law from throughout the world, as husband of his only daughter whom always he venerated and held dear. While there I also saw thousands of bodies of the sacred virgins and, dedicated to those magnanimous women, the soil which, so they say, rejects the remains of degenerates. I saw a Capitoline which was an imitation of ours; except that whereas deliberations of peace and law are heatedly held in the Senate in Rome, here in the evening handsome young men and girls together sing the praises of God in not deny that, the clown added, "therefore you are not a man." Then Diogenes answered, "your conclusion is in fact false, and if you wish to make it true you must begin your syllogism with me." There are many such kinds of ridiculous activities in which they indulge. They perhaps know what they are seeking—whether fame or amusement or a plan for a good and blessed life. I certainly do not. By noble minds, gain ought scarcely to be considered a worthy wage for studies. Such gain is proper for technicians; the goal of the honored arts is more noble. But when these dialecticians hear these things they become angry. This is because the talkativeness of the obstinate man is most like wrath. "So," they say, "you condemn dialectic?" Certainly not! In point of fact I know how much the Stoics respected it, that powerful and manly school of philosophers which our Cicero recalls often in other works of his as well as in his *De finibus*. I know that it is one of the liberal arts and a step forward for those who are striving for the heights and not a useless armor for those stepping into the thorny way of the philosophers. It rouses the intellect, marks a way of truth, teaches the deceits to be shunned. In short, if nothing else it makes men resolute and very keen. I do not deny that all this is true. But a place we pass through once and enjoy is not a place where we can justifiably linger; just as indeed it is insane for a pilgrim to forget the goal of his journey because of the pleasantness of the road. It is to the credit of the pilgrim to find quickly the proper limit, and never linger beyond it. And who among us is not a pilgrim? We all are on a long and difficult journey in a period of time as brief and difficult as a rainy winter's day. Dialectic can be a part of the journey; but it is certainly not its goal. And it can be a daytime rather than an evening part of it. We once did many things honestly that we would now do shamefully. If as old people we are unable to abandon the school of dialectic because we had fun with it as youngsters, we should not be ashamed by that same token either to play the game of odds and evens or ride on a trembling reed or be rocked in the cradle of children. Wonderful indeed are the variety of things and the changes of seasons which nature gladly planned to combat our boredom.

Do not think that you find these things only in the compass of a year. You will find them even more over a long lifetime. Springtime abounds with flowers and leafy trees; summer is wealthy with its fruit, autumn with its apples; winter abounds with its snows. If these things, which are not only bearable but actually pleasing, are distorted when the laws of nature are shaken then they become unbearable. Just as no one will endure calmly the frost of winter throughout the summer, or the heat of the sun raging in strange months; in the same way no one will be found who will not dislike or laugh at an old man playing with children, or be astonished at a gray-haired boy with gout. I ask, what is more useful to all disciplines than the early learning of the letters of the alphabet in which the foundations of all studies are found, indeed what is more necessary? But on the other hand what is more laughable than an old man busy with such things. You therefore rouse up the supporters of your old man with my words. Do not hinder them in any way, but exhort them, not indeed that they hasten to dialectic but that they hasten through it to better things. And tell your old friend that I am not condemning the liberal arts but only infantile old men. For just as there is nothing more unsightly than an old man dealing with elementary things, as Seneca says, there is nothing more deformed than an old dialectician. If he begins to spout syllogisms, my advice is to flee and order him to go and hold a disputation with Enceladus.[2] Farewell.

Avignon, 12 March.

2. One of the hundred armed giants who waged war against the gods.

Fam. I, 8.

To Tommaso da Messina, on inventiveness and talent.

You have asked me what to do finding yourself in that condition usual to almost all the host of writers who, although they either feel unsure of themselves or are ashamed to borrow, yet cannot stop writing because of the pleasure they take in it or because of the desire for glory natural to mortal souls. In such a perplexed and hesitant state you returned to me. First of all you would have done better to have sought a more skillful advisor, one who would have given you either a great many suggestions or the single one, the very best and the most carefully selected. Instead, you are now knocking on the door of a poor man, from whom, however, you will not depart with your hands completely empty. What I have received from others by begging I shall gladly give to you. I must confess, however, that in this matter I cannot give you much more than a single piece of advice. If after a trial you discover that it is ineffectual, you must blame Seneca. But if you find it effective you must render thanks to him and not to me. In short I want you to realize that he is the source of this advice. His loftiest advice about invention is to imitate the bees which through an astonishing process produce wax and honey from the flowers they leave behind. Macrobius in his *Saturnalia* reported not only the sense but the very words of Seneca so that to me at the very time he seemed to be following this advice in his reading and writing, he seemed to be disapproving of it by what he did. For he did not try to produce honey from the flowers culled from Seneca but instead produced them whole and in the very form in which he had found them on the stems. Although how can I say that something another wrote is not mine, when Epicurus' opinion, as recorded by Seneca himself, is that anything said well by anyone is our own? Macrobius must therefore not be blamed because he not only reported but actually transcribed a large part of one letter in the proem of his work. The same thing has sometimes happened to me and to many other greater writers as well. This much however I affirm, that it is a sign of greater elegance and skill for us, in imitation of the bees, to produce in our own words thoughts borrowed from others. To repeat, let us write neither in the style of one or another writer, but in a style uniquely ours although gathered from a variety of sources. That writer is happier who does not, like the bees, collect a number of scattered things, but instead, after the example of certain not much larger worms from whose bodies silk is produced, prefers to produce his own thoughts and speech—provided that the sense is serious and true and that his style is ornate. But in truth, this talent is given to none or to very few, so that we should patiently bear the lot of our personal talents, and not envy those above us, disdain those below us, or annoy our equals. I indeed know what you are saying to yourself silently: "this man is pulling me away from my studies and is discouraging me from being industrious while he teaches me to bear my ignorance patiently." Believe me I think nothing is more to be avoided than to allow laziness to age one's talents. When Cicero writes that men seem to him to be lowlier and weaker than the animals, outdoing them only in that they can speak, I believe we must either be indulgent to the famous orator for the praise he bestows upon his art, or we must take him to assume that speech itself could not exist without intelligence. In general, men seem to me to excel in the ability to understand, to distinguish, and to remember, traits which nature did not allot to animals, although some of them seem able to distinguish and in certain ways to remember. So where are we now? I urge and beseech us all to drive away vigilantly and most vigorously the ignorance in the shadows of our mind and make every effort to learn as much as possible while on this earth where the road may lead us to heaven. But let us remember in our striving that we are not all born under one star, so that because of our natural slowness our road may not extend to the very top. We must therefore be content with the limits of the talents that God and nature granted us. If we do not do this we shall never be able to live without anxiety. And as long as we pursue the knowledge of things, a road we must travel without interruption until our very last breath, new areas of darkness will appear daily into which our ignorance cannot reach. This is the source of our sorrow and indignation and disdain. Since the unlearned multitude will not see these dark areas, they live more gaily and calmly. And this is the reason why knowledge which ought to be the source of sacred pleasure becomes a source of very troublesome anxiety and extinguishes that very life which it promised to serve as guide. Therefore let moderation be present in all affairs. It will induce us to be truly grateful to the Eternal Dispenser not only for what pertains to fortune or to material things, but also for what is good for our soul, however little it may be, for He sees clearly what is good for us, and liberally grants us not what He knows to be more pleasurable but what is more useful. Just as that old man who owned a few acres was justifiably praised for equating the wealth of his mind to the wealth of kings, so will that man be praised who though ugly, dull or stammering, compares himself to Alcibiades for his beauty, to Plato for his genius or to Cicero for his eloquence. Therefore let not the man who lacks talent be lacking in equanimity; as for the man who possesses it, let discretion act as a moderator of all things so that he can judge his true strength with a clear judgment, lest perchance by flattering himself he should weigh himself down with an unbearable weight. This would be against what is written in the *Art of Poetry:* "Select your subject according to your talents, you who write; and consider well what your shoulders can bear and what they cannot." To be sure talent should be assisted by study and should be supported by contemplation, but it should not be compelled to ascend to heights that it cannot reach. Otherwise, aside from the fact that all attempts to do so would be useless, it often happens that while we long for the impossible, we neglect the possible. Now let me introduce a brief and, unless I am mistaken, useful thought, and a memorable one which I read in Quintilian, a very keen man. Since he wrote it briefly and clearly I prefer not to change his actual words: "It frequently happens even to gifted youths that they are worn out by labor and through the desire of speaking excellently they descend into the depths of silence. Concerning this matter I remember the Julius Secundus, my contemporary, and, as is well-known, truly loved by me, a man of wonderful eloquence but nevertheless of boundless diligence, told me what had been told him by his uncle. This was Julius Florus, a prince of eloquence, who practiced in Gaul with a fluency possessed by few men and worthy of his relationship to Secundus. When he happened to see Secundus who was still going to school, he asked him why his wrinkled brow. The young man openly admitted that although it was already the third day, and in spite of all his labor, he could not find a good beginning for his theme topic. As a result not only was he overcome with grief in the present but also felt despair for the future. Florus smilingly said, 'Do you really wish to speak better than you can?' " This is what Florus said to his nephew. And Quintilian in turn says to us, indeed to all of us, "That is the way it is. We should try to speak as well as possible, but we must nevertheless do so according to our ability. In order to improve, study is necessary and not impatience." This advice about eloquence can be extended variously to the other activities of men. But since the subject of this letter has to do with talent and eloquence, we must, as with everything else, learn to bear calmly either an excess or a lack of these qualities. If there be anyone upon whom the stars look with such benign light that he suffices unto himself without outside assistance and can by himself express great ideas, he owes much gratitude to the grace of heaven. Let him avoid arrogance and enjoy the gifts of the Lord with great humility and let him be unconcerned about the ways of the bees. For us, however, to whom such fortunate things do not befall, let us not be ashamed to imitate the bees, remembering what our Virgil has to say about them, "mindful of the coming winter they work in the summer, and, in between seasons, they store what they need." Let us also try to do so while there is time and while life glows and our talents are vigorous. Let us not wait until the cold of old age steals upon us and the winter clouds replace the brightness of the summer. We read in the work of the same poet that the bees also "at the return of summer keep busy among the rural flowers under the sun." And in another place he again says: "During the bright summer they settle upon the various flowers in the meadows and buzz around the white leaves while all the fields echo their murmur." Thus if we wish to apply with advantage the advice handed on by this illustrious teacher of conduct, let us adapt whatever is written about the bees to the activity of human inventiveness. What is our summer if not the flaming period of life? Similarly what is more like the cold winter than old age? What benefit do we expect to derive from this period of our lives and from this leisure, what harvest of talent, if now we stop frightened in the face of toil? What will posterity carry away from our granaries if we stand still in a sluggish idleness? "Naked does the farmer plough and naked does he sow; winter is a lazy time for him." But lest my subject slip from bees to farmers, now in the meadows and through the countryside let us settle on the various flowers of many others. Let us examine the books of learned men and from them let us alight on their very rich and very sweet lessons as though we were lighting upon the white lilies. But we must do so tirelessly as well as modestly and gently. Let us establish an honorable goal for our studies and not the vainglory of the multitude that derives from the witticisms of a windy argument. Let that goal be achieved through the effect of truth and virtue. Believe me it is possible to know something without noisy quarrels. It is not noise that makes the learned man, but contemplation. Therefore, unless we are determined to appear rather than to be, we will enjoy not the applause of the foolish multitude but rather truth and silence. And we shall be happy at the soft sound brought to us sometimes by words of genuine writers. Thus the fields will resound not with sharp noise but with a soft murmur. Since as you can see I have gone much further than the resolution of your doubts required, I shall add something else to what I have said thus far. Flee every place where one lives in a shameful or pompous way and shun the judgment of popular favor. You must know also that that place would be injurious no less to the bees than to you which "either emits a heavy odor of filth or resounds with the blows from a cut-out stone and an offended echo resounds." Do not think that this advice is directed to you alone but to all who are involved in the creation of praiseworthy things. It is primarily by two things that the creative genius of many is choked, namely, the habits of passionate appetite and the distortions of popular opinion. While the former sit inwardly the latter are located outwardly, and the mind becomes weakened and is kept far from the recognition of the truth. These are the things I thought I should say about imitating the bees. From their example, select and conceal the better ones in the beehive of your heart and hold on to them with the greatest diligence and preserve them steadfastly, lest anything should possibly perish. And be careful not to let any of those things that you have plucked remain with you too long, for the bees would enjoy no glory if they did not transform those things they found into something else which was better. You also, if you find anything of value in your desire for reading and meditating, I urge you to convert into honey combs through your own style. From them will flow forth what the present and future ages will ascribe to you with the best justification. Finally, that we may pluck no flowers today if not from the trees of Virgil, let me add the following, "From here you will squeeze sweet honey at certain times of the year, and it will not be so sweet as it will be clear, and will overcome the bitter taste of Bacchus." Farewell.

11 April.

To the same Tommaso da Messina, on the study of eloquence.

The care of the mind calls for a philosopher, while the proper use of language requires an orator. We must neglect neither one, if, as they say, we are to return to the earth and be led about on the mouths of men. But I shall speak of the care of the mind elsewhere; for it is a great undertaking and an enormous labor, though very rich in harvest. At this time in order to avoid slipping into a subject other than the one that I set out to treat, I urge and admonish that we correct not only our life and conduct, which is the primary concern of virtue, but our language usage as well. This we will do by the cultivation of eloquence. Our speech is not a small indicator of our mind, nor is our mind a small controller of our speech. Each depends upon the other but while one remains in one's breast, the other emerges into the open. The one ornaments it as it is about to emerge and shapes it as it wants to; the other announces how it is as it emerges. People obey the judgment of one, and believe the opinion of the other. Therefore both must be consulted so that one will be reasonably strict with the other, and the other will be truthfully magnificent toward the first. The fact remains that where the mind has been cultivated, speech cannot be disregarded, just as, on the other hand, there can be no merit to speech unless a certain dignity is present in the mind. What good will it do if you immerse yourself wholly in the Ciceronian springs and know well the writings either of the Greeks or of the Romans? You will indeed be able to speak ornately, charmingly, sweetly and sublimely; you certainly will not be able to speak seriously, austerely, judiciously and, most importantly, uniformly. The reason for this is that unless our desires first order themselves (and you must know that no one can achieve this except a wise man) it is inevitable that such disorder will be reflected in our conduct and in our words. The well-ordered mind is the image of an undisturbed serenity and is always quiet and peaceful. It knows what it wants, and does not cease wanting what it desires. Therefore, even lacking the ornaments of oratorical skill, it is able to call forth most magnificent and serious words harmonious with itself. Moreover, undeniably the most un-usual often emerges when the movements of the mind are composed. But when these are in agitation little of any signifi-cance can be produced. The study of eloquence requires much time. If we did not need it, and if through its own power our mind could silently display its good traits without the support of words, great toil would yet be necessary for the sake of those with whom we live. For without doubt, our conversa-tions would be of great assistance to their minds.

However, stepping forward, you say, "How much safer for us and more effective for them it would be to exhort them to let us provide for their eyes examples of our virtue. Delighted by the beauty of such examples they would be seized by the urge to imitate. For we are aroused perfectly naturally in much better fashion and much more easily through the stimulus of deeds rather than of words. Through this pass let us advance more readily to the highest reaches of virtue." In truth I am not opposed to this. How I felt about this you were already able to understand just now when I warned that among the first things that must be done is the ordering of the mind. Nor do I think that without good reason the Satirist said: "You owe me first of all the riches of the mind." These would cer-tainly not be first if anything came before them. Further-more, how much help eloquence can be to the progress of human life can be learned both in the works of many writers and from the example of daily experiences. How many people have we known in our time who were not affected at all by past examples of proper speech, but then, as if awakened, suddenly turned from a most wicked way of life to the greatest modesty through the spoken words of others! I shall not re-port here what Marcus Cicero said about this matter at con-siderable length in his books *On Invention*, for what he said there is very familiar, nor would I cite the fable of Orpheus or of Amphion, the former of whom lured huge beasts with his song and the latter plants and stones which he is said to have moved at will, except as one understands that because of their outstanding eloquence both were able to inculcate gentleness and patience in all things, the one into lustful and savage men whose customs make them very like beasts, the other into rustic and rough men who were as unmanageable as stones. Add to this that such study permits us to be useful to those living in distant regions with whom we will never be permitted to socialize but to whom our words may perhaps come. And indeed how much good we will do to our posterity can very well be judged when we consider how much our greater predecessors have left to us.

But once again you remark: "What need is there to work hard if everything advantageous to men has already been written during the past thousand years in so many volumes of a marvelous perfection by god-like talents?" Lay aside this anxiety, I say, and don't ever let it drive you into laziness. This fear was already removed by certain of our great ancients, and I shall remove it from the minds of those who come after me. Let thousands of years flow by, and let centuries follow upon centuries, virtue will never be sufficiently praised, and never will teachings for the greater love of God and the hatred of sin suffice; never will the road to the investigation of new ideas be blocked to keen minds. Let us therefore be of good heart; let us not labor uselessly, and those who will be born after many ages and before the end of an aging world will not labor in vain. What is rather to be feared is that men may cease to exist before our pursuit of humanistic studies breaks through the intimate mysteries of truth. Finally, if no sense of charity toward our fellow men drives us, I would still consider the study of eloquence of the greatest aid to ourselves rather than something to be held in the lowest esteem. Let others hold their own views. I cannot tell you of what worth are to me in solitude certain familiar and famous words not only grasped in the mind but actually spoken orally, words with which I am accustomed to rouse my sleepy thoughts. Furthermore, how much delight I get from repeating the written words either of others or sometimes even my own! How much I feel myself freed from very serious and bitter burdens by such readings! Meantime I feel my own writings assisted me even more since they are more suited to my ailments, just as the sensitive hand of a doctor who is himself ill is placed more readily where he feels the pain to be. Such cure I shall certainly never accomplish unless the salutary words themselves fall tenderly upon

my ears. When through the power of an unusual sweet temptation I am moved to read them again, they gradually take
effect and transfigure my insides with hidden powers. Farewell.

Calends of May

Fam. I, 10.

To the same Tommaso da Messina, a description of an avaricious old man.

You know that your little old man is very well in health. Conduct helps not only the mind but also the body; thriftiness is the sister of good health. Rest assured that this man will become immortal unless he is destroyed by hunger. So thin and emaciated is his little body that neither fever nor gout can find any place in it. His very appearance attests to the nourishment of the man, the pallor of his face, the leanness and cavity of his eyes, the sorrowful eyebrows, and his unpolished austerity. His shoe pulled up in the manner of a cothurnus and his small mantle frazzled with old age must be added to the picture. If he only knew some literature you would call him a philosopher or a poet, for his bare back smacks of the philosophical and his ill-shod feet of the tragic. Whatever might be added to this would be superfluous. So that I might explain in a few words, he is not very unlike the old man whose conduct and mentality are sprinkled with salt by his servant in the *Aulularia* when he says: "The pumice stone is not as hard and parched as this old man. If ever he sees smoke emerging from his kindling wood he cries out quickly for support from men and gods because all his belongings have perished and he himself has been destroyed. Indeed when he goes to sleep he ties a bellows around his throat lest by sleeping he should lose some breath. He even stops up his lower mouth lest by chance he lose any breath through that opening; he laments over the water that he pours forth when bathing, and by Hercules if you ask him for the use of his hunger he would never give it to you. Once indeed a barber cut his nails and he collected all of them and carried off the clippings . . . then a kite snatched some victuals from him and the man came to the praetor crying, and began to demand as he wept and wailed that the kite be bound over to him by bail. There are six hundred other stories that I would remember if there were free time."

Thus did the servant in the play of Plautus speak, but concerning our old man the inquisitive story teller would find six times six hundred such stories. Whoever would see this man or would hear him only once governing the management of a household by rules of economy known to no philosopher would call in contrast prodigal the guest of Apuleus Milo. But we are lingering excessively over the defects of others; let us return to our own. All of us mortals, or almost all, suffer from a certain disease; we are pulled by opposites, and what Flaccus says is indeed true, "when fools try to shun a vice they fall into the opposite one." What do we believe to be the difference between the cakes of Rufillus and the goat of Gorgonius, or between the loss of Aristippus and the epigrams of Staberius? One need not travel on distant byways to seek what makes one happy. Vice dwells in extremes; virtue in the center. Farewell.

Fam. I, 11.

To the same Tommaso, a description of a famished parasite.

I gather that your first request I handled successfully so that you are making a second one. I think you wish to test my capabilities in handling the demonstrative genre. I wish you were testing me in writings of praise rather than the contrary! But since that is what you want and the matter can be handled without names—although the exactness of the circumlocution takes the place of a proper name—I shall comply with this second request of yours. The man you inquire about is a "wandering buffoon" as Horace described him: "one who certainly has no stall and when hungry one who cannot distinguish a fellow-citizen from his enemy." In short he is the most insolent of all who ever devoted themselves to the art of the parasite. Nevertheless he is not at all happier than if he were the laziest of all. The sailor is not as fearful of reefs, nor the farmer of hail, nor the merchant of thieves, as everyone is of him. Everyone avoids him, everyone yields to his passage as if he came loaded down with thorns. Everywhere he finds empty roads, abandoned dwellings, bolted doors. One flees at his approach as if he bore war in his lap. However all these things never befall him more inconveniently than at this time of the year. Summer, however it may be, is the haven of the poor. A single tree suffices as garment, as meal, as roof and as bed.

But now what happens? There is a conspiracy of winter, old age and want. No one offers any aid and what is worst of all his wretchedness finds no compassion. I saw him today being buffeted by a strong north wind. He had his robes tucked up high and he permitted his hair to be blown about by the wind like Maro's Venus. If he had a yellow hat made of wolf skins, he would appear, among other things, to be going to war like a Hernian in his uniform adopted by the Pelasgians; for his left foot was naked. He was driven by such fury that he could admit about himself what that dangerous parasite proclaimed about himself in Plautus: "my fist is a military machine, my elbow is a catapult, my shoulder a battering ram." That is the way he appeared, but in such a manner that among the threats, the traces of a long hunger could be perceived. In short, as Plautus himself says, "I saw neither a more hungry man nor one more overcome by hunger nor one who accomplished less in whatever he began doing." Finally when I had turned aside from his sight into an alley, as though I were evading a pirate's galley in the shadows, I saw him *en passant* exhaling balls of smoke through the mist and it was as though I were passing by the cave of Cacus or one of the Aeolian islands. I heard I know not what quivering and confused sound issuing forth from his throat. I do not know what he wished to say, so broken into pieces were his words. I believe that he would find comfort for his feet and for his shoulders in that utterance of the Satirist: "Be patient and await the crickets." You have what you wanted and you have made me scurrilous. Farewell.

Fam. I, 12.

To the same Tommaso da Messina, the rest of the dispute with the garrulous aged dialectician cited above.

Here we are tempted again. Your dialectician, as you write, cannot be silent. Are you surprised? I would be surprised if he were silent since his fame depends on noise and insults. But it is a good thing that he knows not how to write and that I cannot hear him from here. In this way both my ears and my eyes (because of the intervening sea and land) are safe from his ignorance. So the entire weight of the unfit interlocutor falls upon your head, and deservedly, since you showed my letters to the dialecticians. Admittedly, from all the things that you say you had learned from his coarse barking, the foremost and greatest was that he says that of all the arts ours is the least necessary. Here finally he spews out the venom that was so threatening in the other letters. But is this what he warned that he would use in his assault upon our studies? Very clearly. He said, "Your art is the least necessary of all." First, let us examine this art; although I do not know what art he attributes to us, except perhaps the poetic art. He claims this to be the least necessary. This I do not deny. It seemed so even to our predecessors. "Poetry was born and invented for the benefit of souls." And Horace himself testifies that poetry itself shows it to be for pleasure and ornament and not for necessity. Therefore hurrah for your dialectician. May he abound always with sharp horned syllogisms since he feels as we do and is not ignorant of all things as I thought. But that burning and fiery talent is not restrained within these boundaries. What then? He twists together a swift enthymeme saying: "If it is less necessary it is also less noble." Oh how badly his madness is covered! Now he shows himself not only a dialectician but also a madman. If necessity ennobles the arts, the most noble of all would therefore be the shoemaker's, the baker's and the other lowest of mechanical trades. But philosophy and all the others, the ones that make life blessed and cultivated and decorated, if they do not contribute to the needs of the multitude, are the ignoble ones. Oh new and exotic doctrine unknown to Aristotle himself whose name such arts would disgrace! He indeed says: "All are indeed more necessary but none are more worthy." Let him read the first book of the *Metaphysics* and he will find these words. But I am ordering the old man to proceed in an unknown region of truths and to go along an exacting path, not a light labor indeed! Farewell.

11 December, at the source of the Sorgue.

Fam. II, 1.

To Philip, Bishop of Cavaillon,[1] that he must bear the death of his dear ones with composure.

Your virtue removes from me the enormous difficulty of having to write to you now. For just as the cure of a bodily affliction is more difficult the more serious it is, so it is with the mind. For both, a healthy condition requires no cure or a very light one. And just as with the former there is little or no need for a doctor, with the latter there is little or no need for a consoler. With you, therefore, excellent sir, I should be more careful if misfortune had either crushed or battered you. Since you have borne the blows of fortune with a strong heart, you have snatched from me the role of consoler and have imposed the duty of a praiser and admirer. In this manner, as I was saying, you have cut off from me the need for a more worked-out style. For in order to have consolation pierce the mind of a sorrowing listener, it needs great majesty of words, as well as weighty and bold sentences. For virtue a simple and unpolished witness suffices, nor is it necessary to color the truth of things with fancy colors since virtue applauds itself, and content with its own proclamation, does not need the sounds of a theater audience. I had recently come to you shocked by the bitter report of the premature death of your beloved brother. I measured the extent to which your mind must have been stricken by the anguish of my own heart. Nor did I consider that certain blows which might be fatal to fresh recruits are scorned by strong and proven soldiers, and that certain ones terrified by the flowing of the blood of others would cry out, groan and grow pale and would often collapse in terror, while the ones from whose breast the blood flowed would remain silent, and undaunted, with dry eyes, view their bleeding wounds. Thus I had come a sad and sick doctor approaching a healthy patient. I found your face displaying signs of your having been caught between the affection of a proper piety and the dignity of your own character, between brotherly sympathy

1. One of Petrarch's earliest and dearest friends whose diocese included Vancluse of which he was the feudal lord.

and manly courage. Both attitudes pleased me; one is fitting to your gentleness the other to your wisdom. It is human at the death of one's dear ones to shed tears as evidence of one's devotion; it is manly to place a limit upon them and to control them after they have flowed for some time. The condition of your face indicated that you had fulfilled both these conditions as was fitting. Added to this were words filled with so much depth of feeling that I who had come with the intention of consoling you recognized that you did not need my help, and that I was myself deriving comfort for my sorrows. I shall, therefore, say nothing in the way of trying to console you. I praise, I approve and admire, and I am amazed at the magnanimity of your mind.

You lost a very fine brother. Indeed you did not lose him, but you sent him ahead to the fatherland to which you also must go. Let us speak like the multitude; let us not feel like the multitude. You lost a brother; you would not have lost him unless he were mortal. The complaint therefore is not about the death of one man, but about the mortality of nature which introduced us into this life subject to the rule that we must exit at the command of the one who calls us back. "But he was recalled before his time which seemed the painful result of a too hasty edict." There is no fixed time in this life. We are debtors without limits. If we were bound to a specific day, we could at least delay, evade, and blame the avarice of the overseer. Now we cannot complain about swiftness as we could repayment of what we owe as soon as we accept it. "But he could have lived longer." And he could have died sooner, and he could have died differently, and although no dishonorable death could befall a distinguished man, he could nevertheless have died a more difficult death. He indeed died just as he lived, so that you owe thanks to God because of the kind of brother He gave to you and because of the way He took him away from you. If you consider the destiny and variability of human affairs, not only will you not mourn, but perhaps you may even rejoice that he is dead. For death often intercepts the labors of our present life and often preempts them. Who could enumerate the anxieties and distresses of this world, the afflictions, the tribulations and all the insults of fortune; who could enumerate the dangers of the soul and body and the throng of diseases that vie for both? Although we are not overcome by all of these, we nevertheless remain subject to them until we are removed from their power on the last day. And so your brother is now immune from all of these through the kindness of a timely death. We are wrong, oh kindest sire, and we err too vulgarly when we say that in dying we are snatched from an agreeable life. If we were to consider more deeply, we would realize that we avoid countless evils through death. I could easily show this with the help of authority and rationalization and examples, except that the brevity of a letter does not permit a long discourse. Now the happy youth does not fear those things, for he has escaped from this place and departed from us for a short time, leaving behind him such a reputation that the feelings and heart of those who remember him are charmed by the sweet recollection. Someone might say, "But this is what we are grieving about, that death has snatched from us a good and distinguished man, because the praise of the dead together with the recollection of the harm done to us prompts the tears of the living, and the irreparable loss creates an inconsolable bereavement." This, I am aware, is often said by many. But I, as I recall telling you personally, view it quite differently. Socrates was condemned to punishment by the highly unjust sentences of his judges, and he went to his death in the same state of mind he had always maintained in life. His was a great spirit and firm, and he was not given to yielding to the yoke of fortune. He was happy to leave behind by dying the threats of tyrants whom he had disdained during his lifetime. He serenely brought to his lips the cup of poison which had been given to him by the executioner, but was distracted by the grief of his wife who was influenced by other feelings which made her grieve because her husband was dying a just and innocent man. Upon hearing his wife, Socrates turned to her from his drink for a short while and said: "What then? Did you think that I should die a guilty wrongdoer?" This he said with his usual eloquence. To return to where I had left off, therefore, I disagree with the opinions of most and believe as follows: the death of evil ones must be mourned since it kills the soul and body; but the departure of good people should be accompanied by joy because, mercifully snatching them from this valley of affliction, God has transferred them to more joyful things. Unless perhaps the death of your brother has seemed so much more bitter because it overcame him far from the boundaries of his homeland. But we know better, being acquainted with those highly truthful words of the poet, "Every soil is homeland for the brave," and we also know the even more true saying of the apostle: "Here we have no abiding city, but we seek another." These words seem contradictory but they are not. Each of the writers expressed briefly what he felt but because of the diversity of their speech each spoke in a different way, yet each nevertheless spoke the truth. If you accept the words of the poet, your brother could not die outside his homeland. But if you believe the apostle, everyone dies outside his homeland in order to return at length to it. And indeed if you accept the words of both, you will find nothing to complain about because of the distant place in which a man dies. Perhaps we must grant to the living that, induced by certain either honest or base feelings, they feel one place should be preferred to another. But certainly for the dead there can be no interest in where the best place to die would be. And if someone does not find it so, he should know that he is still wallowing in the errors of his wet nurse or of gossipy women. When the philosopher was asked where he would prefer to be buried, he answered that it really didn't matter, saying: "After all, the nether world is equidistant from any given point." We to whom Christ by ascending to heaven left the hope of ascending with him, maintain otherwise, saying: "What does it matter whether we lie in Italy or in France or in Spain or on the shores of the Red Sea? From everywhere there is an equal distance for ascending to heaven." We must travel that road though it be narrow and difficult. But we have a guide. If we follow him we cannot lose our way. If we consider that road what difference does it make where we rest this burdensome body? Unless, of course, there is reason for believing that on Judgment Day it would be more difficult to reassume a body buried in distant places. But that most pious and truly worthy mother of such a son [2] did not fear such things when at the moment of death, she made arrangements for her burial saying: "Place this body anywhere. Do not let it concern you." And when she was asked whether she feared a death far from her native land, note what she answered: "Nothing is far from God nor is there any reason for fearing that He would not know whence to resurrect me at the end of time." This is what that Catholic woman said. We, who are Catholic and profess to be men, shall we indulge in any more womanish feelings?

But I know what it is that survivors lament so bitterly at the death of friends. They mourn because clearly they will never see again those they loved with the highest affection. Let such credulity be for the pagans, and not even for all of them, but only for those who believe that souls die with bodies. Certainly Marcus Tullius, whose being a pagan is both well-known and lamentable, was not of this opinion believing that the soul was immortal and that famous spirits would find a heavenly dwelling place after this life. Otherwise he would never have introduced Marcus Cato the elder in his book which he calls *Cato the Elder* with the following words so full of hope: "Oh blessed day, when I shall depart for that assembly and meeting of divine souls, and when I shall depart from this tumultuous crowd! I shall be departing not only to join those men about whom I have previously spoken, but to join my Cato, than whom no better man has ever been born, and no one is more distinguished in dutifulness." And later in that same book he says: "I am indeed carried away by a desire to see your predecessors whom I cherished and esteemed; nor will I meet only those whom I knew personally, but also those about whom I heard and read and about whom I myself wrote." These things and similar things which Cato says in Cicero's works testify sufficiently to what both believed. However, whatever they believed, whose hopes had been largely vain and deceptive, a sure hope is offered to us by One who cannot be deceived and does not know how to deceive. This hope is that at

2. Monica, mother of St. Augustine

length we too will go where we trust your brother went. Someone might say, "What shall I do in the meantime? I am torn by a desire, I am overcome by love, and I am tortured by an eagerness to see my brother again." What more should you do than those do who have been torn away by misfortune from very dear ones? They preserve their memory and keep the image of the absent ones deep in their minds; they love them, they speak of them, and they wish them a good journey. You must do the same and I am sure that you have. Keep your brother in that part of your heart which is free of oblivion; and love him dead as much as you did alive, or even much more strongly; compel him to return to you more often through pious and frequent commemoration; pray that his journey be favorable and that he return swiftly to his homeland after having overcome the ambushes of his perfidious enemy. This world was never his nor our homeland. We are but pilgrims here where we awaited him with useless prayers as he hastened to higher goals. This is a place of exile; he has set forth for his homeland. Let us pray that he arrives safely and without hardship. What could be of benefit to him, that let us do. To pray for the dead is a devout kind of service. But tears are for women and do not befit men unless perhaps they are very few and fully controlled. Otherwise they are harmful to those who weep, and they are of no help to those for whose love they are shed. If you still feel the torments of desire, remember that it cannot last long, for the life of man is brief, so that if the lost one cannot return to us, we must soon enough quickly set out for him. As Cicero says, "All short things must be borne even though they may be burdensome." Your brother has been freed from countless labors and has hopefully reached eternal rest or is about to do so. We abide in the battleground of a flowing century. For that reason, if anyone deplores the fact that he has been left behind, let him understand that he may deserve to hear the reproach of Cicero, "To be greatly distressed by one's own misfortunes bespeaks a person who is rather a self-lover than a friend." If indeed he laments because of another's departure, he should be fearful lest, as Cicero also said, "he be guilty of envy rather than friendship." I have said all these things not so much for your information as for your glory, because, as I said at the start, you do not stand in need of any external consolation, thanks to the eternal consoler. Furthermore, what needs could these short letters satisfy coming as they do from the wellsprings of a withered talent?

It is superfluous to add a number of examples of those who are remembered as having borne manfully the death of their dear ones. Nevertheless, that you may understand among whom I number you, and that even in such great company you may confidently hold to your original stance, I shall here enumerate the most noble examples from all of antiquity as my memory permits, for very few of my books have followed me into this solitude. Emilius Paulus, a most magnificent man and the highest honor of his age and of his homeland, from four sons of a most remarkable talent, gave two for adoption outside the family, depriving himself of them, and death seized the other two within the space of seven days. He himself, however, endured his bereavement with such lofty courage that he appeared in public. His misfortune seemed to offer such consolation that when the Roman people heard him speak he seemed to fear that his grief have an ill effect on someone else rather than upon himself. In my judgment he earned no smaller glory from this than from the splendid triumph that he scored at that very time, for he indeed appeared victor over Macedonia as a result of the triumph but over death and fate as a result of his loss. Pericles, an Athenian general, lost two sons in four days and not only failed to lament but showed no change in his regular behavior. The Cato the elder whom I mentioned previously is known by anyone having any acquaintance with history to have been extolled by all who knew him. What is more important, without any historical accounts his fame grew so great among all peoples that once anyone heard him it seemed that hardly anything could be added to the sum of wisdom. This is so true that he is venerated as much in the judgment of the ancients as in the agreement of the moderns as Cato the most wise. And yet among the many outstanding qualities of that man, we admire nothing more especially than the restraint with which he is said to have borne the death of a son, a fine person. Xenophon, upon hearing of the death of his son, did not stop performing the sacrifice that he had begun. Then he removed from his head the crown that he was wearing, laid it aside, and somewhat later began carefully asking questions about his son's death. Hearing that he had fallen in the heat of battle, he replaced the crown on his head in order to show that one should not grieve over the death of anyone unless he has died in a shameful and cowardly fashion which may be the reason why this very wise and indeed Socratic man had laid aside his crown at first hearing the announcement. Anaxagoras at the announcement of the death of his son said, "I hear nothing new or unexpected; for I, being mortal, knew that I had begotten a mortal." Indeed an answer worthy of the man! How many there are, even from the ranks of philosophers, who while pretending to grasp the concept of mortality, nevertheless could not have borne silently the blows of an unexpected death! Nothing unexpected was truly able to affect Anaxagoras for he constantly bore in mind those words we find in Seneca: "All things are mortal and mortal according to an uncertain law"; as well as what Seneca wrote in another place, that he knew all things were in store for him and therefore he would say to whatever befell: "I knew it." Many other examples of similar steadfastness have occurred to me, but the limits of a letter do not permit further inclusion. As I now approach the end, if it seems to anyone that perhaps your resignation is different from these highly commendable examples, inasmuch as you did not lose a son but a brother, I shall calmly allow him to believe as he pleases. Indeed because I myself have undergone the experience not of having suffered the loss of a son but of having felt the hurt of losing a brother, I am more competent to address myself to such a case. I am therefore making no affirmations nor am I trying to compare types of mourning. However I do know this, that often it is easier to replace a lost son than a brother. Farewell.

From the source of the Sorgue, 25 February.

Fam. II, 2.

A letter of consolation on the misfortune of a dead and buried friend and some thoughts concerning the rite. burial.

I grieve that you have lost a good friend but I am more upset that you seem to have lost your sense of judgment. You are consoling yourself neither in a manly nor in a philosophical fashion nor are you mourning one who deserves to be mourned, for the departure of a courageous man must appear enviable rather than sad. If I might summarize briefly the sense of your letter, you do not seem to me so much to be deploring your loss or the unexpected death of your friend (something I could perhaps forgive popular prejudice), but rather the kind of death and the injustice done to his unburied body when it was thrown into the Egyptian Sea. I cannot accept these complaints more typical of old women rather than of the rabble. Indeed I wonder whether against this scrupulous concern about kinds of burial one could not oppose that saying that being cast into a grave is a simple matter? Have you forgotten the short verses of Virgil declaring the same thing, verses that have become so familiar even to young children that they have become proverbial? But if you consider death, you deceive yourself if you believe that it makes one happy or wretched. This verse of another poet is sufficiently well-known: "One is not made wretched by death." It is life that makes people wretched or blessed, and he who has conducted it well until the flight of his last breath stands in need of nothing more, for he is happy, secure, and in port. What sort of person, therefore, do you suppose succeeds in reaching this summit of happiness regardless of whether the earth presses him down or the sea twists him 'round or flames consume him? But since I understand you are particularly disturbed about his burial and are distressed about this more than any other problem, how much happier do you believe is one who is plunged into this earth than another who may be drowned by waves? I believe that you feel as you do because of the horror created in a poem of Virgil where he said, "The waves will bear you, and the hungry fish will lick your wounds." But what if raging dogs tore his wounds, or if a pack of famished wolves tore to pieces his members after having dug up the grave? I believe you will answer, "These too would be unfortunate." Thus the most fortunate of all will be those who enjoy the unshaken, undisturbed quiet of the grave. There is nothing more childish than this idea, for when you have made provisions for all contingencies, those organs that were spared destruction by beasts you cannot deny to the hostile worms. So now please note that what you feared from perhaps most beautiful of animals will happen necessarily from the foulest of animals. In truth the first kind are not to be feared so much since they are a daily occurrence. You see, therefore (and here I shall repeat something which I have said often and not myself only, having shared the opinion with the most illustrious philosophers), that whatever we suffer in this life that is burdensome is not so much a natural thing but the result of feebleness of our mind, or, to use the words of the philosophers, the result of the perversity of opinions. We fear new things, and take lightly customary things. Why should this be except that in the one case the unsuspecting mind is upset by the unexpected appearance of things, and in the other a shield is provided by repeated meditation or reasoning, a shield which opposes all misfortunes. Note the custom of sailors which allows that the bodies of their mates be buried at sea without concern. I cannot avoid mentioning one illustrious example out of many. Lamba Doria, a very rough and strong man, is said to have been the leader of the Genoese in that naval battle in which they first battled the Venetians and which is the most memorable ever fought in the days of our forefathers. Having sighted the enemy fleet he was aware that the hour of battle would be at hand, and although his forces were smaller, when the time came he exhorted his men with magnificent brevity, and joined battle with the enemy. When in that encounter his only son, a most handsome young man, who was stationed on the prow of the ship was the very first to be struck by an arrow and loudly mourning bystanders had encircled the fallen youth, the father rushed forth and said, "This is not the time for mourning but for fighting." Having turned sub-sequently to his son, he perceived no life remaining in him and said, "Dear son, never would you have enjoyed a more beautiful burial had you died in your homeland." Having said this, and though armed, he picked him up still armed and warm, and threw him into the deep. In my opinion, at least, he was most fortunate in that very calamity since he was capable of sustaining such a misfortune so manfully. And in truth that act as well as his words so enkindled the spirits of the fleet with courage that they won an outstanding victory that day. Nor was he held less compassionate than if falling upon the body and mourning effeminately he had become incapable of action, especially in that state of affairs when the country was in such a crisis. You would tear your cheeks with your nails seeing something similar happen to your dear ones; not so much because of the sorrow of death but because of the shameful burial. Sailors, like all other men, also grieve at the loss of friends, but they bear it bravely when they are buried at sea; and this happens because they have learned to endure such things over many years. Why then do I not become indignant with Cicero because custom is stronger than reason? Could an uncultivated sailor have borne such things without tears because he had become ac-customed to them while you, a learned man trained in the fine arts and supported by so great a number of examples, could not do so though relying on reason?

It would appear appropriate to observe how numerous in history are the rites used by men in conducting burial ser-vices and how thoroughly opposed to our customs they have been. Among these, certain ones used to keep the body in the home after having preserved it with the greatest care. In others, people were accustomed to cast the bodies to their dogs for the sole reason that, having bought them and reared them for a long time, according to the means of each family, they considered the stomach of a well-bred dog the best kind of burial. We also read of certain others indeed who ate the bodies themselves. Artemisia, Queen of Caria, perhaps the most famous example of conjugal love, considered noth-ing more appropriate for her beloved husband than upon his death to bury him in a live grave. Having cremated him and having saved his ashes with great care, she carefully sprinkled them on her drink, thereby providing the beloved with the hospitality of her own body. There is little reason for questioning whether she acted properly. What is important is that you understand that all things that distress do so not because of themselves but because of human judgment by which they are produced and reared, and that custom counts very much in the process. The Queen fed upon the man she loved. If you were to see any of our ladies doing the same, you would be horrified and would turn your eyes from the frightening spectacle. But the same done by custom would not be called inhuman or an example of outstanding love but an ordinary act of respect. Nor is it necessary to seek only foreign examples. It was a custom of our ancestors in this very Italy to burn the dead, a custom to which the accounts of history testify as well as the discoveries that have occurred up to our own day of urns buried underground containing human ashes. Nor indeed is that a very old custom. Previously, as now, everyone was buried, until cremation was devised as a kind of remedy against the implacable hatred of the civil wars which raged even in the burial places. In that manner one was spared enemy insult through the power of fire. Thus the Scipios as statesmen who knew that they were truly valued by the state lie buried all together, nor was there anyone of the Cornelian line ever burned prior to the dictatorship of Lucius Sulla. He was the very first who, against the custom of his family and aware that he was widely hated, wished his body to be cremated fearing, as it is reported, that the followers of Marius would venture to do against him what he had done against Marius. The example had served its purpose, and others followed it who had no reason at all for doing so. Subsequently the custom of cremating prevailed and the practice began to assume authority. Eventually what had started as a form of remedy became honorable and it became a serious shame not to abide by the custom of cremating. Hence was praised the patriotism of the man who gathered small pieces of wood on the shore of the Nile in order voluntarily to cremate the body of the great Pompey who had been shamefully beheaded. From this action he acquired a great reputation, for who would know anything about Codrus except that he had burned the body of Pompey? That other Codrus from Athens is, of course, known for another kind of patriotism and a peculiar death. To burn the dead today is considered an act of extreme injustice or vengeance. Whence comes this variety in one and the same people? Of course with the passage of time and the changing of customs we find changes in the opinions of men. Nor am I going to examine again what I have heard great men sometimes discuss, namely, which type of burial is more noble. There is the custom which I recall being our ancestors' and which is known to be practiced by many people even now, but with an added law that restricts burial within the city to only a few who were entirely exempt because of their unusual excellence which absolved them from such laws, and these Cicero recalls in the third book of *Laws*. Then there is this custom of ours which taken up from our ancestors continued as a custom of the Christian religion. To compare these two is not what I wish to do at this time. I would rather complete what I started to say, that many things seem horrible to us because through long habit we conceive many errors which are of no concern to others having different customs. If, indeed, casting aside all else, you ask me, as is appropriate to your profession, for the truth of things not according to the rumors of the rabble but according to careful reasoning, you will find my opinion to be that the wise man turns away from error and that the swarms of fools are either to be pitied or to be laughed at. Farewell.

Fam. II, 3.

To Severo Apenninicola,[1] *a consolatory letter on his exile.*

Although I believe that "exile" comes from *exilio* or, as Servius prefers, from the idea of one who goes *extra solum*, I believe that it is really not an exile unless it happens unwillingly. Kings often exile themselves from their kingdom, doing so especially at the time when the boundaries of a state must either be preserved or defended, or when they devote themselves to the propagation of their glory. No one would ever dare call them exiles unless it were someone whose very reason had been exiled, since indeed they were never more worthy of being called kings. Therefore it is necessary that force and pain of some kind intervene in order to have a real exile. If you accept this, you will then understand that whether you are an exile or a traveler resides in you. If you depart sad and dejected you will know without doubt that you are an exile; but if indeed not forgetful at all of your own dignity nor under constraint, but willingly and with the same appearance and state of mind that you had at home, you obeyed the order to depart, then you are a traveler and not an exile. For you will find in various kinds of things to be feared that no one is wretched except one who makes himself wretched. Thus what makes a poor man is not the scarcity of belongings but cupidity. Similarly in death, which is very similar to exile, it is not so much the harshness of the thing itself as the anxiety and distortion of opinion that is painful. When these are removed you will see many men dying not only bravely but even joyfully and happily. Whence it is certainly understood that the evil of death is not compulsory but willed and is not located in the thing itself but completely in the weak thinking of mortals. Unless this were so, there would never be so great a difference of opinion regarding such a danger. I see the same reasoning applied to exile as I see in all other things. What overcomes us is not in the thing but in us. This is the power of judgment which once deflected slightly from truth soon wallows in countless errors so that it has a very difficult time returning to the truth and, unless greatly assisted, is incapable of

1. An as yet unidentified correspondent of Petrarch.

raising itself to a consideration of the majesty of its own origin. So then, I shall return to the beginning and ask: what is exile? Is it the very nature of the situation, the absence of a dear one, the indignation or rather the impatient desire of a languishing mind that is irritating? But if you firmly believe that whoever is absent from his native land is without question an exile, where are those who are not exiles? For what man, unless he were lazy and soft, has not departed from his home and his native land several times either because he was desirous of seeing new things, or of learning, or of enlightening his mind, or was concerned about his health, or was desirous of increasing his wealth, or because of the demands of wars, or at the command of his state, of his master, of his parents? Why then are such travelers not all wretched except that they resist, and do not allow themselves to be miserable? They too were without their spouses, their children, their kin, their parents, the concourse of friends, and the sight of their beloved city. Nevertheless for all of these the desire was mitigated by moderation and they found some kind of consolation for their absence.

"But their hope of returning was a great help; they would never have gone so bravely had they not believed that they would return to their native land." So be it. But in your case, who took away this hope? Especially since because of its very nature it cannot be taken from one unwillingly? A good man, despoiled of all his goods at the will of a tyrant, can be sent to prison, beheaded, mangled, slain, and remain unburied. While so many threats and blows of fortune may compel us to do many things, no one compels us to despair. We have seen men sent into exile who, before they had arrived at their destination, were called back to the homeland because of the unbearable grief of the citizens. Others, after a long time, returned with so much honor and regrets of the citizens that to me they appear fortunate for having endured such an exile. Others suddenly advanced from extreme poverty to great riches; still others attained thrones after being released from jail, and not a few managed to save their neck from the sharp blade and seemed destined for extraordinary prosperity. No one was committed to such a horrible place that he was not allowed to raise his eyes; no one viewed the loss of his belongings as so deplorable that he was unable to hope for better things. Rome recalled Cicero from exile; she could scarcely be without the presence of such an outstanding citizen for more than a few days. She recalled Metellus also who, having received the most prized letters from the senate of the Roman people while at a theater in Tralles, showing no sign of delight, assumed the same expression with which he had departed from the walls of the city; a man neither too crushed at his departure nor haughty in his return. He yielded to the madness of his homeland in his departure; he fulfilled her desire with his return; modest in the first instant, solemn in the second; but in both truly memorable. Rome tempted Rutilius with a similar recall but he remained more unyielding and considered his homeland unworthy of his return. Marcellus suffered a similar fate, but one which was far different. When he was called back by Caesar, as he returned amidst the joy of all good men, he fell into the hands of the enemy with the result that instead of the pleasant expectations of the public there was deep mourning. I believe that death was no more difficult for him than his exile, for there is only one virtue that arms and teaches men's hearts to bear misfortunes. And indeed such was his spirit during his exile that he offered clear proof of how he would have behaved in the face of death. About this I shall not withhold what Brutus says about Cicero in the book *On Virtue*, namely that he had personally seen him as an exile in Mytilene with such an unbroken spirit and so desirous of good studies, and indeed so happy and blessed, that he did not appear to him so much an exile, although he had been away a long time, as he himself felt himself to be an exile when he departed from him. He also adds that Gaius Julius Caesar, who had been the author of his exile and later of his return, while passing through those places, was so moved by shame over the exile of such a great man that he took care to bypass the city where he was located. Oh glorious exile, whose banishment one of the most powerful citizens of Rome esteemed, and over which the other felt shame! Thus was Caesar frightening to the world and Brutus to Caesar; but both felt respect for the exiled Marcellus. Who would not wish such an exile, indeed who would call it an exile when it is envied by the very fathers of one's country? I have called to mind those whom a repentant citizenry called back; but how many were recalled by fortune! No one called Camillus back to Rome: his way back was prepared by fate and the overthrow of the city and (who would believe it?) by the mad fury of the Transalpine people that spread throughout Italy. As a result he became the one man to be remembered by all exiles as well as an outstanding example of good faith and of an esteemed patriotism toward an ungrateful homeland. To turn finally to examples from our own day, how long did Matteo Visconti remain alone and a fugitive, lacking all things, bewailed by his loved ones, and ridiculed by his enemy after having been expelled from Milan, his native land, by the troops of his powerful enemy! They say that one day while he was wandering on the banks of Lake Garda in deep thought, he came across a messenger of his haughty enemy who asked him, at the request of his master, what he was doing there unattended. His only answer was that he was spreading a net. This answer, perhaps at that time considered contemptuous, soon made clear what mystery it contained. That old man, alone and inactive, caught in the nets of his foresight all his opponents as if they were so many fish deceived by the bait of an empty hope. At still another time when the messenger had returned to him again and had jokingly inquired by what roads or when he would return to his homeland, he answered with a calm look: "Now you go and tell your master that I shall return by the same roads by which I left, but not before his misdeeds begin to outweigh mine." The prediction did not prove wrong since not much later when the misdeeds of the enemy had increased to vast proportions, nourished as they were by an unaccustomed prosperity, he entered Milan as a victor after the enemy had been cast out; and in that city, as you have seen, his grandchildren and sons have ruled down to our day.

I do not want what I have been saying to appear either in your eyes or in the eyes of any good man as though I am in favor of an armed coup against one's native land regardless of how bad it may be (I consider it preferable to die a pauper in exile than to rule unwilling citizens once freedom has been lost), but I wanted simply to show in all the new examples that hope cannot be forcibly taken from exiles. If the recollection of brave men helps minds besieged with difficulties to achieve resignation, here is another outstanding and recent example. Stefano Colonna, a truly outstanding military man, was just as admirable and outstanding in his exile as he was famous in good fortune. His condition was far different from that of other exiles. To certain men it is permitted to live safely anywhere they please outside of the homeland; others when they have left their native land are able to enjoy an even greater freedom. Others are bound by stricter rules that restrict them to a particular place, where, however, they endure no harsh treatment as long as they remain there. But to this particular man his native land was forbidden and no place in the world was safe. There was no port nor refuge anywhere in his stormy existence. And he faced an enemy who was as persistent as he was powerful, Boniface VIII, the Roman Pontiff, who refused to be influenced by humility or flattery; in short the type whom nothing overcomes except death. His rage was inhuman as he sought the head of the undeserving exile in every possible way, with promises, threats, influence, deceit, authority, and money. He promised huge rewards to his persecutors and decreed punishments for supporters inasmuch as Stefano, crossing over the various bodies of water that separated with enormous distance the islands of Sicily and of Britain, often traveled alone around the frontiers of France, in great need of many things, but very strong of mind. Thus when by chance he fell into the hands of explorers near Arles and was asked who he was, he gave his name, which he could have disguised, to the group, and with unshaken voice declared himself a Roman citizen. Good God, how much dignity must have shone in his face to keep the hateful and armed bands of his questioners from angry reprisals! All kings had been urged by public edict not to offer him hospitality. When because of the edict he was ordered to leave Sicily he obeyed with the same spirit he had displayed as an exile in that province, so that it appeared as though a king were departing. Thus did he treat that king and others during the entire period of his persecution, as if indeed he were king himself. With a steadfast courage which feared no hostilities, and standing above the fluctuations of fortune, he held firm so that that poetic saying seemed to apply perfectly to him: "Behold ye the kings fearlessly, without a supplicating countenance." How often was his death announced in Rome and throughout Italy, how often was the reputation of the Colonnas declared undone and how often was it alleged that the distinguished family had collapsed with that man! Nowhere did any hope remain for him, except as it was located in his heart. Moreover, never did he depart from anywhere without bravely spending his days and nights thinking up fearless plans and being engaged in all kinds of toil. Furthermore in the midst of his search for a solution, he sometimes participated in the battles of friends (without either side recognizing him) and by general agreement victory was achieved by the mere presence of this single man. These things are certainly well-known but I believe are most familiar to you yourself and to me. Who therefore would call this exile wretched who was attended by such a retinue of virtues and who after a ten-year trial was able to return to his former state through real magnanimity rather than by chance?

But what is the purpose of collecting so many examples? So that no one, stunned by present misfortune, would be excessively preoccupied with conjecture of things to come, thereby adding to a moderately serious evil, exile, the most serious of all evils, despair. Especially since many things may bring an end to exile: an active virtue, such as the one which brought Stefano himself back to his homeland; often also the changed customs of peoples; the disappearance of feuds; a long lapse of time, something which tames even wild minds; the compassion for a victim of circumstances; the very admiration for silent courage; the services rendered to fellow citizens; the needs of the public or a stroke of good fortune. Furthermore because one has been driven out let him not reject the honor of retaining his virtues, remembering to bring this most precious of possessions into exile since he is not allowed to retain his lesser ones. Nor is it unusual in case of fire to carry off the jewelry and the gold, and to leave behind our home and all the useless or heavy belongings. But if men could be persuaded that gold must be reckoned among precious things, what can they be made to think about courage and virtue? "Silver is cheaper than gold, gold is cheaper than virtue." But anyhow, since we are not permitted always to bring silver and gold into exile, we are permitted to bring the virtues and the riches of the mind wherever we may go. We saw this done by those whom I proposed as examples for you so that you might long passionately to imitate them and so that you might not despair that what had been done so often could not be done again. I say that it is permitted to take your virtue into exile or into prison or even unto death. I said "it is permitted," but indeed it is useful, necessary, and proper. In truth the real exiles are those who depart leaving this quality behind, truly helpless, unfortunate and wretched. Indeed it is not sufficient to take with you as much of this as you may possess; somewhat more is necessary. Note how carefully he who sets forth for foreign lands prepares his provisions; he wishes that they were more the further he travels. Your splendid provisions for this journey will consist of your virtues. By having an abundance of these you will not be poor even if you lack food for the body. Therefore gather these, let these support you everywhere. I know that you have made a remarkable collection of many virtues, which is neither an inconvenient or difficult, but instead a light and pleasant, burden. I realize that your preparation requires much labor; however, once the provisions are ready, they are carried around without toil. You sought them since your youth, and you collected them in your youth, and you collected them in your home. Do not lose them now that you are older and a wanderer. Carry with you as much as you had or more, depending on what need presents itself, although I do know that though you may not want them they will come to you automatically. Indeed these provisions are never consumed by use, but rather increase, for virtue begets further virtues which increase in the midst of difficulties until they have led their possessor to the highest summit of happiness. I shall say nothing about the consolations of your exile, but they ought not to be scorned. If you had been ordered to retire to an inhospitable side of the world in the ice and eternal night of Scythia or under the burning sun, or had been sent somewhat closer but outside of Italy, you would have good cause for complaining about your ill fortune. Instead, consider how unjustified your complaints are! You have been ordered to go to Florence to remain there until the people call you back. Do you not see how much gratitude you owe to the officials who have roused you still half asleep from excessive leisure, and have led you away still clinging to your maternal apron strings out of long force of habit? And finally haven't they decided to send you out of a homeland which, if I may dare say so, is very inferior to a very flourishing city? All this, as I said, I am going to leave out since we are all naturally disposed to feel that the uncultivated and deserted lands where we were born and educated can be considered superior to all others. If that misconception would cease for a while, you would surely pardon fortune and indeed seek forgiveness because you were not previously aware of her kindness. Consider also that you took with you two sons of outstanding character, one a young man and the other really a child, with a fortunate difference in age so that you could share the burdens of your cares with the one and you could forget them with the other; you could find help in the one and consolation for your wandering in the other. These boys made your homeland delightful and you have them with you. What else do you desire? Do you expect your most virtuous wife or your wonderful parents or the flattering of your daughter to return again? It was not exile that took them away from you but death which you overcame so often despite its abuses and despite its overcoming some of your dearest possessions. Therefore, you should not now be overcome by exile, because exile cannot take away from you all the comforts of your former life and especially your boys, remnants of so many happy moments. But as I said, I shall pass over such consolations and all those things that are subject to the blows of fortune for I know that what can take away one's fatherland has power to take away one's children. I shall instead return to the more stable assistance of the virtues which neither the decrees of your citizens nor the power of tyrants nor the violence of plunderers nor nocturnal thefts can snatch away from you. If you did bring these along with you, no one could call you an exile without lying. If however you left them behind, each day will bring something new that you can bewail, every new place will not only be annoying but hostile, and would be not a place of exile for you but a prison. Farewell.

Fam. II, 4.

To the same Severo, on the same subject.

I see that you have lost all hope. Whether you suffer rightfully I have already questioned in my preceding letter. I regret that it afforded you no remedy nor am I certain whether the blame lies with the doctor or with the patient, who must, if he wishes to regain his health, confidently place his trust in the advice of doctors and be most obedient to their precepts. What I tried to do in my letter was to help you save some hope after you had lost your fatherland, since hope has so much power that it does not feel any present troubles and in its promise of happier things projects one's thinking into the future. So what was there that kept you from hoping? Was it the harshness of your homeland because it sent you away? What cruelty? To be perfectly honest about it, aside from exile, what was taken from you or imposed upon you about which you can complain? Were examples of outstanding men lacking? But I paraded many before your eyes, and I would cite more except that they seem to be in vain even though from them you could learn that staunch hope begets happy consequences. Or do you fear that your homeland will be forever angry because it has withheld a little of its usual kindness? But don't you know that fathers have been kinder to those children who had treated them badly; and that no one has burned with greater love than the one who misbehaved toward a truly loyal spouse? Or is your fear the greater because of the edict of your homeland which forbids under threat of punishment any public statement about the recall of exiles? But you must know how the wishes of the people are as loud and varied at the outset as they are uncertain and flexible with the passage of time. But there is a certain something in the minds of mortals that I discern only vaguely and cannot put into words: a sad and destructive perversity, which shuts ears blocked against the salutary voices of advisers, and causes them constantly to do things that make them more miserable and to avoid anything that might lessen their grief. There is nothing that can be imagined that I would call more foolish. Since I now find you disposed to accept the hopelessness of your return with what I might call a kind of pleasure, I shall cease trying to treat a wound which is beyond medical treatment. However, what prevents me from following the practice of those who, having lost one or another limb, in order to prevent the infection from extending through the rest of the body, annoint the surrounding areas of the wound? In imitation I too can go around the boundaries of your wound and quickly prevent with appropriate ointments the grief from extending to the whole mind. But do not be upset, for I shall not touch any sensitive spot with my fingers. I am about to say nothing against your present opinion. Rather, in order to avoid having you turn against your possessions because of one misfortune, or see the tranquillity of your whole life perish, I shall make every effort, provided you are in accord, not to lose any chance of restoring some hope to you. You imagine then that you are living in exile and must die in exile. I believe you now have what you want; that is, my admission that there is no hope of your returning to your homeland. In order to temper your illness even more, I shall concede even more to you. Not only will you die in this exile, but "separated by a whole world you must die far from your homeland and that a barbarous soil will weigh upon you." I have conceded more to your grief than you did, for while you conceded no possibility of happiness, I have proposed things that are even more gloomy. Nor do I really see anything so wretched in this that it could compel a strong man to shed tears. Certainly, if I thought you were burning with the fire of a mod love or of ambition, which seem to blaze more intensely far from one's homeland, or if too few companions followed you when you left, I would have to gather many arguments to soothe either such a flattering possibility or the inconstant evil of ambition, or to offer you comfort in your poverty. Although such arguments ought to have been easy for me to put in words and for you to accept, it is not easy to articulate the remedies for the disease under these limiting conditions. What a sorrowful and mournful thing love is! What wretchedness ambitions leads to, under what a colorful and deceiving light it hides itself, and how little it delivers of what it promises! How poverty may be tolerated with greatness of mind cannot be briefly explained by anyone. But for the present, since the seriousness of your character has not fanned the flame of love, and even if you had felt it once, your age has now quenched it, and since the manner in which you fled honors throughout your life does not allow any suspicion for ambition, and since the devotion of your homeland has helped you avoid poverty, the great labor needed for providing additional consolation is diminished for me. Your homeland afflicted you with no other discomfort than to be without her embraces. All your possessions are either yours or are with you or are under your control. I speak not only of those which could not be snatched from you, such as your modest magnanimity and your other virtues, which either that wise man, Bias, according to Cicero, Valerius and others, or as Seneca would have it, Stilbon, bragged about carrying with him when he fled from his burning fatherland. I refer also to your possessions which, to use a popular expression, you received from the hands of fortune. You departed master of your ancient patrimony as a wealthy exile and as the citizen you had been at home. And I wonder whether you might not be more wealthy than you were because you can be frugal with the riches that now remain. I must add that the greater part of men suppose that they cannot fall before all their possessions have been destroyed. You in truth did not fall but were driven out. Therefore, I believe, you are now feeling in a direct and upright fashion the wavering of fortune; and you understand on what shaky ground you stand when you appear to be great. Furthermore you do not doubt that the ill fortune that drove you out can be overthrown. And so, unlike the great majority of others, you can live on as a wealthy and cautious exile and be comforted by two great and good things against this single and indeed petty evil, if indeed in this life anything can be called good except virtue, or evil except insofar as it is the opposite of virtue. So go forth secure. Your homeland will not call you back, fortune will not return you. Instead the exile that you lament so much and the obstinate injustice involved will make your burden light. Misfortune made many men great, it singled out many others. On the contrary, adversity did not make men wretched but instead it exposed such men and did not allow them to be concealed for very long. Why do you turn pale as if fortune has a great hold on you? It does not play the part of the judge but instead of the witness. Whatever you may be is in your power. It is not in its power to decide what image it would project of you. It can do some of it through talk but it cannot lie. But who is there, unless he be guilty, who fears a witness who speaks only the truth? Fortune does not compel you into cowardice but it does count your steps, exercise your patience, suspect or disdain the cowardice of your heart, and then makes public whatever it finds out about you. Take courage and disperse the shadows of popular error and don't pay heed to the words of gossipy women. You will never be happy nor safe if you surrender yourself to the whim of the people. Whatever the great majority of men admire or fear is ridiculous; whatever they proclaim is false. Entrust yourself rather to the advice of the few. Those things among which one includes exile are not as terrible as they seem. If prolonged reading did not help, perhaps experience will assist you. Do not always look down. Sometimes raise your eyes; truth will be immediately manifest, and you will confess that exile is nothing worse than that a good man must live some distance from his homeland. And in truth he who considers the entire world his homeland cannot live outside it. For what does it matter how different are the lands in which one stops? He may see other valleys and lakes and rivers, but heaven is only one. That is where he projects himself; there is where from all parts of the world he raises his heart and transmits his thoughts believing that he is under a single roof and is crossing from room to room. You also, unless you disappoint the high hopes that I and many others have had for you, would not want to be restricted to a single corner of this huge edifice. In this manner you may call whatever land you walk upon and whatever heavens you see above and wherever you may breathe the sweet air, your fatherland. Therefore, the condition of your exile should not only be easy but pleasant. There are two things which chiefly induce the will of men to kindness: virtue, than which, as Cicero says, nothing is more lovable, and misfortune which is also inflicted on undeserving men. The first of these causes us to love and to admire outstanding men; the second to commiserate with the unfortunate. The first seems to be present in you at this time, the second seems to be approaching. All will judge you a strong man and will call you an exile. And surely if we believe Tullius, among all the virtues, the most brilliant is fortitude. So once again among the tribulations of man exile is not listed last. Unless I am deceived it would be desirable not to have the wrath of your fellow citizens slacken. It is also to be hoped that you do not accidentally lose the name of exile since you can see that in it there is nothing wretched and a great deal that is favorable to your fame. You say, "but my heart dreads toil and dishonor." First of all, I deny that either of these are at stake since I know that the event earned great praise for you since it resulted from your magnanimous opposition to the arrogance of tyrants. Furthermore, in it you found rest and the cessation of your labors as you had always desired. What is more, whoever fears dishonor which is produced by virtue is a friend of fame and not of virtue. In truth whoever flees toil ceases to desire glory to which, unless I am deceived, a difficult but well-known and delightful path leads. As I said, enormous fame awaits you alone through special privilege and without obstacles except perhaps as you may fashion them yourself. What I fear is that you behold the wound that has been inflicted upon you with the eyes of others rather than with your own, and that you measure your situation with another's judgment. This is such a daily curse that at the clamor of others large numbers of men stagger and fall much sooner than they have to, although that man has also fallen whom thousands of men are constantly advising with the worst opinions. But as you may call him very feeble who is cast down by a light breeze, you must consider truly insane one whom you may see judging his own affairs by the rumors of others and especialy of ignorant people. The more numerous these are, the more must the contagious disease which usurps the hearts of so many men be carefully avoided. If you wish to listen to others there is no lack of those who decry your situation with endless complaints and who lament your misfortune although you are safe and sound, and who half-dead sit around the bier of the living. You will hear the mournful voices, and you will see perhaps the tears which are either simulated or almost mad. You will then begin to become wretched because you will become accustomed to listening to these miserable voices. There is almost nothing which a continuous concourse with others cannot accomplish in the hearts of men. But if you choose to consult yourself and to speak with yourself rather than with others, I would never stop expecting great things from you and would call you most happy since you serve as your own judge, and I would consider you worthy of envy rather than of pity. But if you are inclined rather to believe others, then why do you not believe me as I bring to your attention truer and more pleasing things? Believe me, you were never overthrown nor will you be unless you wish it; you will suffer no dishonor, but you have a choice, as you stand on the threshold of eternal glory; you will either progress gloriously or you will retrogress ingloriously. There awaits you not toil but rest; not exile but liberty. What you once sought as it fled from you with astonishing speed you should now embrace as it hastens to meet you spontaneously. "And what was your great desire for seeing Rome? Liberty, which, though late, nevertheless looked upon me despite my indolence." This speaker in pastoral discourse boasts of having left his homeland in order to find liberty. You, a philosopher, complain. You have lived for others a long time. Begin right now to live for yourself. No one will maintain that you hastened too fast since you started off no sooner than that shepherd of Virgil whose "beard fell whiter while shaving." You have always condoned the actions of your fellow citizens since your earliest years. They blushed over your priceless largesse and they decreed that you retain at least the remaining years of a long life. Recognize the spirit of your city and consider your generosity against hers which was so great that despite its real need it permitted you to slip through its hands. Enjoy happily the immunity which is now granted to you and think of the walls of your native land as the unquiet prison of your freedom. You escaped and what is more it happened at the request of your guards who ordered you to go. It would be madness to undertake to return. You should rather turn to those studies to which you had dedicated your youth and which would have made your advanced years certainly tranquil except that your homeland which you now desire had forbidden them. However, they will certainly make your old age peaceful and venerable if it remains a despiser not only of your exile but of all casual things. I speak of liberal studies and especially of that part of philosophy which is the teacher of life. You had never removed these entirely from your mind although for a little while involvement in civic matters kept you from them. Now devote yourself to them completely since nothing prevents it, and give yourself over to the better auspices of a new life by keeping your mind busy with such activities. Read again the history of antiquity. There you will find how many imitators there were of Roman leaders and indeed of illustrious men who wished either to be sent away from their homeland as soon as possible or to be called back after a great amount of time had passed. Why was this so, I ask, if not because it was pleasant to miss the sweetness of the native soil while finding elsewhere greater occasions for the exercise of virtue? Consuls were accustomed to cast lots for provinces after festive celebrations, and the more noble ones would prefer that province in which they saw the greatest dangers, not because they chose the dangers and difficulties for themselves (unless they were mad) but because the splendor of virtue seemed most likely to be present there. Therefore either this exile of yours is a trifling matter and your complaints are out of place among the flattering voices; or it is difficult and burdensome (this the multitude asserts, but I disagree). But if any of the old character has remained in any one man, exile cannot be so bad and his complaints cannot be worthy ones if he laments over something that is desired by others. This place which the magistrates ordained as your place of exile is your province. Not everyone can cross over into Africa with a huge army and having expelled Hannibal from Italy attack beleaguered Carthage. Not everyone can go from victory to victory, at times attacking rebellious Spain and at times freeing the seas beset by pirates, or penerate Armenio or Judea and the kingdoms of all of the Orient. It is not given to everyone, following the slaughter of Numidian troops and the extension of the empire, to transport arms from the South to the North and in a very short time immerse a sword dyed with Libyan blood into the blood of Teutonic and Cimbrian peoples or after thoroughly subduing the Gauls and bringing their leaders to a violent acknowledgment of Roman virtue, pass beyond the borders of the Rhine on the one side and of the ocean on the other and then trample upon Germany and Britain in a single attack. Nor can everyone enjoy the experience of leading captive kings before his chariot. These things are reserved for the Scipios, the Pompeys, the Marii, the Caesars and the Aemilii. Such battles with distant enemies were reserved for men such as these and their likes. Your battle must be with exile whose attack you not only bear but repel and destroy if you wish to achieve whatever is necessary and if you can persuade yourself that the only protection against adversity is patience, and if you will impress deeply in your heart that very wholesome utterance of Cleanthe translated by Annaeus Seneca into Latin poetry: "the fates lead willing men and drag along unwilling ones." Farewell.

Fam. II, 5.

To the devout Giovanni Colonna,[1] that minds suffer greatly from their association with the body.

I received most eagerly your letter which was written during your journey, for I desired even more than usual to hear that things were well with you. For those companions of love, zeal and fear grow with absence. I was distressed and my heart was restless because I had learned that you were disturbed when you departed, and also because I was seeing those who had caused your disturbance, gratified in achieving their abominable desire, parading triumphantly before me the fact that they had you exiled, depriving me of your presence and of your prudent, delightful company. And my visions and dreams had also terrified me as they filled my sleepy mind in extraordinary and troublesome ways. I certainly know that one must not be afraid of questioning dreams, but this is how it is. I have set out on this road, the journey of our life leading to death, on which one must suffer heat and cold, hunger and thirst, and sleep restlessly agitated by threats and ambiguities of dreams. In short, one must suffer many things until that day awaited by the devout and feared by the wicked when this mortal garment and the fetters of this gloomy dwelling are cast off from those minds striving for heaven. Meanwhile I confess that since the road is not long, whatever the philosophers discuss and whatever others feel within themselves about the stilling or acceptance of the blows of passion, I myself have been thus far strongly subject to them. A law was imposed on me together with my body when I was born, that from its association with me I must suffer many things which I would not suffer otherwise. The poet, aware of the secrets of nature, when he ascribed to human souls a certain burning force which he called of heavenly origin, added the following by way of exception: "Insofar as mortal bodies don't slow them down and earthly organs and mortal members do not weaken them. This is why

---

1. Not to be confused with Cardinal Giovanni Colonna who was a nephew of this Giovanni.

they fear and desire and suffer and rejoice but cannot recognize the heavens since they are enclosed in the darkness of a blind prison."

I was wondering, therefore, why no news of you had reached me since your departure when unexpectedly your letter was delivered to me. I recognized the seal and so I read without serious care. However, because the messenger was in an extraordinarry hurry and the affair would seem to need many words for a proper answer, I delayed my response until the next day. Now I perceive that my reply must be in three parts because your various complaints fall into three divisions. One, however, which could be put briefly and which kept me from postponing my resolution was that I, being entangled in the web of my sins, have not yet been able to take refuge in a port, but am being cast about by that same storm in which you left me still battered by the waves. In vain will I try to hoist my sail as I hold on firmly, hoping that a propitious wind will rise up from the West. I am pleased only at your news and am grateful to God because I see that you have at least avoided a great number of labors, since your little ship, emerging from the same perils, "either has reached port or is heading for shore with full sail." Consequently, I can more freely cope with my problems since the desire for succeeding drives me on and I am half free of a double anxiety. Farewell.

Fam. II, 6.

To the same correspondent, that absence is not harmful to friendship.

I was hoping to hear some fine news from you, since your wisdom seemed to me long ago to have overcome the complaints that the stupid and ungrateful multitude loves to mouth loudly. I can see that I was indeed really wrong and I wish I could think that the complaints in your letter were someone else's; instead the writing gave evidence that they were written by your own fingers. In them you bemoan a slight matter with a great number of words more like a woman's than a man's. The gist of your lamentation is that you have suffered harshly and inconsolably because you can no longer enjoy our wonderful presence, either mine or that of our friends. I do not doubt that you have been shaken and disturbed by your sudden departure, for I know the mildness of your mind and the pleasantness of your customs which would never permit any form of sternness or a harsh turn of mind. This is why I do not understand your excessive sorrow. Countless causes might separate friends, but none separates true friendship. When this is present no friend can truly be absent. The more the distance between places separates us from the conversations of friends, by that much do we overcome the woe of absence through continuous recollection. If the power of such recollections were so great that even after death we can honor our dead friends as though they were alive, a lesson we learn from that wisest of all Romans and one of the most famous in matters of friendship, Lelius, following the death of the young Africanus; would it not be just as great if by similarly overcoming absence we can view the faces of friends located in distant places as though they were present? The poet writes "Faces and words cling fixedly in the heart." And in another place he says, "The absent see and hear those absent." Can therefore mad and obscene love accomplish what godly and moderate love cannot? It should indeed be able to do much more, for the same poet says: "First the swift stag will feed in the heavens, and straits will abandon defenseless fish upon the shores; and first, having wandered through the territories of both, the Parthian exile shall drink from the Saône or the German from the Tigris, before his face will slip from our heart." Note the following words that even Lelius, speaking about his very close friend, used: "I loved the virtue of that man which has not been destroyed." Why do you not say: "I love his virtue or their virtue, which is neinther absent nor distant but is always present before my eyes, and will always be honored by me?"

"But it is most pleasant to have friends present and to regard their faces and their eyes, to speak to them, to hear personally their answering words." And since it is helpful in this matter to refer to the testimony of poets, it is with a certain delight of the mind that we read that Anchises, happy at the meeting with his son, said with his palms extended heavenward and with a profusion of tears: "Oh son, it has been granted me to behold your face and to hear and return the familiar words." Now I am not against the idea that the presence of friends is indeed very sweet. Who indeed would deny this unless he is inhuman and even savage? But you will surely not deny that even absence itself has its pleasures unless perhaps we restrict all the beauty of friendship (which is indeed great) to the eyes alone and if we separate it from its abode which is in the mind. But if we did this, a very narrow area would indeed remain where the affection of friends can find delight. I shall remain silent concerning the role of death or prison or illness or trips whether necessary or voluntary; and who can enumerate such daily necessities of nature as sleep, hunger, thirst, heat, cold, weariness, or the innumerable occupations of studies and other responsibilities which prevent us in our very homes, not to say in our cities, from seeing the faces or hearing the voices of our friends? If governed thus, friendship would be found to be of very short duration, whereas it ought to be not only as long-lasting as the longest life but, as I said above, it ought actually to survive beyond. What role because he was blind could Appius not play in the realm of friendship? I won't mention the many others in the same category. He comes to mind first because it is not entirely believable that one who could be such a devotee of a universal state could not have friends because he had no sight. Why is it then that you bewail absence so greatly as if it could take away friendship from you when such absence really has no power in this matter nor in your other affairs except insofar as you permit it to have such power? I ask you to remember not how far you may be from someone (although how can anything be distant in this terribly tight space of which we men scarcely inhabit a tiny part?), but rather how far it is in your power through reflection to be present with absent ones. Here, therefore, is one way in which you can continually see us together: show yourself repeatedly by the frequent interchange of letters. Farewell.

Fam. II, 7.

*To the same correspondent, that anxious expectations must
be eliminated to live a tranquil life.*

You describe in an angry manner the irksome delay that
kept you in Nice for an entire month awaiting a ship to sail
for Italy. But at that time you were in Italy and yet you were
sighing for Italy. I say this because poets and cosmographers
like to say that the boundary of Italy lies on the Varus, while
the city of Nice sits on this side of it, on the shore of Italy.
But of course what you meant was clear. You had in mind
inner Italy and really wished to say Rome rather than Italy.
I can myself perceive the cause of this illness, for youth is
ordinarily full of such expectations which at that age may be
forgiven. In old age, however, when all hopes should be
regarded as being in the past, every lengthy and anxious expectation dealing with this life is detestable. You, therefore,
who are older, probably had your reasons. I, a young man,
speak about myself as a person who, although his adolescence
is passed, sees your age still in the distant future, if anything
can be considered long in this life. However, the more rarely
I experience the annoyance of this sort of sensation, the more
frequently do I complain of the remains of former ills and
the more surely do I understand that a real man does not permit himself to be crushed by present things nor be tormented
by future ones, but instead disdains both periods heartily
and takes lightly whatever time has yielded or promised. I'll
say nothing of the present since I started a discussion of the
future which keeps the minds of men in suspense with great
expectations through which occur, unless I am wrong, many
ridiculous mistakes. Anyone awaiting the arrival of a foreign
ship stares onto the sea every day and, as Lucan would have
it, "is always seeing the sails of the arriving ship off at a distance." Another, on the verge of leaving the shore, invokes
the clear quietness of the heavens through constant prayer.
This one, without concern for appropriate measures, is always doing what the pilot of the Trojan fleet once did. He
rises energetically and, according to Virgil, "he examaines all
the winds and uses his hearing to judge the air currents taking

note of all the stars that are declining in the silent heavens." Another man, trusting to the legacy of a fortunate old man, inveighs against the slowness of death. Still another awaiting his marriage, or the childbirth of his dear wife, or the friendly night, counts the days, the hours and the minutes. What more is there to say. You will remember in my *Philology*, which I wrote only to drive out your cares through entertainment, what my Tranquillinus says: "The greater part of man dies waiting for something." And so it is. You will find very few who are not on tenterhooks because of uncertainty. How many plans were being made by Alexander the Macedonian, by Julius Caesar and by many others of our own foreign leaders when they were removed from this life! And the death that overtook them in the middle of their undertakings was, it seems to me, the more difficult because it was so unexpected. This is why Julius Caesar himself, overtaken by a dangerous storm in a fragile ship, when he had begun to fear death, seemed to complain about this alone, that "the hastening day of destiny cuts short great undertakings." The poet knew what had been especially troublesome to such a man or what ought to have been, when he introduced that remark as the strongest of his complaints. There was really only one medicine for this disease, one which is perhaps at first taste rather bitter but in the drinking pleasant and gentle, and that is if possible to lead the mind away from earthly things; if not, to tear it away and dig it up by the roots. For though this may cause grief and displeasure for many people, once the health of the body is lost, as you know, it is difficult to restore. How much truer this is about the health of the soul in which more violent and more frequent illnesses befall! Therefore, do as follows: be happy with the present and you will not feel yourself being pulled by any expectations for the future. You say, "I wish to go to Italy and I await a ship and a quiet sea." You should say this if your heart continued to adhere to earthly matters and to the snares of unusual delights. But if you tried to rise above this you would say: "I want to go to Italy indeed. But what is more useful for us God knows and men ignore. I am awaiting a ship, but I would not be surprised to see someone who would announce that the ship would not arrive. And I shall receive both reports with equal calmness." You might also say, "But I have something very important to do in Italy." Now, if the study of philosophy did you any good, you would see, I believe, that what cannot be done outside of Italy cannot be very important. No matter how often you may confine me to one place, any undertaking which is restricted by a narrow space ceases to be a great undertaking. "But I wish at least to die in Italy and to be buried in my native land." Whoever says this may be an Italian but not yet a high-minded man. For what is there more childish than to be concerned about where the clippings of hair and fingernails, or where a small container of unnecessary blood may rest, and yet not care where you yourself must rest? Certainly if you consider the body, it does not really make any difference to you where by your permission you abandoned something which formerly belonged to you or when it was carried away against your opposition. But if, on the other hand, you consider the mind, no narrow place can restrict it, nor can any venerable place ennoble it; and whether it's a matter of ascending to the heavens or descending to hell, regardless of where it starts from, the labor and toil required is the same. "But it is sweet to be buried by the hands of one's dear ones." Several things are made sweet not by their own taste but by the corrupt appetite of gluttons. What can you call sweet for either the man who lacks feelings or the man who despises all such formalities? But to return to my main point, the condition of all those who live in the future is always the same: while they look into the future they do not see what is before their eyes, thereby risking certain harm as a result of flimsy hope. The present does indeed pass away while the future rarely comes as hoped for. Furthermore these things that we desire are either almost useless or they are harmful, so that as indignation often follows upon unfulfilled hope, so does disgust or unexpected ill fortune follow upon those hopes which had been agreeably fostered. Therefore, remove all hope, turn away all desire from these deceitful attractions; and begin to desire only one true and greatest good if you have indeed delayed until this age something that is so necessary.

Then will your appetite for running about cease as will your aversion toward long delays. Then, indeed, not only in Nice but, if destiny allows, in the Libyan desert will you remain without annoyance, content with your affairs and demanding nothing more. Some ask: "Can at least that one good you mentioned be hoped for so that it may satisfy the desirous soul with its presence?" Certainly not, for if you desire it fully and sacredly and reasonably (otherwise such a great thing cannot be desired), you will find that what you seek is already with you. Seek and you will find Him whom you desire deep in your soul. You need not wander outside of yourself in order to enjoy Him. If anything perchance still remains that you desire or hope for increasingly, this sense of expectation will be pleasant and agreeable. Whoever fashions himself according to this rule will often and alone among mortals enter into his bed chamber at dusk and say with assurance concerning the past what Seneca said after Virgil: "I have lived and I have accomplished whatever the course of fortune allotted me"; and he can say about the future what Horace said: "Let the heavenly Father tomorrow fill the heavens either with dark clouds or with the pure sun." Nor will he ever in his eagerness for the future be forgetful of the present or live a useless life either for himself or for others. Farewell.

Fam. II, 8.

To the same correspondent, that all things that happen naturally should be borne courageously and that useless complaints should be avoided.

I am tired of your constant complaints; I am beginning to feel a disgust for them, and I can no longer bear your weak character. Indeed your terror before the approach of any particular event is like that of the newly arrived infant. You ought to be ashamed of growing old among laments and indeed of lamenting childishly even though you are an old man. It is childish to become astonished at anything one sees; indeed for children all things are new and astonishing. For old persons and especially for learned ones, there is nothing new or unexpected that happens, nothing to be amazed at, nothing to deplore. Therefore, why so many complaints about things that happen regularly and according to natural law? Prodigies do move minds sometimes. If you see a two-headed boy, or a four-handed one, you react in astonishment. We read in histories of showers of stones, speaking oxen, or a mule giving birth. And yet we disdain daily occurrences. What did you see that has caused you now to display so much astonishment and lamentation? Your astonishment indeed compels me to be astonished; and to pass on to others without too much seriousness this excessive amazement of yours. You who have crossed so many seas and extricated yourself from so many dangers and were saved from the clutches of death so often are now describing, in astonishment and bitter against fate, how you suffered on the sea a great and (to use the words of the Satirist) "poetic storm"; and you relate how being driven by an opposing breeze you were brought back to the shore whence you departed. What you consider an injustice of the sea is instead a natural thing. You would offer a more worthy cause for complaint if what once Caesar's fleet had to suffer between Italy and Greece had happened to you. Because of the frozen Adriatic he was not able to hasten his journey which was stalled because of the numbing cold. Likewise you would have cause for complaint if you had undergone what Pompey's army underwent in Libya when the land shook under their feet, and "no soldier could stand erect because of the trembling sands on which they stood." Now indeed, if you endured sharp stones by land, or even steep hills, and if you bore likewise the fickleness of the sea, you cannot lament as if the elements had been inimical to you, for they were simply obeying the will of nature, not yours. The other portion of your letter relates no less effeminately and weakly how you were struck by illness shortly after landing in Pisa. This you recount as if after so long a life you did not know what illness was. How can any mind prepare itself against death amidst so many daily complaints? We are too quick to accuse nature; no one deplores the fact that he is born or that he lives; yet one complains because he endures poverty, or because he experiences hardship, or because he gets old or ill or dies, as if these things are less natural than those. To be born, to live, eat, be hungry, sleep, be awake, toil, grow old, be ill, and die are all natural, and no mortal avoids them except for those in whom the headlong inevitability of death replaces the inevitability of growing old and the annoyance of hardship. Why then do we pour forth useless complaints? Could it be that since they affect only us, we are permitted to lament? Or is it because we transfer all lamentation from everyone to ourselves, and as if we were bailiffs of human kind we accuse undeserving nature? This is indeed a hateful and unfortunate business, for nature is very gentle and we betray her benefits through impatience, ungrateful to our mother and wicked against ourselves. I plead, therefore, beloved father, and, if it is not unseemly to this young age of mine, I advise you, that whatever may happen let us resolve to bear it manfully, with restraint, without wailing and without any unmanly weeping. For we have the time for deliberating, and thanks to Christ, the time for pursuing our deliberations. Let the rabble go mad. We have a considerable number of reasonable advisors whose warnings we should obey. Don't let my life influence you, however often you may read my letters. And do not let that life persuade you to look up to me personally, for sometimes you have seen a sickly doctor who, unable to cure his own sickness, is able to do so for others. I wish you well.

Fam. II, 9.

A reply to a certain humorous letter of Giacomo Colonna, Bishop of Lombez.

I was aroused from my drowsiness by your chatty letter which I read joyfully and laughingly, crammed as it was with jokes. To deflect your first barb directed at me I ask you, dear father, to note that although you direct many things at me, your very words disagree with your intention. You say that you marvel that at my tender age I can deceive the world so skillfully, that this art seems to derive not so much from experience as from natural abilities. You could have eulogized me in many more, but certainly not more magnificent, words. Whoever travels this journey of life with open eyes knows how often the world, deceiver of human-kind, entangles life in its fetters and with what a bitter sprinkling of sweetness it blesses human life. We continue to look with favor upon the deceits scattered along this journey and eagerly, against the advice of Apollo, we toil against knowing ourselves. Pride inflates one man under the covering of a great and lofty mind; malice and deceit make a fool of an-other man under the garment of prudence or whatever false virtue seems closest. Another man considers himself strong and is instead timid and weak. There is also the man moti-vated by avarice under the guise of frugality, and the man whom prodigality overcomes under the appearance of liberality. The vices are disguised and the huge monsters hide under attractive coverings. Add to these a crowd of delight-ful but transitory and indeed passing and fleeing things. Am-bition overwhelms us with honors, applause and popular flat-tery; dissipation unfurls before us enticing and varied plea-sures; money does the same with an abundance of many things. There is no hook without bait, no branch without some trap, no snare without hope. Add to this human cupid-ity, rash and bereft of council, as well as quick in deceit and opportune in its insidiousness. If, therefore, in this dangerous and fleeting and insidious journey anyone whom nature or effort had made so wary that after eluding the deceits of the world he himself managed to deceive the world by showing

himself outwardly like the multitude but inwardly being unlike them, what would you say about such a man? Where are
we to search for him? In him must be a most excellent nature,
a mature and reasonable age, and a solicitous consideration of
the misfortunes of others. Yet you grant such qualities to
me; very flattering indeed, if you are not joking. But if what
you say does not apply to me today, I pray God, who has
power to free one from the infernal regions, that I deserve
your praise before I die. But where is it that you lead jokingly? You maintain that many people have held magnificent
opinions about me because of my inventiveness! I know that
the art of which you speak gave to certain illustrious men
the kind of talent through which they displayed genuine virtues to their beholders. This is the basis for the divine discourses delivered by Numa Pompilius and this the way in
which the fame of the divine ancestry of Publius Africanus
was established. Such an art does not appeal to me. I know
nothing that I would like to boast of, despite the vain favor
of fate that has pursued me since my birth. I am better known
than I wish to be, and I know that however insignificant I
may be, much is directed against me by both sides for which
I feel neither depressed nor uplifted, for I know that just as
many falsehoods emerge from the multitude as do words.
This is how things have gone thus far, and I am aware that
one need not toil very much to incur the displeasure of the
multitude.

Nor does your politeness cease here. You say that I have
been fooling not only the stupid multitude with my fictions
but heaven itself. You maintain, then, that I have embraced
Augustine and his books with a certain amount of feigned
good will, but in truth have not torn myself away from the
poets and philosophers. Why should I tear asunder what I
know Augustine himself clung to? If this were not so, he
would never have based his *City of God*, not to mention
other books of his, on so large a foundation of philosophers
and poets, nor would he have adorned them with so many
colors of orators and historians. And indeed my Augustine
was never dragged to the tribunal of the eternal judge in his
sleep, as happened to your Jerome; he was never accused of

being a Ciceronian, a name, which was leveled against Jerome and caused him to swear that he would no longer touch any pagan book, and you know how diligently he avoided all of them and especially those of Cicero. But Augustine who had received no interdiction in his sleep not only was unashamed to make ready use of them but openly confessed that he had found in the books of the Platonists a great part of our faith, and that from the book of Cicero entitled *Hortensius* through a wonderful internal change had felt himself turned away from deceitful hopes and from the useless strife of quarreling sects and toward the study of the one truth. And inflamed by his reading of that book he began to soar higher as a result of his change in feelings and abandonment of passions. Oh worthy man and beyond mention great, whom Cicero himself would have praised from the rostrum, and publicly thanked, you are indeed fortunate because among so many ingrates one at least wanted to be most grateful! Oh magnificently humble and humbly lofty man, you do not abuse writers through the use of the pens of others, but rather steering the floating ship of the Christian religion among the reefs of heretics, and conscious of your present greatness without arrogance recall the truths of your origin and the early beginnings of your youth. And so great a Doctor of the Church does not blush at having first followed the man from Arpino who held a different view! And why should he blush? No leader should be scorned who shows the world the way to salvation. What obstacle does either Plato or Cicero place in the way of the study of truth if the school of the former not only does not contradict the true faith but teaches it and proclaims it, while the solid books of the latter deal with the road leading to it? The same could be said about other writers, but it is redundant to bring together superfluous witnesses for something that is so well-known. However, I do not wish to deny that many things in them ought to be avoided since even among our own writers certain things may be dangerous for the unsuspecting. Augustine himself, in a certain voluminous work of his, plucked off with his own fingers the weeds of interfering error from the extremely copious crop of his studies. And so? Rare is the reading free from danger, unless the light of divine truth shines upon the reader teaching him what is to be pursued and what is to be avoided. So long as such a light leads the way all things are secure and those things that could harm are better known than even Scylla and Charybdis or than the most famous cliffs that are found on the sea. And to put an end to this insolent calumny that I am falsely fond of Augustine, Augustine himself knows the truth. For he is in a place where no one wishes to deceive, nor can be deceived. Whence I believe that he, viewing the byways and the errors of my life, is moved to compassion especially if he recalls his own youth which the merciful Almighty brought back to the straight path from its wanderings and deviations. And now He has permitted him to become an eternal citizen of Jerusalem instead of the sandy shores of Africa where for some time enjoyable passion was leading him to death. From up yonder he views me with favor, from there he bestows his esteem upon me. How can I have doubt when I hear him, in that book which he wrote entitled *Concerning True Religion,* saying in the strongest hope: "Any angel who loves God I am certain also loves me?" Therefore if he, through the contemplation of a common God, was not afraid to assign angelic love to himself, I too, since I am a man, should dare to hope for the human love of that most holy soul which is now enjoying the delights of heaven.

But I am leaving myself open for further criticism. You say that to someone like me who even now continues to wallow in things philosophic the words of Augustine must appear almost like a dream. It would have been better had you said that as I reread all those things, my entire life should have seemed nothing more than a dream and a fleeting apparition. Sometimes while reading them I am aroused as if from a very heavy sleep, but because of the oppressive burden of mortality my eyes close again and again, and I arouse myself and continue falling asleep over and over again. My wishes fluctuate and my desires are discordant and, being so, they tear me to pieces. Thus does the external part of man battle against the internal, "now leading with a right and now with a left; without delay or rest." And unless the eternal

Father interrupting the battle with His voice saves the weary Dares from the hands of furious Entellus, the exterior part will win. How much more can I say? Hitherto I have been uncertain of my death and I have lived in anxious hope, often crying out to the conqueror of death: "Oh Unconquered One, save me from these evils; . . . offer your right hand to a wretched man and lead me with you over the waves so that I may find rest at least in the quiet abode of death."

But there is nothing more lingering than jests and nothing more flexible; wherever you direct them they follow. What in the world do you say? That I invented the splendid name of Laura so that it might be not only something for me to speak about but occasion to have others speak of me; that indeed there was no Laura on my mind except perhaps the poetic one for which I have aspired as is attested by my long and untiring studies. And finally you say that the truly live Laura by whose beauty I seem to be captured was completely invented, my poems fictitious and my sighs feigned. I wish indeed that you were joking about this particular subject, and that she indeed had been a fiction and not a madness! But believe me no one can pretend at great length without great toil, and to toil for nothing so that others consider you mad is the greatest of madnesses. Furthermore, while we may be able to imitate illness in our actions, we cannot simulate true pallor. My pallor and my toil are known to you. Therefore, I rather fear that you are abusing my illness with that Socratic playfulness which they call irony in which you yield not even to Socrates. This wound will heal in time and that Ciceronian saying will apply to me: "Time wounds, and time heals," and against this fictitious Laura as you call it, that other fiction of mine, Augustine, will perhaps be of help. For by reading widely and seriously, and by meditating on many of his things I shall become an old man before I will have grown old.

What will be the goal of your jesting? When will it stop? What are you saying? That you were also tempted by my fictions and almost deceived; indeed having been truly deceived, that you had waited some time for me in Rome so that I might simulate a great desire of coming to see you.

Finally, as expert spectators are wont to do with the trickery of mountebanks, opening your own eyes and gaining greater insight into my skill, you discovered the theatricality of my achievement. Good God, what is this all about? By directing such accusations against me you indeed make me out to be a great magician. I begin to feel like Zoroaster, the inventor of magic, or, at least, one of his followers. This would be understandable were I Dardanus or Damigeron or Apollo or anyone else whom such skill made famous. Is it not enough of a trick to be able to become a magician with mere words? But I am afraid we have lingered on this jest too long. I would like you to answer me seriously. Let us set aside my desire for seeing you in person which has occupied me heavily for four years now, during which I thought "he will arrive here tomorrow, you will probably leave the following day"; let us lay aside the sizeable number of any of the concerns which I would share with confidence with no other mortal except yourself; let me overcome my desire to see a very famous father, your worthy brothers, your distinguished sisters, and the strongly desired faces of friends; could you not guess how greatly I would want to see the walls of the City and the hills and as Virgil says, "the Etruscan Tiber and the Roman Palatine?" One could not believe how much I desire to see that city though deserted and but a reflection of ancient Rome, a city that I have never seen, for which I accuse my laziness if it were indeed laziness and not necessity that was the true cause. Seneca seems to me to be rejoicing as he writes to Lucilius from the very villa of Scipio Africanus, nor did he take it lightly to have seen the place where such a great man was in exile and where the bones lay which he had denied to his homeland. If this affected so worldly a Spaniard what would you think that an Italian like myself would feel not only about the villa at Literno or the tomb of Scipio, but even about the city of Rome where Scipio was born, educated and where he triumphed in glory both as a conqueror and as an accused; where lived not he alone but innumerable others about whom fame will never be silent. I speak of that city that has never been equaled nor ever will be; a city which is called the city of kings even by its enemies and about whose people we find written: "Great is the destiny of the Roman people, great and terrible is their name"; whose unequaled greatness of incomparable monarchy both present and future divine poets will sing. Nor will I now continue to enumerate the praises of Rome: it is too great a matter to deal with in haste. But I have touched upon these things hurriedly so that you might perceive that I do not esteem lightly the sight of the queen of cities about which I read infinite things and have written many and shall perhaps write even more unless an unexpected day of death cut short my undertaking. But assume that these things do not affect me whatsoever. How sweet it would still be to see a city with a Christian spirit as an image of heaven on earth united by the flesh and bones of the martyrs and indeed sprinkled with the precious blood of the witnesses of Truth: to see the venerable image of the Saviour of people and in the hard stone the footsteps that shall eternally be worshipped by nations and where may be perceived that saying of Isaiah which was fulfilled clearly and literally: "And the sons of those who humiliated you will come to you bowed, and all those who disparaged you will worship your footprints!" How sweet it will be to wander around the tombs of saints and through the temples of the Apostles pursuing more useful concerns and abandoning the restless anxieties of this life on the shores of Marseilles! Since this is the situation, why do you call me lazy when you know that my journey depends on the will of others? I had offered myself to you as a small but certainly continuous gift. You wished that I should obey another, if indeed a brother such as yours and so compatible with you can be called another. I am aware of no guilt. If there is any blame you must share it with yourself or with your brother.

At the very end of your letter, feeling perhaps that I might be offended by your biting jests (for sometimes the mere flattering touch of a lion of whatever size can crush small animals) you apply a bit of sweet and fragrant ointment where you seemed to have penetrated, urging me to love you and indeed charmingly exhorting me to return your love. What can I say? We impede the saying of many things not only with grief but with joy. This one thing you certainly know without my saying so; I am not so insensitive that I must have someone incite me to so generous and so worthy a love. Would that in loving I had more need of a spur than of the bridle! My adolescence would have been far more peaceful and my youth would have followed far more tranquil. Only this do I ask of you, that you do not feign that I have feigned. Farewell.

Avignon, 21 December.

Fam. II, 10.

To Agapito Colonna.[1]

I am not astonished to see in you what astounds me and all others, and what in myself I lament and bewail. It is a universal evil: those things that could without any danger be disregarded we seek eagerly; what should be sought above all things is openly neglected. We are all concerned about how fertile a field may be, how attractive a house, how obedient a servant, how solicitous a house-staff, how distinguished our clothing, how sleek our horse, how fair our wife, and how decorated the surface of our body. No one worries how beautiful and decorated is our heart. No one pledges or hopes to do anything about it. Instead what ought to be first we defer to last. "Oh people, dear people, money is to be sought first; virtue will follow the coins." Thus it is today, thus was it in the century of Horace, thus will it be in the days of our great grandsons, unless we can perhaps predict something better for our successors. Would that we could really hope for that! As things are presently going I can only predict worse things in the future although worse than they are now I can scarcely fear or imagine. Certainly to live as we do is but a taste of crime and madness so that we could not go beyond without a full collapse of society. Now! now is the time to realize what the Satirist said: "All vice stands on the edge of a precipice." Yet we exert our powers so that something mad is always happening, nor will we ever be satisfied by the older limits of traditional licence; we never attempt to make Horace appear wrong when he said: "Our fathers, who were worse than our forefathers, created us still more worthless, and so we shall create descendants who are even more corrupt." And so that we can put off this serious complaint to another time, I hold that as we continue along this path we shall make ever more true what Marcus Varro, that very learned man, thought, for if we expended upon ourselves a twelfth part of the care we expend in making certain that

1. Grand-nephew of Stefano Colonna the elder who had studied under Petrarch in his youth, and had later been named Bishop of Ascoli.

our baker makes us good bread, we would have been good indeed a long time ago. I say nothing of what we expend on jewelry, footwear, and ornaments. That's the way it will be. The useless will always be sought, the useful will be neglected. However, in your letter, illustrious friend, there was a single token of good hope. You seem to me to be suffering strongly and to recognize the state of your mind which is the first step toward well being. You seem to me to be about to escape from these fetters with magnificent indignation as soon as your body permits. Farewell.

At the source of the Sorgue. the calends of May.

Fam. II, 11.

To the same correspondent, an invitation to a poetic dinner.

Having been invited to dinner with me you will hopefully come; but remember this is not a gathering place for gourmets. What will be offered you is a poetic meal and not as found in Juvenal or Flaccus but as described in Virgil's eclogue: "Ripe fruit, tender chestnuts and an abundance of fresh milk." The rest will be a little rougher: bread which is hard and ordinary, a chance hare or an imported crane (a very uncommon sight hereabouts) and perhaps the thick skin of a somewhat rank wild boar. What else is there to say? You are familiar with the primitiveness of the places and the food here; wherefore I warn you to come not only with fortified feet but as Plautus' parasite says, with well-fortified teeth. Farewell.

At the source of the Sorgue, on the ides of January.

Fam. II, 12.

To Cardinal Giovanni Colonna, a description of another journey.

I have found in a region near Rome a place which is most convenient for my cares if my mind would not hasten elsewhere. It was formerly called the Mount of She-goats because, I imagine, of its being covered by thick brushwood and is considered more inhabitable by goats than men. As the location gradually became better known and its fertile lands became respected, it attracted a number of dwellers who built a kind of fortress on a rather prominent hill. Yet, as greater numbers of houses occupied the narrow confines of the hill it did not lose its ancient name of She-goat. Though an undistinguished place, it is surrounded by places that have a very celebrated reputation. On one side is Mount Soracte, famous for having had Silvester as a resident though it was celebrated even before Silvester in the famous works of poets. There is a Mount and Lake Ciminus, both recalled in Virgil. On this other side is Sutri which is not even two thousand paces away, a very dear abode for Ceres and, as is asserted, an ancient colony of Saturn. One points to a field which is not far from the walls where they say that the first field of grain in Italy was sown by a foreign king and where was yielded the first harvest to be cut by sickle. Having captivated the inhabitants with this miraculous accomplishment, and assuming the office of king, he lived out his life with the public reputation of a god and he is now worshipped through the good favor of men as an old king and a sickle-bearing god. The climate here, as much as I can tell from my brief visit, is very healthy. Everywhere there are countless hills neither too high nor of difficult access and they do not impede one's view. Among these there are shady and sloping hillsides and all around dark caves. Everywhere wooded groves arise keeping out the sun except on one hill facing north which opens its sunny breast to become a flowery dwelling for honey bees. Springs of sweet water resound in the deepest valleys; while stags and deer and doe and other wild forest bears rove over the open hills. Every kind of bird can be heard on the waters or on the trees. I skip over the oxen and the many flocks of tame sheep, the sweetness of Bacchus and the abundance of Ceres which are the fruits of human labor, and the many gifts of nature, the neighboring lakes and rivers and the sea which is not far off. Peace alone (and I know not by what crime of the people or by what laws of heaven or by what destiny or power of the stars) is lacking in these lands. Would you believe it? The armed shepherd watches over the woods fearing not so much the wolves as robbers; the breast-plated plowman turning his spear into an instrument for goading pricks the backs of obstinate oxen; the bird hunter covers his net with a shield; and the fisherman hangs his deceptive hooks and his sticky bait on his hard sword and, what is even more ridiculous, in drawing water from the well he fastens a rusty war helmet on a filthy rope. In short nothing is done here without weapons. The all-night shouting of guards on the walls, and voices calling to arms, have taken the place of those sweet notes I used to play on the lute. You will see that the inhabitants consider nothing safe, and you will not hear them uttering anything peacefully or with humaneness. Instead you will only hear of war and hatred and of things which resemble closely the works of the devil. In these places, dear father, uncertain as to what to do, I have now spent sixteen days and (alas, the power of habit!) you will see me often wandering over these hills amidst the din of soldiers and the sound of the trumpet while others take battle stations, and I constantly meditate on things which might be acceptable to posterity. Although everyone looks upon me with admiration as I go about calmly, undaunted, and unarmed, I am astonished in turn at all those around me who go about fearful, agitated and armed. Here one can see the diversity of human actions. But if I should be asked whether I would depart from here I could not give an easy answer. My departure would be desirable but my sojourn is delightful. I am more inclined to depart, not because anything is bothering me but because I had set out to see Rome. It is perfectly natural that the heart does not rest until it has reached the end of its desires. Because of this I consider that view especially attractive which held that the souls of the dead were kept from the beatific vision of God (in which the greatest happiness of men consists) until the bodies were finally gathered, something which souls could not refuse—although the opinion was refuted by the more rational judgment of many and has long been buried with its author (whom I must say you esteemed very highly, though not his errors). Farewell.

Fam. II, 13.

To the same correspondent, on his lengthy stay at Capranica and on the arrival of Giacomo and his brother Stefano.

On this mount of she-goats, which is indeed a mount of lions and tigers, that Ursus of yours, the Count of Anguillaria, lives more gently than a lamb. He is a lover of peace without fear of wars, fearless in battle but not without a desire for peace, second to no one in hospitality, vigorous in resolution, stern in flattery and unbendingly good toward his own people, a very close friend of the Muses and a tasteful admirer and praiser of distinguished talents. With him, and having a name not contrary to her character as is the case with him, is his wife, Agnes, your very beautiful sister. About her, as Sallust said about Carthage, "I think it is better to be silent than to say too little." For there are certain people who are properly praised in no better way than through admiration and silence, and your sister is one of these. This marriage seems harmonious and gentle like roses or lilies among the thorns and the sharp hedges of animosities. By the pleasantness of these two the harshness of all the rest is tempered. There has now come that wonderful and unique man, Giacomo Colonna, Bishop of Lombez, your brother. When I wrote him to tell him of my arrival, and to find out what he wanted me to do, since all approaches to your home were besieged by enemies, and I did not consider it safe to set out for Rome, he wrote to congratulate me on my arrival and ordered me to wait for him. After a few days, on the 26th of January he arrived with Stefano, his older brother, whose excellence is also worthy of a poet's pen. Both were attended by no more than one hundred horsemen and each advanced amidst the general terror of the onlookers knowing that there were five hundred and more troops bearing the enemy's banners. But their path was strewn with what makes for success in battle, their reputations as great generals. I am now living among these noble spirits with so great a sweetness that often I seem to be elsewhere than on earth and do not greatly miss Rome. We shall go there anyhow although the enemy is once again reported to have blocked more securely the roads to the city. Farewell.

Fam. II, 14.

To the same correspondent, from the city of Rome.

What news can one expect from the city of Rome when one has received so much news from the mountains? You thought that I would be writing something truly great once I had arrived in Rome. Perhaps what I shall be writing later will be great. For the present I know not where to start, overwhelmed as I am by the wonder of so many things and by the greatness of my astonishment. There is one thing that I do want to tell you, however, which happened contrary to what you expected. As I recall, you used to dissuade me from coming for a particular reason, which was that if the ruins of the city did not correspond to its fame and to the impressions I had received from books, my love for it would diminish. I, too, although burning with desire, willingly used to postpone my visit, fearing that what I had imagined in my mind my eyes would belittle at the moment of reality which is always injurious to a reputation. Such reality I am happy to say diminished nothing and instead increased everything. In truth Rome was greater, and greater are its ruins than I imagined. I no longer wonder that the whole world was conquered by this city but that I was conquered so late. Farewell.

Rome, ides of March on the Capitoline.

Fam. II, 15.

To the same correspondent, on the highly justifiable praises of his sisters, Giovanna and Agnes.

There are those who exalt unique Roman matrons of old with unique praises, and indeed ascribe to Lucretia chastity, to Martia seriousness, a holy inspiration to Veturia, the ardor of conjugal love to Portia, a sober joyousness to Claudia, wit and feminine eloquence to Julia, refinement to Cecilia, dignity to Livia, a noble firmness of mind to one of the Cornelias, an attractiveness of conduct and language to the other. Then there are those who have honored other foreign women with their praises, admiring honesty in Penelope, undying love in Artemisia, tolerance in Ipsicratia, fortitude in Thamyras, judgment in Thetis, modesty in Argia, devotion in Antigone, and constancy in Dido. I should like to have these admirers of ancient women see your sisters Giovanna and Agnes. They would indeed find in one home ample matter for praise, nor would they have to wander through all the lands and through so many centuries in their search for feminine honors. Whatever they seek anywhere in scattered form they will find in these two women. You live most happily not only because of your own virtue, but because of the glory of your father, the harmony of your brothers, and the devotion of such sisters. Farewell.
23 March.

Fam. III, 1.

To Tommaso da Messina, the opinions of various people concerning the very famous but doubtful Island of Thule.

The person who loves to wander on the borders of antiquity, which are rough to approach but delightful when you get there, must often tread on paths that may appear highly suspicious. This matter, indeed, that you say you have recently got yourself into, I have been pursuing for a long time, and have likewise been seeking in what part of the world the Island of Thule may be. I seek, but to tell the truth, neither with any certain idea nor with any guesses that would lead me either to a conclusion or to any hope of coming upon one. And so I am writing to you from the very shores of the British ocean and thus close (as rumor would have it) to the very island we are investigating. From here, either with the help of my long study of literature or of my new and careful search of places, I should certainly have been able to write you something reasonably definitive. There is no doubt that Thule was indeed the most remote of lands. Virgil sings of this, Seneca does also, and so does Boethius following both of them, and so do many other writers. There is also general agreement that it is located in the Occident, very far from both the Orient and the South. For us, however, who are located in the West, its very nearness produces curiosity. If it had been situated in the Orient, we should not have been more concerned about Thule than about Thoprobanen. But since we get information about Great Britain and Ireland and all the Orkneys to the north of the western ocean, and about the Fortunate Islands to the south of the same ocean either through actual visitation or through constant testimony of travelers, almost as much as we do of Italy itself or of France, we begin to take notice and to wonder and to inquire somewhat more carefully whether this island celebrated in the letters of all such travelers, emerged anywhere from the waters. The ancients and now even the Orientals and other peoples of the world confirm the opinion that it is situated in our ocean. What more can be said? We see happening to this island what often happens to outstanding men, namely that they are better known everywhere else than in their own homeland. Ask the westerners about the island; the ignorant don't even know its name, while to the learned ones who at least know of its fame, the island itself is no less unknown than to the multitude. I held an interesting conversation about this with Richard, former Chancellor of the English king, a man with a sharp mind and considerable knowledge of letters. Born and educated in Great Britain and incredibly inquisitive from his youth about unknown things, he seemed most capable of solving such obscure problems. However, either because he hoped to do what he said, or because he was ashamed to confess it (a custom which is very common today among those who do not understand how praiseworthy it is for a man who is not born to know all things to be modest and to confess honestly that he does not know what he does not know) or perhaps, as I doubt, because he preferred to keep from me information about this secret matter, he answered that he would certainly satisfy my doubt but not before he had returned to his native land and to his books of which he possessed an extraordinary number. For when I was his friend he was abroad dealing with matters concerning the Holy See for his master; at the very time when the first seeds of the lengthy war between his master and the French king were sprouting, seeds which were subsequently to produce a bloody harvest. The sickles had not yet been put aside nor had the granaries been closed down. But though he left with a promise on his lips, either because he found nothing or because of the serious duties of his pontifical office which he had newly assumed, he satisfied my expectation with nothing but obstinate silence notwithstanding the many reminders I sent him. Thus I learned nothing more of Thule from this British friend.

Several years later there came into my hands a little book on the wonders of Ireland by a certain Geraldus, a courtier of Henry II, king of the English, containing some rather thin matter, but written in a not unrefined style. In considering it for inclusion into my library, I found a small portion that made it deserving to be there. This was the portion which laboriously expressed about the same island the same questions as ours. A similar bent of mind, therefore, made me feel attracted to the author of the work. In his book he touches upon the opinions of several writers who maintain that of the islands in the ocean that are situated near Great Britain and that are between the North and West, the furthest is Thule where in the summer solstice there is no night and in the winter no day; beyond which the sea lies inactive and frozen. He cites the works of Solinus and Isidore in support of this. Nevertheless, he states that that island is not known at all to the West and he confirms that there is none like it or of that name located there. Consequently following conjecture he considers it either a famous but mythical island or separated from the others by an infinite space and thus to be sought only in the very furthest reaches of the North Ocean. He makes Orosius a corroborator of this opinion. He could also have included Claudian when he wrote, "Thule is condemned to the Hyperborean skies." Omitting this fact, he deals with the matter and argues along his own lines. You should consider the witnesses that he uses to see the extent to which they support him, and you will understand how much faith must be placed in his words. I, myself, am very far from all my books and I find this alone the only burden of this trip. Having left home I hear no sound of the Latin tongue, and when I return home I do not have the books which are my companions and with which I am accustomed to speak. All my conversations are through recollection. Therefore I am writing this to you extemporaneously and by memory so that when I see my memory wavering over certain matters I prefer silence than to commit any opinion on paper. Of course there are many things that I remember no differently than if I had books readily available since repeated reflection on such things impresses them upon me deeply and strongly. That author of whom we speak had not perhaps read Pliny the Elder who expressed himself on the matter more strongly than anyone else. I do not dare indicate how truthful his testimony is since I keep wondering, "How can an island so close and so famous be so unknown to everyone?" But I shall report what Pliny the Elder himself thinks about the matter in the second book of his natural history. He feels that Thule is an island distant six sailing days north of Great Britain where he conjectures the daytime lasts six months in the summer and the night an equal amount of time in winter according to a strong argument based on reason, as he sees it, and he furthermore uses as his source a certain Phocea or Pythia of Marseilles. If this is true, how close am I to that very Thule that we seek, whose fame, as I surmise, is great among the Indians and almost unknown among us! Servius himself, although a better grammarian than a cosmographer or poet, following his predecessors in his interpretation of Virgil's statement, "May the farthest Thule be subject to you," remarks as follows: "The Island of Thule is between the northern and western shore of the Ocean, beyond Great Britain, Ireland, and the Orkneys." You will note that almost all writers focus on one point, and seem to agree in various ways that the island lies between the North and the West and not far from Great Britain where, if they had assembled in person, they might perhaps have changed their opinion as the matter demanded. Two of them depart considerably from the opinions of the others, but whether they approach more closely to the truth or whether because of the distance their error cannot be verified directly is uncertain. Of these, one is Orosius who was mentioned above, another is Pomponius Mela, a renowned cosmographer whom Pliny is accustomed to follow in many matters, but here seemed to overlook him. He spoke of only one sunrise during the whole year, at the vernal equinox, and one setting of the sun in the autumnal equinox, and consequently only one day and one night as distinctive times of the year did he grant the Hyperborean peoples, the first inhabitants on the shores of Asia beyond the north wind and the Riphean Mountains. And if we are to believe him they are the most innocent and happy of all mortals. He maintains, however, that Thule is located among the islands of the Ocean opposite the shores of Belgium. He says that the nights are short there, dark in winter, full of light in summer, and none during the solstice. Alas, how much disagreement! Indeed to me the island seems no less hidden than truth itself. But let it be that way because what we seek with hard labor we may safely ignore. But let Thule lie hidden to the North, let the source of the Nile lie hidden to the South, provided that virtue, which is centrally placed, does not lie hidden, and likewise the path of this short life over which a great portion of men proceeds trembling and staggering, hurrying to an uncertain end over an obscure trail. Therefore let us not expend too great a labor in the search for a place which if we found, we would perhaps gladly leave. The time has now come to bring this letter to a close and to expend our time on more useful matters. This is the information that I have been able to unearth as an actual field worker, so to speak, concerning this obscure problem; seek other information from others who are more learned. If it is denied me to search out these hiding places of nature and to know their secrets, I shall be satisfied with knowing myself. It is here that I shall be open-eyed and fix my gaze. I shall pray to Him who created me that He show himself to me as well as myself to me and, as the Wise Man prays, that He make me aware of my end. Farewell.

Fam. III, 2.

To the same correspondent, against the expectations and useless labors of a short life.

How shall I answer your letters? I fear that the swift torrent of human errors has snatched our friend along with everything else and has plunged him into the bottom of the pit. He is growing old, as you can see, amidst the games and illusions of fortune, promising himself many things which, believe me, will never come. However, there is one excuse. He indeed has the same disease that strikes practically everybody. Do you know anyone who does not trouble the peace of today with the hope of tomorrow? This is mortal happiness; this is mortal life. An incredible madness, not any less so because it is universal, is this gaping at fantasies and following doubtful things after having laid aside certain good things. Men do not know how profitable it is to lose empty and false hopes. They are a heavy load, and yet they are laid aside sadly. To that extent do we delight in our own ills. That friend of ours toils and sighs and pants uselessly, and, against the opinion of Flaccus, "seeking lands warmed by another sun, bravely strives after many things during a short life." I do not accuse others of what I excuse in ourselves. The desire of seeing many things also drives us over lands and seas, and especially lately when that passion of mine drove me to the furthest of lands, forced by tedium and repelled by local customs. Hard necessity brought me back. I landed the day before yesterday, and though I had written you things during my trip, I cleaned my dusty pen again with your name first. Our friend, however, that he may return not more learned but richer, avoids no unknown shore of the world and revolves like a flying leaf with each wind current. None of his sighs, as I hope, will ever have an end except with his life. Tell him this for me. It is rare indeed that expectations are realized; but assuming that they are, misery increases with happiness. This is not difficult to understand for the man of experience, except that bad habit closes the ears to admonishing words. But he will see for himself. You stand firm and take care not to be distracted from your goal by the mob of wavering spirits. The advice of Seneca, and indeed of nature herself, is, "There is no need for much, nor for long." Farewell.

Avignon, 18 August.

To Stefano Colonna the younger,[1] *that to have won is point-less for one who does not know how to use his victory.*

You were able to conquer, oh most powerful man. Know how to use your victory, oh wisest of men, nor let anyone accuse you of the reproach which Maharbal once cast in the teeth of Hannibal on the day of the battle of Cannae. If he had followed advice and had turned his banners dripping with our blood from the battlefield toward Rome, you know what in the opinion of the historians was indicated. But the Lord who was favorable to Italy obstructed his wicked daring. That same God, aiding your pious efforts, accompanies you in battle, directs your steps, and His leadership will not desert your banners. He (that same God who once saved the pious though small forces of Prince Theodosius from the barbarian legions) now promises you continuous victories and the final expulsion of your enemies. You certainly uphold a most just cause, and as Christ was witness to the justice of Theodosius, so is He now to yours and calls upon you day and night to bring to a completion what he began. He is not distant from you but near you, with you, and believe me was with you while you were victorious. Otherwise how could you have routed such an army with so few troops and alone, unaware and almost half equipped for an unexpected battle, have crushed so quickly two very haughty enemies though they had been forewarned and prepared? Without doubt celestial assistance was present and will be present, your cause remaining a just one as often as you request it piously and reverently. Go, therefore, secure in such a leader and rest assured that the boy who is born again from the blood of the victims and is adorned with the spoils of the church will be rather a prey than an antagonist. To be sure, your former victory was glorious but hollow; this one may be as rich as it is easy. Go, therefore, to certain

1. One of the Colonna brothers who were very close to Petrarch, he was a Roman senator and military commander deeply involved in the battle between the Colonnas and the Orsinis and in the struggle against Cola di Rienzo which resulted in his death in 1347.

victory rather than to an uncertain struggle, and go relying not so much upon your own power as upon divine assistance. The very elements will fight in your behalf as they fought for Theodosius, and, as Claudian says, Aeolus will send you from the stars your armed winter winds; heaven will serve you, and the conspiring winds will descend upon your fleets. For you too will be waging war with the enemies of the cross although they be usurpers of the name of Christ. That this is so and that the new Eugenius has turned from a lamb to a wolf, and from a priest to a tyrant, the oppressed and plundered churches of Italy bear witness. The offended Godhead seeks you as an avenger not only of the offenses committed against you but those committed against Him. Do not fail in this twin vengeance, and do not place so much confidence in deeds already accomplished that you fail to see what remains to be done. Whether a little, a great deal, or an enormous amount has been done, it adds up to nothing if the beginning has no end. And I beg you not to prefer enjoying a victory to using it properly; something in which the great master of military science is declared to have erred to our very good fortune but to his very bad misfortune. Although that one example ought to furnish sufficient caution and proof to all the generals who have existed and will exist in the future, I shall refer to others from among our own as well as foreigners so that you will not be influenced in such a great matter by the recalling of only one example. Pompey the Great, victor at Dyrrhachium, let Julius Caesar get away when he almost captured him and could have held onto him. Whether it was his ignorance of warfare, or the clear superiority of the antagonist, or fortune assisting her follower in an extreme moment, or whether (which is the general view) it was an utterly astonishing example of humanity (would that it had turned out well!), it was soon followed by a public calamity in Thessaly and the miserable death of the commander himself in Egypt. And in Africa at the same time the destruction of Cato and of freedom, in Spain the sad destruction of the relics, in Rome the plundered treasury, the suppression of the laws, and the Senate ready with concealed sword, and the conqueror killed on the Capitoline which he had honored with four triumphs. Then there was the harsh siege of Perugia and of Modena, and the cruel slaughter of the residents of Parma which Cicero recalls in his *Philippics*, and Pharsalia once again flowing with our blood, and those huge naval battles fought under the summits of Leuca and Aetna. Finally from that time down to our own century a series of so many misfortunes has flowed from those actions that their enumeration is impossible and their recollection unpleasant and there seems to be no end to the afflictions. What should I say about Cyrus, the king of the Persians, who, to speak the truth, was a victor in battle and a loser in victory. What should I say about Alexander, the Macedonian, who, having lived safely through war, perished at a banquet? Agamemnon destroyed that famous and proud Troy; Africanus the younger (our Policertes, so to speak) completely destroyed Carthage and Numantia; and both were safer in war than after the victory, and happier in military service than at home. Knowing that they are distant no less in character than in time and place, I have joined them in this portion of my brief letter because their fate and end seemed to be almost the same: conquerors of the enemy, each having subdued and overcome the foreigner, they perished amidst the caresses of their most abominable wives. I confess that this has nothing to do with our subject, so that I shall lead the entire matter to a single end in order to show that there is much to fear even for victors. Deeds accomplished should never satisfy, and one should persist long and continually in the fashion of Caesar pressing on energetically to success and pursuing the favor of the gods, and believing that nothing has been accomplished as long as anything remains to be accomplished. Otherwise many people will consider victory more suspect than war, and seriously wonder whether it were better not to have begun than once begun to have deserted beckoning destiny in the middle of the road. Farewell and take care.

Fam. III, 4.

To the same correspondent, that there is nothing new under the sun.

How I felt concerning the general state of your activities I had written to you, oh most courageous man, some time ago in the vernacular so that it could be understood even by your soldiers who will in part avail themselves of your trials and of your glory. Soon afterwards, however, with my inventive impulse always providing me with something new, I composed a poem for you containing matter from my own work and from others. I followed that rule whereby the first verse was mine, and the second was taken from some talented poet, so that not only the ingenious connecting of ideas but the harmony of the words would also delight a reader. In doing so I gloried in the thought that I had invented a new poetic form, until after having sent my poem I discovered that others had handled this type of poetry before me and that what the wise men of the Hebrews had said was indeed true: "There is nothing new under the sun"; and also what the comic poet had written: "There is nothing to be said that has not been said before." Recently through the messenger of your magnanimous father, Stefano the elder, I wrote in a free style prose something with which I thought I could strike several chords of your valor. If you have received it, there is nothing that I would change, nothing that I would add. Although many things offer themselves, it is sufficient to have alerted a wise man. Farewell.

To an unknown correspondent, that the solitary life cannot be fully commended except by an expert.

You request that I explain briefly the state of the solitary life which I seem to be living at this time, as you say, beyond the custom of our station. Whether you ask this because you are eager to imitate or to ridicule, you alone know. Perhaps you do not realize how great a matter you wish to be expressed briefly and compressed into a very narrow framework. Eloquent writers have written books on this very matter, but none in my opinion has hitherto praised such a life sufficiently. I confess that I was driven often to write about the subject, and would have done so except that I did not yet trust sufficiently either my talent or my style or my information about the matter. As for your request, I feel strongly that I would never listen seriously to someone praising the solitary life unless he had enjoyed first its sweetness in some form, for it abounds in new and countless advantages that are learned not by listening or by reading but only through experiencing. Thus I believe that one cannot learn about this except through experience. And what good is it to deal with the matter with great eloquence when those who listen either will not understand or will believe minimally. You, therefore, if, as you declare, the admiration for my solitude and the desire for imitating it attract you, you should not weary me, busy as I am with other cares, you should not implore an exposition which would be inadequate to the task. But if you (to repeat something that I say often because I believe it so strongly) make your request with a pure mind and with a desire for learning and not for testing my mind, come and see, and you will not be indebted to others for something you can do by yourself. Stop scratching the itch on your ears with the nails of another's words. Nothing prohibits you from accomplishing the same thing with fewer words. That will be more respectable than if you wrenched from me a treatise on so important a matter. This will benefit neither the giver nor the seeker except to render suspect the intention of the reader and contemptible the work of the writer. Farewell.

At the source of the Sorgue, 4 May.

Fam. III, 6.

To a friend eager for a questionable undertaking, that not all profit is useful.

Think what you will concerning the question that you have proposed. You lack neither age, nor the knowledge of books, nor the experience of life. As for me, the very consideration of dishonest matters is shameful. I do not find the highest good or any kind of good in riches or in pleasure (an opinion of the Stoics, not of the Peripatetics, with my preference being Stoic rather than Epicurean in all things). Riches and pleasure are comfortable and helpful in a mortal life; wherefore the former are called Fortune's good, the latter the good of the body. But the good that we seek lies in the mind and serves neither the body nor fortune. Though I admit that the others are called goods, I contend that they are not. Nor should you think that perhaps I have inadvertently slipped into an error by saying this. I am not ignorant of what Aristotle has to say about it, or what Epicurus felt, but the authority of philosophers does not prevent freedom of judgment. For me that opinion of philosophers seems more inspired and true which says that those who divide goods into three parts cannot be happy. The good is one, and one is that which makes us happy. Yours is far too empty and forced a happiness which involves, or rather requires, not only the beauty of the body and its total health but even riches. It is too exposed to the snares of thieves, and ultimately to excessive worry and agitation, qualities that certainly do not lead to true happiness. The happiness of Epicurus which consists in pleasure is not happiness but extreme misery. For what is more wretched for a man than to surrender the human good, reason, to an animal good, the senses? But do I seem to have lost my mind when among such great judges I should take on the controversy unasked? Well, then, let everyone believe as he pleases; it is difficult to give up inveterate beliefs. Philosophers whose names can scarcely be enclosed in the narrow confines of a letter have written a great many treatises on these beliefs. There is an entire book of Cicero which discusses the limits of good and evil. When you read it I doubt that there will be much more that your hearing or your intelligence would have to know. But since you asked from me not the truth of the matter (for that perhaps is hidden) but how it appeared to me, I shall bring the entire matter to a conclusion briefly. Do not listen to unjust advisors; they care neither about your name nor your welfare and offer you only what they themselves believe in or what they think would please you. You must consider nothing but noble things as worthy of being counted among good things. "But profit is useful." True, if joined with honesty. Otherwise you must know that there can be nothing more harmful. What Cicero himself says on this matter in his book *On Offices* is generally known. However, a large part of his readers, indifferent to the contents, examine only the words and embrace the precepts of life on hearsay as if they were tales. Remember that those books treat matters relating not to the tongue but to the mind, and contain not rhetorical but philosophical lessons. And keep in mind constantly what was once well-known to the Attics in Athens; namely, the advice of Themistocles, the explanation of Aristides and the judgment of the assembly. In like manner, despite the multitude's ridicule, I do not disdain profit, but with this proviso, that it involve nothing that appears dishonest; otherwise I shall avoid gold no less than a cliff. For gold, as Plautus says, "often advocates wrongly many things for many people." Finally, so that I may end with that same author, "I do not believe that all profit is generally useful to man." Farewell.

Fam. III, 7.

To Paganino da Milano,[1] that the appetite for power must be controlled, and on the optimum condition of the state.

Although I am not ignorant of how much more the Roman state increased under the rule of the many than under the rule of one man, I know that it has appeared to many and even to great men, that the happiest condition of the state is under a single and just ruler. Thus authority and experience seem to be a odds. But the question is greater than can be discussed in such a short letter. Certainly, as the present state of things is for us, amidst such implacable discord of minds, there is hardly any room left for doubt that monarchy is the best for regrouping and restoring the power of Italy which the madness of civil wars for a long time has diminished. I knew these things, and I confess that a royal hand is necessary for our ills. Similarly, I have no doubt you believe that I prefer no king more than this king of ours under whose power we live so agreeably and quietly that we do not need the kindness of Pyrrhus, the fortune of Alexander, the justice of Zaleucus, or to use instead examples from the Romans, the ardor of Romulus, the religion of Numa, the military prowess of Tullius, the grandeur of Ancus, the comportment of Tarquinius, or the prudence of Servius. Certainly if justice alone distinguishes a king from a tyrant, our king is a true king, however much the most genuine tyrants of all call him tyrant while they wish to be called fathers of their country. With these no Phalaris, no Agathocles, no Dionysius, in short no Gaius or Nero and no Heliogabalus, most loathesome of all, can contend in lewdness and roughness. Therefore, since it is part of the prudent man to preceive not so much what delights as what sets free, and in this very process to consider carefully not the beginnings of things but the results, I would

---

1. A close friend of Petrarch and firm supporter of the expansionist policies of the Visconti, Lords of Milan, during the decade 1339–1349. Served as governor of various cities for Luchino Visconti, and probably met Petrarch while serving as governor of Parma in 1348. The "king" referred to in the letter is Luchino.

like to ask you whose excellent advice he accepts, and whose prudence and trust you let no one doubt; I would, I say, like to ask you, dear friend, who know my mind, to give him this perhaps homely but sincere piece of advice; persuade him that he has extended his borders sufficiently with regard both to his wealth and his fame. Nothing ever satisfies cupidity and I hope that she will not deceive him with her enormous promises. Moderation in all kinds of fortune is like gold; and human happiness without setting a limit to itself is eager to advance, and extending into infinity brings with it not only a great deal of anxiety, but nothing enduring, nothing certain, nothing peaceful. Therefore, I have always liked the modesty of the younger Africanus, who, as Censor, ordered that the lustral song be changed because it sought from the gods an increase in the happiness of Rome and thus seemed too full of cupidity and unfit for the gods themselves, and that thereafter the Romans would implore nothing more than the present state of things and stability. This was certainly wise and prudent if mortal affairs were consistent and if what they sought from their false gods could have been sought from our omnipotent God. I see that many more things could be said here but what need is there of words? You know my mind; you know what I desire and what I fear. I hear that he is undertaking new enterprises. I wish him well if he continues but would prefer that he cease, for that path would be safer. Declare your opposition, I beg you, to his ambitions. Remind him of the saying of that most temperate commander: "That the Romans wished not so much to possess gold as to rule over those who possessed gold." If this is said correctly about gold, which can be hidden, what could be said about lands and cities? Likewise, if this can be said rightfully concerning enemies, what would you say about friends whom you control not by compulsion but by spontaneous agreement and of whom you may possess with full justice not only the lands or the gold but their bodies and minds? It is both more noble and safer to have friends than the possessions of friends; and where you may control those who are willing, it is foolhardy to wish to control those who are not. It is the advice of philosophers, and indeed of nature which says: "Nothing achieved by violence is long lasting." It is easy to defend the borders of a modest kingdom; the huge kingdom is difficult to achieve and very difficult to watch over. Farewell.

Fam. III, 8.

To a friend, an exhortation against putting faith in the answers of soothsayers or any kind of diviner.

I beg you, let us lay aside, if we can, both the sad memory of past events and the anxious uneasiness about future ones. They torment us over nothing, and like double stings disturb the peace of our life on both sides. What are we striving for, over what are we tormented? What's been done cannot be undone, nor can the future be foreseen. What need is there for astrologers against whom the authority of the saints, of philosophers and poets, and of all those who perceive the truth clamors? To skip over the words of many philosophers, who does not know the famous testimony of Virgil that the minds of soothsayers are ignorant? What Attius said is also known: "I believe nothing said by the fortune tellers who enrich the ears of others with words so that they can enrich their homes with gold." No less interesting is that saying of Pacuvius, that very ancient poet: "If they were to foresee what lies in the future they would be similar to Jupiter." Nor should you believe that the poet is much different than the soothsayer in this regard. As Isaiah says: "Proclaim what will come about in the future and we shall understand that you are gods." I therefore believe that that advice of the very learned Favorinus, mostly taken from Cicero, with which both dissuaded us from all these illusions and deceits, should not only be accepted but amplified. For either these who promise news of the future foretell adversities falsely and fill us in vain with empty fear, or, if what they foretell be true, they make us wretched beforehand. Or again, they may deal with things that do turn out, thereby doubling our suffering with the weariness that comes of waiting than which I know no greater, and with the removal of joy when achieved, or its "deflowering," as Favorinus called it. And indeed, before such joy appears, it will already have been destroyed by the preoccupied mind full of hope. If the prediction is false it is certain that the empty and absurd joy ceases in the grief and shame of a lost hope. Therefore they are not to be taken seriously who promise impossible things even for themselves and useless things for us. And so? Let everyone believe that Christ said for him what Jupiter says to Amphitryon in Plautus: "Be of good heart; I am present, oh Amphitryon, with help for you and yours. Let there be nothing you fear; send away all sooth-sayers and diviners; I can speak of future and present things much better than they," adding not "because I am Jupiter," as he says, but because I am God. He doubtless speaks many things to us constantly through the ears of our heart. If we were willing to listen to Him, we could easily disdain the promises of these mountebanks. Death is certain; the hour of death is uncertain, so that we await each hour as though it were the last; it is sufficiently beneficial to know these things. Therefore what ignorance in these men, what madness is ours, that we should be tortured by predictions that are covered by thick darkness and can be seen in the future only by God? I confess that there is only one extraordinary thing in all of this vain activity, and that is that anyone who is right in most other things will be called a liar if he makes only one unusual mistake, whereas soothsayers, however false they may be, acquire the fame of prophesying truly in making a single accidental guess. Cicero marveled at this, although with different words, in that book in which briefly he builds up the art of divination in order to destroy it. Augustine in a variety of places, and especially in the book *On Various Matters*, speaking against those "who now," as he says, "are called astrologers, wanting to subject our acts to celestial bodies and to sell us to the stars and there receive the price for such sale from us," reasons as follows: "When it is said that they have predicted many true things, it happens because men do not keep in their mind their errors and false-hoods, but instead, paying attention only to those things which happened according to their predictions, they forget those that did not happen. And those things are remembered which happen not because of knowledge, which they do not possess, but by some obscure combination of circumstances. But if they wish to yield to their skill, let them say that any of the dead and written parchments which many believe contain prophesies also foretell things skillfully. And if a verse foretelling future things often emerges from manuscripts without skill, what is so extraordinary if even from the mind of a speaker there emerges some prediction of future things not through skill but through chance?" These last words are Augustine's which apply here because of his authority and because of his faith. What else do you think opened the road to all of these deceitful doings except the ignorance of the multitude and their infinite cupidity, not to say their madness, wanting so badly to know those things which cannot be known and which it is not useful to know? You, therefore, avoid these kinds of rash and impudent men who oppose the peaceful life so that, as much as possible, you may spend this very brief time without unnecessary and inane cares. In short, be sure of this: Until you throw aside the burden of super-stitions, you can desire but not pursue the blessed life. Op-posites repel; fear and happiness will never live happily to-gether. Farewell.

Fam. III, 9.

To Matteo da Padova,[1] against drunkenness.

I shall not mention what can be said at great length against drunkenness; how detestable, how dangerous, how sad an illness it is, and how much madness there is in skillfully drowning and killing off in a foaming glass one's reasoning powers with which nature has endowed man uniquely and specially. Through drink, one has no control over his feet, tongue, and mind; his head trembles as do his hands, his eyes tear, his body smells and the lingering traces of the previous day are offensive on the following day. I will not mention the way in which the passions rule, the loss of control, the stories and laughter of the people, the hatred and contempt of good friends. I also pass over the sudden alteration in mood and the ignorance of even learned men and the childishness of the man of any age, a childishness exposed to the joking and deceit and mockery of everyone. Nor shall I mention cracks in the mind crushed and weak because of a heavy burden, letting out secrets often harmful to one's self or to others and the cause of actual death to many and of utmost misery. Furthermore there are the lamentations and the inane joy and struggles and quarrels and rifts and the heedless encounter of armed men with unarmed ones. All these things I pass over since they are known and common. There is a book of Apuleius of Madaura entitled *Florida*. In it he discusses humorously what the first glass and second and following ones do to a drunkard. I shall not enlarge upon his opinion. For I know not why or how one drinks more today than formerly. Indeed, would that this were the manner in which dissipation worked. In any event, wherever we turn, we seem to have become weaker toward virtue and stronger toward vices. In my opinion, therefore, the first glass pertains to thirst, the second to pleasure, the third to passion, the fourth to drunkenness, the fifth to wrath, the sixth to quarreling, the seventh to madness, the eighth to sleep, the ninth to illness. Tell all this to that Marcus Bibulus, not the associate of Julius Caesar but yours, with whose vices

1. Unknown correspondent.

and wantonness you constantly quarrel, if you believe that it may be useful. If by chance he appears irreproachable to himself because he has not yet reached the extremes of drunkenness, tell him that it is better to have descended even slightly from the heights of moderation and restraint than to hit bottom once you have started to slide. Both virtue and vice approach slowly; no one is made excellent or evil overnight. Farewell.

Fam. III, 10.

To a Transalpine friend, a man of great repute, that cow-ardice does not delay death and that he should do nothing base in order to attempt to live longer.

Faith breaks my silence and charity compels me to speak. Christ is my witness that I feel compelled to write things which, if you read them in the same spirit in which they were written, would increase your good will toward me and your glory among the people. How could I pretend, if I wish not to be a false friend, that you, surrounded by great dangers, need not be roused if asleep or forewarned to be vigilant? You see what serious warfare has arisen between the kings of France and Britain. Without doubt there has been no graver situation since the days of our forefathers, not indeed in Europe since antiquity, nor was such a great opportunity ever offered to strong men to achieve glory. All the kings and all the people, uncertain about the outcome of such a struggle, and especially those who inhabit that territory from the Italian Alps to the ocean, whom the frightful din of approaching battle terrifies, have taken up arms. You alone, in such a whirlwind of happenings, sleep. The Virgilian rebuke should press upon you and like a messenger sent from heaven should exclaim: "Can you indulge in sleep under the present circumstances and be blind to the dangers that surround you?" Indeed even if nothing more than shame could bother you, you ought to have roused yourself more quickly. With what nerve and with what spirit, while others spend their time under the helmet and bear the shield in the hot sun, do you, far from the battle lines of men, and attended by retinues of women, nourished with rare dishes and covered with soft garments, remain inert in the shade and in leisure, you whom I formerly considered a man eager for honor and glory, a powerful and noble man, a youthful and strong man? I ask you, what is keeping you? Do you like elegance? Are you fleeing from labor? But listen to the words of a very strong man offered by Sallust: "Arrogance is becoming to women, toil to men." Do you fear thirst and sandy paths and terrible serpents during the dog days? But listen to the words of another man who, though less warlike, was no less strong: "The serpent, thirst, heat, battlefields are sweet things to virtue; patience enjoys hardships." But perhaps you fear death and the sword? But even here the words of another brave man come to mind: "Death is a final punishment and ought not to be feared by men." I say it ought not to be feared any more than sleep or rest. What is there of real consequence between the day of birth and death? Basically a great deal. Our birth envelopes us in the labors of human life, death sets us free. Whence that custom, taken from the innermost heart of philosophy, of grieving at the birth of one's dear ones and rejoicing at their death. But not to stray from the opinions of the multitude (from which we should indeed be retreating as much as possible if we desire salvation), let it be granted that death is to be feared, and let that notorious saying of Aristotle be produced, that death is the ultimate dread (note that he took pains not to say "the greatest" but "the ultimate"); leaving it, however, as "the greatest," do you think that by keeping away from war or seas you can really avoid death? Well known are the words of still another poet: "In vain do we avoid bloody Mars, and the crashing waves of hoarse Hadria; in vain do we fear the south breezes which are considered harmful to bodies in the autumn." Even with the greatest care given by a human to his body, he must die. "But the desire to postpone death is a drive of mortals." I confess this and I recognize the excuse of public foolishness. But first I ask you, how small indeed is such postponement! Then to how many misfortunes is it exposed! For how many people who managed to live longer did a postponed death do harm and indeed diminish the glory of their life! We abound in daily examples, but I call to mind ancient ones with greater reverence, and our own more willingly than foreign ones. If Tullius Hostilius had lived a little less long, he would not have suffered the blow of the thunderbolt. Remove a few years from Tarquinius and he will have died a king and not an exile. A longer life produced blindness for Appius Claudius, imprisonment for Marius and shameful flight and a slimy hiding place in marshes. Who more illustrious than Pompey the Great, except that the prolongation of his life obscured the splendor of so great a name? What followed such splendor but the indignity of death? What shall I say about the two Africans? How much better do you think it would have been if one had perished before the walls of Carthage and the other before the gates of Numantia? The first one would not have condemned his homeland in a famous epigram for an unworthy exile, and the second would have avoided the injustice of an unavenged death. Caesar Augustus himself, whom you would judge the happiest of all, how much more happily would he have died prior to the adultery of his already aging daughter and before he began counting her "tumors" as he used to call them with bitterness. I bypass Regulus and Cato and the others whom a noble death illumined, although I am compelled to feel differently about them than about our own (I refer to Cicero and Seneca). I would not want to have had Cato die before the Civil War lest the highly trustworthy witnesses of his steadfastness as well as his renowned toil and distinction might never have been known. I admire him with undaunted spirit, I admire him struggling with the serpents, I admire him wandering over the Libyan sands; I praise the firmness of his mind, I praise his stubbornness, I praise his freedom; I do not praise his willed death and his despair. And so that you may not think that I am perhaps neglecting foreign examples, Pyrrhus and Hannibal would have died with greater fame if they could have had their burial in Italy. For both, their return to their fatherland was unfortunate. Cyrus could also have been more famous had he died before touching the Scythian shores. Your Brennus would have been more famous if he had died before touching the threshold of Delphi. What should I say about the poisoning of Mithridates, the vicissitudes of Alcibiades, the exile of Themistocles, the chains of Aristides, the fire of Croesus? Rarely does a long life enjoy an equally long happiness. When happiness ceases it is not just a matter of being unhappy (unless a present disaster becomes even worse by the memory of past happiness); were nothing to happen to us while alive, we are nevertheless compelled to behold many things happening to our dear ones which do not permit us to call ourselves happy. Happily would Priam have departed this world, or Peleus, or Nestor, if they had preceded their children. To include a different type of example, the poisonous cup would not have killed Socrates, nor dogs Euripides, nor swords Demothenes and Cicero, nor forgetfulness Messalla, nor would leprosy have overcome Plotinus if an opportune death had preceded their overwhelming afflictions.

But enough of such examples, and especially in a matter which is clear. You see, therefore, that the desire for a longer life is blind, that a good death is to be preferred in which one can readily see that no one can be deceived, and no one can be displeased. But since custom has continued to desire harmful things indiscriminately as well as those which constantly overcome us, one may prefer to opt for the majority. Or do you hope to achieve the desired goal through sloth? You are indeed terribly wrong. How many did an excessive laziness crush whom toil and vigilance might have preserved; how many did either hangovers kill or drunkenness strangle who would have been saved by fasting! It is generally known that more are killed by food than by the sword. Whatever food people eat, in whatever corner of the earth they may try to hide, death finds them and demands, requires, and extorts its tribute. In vain do we try to evade; if we do not proceed toward death, it will follow us. Consider, therefore, what is more noble, what is more worthy for a man, either to hide and flee what one cannot avoid, or to oppose whatever comes and do what one should and follow one's fortune voluntarily lest, if one were to linger, one would be drawn forward by force. Oh pitiful sweetness of very brief delays! Who is so anxious to live that he would not prefer to die forthwith than to prolong his life the space of a single year with dishonor, destroying the dignity of all his past years? How more obscene will it be to do something unbecoming for fear of death when all that is promised is the uncertainty not of a year but of a day? You say to yourself: "I would go if only I did not fear the danger of death's approach," something that could be said anytime you are able to remain without danger. However, is it not true that either a sudden fever or some other illness (for the fate of humans may take many forms and an astonishing variety) could perhaps snatch from you the life that you denied your king? If this is so, I urge and implore you to take heed right now and raise your eyes. You will see a vast array of kings and of people tottering under overwhelming preparations, and about to collapse under the pressing power of fortune. This is no time for pretending. Your enemies are vigilant and they surround their king with a yoke of submissiveness. If he were to enjoy victory, and were to see how inactive you are now in his moment of need (and you should know that he has been hostile to you for some time), how do you think he would react? But if it were to happen otherwise, since fortune disposes of all things as it pleases, do you perhaps hope that the security you enjoy in your present repose would continue in that ardor of conquest? You will indeed appear to have held back not because you wanted to but out of fear! And the general collapse will envelope you equally with everyone else. Believe me, both sides will call you a spectator of the struggle, prepared to change directions at the nod of fortune and the will of the victor. Therefore good will appears nowhere and danger everywhere. It will be useful to recall Metius, a leader of the Albans, who was quartered with a team of four horses pulling in different directions at the order of Hostilius, king of the Romans, because he had remained neutral in the middle of two armies. Hurry, and wake up, I beg you; return rapidly, while there is still time, to your duty which has been so long neglected. To sleep in a quaking world resembles death much more than sleep. I wish you well.

To Guido Gonzaga,[1] *lord of Mantua, that love equates unequals.*

Truly great and wonderful is the power of love which so powerfully and tenaciously and with invisible, although by no means imperceptible, ties binds the smallest things to the greatest, and despite their inequality controls them with equal power. And why should it not have this dominion over the minds of men vigorous in their feelings and in their rational powers, if it can bind insensitive and contrary things with strong ties? The air would not cling to fire nor earth to water, nor would rivers recognize their banks nor the sea its shores nor the stars their paths, were it not that the almighty or, as people call it, sacred love of the world binds all things together in the world. Therefore He who regulates heaven and earth with equal justice did not discriminate between my humble status and your lofty one. He observes this principle: He knows how to make unequals equal, and does not allow a faithful lover not to be loved. In times past through your sensibility, and through no particular doings of mine, but only through the perception of the mind, as one says (for minds have their eyes with which, once the veil of the body is overcome, they see one another), through your sensibility, as I started to say, oh outstanding friend, you felt the extent of my devotion toward you. Love compelled you to love in return; something which a number of indications but especially two recent letters of yours which Giovanni d'Arezzo, your chancellor, showed me, made me recognize very plainly. In these letters, amazing as it may seem, while you may have sent your messenger here on many matters of high importance, you inquire not about the state of the Roman Curia (than which there is nothing more base or incredible in this day and age), not about the condition of your closer friends, not even about the transactions of your affairs,

---

1. Son of Luigi I, initiator of the greatness of the Gonzaga family. Following his father's struggles against the Estes, the Scaligers, and the Visconti, he recognized the authority of the latter, and was made Lord of Mantua from 1360–1369.

in fact about nothing except about me and my doings. And you berate Giovanni because, although you were curious about other things, he was silent about that particular one which alone and above all others you wished to know about. And furthermore to be certain that no one might think that you had spoken casually, you asked the same favor in two letters. I omit other things you say that would perhaps provoke marvel in those who do not know on what friendly terms Caesar Augustus held above all others Virgil, your fellow townsman, of peasant origin but hardly a man of peasant genius; and also Horace, a freedman by birth but free-born in literary skill; and in those unacquainted with the letters often filled with pleasant flattery that this ruler sent to those humble friends as if to equals. The recollection of these things, while they may diminish the wonder, increase my joy so much the more because I feel myself becoming associated with such examples, and because the road to such glory is being opened to me. As another of these friends of Caesar says, "To have pleased princely men is not the least of praises." And here indeed a new miracle emerges; namely, that while there was much to be pleasing in them I must confess there is nothing pleasing in me. For how can I hope to be pleasing to others since I am not pleasing to myself? We call a woman fortunate who is not beautiful but appears to be so to her husband; we call a slave fortunate not because his work is superior but because the love of his master is deep. Thus with me, whoever I may truly be, if I seem worthy of your esteem, I would call myself happy in your opinion, and if I possess nothing that makes me likeable, nevertheless, if I do please, that is sufficient. I would render thanks to you except that I distrust my ability to use words worthy of your kindness; and it is wiser to be silent about those things that exceed one's ability to speak.

On the bank of the Rhone, the ides of January.

Fam. III, 12.

To Marco Genovese,[1] that even those who serve the state can love piously and honestly and can also aspire to the silence of a loftier life above the din of the active life.

You have, most excellent man, made your mind perfectly clear in your letter; for no one can speak in such a manner unless he feels strongly. I feel the strength of your style (your great love dictated your words), and I gladly and eagerly hasten to open the doorway of my friendship. Why do I say "open" when more than four years ago I offered it to you at your own most welcome request? I recognize my Marco, and I embrace him with delight in these letters of yours as after a long silence he rightfully returns to me. I now perceive the extremely rich and pleasing benefits of your blossoming character. Indeed, I always hoped that from the young man you were you would become a great man. But I confess that I did not believe that it could happen so soon. Your virtue, being premature and for that reason more pleasing, surpassed my hope. I also recall that most glowing proposal of yours which in those early days of our friendship in extended discourse you trustingly revealed to me. I do not regret that now that proposal is either modified or, hopefully, merely postponed, provided you tell me, as you had promised at that splendid beginning, that you would love God in all circumstances, that you would adhere to Him, worship Him, and long for Him with your entire mind. I am not imposing an impossible rule upon you. Where I am bidding you to go is a much trodden road. How many outstanding men arrived gloriously from the storms of public life to the silence of cloistered gates; how many also, having dropped anchor far from such gates, have completed the voyage of this life most happily! The Divine Potter knows our true image. He knows what is good for us and for our soul. Often He indicates in indescribable ways the paths on which He wishes to be approached. Do not despair, therefore, that you seem to be entering a byway, or as the Pythagoreans call it, the sinister path; or that your concern for your citizens,

1. Unknown correspondent.

which requires so much of your time, appears opposed to that divine grace which you seek. Persevere, proceed, do not hesitate, do not abide nor fail in your own salvation. He is present who foresees all your time infallibly and eternally (regardless of how you arrange it). Nor is there any reason why you should meanwhile think that you were born in vain if you were to assist your fatherland with your labor and with your counsel, especially in these times when it needs you so badly and, as Plato indicates, rightfully demands a part of your birthright for itself. Heavenly is that saying of my Africanus in Cicero's work: "For all those who have preserved, assisted, and supported their fatherland, there is certainly a definite place in heaven where the blessed experience joy eternally." Well known also is what follows: "There is nothing that may be done on this earth that is more acceptable to that supreme God who rules over all this world than the assemblies and meetings of men united by law and forming what is known as states." The time will doubtless come, my friend, which you long for, when you can raise yourself from the ground not so much as did Maro or Ennius but like Ambrose or Arsenius with wings powerful enough for flight. You will at length do what you have long done in your mind, and with the same Helper who was your inspiration; and you will accomplish it, as I hope, in the security of a more perfect age and of a more mature judgment rather than in the attempt of a youthful indiscretion and impetuousness. For just as the road is safer for the pilgrim over land free of highwaymen and over plains and solid roads under a calm sky, so when the passions are quiet, the judgment secure, and the ferment of youthful pride restrained, through the more moderate and serene years of life, one proceeds in greater safety to salvation. No age is rejected, however, as I have said, no one who participates in honorable activity may be excluded from this path. It has also been established, according to the opinion of Plotinus, that one becomes blessed and is cleansed not only through the penitential virtues but also through the political ones. To speak of a Christian example, Martha's active solicitude is not to be scorned even though Mary's contemplation may be superior.

There you have within our narrow limits of time, dear friend, as much as can be said about one of your requests, that I write you some useful information about life. What I send you came from a brief period of time before dawn and is indeed very short, but is in itself, I believe, complete if I were to add the following: a shortened path to virtue has been seen by philosophers as undertaking to become what we wish to appear. And nothing is more effective, I believe, than another saying since it pleased the same philosophers: the entire life of learned men is nothing more than a preparation for death. So far I have tried not to instruct you but merely to advise and exercise your memory. Still remaining is your request that I keep you always in mind. I find it helpful here to use your own words. Be assured that I have been doing so a long time. From when I first saw you I fixed your image indelibly deep in my heart like a faultless diamond which no time can remove, nor any place. Finally, I would like to congratulate you for the virtue and good fortune by which you deserved the friendship and kindness of so great a prince. And for the esteem granted to this little old man I express my gratitude. Farewell.

At the source of the Sorgue, the calends of January.

To Friar Giovanni Colonna, that the gout is common among the wealthy.

I am going to babble an old maid's tale to you but one that is apropos. A spider once on a journey met the gout and said, "Where are you heading so sadly?" The gout answered, "I met a rural and shaggy guest who tortured me with perpetual hunger and labor, and who after having kept me roaming until night among clods and stones, would scarcely allow us both in our wretched state to go back to his dusty and empty home. He would never wear shoes without holes nor be without a very heavy bundle on his back. The evening that followed would be no better than the miserable day. He would comfort me with a dinner that was dismal indeed, with old pieces of moldy and hard bread and with garlic and very strong herbs, and he would pour vinegar into his murky drinking water. It was indeed a feast day whenever some Sardinian cheese was available. Having welcomed me in this manner he would have me rest on a couch whose hardness exceeded that of his little field. Arising then at dawn he forced me back into the hated work of the fields; and thus one day followed another with no respite and no hope of repose. On Sunday he would wash the sheep of his master or repair the bed of the stream or stretch out the hedge around the meadows. I therefore am fleeing this unending evil and the home which is so unfavorable to my way of living." Having heard these things the spider said, "Goodness, how different my condition is! I had a host who was effeminate and soft and for whom pleasure was not only the greatest but the only enjoyment. Rarely did he lead his feet outside the house; and he prolonged his dinner until dawn and his lunch until evening. Sleep, which possessed his remaining activities, was sought under fancy coverings, and to sleep was devoted whatever time remained beyond banqueting and dissipation. There were costly festive dishes, all kinds of foreign perfumes, fancy wines, golden utensils, jeweled drinking cups, walls covered with silk tapestries and floors with purple carpeting, and together with all this a host of servants always in movement, running to and fro and yet present everywhere. While this throng sweeps with brooms, and while it shakes out the dust from the paneled beams, I can scarcely spin my skillful webs, and, even when I started sadly to do so, at the very beginning of my work I would see my hopes dashed and my labors useless. When I was most unfortunately driven out headlong, I sought the shelves, but without success. The solid walls of snow-white marble left no lodging for miserable me. Therefore, I fled from the presence of these pursuers preferring a peaceful exile anywhere to the endless domestic labors." When the spider had finished speaking, the other answered: "My, how many are the good things which are lost either through ignorance or through neglect! Ignorance is the blindness of the mind, negligence is the sluggishness of the soul. One must keep his eyes open and must not put off those salutary things that offer themselves. It is clear from what I have said and heard that those things which may have appeared most unfavorable to us would have been most favorable if we exchanged quarters. My host would have been most suitable to you and yours to me." This plan appealed to both and they exchanged homes. As a result it came about that the gout lived among delights in the palaces of the rich and the spider in squalor and poverty in the hut of the peasant.

I understand, my friend, that the gout has sneaked into your home, and I am astonished. I did not think that there would be room for it in such a frugal home, and I fear lest it found there something appealing. But if it is true, I shudder no more at the evil than at the cause of it. I would prefer that you would have the spider as your guest. You must resist such beginnings. There is nothing more useful for resistance than vigilance, toil and fasting. As a boy I saw a young man with the gout, and I saw the same one as an old man free of the gout. I asked him how it happened, and he answered simply that he had done nothing other than to renounce wine altogether. Cicero recounts, and after Cicero others, that certain wealthy men having become hopeless with the gout returned to health when they became poor. I dare not order you to become poor, although if you understand, it would not be necessary to command. As I hear, you profess, among other things, to be a voluntarily poor man. Do I lie? Certainly within the dwelling of the religious and especially in the hut of the beggar there is no place for wealth. Wealth and indigence do not dwell together. Poverty being excluded I fear not so much that you store gold than, as the apostle says, that you store wrath on the day of wrath. Meditate on this since you have an understanding with Christ which you should recall very well. If you have forgotten, reread the text of the agreement and you will find what you promised Him and what He promised you. As I said, I am not forcing you to become poor, not because it would not behoove you to accept and me to give friendly advice, but because it displeases me to pour forth words and to speak in vain. For I see that the very name of poverty is horrifying and shameful to you and you cannot voluntarily lay aside what you have voluntarily embraced. This was a voluntary poverty which is called thriftiness by philosophers. This I urge you to adopt. This is the one road that I hold out to you for the health of your body. As another Hippocrates I offer you this perhaps bitter but healthy drug. If you wish to be healthy, live like a poor man. Gold which is hidden in a strongbox harms only the mind, the more delightful food harms both the mind and the body. Therefore, if you wish to eliminate the gout, eliminate pleasures; if you wish to eliminate all bad things, eliminate wealth. Farewell.

At the source of the Sorgue, 22 June.

Fam. III, 14.

To an unknown correspondent, an explanation for the turning down of a loan sought in the correspondence of a certain important friend.

I disdain with unrestrained indignation the yoke of money which weighs down kings. I shall not allow, God willing, that the soul become a servant of metals when it is disposed to greater things. However, although I forbid money to dominate, it refuses to submit and the one it cannot add as a slave it scorns as a master. I shall say even less: money is more proud than I have said and wishes to have me neither as master nor as a companion. It refuses my control, and does not admit my friendship. It breaks the crowbars, it unties all knots, it scorns the lock of my strongbox. When I seem to have locked it up, it seems to slide away through invisible cracks. As often as I consider that matter irksome, I also look upon it with favor when I look around me and observe those whom it has usually made its slaves or given hospitality to.

Since this is so, you will forgive me if I do not relieve your present financial plight, something that is more painful to me than to you. But so that you do not think that by writing you gained nothing, know that there is an abundance of excellent pledges that I have ready for you. However, I was not able through any expedient to persuade your servant to bring them to you. Order him to return to me, but with less stubbornness. Otherwise my own servant will come to you, although I would like our wound to be known to no one except the doctor. Furthermore, I should like to add that from your letter things appeared for both of us more humorous than pleasant. I received comfort for my condition, not because I delight in having your company in my poverty, but because it is not right for me to be indignant since so great a man has so much in common with me, and because you no longer have to seek an excuse. And so that you may not become too concerned, I already had my pen in hand, and in order to keep any information from reaching the ears of the greedy usurer concerning my affairs, I had determined to ask whether you could offer assistance to my needs. What should I say? I am not unaware of the fertile areas of philosophy and the very plentiful matter with which minds can be armed against the webs of fortune, among which poverty is not the last. And while such things are not permitted to dwell with us, because as Flaccus said so elegantly, "Something is always lacking to a meager patrimony," there are also many things that can be said to be healthy not only for us but generally. Although I could speak about them, I shall not do so in order to avoid following that public custom of exchanging words for things. It is an easy friendship to offer advice in place of help. In such cases which are common in my house (and they could have been very rare except that I am careless about my patrimony because of my more noble cares) when I have found many kinds of remedies either concocted by myself or by more learned men, then I try that most effective solution of all which says that all fortune has its annoyances; or that other one which may be very true if one were to undertake some serious investigation, that every life even though it may appear very happy on the surface, is tormented; or finally that the most troublesome and demanding, and if you want to look more deeply, actually the most miserable state of all is that of wealth. On the other hand, though difficult, poverty is extremely safe and unimpeding, while the intermediate condition is best of all, and I rejoice that among the rarest gifts of God this has befallen to us. If sometime we lack anything, heavenly generosity compensates us with great numbers of gifts for what we lack and causes our good fortune to be sweeter for us because of the brief taste of bitterness. But if we lack many things, indeed all things, I nevertheless feel that I am happier being needy in a praiseworthy fashion than abounding with riches in a base fashion, and that those who place dishonest wealth before honorable need do not enjoy true wealth. Farewell.

31 December.

to a quarrelsome friend, that just as the friendship of good people is to be sought, so is the enmity of evil people to be shunned.

Try to be liked by all good men, and do not fear that you may have too many friends or that I am suggesting too much of a task for you. Wherefore I say that if you were to make none but good friends, they would be few. "Good men are indeed rare; they are rarely as many as the gates of Thebes or as the sources of the wealthy Nile." You ask, "Who says so?" What does it matter? If you approve the saying, why do you seek the answer? As Augustine says, "All truth partakes of the truth." I agree. Would you perhaps deny it? Experience speaks, which is not accustomed to lie; the truth speaks, which cannot lie. But if you want to know the human author, it was Juvenal who said it, most skillful in such matters and acquainted most deeply with the ways of men. If you do not believe him, listen to another one, through whose mouth speaks One who not only knows but created men. And what did he say? "There is no one who does good, not a single one." The poet said few, the prophet said no one; and according to each one's perspective, they are both right. Since one must not despair that good men can be found, and since when we begin to despair of all we must necessarily also begin to despair of ourselves, consider that some men are not only good but excellent. For the sake of harmonizing these differing opinions, listen to Flaccus who speaks out arbitrarily: "No one is born without defects; best is he who is marked by fewest." And indeed it is so. The stoics certainly clamor in their pledge to remove all disease that is rooted in souls. They would become the most outstanding of doctors if they could only deliver on their promises. But in this life of men, from among whom we must choose our friends, experience shows that there is no mind, regardless of its serenity and tranquillity, which is not sometimes moved by light concerns and shaken by upsetting human affairs. Just as an armed ship blown about the high seas is not overcome, so also for the mind the best praise is that it does not succumb. So that, though the Stoics disagree, it happens that in this life in which we know nothing to be perfect, we consider a healthy state any light and curable disease. Therefore, to return to the main subject of this letter, with this kind of man try to make friends by whatever means possible, not with those having no defects at all, but with those whose defects are inferior to their virtues (a group that you will learn is in itself very small). However, you will accomplish this in no better way than through the imitation and practice of their conduct and zeal. On the other hand, however, be neither friend nor foe nor acquaintance to the evil ones whose number is countless. They focus on your looks and ignore your mind. Pay heed to the advice of that man who warned: "Let all things be different within, but let our looks adapt to the people." Let them believe that you do what the people do. But you should do the tasks that are yours and something always a little greater in your own eyes. In such a way you will most likely avoid safely the hazards of the world, being dear to the few, unknown to the many, and hateful to no one. And do not think that today I have been philosophizing without basis. I hear that you have undertaken a huge war and a severe feud against wicked opponents and are wavering as to whether to reform them or destroy them. To do both things is of course impossible, and I consider it somewhat easier to destroy them than to correct them. I praise the stings of a generous indignation, but I do not praise an indecisive contest and vain zeal. If, in fact, it is wise to shun useless toil, what do you think about that toil whose only fruit is hatred? Therefore sound a retreat, I beseech you; otherwise be certain that you will be needing many legions. Farewell.

Fam. III, 16.

To Paganino da Milano, that patience is the only remedy in adversity.

My, how many things can be said now in answer to your letters! But neither have I the free time nor do you need the help of words. I am considering another kind of remedy. The power of fortune is great, as is its speed. Without doubt, of all those things which happen either in books or in the midst of the life of men, and they are indeed many and varied, this is the most important. I confess that there are some difficult and serious and unpleasant things that you are undergoing. There is only one consolation in adversity: patience. And especially if you disdain earthly things, if you keep in mind that you descended into this arena of life not for pleasure but for toil, if you endure adversity with great effort, and recall that a soldier's courage is tested in war, the sailor's in the storm, and a good man's in adversities. Farewell.

Fam. III, 17.

To the same correspondent, the time to think is before acting.

Far be it for me to dissuade anyone from complying with a reasonable request; but I remind you to observe foresight just as I thus far have observed hindsight. There is nothing more pleasant or more sweet than to be a partaker in helping someone who is deserving and needy. On the other hand, there is nothing sadder than unexpected ingratitude. It is indeed a sign not only of great knowledge but of great fortune to discern among so many hiding places of the heart the pure minds from the false ones, and to recognize before becoming acquainted whose prayers are sincere and whose tears are wretched, whose need is fictitious and whose flattery is feigned. It is common for most men to be mindful of those things that they wish to come to pass, and forgetful and slow when it is time to express gratitude. Men's minds are subject to so great and so sudden change that someone you may see entreating you in the morning you would not recognize in the evening after his request has been granted. About these *Ecclesiasticus* says: "As long as they may receive, they kiss the hand of the giver and they lower their voice in promises; and at the time of restitution they will request time and will speak words of weariness and complaint." You know the rest. But since we live among ingrates, we should not stop for that reason, otherwise virtue will seem to have been overcome by vice. I believe we should go a little more cautiously.

Farewell, and for whatever you are to do, think carefully while there is time for changing your mind; for subsequent deliberation is too late.

Fam. III, 18.

To Giovanni dell' Incisa,[1] to whom he has entrusted the search for books.

What formerly forgetfulness or laziness often kept me from doing, I want now to deal with, dear brother. And if I may be allowed to brag I shall do so in the name of Him in Whom alone it is safe to brag. Divine mercy has now almost freed me from the throes of human cupidity, if not perhaps altogether, for the most part at least. It was from heaven, therefore, that this was granted to me either through the goodness of nature or through age. Having indeed seen so many things and considered so much, I have finally begun to understand how many are these desires with which the human species burns. Lest you consider me immune to all the sins of men, there is one implacable passion that holds me which so far I have been neither able nor willing to check, for I flatter myself that the desire for noble things is not dishonorable. Do you wish to hear the nature of this disease? I am unable to satisfy my thirst for books. And I perhaps own more of them than I ought; but just as in certain other things, so does it happen with books: success in searching for them is a stimulus to greed. There is indeed something peculiar about books. Gold, silver, precious stones, beautiful clothing, marbled homes, cultivated fields, painted canvases, decorated horses, and other similar things, possess silent pleasure. Books please inwardly; they speak with us, advise us and join us together with a certain living and penetrating intimacy, nor does this instill only itself into its readers, but it conveys the names and desire for others. To cite some examples, Cicero's *Academicus* made Marcus Varro dear and attractive to me; and the name of Ennius I heard in his books on *Offices;* from a reading of the *Tusculan Disputations* I first felt my love for Terence; from the book *On Old Age* I became acquainted with the *Origins* of Cato and the *Economics* of Xenophon and I learned that the same book was translated by Cicero in his same *Offices*. In the same way

1. Theologian and Prior of the monastery of St. Marco in Florence. A relative as well as a close and trusted friend of Petrarch.

the *Timaeus* of Plato made me aware of the talent of Solon; the death of Cato made me know the *Phaedo* of Plato, while the interdict of Ptolemy made me know Hegesia of Cyrenaicus; and I believed Seneca even before I ever saw the letters of Cicero. Augustine prompted me to start looking for Seneca's book, *Against Superstitions.* Servius revealed the *Argonautica* of Apollonius; Lactantius as well as others made me long for the books on the *Republic;* Tranquillus the Roman history of Pliny; Agellius the eloquence of Favorinus, and likewise the budding brevity of Annaeus Florus prompted me to seek the remains of Titus Livy. To pass over the most famous and widespread works which do not need witnesses, the fact remains that when a more famous witness testifies, such works sink more deeply into the mind. For example, it is in the *Declamations* of Seneca that the eloquence of Cicero is praised and that an unusual announcement of his genius is made; while Virgil's prolific eloquence was shown by Eusebius in the *Saturnalia.* It was the respectful and humble testimonial by the poet Statius Pampinius to the *Aeneid* of Virgil, whose footsteps deserved so much to be followed and worshipped, that informed his *Thebaid* as it was about to be published; while the judgment, universally unquestioned, proclaiming Homer the prince of poets, was given by Horace Flaccus. I am citing more writers than is necessary, for it would indeed be much too long to recall everything I learned in my youth in reading Priscian, the grammarian, as, for example, how many foreign names of books he compiled, and how many later ones by Pliny the Younger, or how many contemporary ones I found in Nonius Marcellus, and how often they truly excited me. Therefore, to return where I left off, no one will be astonished that minds were inflamed and deeply shaken by those books, each of which openly displays its sparks and its stings and also bears hidden within it other qualities which reinforce themselves in turn. Therefore—while it shames me, I must openly confess it and yield to a truth—the passion of the Athenian tyrant (Pisistratus) and of the king of Egypt (Ptolemy) always seemed to me more excusable, not to say noble, than that of our leaders, because the zeal of

Pisistratus and that of Ptolemy Philadelphus seemed more noble than Crassus' lust for gold although he had more imitators. But in order not to have Alexandria or Athens downgrade Rome, and Greece or Egypt downgrade Italy, outstanding thinkers are part of our heritage as well, and they are so numerous that it is too difficult even to name them. And they were so dedicated to these things that there may be found among them those who held the name of philosopher more dear than that of empire, and I might add that they were eager not so much for the books themselves as for the contents. There are those who accumulate books like other things with no intention of using them, but with the sole pleasure of possession, and not so much to aid their thought as to ornament their rooms. To mention but a few examples, the Roman library was the care of the divine Emperors Julius Caesar and Caesar Augustus. In choosing an overseer for such an enterprise the former appointed a man who was not inferior to, and perhaps (without intending any slight) superior to Demetrius Phalerius who had been famous in Greece for this activity, that is to say, Marcus Varro; while the latter emperor appointed Pompeius Macer, a most learned man. Asinius Pollio, the very famous orator, also displayed the greatest enthusiasm for the Greek-Latin public library and is said to have been the first of Rome to make it public. Of private concern, on the other hand, was Cato's insatiable desire for books, to which Cicero testifies, and Cicero's own passion for acquiring books about which ample testimony may be found in his letters to Atticus of whom he makes the same request with great urgings and prayers as I do now to you. If it is permitted to a very great talent to beg for the services of books, what do you think should be permitted to a poor one? I have not achieved what I had considered most important in this portion of the letter and what seems scarcely credible without citing the zeal of a very learned man and the friendship of princes which calls one back to reality. Amonicus Serenus is remembered as having a library containing 62,000 books all of which he left to Gordian the Younger who was then emperor and a disciple of his, a matter that made him no less famous than the empire. I say all these things as an excuse for my vice and as a comfort to such renowned colleagues. As for you, if you care for me, make this request of some trustworthy and lettered men: let them search throughout Tuscany, let them roll out the closets and chests of their church people and other men of letters in case something might emerge that might be suitable to soothe or irritate my thirst. On the other hand, although you know in what lakes I am accustomed to fish or in what thickets I am accustomed to go bird hunting, to avoid having you be deceived I insert as a separate enclosure those things which I especially desire. And so that you might be more vigilant, know that I sent the same requests to other friends in Great Britain, France and Spain. Make an effort not to let anyone surpass you in faith and industry. Farewell.

Fam. III, 19.

To his Lelius,[1] concerning the stubbornness of human expectation.

Hope in men is so obstinate and determined even against proven misfortunes that none is deterred from his undertaking: not the farmer facing bad crops, not the sailor facing the storm, not the architect facing the destruction of buildings, not the father facing the tragic destruction of his children. Because all these have the same things in common we see the famished sowing, the shipwrecked sailors sailing, those barely saved from ruins undertaking to rebuild upon the same foundations, and childless adults undertaking further procreation among the very graves of their children. I have before my eyes here some fishermen exhausted from cold and hunger. It is extraordinary and utterly unbelievable that though hungry and naked all day, they yet spend their nights awake until dawn with the same lack of success whether they use hooks or nets. They accomplish nothing, they suffer uselessly and in vain, and they lose time which could perhaps more usefully be spent differently. Nor, obstinate from the beginning, are they minded to turn away from the dangerous eddies. Thus a long-lasting habit of undertaking bitter activities becomes pleasant. Sweeping the unproductive sands in the deepest stream beds, they discover the poverty which they flee amidst the waves and the reefs, never finding perhaps what they so obstinately seek. Indeed I'm not sure whether still other examples which may be simpler to relate are not more worthy of admiration. I speak of the striving of beasts, which, though they leave their lairs very often, are never still. The tiger never ceases to produce new offspring and, if they are lost, to feed older offspring; doves deprived of the comfort of their young lose none of their drive in their remaining activities; Philomena, after the theft by the shepherd, follows her lost young

---

1. Lello di Pietro Stefano dei Tosetti was a very strong Roman supporter of the Colonnas. Petrarch first met him during his journey to Rome with Giacomo Colonna in 1330, and he became, with Socrates, one of Petrarch's most intimate friends. Petrarch classicized his name in memory of Scipio's closest friend, Laelius.

with a long sigh and very sweet plaints, and suspends the nest from the very same branch, tempting fortune with subsequent births. I shall now tell you something which is unknown to you but widely known by all the inhabitants of this valley. For some time an eagle has been living in these mountains. A foreign swineherd, not less shaggy than the swine he feeds but even rougher than the wild boars, secretly lay in wait at the eagle's nest considering his soul worth no more than it perhaps really was. Having let himself down with a rope (I remember all this with horror) from the very high cliff which from the clouds overhangs the source of the Sorgue, he approached the lofty home like a rash hunter and removed from the concerned mother her featherless young which were her hope. He tried it once, twice, and other times, and finally forced the eagle to move, for having seen her nest emptied so often, she after a while carried away her nest and all its holdings to another portion of the cliff. There she revived again the hope of replacing her lost offspring, but I'm afraid with no better luck than before. For that persistent enemy of hers, desirous of petty gain, extravagant of his life, is already preparing more rope and knots with which hanging in the void he may capture the usual spoils from the unusual perch.

In our discourse we have now slowly descended to the smallest of subject matters. Neither does the wrong done to the bees when their honey has been stolen remove the sweetness of making honey, nor does the flooding of the underground stores of the ants lessen their industry and their pleasure in constant going to and fro, nor do they despair of being able more happily to undertake what had already been undertaken unhappily. Otherwise, if the heart's hope perishes with the succession of events, human motivation which we perceive on all sides will become inert as fortune interferes regularly in all human actions. A life which is already withering can lead only to an inglorious end. And perhaps so that this would not happen to any living being, and especially to man, tough and determined hearts were given to humans. To climb back again in one easy step from lowest matters to the loftiest, the elders rebuilt the city of Rome which had been burned by the Gallic Senones, a matter in which the authority of Camillus with the help of omens prevailed against the resisting tribunes. Similarly those elders of ours returned to the battle lines after the defeat of Allia, and after the defeat of the Ticino, and after Trebbia, and after Lake Trasimeno. And following the disgrace of the Caudine peace they won a most glorious victory. And after Cannae, a most serious and almost fatal wound to the republic, in order to avoid having Italy abandoned by its cowardly citizens, the flashing sword of Africanus won the day despite the advice of Cecilius Metellus. And if the unbending hope of one man, and indeed of a very young man, had not supported the wavering minds of many old men, the empire would have been finished, and there would have remained no memory of the Roman name and no trace of Roman power. For Hannibal, to use the words of the historian, Florus, would have made an Africa of Italy, and indeed not Latin but African colonists would possess Italy. And if anyone of Italian blood would have survived after so many disasters he would have been nothing more than a small stream of water mixed with the open sea among the foreign customs and victorious foreigners. Therefore what we are not and what we are, I confess openly, we owe so far to the positive hope of a single man. So much for now about our own. What should I recall about the Spartans or about the Carthaginians who never ceased hoping as long as they existed? What about the Saguntini who, while hoping until the very end for help from us, accepted incredible afflictions from a very cruel enemy? It would be tedious to discuss all such examples. Therefore, so that my discussion may cease where it started, hope is the last anchor of a threatened ship. If this anchor tears away from those who are struggling in the stormy sea, there is no way left in life, no port for rest, no return to safety. You may now wonder what such a long disquisition wished to show. Only one thing: that you count your friend among that number whose hopes are few and perhaps vain, but always strong. For me these things needed to be explained more carefully so that you might be aware of the affection of the writer. Other things you understand without mention. Farewell.

Fam. III, 20.

To the same correspondent, a complaint about his silence and what a relief it might be to be freed from useless expectation.

I have often labored with my letters to entice you to write, but I have thus far failed. I shall continue to interrupt your silence hoping that you will be ashamed to listen to so many noises of your friend in silence. I shall force open your lips either in indignation or perhaps in a smile or in a flow of words. I will not care too much about what you will reply; by your simply beginning to speak I shall be the victor. If old concerns hold you, I shall add new ones; if you have lost the pen of laziness, I shall give you back the pen of assiduity. But if perchance you are puffed up with pride and, to confess something which I cannot possibly suspect, you consider it unworthy of you to correspond with your friends, I feel that I must drag you from that extremity of mind and bring you back into the even fold of friendship. Therefore be assured of this: I shall not stop directing complaints and laments to you until you return to your former level of interchange of correspondence with me—at least as long as we continue to be so close that neither can claim a lack of messengers and the exchange of letters amounts almost to handing them to each other—or until such time as you make clear the cause of such a great change. The footsteps of one messenger will be followed by those of another; heaps of my letters shall appear before your eyes; you know the writing and the seal of your friend, and your love and respect will not permit you to throw them away untouched. You will open them despite yourself, and they will flatter you to read them thoroughly. Thus, you who are avoiding the labor of writing a brief letter will not avoid the trouble of a lengthy reading. Therefore, believe me, free your eyes with the aid of your fingers and teach the more ignoble parts of your body to serve the more noble ones. Take your pen; what I ask you is not unusual. The pen has been your sword since your childhood. Your adulthood and the condition of your homeland later forced you to bear other arms. Finally you returned to the more peaceful halls of the Roman pontiff and to your former studies, as your destiny wished. What am I therefore asking? Do what you do daily, write something, and do what you likewise never do, write to me. Soon, of course, I shall take a stand and either myself write more seldom or more briefly. I shall be happy with having triumphed and with having cast you down from that stronghold of your silence. At this point, however—and I know with whom I speak—you find cover under that old and common shield: "Oh brother, what do you expect? I have nothing to write." But I, although I could never believe that in such an abundance of possibilities and for such a talent and eloquence there could ever be lacking any subject matter to write about, I am much more prone to believe that some other cause, whether true or fictitious, has imposed such silence upon you rather than a cloak of forgetfulness. Therefore, I ask of you at least this which many have asked of their friends, but among those whom I have read Cicero comes to mind first: write that you have nothing to write; write this very fact but somehow in other words, otherwise I shall have indicated to you a path which was much too short and open to escape, which was not my intention. You will escape, if I know you, with a single leap and redeem yourself with a single word of which I was author. And I, as it happens to many, shall have fooled myself with my own advice.

But now enough of excessive complaining lest in trying to achieve revenge I punish your silence with loquacity. And to be certain to include in this letter something about my domestic problems, I ask you to intercede with our common lord for a successful conclusion of my affairs and I would consider any of them successful provided that at least one is brought to conclusion. It is a great thing, dear brother, to be freed from a vain expectation. Men do not know what an advantage it is to abandon superfluous and infinite desires. Once lost they satisfy and once possessed they torture the minds of wretched men busy with more vain things than with firm ones. And such is this madness, that they fear to be freed from their errors to make place for the truth while they promise themselves a successful conclusion to huge undertakings. Indeed, being self-indulgent, haughty, and bad judges of their affairs, they imagine themselves worthy of having all things happen at their command. Thus as Ovid said concerning affairs of love, "While each of us is pleased with himself, we are nothing but a credulous mob." Already we have lived half of our lives amidst widespread madness. As Cicero has elegantly stated: "Everyone wishes for himself the good fortune of Metellus." How many, however, are deceived by this empty hope, indeed how very few are not so deceived! Hence we must point out that if we accept the testimony of ancient writers Metellus who was forever happy had only one friend, and that friend is said not to have been at home but far off and outside the boundaries of Italy. The reference does not describe the extent to which these two actually usurped the vain name of happiness. Perhaps there will be another time to speak about this. For now, so that I might complete what I began, if no one achieves what everyone hopes, consider how many there are who deceived by the dreams of life and waiting for their fulfillment were overtaken by death, and how many will ultimately be overtaken. Terrified by this I became determined to pursue the following rule for myself: that I would not seek things that were loftier than I, that I would indeed modestly seek a few things equal to my powers, and that I would enjoy them and should I lose them that I would bear it bravely and would not be torn by sorrow. I fashioned myself according to this rule, that in order not ever to dread any coming event I had to eliminate the brother of anticipation. Wherefore I beg you, dear brother, in the name of the Heavenly Host to free me as soon as possible from this perplexity. Free me from my strong anticipation. Whatever will happen I shall bear patiently. I shall come to a close by citing that writer whose following words I particularly like: "It is a part of kindness to deny quickly what is being sought." Farewell.

Fam. III, 21.

To the same correspondent.

There clearly came to pass between us what is written about your Pompey and his Cornelia: "As they departed, neither found the strength to say farewell." But there was no need for too many words to be exchanged between us since they are mere conveyers of the spirit and feelings that they symbolize, and as such they are known to us, since our hearts are mutually accessible in silence. There is one thing which I would like you to do if the possibility presents itself. A certain young man knew a young maiden with whom he was madly in love and who did not discourage him when he proposed marriage to her. And all this (and please note this in particular) happened either *in thoro* or *in Thor*. The lord of the place—should I call him noble or uncouth?—called for the death of the young man whom he had persecuted with a grievous and ancient hatred. The young lady publicly forgave the young man saying that nothing had happened between them contrary to her wishes, and asked that her promise of marriage be carried out. He agreed if this were possible, but being presently confined in a prison he knows that he will be tried before a prejudiced judge. However, were the fetters to be removed and both parties exonerated, being of the same age and attitudes and wealth, they would be able to celebrate the highly desired marriage. When all these things were reported to me first through the outcry of indignant people and then through the entreaties and complaints of friends, you came to my mind first of all as someone who should be sought out to render assistance in such a distressful situation. We too, dear brother, were victims of love at some time, and it behooves us to render assistance to others in love. Although such things do not affect our master or his lofty spirit, I do not believe that he is so hard or inhuman that he would not commiserate with such human weaknesses. Nor should we suppose that rural types undergo passions with less suffering. That bow-bearing Cupid has equal power over all kinds of men. I know that Virgil writes that "a sudden madness overcomes the incautious lover," and adds "indeed pardonable," but then finally adds something frightening, "if the Manes knew how to pardon." For I fear lest that more cruel Bellerophon possessing no human traits and furthermore inflamed by anger might not be more thirsty for blood than is proper. However it turns out, let us fulfill our duty, I by appealing to you, you by appealing to our master that he seek through his letters from the previously mentioned lord of Thor the liberation of his prisoner as a voluntary gift. My steward whom I have sent to you for this one purpose will inform you of the man's name and of all the particulars. You will find him no more urbane than the lover for whose madness we are asking indulgence.

At the source of the Sorgue, 26 April.

Fam. III, 22.

To the same correspondent, on the notable effects of elo-
quence and of music and the fact that the most savage beasts
are soothed by flattery and sweetness.

What do you wish me to say to you? It is as I have heard
and read. No nature is so rough that it is not soothed by the
sweetness of customs and words. So did that elder Africanus
of mine pacify with speech Syphax, the king of the barbarians
unaccustomed, as Livy says, to Roman ways; and even more
surprisingly pacified Hasdrubal, the Carthaginian leader, a
barbarous and savage enemy to Rome, during the progress of
a banquet and a pleasant and friendly meeting. Thus did Julius
Caesar begin speaking so mildly and caught in the nets of his
Caesarian eloquence Amycla still covered with seaweed and
foam, a mere naked and helpless fisherman. As a result, attracted by the unusual sound of Caesar's words and because of
his admiration for his unknown host, Amycla, at Caesar's
command, untied his fragile and unseaworthy boat from its
safe mooring, and wanting to appear eager to obey, hastened
to certain destruction. But the Africani and the Caesars aside,
that prince of philosophers, Plato, was able to win over
Dionysius, the tryant of Syracuse; as the poet, Euripides, did
Archelaus, the king of Macedonia; the unbending, tyrannical
spirit of the first and the barbaric excess of the latter could not
resist, and the hardness of both was softened by talent and eloquence. The orator, Antonius, offers another example of this
kind, one which surpasses all wonders, for he held in check
with a flattering speech the cruel executioners sent to kill him
when they had already drawn their swords. His eloquence
conquered their cruelty except that one of them, not having
heard him speak and arriving after the others had left, like an
asp not hearing the voice of the enchanter, struck him with
the venom of his wicked deed. But why do we search for examples from among men? We see bears, leopards, lions and
other fierce, powerful beasts, softened by flattery, patiently
obeying the command of a weak master and accepting chains,
prison, threats and blows. And we see birds who roved the
skies, against the primeval law of their nature, preferring

human companionship to their own liberty, and we see them spending their life in fetters with a covering over their heads, with no further hope of seeing their native land, controlling their hunger, following the will of their feeder, taking food from his hand, recognizing the voice of their captors, obeying their calls, going and returning according to the order of their owner, and bringing back excellent catches not for themselves but for their master. Concerning fish I do not remember reading anything similar except that dolphins have an affinity for humans by some strange kind of attraction. And there is a historical or rather a fabulous story about a certain Arion who seated on the back of this fish rides about the crashing waves of the sea. And it is said that this unusual passenger sings to the lyre, the instrument making the voyage easier, the music charming the ears and lifting the unusual vessel over the surface of the water. Such a story, it appears, could not be accepted except as fable, for instead of rudder, mast, sail, and oars there was only the sweetness of music.

But you will ask to what purpose all these strange allusions. So that you may understand that I consider your talent among the greatest since, having freed your bait from the rocks, you have succeeded in capturing with your words and presence the friendship not of men, beasts, or birds, but of this aquatic animal which was brought up among fountains and rivers. He did indeed return to me unmindful of himself and mindful only of you. When I asked him questions about his master and his friends, his answers concerned Lelius alone; how he had admired his handsomeness, his conduct, his speech, his dwelling, his clothing, and as if he were one unknown to me he praised him in his rude and atrocious speech. When he wove very long stories about him to me which I often interrupted with Terence's question, "Alas, do you praise him to me?," he would start all over again from the beginning. What more can I say? I understand that you have taken away from me with your skill my farm hand. I confess that I did not grieve nor was I envious; I was astounded that you in one hour were able to do more than I in all of ten years. It is truly astonishing unless you blend in your conversations some form of magic art. Now, therefore, captured by love for you he is returning to you once more with this letter. At the same time he is counting on you for some kind of assistance through the intervention of our master in order to set free his friend about whom I wrote you the day before yesterday and who now is threatened with a desperate situation. However, the mind of the judge which I have feared from the very beginning, obstinate in wanting the young man to be punished, may not be open to entreaty. Rumor has it that he is going mad with grief and envy, according to what they say, over the plucking of the maiden's flower to which he himself greedily aspired; furthermore, that he is most indignant because in this love affair the flattery of a nobody accomplished more than his own useless riches. But though words may, perchance, be wasted on deaf ears, the merit of compassion nevertheless will remain unblemished with our lord, and the fruit of goodness with you. The young man, with my help, will also pay off the debt of his gratitude. As for that unfortunate lover, if it cannot be otherwise, he will repay the sweetness of his love as many have done with the bitterness of death. Meanwhile you will reckon this messenger among your humble friends, for he considers you among his foremost masters. Indeed he seems to me to be more desirous of your favor than of the life of his former friend. Therefore in order to impress you deeply and to indicate with a symbolic little gift that his soul is most delightfully devoted to you, he brings you a small bottle of the softest of all liquids, oil, which flowed from the fruit of our trees covering these hillsides perfectly naturally and, as they say, virginally because not subject to force. Here I would say that the inventor of the olive, Minerva, dwells after having deserted Athens, except that sometime ago in my *Africa* I had already placed her on the shore of Genoa in Porto Venere and in Lerici. Farewell.

At the source of the Sorgue, 29 April.

Fam. IV, 1.

To Dionigi da Borgo San Sepolcro [1] *of the Augustinian Order and Professor of Sacred Scripture, concerning some personal problems.*

Today, led solely by a desire to view the great height of it, I climbed the highest mountain of this region which is appropriately called Windy Mountain. The idea for this trip had been in my mind for many years. As you know, my destiny has been to live here since childhood. This mountain visible from any direction has always been in my sight. The drive to do what I did today finally overcame me, especially after having re-read some days ago in Livy's history of Rome how Philip, King of Macedonia—the one who waged the war against the Roman people—ascended Mount Hemo in Thessaly from the summit of which he believed two seas were visible, the Adriatic and the Black. Whether his belief is true or false I have been unable to ascertain, both because the mountain is far removed from our land and because the disagreement among the authorities makes it a doubtful matter. To mention but a few, Pomponius Mela, the cosmographer, asserts without hesitation that it is true; Titus Livy considers it false; as for me, if I could climb that mountain as readily as I can this, I would quickly clear up the uncertainty. But putting this matter aside, I shall return to my mountain, and tell you that it appeared excusable for an ordinary young man to do something considered appropriate for an old king. Yet in thinking about a companion to accompany me, I found no one, alas, who seemed to qualify for the undertaking, so rare even among dearest friends is that perfect harmony of inclination and of custom. One seemed too slow, another too careful; one too deliberate, another too rash; one too gloomy, another too joyful; finally one too foolish and one, whom I wished to have come along, appeared too prudent. The silence of this one, the impudence

1. A professor at the University of Paris whom Petrarch met in Avignon probably in 1333. His extraordinary learning and abilities prompted King Robert to appoint him professor of theology at the University of Naples in 1338–39.

of that one, the size and weight of another one, and the thinness and feebleness of still another terrified me. The cool incuriosity of this one and the burning concern of another dissuaded me. Although they are serious, such faults may be endured at home—for charity supports all things and friendship rejects no burden. But on a journey the same faults become very serious. Therefore my delicate mind, seeking honorable delight, carefully considered each quality individually without detriment to any friendship, and it quietly foresaw and rejected whatever seemed to be troublesome for the proposed trip. What do you think? I finally turned to a strictly domestic assistance, and I disclosed my plan to my only brother who was younger than I and whom you know well. He was delighted at the news and rejoiced that he was considered both a brother and a friend by me.

On the determined day we left home and came to Malaucène in the evening, a place at the foot of the mountain, looking north. We lingered there for a day and finally the next day with our individual servants we climbed the mountain after considerable difficulty. It is a steep mountain with rocky and almost inaccessible cliffs. It was well said by the poet, however: "Persistent toil overcomes all things." The day was long, the air was mild, and the determination of our minds, the firmness and readiness of our bodies and other circumstances were favorable to the climbers. The only obstacle was the nature of the place. We came across an elderly shepherd on a slope of the mountain who made every effort with many words to keep us from continuing our climb, saying that fifty years earlier, driven by a like youthful motivation, he had climbed to the very top and had brought back from there nothing but repentance, weariness, and his body and clothing torn by stones and bushes, and that no one had been known before or since to dare undertake a similar climb. As he shouted all these things, we, like all young people who refuse to heed warnings, felt our desire increase as a result of the prohibition. When the old man observed that he was arguing in vain, he accompanied us a short way among the cliffs and pointed out the steep path, giving and repeating many warnings as we turned our backs to him. Leaving behind with him our extra garments and whatever else might have been a hindrance, we made ready to start the climb alone, and began to do so cheerfully, but, as usually happens, weariness swiftly followed our extraordinary effort. Not long after our start, therefore, we stopped on a cliff. From there we once again began our climb but more slowly; and I, in particular, pursued a more modestly inclined mountainous path. My brother proceeded to the heights by shortcuts over the ridges of the mountain, but I, being weaker, turned toward the lower reaches. To my brother, who would call me back and indicate the most direct path, I would answer that I hoped to find an easier passage on the other side of the mountain and that I would not be afraid of a longer road if I could advance more easily. Having offered this excuse for my laziness, I was still wandering through the valleys without finding a more gentle access anywhere by the time the others had reached the summit. The road got longer and my burden grew heavy. Meanwhile, exhausted with weariness and troubled by the confused straying I was determined to seek the heights. Finally after I had reached, tired and distressed, my industrious brother who had refreshed himself with a long rest, we climbed along for some time side by side. We had scarcely left that hill, however, when I, forgetful of my former wandering, pursued the easy length of the paths and headed down hill to end once again in the valleys. Thus as before, I encountered serious trouble. I had tried to put off the annoyance of having to climb, but the nature of things does not depend on human wishes, and it is impossible for a body to arrive at a summit by descending. What more need I say? This happened to me three or more times within a few hours, not without my annoyance or my brother's laughter. Having been thus frequently deluded, I sat in one of the valleys and there proceeding from the physical to the metaphysical in mental flights I reproached myself with these or similar words: "What you have experienced so often today in trying to climb this mountain you should know happens to you and to many others as they approach the blessed life. This is not easily realized by men, however, because although the movements of the body are visible, the movements of the mind are invisible and concealed. The life we call blessed is certainly located on high, and, as it is said, a very narrow road leads to it. Many hills also intervene and one must proceed from virtue to virtue with very deliberate steps. At the summit lies the end of all things and the limit of the path to which our traveling is directed. There everyone aspires, but, as Naso says, 'To wish is not enough; you must long for something so that you may succeed in anything.' You yourself certainly—unless as with many other matters, you are deceived in this too—not only wish but long for it. What detains you? Certainly nothing except the more level and, as it looks at first confrontation, less impeded road of earthly and base pleasures. Nevertheless, after you have wandered widely, you must ascend to the summit of that blessed life burdened by labor ill-deferred or you will sink slowly into the pitfalls of your sins. And if—God forbid—the darkness and shadows of death should find you there, you would lose the eternal light in perpetual torments." Incredibly such meditation brought new strength to my mind and to my body and made me willing to face whatever remained. How I wish that I could complete with my mind that journey for which I sigh day and night as I overcame all the difficulties of today's journey with my physical body! And I wonder why what may be done through an active and immortal mind without any physical action in the blinking of an eye should be far easier than something done over a period of time at the indulgence of a mortal and perishable body and under the cumbersome weight of heavy limbs.

The highest slope of the mountain is one which the inhabitants call "Sonny." Why I do not know, except that I suppose it is said by way of antonymy, as in some other cases, for indeed it seems to be the father of all neighboring mountains. On its summit there is a small plain. There finally we paused in a state of exhaustion. Since you have heard what thoughts ascended into my mind in the ascent, hear, father, the rest, and please grant one hour of yours to the reading of what happened to me in one day. First of all, moved by a certain unaccustomed quality of the air and by the unrestricted spectacle, I stood there as in a trance. I looked back. Clouds were beneath me. And suddenly what I had heard and read about Athos and Olympus became less incredible to me when I looked out from this mountain of lesser fame. I then directed my sight toward Italy where my heart always inclines. The Alps themselves, frozen and snow-covered, through which that wild enemy of the Roman people once crossed and, if we believe the story, broke through the rocks with vinegar, seemed very close to me although separated by a great distance. I confess that I heaved a deep sigh toward the sky of Italy which was visible to my mind rather than to my eyes, and I was overcome by an overwhelming desire to see once again my friend and my homeland. However, the way this happened led me to feel shame for my as yet unmanly desire for both these things, even though I did not lack either an excuse or the aid of scores of great examples for wanting both. My mind thus was overcome by a new thought and was transferred from those places to these times. And I began saying to myself: "Today completes the tenth year since you departed from Bologna after completion of your youthful studies." Oh, immortal God, oh immutable wisdom, how extensive and how many changes within me during this interim! I shall skip an infinitude of them since not yet being in port I cannot recall in security the storms through which I have passed. The time will perhaps come when I shall enumerate all of these storms that beset my life in their appropriate order, prefacing it with those words of your Augustine: "I wish to recall all my past foulness and the carnal corruption of my soul not because I love them but so that I might love you, my God." As for me, there still remains indeed a great deal that is uncertain and troublesome. What I used to love I no longer love. I am wrong, I do love it but too little. There, I am wrong again. I love it but I am too ashamed of it and too sad over it. Now indeed I have said it right. For that is the way it is; I love, but something I would like not to love, and would like to hate. Nevertheless I love, but unwillingly, constrainedly, sorrowfully and mournfully. And in myself I miserably experience the meaning of that very famous verse, "I shall hate if I can; if not I shall love unwillingly." The third year has not yet passed since that perverse and worthless inclination, which held sway over me and ruled over my heart without opponent, began to be replaced by another inclination which was rebellious and reluctant. Between these inclinations a very insistent and uncertain battle for control of my two selves has been going on for a long time in my mind. Thus I pondered the decade just past. Then I began to project my troubles into the future and asked myself the following: "If it chanced that this transitory life would be extended another ten years for you, and you were to approach as far toward virtue as during the past two years—through your new inclination doing battle with your old—you retreated from your former obstinacy, could you not then, although not certainly but at least hopefully, go to meet death in your fortieth year or disregard calmly the remainder of a life which is vanishing into old age? These and similar thoughts were running through my mind, dear father. I was rejoicing in whatever success I had enjoyed, I was weeping for my imperfections and I was bewailing the general mutability of human actions. And I seemed somehow forgetful of the place to which I had come and why, until, after laying aside my cares as more suitable to another place, I looked around and saw what I had come to see. Having been reminded and almost awakened to the fact that the time for departure was at hand because the sun was already setting and the shadow of the mountain was growing, I turned to look behind me toward the West. The boundary between Gaul and Spain, the Pyrenees, cannot be seen from there not because anything intervenes as far as I know, but because the human sight is too weak. However, the mountains of the province of Lyons could be seen very clearly to the right, and to the left the sea at Marseilles and at the distance of several days the one that beats upon Aigues-Mortes. The Rhone itself was beneath my eyes. While I was admiring such things, at times thinking about earthly things and at times, following the example of my body, raising my mind to loftier things, it occurred to me to look into the *Book of Confessions* of St.

Augustine, a gift of your kindness, which I shall always keep on hand in memory of the author and of the donor, a handy little work very small but of infinite sweetness. I opened it and started to read at random, for what can emerge from it except pious and devout things? By chance it was the tenth book of that work to which I opened. My brother stood by attentively to hear me read something from Augustine. May God be my witness, and my very brother, that my eyes happened to light where it was written: "And they go to admire the summits of mountains and the vast billows of the sea and the broadest rivers and the expanses of the ocean and the revolutions of the stars and they overlook themselves." I confess that I was astonished, and hearing my eager brother asking for more I asked him not to annoy me and I closed the book enraged with myself because I was even then admiring earthly things after having been long taught by pagan philosophers that I ought to consider nothing wonderful except the human mind compared to whose greatness nothing is great.

Then indeed having seen enough of the mountain I turned my inner eyes within, and from that moment there was no one who heard me speak until we arrived back at the foot of the mountain. The passage had tormented my silence, nor could I believe that it happened by chance but rather thought that whatever I had read there had been directed to me and to no one else. On recalling how Augustine had supposed the same thing happening to him when in his reading of the book of the Apostle, as he himself relates, he first came across these words: "Not in banquets nor in drunkenness, in beds or in rudeness, in strife or in envy, but put on the Lord Jesus Christ and do not provide nourishment for the flesh in your lusts." Something similar had already happened earlier to Antonius when he heard these words written in the gospel: "If you wish to be perfect, go and sell whatever you own and give to the poor, and come and follow me and you will have your treasures in heaven." And believing that these words of Scripture had been read particularly for him, as his biographer Athanasius says, he gained the Lord's kingdom for himself. Just as Antonius upon hearing these words sought nothing more, and like Augustine, who having read went no further, so did I find in the few words which I have given the main point of the entire reading, and silently considered the extent to which true judgment was lacking to mortals who in overlooking the most noble part of themselves scatter their interests in various directions and become lost in vain speculations. What could be found within they go seeking without. I admired the nobility of the mind except as it had voluntarily deteriorated and wandered from its first beginnings and had converted into disgrace what the Lord had given to it for its honor. How often, do you think, upon returning home that day, when I turned back to look at the summit of the mountain, it seemed to me scarcely a cubit high in comparison with loftiness of human meditation if only it were not plunged into the mire of earthly filthiness. This thought also occurred to me at every step: if I had willingly undergone so much perspiration and toil to take my body a little closer to heaven, what cross, what prison, what torture rack should frighten the mind drawing nearer to God and willing to conquer the extremes of insolence and mortal destiny? And this thought also occurred to me: how many are there who will not divert the mind from this normal path either from fear of hardships or through desire for pleasures? Too happy man!—if there is any such person anywhere, I would think it is about him that the poet gave his verdict: "Happy is he who could know the causes of things and submitted his fears an inexorable fate and the rumblings of greedy Acheron to his scorn!" Oh with how great zeal one must toil, not to achieve a more lofty place on earth, but to trample underfoot our appetites which are exalted by earthly impulses!

Among these movements of my searching heart and without any sense of the stony pathway, I returned late at night to that little rustic inn from which I had set out before daylight, the full moon offering a welcome service to the wayfarers. And meanwhile, therefore, while the duties of preparing the meal occupy the servants, I have gone alone to a hidden portion of the inn in order to write this to you hastily and extemporaneously lest with delay my determination to write might subside with the change of place or of our feelings. See, therefore, beloved father, how I wish that nothing of me be hidden from your eyes, having carefully opened not only my entire life to you but even my simple thoughts. I beg you to pray for them so that having been rambling and unstable for so long, they may sometimes find rest, and having been tossed about hither and yon, they may be directed to the one, the good, the true, the certain and the stable. Farewell.

Malaucène, 26 April.

To the same correspondent, congratulations on his trip to Robert, the greatest king and philosopher, and the salutary effect that the conversation of famous men has on one's peace of mind.

My ears have heard nothing sweeter since they heard you announce that, upon summons, you visited the king. "I await your comment," you say. Since I cannot respond briefly, I shall respond at length. Your mother once wished for you a long life which turned out to be exposed to countless dangers and misfortunes. At other times she wished you wealth, that extraordinary snare for human minds and deadly burden upon freedom. At still other times she wished for you beauty of the body which is very often the cause of deformity of soul. What can I say about your comrades or about your nurse? A single law governs all females: they desire silly things, and they dread things of small account. Your father, it is proper to believe, wished for loftier things. He desired for his son what the Satirist said, "The eloquence and fame of Demosthenes or of Cicero," things which are often full of danger as is attested by the fate of both men. The ears of the Lord are therefore fatigued by the many empty prayers either your own or of others on your behalf. I do not desire any of these things for you. Why? Because it is foolish to seek furiously what can lead to a bad end. I wish for you what I wish for myself, a blessed life, to which many aspire but which few achieve. For the path leading to it is rugged and narrow and difficult, while the byways leading away from it are pleasant and smooth. As with archery, in a number of human activities, to stray from the mark is very easy. Hitting the mark is the goal, and because there is only one path to the mark but countless paths away from it, the object is difficult to attain. Indeed what I call the blessed life, which may perhaps have been viewed differently by very gifted and learned men, may be perhaps deserved and hoped for by human endeavor while enclosed in the prison of the body, but it can never be embraced and possessed. It is thus that one runs in this race-course:

the goal lies where all desires are appeased. This conviction is not held by us alone, for must not Cicero have been alluding to something like this when he said that this life is a passageway to heaven? Yet there are times when mortal life has some similarity to eternal life, so that while it may not be truly blessed (for that is truly blessed to which nothing more can be added), yet at times it may look upon human miseries as far beneath it, and even from the lowest depths it may gleam with the light of celestial happiness. This light certainly cannot be provided by weath nor by the applause of the maddening rabble, nor by power or pleasure, but only through the aid of virtue and peace of mind. While others may disagree with me on how best to achieve such peace, it is my considered opinion that nothing contributes more than familiarity with noble talents, and conversation with outstanding men. You perceive, I think, what I mean. Nevertheless I shall speak more clearly. "Who is more outstanding than Themistocles in Greece?" said Tullius; and I faithfully repeat: "Who in Italy and indeed who throughout Europe is more outstanding than Robert?" When thinking about him I find I admire his character more than his crown and his mind more than his kingdom. Him do I indeed call king who rules and controls not only his subjects but himself, who takes command of the passions which rebel against the mind and would crush him if he yielded. Just as there is no clearer victory than to overcome oneself, so is there no loftier king than the one who can rule himself. In what way could any man be my king who is ruled by ambition? In what way could he be invincible when misfortune overwhelms him? In what manner could he be serene whom sorrow beclouds? How could he be magnanimous whom the fear of the least things frightens? And to forego the shining names of the virtues, who can convince me that that man is free whom the multiple yoke of various desires weighs down? I shall descend and ask how we dare call someone a man who preserves only the outward aspect of a man, but is as ugly and as frightful as a raging beast because of his ferocious character? Therefore it is only by an astonishing if general folly that a man is called king who is not a ruler, not free, and often not even a man. It is a great thing to be a king; it is a very small thing to be called a king. Kings are far more rare than the multitude believe; the title is not an ordinary one. Sceptres would use up less jewels and ivory if only true kings carried them. True kings carry within themselves what makes them vulnerable. They are truly kings when their guards are gone and their trappings are removed. Only the worship of exteriors makes the others terrifying. Robert is truly illustrious and truly king, for his true might is indicated by his many examples of incredible patience and moderation about which it would perhaps be better to speak another time. How widely he rules is made evident in the multi-lingual and multi-customed people and the large range of separate regions he controls. In a certain tragedy of his, your Seneca summarized what a king ought or ought not to do: "Wealth does not make a king, nor purple vestments, nor a royal aspect, nor royal quarters of gold; he is rather king who lays aside fear and the evils of a cruel heart." A little later he adds: "A good mind possesses royal power; it has no need for horses nor for arms nor for the useless weapons which the Parthian hurls from afar when he simulates flight. Neither does it have need to overthrow cities with machines that have been moved into place in order to hurl rocks from a distance. A king is he who fears nothing." These are the words of Seneca. To this king, therefore, to bring an end to what I started to say, you proceeded upon being called. That he should send for you, and that you should obey, could only have resulted from the very great similarity of your desires. Indeed how much comfort for his great cares he has garnered I would reveal if I were speaking to anyone else. As for you, there was no manner in which you might proceed more quickly to that internal peace which you often sought and to which the troubles of Tuscany drove you. I therefore congratulate both your prudence and your good fortune, and I repeat somewhat more confidently those words which I spoke at the time. When first hearsay and then your own letters told me that you had left Florence for Naples I said to myself and to my friends: "Our Dionysius is striving for peace of mind with great steps and he has entered upon the straight path to the blessed life."

As for myself I send you only the following news: I shall be following you shortly for you must know what I think about the laurel crown and how upon balance I have determined that only the very king of whom we speak and no other will bestow it upon me. If I shall be considered sufficiently worthy to be called, all well and good. Otherwise I shall pretend to have understood differently the sense of his letter which he himself sent me with the highest and most friendly courtesy though I am unknown to him; and as if in doubt I shall play primarily the role of seeming to have been summoned. Indeed I have answered his royal style in a very common manner as if stunned by lightning, for our talents were too different, and our lutes, as they say, too unequal. Farewell.

At the source of the Sorgue, 4 January.

Fam. IV, 3.

To the famous king, Robert of Sicily.[1]

A highly unusual brightness has blunted my eyesight. Happy is the pen capable of writing with such magnanimity. What shall I admire first? The exceptional brevity, the majesty of the ideas, or the divine charm of the eloquence? Oh illustrious king, I confess that I never believed so great a matter could be said so briefly, so seriously, so elegantly, and truly I never expect anything again like it from a human mind. So that one might know that you hold the hearts of men in your hands, a power to which the effort of all illustrious orators aspires, you move the mind of the reader with such a variety of emotions that without effort one can follow the train of your thought everywhere with a wonderful ease. At the very beginning of your sober discourse while you deplored most magnificiently the greatest of human miseries and the most bitter burdens of hardships and that most harsh inevitability of death as it gradually creeps from the roots of the tottering trees and branches, I was moved so deeply that frequently sighing as I read, and terrified by our inevitable destiny and even detesting this name of man, I found myself nearly wishing not to have been born or ever to be born. When this happened, and I thought all my peace destroyed, the hand that had inflicted the fatal wound soon began to offer a pleasing remedy. I recognized that the author of the unexpected grief and of the sudden consolation was one and the same, and I was never more certain of the power of eloquence. So powerfully through the choice of a few words and under the pretext of the immortality of the soul and of future rebirth did you uplift my sick and wavering mind that I was soon rejoicing at having been born a mortal. For what greater blessing can one conceive than, once divested of our garment of flesh and thus free from these chains, reaching the day (following the completion of certain cycles of time) when we, having overcome death, put on immortality, thereby restoring in-

1. Ruler of southern Italy from 1309 to his death in 1343, and scion of the French Anjou family.

dissolubly and reforming the rotten garment of our flesh half eaten by worms and altogether rotten? Although none of the classical philosophers ever achieved this hope, the belief in immortality is nevertheless very ancient, not only among our own thinkers but even among those who have never heard the name of Christ. Except for Epicurus and a few others from his notorious flock, there was no one who denied the immortality of the soul. I shall bypass in this matter people such as Pherecydes who was the first proclaimer of this belief among the Syrians and his disciple, Pythagoras, and all of his following, as well as Socrates and all his followers. Plato, a very great man, published a notable book which Cato of Utica used, it is said, as a comfort on his very last night so that he might more boldly approach contempt for this life and love for his decreed death. Later Marcus Cicero in his *Tusculan Disputations* and in the sixth book of his *Republic* with his divine sort of oratory proclaimed the same beliefs; and again in his dialogue, *Lelius*, on true friendship, and in that book which is called *Cato the Elder* dealing with the defense of old age, and in many other places he touched on this belief. Thus it troubles me terribly that so much revealed truth should remain unknown. But to whom am I speaking these things so foolishly? Surely not only to the king of our day but to the king of philosophers. Please forgive me if the heat of discourse has driven me not only to embracing your royal teachings to which I owe so much but to confirming them with appropriate support, because they have affected me so deeply that I now confidently and full of hope await that day of death so dreaded by the human race.

Such a day has been experienced by your granddaughter whom you celebrate and refer to at the end of your letter. It appears to me that she is rather to be envied than to be mourned for her sad fate. For although she was snatched away in the flower of her age and of her beauty, and with the lament of almost the entire world and especially of the two kingdoms where she was born and where she was transported amidst tears and weeping as a rare and select object of distinction, she herself is happy not only because she has crossed over the frightening threshold of death to the pleasures of the eternal life but because you have glorified her for all time in your highly noble praises. For who can really dare to declare dead and indeed not gloriously alive the one whom God in heaven and you on earth wish to have live? I say, oh doubly fortunate lady who, in place of one temporal life which in itself was brief and uncertain and exposed to a thousand misfortunes, has attained, as it were, two eternities of which one is owed to a celestial king and the other to an earthly king, the former to Christ and the latter to Robert! Receiving these two gifts from such generous givers, she should for that reason seem more fortunate because she has been favored by those who are most worthy of favor both in heaven and on earth, for a great deal accrues to such gifts from the character of the donor. It matters a great deal from whom you receive a kindness and to whom you may consequently be subject. I shall of course not touch upon the condition attained in the blessed immortality of heaven, nor upon the most blessed alteration of such a life, for my strength is not sufficient to pursue such ineffable matters. How great, in short, is the glory which you have acquired for her with your highest praises? There is little doubt that as long as the epigram or epitaph, however you prefer to call it, lasts (and I am confident it will be eternally) in which you honor the memory of your departed granddaughter, so long will she survive with you and with the most famous names of all the ages. There are those who might wish that a similar eulogy for an untimely and lingering death could serve as compensation for a limited life, and those who with endless sighs will repeat the words presumably spoken by Alexander the Macedonian about Achilles: "Oh fortunate one to have found such a singer for your virtue!" But I fear that the length of this letter may displease you, and besides, your highly elegant brevity warns me not to ramble any longer. I therefore stop, praying to God and all heavenly creatures, to ordain that your serenity, decorated with the twin laurel crown for military triumphs and for letters, continues to flourish most happily.

At the source of the Sorgue, 26 December.

Fam. IV, 4.

To Giovanni Colonna, Cardinal of the Roman Church, where best to receive the laurel crown.

I find myself at a difficult crossroads, and do not know the best path to take. It is an extraordinary but brief story. On this very day, almost at the third hour, a letter was delivered to me from the Senate, in which I was in a most vigorous and persuasive manner invited to receive the poetic laureate at Rome. On the same day at about the tenth hour a messenger came to me with a letter from an illustrious man, Robert, the chancellor of the University of Paris, a fellow citizen of mine and well acquainted with my activities. He, with the most delightful reasons, urges me to go to Paris. I ask you, who could ever have guessed that anything like this could possibly have happened among these cliffs? Because the affair does indeed seem almost incredible, I have sent you both letters with the seals still attached. The one letter calls me East, the other West; you will see with what powerful arguments I am pressed hither and yon. I know that in almost all human affairs there is hardly anything enduring. If I am not mistaken, in a great portion of our cares and actions we are deceived by vain shadows; nevertheless just as it is the spirit of youth to be more desirous of glory than of virtue why (since you afford me permission to brag confidentially) should I not consider this as glorious for me as did the most powerful African king, Syphax, when he was called into an alliance by two of the greatest cities of the whole world, Rome and Carthage? That was indeed a tribute to his rule and to his wealth. This is being granted to me personally. His devotees found him amidst his gold and his jewels seated on an exalted throne and attended by armed guards. My friends found me in the morning wandering in the forest, in the evening over the meadows or walking on the banks of the Sorgue. I was offered an honor, whereas aid was sought from him. But since pleasure is hostile to reason I confess that though happy about the event, I entertain grave doubts in my mind, being driven on the one side by the charm of novelty, and on the other by reverence for antiquity; on the one side by a friend, on the other by my native land. The fact that in Italy there is the king of Sicily, whom among all mortals I accept as a judge of my talents, turns the scales in one direction. So you can see the flux of my uncertainties. You who did not hesitate to extend your hand in their behalf, help my fluctuating mind with your counsel. Farewell, oh glory of ours.

At the source of the Sorgue, calends of September, at eventide.

Fam. IV, 5.

To the same correspondent, acceptance of proposed advice.

Not only do I accept your advice, I embrace it. It is magnificent and most worthy of your wisdom and humanity. I am not troubled by the fact that you are a friend of my native land, for you are a greater friend of truth. I shall go where you order. If anyone perchance should wonder about the choice I shall refer first to the reasons and then to your name, for quite often authority is accepted in place of reason. There now remains only the determination of what words I should use to excuse myself to my dear Robert of Paris who will, I know, understand my action, so that not only he but that famous university will realize, when the news becomes public, that its case was well-presented. But concerning these things I shall speak to him more at length personally; for I hear that he is himself coming to me for the express purpose of taking me to Paris. If that is the case, I shall conclude the affair at that time. To what you ask at the end of your letter, until I have had sufficient time to mull it over, I cannot respond unless I were to fabricate an answer. It is a story which is foreign to my nature, and what makes it even more so is the fact that in the meantime I have been involved in matters that are totally extraneous. It is as Sallust says: "When understanding is involved, the mind is king." Furthermore, the matter is very old and has been absent from my memory for a great number of years. Therefore, to use the words of Plautus, "A long day makes the mind uncertain." But we shall discuss that at greater length in person.

At the source of the Sorgue, 10 September.

Fam. IV, 6.

To Giacomo Colonna, Bishop of Lombez, on the same matter.

Not for the first time today do I understand the tricks of fortune. She does not so much attack us as scatter and separate us lest we offer each other consolation in happiness or adversity. She knows how many cares once troubled my heart, cares which only you could help to alleviate. Then in my frantic search for advice upon returning from the North I discovered that you, the only comfort of my heart in that pressing affair, had departed. Even though you had departed for Rome, your homeland and the homeland of everyone, always longed for by me above all other places and at that moment desired not only for itself but because of your presence there, my heart was sad and downcast because of the difficulty of joining you. I appear to be in exile wherever I am without you, and at that particular time being especially distressed and burning with love, I envied Rome for you and you for Rome. I was in such a state that with fate opposing my youthful enthusiasm the few years in which we lived apart seemed like many centuries. As you saw, I finally came to you despite the rigors of winter, of the sea, and of war. Love does indeed overcome all difficulties, and as Maro says, "devotion conquered the difficult journey." While my eyes sought their venerable and delightful object, my stomach felt no disturbance from the sea (although naturally very impatient about the uncomfortable condition), the body felt no rigor of winter or of the land, and the mind felt no threats of danger. Thus I proceeded to you completely committed, thinking only of you and not seeing other things. Once I found you, no memory of the lengthy road remained. And now that same fortune turns her sneers against me so that as I head for Rome you have gone to Gascony and the furthermost shores of the West. It appears that we are most separated when I most desire you, oh supreme token of my glory. But the very nature of human desires is such that what is longed for most is achieved with greater difficulty. But so that you may be mentally present, if not in person, know that driven by the desire for the Delphic laurel!—which once was the unique and special object of desire of outstanding rulers and of sacred seers, but now is either scorned or forgotten—I spent a great number of sleepless nights as I often revealed to you. And when I in my insignificance was eagerly implored by two of the greatest cities, Rome and Paris, one the capital of the world and queen of cities, the other the mother of the studies of our time, after careful consideration and thanks primarily to your great brother who above all others served as my advisor and counselor, I determined finally to receive it nowhere else than in Rome on the ashes of ancient poets and in their dwelling. So on this very day I have begun my journey. It will require more time than usual for I must first go to the king, visiting Naples, and only then take the road to Rome. There I shall remain a few days, and if I am right, the affair will take place on the Capitoline on Easter, April 8. You ask why so much trouble, enthusiasm and care. Will the laurel make me the more learned or better? You say I will become perhaps more famous and therefore more exposed to envy; that the mind is the seat of knowledge and of virtue which find their proper seat there and not in leafy branches like little birds. "To what purpose therefore this pomp of foliage?" What will I answer, you ask. What else except those words of that learned Hebrew: "Vanity of vanities, all is but vanity"? Thus are the ways of men. Farewell, and do let your thoughts accompany me with favor.

Avignon, 16 February.

Fam. IV, 7.

To Robert, King of Sicily, on his laurel crown and against those who praise the ancients while always despising things of the present.

How much the study of the liberal and humane arts owe you, oh glory of kings, which you yourself preferred to pursue with considerable industry, if I am not wrong, rather than attempt to become more famous through the crown of a temporal kingdom, has been known to the world for some time. Recently you obliged the abandoned Muses with new kindness by solemnly consecrating to them this talent of mine, however small. To this end you decorated the city of Rome and the decaying palace of the Capitoline with unexpected joy and unusual foliage. "A small matter," someone will say. Nevertheless it is something very conspicuous because of its distinguished novelty and because of the applause and delight of the Roman people. This custom of the laurel crown, which has not only been interrupted for so many centuries, but here actually condemned to oblivion as the variety of cares and problems grew in the republic, has been renewed in our own age through your leadership and my involvement. I know many other outstanding talents throughout Italy and in foreign countries which nothing would have kept from this goal except for its long disuse and the ever suspect novelty of the affair. After my personal experience with it I am confident that the novelty will wear off in a short time and the Roman laurel will be vied for through competition. For who could seriously hesitate when King Robert is one of the patrons? It will be of help to have been first in this competition in which I do not consider it to be inglorious even to be the last. I myself would not have been imbued with such a desire feeling so unworthy of such an honor unless your support had provided me with strength and courage. And would that you could have adorned the joyful day with your most serene presence which in fact, as you yourself were accustomed to say, were it not for your age which did not allow it, your royalty would never have stood in the way. I actually felt through many signs that you enjoy testing for yourself certain customs of Augustus Caesar and particularly the one which caused him to show himself not only gentle but friendly and warm to Flaccus, son of a freedman who had previously been an opponent; and not to despise the plebeian origin of his Virgil in whose talents he delighted. An excellent trait indeed, for what is less becoming to a king than to expect an artificial nobility in those of outstanding virtue or talent who actually possess the kind of true nobility with which you yourself could provide them? I am not ignorant of what certain contemporary men of letters who belong to a haughty and lazy group opposed to this would answer. They would say: "Maro and Flaccus are now buried; to waste fine words on them is in vain: distinguished men have long perished and only the mediocre remain as with wine only the dregs remain at the bottom." I know what they might say and what they might think; nor can I oppose them on every count. It seems to me that those words of Plautus applied not only to his age when a taste for such things had barely begun, but even to ours. He says, "The flower of poets lived at that time, and they have departed hence for a common abode." We indeed can more worthily complain in such a way, for in those days there had not yet arrived those whose departure he laments. However, the intention of these men is most suspect, for they do not say what they do in order to lament the destruction of knowledge, which they wish to remain destroyed and buried, but in order to discourage through despair the contemporaries whom they are unable to imitate. Doubtless the despair which holds them back motivates us, and the bridle and chains which affect them, are goads and spurs to us so that we try to become what they believe no one can become except one of the ancients. Although I confess that such men are rare and few, there are some. And what forbids one to be one of the few? If this very rarity deters everyone, there would be in a short while not a few but none at all. Let us make an effort, and in keeping our hope alive perhaps we can achieve the goal. Maro himself says: "They are able because they know they are able." Likewise, believe me, we too will be able if we truly believe it. What is your opinion? Plautus deplored his age, grieving perhaps the death of Ennius or perhaps of Naevius. The age of Maro and of Flaccus was also not just to such great talents. The one, poet of divine inspiration, while he lived, was harassed by endless contentions among his rivals who slandered him as a plagiarist. The other was accused of insufficient admiration for the ancients. It has always been and always will be true that veneration is accorded the past and envy to the present. About you, however, oh greatest of kings, worthy to be numbered among philosophers and poets, one can say with even greater truth, what Suetonius says about Augustus: "He fostered the talents of his century in every possible way." And you foster the talents of your century and always favor them with your kindness and indulgence. And I speak as one who has experienced also what follows in that author: "You listen kindly and patiently to writers reciting their works, not only poems and histories but orations and dialogues. But you feel offended that anything he composed about you unless it is done seriously and by distinguished writers." In all these things you have imitated that same emperor, and you have turned away from those who are unhappy with everything unless they are attracted by the impossibility of ever achieving it. I have recently been honored by these ways of yours and by your courtesy just as many others have, by mere chance and without deserving it. Not, as I said, would your royal esteem have stopped here if either old age were more distant or Rome closer. This messenger of your majesty, who intervened in your behalf in all the functions, will tell you personally what happened to us either in Rome or after our departure, whether joyful or dangerous. As for the rest, your very last words urging me to return to you as soon as possible shall remain forever in my memory, and as God is my witness, not because I was taken by the splendor of your court as much as by your talent. I expect from you riches different from what are usually expected from kings. Meanwhile I pray that He who is the fountain of life, and the King of kings, and the Lord of lords prolong the years of your life and ultimately transfer you from this mortal throne to an eternal one.

Pisa, 30 April.

Fam. IV, 8.

To Barbato da Sulmona,[1] royal secretary, on the same laurel crown.

On the Ides of April, and in the 1,341st year of this age, on the Roman Capitoline, in the presence of a large multitude and with great joy, there occurred what the King of Naples had decreed for me the day before yesterday; Orso dell' Anguillara, a friend and senator, a man of lofty talents, honored me with the laurel crown as approved by the King's judgment. The King's hand was absent, though not his authority nor his majesty; his presence was felt not only by me but by all who were there. Your eyes and ears were also absent, though your mind is constantly with me. The magnanimous Giovanni was likewise not there who had been sent by the King and was hurrying with astonishing speed when he fell into a Hernician ambush beyond Anagni. I rejoice that he was able to escape, but, though he was expected, he could not arrive in time. You will be informed about the other things that happened beyond all hope and expectation. But so that I might learn from fresh experience how sad things always accompany joyful things, we had scarcely left the walls of the city when I, together with those who had followed me on land and sea, fell into the hands of an armed band of thieves. How we were freed from them and were forced to return to Rome, how upset the people were because of this, how we left on the following day supported by an escort of armed men, and the other events on our trip would make too long a story for me to attempt to relate here. You will know everything from the bearer of the present news. Farewell.

Pisa, 30 April.

1. A member of the distinguished circle of humanists in the court of King Robert, he met Petrarch during his first visit to Naples in 1341. He was appointed royal secretary the following year, and upon the death of King Robert in 1343 he became head of a "school" of Petrarchists in Southern Italy. Petrarch dedicated his *Epistole metrice* to him.

Fam. IV, 9.

To Cardinal Giovanni Colonna, on the liberation of the city of Parma.

Returning from Rome, in possession of my long-desired laurel crown, and like a victor bearing with me the title of Laureate, which I modestly wish to announce to you knowing that it will delight you, I, today (to give you further news which will also delight you), entered Parma in the company and under the auspices of your friends from Correggio. As you know, we have been excluded from the city, but on this very day they too entered the city which had been returned to them after the garrison of tyrants had been expelled. Following the sudden shift in fortune and with the incredible rejoicing of the freed people, peace, liberty and justice have returned to the city. Overcome by their entreaties with which they accompanied their hope for your approval (about which I have no doubt), I determined to spend the summer here. They maintain indeed that they really need my presence which was certainly an indication of flattery rather than necessity. For in truth, of what use could I really be in this state of affairs? I take pleasure not in the noise of cities, but in the silence of forests. I hwas born not for legal cares or military matters, but for solitude and quietness. Indeed they themselves, aware of my desire, promise me real quiet when the din and ardor of exulting joyfulness diminish from sheer exhaustion. For whatever it might have been, I simply had to surrender to their kindly requests. You will see me at the beginning of winter. I say so unless you prefer it to be sooner or fortune later. Farewell.

23 May.

To Pellegrino da Messina,[1] on the sad case of the untimely death of a friend.

I feel impelled to defer my painful grief which cannot be contained within the boundaries of a letter. The blow is not one to which my mind is accustomed and cannot be lightened by ordinary remedies, it has descended very deeply into my heart. Untamed fortune watched the place and time for the blow and waited for it to have its fullest effect. In what might be called the springtime of life she snatched away my Tommaso whom I can never mention without tears, with the best flower of his rare talent still promising the richest fruit of virtues and great accomplishments. His premature death, I must confess, makes all mortal things worthless to me. I see now how great is the strength of our existence and what I can hope for now, and I am warned by the example of that very close brother of mine. Our ages were the same, as were our minds, and our desire for knowledge, not to speak of an amazing sameness of inclination. We were truly one, we progressed on one path, we sought a single goal. Our work was similar, as were our hopes and our goals. Would that our end had come at the same time! I intend to lament this most bitter blow of the fate with myself, and, if I can, to apply the necessary remedies to my very deep wound and to console myself with my letters and with an appropriate volume. This is what Marcus Cicero first did at the death of his most beloved daughter in that divine and indeed inapproachable style of his. Many centuries later Ambrose did the same thing at the death of his brother. If only my affairs allow, I too should like to attempt the same with a more humble style for the death of my friend. In the meantime please accept the epitaph which you requested, still moistened with tears, and let my brief song appear upon the tomb and my grief upon the body of my friend. Farewell.

"Behold Tommaso, fortunate in talent and in mind, whom the hastening day of destiny snatched away. The land near

1. Brother of Tommaso Caloiro.

Pelorus gave him to the world, and the same land greedily took him away, and a death hostile to wretched me suddenly cut down the flower still young with fresh vigor. Shall I therefore express my gratitude for so great a gift by celebrating through song the Sicilian shore or should I rather lament the shameful theft? I weep. There is nothing sweeter to sad people than weeping."

Fam. IV, 11.

To Giacomo da Messina,[1] on the death of the same friend.

After the death of my dear Tommaso, I confess that I wanted to die but could not; I hoped for it but I was denied. I know what Annaeus Seneca would have answered had he heard this: that it is useless to wish for something that is in our power to attain. But I, though I follow the ideas of such a man in many things, disagree with him in many others and especially in this hasty and rash opinion which would not be difficult to disprove through the authority not only of our own philosophers but also through the testimony of foreign ones. But now is not the time for me to do so. Therefore, to come to the matter at hand, deeply shaken by the very sad announcement that I had lost the best part of me, and detesting a solitary and uneasy life without him, I was conveniently stricken with a fever that caused me most willingly to approach the very threshold of death. But when I desired to cross over the threshold I saw written on the gates: "Not yet, not until your hour has come." I continued worrying, but when I was finally repelled I suddenly returned to this life and now live so that anyone can see that I am living most unwillingly. However I do live hoping only for what others fear, and I cultivate my grief with the idea of the brevity of life. For I know that I have a treaty with death and a business agreement with the flesh. Would that I could spend whatever time remains in my life in such a way that I will be in readiness at all times and, as they say, hold what I owe always in hand in order that the words of the Psalmist will apply to me, "My soul is always in my hands." Farewell.

1. Brother of Tommaso Caloiro.

Fam. IV, 12.

To Cardinal Giovanni Colonna, a consolatory letter on the death of his illustrious brother Giacomo.

Grief impels me and love urges me to write something. Only despair of achieving anything positive dissuades me; for I believe that you do not need such help with the most recent anguish inflicted upon you. Will grief overcome? Will love conquer? Will despair yield? Impelled by an innate devotion I return to my pen which I had hitherto rejected and cast aside, for no other reason than that thereby the sorrow which burns within and oppresses my mind will cease for a while. And would that I could become—though untimely and unfit—the consoler of your grief! I know that Tiberius jeered at the envoys of the Trojans when they came somewhat tardily to console him on the death of his son; after hearing their message, he answered that he too was grieved at the death of their most notable citizen, Hector. But your mind is not on such things, nor are these your ways. Your devotion is very well known, your kindness common knowledge, not only to your own but to everyone. I am aware of how many sighs restrained perhaps by the strength of your mind or assuaged a little by the passage of time I may be renewing with these words of mine. I shall never attempt to lessen your misfortune with mere words. I shall rather confess that no one of all whom I have seen, heard or read about has lost more in the death of a single brother. See how abundantly I surrender to my tears and how I leave wide open a path for my sighs even as I eagerly try to eradicate completely your distress. Meanwhile let the sorrows flow in whatever way they can, recalling, however, that soon they will be able to emerge by hidden exits and, as happens with mournful minds, will continue to search constantly for different outlets to your grief. I see that your loss is enormous and in many ways extraordinary because of the death of so great and so beloved a brother. But I would consider it an infinite and inestimable loss only if death had destroyed him and not merely separated him from us for a short space of time. However, while he was here how little was the part of his life he spent under your eyes? I ask you, reckon the time as do the most devoted lovers, and recall the time from the end of your infancy to the present. Far from his homeland during the most glorious exile of his father he was brought into life. He uttered his first cries in a distant land; then, a boy of respected ability, he spent much of the more tender years of his life apart from you, but even when he was with you, you were both of an age when you were incapable either of sound judgment or of founding an enduringly solid love. Thus he was either far from you or he was in effect absent from you. Then, as he approached the end of his adolescence, because of his great and unequaled love of letters, he wandered far and wide sometimes through Italy, sometimes through France. And so, while busy satisfying his noble thirst by traveling through different lands, he plunged into almost every type of study, and thereby obligated himself until his manhood to live in voluntary exile.

After this, through admiration for his virtue, which earned him dispensation without any trouble, he was early raised to the bishopric. He performed his duties in such a way that all prominent men except himself felt shame that he did not occupy a more lofty position. He was completely free of any ambition or avarice, and happy in his fate he notably occupied the rank of bishop. Not only did he not desire a loftier position but rather indeed detested and hated such elevation and feared the heights of supreme good fortune as if they were a precipice. Witness to all of this is not only the tenor of his entire life and his language which he did not change even in the most intimate moments, a sign of his lofty and tranquil mind, but the letter which he wrote you with his own hand and which testifies fully to his seriousness, modesty, and contempt for earthly things. As I reread it I do so always with many tears of happiness, for that letter is with me since you considered me worthy of being its custodian and capable of replying to it. Now I even seem to behold him as if he were present and seem to hear his living voice; indeed because he so completely covered in the letter with very few words those things that pertain to sobriety of the mind and to the blessed life, there remains little need for the special learning of philosophers. Among other things, amazing as it sounds, while we were trying so hard to have him occupy a loftier position, he affirms with a religious oath that he is far happier with his state than one might believe, that he did not wish under any condition to rise higher, and that he not only hoped but desired to die in the very state he found himself. Yet, however unwilling, he would have risen to the height to which his renown and the merit of his blood entitled him, had envy, which rules courtly minds, not intervened; and after such envy had yielded to his glory and to his virtue, had an ever ready death not outstripped the course of his most vigorous youth at midpoint. But I shall return to my main line of thought. Having been made a bishop, and feeling the very demanding care of the office which had been entrusted to him, he forthwith departed from you and hastened to his own see, not at all alarmed by so great a change of affairs and of place. He who had been nourished amidst Roman wealth and charms, very serenely and calmly crossed to the heights of the Pyrenees. His arrival brought changes not as much to his features as to those of the region, nor did it seem that he himself had crossed over into Gascony, as that all of Gascony seemed to have passed over into Italy. Having journeyed with him, I find the very recollection of that trip makes me happy as I recall his gentleness in his good fortune, his humility over his many natural endowments, the respectability which is so much to be admired in that kind of person, finally his constant thoroughness in his observance of all his rites, and his seriousness which is more to be desired than hoped for, not so much in a young prelate as in an older one. Interrupt me, whenever you find me in error; but in all that time, you did not see your most beloved brother. On returning he perhaps stopped to enjoy for a while the highly desired company of his brother. I truly believe that he hoped to do so, for I am certain that he desired it. But that lady who controls the actions of men, Lady Fortune, prohibited it. Being summoned by the troubles and cries of his home and of his homeland, he felt obliged to go to Rome where I too after a long period of absence followed him, as you know, having been charmingly invited and having finally received your permission. I believe that God brought all this about so that as an admirer and witness of his twin virtue in peace and law I would take an active interest in the deliberations of that most prudent soul. After seven years in his homeland where he observed that steadfastness of patriotism and of mind which makes Rome recognize that he alone preserved what remains of her, and even while confessing that she owes her preservation to his ashes, he came back to you but remained no longer than to direct to you his very last salutation and farewell. He departed at once feeling distress because of the vacancy left in his deserted see and being desirous of a solitude which he felt would compensate for the long time he had spent in the press of a great many people. And so, having decided to live for himself as he had lived for his homeland and for his friends, he once again returned to his bishopric. There, living with great honor and becoming a victor over himself as formerly he had conquered others, he entrusted his life most exemplarily to God and to man. At length having spent one year there, and still a young man, he was transported from the storms of this life to a port of rest and to a happier kingdom.

Review with me each one of these moments, dearest father, and do not be displeased to talk about your brother with one who mourns in him the loss of his own honor. And as nurses are accustomed to do with infants who have fallen let me try after such a grievous misfortune to find whatever comfort there is in words. Examine with me therefore the total time of your brother's life. You will admit that he spent a very small portion of his life with you and that you tasted his sweet brotherly company always in haste and, as they say, barely skimming its surface. And if you did not thus far grieve his absence, cease to do so now. However, what your wounded and torn mind will now answer me in silence I understand and know, for through frequent injuries by death I have become highly experienced. Your mind will say, "Are you not trying to convince me that the condition of death is the same as being absent? When he was absent

I hoped longingly to see him again, I knew where he lived and through constant reports I was comforted over his absence. But now that comfort and all hope has perished." I confess, indeed, that death and absence do not appear to me the same, but I do find a certain greater comfort in death. Both conditions do indeed remove the body; neither one removes the soul. Yet absence constantly holds distressed minds in suspense whereas death removes all needless anxiety from them. For who can withstand the absence especially of brothers or friends and feel secure unless he is completely unaware of human misfortunes and has no regard for the power and fickleness of fortune? Others can see for themselves, but from the time I have been here I have never received a letter from a loved one without trembling and fear. Even when I learn that all is well I am not free of concern. For who assures me that while the letters were reaching me across the Alps and over the sea some misfortune might not have befallen since it usually occurs in the blinking of an eye? Nor does it shame me to boast to you in friendship that I have devoted a great deal of time and study to this so that I would have my mind armed and prepared for sudden onslaughts of misfortune, and so that I might attain, if possible, what Seneca says: "The wise man knows that everything remains to be seen; whatever happens, he says: 'I knew it'." In truth, not feeling myself wise in countless other things, I feel the same way about this particular distress which to this day no matter how hard I try I have been utterly unable to overcome. Death must have freed you from such anxiety, and, unless I am wrong about the greatness of your mind, it truly did so. You know where your brother is and how he is, and you need not be fearful, as usual, of change in his fortune. If justice, if faith, if devotion, if charity clear the path that leads above; if the mind set free from earthly fetters is borne upward in freer flight; if heaven is the ultimate and eternal abode of good and well born spirits, we can be sure that your brother has ascended there. And unless some contamination of our mortality should be impeding him, which I certainly do not believe, he is on his way and now hastens freely and cheerfully to his fatherland. Moreover, wherever he is, he often turns his eyes to you and beseeches you not to impede his most happy departure with your mourning. Nor should the desire to see your brother upset you. You will see him in good time much more honored than before and much more joyful. Why not, since I myself do not despair of seeing him? Otherwise, I must confess, I would be inconsolably distressed. For who would deny me, a Catholic although a sinner, that hope which I find the Gentiles possessed? You understand to what I refer. I speak of Cato and Socrates whose opinions on this matter it is not necessary to recall since I believe they are better known to you than to me. Death, therefore, cannot forever take away from you the sight of your brother's presence, but has simply postponed your seeing him. Even if she had carried him off forever, there would still be no proper occasion for unbridled mourning; you mourn him either because he has been freed from toils and dangers, in which case your tears, I ask you to consider, are rather those of envy than of compassion, or because you have been deprived in the middle of this journey of pilgrimage of an important escort and have been abandoned by a most pleasant and delightful companion. It is a valid, but by no means sufficient, reason that distinguished minds are overwhelmed through such losses by the affliction of their own misfortune. Moreover, it is most fitting that as often as the memory of your loss returns before the eyes of your mind, so often should it also recall divine grace; for he is an ingrate who mindful of losses is foregtful of benefits. Therefore, while that bitter reflection which says, "Alas, what a brother I have lost!," stings the mind, let that other thought soothe it: "Oh what a brother I had, indeed what a brother I have and shall have eternally! Although he did not enjoy a stay here only as brief as was necessary for him, for me, for the fatherland, and for the world, it became of greater advantage to him alone to be separated from evil; thus God took him considering clearly his welfare and not ours." Indeed He might well have considered our welfare also, for who is capable of contemplating the hidden and inscrutable causes or effects of divine providence, when the Apostle himself, if I am not mistaken, said: "Who knows the judgment of the Lord, or who was his advisor?" What man dares to judge whether it is possible to answer anyone who is lamenting the death of another what was once answered in 3 verses on a tablet to a father concerning the death of his son: "Men wander through life with ignorant minds. Etynous enjoys the happy consent of the Fates. Death was good for both you and him."

Human rashness resists all goading and with the horns of its pride vainly opposes attacking fate only to be finally vanquished. What can I now say about the empty vows, the joy or the complaints of men? Concealed truth lies hidden on high; we are surrounded by a dark cloud; we are ruled by chance; blind we are led by the blind, nor do we know what is to be wished or feared by us, perceiving only through the shadow of the flesh. We groan at what is good for us; we rejoice at our wretchedness; we weep and we laugh without reason. Let each one follow his own opinion, to me the greatest of errors appears to be that we do not freely commit ourselves and our goods to God, that we put any trust in our own counsel having so often been deceived by it; that we are taken by so great a love for this mortal body of ours that we are hardly ever able calmly to depart from here or see our beloved ones depart, as if we were born for no other reason than to cling to the thick filth and to the dregs of our flesh, wallowing in the eternal whirling of the world's vicissitudes and the mockery of fortune. This would certainly not happen to those who meditate upon the many dangers of our desires. First of all, life is brief and the time of life is most fleeting. The sea of human affairs is made rough and stormy by adverse blows. Ports are rare and hardly accessible to men. Reefs are countless on all sides among which navigation is difficult and utterly uncertain. Hardly one in a thousand can swim his way to safety. Thus does Fortune rule us, lying in wait for every level of man. Thus does the fragile boat of our mortality strike against each obstacle. And can we among these obstacles wish for ourselves or for our loved ones a little longer life, when indeed, to tell the truth, this means but a longer exposure to peril?

Let whoever wishes to pretend that having once entered upon the journey of this life under favorable stars and with favorable fortune and finally with God on his side, he can have nothing harsh and troublesome happen to him. I declare that it is an impossibility, certainly unheard of through the centuries. Besides, even though danger may not be present, fear does not vanish. Therefore it would perhaps be more fortunate and less ill-advised, if it were up to us, to act like sailors who in a suspicious body of water are accustomed to turn their helms cautiously and lower their sails long before sunset, and thus seek the port of life and die while still in a budding age and in strength of mind and body and before reaching the point where longer life leads to the last difficulties of old age. Oppressed by such difficulties people complain about living and fear dying and thus often accuse the very time for which they had wished. Finally, they do not know what they do and do not wish to, so great is their uncertainty. Meditating on these and like things we have reason to abstain from blaming the decrees of heaven or the hastiness of death; otherwise our anguish and complaints will appear to be entirely selfish. Indeed I do not doubt that your brother, so dearly recollected, neither lived more than was necessary for himself nor was called when the time was least opportune, although for many, among whom I count my wretched self, he departed long before we wished or suspected.

I refuse to believe that you would find any consolation in those very unmanly expressions of feeling appropriate to inferior minds, such as: "Why did death overtake him so far away? Why is he not buried in his fatherland? Why could we not see him die?" Things such as these even that strong man who was nevertheless prone to tears seemed to lament in the works of our poet when he said: "I was unable to see you, oh friend, or to offer you, before my departure, a resting place in your native land." I shall not allude to popular sayings or try to show how truly small this earth is through geometric demonstrations, or that from whatever place one departs, the path to heaven is one; or that all our lands are not only a homeland for the strong but the birthplace of man. Who does not know such things? I shall rather refer to two things, both determined by divine providence. First of all, of course, that two cities although very dissimilar but extraordinarily honored by him while he lived should both courageously share the deceased, with Rome retaining the perpetual and eternal reputation of his citizenship, and the venerable church of Lombez the remains of its lord, a church which unless I am wrong in my prediction will never possess a more renowned inscription in all the centuries to come if of course you permit his remains to be in its possession in perpetuity. I hear in fact that you are considering having the remains transported to Rome, a matter concerning which I do not intend to influence you in so as not to seem unfair either to the city of which I am a citizen or to the church in which I am a clergyman. A second providential touch seems to be that only one of us was present to receive his departing embraces and words, thereby sparing the other such a sad experience. As everyone knows, wounds are less disturbing to the ears than the eyes.

I have prolonged this letter more than is proper, and I hope that, furnished with far stronger weapons against all misfortunes, you will find nothing in him to praise more highly than his faith. So let the matter come to an end; let the weeping cease; let the tears dry and lamentation be silenced. Do not consider your brother dead, for he lives. We instead die daily without being aware of it, and, oh human blindness, we fear death, beginning of the true life. Let him, therefore, be present not in your mourning but in your thoughts and in your conversations as though he were alive. Outlaw in your halls that silence of the pusillanimous which so many observe in homes which are in mourning where they avoid even the name of the deceased as though it were something sorrowful. Indeed, let his name resound gloriously and let it sink its roots in your home and stretch out its branches widely, especially because tombs need not fear the cloud of envy which eagerly settles on men of great reputation. If death made many who were hated and unknown at home and in the forum famous and popular, imagine how much more we can expect for this man whose life was always most delightful and remarkable, and if there is anything loftier than a superlative, whose death was even more remarkable? I urge you also to keep far from your door that other abuse of the rabble which I notice many following, especially Romans, that abuse which I have sometimes reproved, of never mentioning the name of the deceased without prefixing it with some expression of affliction like, "That poor man, that victim of misfortune!" They then drag out the unfinished name whose very first syllables can hardly be understood. Your brother unquestionably lived happily in this world and departed even more happly and now lives elsewhere most happily and should, therefore, be mentioned without hesitation. Lucan reports the words of the dying Pompey: "Let one not become wretched because of death." Well said, otherwise all men who have been born as well as all those who will be born in future centuries are miserable. Finally, I wish to stress one point again and again, and that is that certain distinguished men to whose names I need not refer, were not more praised for anything than because they bore the death of their beloved manfully. To this you ought to apply yourself more diligently since if you look around you, you will see that your actions are regarded as examples, that you are, as it were, among the loftiest mirrors, and the eyes of all are fixed on you. This your industrious dignity and the majesty of your very large family and the temperance of your past life acquired for you.

On the nones of January.

Fam. IV, 13.

To Lelius, not a consolation but a lament over the same death.

We have lived too long, dearest Lelius. We should have died before God snatched away our most kind and considerate father, comfort of his sisters, joy of his brothers, hope of his friends and terror of his enemies; a model of conduct, a temple of virtue, an image of respectability, patron of literature, lover of studies, herald of talent and infallible judge of merit; envious of no one, envied by all men of note; pious, gentle, modest, moderate, courteous, stable, strong, just, liberal, generous, high-minded, foresighted . . . alas, I fail in my praises and cannot find what I may say worthy of so many virtues. I am either beguiled by love or the sudden veil of death has been drawn over the most radiant and visible light of the clergy in this age. When I received the announcement my heart alone knows in how great an eclipse I was plunged in my wretchedness, but my eyes are witnesses thereof. However, except for the tears of the parents and of the brothers, I think none can flow more copiously than yours. This is suggested to me by the gentleness of your mind and your deep devotion which you inherited but in which not satisfied to equal your father, you excelled. Alas, how often and with what joy do I think of that day which I hoped was approaching, when, yielding to the kind letters of the deceased, and crossing from the Apennines into the Pyrenees, I would stand unexpected before his desired presence and would reverently offer him my Roman laurel crown which, though unworthy, I wear, and which long before his simply hearing of it from a distance had afforded him occasion for great delight, expressed in a very elegant gift, a personally composed poem. Furthermore, I also hoped to offer him the new foundations of my *Africa* which would have been the second of two small but devout gifts. The Almighty forestalled my desire and I was not worthy to see such a happy and joyful day. How shall I now resolve my difficulty? How shall I make future plans for myself? What shall I do? Often I say these things to myself with tears: "Where are you preparing to go, oh unhappy one? The one you sought has departed. Where will you go? To his brother's palace which is in mourning and has been widowed of so great a splendor? Or to his tomb where your hopes are buried? Both would be places of anguish. Has not misfortune brought you enough mourning without your indulging in further tears, either by intermingling with a throng of grieving mourners or by kissing the fond hand of a haughty pope?" Such is my condition until you provide a sail for my feelings and give a definite direction to my shaky resolve. Farewell.

Fam. IV, 14.

To Sennuccio di Firenze,[1] *concerning the condition of his domestic help.*

I have in my home three pairs of servants, or, to speak more modestly, of lower class friends, or to tell the truth, of domestic enemies. Of the first pair one is far too simple and the other is far too shrewd. Of the second, one is rendered useless by his childishness and the other by his age. Of the third, one is mad and the other shamefully lazy, and as in Cicero's saying in a letter to Socrates, one is in need of a bridle, the other of a spur. Faced with such opposition I used to attempt to correct the situation, but now I sit as a simple spectator, nor can I stop wondering at the minds of those who regard mobs of servants as something glorious, and are commonly found in the company of those whom they feed, delighting, that is, in the company of their domestic underminers. It is enough for you to know my need, nor do I believe that you expect me to beg you for help. If by chance there should appear anywhere in rather humble straits a spirit whose age and conduct are moderate, you will have found a man in whom such qualities as I seek are to be found—I would not say perfectly but tolerably—and who could be not my servant but my colleague, friend, and master. Yet I fear that I seem to be committing you to a search for a Phoenix which usually is reborn only after 500 years, exists singly in all the world, and isn't known to us in the West. Farewell.

1. A popular though minor poet of Florence, friendly with both Petrarch and Dante. Born around 1276, he was exiled in 1313 for having accompanied Henry VII to the very walls of Florence. He then joined the papal court in Avignon where he met Petrarch.

Fam. IV, 15.

A controversy with a certain famous man against vaunters of knowledge which is not theirs and against excerpters of literary ornaments.

It is difficult for me to say how much my ears, weary of the rabble, were charmed by your letter which I read over and over again. Although the letter appeared to you too wordy, as I learned from its ending, I myself found nothing wrong with it except excessive brevity. Therefore, I was unhappy to read that you threatened hereafter to be more brief. I would prefer that you would be more lengthy. However, you are free to do as you please. You are the father; it is not proper for you to yield to me, but for me to yield to you. But do you believe that it will all depend on you? Do you not know that the fact is often different from the intent? You will perhaps hear things which, though you are desirous of silence, may compel you to speak. Would you like me to follow through since I seem only to be threatening? I start by saying that I hold the same opinion of you which Macrobius held of Aristotle regardless of whether it was based on love or on truth. I believe that there is hardly anything that you do not know. If anything emerged from you opposed to truth, I surmise that either you gave it too little thought or that you were joking, as Macrobius also says about Aristotle. Of course what you say about Jerome, that you prefer him among all of the doctors of the church, is not new to me at all; this opinion is quite old and widely known. Indeed, you dispute in vain when you speak of comparisons where superlatives are involved. You cannot be wrong, for whatever choice you make will be the greatest and the finest. I recall having many discussions with your dear friend from Lombez, Bishop Giacomo. He, following your footsteps, constantly preferring Jerome, and I Augustine among Catholic writers. If indeed I were not afraid of offending either you or the truth, I would say, dear father, what I feel. Just as the stars are many and varied and bright, and this one is called Jupiter, another Arcturus, and another Venus, yet is Augustine the Sun of the church. But, as I said, I hardly attach any importance to this since the choice is a safe one and judgments must be left free. But as for what follows, namely, that you prefer Valerius among the moral philosophers, who would not be astounded if it were said seriously and persistently and not for stimulation and jest? If Valerius is first, where does Plato fall, or Aristotle, or Cicero, or Annaeus Seneca whom certain great judges in such matters place before all? Unless perchance that judgment of yours excluded Plato and Tullius as I was greatly surprised to read in that part of your letter where, for some reason, you asserted that they are poets and are to be included in this group. If you can prove this, you will achieve more than you perhaps think, for with Apollo's support and the approval of the Muses, you will have added two inhabitants to the shady peaks of Parnassus. I ask, what moved you to believe that, or to say it when Tullius appears as the greatest orator in his first books and as a famous philosopher in his last ones? Just as Virgil is everywhere a poet so is Tullius never one, since, as we read in his *Declamations*, "Virgil lost all felicity of talent in his prose; Cicero in his poems." What shall I say about Plato when he has deserved the name of prince of philosophy by consensus of the greatest men, and when Cicero and Augustine and many others always except Plato in all of the works in which they declare their preference for Aristotle over other philosophers? Plato might be thought of as a poet if regard is paid to Tullius' account of Panetius' calling him the Homer of philosophers, but this was intended to mean no more than the prince of philosophers, making him among them what Homer is among poets. What are we to reply to Tullius himself who somewhere in his letters to Atticus calls Plato his god? In a variety of ways all of them attribute to Plato divinity of talent, at times using the name of Homer, and, what is even more distinctive, the name of god.

Therefore, availing yourself of this opportunity, and considering the extraordinary pleasure derived from speaking about unknown things, you should plunge deeply into an examination of the great poets. You should discover of each poet who he was, in what period he was born, his particular poetic style, and the status of his reputation. It would take too long to pursue other individual details in your letter, many of which have never been heard of and others which you could have taught all of us in our desire to learn from your eloquent letter. But, if it is permitted to my profession to interject a thought, I marvel at why you are so unfamiliar with the name of Naevius and of Plautus that you thought I was saying something quite strange because I cited them in my letter to you, and you imply, although with concealed admiration, that, as Horace says, I dared "to form a new person." So thoroughly do you dwell on this matter that the only possible answer appears to be that I be condemned for my boldness in introducing upon the stage new and foreign names. You halted your attack, however, and finally felt it best to blame your own lack of knowledge. This you did most modestly and politely. Yet although your words suggest one meaning, your true meaning, unless I am mistaken, seems to be different, once again most surprisingly since you seem to be so familiar with Terence. For he almost at the very beginning of his proem to the *Andria*, recalls Naevius and Plautus together with Ennius in the same verse. And again in his *Eunuch* he mentions Naevius and Plautus, while in his *Adelphis* he makes mention only of Plautus. Both of them were recalled by Cicero in his *On Old Age*, and by Gellius in his *Attic Nights* where he transcribes the epigrams of both in a very ancient language. But what am I doing? Who, may I ask, ever hears the name of poetry without the names of these men? That is why, dear father, I marvel with good grace at your astonishment. I beseech you not to let this fall into strange hands, for where your fame is most acclaimed, there is where it must be guarded most zealously. With me of course you can speak as if to yourself, and, as the learned do among themselves, change and retract what you may have said. But after your words have reached the public, that possibility is gone and you must undergo the judgments of the many. Thus I am returning your letter to you by a trustworthy messenger, and this one along with it, a copy of which I shall be keeping for no other reason than to refresh my memory by consulting it should you decide to answer. You introduce one further unusual and unknown opinion

(I speak quite freely since I cannot do otherwise having started this way), when you state that Ennius and Statius Papinius were contemporaries. I ask you, dear father, how you ever arrived at such a chronology? Who ever sought such information from you? Anyhow, check this more carefully. You will find that Ennius flourished under Africanus the Elder, and that Statius, after several centuries, flourished under Prince Domitian. Unless I am mistaken, you now have reasons for wanting to answer and will not be able to do so as briefly as you thought.

By your leave let me add one thing in good faith. I recall having written you what I am about to say some time ago while I was spending my youth somewhere in Gascony, and I did so rather bashfully, as behooved my age, because I expressed my displeasure at the vernacular writings which during that period you had occasionally sent to Giocomo Colonna whom I mentioned before and whose love attracted me to those lands as it would have attracted me to Ethiopia. But at that time I spoke childishly as one who had scarcely been weaned. The time has now come for my words to be manly, and therefore, as I said, if you will give me leave . . . what are you saying? I believe you are laughing. Fine, you have given me such leave. Listen, therefore, dear father, and observe and take particular care that no outsider intervenes. I am speaking to you, and I desire that you be judge of your writings which, although I seem to attack, I would defend against any detractors. Nor am I unaware that this letter of censure of a son to a father appears too strong and insolent, but love forgives boldness. Just as I wish my reputation to come to me through real worth rather than through unclear popular approval, so was your reputation of particular concern to me since my young years. This is what is compelling me to speak, lest, if I remained silent, you might hear the same from others, or, what is even worse, might be torn to pieces by anonymous critics. Certain unjust judges of such matters would measure your abilities by such small things as you playfully include through the oversight of the wandering mind. I have noticed that in all of your writings you try your very best to be clear. This explains your searching through unknown works so that in borrowing some things from some writers you insert them among your own thoughts. Your disciples applaud you, astonished by the countless names of authors and call you omniscient, as if you were an expert on all those whose works you quote. Learned men, however, easily discern what belongs to you and what to others, and even what has been interchanged, what has been borrowed, what has been stolen, what has been drawn in considerable substance and what has been borrowed unconsciously. It is childish glory to show off one's memory. As Seneca says, it is shameful for a man to search for little flowers, for it becomes him to enjoy the fruit and not the flowers. You, who are so venerated in this age and so famous in your profession, and indeed (to soothe your feelings rather than to be constantly stinging) being the only prince without comparison in our time interested in scholarly matters to which you are dedicated; you, I say, for some strange and childish reason went indifferently and blindly beyond your limits into foreign areas, and with the day coming to an end, you wasted your time plucking little flowers. You like to test unknown fields where, often failing to find a path, you either wander endlessly or sink.

You like to follow in the footsteps of those who display their knowledge as though it were merchandise in the marketplace, while in the meantime their home is barren. It is certainly legitimate to strive for what may make of you more than you seem to be. But boasting is always painstaking and dangerous. Remember also that while you may wish to appear great, countless other things occur which not only reduce you to your true size but sometimes even reduce you to inferiority. To the unique mind it is sufficient to deserve the glory of one field of knowledge. Those who pride themselves in being honored in a great number of arts are either divine or impudent or insane. Who among either the Greeks or the Romans can be remembered as having presumed so much? New customs bring new rashness. Such men carry before them glorious titles so that, as Pliny says, "they may deserve recognition, but when you look underneath, dear God how little you find there of any substance." You, therefore, so that I may now end, if you believe me at all, be satisfied with your limits, do not imitate those who promise all things, who deliver nothing, and who, handling all things and, as the comedian says, perceiving all things, understand nothing. There is an old and helpful Greek proverb which says, "Let him who knows some art exercise his skill therein."

Farewell, and I beg you to forgive me if you feel offended.

17 August.

Fam. IV, 16.

To the same correspondent, additional thoughts on the same argument and concerning the University of Bologna.

It is just as I thought. Openness begets anger, truth begets hatred, advice begets scorn. So what shall I do? Words cannot turn back. I would have been more flattering if I had thought you enjoyed flattery . . . nay, I would have been even more harsh and would have freely condemned your present reaction which I consider effeminate in a strong man. Since I now realize that openness is hostile to friendship, perhaps silence is my wiser course of action. But fearing that also, since silence may also produce anger, I shall speak so as not to offend again. However, I shall do so as briefly as possible that you may realize that I speak under compulsion. First of all, I make you the judge of all that I said or shall say. You claim in a brief opinion that, "I erred in certain things, in many things, in all things." I certainly rejoice that it was I who erred rather than you since deformity is more apparent where there is more light, and error is more hopeless in an old man. Nevertheless there is something further that I must ask. You are present; therefore I appeal to your tribunal; there is no need of counsel, for you alone sit in judgment. You prefer Jerome to Augustine. This I knew, but what you offer as a reason for your preference I confess I do not understand. What, I ask, does it mean when you say that you prefer him not because he is greater, but because he is more useful to the Church? You say that you have proven this with a very long argument in a certain work of yours which I wish you would have sent with your letter. But apparently you wished either to spare your messenger or your letter. You did, however, add what you considered particularly pertinent to the proof of your demonstration, that is, that your conclusion was verified by Augustine's own authority. But are you not aware that in his conversation a person generally avoids mention of himself? "But really," you say, "Augustine openly confesses that he preferred Jerome to himself." Who cannot see the obvious answer? Here alone, I say, I cannot agree with the judgment of that most holy soul who was admittedly accustomed to speak about and judge others very favorably and himself humbly. I indeed gave to Augustine the palm for fruitful labor within the Church. I did not do so obstinately however like one who feels bound to a particular opinion, or school, or man, so that I could not change my opinion once the truth were disclosed. I had learned this from Marcus Tullius, and from father Augustine himself who does not deny that he himself had learned it from the same Tullius. For as a boy I had carefully learned from Horace not to swear on the word of any one teacher. You yourself do not hide how many such sources there are, and having abandoned this part of your defense, you soon slip into another one saying that after considering everything, there was nothing that had drawn you into this opinion except the undeserved and extraordinary ingratitude of the Italians toward Jerome. This remains the only defense of your opinion; but this is, I repeat, an argument which I cannot at all understand or grasp. What is this ingratitude you speak of? I confess that we are ungrateful not only to saints but to the Lord of all saints. Why is there special reason for complaining particularly about Jerome more than about any of the others? Or what fault is it especially of the Italians rather than of men in general since he himself was not of Italian extraction and dwelled mostly in the Orient? Turn, dear father, to whatever argument you like; your reason, in my opinion, will not suffice to prove your point unless it be perhaps the silent impulse of the mind which substitutes for reason a pious rather than a carefully weighed devoutness. But I shall avoid lingering on things which degrade and in a certain way profane such holy names in the trivial disputes of a sinner, something which I consider very close to sacrilege. Therefore it would be wiser to be silent about these things, for excessive rubbing and striking together of precious things is dangerous.

I pass on to Plato and Cicero whom you try to make poets because they wrote two fictitious stories containing lessons of conduct and, as Macrobius testifies about one of them, because these stories seem to be rounded out with a touch of the three parts of philosophy and are, without concern for the rules of metrics, inserted in the midst of books dealing with politics and the state. To no purpose Macrobius defends both of them against their attackers who maintain that fictitious stories should not be invented by a philosopher; whereas I congratulate these two, and if possible Aristotle, and Seneca, and Varro, for being included in the rolls of poets; for these latter could perhaps more properly be so included rather than Plato or Tullius. For Aristotle wrote about poetry and poets, and Varro wrote books of satires and about poets; he also composed a fairly good poem on Jason and the Golden Fleece. Seneca, however, wrote tragedies which certainly deserve the next to the highest rank if not the highest in literary merit. But why, I ask, did you not make them actors since during their lives they perhaps said or did something silly, especially Tullius who wrote so many laughable things in his *Saturnalia;* while his freedman, Tiro, wrote a book on the jokes played by his master? Why not make them fishermen or boatmen or something similar because they relaxed themselves by casting fish lines or by rowing when off on vacation? Do you wish in the dispute to make an analogy with a military custom so that just as a single duel produced the Torquati and the Corvini, one story would suffice to produce a poet? To be a great writer requires perseverance; a single sample does not suffice. Enough of this. In your last letter you make no mention of Ennius and Statius. And I believe that you recalculated the number of years on your fingers. Finally I shall say nothing about that long and drawn-out portion of your argument where you attempt to argue that my advice is unjust because nothing is lacking to your judgment—except that I am happy for you that you hold this opinion of yourself. Oh happy you who are satisfied with your own personal judgment! Oh how I wish that you could teach me this art so that I would know how to flatter myself with similar judgments! I really do not know whether it might not sometimes be better to enjoy error than to grieve always over the truth.

To your argument that makes me appear almost to have violated a military oath because at the height of my powers I started to abandon the study of law and Bologna, the answer is simple; although I believe that as one who made that city and that university particularly illustrious, you would not like it. Since therefore I have disturbed you enough, I shall not make mention of the defenses I have been accustomed to use to justify myself, for this problem I have often discussed with many people and especially with Oldrado of Lodi, a very well known jurist of our day. There is only one thing that can be said without hurting any feelings. Nothing which is counter to nature can lead to any good. Nature begot me as a lover of solitude and not of the marketplace. In short be certain of this much: that I never did anything prudently (which I tend to believe), but, if I did, this is among the first things which, if not wise, has certainly been fruitful, namely, that I saw Bologna and that I did not remain there. Farewell.

31 August.

That one's life style must be controlled by one's capabilities and that nothing encourages an enthusiasm for lavish entertainment like bad examples.

I do not wonder that you find delight in lavish entertainments. Once this was the bane of only a few homes, but now it seems a custom residing perpetually in all of them, except when poverty obstructs the entrance. The cause of this is not our nature which would thrive long and pleasantly on too little rather than too much: rather it is habit and even more so imitation that are the real culprits. For who possesses so much self restraint that his eyes are not sometimes attracted by the extravagance, the elegance, and the fame of a neighbor? The advice given by the old man of Plautus in his *Aulularia* is useful: "Let elegance be according to means, and glory according to desert." If men would remember this, the road to lavish extravagance and unjust profits would be closed and men would live much more peacefully. Now selfishness begets blindness, and the blows of ill will crush the control of reason. I beg you, however, to try as hard as you can to be a follower of your own inclinations rather than an imitator of the intemperance of others. Avoid destructive examples; we possess minds that are too prone to evil. One teacher of selfish pleasure suffices for a great number of people. Frugality quickly gives way to excess unless our firm reason strengthens the resistance of our thoughts, teaching them to follow the true good and to avoid false good. Why do you admire the bright garments and the glittering stones on the fingers of your neighbor? It is a masked happiness. Expose the man himself and you will not deny that he is most unhappy. Misfortune hides under the gold and he is both envious and wretched, something which I consider an extreme form of evil. I shall conclude differently than did Plautus about his Epidichus: "This," he said, "is that man who found his freedom in wickedness." As a matter of fact, this wickedness found him wealth, power, and the friendship of kings, but it destroyed him and his freedom. Let him keep for himself without envy those many things he possesses which are so great in the eyes of the multitude. Do live happily and contented with your possessions and especially with what he lost, and farewell.

Fam. IV, 18.

A rebuke to a friend.

I am a friend to you and not to your ways. However, since you ask what my opinion is of you and of all your affairs, I shall let Plautus answer for me very briefly and truthfully, answering each point with almost single words. First of all, I do not like your love affair which is an unfortunate burden to the soul. You are becoming involved in an obscene fire. I ask you like the servant of Plautus in the *Asinaria*, "Is this woman whom you embrace but smoke?" If you ask me why I inquire, I answer because your eyes are always misty with tears. So much for you. As for your little woman, you can read for yourself what is said in that comedy known as *Curculio:* "two women are worse than one." As for the servant, I say what the same poet says in the *Epidichus:* "He is too expert in evil doing." I add this on my own: you are too quick to believe, too inclined to comply. If these things are false, my friend, scold me; but if true, correct them, and farewell.

Fam. IV, 19.

To the same correspondent.

You do not deny the accusation made by your friend, and you do so frankly. This modest confession of guilt affords great hope for the improvement of your life. Your being silent concerning your servant is also a sign of caution. Indeed anyone you do not wish to accuse you cannot excuse. But that you should try to excuse the little women I consider either improper politeness or blind judgment. You yourself appear to be what you think you should feel about them, when you call one of them excellent and the other bearable. I consider what Plautus says in his *Aulularia* much closer to the truth: "There is no excellent woman; one is really worse than another." Farewell.

Fam. V, 1.

To Barbato da Sulmona, on the death of King Robert of Sicily.

What I feared has happened. What I dreaded I am suffering. My fear has turned into grief and my prayers into tears. Not long before I foresaw it, our illustrious king has abandoned us; and his age, though well advanced, made his death no less hard to bear. Alas, dearest Barbato, how I fear that those other presentiments of mine may also come true, presentiments which my distressed mind, always a too certain prophet of evils, now suggests to me. I am really alarmed about the youthfulness of the young queen, and of the new king, about the age and intent of the other queen, about the talents and ways of the courtiers. I wish that I could be a lying prophet about these things, but I see two lambs entrusted to the care of a multitude of wolves, and I see a kingdom without a king. How can I call someone a king who is ruled by another and who is exposed to the greed of so many and (I sadly add) to the cruelty of so many? Therefore, if on the day when Plato departed from human affairs the sun was seen to fall from the heavens, what should be seen in the death of that man who was by nature another Plato, and in his wisdom and glory second to no other king, and whose death furthermore has opened the way to so many dangers on all sides? May almighty God assist in these matters and prove that my pious solicitude is greater than necessary. But granting that for others all things come to pass beyond all expectations and that my fear prove useless, who will console me, dear friend? Or who will alleviate my grief? For whom shall I stay awake nights henceforth? To whom shall I dedicate these talents or this zeal however small they may be? Who will raise once more my collapsed hopes, who will rouse my sluggish mind? I have had two motivators of my abilities; this year has taken both from me. Over the first I grieved with Lelius during my recent stay in Italy where I sought in either place a suitable partner in my grief—and over the second I grieve today with you, and I shall continue to grieve as long as I live. And I who sometimes console others, do not now find any argument or words to console myself. From this therefore my despair of consolation, my shame in weeping, and my distrust that the power of style is adequate to dispel either. Yet conquering all, my hope of seeing you soon bids me be quiet. I shall obey, and shortly when I am with you I shall weep freely. Meanwhile I am writing these words to you as I weep at the source of the Sorgue, a port which is known as a haven for the storms of my mind, where yesterday evening I fled alone after receiving the very sad news in the morning on the shore of the Rhone.

29 May.

Fam. V, 2.

To Giovanni Colonna, an expression of gratitude for the great honors rendered him.

I express my gratitude for many other favors and for the extremely valuable favor of your letters which always precede me whenever I come to Rome. I recognize the traps of your love, for I was received more in the manner of an angel than of a man. There is nothing more energetic than a lover. Even borne on the wings of the North Wind I have never found everything not prepared for me. I will be astonished if I do not become accustomed to your feelings toward me, for a habit prolonged lessens the wonder of things, alleviates pain, and diminishes pleasures. Who can enumerate the many honors which throughout my life you showered upon me? It would take too long to repeat examples of how you have treated me almost as an equal although you were my master; extending to me the courtesy of conversing with me; granting me freedom as a man though I lived under the rule of a master; your sharing of secrets; your according me privileges, honors and esteem, all of which are so pleasing to recall. Out of a thousand I shall refer only to one which will amaze you in seeing how deeply it is rooted in my heart and blood. Remember when following some serious trouble which arose among certain servants of yours, recourse was made to arms, and you, angered by a just indignation, and proceeding as though in a court of law, assembled your servants and bade all of them to take the oath of truth, including Agapito, bishop of Luna, your brother. I too raised my right hand, but you, though still harboring your feelings of anger, withdrew your Bible, and with everyone listening, said that you would be satisfied merely with my word. And to show that you did not regret this, nor felt your kindness to have been unwarranted, whenever similar cases arose, though having all the others take the oath, you never allowed me to do so. What can be more distinctive than this judgment of so great a sire? Let as many greedy people as wish to consider gold and precious stones highly valuable, they cannot value an honor such as this. You have renewed in me, most esteemed father, the ancient honor of the philosopher Xenocrates which Cicero mentions in his letters to Atticus. When he was required by the law to take an oath in order to act as witness, he was excused from having to do so by the Athenians who believed in his respected trust. I say that this is what you renewed in your dealings with me, except that what happened to him when he was in an advanced age, you did to me while still a youth, and what happened to him but once, you do for me continuously. Do you think that I could ever forget such things? The account would be terribly long if I were to adduce additional examples, and neither the time nor the place is appropriate. I hear the voice of your great father who has decided to follow me outside the walls of the city although I do not want him to do so. Today I shall be a guest at his Preneste. There I shall find waiting for me that very famous man who is his grandson and your nephew through your brother.

Rome, nones of October.

Fam. V, 3.

To the same correspondent, on his journey and the horrors of the ruling Council of Naples.

That I should break my word was almost necessary for me and certainly useful to you. I promised that I would undertake a sea journey for no other reason than the common belief that it is more expeditious and fast to go by sea than by land. I boarded a ship in Nice which is the first of the Italian cities in the West, and I arrived at the port of Monaco when the stars were high in the sky. There I became silently angry, for on the following day we unwillingly stayed on after having tried several times to depart in vain. The next day we raised anchor in a dangerous storm, and, after being tossed about for the entire day by the large waves, we arrived at the port of Moritz during the stormy night. We did not therefore enter the city. I stayed in an inn on the seashore sleeping on a kind of sailor's couch and had to take my meal as my hunger dictated and my sleep as my weariness demanded. There I became still more indignant as I perceived the tricks played by the sea. Why say more? After considering several plans throughout the night, I decided at dawn that I would prefer the rigors of a trip by land rather than subjection to the waters. Therefore, after having my servants and all my baggage placed back into the ship, accompanied by only one servant I started along the shore. Fortune intervened favorably in my decision. Among the hills of Liguria for some unknown reason some German horses were on sale which appeared lively and powerful. Having hastily purchased some, I continued my proposed journey but once again not without being bothered by sea-like troubles. A serious war is presently in progress between the Pisans and the lord of Milan, caused, as you know, rather by the arrogance of minds than by territorial problems, for the Apennines have separated the borders so that the ancient boundary of the Po no longer applied. But arrogance knows no bounds, and ambition is satisfied with no limits. So although I had started out on a straight path, the fact that near Lavenza both armies had encamped, with the lord pressing forward seriously while on the other hand the Pisans defended their Mutrone with all their might—I was compelled at Lerici to believe myself once again on a sea journey. Passing by Corvo, the huge cliff so called because of its color, and then the white cliffs and the entrance to Macra and then Luni, once famous and powerful but now carrying an empty and insignificant name, I spent the dead of night in Mutrone itself in the care of the Pisans and then managed to make the rest of my journey overland without serious obstacles. I shall not continue with an account of where I ate and slept or what I saw or heard in any particular place. I shall hasten instead to my conclusion. Through Pisa after leaving Florence on my left I came to Siena and then to Perugia. Then I arrived at Todi where I was received by your men of Clairvaux with great joy. Under their guidance I entered Rome by way of Narni on the fourth of October when the night was already well advanced. My precipitous haste thus made me at this time a night traveler. I nevertheless determined to visit your great father before I retired. Good God what human majesty, what a voice, what a presence, what a face, what clothing, what mental power for his age and what strength of body! I seemed to be looking at Julius Caesar or Africanus except that he is older than either of them. Nevertheless he seemed to have the same appearance which he had seven years previously when I left him in Rome, or as when I had seen him for the first time twelve years before in Avignon. It was amazing and almost incredible that this man alone does not grow old while Rome itself does! With fatherly affection he asked a few things about you and your situation, though I had found him half undressed and ready to go to bed. What remained to be said we postponed until the following day. I spent that day with him from morning to night, and there was hardly a single hour that was spent in silence. But I shall tell you about the other things in person. He was gladdened in an extraordinary way by my arrival, hoping, as he said, that your friends would find an end to their imprisonment and distress through my diligence, the hope of an old man which I am sorry to say proved false.

But not to keep you any longer, having departed from him

in Rome I came to Naples where I visited the queens and participated in their Council meeting. Alas, what a shame, what a monster! May God remove this kind of plague from Italian skies! I thought that Christ was despised at Memphis, Babylon, and Mecca. I feel pity for you, my noble Parthenope, for you truly resemble any one of them since you reflect no piety, no truth, no faith. I saw a terrible three footed beast, with its feet naked, with its head bare, arrogant about its poverty, dripping with pleasures. I saw a little man plucked and ruddy, with plump haunches scarcely covered by a worn mantle and with a good portion of his body purposely uncovered. In this condition he disdains most haughtily not only your words but also those of the Pope as if from the lofty tower of his purity. Nor was I astonished that he carries his arrogance rooted in gold. As is widely known, his money boxes and his robes do not agree. To be sure you know his sacred name; he is called Robert. In the place of that most serene Robert who was recently king, this other Robert has arisen who will be an eternal dishonor of our age just as the other was its only glory. I shall now consider it less unbelievable that a serpent can arise from the remains of a buried man since this insensitive asp has sprung up from the royal tomb. Oh supreme shame! See who has dared invade your royal throne, most excellent king! But this is the trust one can have in Fortune. She not only turns human affairs around but overturns them. It was not sufficient that she should remove the sun from the world, thereby superimposing dark shadows over it, but after having snatched away our unparalleled king she did not simply replace him with someone inferior in virtue, but instead with a horrible and cruel monster. Is this how you look upon us, Lord of the stars? Is this a suitable successor for such a king? After the Dionysii and Agathocles and Phalaris, was this person (who is more repulsive and underneath more monstrous) a proper legacy of destiny to the Sicilian court, this "most unmerciful oppressor," to use the words of Macrobius? With an extraordinary type of tyranny he wears not a crown, or a habit, or arms, but a filthy mantle, and, as I said, not completely wrapped in it but only half way, and curved over not so much because of old age but because of his hypocrisy. Relying not as much on eloquence as on silence and on arrogance, he wanders through the courtyards of the queens, and, supported by a staff, he pushes aside the more humble, he tramples upon justice, and he defiles whatever remains of divine or human rights. Like a new Tiphys and another Palinurus he controls the helm of the unrestrained ship of state which, in my opinion, will soon perish in a huge shipwreck. For there are many people of this stamp, indeed almost all, except for Philip, bishop of Cavaillon, who alone takes sides on behalf of foresaken justice. What can he do, a single lamb in so great a flock of wolves; what can he do except to flee forthwith, if he can, and seek out his sheepfold? This is what I believe he is thinking of doing, but out of pity for the collapsing kingdom and in memory of the last entreaties of the king, he is detained by a double set of chains. Meanwhile how clearly do you think his voice can be heard in the seductive band of courtiers, invoking the faith of God and of men, attacking the terribly unjust plans that are proposed, and checking the impudence of many with its authority, parrying Fortune with his wisdom and placing his own shoulders against the destruction of the state which he can delay but cannot change. Would that such destruction not envelop him also! The matter has now reached the point where I have no hope in human assistance, especially with respect to the surviving Robert who in his excessive treachery and because of the strangeness of his dress deserves the name and rank of the foremost monster in courtly circles. And you will have to share some of the blame if from the information that I sent at some length in other more confidential letters you do not keep the Roman Pontiff better informed. As a fitting conclusion, pass on to him this one particular thought of mine: would he believe that the Saracen centers of Susa or Damascus might receive his apostolic exhortations more reverently, as I believe they would, than Christian Naples? If my respect for his holiness did not prohibit it, I would add those words of Cicero: "We are being punished justly, for had we not permitted the crimes of many to go unpunished, the thought of so much license would never have occurred to a single man." In truth while I am trying to relieve my angry stomach with these sputtering words, I fear that I might also be moving you to anger. If this proves of no avail, and if the temerity of such people and your patience can lead to nothing more than our getting upset, of what avail is it to try to relay the insolence of the matter with our words, something which neither Cicero himself nor Demosthenes could accomplish? Even if it were possible, such damage would accrue to the person who undertakes it that he would lose his peace of mind while the perpetrators of the crimes remain unpunished. Therefore it would be wise to bring our words to a conclusion.

Perhaps three or four times I have visited the prison known as Camp Capua, where I saw your friends who have lost all hope except in you since the rightness of their cause which should have been their primary protection has thus far proven damaging to them. As everyone knows, it is most dangerous to try to uphold a just cause before an unjust judge. It might be added that there is no greater enemy for unfortunates than the man who haughtily enjoys the spoils of their belongings, since he naturally would like to remove those who may find occasion to demand the return of what is rightfully theirs. Thus, cruelty always follows upon avarice, and it might also be noted that when there is a pirating of one's inheritance there is always the potential danger of loss of life. It is certainly a difficult lot of man not to be able either to be poor in safety or to regain his riches! If ever this happened to anyone it is now happening to your friends, for as captives there is no one who has not had some portion of their personal belongings plundered. How could such grasping plunderers possibly be concerned about the liberty or safety of someone who seems to be closely connected with their own poverty? Therefore they would have been safer had they possessed nothing. But the situation is such that they made bitter enemies with serious harm to themselves. I saw them in fetters; oh shameful sight! oh unstable and onrushing wheel of Fortune! However, just as there is nothing more ugly than that kind of captivity, in the same manner there is nothing more elevated than the minds of the prisoners. As long as you are safe, they continue to have the greatest hope in the outcome. I for my part can hope for nothing unless some greater force intervenes, for if they expect the clemency of deliberations, the die is cast: they will waste in the squalor of prison. The elder queen, formerly the royal spouse, now the most wretched of widows, has compassion, as she says, affirming that she can do nothing more. Cleopatra with her Ptolemy could also show compassion if Photinus and Achilles would allow it. This is what I see. I need not tell you with what spirit I behold it all. What can I do? One must have patience. And although I am certain of the answer, I nevertheless expect an answer, having been ordered to seek one. Farewell.

29 November.

Fam. V, 4.

To the same correspondent, a description of Baia and of the female warrior from Pozzuoli.

I have known your attitudes for some time; you cannot endure not knowing about things because an implacable desire for knowledge stirs your noble spirit. I have tried to satisfy your desires whenever my fortune had me travel to the North or to the West. I have now made a different journey, but in the same frame of mind and with the same intention of obeying. You have indeed heard the account of my arrival and of the mishaps that happened to us on our journey, and then what transpired in Naples in the negotiations on behalf of your prisoners and the kind of hope that remains. But listen now to the rest which contains nothing to upset but rather something to delight you. Influenced by the useless waiting and the long weariness, I had decided to explore Mt. Gargano and the port of Brindisi and that length of sea that lies above, not so much for the sake of seeing those places as from a wish to leave this place. Through the persuasion of the elder queen I did not do so but instead changed my plans for a longer trip and decided to visit closer and certainly more wonderful places. But if when I depart from here the time of year does not prevent my seeing those other places, I shall take comfort in the effort to get to them, for although I shall have achieved nothing in those matters for which I had come here, I shall nevertheless see many things which I never expected to see. But concerning those places, upon my return to you after my lengthy journey through almost all of Italy, health permitting, I shall tell you in person. What I have seen so far I have committed to writing so that you may know about these things as speedily as possible.

I saw Baia along with the very famous Giovanni Barrili and my Barbato. I do not recall a happier day in my life, not only because of my friends' company and the variety of notable sights but because of the recent experience of many sad days. I saw in the winter months that very attractive bay which if I am not mistaken the summer sun must overwhelm.

This is nothing but an opinion, for I was never there during the summer. It is now three years since I was first brought here in the middle of the winter with the north winds raging, a time when one is particularly subject to danger in a sea journey. Therefore, I was unable to view from up close the many things I wished to see. However, I have today finally satisfied the desire which has occupied my mind as a result of that brief taste of things and of wishes that have been with me since my youth. I saw the places described by Virgil; I saw the lakes Avernus and Lucrinus as well as the stagnant waters of Acheron; the laguna of Augusta rendered unhappy by the fierceness of her son; the once proud road of Gaius Caligula now buried under the waves; and the obstacle against the sea built by Julius Caesar. I saw the native land and the home of the Sibyl and that dreadful cave from which fools do not return and which learned men do not enter. I saw Mt. Falernus distinguished for its famous vineyards and the parched soil exhaling continuously the vapors that are good for diseases. There I also saw balls of ashes and boiling water as in a boiling copper vessel spilling over with a confused rumbling. I saw the wholesome fluid which the cliffs everywhere dripped and which as a gift of mother nature was once employed for all kinds of illnesses and later, as the story goes, mixed with the regular baths because of the envy of the doctors. Now many people of all ages and of both sexes throng from neighboring cities to the waters. I saw not only what is called the Neapolitan grotto which Annaeus Seneca recalls in his letter to Lucilius, but everywhere mountains full of perforations and suspended on marble vaults gleaming with brilliant whiteness, and sculpted figures indicating with pointing hands what water is most appropriate for each part of the body. The appearance of the place and the labor devoted to its development caused me to marvel. Henceforth I shall be less astonished by the walls of Rome and her fortresses and her palaces, when such care was taken by Roman leaders so far from the homeland (although the homeland for outstanding men is everywhere). They often took winter pleasures in places more than a hundred miles from home as if they were suburbs. Their summer delights included Tivoli and the lake of Celano and the wooded valleys of the Apennines, "and Lake Cimino with its mountain," as Virgil says, and the sunny retreats of Umbria, and the shady hills of Tuscany, and the mount rightfully called Algido, and the gushing springs and clear rivers. Their winter delights included Anzio, Terracina, Formia, Gaeta, and Naples. However none was more pleasant nor more popular than Baia. This is attested to by the authority of the writers of that period and by the huge remains of the walls, although I am not ignorant of the fact that this was a place of dwelling worthy rather of human pleasures than of the gravity of the Romans. For that reason Marius, naturally a rather rough man, and Pompey and Caesar, more noble in character, are all praised for building on the mountains from where, as was fitting for such men, they were not immersed in but rather protected themselves from effeminate elegance, the obstreperousness of sailors, and disdained the pleasures of Baia from aloft. Scipio Africanus, however, an incomparable man, who did all things virtuously and nothing for pleasure not only disdained life on the hills of Baia, but determined never to see this place which he considered inimical to his ways, a resolution very much in keeping with the rest of his life. He therefore avoided even a view of the place and preferred to live in Literno rather than in Baia. I know that his small villa is not far from here, and there is nothing that I would look upon more eagerly if I could visit with some guide places renowned because of so great an occupant.

While many marvelous things have indeed been created by that God "who alone creates great wonder," He nevertheless created nothing more wonderful on earth than man. Thus of all things I saw on that day that I am describing to you in this letter the most remarkable was the strength of mind and body of a woman from Pozzuoli. Her name is Mary. Her outstanding trait is the preservation of her virginity; although she is a constant companion of men who are often men of arms, no one, as almost everyone is ready to attest, has assailed the virginity of this strict woman either seriously or in jest, more out of fear, as they relate, than out of respect. Her body resembles rather that of a soldier than a virgin, her strength is such as to be desired by veteran soldiers, her dexterity is rare and unusual, her vigorous age, condition and enthusiasm are those of a powerful man. She practices not with cloth but with weapons, not with needles and mirrors, but with bows and arrows. She is marked not by the signs of kisses and the lascivious signs of the bold teeth of lovers, but wounds and scars. Her primary concern is with arms, and her mind disdains the sword and death. She wages an hereditary war with her neighbors in which already a large number have perished on both sides. Sometimes alone, often attended by a few others, she came to grips with her enemy, and to this day she has always emerged the victor. She is quick to engage in war, slow to disengage, she attacks her enemy boldly, as she weaves ambushes carefully. She endures hunger, thirst, cold, heat, wakefulness, and weariness with incredible patience. She spends her nights under the open sky and travels fully armed; she rests on the ground and considers among her delights the grassy turf or her shield on which she lies. Among such continuous hardships she has changed considerably in a short time. Not too long ago when my youthful desire for glory led me to Rome and Naples and to the King of Sicily, she attracted my attention as I saw her standing there unarmed. When she approached me today armed and surrounded by armed men to pay her respects, I was taken by surprise and returned her greeting as if to an unknown man until warned by her laughter and by the gestures of her companions I finally managed to recognize under the helmet the fierce and unpolished virgin. There are many fabulous stories told about her; I am repeating only what I saw. Powerful men from different parts of the world had assembled, men hardened by warfare whom chance had caused to stop there although they were directed elsewhere. Having heard the reputation of the woman, they were driven by the desire to test her strength. Hearing about this, we all agreed to ascend to the fortress of Pozzuoli. She was walking in front of the doors of the church in deep meditation which caused her not to notice our approach. We approached to ask her to supply us with some kind of proof of her strength. At first excusing herself for some time because of pain in her arm, she finally ordered that a heavy stone and an iron beam be brought to her. After she had thrown it into the center of the group she urged them to try lifting and competing. To be brief, a long contest ensued among equals, and everyone tried his hand as if in great rivalry while she acted as observer judging the strength of each of the men. Finally, with an easy try, she showed herself much superior to all, causing stupefaction in the others and shame in myself. We eventually left, being in a condition which prompted us to give less faith to what our eyes had seen than to the belief that we had been subjected to some kind of illusion. It is said that Robert, that greatest of men and of kings, once sailing along these shores with a large fleet, stopped at Pozzuoli intrigued by the wonders of such a woman and desirous of seeing her. In my opinion this does not seem to be quite believable because living so close to her he could have summoned her. But perhaps he landed there for some other reason, being desirous of viewing something new and being naturally eager for all kinds of knowledge. But let the burden of proof for this matter, as with everything else I heard, lie with its tellers; as for me the sight of this woman has rendered more believable whatever is narrated not only about the Amazons and that once famous female kingdom, but even what is told about the virgin female warriors of Italy, under the leadership of Camilla whose name is the most renowned of all. What should keep one from believing many instances of something which I would have been perhaps slow to believe if I had not had personal experience? Indeed, just as that ancient heroine who was born not far from here, at Piperno, at the time of the Trojan downfall; this more recent Camilla, was born at Pozzuoli in our times. This is what I wanted to have attested in my short letter to you. Farewell and enjoy good health.

23 November.

Fam. V, 5.

To the same correspondent, a description of a storm without equal.

To describe a remarkable storm in a few words and much imagery the Satirist wrote that a poetic storm had arisen. What could be more brief or more expressive? For neither the angry heavens nor the sea could do anything which could not be surpassed in words and poetic style. To avoid superfluous examples of something that is obvious, I remind you of Homer's storm and of the leader who was dashed against the cliffs and of all the misfortunes caused by Mt. Caphareus. In imitation, our poets have maintained that mountains of water are raised to the stars. But nothing can be described by eloquence or can be imagined which yesterday was not equaled and even surpassed close to here. It was a disaster unique and unheard of in history. Therefore let Homer sing of his Greek storm, and Maro of his Aeolian, and Lucan of his Epirian, and others of other storms. As for me, if ever there is a sufficient block of time, the Neapolitan storm can provide me with abundant material for a poem, although it was not only Neapolitan but spread throughout the upper and lower seas and according to hearsay was almost universal. For me it was Neapolitan because it caught up with me during a painful delay in Naples. As much as the press of time before the departure of the messenger will allow, I shall try to persuade you that truly nothing more horrible or more violent has ever been seen. Amazingly, there had been preceding warning of the approaching blow, for a certain bishop from a nearby island and interested in astrology had announced the danger several days earlier. But since such people almost never get to the truth by their guesswork, he predicted that Naples would be destroyed on November 25, 1343 not by a sea storm but by an earthquake. Furthermore he surrounded everything he said with such extraordinary terrors that a large portion of the populace, under the threat of death and thus desirous of changing their manner of life, were intent on doing penance for their sins, and abandoned all other kinds of activity. Many others made fun of such idle fears especially because of the considerable number of bad storms which had occurred at that time. Therefore, they considered the prophesy wrong as to date, and gave many good reasons for having no confidence in it. I myself was neither hopeful nor fearful, and, though favoring neither side, I inclined somewhat toward fear, for the fact seems to be that things that are hoped for come less readily than those that are feared. I had also heard and seen at that time many threatening signs in the skies which for one accustomed to living in northern climes resembled the supernatural events that occur in the cold of winter, and make one prone to turn to fear and indeed to religion. What more need I say? It was the night before the predicted day. An anxious crowd of women, concerned more with the danger at hand than with modesty, ran to and fro through the alleys and streets, and holding their children to their breasts they tearfully and humbly crowded the doorways of the churches. Worried by the public alarm, I returned home in the early evening. The sky was calmer than usual which caused my comrades to go to bed with considerable confidence. I had decided to wait, wanting to observe the manner in which the moon would set. However, because it was in its seventh day, if I am not mistaken, I stood at the windows which looked toward the West until the nearby mountain hid it in a covering of clouds, and before the middle of the night it assumed a sad look. Finally I, too, in order to make up for lost sleep, went to bed.

I had scarcely fallen asleep when not only the windows but the walls themselves, though built on solid stone, were shaken from their very foundations and the night light, which I am accustomed to keep lit while I sleep, went out. We threw off our blankets, and in place of sleep the fear of imminent death overcame us. Here is what happened next. Each one of us sought out the other in the dark and encouraged one another with our voices as we recognized each other by the aid of the ominous light in the air, while the most holy Prior David, whom I here name out of respect, and the religious of the dwelling in which we were living and who regularly used to rise for the nocturnal adoration of Christ, frightened by the unexpected danger, and bearing their crosses and their relics of saints, and invoking the mercy of God in a loud voice, all marched with their torches into the bedroom I occupied. This made me feel somewhat relieved. We then all proceeded to the church, and there we spent the night prostrate with much wailing, believing that our end was imminent and that everything around us would shortly lie in ruins. It would take too long to try to describe in words every horror that surrounded that infernal night, and although my words may fall short of the truth, they will transcend any plausibility that can be placed in truth itself. What a downpour! what winds! what lightning! what deep thunder! what frightening tremors! what roaring of the sea! what shrieking of the populace! In this state which made the evening as if by magic appear twice as long, when we finally began to glimpse the dawn, the daylight appeared imminent rather through conjecture than in actual fact. The cloaked priests repeated their sacrifices at the altar and we, not daring to look at the heavens, threw ourselves prostrate on the moist and naked floors around them. When no doubt remained that it was indeed daylight (though it continued to resemble the glow of night) and the shouting of the populace suddenly became silent in the upper part of the city, although it seemed to be increasing more and more from the direction of the shore, and we could not learn what was happening by inquiring, our despair, as often happens, became boldness, and we mounted our horses and descended to the port determined to see for ourselves and to perish if necessary.

Good God! When was anything like this ever heard of? The oldest sailors asserted that what had happened was indeed without parallel. The port was filled with frightening and dismal wreckage. The unfortunate victims, who had been scattered by the water and had been trying to grasp the nearby land with their hands, were dashed against the reefs and were broken like so many tender eggs. The entire shore line was covered with torn and still living bodies: someone's brains floated by here, someone else's bowels floated there. In the midst of such sights the yelling of men and wailing of women were so loud that they overcame the sounds of the seas and the heavens. To all this was added the destruction of buildings, many of whose foundations were overturned by the violent waves against which that day respected no bounds and respected no work of man or nature. They overflowed their natural limits, the familiar shoreline, as well as that huge breakwater which had been constructed by zealous men and which, with its outstretched arms, as Maro says, constitutes the port, and all that portion of the region which borders the sea. And where there had been a path for strolling there was now something dangerous even for sailing. A thousand or more Neapolitan horsemen had gathered there as if to assist at the funeral of their homeland. Having joined this group, I had begun to feel somewhat less frightened of perishing amidst so many. But suddenly a new clamor could be heard. The very place on which we stood, weakened by the waves that had penetrated beneath, began to give way. We hurried to a higher elevation. No one raised his eyes to the heavens, for the band of men could not bear to look at the angry faces of Jove and of Neptune. Thousands of mountainous waves flowed between Capri and Naples. The channel appeared not dark or, as is usual in great storms, black, but greyish with the frightening whiteness of sea foam. Meanwhile the younger queen, barefooted and uncombed, and accompanied by a large group of women, departed from the royal palace unconcerned about modesty in the face of great danger, and they all hastened to the Church of the Virgin Queen praying for her grace amidst such dangers. Unless I am mistaken, I imagine that you now fearfully await the outcome of such a calamity. On land we could scarcely find an escape and neither on the deep nor in port could a ship be found to equal those waves. Three long ships from Marseilles, called galleys, which had returned from Cyprus after crossing wide expanses of the sea and were anchored there ready to depart in the morning, we saw overcome by the waves with a universal outcry and without anyone being able to offer assistance and without a single sailor or passenger saved. In the same manner other even larger ships of all kinds which had taken refuge in the port as if in a fortress were destroyed. Only one of so many survived. It was loaded with robbers who had been spared their rightful punishment so that they could be sent on an expedition to Sicily, and who, having been spared the sword of the executioner, were to be exposed to the sword of battle. This huge and powerful ship, armed with the hides of bulls, although it had suffered the blows of the sea until sundown, also began to be overpowered. The exhausted prisoners hastened from all sides to the keel because of the threatening dangers. It is said that they were four hundred in number, a group large enough for a fleet, let alone a single ship. Furthermore they were powerful persons who, freed from death, feared nothing more than death which they resisted even more obstinately and boldly. In postponing the outcome by slowing down the sinking of the ship, they prolonged the disaster well into the following night. When they were finally overcome, they abandoned their tools and dashed to the upper portions of the ship. Suddenly beyond all hope the skies began to clear and the exhausted sea began to slacken its roughness. Thus, so many having perished, only the worst seemed to escape, whether because "Fortune saves many guilty ones," as Lucan says, or because "the gods thought otherwise" as Virgil says; or, as may be the case, those are most free from the dangers of death who consider life worth little. This is a digest of yesterday's happenings, but in order not to take up any more of your time and of my energy—although the account does offer ample matter regarding human behavior in times of crisis about which much has often been said but very little by wise men in view of the subject's importance—there is one thing I want to be certain does emerge: that is, I beseech you not ever again to order me to place my trust in winds and seas. This is something in which I would obey neither you, the Pope, or my own father if he were to return to life. I shall leave the air to the birds and the sea to the fish; as a terrestrial animal I shall prefer land trips. Send me where you will, even to the Indies, as long as my foot tramples the soil. I shall not refuse to approach either the Sarmatian with his bow and arrows, or the perfidious Moor. Otherwise (and pardon me for confessing it) I shall be free not only during the Saturnalia of December but throughout the year. How else could you persuade me, I pray, or with what words would you ever solicit me to sail again? "Choose a stout ship and skilled sailors." But both were available to these men. "Search for a port while the sun is out, cast your anchor at night, beware meeting with enemy, hug the shoreline"? But these people, in the full light of day, with their anchors cast into the clinging sands of a port, and being able almost to touch the shore itself with their oars, perished among thousands of grieving friends. I did not read about this, nor hear about it, but saw it with my own eyes. Therefore do stop now and let your decency at least on this occasion forgive my fear. I know what arguments are used against my position by learned men: danger is the same everywhere although it may appear more likely on the sea. So be it. Do you however behave generously and permit me to die on land since I was born on land. There is scarcely any sea between us in which I have not been often shipwrecked, although among the sayings attributed to Publius is the one which says: "He who undergoes a second shipwreck accuses Neptune wrongfully." Farewell.

Naples, 26 November.

Fam. V, 6.

To the same correspondent, a complaint about the nocturnal prowlers in Naples and about the disgustingly bloody gladiatorial games that are permitted there.

I was hoping to be free of the heavy fetters of business, and I believe would have been if the poisonous serpent had not overcome the minds of the judges who had been restrained by pity. One of the Psylli would not have been more capable of recognizing poison with his mouth than I was in recognizing it with my ear. I continue my opposition, but now I fear that the damage is fatal. However, I shall continue trying as long as any shred of hope remains. Perhaps last night I might have obtained the courtesy even of rejection had the Council not adjourned because of the approaching darkness, and had not the incurable disease of the city compelled everyone to return home early. Though very famous for many reasons, the city possesses one particularly dark, repulsive, and inveterate evil: to travel in it by night, as in a jungle, is dangerous and full of hazards because the streets are beset by armed young nobles whose dissoluteness cannot be controlled by the discipline of their parents, by the authority of their teachers, or by the majesty and command of kings. But is it any wonder that they act brazenly under the cover of darkness without witnesses, when in this Italian city in broad daylight with royalty and the populace as spectators infamous gladiatorial games are permitted of a wildness that is greater than we associate with barbarians? Here human blood flows like the blood of cattle, and often amidst the applause of the insane spectators unfortunate sons are killed under the very eyes of their wretched parents. It is indeed the ultimate infamy to hesitate having one's throat pierced by the sword as if one were battling for the republic or for the rewards of eternal life. I was taken unknowingly the day before yesterday to such a place not far from the city which is called appropriately "The Furnace" where indeed a workshop full of soot and of inhuman fierceness darkens the bloody blacksmiths at the anvil of death. The Queen was present as was Prince Andrew, a boy of lofty mind, if ever he were to assume the long-deferred crown. All the militia of Naples was also present in all their elegance and propriety. All the rabble had eagerly flocked to that place. And so I, curious about so great a crowd and about the passionate interest of well known people, thinking that I was about to view something great, focused my attention on the spectacle. Suddenly, as if something very delightful had occurred, thunderous applause resounded. I looked around and to my surprise I saw a most handsome young man lying at my feet transfixed by a sharp pointed sword which emerged from his body. I stood there astounded, and my whole body shuddering. I spurred my horse and fled from the infernal spectacle, angry at my friends' deceit, at the cruelty of the spectators and the continued madness of the participants. This twin plague, dear father, as if inherited from our ancestors has reached subsequent generations in an ever increasing tempo, and the reason for it is that the license for committing crime has now acquired the name of dignity and freedom. Let this suffice, for it is a tragic matter and I have already wasted many words speaking of it with the obstinate citizens. Indeed we should hardly be astonished that your friends, offering as they do such a prize for greed, should be prisoners in that city where killing men is considered a game, a city which Virgil indeed does call the most delightful of all, but as it stands now would not be considered unequal to Thrace in infamy: "Alas flee the cruel lands, flee the greedy shore." I certainly accept those words as relating to this city; and unless you hear otherwise, expect me to leave within three days to flee, even if my business remains unfinished, first to Cisalpine Gaul, and then to Transalpine Gaul and to you who always cause all my trips to be delightful unless they are by sea. Farewell.

Naples, calends of December.

Fam. V, 7.

To Giovanni Andrea,[1] *professor of Canon law at Bologna,
how much faith one should have in dreams.*

You write me that you have been so deeply disturbed by a
dream so real that you almost believed having seen it while
awake. You were now seeing it a second time, except that
what you dreamed was of something that could not happen
more than once. However, even while thinking that the
dream event could not be repeated, you became aware that
the dream was of something you had seen before. Now
you ask whether anything like it had ever happened to me,
what I believe about such matters, and what learned men
have said about them. The subject is indeed as vast as are the
sources of disagreement, especially because this problem has
not only been tackled by men of letters, but popularly, with
everyone giving evidence of his own experiences of dreams.
As a result it is difficult in the debate to separate the truth
from the chatter. Not only do the people disagree, but
learned men also, yet their opinions which you know very
well you nevertheless deliberately tempt me to discuss. You
know the commentary of Chalcidius on the *Timaeus* and the
commentary of Macrobius on the sixth book of the *Republic*
where he presents a clear and brief distinction between types
of dreams. You have Aristotle's book on these and related
matters. Finally you have Cicero's book on prophesy, in
which you will find how he himself, as well as others, viewed
the matter. Why do you want me to repeat what is very well
known? It is indeed curious that anyone knowing the authority of the ancients should want to hear my opinion, but
I suppose friendship does curious things. If you really place
any importance in my judgment and believe that my opinion
is valid for the matter at hand, I agree in this with my Cicero
as I do in so many other things. However I do so without

1. A learned and famous law professor at the University of Bologna and considered one of the outstanding specialists in canon law.
He held the chair in canon law at Bologna for forty-five years, and
was a teacher of Petrarch. As an admirer of St. Jerome he wrote a
carefully researched biography of the saint.

obstinacy and am ready to alter my agreement with him if anything more certain should appear, refusing to assume the arrogance and rashness of asserting anything with finality, something he himself advises in his book *Academic Questions*. There you have it. If you should wish to hear me dealing with this matter in a more elaborate fashion, I have in hand a book entitled *Liber memorandarum rerum* which if it is ever published will deal in a first part more fully with these matters. However, to the many examples of the experiences of others which I have collected in that book, I shall add as you request two personal experiences of dreams, one pleasing, the other sad, but both about a verified event. To both of them there are witnesses whom I told of my dreams after I had them and before they came true. My recollecting both will thus give satisfaction to you and be pleasant to me.

I had a friend in my early years than whom at that time neither nature nor fortune had given me any dearer. Being suddenly stricken by a serious illness he was given up as lost by his doctors and I despaired for my own life. There was only one kind of consolation I could find, and that was to weep. I wept constantly day and night. Then one night, having been awake until dawn, I finally submitted my weary eyes to a sad dream. I suddenly saw him before me and the sight made me emit terrible groans which awoke my colleagues. As I later learned from them, when they saw me asleep, though they perceived I was having some kind of troubled dream, feeling sorry for my many hours of sleeplessness, they preferred to let me have a disturbed rest rather than none at all. However, my sick friend seemed to approach me and to gently wipe my tears pleading that I put an end to a grief which had no basis in fact. And when I set about refuting his words and complaining about my fate, I seemed to hear him interrupting my complaints saying: "Be silent; whatever you are about to say I know; but here is someone approaching who will put an end to our conversation; I beg you to renew your hope for my health through him, and rest assured that I shall not perish at all from this disease unless I am forsaken." As he was saying these things there was a loud knock on the door of my bedroom which caused both sleep and the vision to vanish. I looked around, and in the light of daybreak I saw standing at my bed one of the doctors who had been very friendly to both of us, and who, despairing of my friend's health, had turned all his attention to comforting and consoling me. I approached this very dear and courteous man with many prayers, urging him to return to my friend and not abandon hope (especially in the case of a man who was so young), so long as any sign of breathing remained with him. However, as he pointed out very sadly, he admired my grief and useless anxiety, but could profess only the art of curing and not reviving, being a doctor and not God. I, in turn, with my eyes still wet with tears shed during the night, with sound mind though somewhat upset, explained to him what I had seen and I warmly sought his assistance in this misfortune. What else can I say? I convinced him even though he was highly reluctant. He went and soon returned bringing news of somewhat better hope. All the others who had deserted the sick man likewise eagerly returned, and in this fashion my friend was returned to me from the hands of death herself. Even though I am attracted by the sweetness of such recollection, and may linger too long on personal matters, I shall not refrain from relating the following.

Giacomo Colonna, the younger, a man in our time of the greatest note and endowed with a nature that would easily have been truly superior in any century, was a person who valued my friendship and with whom I lived on friendly terms. Only in one matter have I felt that fortune had not been as unfair as she might have been with me; very rarely has she permitted me to be involved directly in my griefs, but rather caused me to be hurt from a distance and preferred to have my ears feel the blows, thus sparing my eyes. Many things can be said about that man which I shall pass over, since they have no bearing on present matters and there is nothing indeed that you could hear about his ways that would be new to you inasmuch as, of all the bishops, it was this one that you preferred cultivating and honoring for yourself. You cultivated the outstanding talent of a truly noble youth during his adolescence, like a skillful cultivator of talents capable of extracting the fruit from the flower. You soon came to love the excellence of his virile mind which was best known to you; then you bestowed upon him honors worthy of his merit and priesthood which he so truly deserved; finally you accompanied him with compassionate tears and deep human affection even though in his exit from so many concerns and from the midst of the labors of life he proceeded to better things, and you did so like a father insofar as dignity was concerned, like a son insofar as age was concerned, and like a brother insofar as intimacy was concerned. But I shall return to the matter at hand. He, then, hating the hubbub of worldly life, fled his venerable father, brothers, and native land and like a distinguished patron he once again sought his see and withdrew to the retreats of Gascony. As he had everywhere lived the rest of his life magnificently, he there now lived the last portion, in an utterly episcopal and dedicated manner as if aware of his approaching end. However, being in Cisalpine Gaul divided from him by a considerable expanse of land, I was at that time enjoying some rest in this very garden from which I am writing to you. Rumors brought me gossip about his illness, but it was such that fluctuating between hope and fear with great anticipation I used to await more certain announcements. I shudder even as I recall those moments, for the very place where I saw him clearly in the quiet of the night lies here before my eyes. He was unattended, and was crossing this very brook in my garden. I went to meet him in a state of astonishment asking him many things: where he came from, where he was going, why in such haste, and why he was traveling alone. He answered none of my requests but as he was most pleasant in his conversation, he said smilingly: "Do you remember when you lived with me on the other side of the Garonne how annoying the storms of the Pyrenees were to you? Weary of them and determined to depart for good, I am on my way to Rome." Saying these things he had already hastened to the outskirts of my residence, as I was urging him to take me with him. Having gently denied my request time and again with his hand raised, he finally said with a change of voice and in another tone: "Stop, I do not wish to have you as a companion at this time." I fixed my eyes upon him and I recognized from his paleness that he was dead. Overcome by fear and sadness I cried out so loudly that awakening at that very moment I heard the very last sounds of my cry. I marked down the day and recounted the whole story to my local friends and wrote about it to absent ones. After twenty-five days the news of his death was brought to me. When I check the dates, I note that he had come to me on the very day on which he had passed away. Finally after three years his remains were brought back to Rome (which I did not know and did not even suspect), his soul, as I hope and desire, having returned triumphantly to heaven.

But enough about dreams; let us rouse ourselves. This much I point out. I have faith in dreams not because Caesar Augustus, that very great man both as a ruler and as a learned person, may be said to have been of contrary opinion, and there are many today who agree with him; nor because a dream made either my master or my friend appear before me in my anxiety, nor because one died and the other lived, for in both cases I saw either what I wished for or what I feared, and fate happens to coincide with my visions. My faith in dreams is no more than Cicero's who considered that the accidental truth of one of his dreams did not undo the ambiguities of many others. Farewell.

27 December.

Fam. V, 8.

To the same correspondent, on the condition of a lustful young man.

You would like to know what I think of and what I hope for this man of yours? A prisoner of a harmful and, what is worse, a shameful passion, he is completely entangled in a net of evil. Meantime he may appear angry, and indeed oftentimes is forced to be. Such is the nature of love, such the life of lovers. They become angry and they quarrel, and conclude their many battles in repeated truces, hardly ever keeping even for a moment to a single purpose. Of life's difficulties there is nothing worse than this fickleness and fluctuation. In consequence you will rarely find them happy, but often sad; you will always find them changeable, but never consistent. You write that this young man of yours has now become revolted by his pleasures. I believe it, since I am certain it could not be otherwise. For who is so obstinate that he may not sometimes open his eyes and, seeing his wretchedness, hate it? However, I do not agree with what you add, for you express the greatest hope that such signs indicate he can loosen himself from his chains. I myself believe that considering the age and mental bent of the man, he will become more embroiled unless God's help is very close. Since it is the custom of a snared bird to become more entangled by trying to shake itself loose, I would be more optimistic if his love seemed to be ending in oblivion and silence rather than in animosity and quarreling; the former is a sign of a restored mind, the latter of offended love. I fear what Terence says in his *Andria:* "The anger of lovers is but a renewal of love"; I fear what Seneca said to his Lucilius: "Nothing revives more easily than love"; I fear those words of Virgil: "Oh wicked love, what do you not compel mortal hearts to do?"; I fear everything Cicero has to say about this matter in the forth day of his *Tusculan Orations;* finally I fear the general agreement on this matter of all the philosophers, and the opinions of poets. But above all things I am frightened by the abominable skill and inextricable snares of the panders and the harlots; I shudder at the flattery of the sirens and the clinging snare of passion; I tremble at this harborless Charybdis, notorious for the shipwreck of so many, in which he is now navigating. In short there is nothing, as matters now stand, which I do not fear. For what he now threatens cruelly, or angrily imagines as he blurts: "Am I going to let her. . . . Why she! that fellow! and me, too! she doesn't!" and those other things that follow, the ending will be as Terence expresses it: "All she has to do is rub her eyes hard and squeeze out one little make-believe tear, and that will be the end of (his) talk. She'll blame it all on (him), and (he'll) be the one who pays." * Let him rage with loud clamor and let him noisily declare himself free, but if I were to be the judge, I would agree with the judgment of the old woman who murmurs that he has fallen into slavery. Why? Because I know in what way her murmur is more potent than his clamor, and to what extent some skills surpass others. Between them there is neither equality nor similarity. One is made of iron, the other of clay; one is like fire, the other is like stubble; one reflects swiftness of feigning, the other ease of believing; one is composed of countless hooks, the other of as many hook-eyes. You know everything, and although your age excludes you from these concerns, I speak of nothing which is really unknown to you. Doesn't the old woman in the *Asinaria* of Plautus appear to you rightly confident in these matters? You will recall that she speaks thus to the angry and menacing young man: "Your mind here at home is held fast by the nails of passion; hurry as much as you can with oars and with sails, and flee, for the more you attempt to gain the open sea, the more the waves carry you back to port." The witch was certainly sure of herself since she had learned of such youthful adventures through the experience of a full life. To these things I shall add only this one: that you give thought to the fact that by the passage of time cities are destroyed, kingdoms transferred, customs changed, and laws altered; yet those things that pertain to minds of men and the diseases of the mind are almost all the same as they were when Plautus imagined his stories. What you say is pro-

* Trans. of F. O. Copley, *The Comedies of Terence* (New York, 1967).

claimed quite frequently by this man, if he does indeed proclaim it everywhere, namely that he did burn with passion
once but no longer was its victim, is indeed a fatal sign of this
disease. The short verse of Naso is well known: "He who says
too often 'I do not love,' does indeed love." I do not believe
in words but in deeds, and not quickly in these unless an
opposite way of life is tenaciously pursued in order to wash
away the stains of the previous life. A quick remedy does
not help a lingering illness. What we learn through long
practice must be unlearned through long disuse. You now
have this prediction of mine concerning your young man,
and would that events will prove it false, for certainly the
right hand of the Almighty is powerful, and as with the conversion of David He could in His forgiveness and in less time
than it takes to say it raise one from the lowest depths of
misery.

But you know that holds very rarely and for very few
men. Farewell.

13 May.

Fam. V, 9.

To the same correspondent, on the condition of a dissolute old man.

You have brought up a subject unlike the one in your first letter, that of a dissolute and lustful old man, yet more appropriate for satire, for, according to the rhetorician, "A lustful young man sins, a lustful old man is mad," and in confirmation Plautus: "We sometimes rave as old men,"—not only sometimes but in fact very often. This was true in ages past; now however we crawl as infants, we play as children, we go mad as youths, we do battle as men, we rave as old men. Thus missing no portion of life, we bring some form of folly into each age through a graded series of errors. I know not what to say except that were it not for some ray of light shining among so many shadows I would certainly agree with the ancients who believed that next to dying the best thing is not to be born. There is one excuse, however, that this kind of old man seems to have: their need for consolation in their feeble age; and now indeed such liberty is openly accepted. Thus in his *Asinaria* even Plautus excused his lascivious old man saying: "If unknown to his wife, this old man enjoyed some pleasure, he did nothing new or astonishing, or different from what others have been accustomed to do; there is no one of such an unyielding temper or firmness of mind who would not, should the occasion arise, indulge himself." This is what Plautus said, and this is what we all say either as young men for whom lust is an honor, or as grown men for whom lust is a habit, or as old men for whom lust appears as a venial sin. How often will you find an old man who, when an opportunity presents itself and there are no witnesses present, would not immediately forget his lack of virility and rush into an affair like a young person, flattering himself with the thought that delight and pleasure are both beneficial and proper, and that the only comfort of old age is lust, which is, in truth, the disgrace and destruction of old age? You must speak to our old man and make him pay attention to what he is doing, where he is going, and how contrary to his age, how unbecoming and how dangerous and inconvenient his lust really is. Perhaps modesty and fear may be effective in accomplishing what reason and satisfaction ought to have done long ago. But if he continues, convey to him only these words of mine: that he must stop soon because as the lust of youth leads to old age, the lust of old people leads to the grave. Farewell.

Fam. V, 10.

To Barbato da Sulmona.

As is our custom I am moved to share with you my circumstances and my hardships. As you know, warfare has ceased in Parma; we are surrounded by the great rebellions not only of Liguria but of almost all of Italy, and we are confined within the borders of a single city not because of a lack of courage in our men (which they have often proved in bold sallies), but because the cunning of the enemy is such that it reveals neither the road to peace nor the road to battle, but is confident that it will conquer by weakening our spirits through patiently subjecting us to the slow weariness of a siege. Therefore, under the often varying hand of fate, the besieger himself becomes besieged and the outcome is not yet certain. In any event, the issue is being fiercely fought by both sides, and, unless I am wrong in my prediction, the ultimate day of reckoning approaches ever closer. I waver in my mind and do not lean completely toward either side, striving not to fall prey either to empty hope or to useless fear. In this condition we have been experiencing the siege not for a few days only but for many months, certainly not the least of military misfortunes. In this predicament I have recently felt a desire for freedom, which I pray for and seek to embrace enthusiastically and, as it flees from me, pursue through the world. For some time a desire for my Transalpine Helicon has gripped me because my Italian Helicon is aflame with war. And so I have been driven on the one side by hatred, on the other by longing. But what could I do? The road leading West had become completely inaccessible. I turned to the East, and although all the roads there seemed full of enemy, yet a short trip in that direction seemed safer than the longer route through Etruria. What more need I say? Departing with a few men through the enemy positions, I undertook a journey at sundown on 23 February. When in the middle of the night I arrived at Reggio, a hostile city, a group of bandits suddenly emerged from ambush with loud shouting threatening death. Deliberation was not possible, with time, place, and the surrounding enemy threatening.

What could a few men unarmed and unprepared do against a great number who were armed and experienced in violence? Our only hope lay in flight and darkness. "His friends flee and are covered by the darkness of the night." I confess that I too removed myself from the danger of death and the resounding weapons. Just when I thought I had evaded every danger (I ask you, how can any man consider himself safe?), whether because of a ditch or perhaps a tree trunk or a rock barrier (for the darkness of that cloudy and blinding night made it impossible to see anything), my most faithful horse fell headlong to the ground with such a blow that I was stunned and felt broken into pieces. Nevertheless I managed finally to collect my courage and rose to my feet, and I, who despite the many days that have elapsed cannot yet bring my hand to my mouth, at that moment supported by my fear sprang once again upon my horse. Some of my companions returned home, some, undaunted by their vain wanderings, did not abandon the undertaking. Our two guides having lost track of the road markers provided by heaven and earth, exhausted and disturbed, compelled us to stop in an out of the way place from which, to add to our terror, could be heard the voices of enemy guards of some close-by camp. Heavy rain, too, had begun to fall, mixed with raging hail, and amidst heavy thunder we felt a constant fear of a more dramatic death. My report would take too long if I covered every point. While we spent that night, which was truly hellish, lying under the open skies on the wet ground, the swelling and pain of my injured arm increased more and more. There was no grassy turf on which to sleep, no branches of a leafy tree or protection of a cave, only the naked earth, the agitated air and raging Jupiter, and, along with the fear of humans and of beasts, the many discomforts of an ill body. Among so many difficulties only one reason for consolation existed which perhaps you will be astonished at and pity: having placed our horses crosswise on the road, we used them as tents and as a covering against the storm. At first they snorted and were restless, but they soon became silent and quiet, as though they were not without some feeling for their wretchedness. They thus provided us with a double service on that awful night. And thus after so much hardship and anxiety dawn finally arrived. As soon as the weak light indicated a path among the bushes, we hastily left the unsafe places. Arriving at a friendly town called Scandiano, we learned that throughout that night a large band of horsemen and foot soldiers had lain in ambush around the walls to capture us, and because of the great storm had departed shortly before our arrival. Try now to deny that fortune is indeed mysterious and powerful enough to change careful plans into destruction, and errors into wise actions. I am fooling with you, dearest Barbato; you know my feelings about fortune; it is but a formidable word. However one wants to look at the matter, our mistaken path proved to be useful as was the storm; we avoided worse things by means of bad things. In that place, therefore, at the arrival of dawn I revealed what had happened amidst many tears on the part of my companions; and since a delay in that place did not seem too safe either, wrapped in tentative bandages, I arrived over mountainous paths in Modena and on the next day in Bologna. From here I am writing these things not as I usually do but with the hands of others so that you will not worry about my condition and my affairs. Regarding the care of my body, all that can be humanly done is being done. While there is much hope for my recovery it certainly will not be swift. The doctors expect help from my age; I expect assistance only from almighty God. Meanwhile my numb right hand does not obey me, but my courage becomes more resolute in adversity. Farewell.

25 February, Bologna.

To Andrea da Mantua,[1] *that the words of detractors should be despised, but their writings should be refuted with writings.*

Hardly ever have I been given a more just reason for complaint or richer occasion for self-defense: I am being maligned at every crossroad. What shall I do? My attacker has attained the point of injustice; disreputable people are slandering my reputation. My detractor deserves to be despised, for he is the more annoying the more he is vile. It is difficult to pretend, yet the dignity of silence is preferable to justified complaints. Let them sharpen their tongues, for I do not fear words. If they express themselves in writing, I will reply, for so long as I live I shall repel the attacks of living critics. But what if they threaten me after I die? For, as I hear, they constantly give birth to a ridiculous mouse or an Indian elephant. But when I ponder the matter, I can only say that should they wait until I am no longer present, they would be behaving in a vile fashion and would be heaping upon me accusations that could hardly be called magnanimous. What else shall I say about their opinions except what I usually say, the same as was said by Plancus against Asinius Pollio which Pliny the elder recalls at the beginning of his *Natural History:* "With the dead only ghosts can contend"? Therefore, if they have something to say, let them reveal it while there is someone who may answer. You will see the offended party become popular because of the insults. Thus Aeschines made Demosthenes more famous, Galba did the same for Cato, Sallust for Cicero, Emilianus for Apuleius. Otherwise they choose an inglorious type of battle when they speak against an absent person and battle with silent ashes; although in this age of ours that is precisely what in their impudent way they hope to do. Farewell.

1. Little is known about this admirer of Petrarch who presumably defended him against his detractors and critics.

Fam. V, 12.

To the same correspondent, on the same matter.

That Theon of ours, or if you prefer Bion, is looking for trouble; I recognize the hissing, the asp must be close by. Should I be indignant or astonished that he does not spare me who would not spare even Homer himself? I think he believes that I get the same pleasure he does from such doings. He is indeed very wrong; nothing is more pleasing to me than silence; after that, nothing is sweeter than a conversation with a friend. If he persists, I shall flee; but you ask what I would do if he does not allow me to do so? I shall remain silent. If he does not permit even silence? I shall speak. How much will I say? Nothing will be briefer. And what shall I say? I shall threaten him with a kind of insult he has never heard; he will be upset and shocked and perhaps, as may happen, disturbed by his conscience, he will be silent. And this will be the end of the dispute because there is nothing that checks the tongue of a critic more than the fear of a sharper tongue. If this does not stop him, with what other arms shall I drive out this gnat? I shall take vengeance like an old woman and shall say to him what one old woman is said to have said to another: "Oh greatest of men and more modest than all, oh cultivator of the virtues, oh ornament and hope of the fatherland; you certainly have never heard anything like this." Now what do you say? Have I not tried hard enough to keep my promise? Either I am mistaken, or though his ears have become hardened to insults, he never heard one like it before now, not from the mouth of a lover, or of a flatterer, or of a mocker, or of a devotee regardless of his impudence. I believe that that unusual style will astonish him; you will laugh, and I meanwhile shall escape. Farewell.

Fam. V, 13.

To his Socrates, the desirability of not delaying salutary advice.

If you have not yet put to rest your heart's anxieties (I being aware of my own troubled state), and if my entreaties can be of any avail for either of us, I beseech and implore us both to drive away at once all the things that torment us and to suppress finally the restlessness of our minds. And let us not be troubled because we have delayed too long or have begun too late. You will not persuade the traveler who gets up late one morning that though the sun may be high he should return to his bedroom in order to prolong his sleep until that evening even though he feels heavy from sleep, or feels distress from excessive drinking, or feels exhausted with weariness. You will rather persuade him that it will be much better to hasten, to double his speed, and to try hard to compensate with energy for what sleep had done. We too, if you reflect, are wayfarers, and an endless journey awaits us, and the hour is already late, for we have been wasting our morning in sleep. We should therefore rise much more vigilant lest perhaps the night should press upon us as we loiter. The matter invites many more considerations but time is short and what has been said certainly suffices for men of good will. Farewell.

Fam. V, 14.

To the same correspondent, on the annoying relations with servants.

Recently I was reading some charming stories by Plautus for the sake of fleeing boredom and relaxing my mind, and thereby for a short moment with the help of the ancient poet avoided the heavy cares of life. It is certainly astonishing how many pleasant stories and elegant pieces I have found therein, and what trickery of servants, what old wives' tales, what flattery of harlots, what greed of panders, what voraciousness of parasites, what anxieties of old men, and what youthful loves. I now am less astonished at Terence for having achieved such great elegance following such a leader. But we shall speak about other things in due time, for there is much to be said, and for those who have abundant free time (if by chance such a thing should ever happen to us), these are very pleasant matters. For the present I shall include only one which most appropriately happened on this very day. There is a comedy of his entitled *Casina*. In it a man and lady disagree over the marriage of their young maid. A domestic war ensues; indeed one that you might call a civil war. As a result all things seem to fall apart for the two married people who appear so united. They agree on nothing whatsoever: the father pursues his own love affairs, and the mother those of her son. Two servants, who are very obstinate rivals, eagerly aspire to marry the girl, one supported by the father and the other by the mother. The servant who is abetting the lust of the master proved unmovable when the mistress of the house begged him to desist from helping his master. When he was asked by his master, who had overheard the final words of the dispute, with whom he was quarreling, he answered, "With the one with whom you are always quarreling." "With my wife, then," answered the old man as if understanding the matter in a roundabout way. To this the servant answered in a manner which was neither servile nor impolite and which, as I read today, seemed to be directed in a certain way to myself. "How can you speak to me of your wife?" he said, "You are indeed almost a hunter since you fill your time night and day with a dog." This is what that servant replied. What can be said that would be more suitable for me? My life has certainly not included a wife and though subjected to a variety of storms it has remained immune from this Charybdis. But there is another kind of trouble for which the words of that servant could be suitable; and while I have undergone the experience for quite some time I was not aware of his words. I knew that I was living with dogs, but that I was a hunter I did not know unless reminded. Servants can be called dogs, being, as they are, biting, gluttonous and barkers. I can bear all these qualities except the last, for barking is too averse to the tranquillity I seek. But of all that bands of dogs there are two that are absolutely unbearable to me, for I have managed to bear with the others up to now. One of these is the one whom I sent to you today with many letters of friends (among which I added this letter after reading Plautus). You can therefore keep this one for yourself if you wish to become a hunter or send him into the woods or into the slaughterhouse, provided that he never returns to me. The other is that other raging old man whom you know very well. Decency prevents me from driving him out, not so much out of respect for him as for his age and long friendship. Therefore since my Plautine servant declared that I was a hunter I shall do what considerate hunters do. I shall not drive a loyal dog from the house although he has become useless because of his old age and his mange, and most troublesome because of his barking. However if I cannot send him away, I shall flee myself and leaving the empty house for him to enjoy I shall seek other regions. Since I have not yet decided where this shall be, you will read my decision in a more confidential letter. In sum, I can become a fisherman at the source of the Sorgue, as my thinking goes for now, but I certainly shall not be a hunter nor shall I spend my life with dogs such as these. Farewell.

Fam. V, 15.

To the same correspondent, an exhortation.

All of us who are born are called to the Campus Martius; some however for no other reason than to make noise and to add to the number; others to enjoy the honors and rewards of hard effort. To belong on the side of these we must make a deliberate choice and effort. The outcome He alone will see in whose hands we have placed ourselves and our affairs. The will for it rests indeed with us. Therefore it behooves us to make up our minds, to become candidates, and to implore the approval of the Supreme Commander and of His friends, for such assemblies are intended not to determine a consulship or a praetorship but, as the young man in Plautus says, our very existence. Farewell and be vigilant.

Fam. V, 16.

To Guido Sette, Archdeacon of Genoa,[1] an excuse for not writing.

I have lost a letter that I had addressed to you. This has resulted from the messenger's delay, and the brash desire of my companions who, in their constant desire for novelties and, to use the words of Solinus, in their usual wanderings through my library, driven by impatience rather than zeal, must have come across that letter, read it and taken it without my knowing. They said that they feared lest a copy of it also perish, as had happened in many other instances when my friends became upset and condemned my carelessness. When I had learned this, I urged them to return it to me, and they hurried to search for it. Why take any longer in explaining what happened? The truth is what someone once said: "Haste does all things badly," for while all desired to find it no one succeeded; and while it was handed to one of them with the consent of all in order to be transcribed, to everyone's sorrow he either lost it or pretended to have lost it—I do not know how except that I never saw it again. I shall confess one thing which I am not ashamed to do with you: it is hard to believe that I could have become so concerned over anything so small. Rarely on other occasions have I perceived my frailty so clearly. I turned everywhere and for many days and nights I sought the lost letter while I complained, at times rebuking the rash confidence of my companions, at times my own casualness, accusing them because in admiring my style more than it deserved they acted inappropriately, and myself because in my search for an untimely glory from the first fruits of my studies I was perhaps becoming too harsh with my friends. Of course even the greatest mental blows are mitigated in time. I have now stopped complaining, and modesty has expelled sorrow; I am indeed ashamed to have complained so bitterly. Since no remains of that letter survive except the loving recollection, as Augustine says, let it indeed have per-

1. One of Petrarch's earliest friends whose father had moved his family to Avignon at the same time as Petrarch's father. Reared together in the papal court their friendship lasted their entire life.

ished so long as my pen remains. Meanwhile, as I return to my usual habit of writing, I wanted to let you know the reason for the interruption lest you be upset by my unusual silence. Farewell.

To the same correspondent, that the works of ugly people can be beautiful.

I am not unaware of your astonishment that I should appear to bear so badly the loss of a single letter. For it is not evidence of great talent to hope for glory from one's letters. The followers of true philosophy do not doubt that true glory proceeds not from words but from deeds. For me glory is not what is acclaimed by the rabble whose praise noble minds find almost disgusting, but rather that which flourishes and is nourished by the serious and pleasant recollection of virtuous works in the heart of distinguished men, and of which God and one's conscience are witnesses without theatrical applause or the support of the multitude. This alone is real glory because its roots are deeply implanted in firm soil, and it is not subject to chance. The kind that is based on the prattle of men is, to begin with, of short duration, is very easily overthrown, and then is forever tossed about by those very blasts that raised it on high, so that it eventually falls to destruction. Furthermore, even if it could last forever, the fact that it is sought only with the most vulgar and least noble means made it unattractive to the truly noble minds, being but the cheap wages of servile labor. Mulling over these things in my mind, I confess that I was astonished at myself and reproached myself severely. On the other hand as I recalled how pleasant the reading of that letter had been for me, I softened my self criticism and I acquitted my longing for it of all fault. I am not certain whether true or false, but I persuaded myself with a number of arguments that I had deplored its loss without any reference to a desire for windy praise, but rather because I had felt that it was useful to me. And what made me so confident was not any skill or talent, but that true Teacher of the arts and Master of skills who made me dare to hope that that letter composed by the hand of so great a sinner would not only be pleasing to readers (which would be of little account) but perhaps even beneficial. In it I had said many things against fortune, against the softness of men and especially my own; and with many exhortations to virtue and not a few attacks against our century and against the vices that now seem to rule over all the world, I had provided the letter with a double spur. So true was all of this that upon rereading it I scarcely thought it was my work and I felt far more respect for it than I usually do for my writings.

Nowhere is it written that Phidias and Apelles were handsome; nevertheless the remains of the outstanding works of one survive, and the fame of the other has come down to us. Therefore, despite so many intervening centuries, the remarkable talent of both artists lives on in different forms, of course, because of the different materials used. The work of the sculptor is of course more durable than that of the painter whence we learn about Apelles in books and about Phidias in marble. I believe the same about Parrhasius and Polyclitus and Zeuxis and Praxiteles and about all the others concerning whose personal beauty nothing is said because of the outstanding beauty of their works and their distinguished reputation. To move now from the ancients to new things, and from foreign artists to our own, I know two outstanding painters who were not handsome: Giotto, a Florentine citizen whose reputation is very great among the moderns, and Simone of Siena. I also know several sculptors but of lesser fame (since our age is truly mediocre in that art form). In any event I noticed with them something about which perhaps I shall say more in another place, namely that the works of single artists differ a great deal from their creators. If anyone were to seek the cause of such difference from them, they would answer, I think, not what Mallius the painter who, having been asked by his friends at a dinner why he had produced such ugly children when he had painted such beautiful forms, answered: "because I paint in the light and I conceive in the darkness." His answer is of course facetious. More truthful would be the answer of those who would say that both the appearance of a body and the possession of talent (which is the form of the soul from which these works which we praise and admire emerge as if it were a fountain) are gifts of almighty God, not of men, and they must be received not only naturally but gratefully, whether they are bestowed liberally or sparingly, since they are free and always exceed human merit. Nor ought any man question the reason why anything is done to a greater or lesser extent by Him whose will is the highest and inaccessible cause which no human efforts may grasp; for the more "man strives to achieve the great heights," the more "God will be exalted," and mortal insights are frustrated in the depths of His council.

I enter gladly upon this argument even though I could have bypassed it so that you would not marvel if I too were to write a beautiful letter though ugly myself; and if in that letter, to use the words of Gregory, I an ugly painter depicted a handsome man. Consequently its very form in which it outdid its sisters was the reason for its loss and my grief, so that I would understand why sometimes outstanding beauty is harmful not only to bodies but to writings and why one should seek moderation in all things. Thus my letter, which I had begotten but not yet adopted, caused me to grieve over its loss as if involved in some kind of funeral rites, and in my memory I celebrate its anniversary grieving that it had been removed so swiftly from my very presence and, so to speak, had been destroyed in its very cradle. My plaint in this matter is deeper because any hope of seeing another letter arise from the bones of that one, as if it were a Phoenix rising from its ashes, is very small. None of its remains have survived, for against my custom I had entrusted all of it to writing and none to memory. Therefore when I now search for it in my memory I do not find it nor do I recognize any imprint of the departed one. All I retain of it is the recollection that it was very pleasant for me to write it, even more pleasant when I read it, but most unpleasant when I think about it, just as happens when a bit of honey taken from a tasty honeycomb is brought close to one's lips and then suddenly drawn away. With the removal of the sweet taste only the bitter remembrance of the sweetness would remain. Being upset over these things, I stopped writing for a long time. I detested my waking hours and judged everything by what had happened in that single event. I finally realized that it was not wise to act like a sailor who leaves sailing for fear of a single shipwreck or a farmer who destroys his plow because of one bad year, and so I returned to my pen. But again I ask, what shall I do? Your letter has also perished and followed its companion. As far as my memory helps me, there were two things that I especially enjoyed in it. I rejoiced, as is the custom among men, that fortune had been more kind to you than usual, although I am aware that the joy that comes from believing in the propitiousness of fortune is frivolous, since fortune was never friendly to anyone without preparing even more intimate deceits, and she exalted no one except to prepare his fall from greater heights. But this is one of those human errors which are countless and which, to use the words of Cicero, "we seem to have sucked with the milk of our nurse," and which we all wish we could lay aside in our old age. I received greater joy from the end of your letter where you seem to be acquainted with the uncertainties of fortune and to have your mind ready for any eventuality. This is what I wished, this is what I hoped, this is what I sought from God, that He would provide me and my friends with strong minds that disdain the inconstancy of things. To request that we undergo no adversity in life is to no purpose; but that we should bear patiently whatever happens is indeed a worthy prayer. Indeed, unless I am mistaken, I saw your mind in your words, and I said to myself: "Now he is a man, he stands erect on the earth and contemplates the heavens." Farewell.

Fam. V, 18.

To the same correspondent, on his present condition.

I send you briefly news of my condition about which you inquired. Although among true philosophers there is only one good for men to pursue and not three, namely the one found in a mind which is well disposed by heaven and distinguished by the possession of noble habits (since those of the body and of fate are not truly to be considered goods but merely conveniences of small utility), because I believe that you wish to hear about all three goods, I shall do what you desire. In what condition my mind is, I neither know fully, nor is it for me to declare. As Augustine says, "Those shadows in which my possibilities are hidden from me are to be regretted since my mind questioning itself about its own powers believes that it should not easily trust in itself." As far as I am able to say, however, human distress holds me thus far either sitting or lying in the mire of the flesh and in the chains of my mortality. I seem, however (unless I falsely feign to myself to appear this way), to be most willing to emerge from this condition. But I am weighed down by my burdens, and the unyielding yoke of inveterate habit prevails over me. Who will free wretched me from its slavery unless that Lord who "frees the chained slaves and enlightens the blind"? Fate has waged a continuous war against me thus far. Knowing that communing produces discord I labor not to have anything in common with her in order to live in peace. Empires, kingdoms, wealth, honors, and other such things are hers and let her keep them. None of them appeals to me. Let her leave for me those things which are good for my soul if there are any left. These are not her gifts and I require that they be free of her control. Why does she rage, why does she threaten? For too long have I been her debtor. Let us total up all our accounts and let her take back what is hers. Too long have I watched over her depository. What is she weighing? There is no reason for delay or struggle; let her take back whatever it is and let her depart and never return. She has already taken a large share, and whatever little remains is a troublesome burden for shoulders striving for loftier things. Insofar as the body is concerned, I am not the one you left behind. The guest of my body, disagreeing sharply with it, wages an implacable struggle. Anxiety over this struggle has caused a change in my appearance which is premature, so that you would scarcely recognize me at our next meeting. This sort of thing, however, does not disturb me. As long as I was healthy I had believed with Domitian: "Nothing is more pleasing or shorter than beauty." I was indeed born for greater things than to be the slave of my body. "Seneca," you say, "said this." Who denies it? And I say it as will many after me and as perhaps many did before him, and whoever will have said it, provided he did not lie, said a distinguished and splendid thing. I said not only that, but I shall say what follows and in both things I know I am not lying; would that I were not being deceived. Let it not be said that because of the love of my body or the desire of this life I fear the day of death, for I have appropriated this other saying of a very deep truth for myself, namely, that what is called this life of ours is really a death. Farewell.

Fam. V, 19.

To Clement VI, the Roman Pontiff,[1] that he must flee the mob of doctors.

The announcement of your fever, most blessed father, brought trembling and horror to my limbs; nor shall I speak to flatter you or to say the same things as that man about whom the Satirist says: "He cries if he sees the tears of his friend," or elsewhere: "If he says, 'I feel hot,' he perspires." But rather do I resemble him who, as Cicero says, was concerned about the welfare of the Roman people in which he saw his own included. My welfare indeed and the welfare of many others depends upon your health. My trembling therefore is not pretense, for I am not concerned about the danger of another but about my own. All of us who depend upon you and hope in you may perhaps appear healthy when you are ill but we are not. Since speech deserves to be brief always but especially in those things which are transferred from a human mouth into divine ears, I shall say a few things to you now with humble mind and respect. I know that your bed is besieged by doctors; this is the first reason for my fear. They all disagree purposely, each considering it shameful to suggest nothing new or to follow upon the footsteps of another. "There is no doubt," as Pliny says elegantly, "that all of them strive for a reputation with some kind of novelty and they regularly use our souls as an item of trade . . . and it happens only in this profession that whoever professes to be a doctor is immediately believed although it is impossible to imagine a more dangerous falsehood. We do not, however, reflect about this because everyone is flattered by the pleasure of his hope for himself. Furthermore, there is no law to punish this dangerous ignorance, and no example of such a wrong being punished. They learn by submitting us to dangers and they experiment unto death itself. Only for the doctor is there maximum im-

1. Pope from 1342–1352. During his serious illness in 1352 Petrarch sent him advice through an intermediary suggesting that he beware of doctors. When the Pope expressed his wish to have the message in writing, Petrarch obliged and was thenceforth mistrusted and attacked by the medical profession of the day.

punity for murder." Most merciful father, look upon their multitude as if it were a battleline of enemies. Learn by remembering the epitaph of that unfortunate man who ordered only the following words to be inscribed on his tomb: "I perished because of a mob of doctors." In our own time the prophesy of Marcus Cato the elder seems to apply to our times best of all: "Whenever the Greeks transmit their literature and especially their doctors to us, we shall be corrupt in all things." Since nowadays we do not dare live without doctors (although without them innumerable nations survive perhaps better and more soundly, the Roman people living thus for over six hundred years in a flourishing manner according to Pliny), choose for yourself, however, only one who is outstanding not because of his eloquence but because of his knowledge and trustworthiness. For now, unmindful of their profession and daring to emerge from their own thickets, they seek the groves of poets and the fields of the rhetoricians, and as if called not to heal but to persuade, they dispute with great bellowing at the beds of the sick. And while their patients are dying, they knit the Hippocratic knots with the Ciceronian warp; they take pride in any unfortunate event; and they do not boast of the results of their cases but rather of the empty elegance of words. And, lest your doctors think that I have invented any of this today which I often ascribe to Pliny because he said many things about medicine and spoke more truth than anyone else about doctors, I have indeed followed him in most parts of this letter, and let the doctors therefore listen to him. "It is obvious," he says, "that whoever succeeds in speaking among them should instantly become the arbiter of our life and of our death." Because I have gone further than I intended with fear urging on my pen, I shall stop now by saying that you ought to avoid the doctor who is powerful not in his advice but in his eloquence, just as you would avoid a personal attacker, a murderer, or a poisoner. To such a doctor one can most justifiably say what that old man in the *Aulularia* of Plautus said to his loquacious cook: "Go away, you were brought here to work in your specialty and not to make speeches." For these reasons, take good care of yourself and have high hopes and a joyful mind which help in wonderful ways the health of the body if you wish to save yourself, all of us, and the church herself who is ill together with you.

12 March.

Fam. VI, 1.

To Cardinal Annibaldo, Tusculan Bishop,[1] against the greed of the Popes.

Maro called envy an unfortunate thing, and rightly, for what is more unfortunate than to be tormented both by one's own ills and by the good fortune of others? Indeed the remark a certain Publius jokingly directed against a certain Mutius who was renowned for his envy and his maliciousness was elegantly put; for as we read, when he saw him sadder than usual, he said: "Either something disagreeable has happened to Mutius or something good has happened to someone else." That is exactly how it is; the envious person blames his own problems on the good that has occurred to someone else, and, as Flaccus says: "He grows lean because of the wonderful things that are happening to someone else." To grow lean by the abundance and prosperity of others as much as by one's own hunger or starvation is certainly a great wretchedness. But I would not fear to assert that avarice is a more unfortunate vice than envy or than all of the other vices. Although envy frequently produces dejection, it is inactive, whereas avarice is both sad and active. Although pride always thinks something great about itself, it still takes pleasure in its false opinion; avarice always feels itself famished and wanting, nor is it ever deceived. That poetic verse is indeed very true: "The miser is always needy." For if he is a miser, he desires, which the very name of the vice indicates. As Seneca says, there is no doubt that "it is not the one who has too little but one who desires more who is truly poor." And in consequence it may be concluded that the scarcity of possession does not cause need, since nature is satisfied with a little; one who properly satisfies his needs is indeed wealthy, for he lacks nothing. But an unsatisfied desire for possession feels that it lacks whatever it desires;

1. A descendent of an illustrious family and very learned in canon law, he was appointed by Pope John XXII as Archbishop of Naples and later Cardinal of Tusculum, near Rome. He was also sent as emissary to seek to expedite peace between the kings of France and England. His taste for pomp and splendor had become almost legendary by the time of this letter.

yet because it desires all things, by its wishing it makes even unnecessary things necessary. Avarice thus makes one's property, which before had been minimal and easily manageable, an incurable and immense problem. Once again that saying which is so popular with philosophers is indeed true: what misers possess they lack just as much as what they do not possess; except that in my view the miser seems to lack more what he has than what he does not have. In the former case he undergoes nothing but constant anxiety and well-grounded fear, while in the latter he sometimes enjoys a brief though false joy which delights him and makes him preempt the desired good through false hope. Wrath is sometimes overcome by a certain wild and, as they say, inhuman sweetness; avarice is never assuaged, for it burns still more with success and, as the Satirist says: "The love of money increases as the money itself increases," and whoever does not have any, desires it less. Whoever does not have it has less longing for it. In one of his letters Annaeus Seneca attributes one cause to this phenomenon for which many causes can be found. He says: "money makes no one wealthy; in point of fact there is no one in whom money has not inspired a greater desire for it"; and he continues: "You ask what may be the cause of this? He who possesses more begins to be able to have still more." This argument considers the fact that those things that cannot be possessed are neither desired indiscriminately nor hoped for because the difficulty of possessing them is so great as to render them almost impossible. Unless he is insane no one wishes wings with which to fly, and only a mad person hopes for them. But for a journey many people wish for a horse, a vehicle, or a ship, and all wish for the soundness of their legs. If such soundness should be irreparably lost, all hope and desire cease. I often add another argument to Seneca's, which goes as follows. The poor man seeks land or money only as a result of natural need which is usually very small and modest, and he seeks them only for those uses for which they are intended. Concerning these Flaccus says: "Do you not know how much money is worth? Of what use is it? It purchases bread, vegetables, a sixth of wine and whatever else human nature cannot do without." Human desires are thus restricted to such narrow limits; the rich man, however, abounding in necessities *ad nauseam*, roves through luxuries with his insatiable mind and provides it with extensive land holdings which are not intended as fields to relieve wants but as kingdoms to support pride, and is wont to view large quantities of money not as money but as mountains of gold. In these things, of course, lies the endless kingdom of avarice. Nor indeed is there any way of selecting since there is no limit to growth. Whether such limit is stretched out to the outer boundaries of a region by trading and plundering, or whether all the gold were made level with the mountains, as the other Satirist says, he would find no reason to stop. For he can go on wishing until with the boundaries of his fields he will have crossed the seas and the mountains to the ends of the lands, until the quantity of gold exceeded the Alps and he touched the stars with his head. He would be to such a degree more powerful than Caesar that he would not only bound his empire with the ocean but it would extend across the ocean, and finally he would be wealthier than Midas so that not only what he touched but also what he saw would become gold. We have seen many men who, when after their search they had arrived somewhere they had never imagined, had left all of their hopes and their original desires far behind them, become mad over again as they entertained new desires and new hopes. If you would recall to them their former condition, they would become angry and behave as if modesty might be something plebian or as if they themselves had become better because they were more greedy. Their dissoluteness having increased with money and desire, they are ashamed of humble desires. What hope can you therefore entertain for these, either of expectation or of desire, except that there may be nothing left anywhere that would be desirable? For as long as something does remain to be desired, they will hope for it and desire it, and when they have achieved their closest hopes others will constantly appear. Therefore, there will be no end except death itself. It would not happen this way if they did not always think of things to be sought, but sometimes looked closely at themselves and the things they did seek. But those things that appear precious to seekers become meaningless to those who obtain them, thus making desire infinite because it has no boundaries in which such gains may be contained, and sadly avarice is never satisfied, for as the prophet Aggeus said: "He who collects wealth puts it in a perforated sack." I come now to the other plagues. Concerning the one which we call *accidia* (sloth), the same things may be said that were said about envy. However, gluttony and lust often enjoy their own delights in which they rejoice and receive fugitive joys. Avarice enjoys nothing except the most bitter anxieties, for while it covets those things that it desires it neither possesses them nor sees them once acquired except as punishment, whence its restlessness and agitation. Since this is the case, avarice can justly be called the most fatal of all the "sisters" and is called by the Apostle the root of all evils.

I am aware that you wonder why today I wish to linger beyond custom on what some call a troublesome philosophy. However, I do not speak to you any more than I do to almost all mortals who are of your kind, and especially to those upon whom that mighty passion, as I perceive, has placed its throne and as a victor implanted its standard. I become more indignant the more unlikely appears the reason for your being a victim of cupidity. For whom do you amass these piles of gold? A legitimate posterity is denied you. A frugal and moderate existence befits you best; what remains belongs to Christ's poor whom you do not fear to cheat and plunder while their lord observes from above and threatens vengeance. And you know not for whom your crime may be useful in the future because meanwhile it has become laborious and destructive and even fatal. Many excuse their conduct in the name of their children, and they cover the vice of their mind with a curtain of devotion. So do the expectant lioness and tigres become wilder after giving birth, and love of new offspring arouses even tamed beasts. For you there is no excuse and no covering up of your vice. You stand naked before the eyes of the entire world, and you are pointed to with the biting reproach of all the peoples. They say, "Behold the heralds of virtue who speak splendidly about eternal life and at length about the liberty of the mind, and are nevertheless beyond reason pledged to earthly things and are slaves of avarice." For in truth although his reference may be general, does David not seem to be referring especially to you when he says: "Only a breath is any human existence. A phantom only, man goes his way; like vapor only are his restless pursuits"? And to signify the madness of a pontifical avarice to come after many centuries, he said more specifically, "he heaps up his stores, and knows not who will use them." * These things are certainly said of you more than of any others, oh greedy Pontiffs. We both see and read of parents who pile up treasures for their children, although fortune often prevents their parental intentions when what was due for certain ones falls to others. However, the purpose of parents is well known. I ask you what indeed are your intentions? What do you accomplish? For whom do you pile up treasures except for the devil and for his angels, who anxiously observe you, count the days, and eagerly await your inheritance in order to erect on the threshhold of hell with the booty taken from the plundered poor the highly pleasing trophies bearing your name? You inquire in astonishment: why do you bring up those things today rather than earlier? Is is possible that until now we have not been avaricious or that avarice was not a vice? Or must I believe that you are now for the first time opening my eyes to something that you yourself had not seen before? I shall reply to your wonderment. I knew that you were all greedy and that avarice was a vice, and I knew that there is no one anywhere who did not know this and that this is not the first time I open my eyes to both things. But when the day before yesterday I came to visit you, and I saw your altars, indeed the altars of the Lord of virtues, loaded with silver and gold and jewels, and I stood there in amazement stricken by the maddening brilliance, I said to myself: "Here are the new arms of avarice, a new way of perishing. It is not sufficient for us to be avaricious, but we must also make Christ so and 'we call the gods and Jove himself to a share in the booty,' " as Virgil says. Indeed you appear to justify these riches, which have been

* Douay version

badly acquired by making the poverty-stricken Christ a participant in your plundering and theft, and setting him unwillingly amidst your gold. This is not the way to soothe divinities. Have you not read in Seneca that the gods were propitious when they were of clay? And yet the gods were certainly never propitious nor even can be, for how can one be propitious to others who is wretched within himself? I therefore do not like Seneca's opinion, only his words which I would like to apply to a happier subject. Surely Christ has always been propitious to the human race; but he was far more real when he was made of clay. Now that he is made of gold and jewelry he is angry and does not hear our prayers because of his most understandable indignation. He does not dislike gold, but those who are hungry for wealth and whose desire and search has no end. The earliest men openly confessed what they really felt: they sought riches in order to abound in them. You seek in order to adorn Christ: a pious work indeed if he wished to be adorned with the spoils of the unfortunate rather than with the virtue and devotion of the faithful, and if cupidity joined to lying were not more hateful to God. I have often noticed something similar among the rulers and the masters of the earth who seek books with great zeal, and search for them, seize them, buy them, not because they love letters, of which they are ignorant, but because of avarice. They seek rather to ornament their bedroom than their minds; their concern was not for knowledge but for reputation, not for the thoughts expressed in the books but for their prices. In truth they do not lack an excuse which is somewhat colored but nevertheless false. They say that they are considering their offspring and posterity, and that huge libraries are compiled, according to what they say, for those who are not yet born and are uncertain about the kind of a life they may have to lead. In truth, however, they act because of their own greed and ignorance. What is the purpose of your attempts at collecting so much? You will answer that it is to fill the temples of Christ with gold. But what do you say to the exclamation of Persius: "Oh souls bent toward earthly things and empty of celestial things, of what benefit is it to introduce your customs into the temples?" And so that you should not believe that

these words are for others, hear how he immediately afterwards calls you by name: "Explain, oh Pontiffs, what gold
does in the sanctuary?" Answer, oh Pontiffs, for he is speaking to you. Answer this one young man, all you elderly ones;
answer this one poet, all you theologians; answer this one
pagan, all you Christians. What can you say? What is gold
doing in the sanctuary? If you prefer not to answer a poet,
should you not at least answer the prophet who requires of
you not gold but other kinds of ornaments for the temples?
You read in Malachias: "The son honors the father and the
slave will fear his master; if therefore I am the father, where
is the honor owed me? And if I am the master, where is the
fear owed me: The Lord of hosts speaks." And to let you
know that he is speaking to you, he adds: "To you, oh priests,
who disdain my name, do I speak." I indicate this unless there
is someone who thinks that this complaint would apply more
worthily to other times than the present. As I said, I see the
multitude burning with avarice, and I confess that nothing can
serve as an excuse, for there is no excuse for sin; if the excuse
is valid, it is certainly not a sin. But the dearness of children
and the manifold needs and ignorance of the multitude miti-
gate the crime. Oh Pontiffs, I beg you ask yourselves: what
does this madness for possession avail one who lives among so
many certain riches, amidst so much knowledge of human and
divine things, and in a solitary and celibate life which prohibits
considering the morrow? You will probably refer me to those
well known words: "The Church possesses the gold." It is
good if it does possess it, but very bad if it is possessed by it.
The riches of men can please; men of riches definitely do not
please, those men who having completed their sleep find nothing left in their hands. Therefore the answer which Persius
gives to his own question is perhaps closer to the truth. When
he asked a second time: "What is gold doing in the sanctuary?" he concluded: "Indeed only this, the same thing that it has
done for Venus when dolls are consecrated to her by a young
girl." I beseech you, therefore, let the useless gold depart from
the temples and let it be contributed to the other temples of
the Lord, that is, for the use of men in want; let it become the
love of Christ rather than the ostentation of the century; and

let it not always serve idolatry under the pretext of devotion. Do you not know that avarice is the slave of idols? No people abound among so many idols, and to no one can it be said more fittingly: "Beware of idols." Believe me, oh Pontiffs, Christ could have had gold but refused it; he could have been rich when he lived among men, but he preferred poverty; he could have used vases from Corinth, but he preferred earthen jars. Do not, oh Pontiffs, seek frivolous excuses or increase the fodder of avarice in the name of Christ or as nourishment for your madness. Christ does not need your gold, nor does he take delight in your superstitions. He seeks rather the pious acts, the noble thoughts and the humble wishes of the pure and naked heart. What place is there for gold among such things? Do not, oh unhappy ones, be concerned about how proudly you sacrifice, how elegantly, how brilliantly, but rather how piously, how humbly, how chastely, how moderately. Sacrifice rather what the prophet king after having broken his chains sacrificed to his liberator, namely, the host of praise, and call upon the name of the Lord. Sacrifice, I say, the sacrifice of praise, the sacrifice of justice and hope not in gold but in the Lord. Hear the Psalmist, oh you who are hard of hearing, as he calls out day and night: "The contrite spirit is the sacrifice worthy of God." What need is there of gold in this? The need is for the spirit, but only if it is contrite; the need is for the heart, but contrite and humble. This is the sacrifice which is pleasing to God and achievable to man without digging under the earth. The need is for a humble and unstained mind, but there is no need for either pure or unprocessed gold. I know not what more to say and I fear wasting my words. But if, after the Prophet, you would not mind hearing Persius once again, see what that pagan said to his Pontiffs in those days: "Why do we not offer to the gods what great Messala's blear-eyed offspring could not offer even out of his great dish?" And in order not to leave any doubt as to what this offering to the gods was which those who were proud because of their birth and wealth, the blind sons of the wealthy, are not able to make, he subsequently defined it as "the ordered justice and right of the mind, and the holy recesses of the intellect, and a heart imbued with nobility and virtue." Striking words indeed and worthy to have been said about Christ himself. Farewell, and lend a fair ear to these faithful criticisms.

Fam. VI, 2.

To Giovanni Colonna of the Order of Preachers, that one must love not sects but the truth, and concerning the remarkable places in the city of Rome.

We used to walk widely by ourselves throughout Rome, and you are indeed acquainted with my peripatetic habit. I enjoy it very much and find it most appropriate to my nature and personal habits. Of the opinions of the Peripatetics certain ones please me, others hardly at all, for I do not love sects but the truth. Therefore I am at one time a Peripatetic, and at another a Stoic and sometimes an Academic. Often however I am none of these, especially at those times when something suspect appears in their writings which is opposed to our true and blessed faith. For we are permitted to love and approve philosophical schools if they are not opposed to the truth, and if they do not turn us from our primary purpose. When by chance they attempt this, whether it be Plato or Aristotle or Varro or Cicero, they are all to be disdained and trampled upon freely and steadily. Let no sharpness of disputation, no mildness of words, no authority of names affect us. They were men, and to the extent that they could accomplish this through human curiosity, they had both knowledge of things and clarity of expression and were fortunate in natural genius. But they were wretched in their lack of the knowledge of the highest and ineffable good, and like those who trust their own strength and do not desire the true light, they often stumbled over an immovable stone in the manner of the blind. Therefore let us admire their genius in such a way that we venerate the author of such genius; let us have compassion for their errors as we rejoice in our grace; and let us realize that without any merit we have been honored and have been raised above the greatest thinkers by Him who deemed worthy of revealing to children what he had hidden from the wise. In short let us philosophize in a manner which the very name of philosophy suggests, for the love of wisdom. Indeed the true wisdom of God is Christ so that in order to philosophize rightly we must first love and cherish Him. Let us be such in all things that above all things we may be Christians. Let us thus read philosophical, poetic, or historical writings so that the Gospel of Christ resounds always in the ear of our heart. With it alone are we sufficiently happy and learned; without it no matter how much we learn we become more ignorant and more wretched. To it all things must be referred as if to the loftiest stronghold of the truth; on it as if on a single immovable foundation of literary truths, human labor can safely build. And we must not restrain ourselves from diligently cultivating other teachings which are not contrary to it, for although the returns may be limited in so far as any real accomplishment is concerned, we shall appear to have added a considerable measure to the enjoyment of the mind and the cultivation of life. I have said these things at random as far as they seem to befit a letter of this type. Now I shall proceed.

We used to wander together in that great city which, though it appeared empty because of its vast size, had a huge population. And we would wander not only in the city itself but around it, and at each step there was present something which would excite our tongue and mind: here was the palace of Evander, there the shrine of Carmentis, here the cave of Cacus, there the famous she-wolf and the fig tree of Rumina with the more apt surname of Romulus, there the overpass of Remus, here the circus games and the rape of the Sabines, there the marsh of Capri and the place where Romulus vanished, here the conversations of Numa and Egeria, there the battle line of the *trigemini*. Here the conqueror of enemies who was in turn conquered by a thunderbolt, and the builder of the militia; there the architect king Ancus Martius; here the organizer of social classes, Priscus Tarquinius, lived; there the head of Servius glowed; there sitting in her carriage cruel Tullia crossed and made the street infamous because of her crime. Here however is *Via Sacra*, while over there are the Esquiline Hill, the Viminal, the Quirinal; here the Campus Celius, there the Campus Martius and the poppies cut down by the hand of the proud one. Here one can still see the wretched Lucretia lying upon her sword and the adulterer fleeing his death, as well as Brutus the defender of violated chastity. There is threatening Porcina and the Etruscan Army, and Mutius beset by his erring right hand, and the son of the tyran competing with liberty, and the Consul pursuing (to hell itself) the enemy expelled from the city; and the Sublician bridge broken behind the brave man, and Horatius swimming, and Cloelia returning on the Tiber. There may be seen the house of Publicola which was fruitlessly suspected; here Quintius used to plow until through his merit the plowman was made dictator; from here Serranus was led away to become Consul. This is the Janiculum, this is the Aventine, that is Monte Sacro, on which the angered plebians withdrew from the rulers; here the lustful tribunal of Appius stood, and Virginia was rescued from violence by the sword of her father, and there occurred a worthy end to the dissipation of the Decemvirs. From here Coriolanus, who was perhaps about to triumph with his arms, departed after having been conquered by the devotion of his supporters. This is the rock that Manlius defended and then fell from; here Camillus repelled the Gauls as they gaped at the unexpected gold and taught the despairing citizens how to recover a lost fatherland with a sword and not with gold. Here armed Curtius descended; there was found underground the head of a man with an immovable face which was viewed as a prediction of the highest and firmest form of empire. There a deceitful Virgin fell under arms after having been deceived by her own deceits; here is the Tarpeian fortress, and the wealth of the Roman people collected throughout the world; here is the silver goose; there is Janus the guardian of arms; here is the temple of Jupiter Feretrius; this was the temple of Jupiter, this was the home of all the triumphs; here Perses was brought, from here Hannibal was driven away, here Jugurtha was destroyed as some believe, others indeed believe that he was slain in prison. Here Caesar triumphed, here he perished. In this temple Augustus viewed the prostrate kings and the whole world at his feet; here is the arch of Pompey, here is the portico, here is the Cimbrian arch of Marius. There is Trajan's Column where he alone of all the emperors, according to Eusebius, is buried inside the city; here is his bridge which eventually assumed the name of St. Peter, and Hadrian's fortress, under which he also lies buried and which they call Castel Sant'Angelo. This is that massive rock surmounted by two bronze lions which was sacred to the deified emperors, and on whose summit, rumor has it, rest the bones of Julius Caesar. This is the shrine to the goddess Tellure, this is the temple of Fortune, this is the temple of Peace, which was rightly destroyed at the arrival of the King of Peace; this is the work of Agrippa taken from the false gods to be dedicated to the mother of the true God. Here is where it snowed on the fifth of August; from here a stream of oil flowed into the Tiber; from here, according to tradition, the old Augustus, following the Sibyl's advice, saw the Christ child. This is the insolence of Nero and his raging extravagance in the buildings he raised; there is the house of Augustus, on Via Flaminia, where some maintain is the tomb of the Emperor himself; this is the Column of Antoninus; this is the palace of Appius; this is the Septizonium of Severus Afrus which you call the temple of the sun but whose name I find in the form I use written in history. On these stones still survives after so many centuries the great rivalry in talent and skill between Praxiteles and Phidias; here Christ appeared to his fleeing Vicar; here Peter was crucified; there Paul was beheaded; here Lawrence was burned, who after being buried here, was succeeded by Stephan. Here John scorned the burning oil; there Agnes after her death came back to life and forbade her kin to weep; here Sylvester hid; there Constantine got rid of his leprosy; there Calixtus mounted his glorious bier. But where shall I end? Can I really describe everything in this short letter? Indeed, if I could, it would not be proper; you know all these things not because you are a Roman citizen but because since your youth you have been intensely curious especially about such information. For today who are more ignorant about Roman affairs than the Roman citizens? Sadly do I say that nowhere is Rome less known than in Rome. I do not deplore only the ignorance involved (although what is worse than ignorance?) but the disappearance and exile of many virtues. For who can doubt that Rome would rise again instantly if she began to know herself? But this is a complaint to be dealt with at another time.

We used to stop often at the baths of Diocletian after the weariness which ceaseless walking about that city had produced in us, and indeed we would often ascend to the roof of that building, once a home, because only here could we enjoy the healthy air, the unimpeded view, silence and desired solitude. There we did not discuss business, household problems or public affairs of which we had previously sufficiently unburdened ourselves. And as in our travels through the remains of a broken city, there too, as we sat, the remnants of the ruins lay before our eyes. What else may be said? Our conversation was concerned largely with history which we seemed to have divided among us, I being more expert, it seemed, in the ancient, by which we meant the time before the Roman rulers celebrated and venerated the name of Christ, and you in recent times, by which we meant the time from then to the present. We also spoke much about that part of philosophy which deals with morals, whence it gets its name; and sometimes indeed we discussed the arts and their authors and rules. Thus once when we had entered into this latter subject you asked me to explain clearly where I thought the liberal arts and the mechanical arts had their beginning because you had from time to time heard me talk on the subject. I responded quite simply because the hour, the absence of trivial cares, and the very place encouraged me to go into the subject at some length, and because your attentiveness suggested that the subject was indeed pleasing to you. I assured you, however, that I would say nothing new, nothing that was really mine, and yet nothing that was basically borrowed, for from whatever source we learn anything it is ours unless by chance forgetfulness takes it from us. You request now that what I said that day I repeat and commit to a letter. I confess that I did say many things which I can only repeat with different words. Give me back that place, that idle mood, that day, that attention of yours, that particular vein of my talent and I could do what I did then. But all things are changed: the place is not present, the day has passed, the idle mood is gone, and instead of your face I look upon silent words, my spirit is impeded by the din of the business matters I have left behind, matters which until recently roared in my ears, although I fled as soon as I could in order to answer you more freely. I shall, however, obey as best I can. I could send you to some ancient and modern writers from whom you can learn what you seek; but you made provisions for me not to do so when you asked that I say whatever I have to say on the subject in my own words because, as you observed, everything I say appears most pleasing and clear to you. I thank you for this opinion whether it is really true or whether you do it by way of stimulating my mind. Here is then what I said at that time, perhaps with the words of others but certainly the same thoughts. But really, what are we doing? The subject is clearly not a small one, this letter is already too long, and we have not yet started, though the end of this day is at hand. Would it not be a good idea for me to give some rest to my fingers and to your eyes? Let us put off what remains until another day; let us divide the labor and the letter, and let us not cover two very different matters in the same letter. But what do I have in mind? What am I promising you when I say another letter tomorrow? This is neither the work of a single day nor a task for letters, it requires a book which I shall undertake (if I am not impeded and frustrated by major cares) when fortune returns me to my solitude. Only there and not elsewhere am I myself; there lies my pen which at present rebels everywhere I go and refuses my orders because I am preoccupied with burdensome matters. Thus, while it is constantly busy when I have plenty of leisure, it prefers to have leisure when I have much to do, and almost like a wicked and insolent servant, it seems to convert the fervor of the master into its own desire for rest. However, as soon as I get back home I shall compel it to take on its duties and I shall write about what you seek in a separate book, indicating what has been written by others and what are my own ideas. Indeed just as I am accustomed to writing these friendly letters almost as amusement in the very midst of conversations and bustle, in the same way I have need of solitary quiet and pleasant leisure and great and uninterrupted silence in order to write books. Farewell.

30 November, in transit.

Fam. VI, 3.

To the same correspondent, consolation against certain difficulties of life.

Though we agree fully on almost everything, there is one basic disagreement between us, and that is that you are too querulous, too self indulgent in lamenting your lot, too complaining about your affairs, excessively involved in excusing yourself and accusing fortune, and finally too soft in tolerating the human condition because you are yourself a man. I must confess that the beginning of your letter moved me to tears; for why should I consider hiding my own feelings, and where I demand firmness from you why disguise my own softness? Where I order you to be happy, I cannot deny that I myself am sad. But I flatter myself in this; tears shed for the misfortunes of others are more noble than those shed for ourselves—even though all things being common to us nothing can be said about one's own situation that does not apply to another's, for what is another's is ours. This is true not only in close friendships but even in the general society of men, as the Satirist said in teaching that no evil is foreign to the good man and that cares are given to human beings for an indication of their natural compassion. This the Comic had said somewhat earlier: "I am a man; I consider nothing human alien to me." I do not deny the truth of this, yet in this public duty of sharing one's humanity there are degrees whereby from the widest concept of humanity, so to speak, we narrow down the scope to kindred and friends, and universal love of all is gradually compressed into a certain individual love and kindness toward the few. Therefore, why should I once more hide from you what follows? Just as the beginning of your letter moved me to tears, the ending of the same letter moved me to laughter. "But those are opposites," you say. I know, but sometimes both laughter and tears do emerge from a single source. No less sorrowful was Democritus, perhaps, who "used to exercise his lungs with a perpetual laughter," as he says, than Diogenes who was continuously wet with teardrops. Nor was Hannibal more happy in the misfortunes which befell his fatherland when he laughed over them, than the people who mourned. On the other hand, if we are to believe Lucan, Caesar was no sadder when he wept over the death of his son-in-law than the army which applauded him. But let us return to you. The first part of your letter pointed out how huge an accumulation of many, indeed almost all, tribulations had fallen upon you, and it did so in a style which was both wretched and distinguished. Upon reading your account I could not restrain my tears and I shed still others when I saw what you called the stains caused by your own tears. I do not know why we have greater compassion for the man who laments his misfortunes manfully than for one who does so effeminately. I continued to read attentively with my mind and eyes and felt charmed by the very sweetness of the style as I read, even though the letter was quite long. However, having read the rest of the letter with moist eyes waiting to discover what it was that you had endured about which you very greatly complained and grieved, I suddenly found your explanation of the entire matter in three or four words near the end of your letter. You were in Tivoli, you explained, an old, gouty, poor man and among the many ills you had to bear the worst was that you had lost all hope of ever seeing me again. Restrained by illness, you say, you cannot move from where you are or dare to call your friend to come to you from so great a distance caught as he is in the burdens of his infinite duties well known to you. This is the ending that you give to your tearful letter. Here, I must confess, is where I laughed. Someone might say. "But indeed do these things seem insignificant or unimportant to you?" Certainly not, but they are so ordinary and so common that it is scarcely discourteous but truly laughable that a man should be either indigent or astonished at such discomforts.

To start from the beginning, what man ever lived who did not grow old by living? We read that our earliest fathers lived for many centuries but do we not also read that they grew old? But I disregard those who lived at the beginning of time who were brought forth to the light, as it were, in the childhood of time itself as if confirming their vigor and durability which enabled them to reach almost the thousandth year of life, and yet grew old, even though more slowly. I repeat that I am disregarding these about whose age there usually is much disagreement among great thinkers and who are unrelated to our present purpose. So I turn to those whose age is both less extraordinary and more suitable to our purpose. Abraham grew old, Isaac also, and so did Jacob. Concerning the first one it is written: "And Abraham was an old man and had seen many years," and later: "failing he died in a ripe old age and advanced in age and in the fullness of days." About the second it is written: "And Isaac grew old and his sight grew weak and he could not see," and later: "He died an old man and in the fullness of his days he was gathered to his kinsmen." Concerning the third it is written: "The eyes of Israel grew weak because of his very old age and they could not see clearly." You can hear for yourself that it was not only old age but also the fading away of and failure of the eyes. Moses was perhaps stronger about whom when he died after one hundred and twenty years of life we read: "His eyes did not grow weak nor did his teeth fall out." Did he nevertheless not grow old because he happened to be a stronger old man? His successor Joshua, an outstanding soldier who killed so many kings and scattered so many people, was not able to resist old age but rather heard the Lord say to him: "You have grown old and are an old man": and he himself said to the assembled people: "I have grown old and am at an advanced age." That is the man whom, because of his incomparable faith, God obeyed and instructed the sun and the moon to be still, and they were. But was he able to hold back even a single day of his swift life or hasten it or slow down uncoming old age? What shall I say about King David? Is it not true that he also "grew old, and reached a ripe old age, and however much he covered himself with clothing he could not keep warm?" He who had been so inflamed with the love of God and men became so cool in his brief old age that he lay with a maiden for protection against the cold. And he said concerning himself: "I was a young man," and immediately added; "for I have grown old." You may find perhaps someone whose days you envy but no one enjoying perpetual youth. Everything that has risen must of necessity either set immaturely or set in maturity by growing old.

In secular histories you will find no like spans of human life and if you should by chance come across one, you may be sure it was intended to be taken humorously rather than historically. Indeed the history of distinguished deeds previous to Ninus, king of the Assyrians, who seemed to be a contemporary of Abraham, as Macrobius likes to point out, is prior to the time of the Greeks. Thus all the historians who go back in their writings to very early times begin with Ninus, and only after many ages have we begun to gather examples from our own ancestors. Some think that this should not appear too surprising while other argue, as I have pointed out, that with the aging of the world life becomes shorter and bodies become more fragile. Among foreign people indeed, to touch briefly upon the most famous example, Nestor lived a very long time, having survived, according to what is written, even unto the third age of men, although Seneca limits his age to ninety-nine years while Ovid extends it to beyond two hundred, which is more in accord with Cicero and Homer. Hiero of Syracuse also lived a long time as did Masinissa, king of the Numidians, the first seeing his ninetieth year, the other surpassing it. Highly praised was the old age of Solon and of Sophocles: the first grew old without interrupting his studies and constantly learning something more; the second being close to death wrote a very noble tragedy at an age when those who do reach it are scarcely in full possession of their mental faculties. Isocrates, the orator, after he had published his outstanding work almost at the same age, that is ninety-four, survived five more years and was able to enjoy the late pleasure of the success of his work. I have read not only about Homer's old age but about his blindness; whether old age or some other cause lay behind his blindness I do not know if you have discovered in your readings, but I have not found the answer. Nevertheless, what kind and how pleasant must we consider Homer's old age accompanied and made richer as it was by all his pleasant cares and duties? What remains of these cares after thousands of years affects and fills me with so much sweetness (and I believe the same must happen to others) that often, unmindful of my own cares and forgetting my present ills, I find complete rest in recalling that blind old man. Carneades achieved a peaceful old age at ninety, Xenophanes Calophonius at past one hundred, Democritus and Cleanthes at ninety-nine, Gorgias Leontinus at one hundred and seven. Chryssipus undertook a work of astonishing brilliance in his thirtieth year and left it behind when he died in his eightieth. At the same age Simonides recalls that he entered a poetry contest. We read that Socrates reached an advanced age and would have lived longer if the poisoned cup had not prevented it. His outstanding student, Plato, having completed his eighty-first year, died on the very same day as that of his birth, and in those studies in which he had for a long time exercised his mind he achieved the proper limit of a human and perfect life as established by himself. Indeed many illustrious philosophers achieve the same limit, among them Dionysius Heracleontes, Diogenes the Cynic, Eratosthenes, Xenocrates the Platonist and the prince of all, as we have said, Plato himself. His own student Aristotle did not go beyond his sixty-third year, a number which is dangerous and they say frightful for the human species in that it brings either death or extraordinary calamity. Why this is so, some try to rationalize, others allude only to personal observation of long experience. Which of the two arguments is the more forceful, let those decide who present them. If they relate truth, our own Cicero was not able to cross this barrier of human life not because of old age but because of the wicked command of cruel Anthony. And since we have reached our own Romans by way of Cicero, we might recall how venerable was the old age of Numa Pompilius the Roman king, but even more venerable that of Cato, of Camillus, of the Fabii, of Metellus, of Valerius Corvinus, almost all of whom achieved the same age, one hundred years, as did the blind Appius from whose blindness all the citizens of the entire republic expected leadership. Augustus grew old in a most glorious fashion, Pompey in a more unfortunate one; but we are not here talking about fortune but about age. Certainly Augustus himself, the greatest and most powerful of all monarchs, after the founding of the empire, as some like to believe, and after having governed it for a long time in the greatest peace, which no one denies, passed away peacefully in the seventy-sixth year of his life among the many tears of the Romans and in the embrace of his most chaste wife. Augustine achieved the same age so that there is a great similarity both in their names and in the period of their life. Jerome, on the other hand, having reached his ninetieth year lived longer; Origen, and also Ennius the poet, reached seventy; Bernard sixty-three; concerning Ambrose and Gregory I am not similarly informed. Without a doubt, however, they all achieved a ripe old age since God Himself who is the fountain of life watched over them to avoid letting such men whose life was to be of such benefit to the Church not live long enough. Asinius Pollio reached the eightieth year; Marcus Varro lived beyond the space of a single century leading a rich life and writing. Seneca has spoken a great deal about his old age, although an old man, and would have lived even longer were it not for his mad disciple who forbade it.

I now ask your indulgence, dear father, to permit me to interpolate here a subject which is much occupying my mind, and to add to the illustrious examples of so many glorious elders a unique example which though indeed humble and recent is truly noble and which it pleases me much to recall with veneration, something I would not dare do if I were addressing anyone but you. My paternal great grandfather was a very holy man and of considerable ability to the extent one may be so without cultivating letters, so much so that not only did his acquaintances consult him about family matters, about business affairs, about legal affairs, and about the nuptials of their children, but also officials about affairs of state (as we learn about Appius Caecus), and even men of letters both at home and abroad consulted him about matters of high, even philosophical, import. All marveled at his answers, the fairness of judgment and the sharpness of his mind. His name was Gattius and he was endowed with a character and a devotion that lacked only a strong promoter in order for his memory to be consecrated. Even after I had passed adolescence there were many who continued to speak about the wonder of that man, but I prefer to pass over these and would not even have mentioned him in order not to bother you with excessive examples. In any event, that man after having lived a harmless and happy life, as I heard our elders relate, in the one hundred and fourth year of life, also, like Plato, on his birthday, but older than Plato by twenty-three years, and furthermore in the same room in which he was born, on the hour which he had predicted long before to many friends as the hour of his passing away, amidst his sons and grandchildren, with no suffering either of body or mind, and speaking of nothing except God and goodness, simply dozed off, as it were, while he spoke. And they say that among his very last words were those of David: "As soon as I lie down, I fall peacefully asleep," and having scarcely uttered these words, he became silent and fell asleep peacefully. I thank you, dearest father, that you have allowed me to recall the memory of my great grandfather, and to include his name in this short letter to you, because I do not know any worthier place in which he deserved to be recalled than among distinguished elders.

But what am I doing? A short letter of consolation has turned into a long history. However, you will grant me your indulgence if you know with how great a pleasure I have dwelled upon these excellent and selected elders to whom I wish that you at this moment, and myself not too much later, should be added. Although we may be dissimilar to them in other qualities, we are at least similar to them in equanimity. Do not believe that I have completely strayed from my subject, for the question is whether one should complain about becoming an old man when one recalls that such outstanding men became old? Indeed, who will not share with even greater joy the fate of these most fortunate men, and accept old age in common with such men? Who indeed of all these men lived for a long time and did not grow old? Is there anyone whose long life we read about who did not end up with old age? But we, with a contrary desire and battling with ourselves, wish to live a long time, indeed always, never growing old and never dying. I know what you will answer: that you were not ignorant of all these things but that you were complaining about growing old before your time. All who are growing old have that common complaint; and Numa Pompilius, whom I mentioned above, was grey haired at a very early age, as was the poet Virgil; all who live in these times have the same complaint. I myself am wont not so much to complain as to be astonished because I had grey hair considerably before my twenty-fifth year; although I won't forget how once my father, in other respects neither healthier nor stronger than I, having looked in the mirror and having seen on his head perchance one hair becoming truly white rather than a pale grey, although being older than fifty, gave vent to his amazement and to his complaints by upsetting not only the entire family but the entire neighborhood. This is what pains our times; this is what our youth bewails: that in a short time ways of living and of growing old have changed a great deal. While I perhaps agree with the latter assertion, I deny the first: one does age more quickly than usual. It may be that that is not true generally; but I affirm without hesitation that one does indeed acquire white hair more quickly than usual, whether the cause lies in an earlier aging or in the large number of worries that one has today. There is little doubt that where our ancestors were involved in more useful cares we are involved in too many cares. And there is nothing which causes the flower of youth to wither more rapidly than the anxiety of cares and a troubled mind. Otherwise the ways of living, unless misfortune or guilt cuts them short, continue to remain almost nearly the same, as is stated in the *Psalms*. But since your religious modesty makes me certain that you do not complain about your hairs which you indeed gladly accept, though they may be untimely, I doubt not that you would enjoy them if as Claudian has his Stilican say, "White hair comes in haste making appearances venerable." I am therefore sure that you complain about other inconveniences of old age which some writers consider in great numbers, but which Tullius limits to four as follows: the diminution of strength, a weakening in the ability to apply oneself, less desire for pleasures, and approaching death. I can indeed say many things here to offer you consolation, except that it would be rash to review what Tullius has treated formally. You have his book *On Old Age* which contains a section on Cato the elder. Once you have read this you will find that nothing more need be added, I feel, to make old age less troublesome and even more pleasing to you. As for old age coming too rapidly and ahead of time, I shall say only this: abiding infirmity of the body is present there too is our old age (according to the most learned men), thus wherever an abiding infirmity of the body is present there too is our old age. For just as at the end of life is death, so a lingering weakness whenever it befalls is the end of a blooming and healthy youth. Therefore the term old age must be applied either to the end of life, or to the end of the fuller life, regardless of the stage in which it occurs, we have fulfilled the time granted us and old age is the legitimate consequence.

What, think you, should I say about poverty? Who is not poor except for someone who desires nothing? Those who seem extremely wealthy are really poorer than others because they need more things and poverty is nothing else but the need of necessary things. But those who are seemingly wealthy, driven from the truth by false opinions, create for themselves the necessities which appear merely excessive to those who are not quite so mad, and even superfluous to the sane, and in truth to the learned appear harmful even and deserving to be fled from at any cost. The wealthy are therefore the poorest of all, needing and excitably pursuing countless things, even twisting their need into desire. I am not unaware of their response to such charges: namely, that poverty is despised with more difficulty in fact than in word. I do not disagree; I confess it is a difficult thing, but, good grief, how safe, how secure, how convenient, how free and finally how pleasant it would be if we could be induced to love poverty in our mind! But let us stop praising poverty lest we be justifiably ridiculed by the people. They say (and I wish they were lying) that we praise poverty but love wealth. How common it is to find men who, having much praised poverty, flee from it with all their might? Cupidity will be overcome and eternally rejected by the minds of men, or rather completely destroyed, only when poverty has as many lovers as it has praisers. However, it would have many more lovers if the good it does along with the peace and happiness it brings were more widely known. Thus far, however, it remains as it was in the age of Lucan, a gift of God except for rare cases not yet understood by mortals. Among illustrations the exceptions are Valerius, Cincinnatus, Curius, Fabricus, Regulus, examples which touch minds blinded by avarice and cupidity only so long as the time it takes to read or hear about them, and then only superficially. But much more notable are our most holy elders who traveled around the world introducing truth into the hearts of men, very happy in hunger and nakedness, triumphant in overcoming and treading upon the necessities of life, and with whose bare feet the earth was not worthy to be tread. Venture to follow their examples yourself, "Dare, oh stranger, to condemn wealth." It was not accidentally nor without due consideration that he said: "Dare do so." More great men have disdained life and shed their blood and risked their souls than have despised riches. Dare, therefore, you too, oh stranger who do not have a permanent abode here; lay aside your burden, which is unfit for lovers of liberty, and you will arrive in your fatherland the more safely the more freely you advance. Dare, I say, to despise wealth and (to quote what follows), "Mold yourself also in the image of God." Who will hesitate to despise wealth and power when he recalls, to mention but a few examples, the sacred and humble poverty of Christ, especially if such recollection is supplemented by the awareness of how many calamities or hazards those riches which are so greatly desired and sought in every way bring with them? Certainly Solomon himself, who was considered a wise man by the Hebrews (as was Lycurgus among Spartans, Solon among the Athenians, Cato or Lelius among our Romans), sought neither wealth nor poverty from God since he considered them causes of pride and despair. What then is the answer? He said, "Grant only what is necessary for sustaining life." Our apostle followed him when he said: "Let us be satisfied with the possession of nourishment and a roof." Yet we not only seek riches, but we desire most what is harmful among them, namely extravagance and excess. I ask you, what is there in avarice that is so delightful? Certainly nothing more than the toil of seeking and the fear of preserving; nothing more, I say, than fearing catastrophies, fires, theft, robbers from within and without, and finally mice and moths; in addition, being always deeply concerned, sad, in constant state of anxiety, and burying the heart itself, though still alive, in gold, as it is written: "Your heart is where your treasure is." It is certainly true that "guarding great wealth is indeed a wretched thing!" But these things happen to us unknowingly; as Flaccus asks, "What worth does money have; what good does it serve?" To those who believe in wealth, a modest amount of it will appear like unbearable poverty. There may exist without any interference by fortune the two grades of wealth described by Seneca: "To possess what is necessary, to have what is sufficient." Let one approach the third step which is possessing in abundance, and let the fourth be added which is possession of a great deal: then one will think that nothing has been achieved until one arrives panting and raging to the possession of what is excessive. Then unless possessions begin to do harm, unless they cause unhappiness, hardship, and perhaps an early death, they are not viewed as riches. But to repeat, what am I doing in this search to help you find a defense against poverty? Whatever anyone has been able to say or to think about this matter is already known to you. There is one thing in my mind, however, besides these many well known ones, which I shall not withhold from you: namely, that just as lightening the burdens of a heavy body is necessary, so is poverty necessary for you. Indeed, though I hear that certain of your followers are turning their back upon poverty without even a quibble, you did, nonetheless, take the vow of poverty whether openly or silently. It is good that you used to flee it, that it pursued you, and that now the need of facing your vows has caught up with you, and has seized you so that you are compelled to satisfy what you owe. You are the servant of Christ; you know what pleases him. And you know what you promised him. Be silent and have patience; I cannot listen to you with objectivity. You lament about poverty to me as if you did not know that you had entered into this life naked and will leave it naked; and also as if you had professed not the poverty of Christ but the riches of Croesus. Believe me, dear father, poverty was often used to the welfare of many people, it was never useless to anyone, except to those who made it unbearable through their impatience and laments. For you, indeed, it is not useless but necessary and healthful, so that without it you will not be able either to expect salvation or to keep your agreement with your Creator. These are the points I wished to mention regarding a noble and reasonable poverty. The type which is inconvenient and lowly and is called "foul indigence" by the poet, does not affect you, thanks be to God, a type which requires the power of greater eloquence to justify.

Let us now turn to remedies for the gout. Oh, if only anyone touched by that disease were by chance to cast his eyes upon this part of this letter, what hope do you think he might have of receiving any lotion, powder, or soothing counsel? Let him cease hoping for such things from me. I wish to spare him any toil, for if he hopes for this by reading what I write let him read no further. Indeed such remedies are despaired of by most of the more learned physicians. If you consult the others, you will learn that men of wealth need not despair at all, whereas the poor ones can hope for nothing, since very often this plague inhabits the homes of the wealthy. And if you should wish to listen to these men they will enable you to yell constantly, entirely bound up in the sufferings of present pain and the hope of future recovery, and to groan constantly besmeared with the oil of sadness and soaked with ointments. I instead would prefer that you suffered while you were dry, unbound, and unrestrained, and by dieting, exercising, and work make your weak body become strong against a new enemy. In such matters one can hope for nothing beyond words from doctors. If there is any form of help against the gout, it is to be sought entirely in poverty, or if this is difficult, from temperance of the mind. Poverty is an excellent medication against the gout, whether it is created through necessity or through choice; this latter path is called thriftiness which one defines as voluntary poverty. Concerning these things, however, I seem to have said enough in a previous letter to you when news of your condition had not yet reached me except for your problems with the gout. I should add one thing however which I was not aware of at that time: believe me it was divine permission that coupled poverty with the gout so that, just as a remedy for poison is taken from poisonous animals, and just as the bees prepare the sweetest honey out of certain very bitter herbs, in the same manner you can produce remedies for your ills from no other source than those very ills. But enough about poverty and the remedies that it provides. Concerning the moderation and the patience of the mind a longer discourse is necessary in order to provide it with authoritative reasons and examples. Here Marius and Atilius and indeed all the Roman legions come to mind for there has been no people equal to them in this kind of glory. Here also come to mind, to take another type of people, Possidonius, Anaxarchus and (though a more lowly, nevertheless I believe, a more effective example) the African slave, avenger of his master, spoken of by Titus Livy, who, though mangled by tortures, not only refused to groan, but because of his joy in overcoming his pain, gave an outward appearance of almost laughing. Such examples are almost infinite and with them one would fill not only a letter but a book. Nevertheless, as I have said, modesty and restrained silence appear best when dealing with Cicero. I have heard several notable men admitting that the second book of his *Tusculan Disputations*, which I often found helpful in my sorrows, has been of similar aid to them. I would like you to become familiar with it and have it at hand whenever you feel the pain of gout approaching with its usual symptoms. Yet for a learned and religious man in dealing with all the hardships and griefs which cannot be avoided in this mortal life it is an admittedly much sweeter, more pleasant, and more worthy medicine to recall the hardships and griefs that Christ suffered for us. Likewise it is appropriate to recall the wounds with which our wounds were healed, and that we were snatched from the danger of an eternal death; to recall the nails and the spear and the most precious blood in which our filth was cleansed as in a bath and through which we were reborn and were mildly warned to spurn earthly burdens with a lofty mind and to fear nothing except the punishment of eternal damnation with its infinite sufferings. It would be useful further to recall not only Christ for whom all things were auspicious and simple because of his divinity, incomparable glory, and unapproachable power, but also the shining host of those who are called martyrs, many, like ourselves, mortal men, not only strong men, but what is still more miraculous, often even tiny women and maidens who, insipred by the divine spirit, endured those sufferings in comparison with which whatever you suffer can be called peace and comfort. But because these examples are well known and very familiar to you as part of the core of knowledge appropriate to your calling, lingering no longer, I shall hasten to less well known matters.

There is a type of remedy which perhaps you have not thought about and which occurred to me suddenly as I read your letter and caused me to laugh, as I have pointed out. However I do not want you to be angry with me because I jest at your ills as I am accustomed to do with mine. We know that strong and learned men were accustomed to jest not only about their ills but about death, witness Prince Vespasian and the philosopher Socrates. Allow me therefore to do the same regarding the pains in your feet although my jest is not facetious but touches upon the truth. Examine, dear father, your journeys since your youth and your propensity not to stay still; you will see that like the bridle for the untamed horse a gout was required for you. Perhaps it ought to be required for me too so that I might now learn to stay in one place and settle down. Without doubt, however, it was required for you more than anyone else I know. You would, if you could, have gone beyond the boundaries of the inhabited world; you would have crossed the ocean; you would have gone to the antipodes, and your reason would not have helped you seek a halt though it is powerful in other matters. What more need I say? You were able to stay still only with the help of the gout; it alone provided a halt for you and caused you to stop. What can you say? You will obey whether you want to or not. However, do not consider it an injustice: nothing more appropriate ever happened to anyone, nor anything more suitable. The master of a ship controls its movement either by a line or an anchor, and an anchor was cast for you near the land from which you first sailed for the deep. Your fate allowed you a rambling and laborious youth. Nor did you appear to let up with old age. You slowed down only with the help of the gout. The careful herdsman collects his cattle where there is a possibility of rest and grazing once all possible escapes have been closed off. Recognize the prudence of your Herdsman: he has restricted you to very pleasant and fertile pastures, not in Persia, or Arabia or Egypt, where you could wander as if in your own suburbs, but in your own homeland with the full submission of your limbs, and after countless trips which, were it up to you, would never have ended. You enjoyed the culmination of heavenly grace when He enclosed you not in Rome, a place which honors you for your own titles and for those of your family but is not propitious for your rest, but rather he located you not far from or beyond the sight of your beloved city. What more need be said? The Tiber was assigned for the leisure of your old age, and He provided against any possibility of flight. You grieve where you should rather render thanks to the Lord who, having snatched you from so many earthly and maritime dangers and so many lengthy byways, wished to locate you finally in this land, as Maro says, where there is no lack of food either for the soul or for the body; where your books, your fervor, your abilities and the very kind of air and water and the pleasantness of the beautiful landscape can charm both the harsh and the rustic mind; where the sweet sight of your fatherland is always present as well as the moderate proximity of our friends; and where boredom and disgust exist no longer, conditions which the noise of a huge city or perhaps the perpetual conversation of so many acquaintances could produce in you. Enjoy the good things you possess, therefore, joyfully, calmly, and peacefully. You are better off than you think; you would be unable to choose a more convenient place in the entire world than the one which your fate has offered you. But you will press the argument and you will say, "Why not without these illnesses of the body?" You ask me to answer what I feel: your mind needs fetters. I beg you to accept this not as something offensive but as praiseworthy; for wherever there is more fertile ground, there we find an abundance of things whose growth must be checked and rooted out so that the crop will grow more freely; and often, where you find a more noble and more powerful horse, there will you find a wilder horse which needs much stronger chains. You would now be, as I surmise, in some other corner of the world: you would be swimming at times in the Nile, at times in the Indian Ocean or the Tanais, or you would be climbing the Rhiphaean mountains or the thickets of the Hercynian passes, an eternal wanderer and fugitive on land. There came to your assistance the devotion of Him who alone knows our ills and the remedies for them which are not on that account any less useful than they are bitter. The complaint in which you most graciously express your desire for my presence and companionship seems to be more noble and worthy of your kindness. Only in them, you say, did you find real pleasure, and you lament that these were taken away from you at a time when they were affording the greatest pleasure. To tell the truth, this is not a serious matter. If you are a friend, and indeed a father (nor have you ever proven otherwise in your special devotion and constant paternal affection), no place and no time can snatch me away from you. Place me on the highest summit of Mt. Atlas which was changed to stone by the eyes of Medusa, and place yourself on the Caucasian cliff where the bound Prometheus complained about Jupiter; and we can still sit together, eat together, chat together, and deal with serious matters. Nothing will ever intervene which will restrain us from seeing and hearing each other. Love is winged, and it crosses not only lands but the heavens and the seas; it recognizes neither the gout nor chains; and even with the opposition of fortune, it can be where it wishes. Are you astonished? It does not even recognize the power of death, and whatever seems to have avoided her it embraces. That is why you will find those who had been turned into ashes once again become whole under its power. You will find Octavia with her son, Artemisia with her husband, Lelius with his friend, despite death and, as I was saying, free of their graves, alive and present. Therefore enjoy me, for I also enjoy you. No normal day of mine passes without you, no night, no journey, no meeting; I am with you everywhere. But if by chance (since I cannot deny that it is most pleasant and delightful to enjoy the actual presence of friends provided it is not denied that often their presence is sweeter in memory than in actuality which may often be uneasy—something I myself dislike), if, I say, you perchance consider my presence useful as a comfort for your life, there is a double road that leads to it: on the one hand I would not refuse to come to you, as unlikely as that may sound, and see your summer dwelling and that of Horace the poet, and to remain as long as it is necessary to satisfy your desire; on the other if you yourself prefer to come to see me (since the human mind is accustomed to enjoying with a greater sweetness those things which it seeks with greater toil) I will not hesitate to give you such directions that you will neither be slowed down because of the defect of your feet or indeed be compelled to touch the earth with them. Let your servants carry you to the Aniene, which flows along the walls of Tivoli. There have them place you on a boat and descend downstream lying in the hold of the boat until it arrives, on the right hand, at the Tiber. Then, being now on a broader stream, you will reach the sea through the walls of the city of Rome itself. From there, still keeping to the right, but now entrusted to a stronger boat, you will enter the heart of the Tyrrhenian Sea until, having left Marseilles far behind, and, having taken a river boat, and again bearing right, you are transported to the entrance of the Rhone River where you will enter into the marshes and stony plains of ancient Arles. Soon you will see on a frightening cliff dismal Avignon, formerly called Avegnon, where now the Roman Pontiff, having deserted his proper See, despite, I believe, the nature of the place, strives to make it capital of the world, unmindful of the Lateran and Silvester. From there still traveling upstream, ascending some three miles more, you will find at your right a silvery stream. Turn into it, for it is the Sorgue, the most peaceful of rivers. After ascending its waters for about fifteen miles you will see a spring second to none and the source of the extremely clear river, as well as a very high cliff overhanging the bubbling waters so that one cannot and should not try to penetrate any further. And so that all things will continue to go expeditiously and favorably, being finally carried to land at that spot, you will see me on the right shore. For where outside of Italy could I find a more peaceful place? You will see me contented with the hospitality of a modest but shady and narrow garden, and my little house, perhaps too little for the visit of so great a guest. You will see me as you wish me, in very good health, lacking in nothing, and expecting nothing in particular from the hands of fortune. You will see me from morning to night, wandering around alone, roving over the meadows and mountains and fountains, living in the woods and in the countryside, fleeing human footsteps, following the birds, loving the shadows, enjoying the mossy caves and the blooming meadows, cursing the cares of the Curia, avoiding the bustle of the cities, shunning the doors of the exalted, mocking the undertakings of the multitude, and keeping equal distance from joy and sadness; enjoying my leisure all day and night, glorying in a partnership with the Muses, amidst the sound of birds and nymphs, and accompanied by few servants but many books. At times you will see me at home, at times out, at times standing still, at times resting my tired head and weary limbs on the babbling river bank and at times on the tender grass, and, to mention something which is not the least part of my pleasure, meeting no one except rarely someone who might want to relate perhaps a thousandth part of his cares. You will see me at times taking a stand against these things or remaining silent, at times speaking at great length with myself, ultimately disdaining myself and all things mortal. So you see, dear father, that while I summon you I seem to remove the labor of the journey. If indeed you read this and have faith in me, you will be seeing enough of me. Farewell in the meantime, for while I seem to be conversing with you, I have forgotten that I am writing a letter.

At the source of the Sorgue, 30 May.

Fam. VI, 4.

To the same correspondent, what examples are worth is shown by examples.

I do use great numbers of examples but they are all illustrious, true, and, unless I am mistaken, contain both pleasure and authority. People say that I should try to use fewer. I confess I could get along without any examples. I do not deny that indeed I could remain totally silent and perhaps be better off for it. But amidst so many evils in this world and so much infamy it is difficult to remain silent. I seem to have practiced sufficient patience in that I have not yet applied myself to the writing of satire since long before these monstrous days of ours I find written: "It is difficult not to write satire." I speak a great deal, I even write a great deal not in order to be of any particular use to my times, whose wretchedness has reached the point of despair, as to unburden myself of ideas and to console my mind with writing. Nevertheless if anyone asks why I sometimes overflow with examples, and seem to linger lovingly over them, I shall answer as follows: I believe the reader is of the same mind as myself. There is nothing that moves me as much as the examples of outstanding men. They help one to rise on high and to test the mind to see whether it possesses anything solid, anything noble, anything unbending and firm against fortune, or whether it lies to itself about itself. Next to experience itself which is the best teacher of things, I would wager there is no better way to learn than by having the mind desire to emulate these greats as closely as possible. Therefore, just as I am grateful to all those authors I have read who afford me this opportunity to test myself with appropriate examples, so do I hope that those who read me will be grateful. I am perhaps wrong in hoping for this; but I am not deceiving you with these words, for in this hope rests the one true reason for my practice. There is another, however, because I also write for myself, and while I write I become eagerly engaged with our greatest writers in whatever way I can and willingly forget those among whom my unlucky star destined me to live; and to flee from these I concentrate all my strength following the ancients instead. For just as the very sight of my fellows offends me greatly, so the recollection of magnificent deeds and outstanding names gives me such incredible and unmeasurable delight that were it known to everyone many would be stupified to learn that I find greater pleasure in being with the dead than with the living. To these truth itself would answer that those men are alive who spent their days virtuously and gloriously; these, rejoicing amidst pleasures and false joys and enfeebled with luxury and sleep, heavy with drinking, although they appear to be alive, are instead nothing more than breathing and obscene and dreadful cadavers. This continues to be, in truth, a source of endless controversy among the learned and the ignorant. So I shall continue from where I began. You therefore now have my reply to your question and to the astonishment of those who surround you as to why I use an excessive number of examples of famous men of antiquity; namely, that I hope that it will profit others as I know for certain it has profited me as a reader and writer. Furthermore, since no single individual can do anything to please all men, let them wonder and disapprove if they care to. Certainly in order that I may not seem to abandon my usual habit because of the rumbling of others, I shall not desist from including even in this letter several examples and in the examples showing what examples can accomplish.

Before Marius, all those who had to undergo amputation at the hands of doctors used to be bound, for since they were persuaded that the pain of the body could not be overcome by the strength of the mind, they used cords for assistance. Marius was the first to be amputated untied, but after him there were many others. Why was this so, I ask, if not because the example of a very resolute and strong man fired minds to imitate him, and, to use the words that were used by a fellow citizen of his, because his authority prevailed? In the war in Latium the Consul Decius sacrificed himself for his legions and for the victory of the Roman people at Veseris. Voluntarily to seek death so that you may achieve victory for others is something easier to do with words than actions. The example, however, was so effective and powerful that his son Decius in the war with the Samnites and Gauls, being himself also a Consul, determined to imitate his father, and calling him by name went in behalf of his fellow citizens fearlessly to death which he had learned to disdain after the manner of his father. In the war at Taranto against Pyrrhus the grandson imitated both, and fell finally as a third victim from the same family although not wearing the same insignia, but nevertheless with similar courage and devotion to the Republic. Never would Themistocles have been the great man he was had he not been incited by the examples of Miltiades and induced to become of equal courage with him. Never would Julius Caesar have ascended to the summit of glory had he not learned to imitate and admire Marius from his youth. He was even inspired by the statue of Alexander which he saw in the temple of Hercules at Cadiz and which soon not only incited him to a desire of achieving great deeds but according to Tranquillus caused him to groan. For indeed if statues of outstanding men can kindle noble minds with desire for imitation, as Crispus relates that Quintus Fabius Maximus and Publius Cornelius Scipio were accustomed to say, how much more should virtue itself directly bring this about since it would be reflected not from shiny marble but from direct example? To be sure, the outlines of bodies are contained more distinctly in statues while descriptions of deeds and customs as well as the condition of minds are undoubtedly expressed more fully and perfectly by words than by anvils. Therefore I feel that it would not be improper to state that statues reflect images of persons while examples reflect images of virtues. What shall I say about great talents? Imitation gave us a pair of outstanding stars in the Latin language, Cicero and Virgil, and brought it about that we would no longer yield to the Greeks in any area of eloquence. While the latter followed in the footsteps of Homer, the former followed Demosthenes, and while one equaled his leader, the other left him behind. It would be possible to point out the same thing in all men but I do not wish to appear today to proceed too far in that for which your supporters criticize me. However I am unable to keep myself from including one example which is well known to you. For indeed the example of Antonius the Egyptian and of Victorinus the rhetorician and martyr really helped Augustine who had been hesitating for a long time about which path to follow, as did the sudden conversion of those two public agents near Treves, a conversion which when Pontianus an imperial soldier described it to him (and you will find the words of Augustine himself in the eighth book of his *Confessions* if my memory serves me), he cried out, "I burned to imitate them; and it was for this reason that he told the story." This therefore is the reason for my advice that must be repeated often because of my critics and admirers; for I see how examples lead many men to virtue, and I feel how they operate in me, and I hope the same for others. If I am mistaken, the matter can do no harm; those who do not like examples need not read them; I compel no one, and besides, I prefer to be read by few. Farewell.

Avignon, 25 September.

Fam. VI, 5.

To Barbato da Sulmona, on the sad and undeserved death of King Andrea.

Alas, how violent and how inevitable are the blows of fortune even when foreseen! As you know, dearest Barbato, I am accustomed to speak often about fortune and other matters in the manner of the multitude, in order not to appear too withdrawn from common language. If I were to be asked about such matters privately I would perhaps answer in a far different manner. But I pass on, for if I adhere to this subject I shall be entangled and drawn into useless and trivial disputes. However, to continue where I left off, the idea that "fortune is omnipotent and fate is inevitable" may be seen held not only among the multitude but even in the opinion of certain very great and most learned men, and among the first Virgil. The words "omnipotent" and "fate" in such context, however, would appear suspect coming from a Catholic. Well, whatever that power may be, whether it influences human affairs through the judgment of God or through his leave, it is doubtless a great force and utterly invincible and one against which the foolishness of our efforts battles in vain. For inexorable necessity smothers human counsel easily; it destroys all the defenses against evil and all mortal remedies. And it is clear that this fact, if it has ever been understood, is especially understood and grasped now. I ask, what new or unexpected things have happened? Who had not foreseen them? And of what benefit was foreseeing them? The awful slime of evil had penetrated so deeply into all the veins of the kingdom as now to be fatal, so far advanced are the boldness and the dissoluteness of the evildoers, and the despair and grief of the pious. Everywhere the signs of the approaching storms were numerous: disturbing clouds shaded serious faces; stubborn winds pressed upon disturbed hearts; glowing eyes flashed; mouths thundered and uttered menaces; it was almost as though ungodly hands were hurling lightning. The seas of the royal court at times were swollen with anger; at times a horrible glow and crashing of waves resounded and foul birds and strange portents seemed widely to encompass your shores. With the death of its king the face of the kingdom has changed and with the soul of a single man the vigor and resolution of everyone seems to have vanished. We witnessed all these things and were distressed no less by future than by present evils. But who dared to speak up when thought itself scarcely enjoyed freedom, and punishments were meted out not only by mouth but by nods of the head? For that reason everyone was silent on the roads; soft whispers could be heard in homes, sad forebodings and previsions of impending evils, and all accompanied by those silent presages, fear and grief. In short, minds were benumbed by the eyes as if struck by the dreadful light of a close thunderbolt. Unless I am mistaken, no one feared more openly than I and grieved more freely. No one looked more closely at those portents of the court, and struck out more obstinately either with his tongue or with his pen. Alas, how great and how evident is the truth of Proverbs! "Let him who wishes to be a truthful prophet prophesy evil." Another one says: "It is rarely that a calamity strikes singly." It is really so: this is what we learned from the ancients and this is what we really see. The series of tribulations is always great; afflictions never go unattended; he who is struck by one of them knows that he will stumble into many. And indeed, just as in so great an abundance of evils there must be great numbers of wretched people, likewise in so great a scarcity of good things there must be few happy people. Doubtless, the entire world is filled with wretched people and with the groans and complaints of such people. On the other hand, who does not see how rare happiness is among mortals when one considers deeply our journey in this life and carefully shakes off the hold of fortune? One finds no one to be ever truly happy or fully in control of his desires, for as we learn from historians, even that habitually happy Metellus was unable to find one companion in the most remote hiding places of the Arcadians.

Who therefore among those who hold these views should be surprised that just as a spear hurled within a crowd of people cannot stray, the same holds for a prophesy released amidst such an accumulation of evils, and that just as the spear would strike something alive, thus would the prophesy strike the truth? You will remember, dear friend, how when the king was alive but near his death (and I refer to that king who alone deserved such a name) I either orally when I was present or through letters when I was absent, and not long after his death, again orally, revealed not without visible disturbance what I felt and what I feared would be coming as if I were certain of the future. For I saw the foundations of the kingdom being shaken from the top, and I saw before my eyes the serious misfortunes befalling the collapsing kingdom. I confess I did not see that the head of an innocent youth would be the first victim of that collapse. I cannot imagine what concealed from me amidst so many gloomy conjectures that one possibility which perhaps was the worst of all evils; although as I now seem to recall, I did speak to you in my earliest letters about the lamb being thrown among the wolves. Would that my prediction had been less true! Of course I viewed the rage and gnashing of the wolves as things common to doomed men—contempt, envy, deceit, theft, prison, and exile. But I had never learned to conceive of nor fear such a death for such a man, and indeed could not recall in any tragedies I had read such abominable and insidious savagery. Imagine! Our age, which is so prolific in crimes, has now committed one in which antiquity would glory and posterity find consolation; and so that every age may find an excuse for its misdeeds, a crime that might be considered the *summa* in fierceness and in inhospitality was committed in these times. Oh Naples, so suddenly changed! Oh unfortunate Aversa, indeed averse, a name which you seem to have assumed from the event that was totally averse, I say, to humaneness and trust, qualities which were owed first to the man, secondly to the king and just lord! You disdained observing any reverence for both titles, and your people broke their sacred obligation to both his capacities. Within your walls your king perished at the hands of impious fraud. Would that he had been killed by a sword or through some other form of manly death so that he would appear to have been killed at the hands of men, not mangled by the teeth and claws of beasts. Oh city, founded under an evil star, inscribed by an unpropitious boundary, constructed on bloody mortar, and inhabited by cultivators of snakes, master city of cruel examples! It was a grave enough irreverence and crime to violate so cruelly and so arrogantly the sacred person of a public servant made in the image of the Lord. You perpetrated that crime not against an ordinary man but instead you tore to pieces a most mild and innocent man who was your lord and concerned about you far in advance of his years, in love with you, a boy of rare talent, promising great hope. Alas, not you, but those harsh and savage—I don't know what to call them—men or beasts or some other kind of rare monster living within your walls who, defiling the Italian lands with their barbaric cruelty, destroyed your king and theirs not with a sword, not with poison, certainly the usual and difficult death of kings, but with an infamous noose as if he had been an incendiary or a bandit. They had not only delayed granting him the crown (through long and perfidious evasion) which his head deserved and hoped for, but they threw around his neck the unkindly knots of a cord. If perhaps such news might not reach posterity because of our silence, I would pass over the unworthy mockery that was made of his body which was most worthy of another kind of funeral service and of a longer life. But you, wretched city, carry within you things which are sorrowful in all lands, in all centuries, and which befoul memory. However, you are really without blame except that resignation to crimes often implies agreement, and besides, if you are unable either to resist or avenge such crime, you are more worthy of pity than hatred. But you, oh Christ, sun of justice, who see all and illuminate the universe with your eternal rays, why did you suffer this cloud of infamy to lie upon our lands when you could so easily (unless these transgressions of men are obstacles for you) have broken through the offensive vapors of hatred hardened by the misty cold of the night with the glowing brilliance of your love? You, however, dear Robert, greatest of all kings of our day who I believe behold and commiserate with our affairs from some portion of the heavens, with what eyes did you behold this abomination? And how were you able to endure this horrible injustice to your blood? Could you not have averted the wicked deed with pious prayers? Or was it that although able you were not willing? This is a somewhat difficult conjecture, for although it may be somewhat close to the truth that you are not moved by earthly grief because of the celestial joy that surrounds you, could it really be that you were not touched by love of your creatures and your essential piety? However that may be, you are fortunate indeed that you did not see this day in person! On the other hand, had you been present, that most unfortunate day would never have dawned nor would so much envy have been allowed. For indeed your regal presence would have been the salvation of the kingdom, the conciliator of minds, the fountain of justice and the expeller of treachery, and like a salutary shade over your flock you would have been as propitious to shepherds as fatal to serpents. But if human virtue was of no avail by heavenly decree, then your death was indeed propitious and deeply opportune, for it kept your eyes, indeed those eyes that by natural law were able to observe horror and suffer tears, from having to witness such a sad spectacle. Oh grief! Your chosen, dear, pious sweet trust whom you had committed to people who ought to have watched over him and honored him was instead destroyed by them not because they were overcome with sleep or cowardice, but because they were inflamed with hatred and goaded by envy! Dear justice against all crimes! Neither his innocence, nor his blood, nor his majesty availed him, no one among men or gods, nor any memory of you which was expected to be most effective afforded him any aid. The winds of rash and desperate negligence dispersed your words and unusual warnings of a pious father and excellent king with which on your deathbed you tried to protect the future of both your family and your kingdom as much as was allowed to mortal counsel. Now the oblivion of all human and divine justice has covered them over. But enough weeping, if only because where we may think we see an end, there we may find a beginning; since, as I was saying, evil usually comes in quantity, attended by more evil, and since the good is a rare and solitary thing, I sense in this particular evil that a number of other evils may follow, for which reason in order to avoid once again being more correct than I wish to be or appearing to be a prophet of doom I prefer to remain silent. Everything may turn out better than I hope, and the anger of a few may not harm the Republic, an anger which I hope will not remain unavenged on those who possess it; for although divine justice often yields to compassion, nevertheless this happens to those who are ashamed and repent their sins, and not to those who glory in disgraceful acts. I send you these words from the fountain of the Sorgue where once again I have fled from so great a storm in Italy as if to enter a safe port, grieving over the past and frightened over the future, on the calends of August, during a stormy night. Farewell, take care of yourself and remember me.

Fam. VI, 6.

To an unknown correspondent, vices that cannot be over-come ought to be forsaken.

Leave him alone and to himself; he is old enough. The roads stand open and he can go wherever he pleases. Let go the reins of that untameable man. You strive in vain. I repeat, leave him alone; let him go where his mind directs him; believe me he will not climb. You have seen horses who are too lazy for a journey and for climbing, afraid of battle, but nevertheless impatient with others and constantly snorting. It is the mark of a degenerate mind to abuse minors, not to be able to suffer associates, to hurt when one can, and to await the occasion rather than a reason. Flies annoy the leanest oxen, the dog molests the poor traveler; number our little man among these examples. His passion for harshness and hurting becomes greater where there is either mourning or bereavement, or extreme poverty, or where there is the least possibility for defense. For this reason he does not limit himself only to those things for which he has skill, for his will is never insufficient and is always the same. Why therefore do you reprove him? You are wasting time. This evil calls for something other than words. Give him an equal opponent and you will see that drive of his lessen. A wolf will always be a wolf while the sheep is present; bring in another wolf and he will be a sheep. Why, therefore, as Flaccus says, "do you pour forth prayers into closed ears?" Why not then leave him alone crushed and buried by his own vices, swollen with pride, burning with avarice, raging with wrath, wild with passions, a slave to his mouth and stomach, always consumed with very deep stupor and, as Maro says, buried in sleep and wine. What would you do for this man? What would you say to him? You will be speaking to a barrel and indeed a full one and one which can answer nothing from within, can understand, and even hear, nothing. Licinius Crassus seemed to have been speaking precisely about one like him in saying that if only he had a bronze beard he would be lacking nothing else, for he has an iron mouth and a lead heart. He certainly has hardened ears and a calloused mind; real words do not penetrate the thick covering that conceals lies. I do not know whether you are one of those who do not mind wasting words lightly; but this I know for sure, that with this man words are wasted. Perhaps such wastage would be tolerable except that in this case hatred and contempt are the result. Farewell.

Avignon, 29 April.

Fam. VI, 7.

To an unknown correspondent, on the difference between eloquence and loquaciousness.

I do not deny that in enthusiasm for domestic affairs and for amassing wealth he is a most accomplished man and the most cautious of all I have ever known, and one who, like Plautus' old woman, has eyes not only in his face but in the back of his head. However, concerning what you said about his eloquence I most certainly disagree. A great distance separates eloquence and loquaciousness: one is a matter of quality, the other of quantity; one calls for talent and skill and moderate practice, the other for rash attacks and impudence. They are indeed opposites; and yet many people fail to see the difference. If you were to apply your mind more carefully when he speaks, you will confess that just as you have heard nothing more resolute, in the same way you will confess that you have never heard anything rougher than the speech of that man, nothing more uneven, and nothing more untimely. Please understand these words as being said not so much that I might destroy the false reputation for eloquence of someone whose name I will not mention, but so that I might correct your judgment. Farewell.

Fam. VI, 8.

To a friend in need.

How poor or how wealthy you may be I do not know. I am speaking of your money box; for without doubt you are wealthy in mind, which in the fashion of Bias carries all its goods with it, not fearing destruction either by fire or shipwreck, and which, like those who fear nothing at all, does not fear the danger of plunderers, the deceit of thieves, rust, moths, disease, death, old age, or catastrophe. But concerning your money box I have some doubts, for while I esteem your mind and your conduct and your good fortune, I suspect that just as you do not need much, so you must lack something. For just as it is mad to need countless things, so is there real truth in that Socratic Xenophon's saying: "To lack nothing is appropriate for the gods, to lack very little means being close to them." Wherefore, because I recently heard certain things about your money box from someone who was aware of the situation, I determined to be of assistance according to my means. Here therefore is a little something to which I can hardly refer as remnants of my fortune since I would be speaking more arrogantly than I wish. Similarly, to call them gifts is to say something other than I feel. I shall call it therefore one of the gifts of God for which, though I do not care for such things, He deemed me worthy of accumulating beyond hope and prayer. It is a bit of this that I send you and that without doubt you will accept courteously. In this meager thing, as if in a small mirror, you will recognize the great affection of the sender and you will think rather of the wish of his mind than the smallness of the gift. I am aware that certain strong men and certain learned men possessing the same strength of mind as yourself were once tempted in vain by similar gifts. Among these are the famous names of Fabritius and Curius, Roman leaders, one of whom is praised for having disdained the gold offered by King Pyrrhus and the other the gold offered by the Samnites. Each was acclaimed because of such disdain but one was made even more famous by the splendor of his answer. For although certain scholars confuse history after their fashion, the fact remains that the noble and famous reply, "Romans do not wish gold but to rule the owners of gold," was not made by Fabritius as the multitude believe, to the king, but was given by Curius to the messenger of the Samnites. Xenocrates had a similar experience with the envoys sent to him by Alexander of Macedonia when they were sent with fifty talents for him by the king himself. He invited them to dinner in the grounds of his academy and philosophically offered them a mediocre and quickly prepared dinner, and dismissed them. On the following day when they had returned to seek whom he wished to have count the money of their king, his rebuttal was: "Did you not understand from yesterday's dinner that I do not lack money?" When he noted that they were dejected, in order to avoid the accusation that he had scorned the gift and the legation of the king, he accepted a very small part of the large amount of money, and ordered that the remainder be returned to the king. The story is also told about the contempt of Diogenes the Cynic for that same king. When Alexander, desirous of seeing him living inside his versatile barrel after having admired the man, asked whether he wished to have something given to him by the king, Diogenes answered: "Other things at other times; right now I would like to have you move out of the sun." For it was winter, and having by chance turned the bottom of the barrel toward the north, he kept his face to the south and in such a manner the little old man sunned himself half naked but with a burning mind. This was a joke compared to the much rougher and almost arrogant answer of Demetrius who so disdained the gold that had been sent to him by the Roman emperor that he laughingly said: "If he wished to tempt me he should have tested me with his entire empire." The Indian, Calanus, while he went to a voluntary death naked on the huge pile of wood that had been raised and fired according to the custom of his native land, said to Alexander of Macedonia who had come forward asking whether there were anything he wished: "There is need for nothing; I shall be seeing you in a short time." But indeed there is nothing very astonishing about this; for what would that man not scorn who scorns that very life on account of which we desire all other things? Indeed that amazing contempt was supplemented by the fulfillment of the prophesy, for within a few days Alexander was destroyed by that cup which became the avenger of the Persians and the Indians. Somewhat more sophisticated was Dindymus who, when the same Alexander came to visit him without all his regal splendor and found him naked in a remote solitude, chose from all the gifts that had been brought to him by the very wealthy king nothing but the smallest and least expensive lest his contempt might appear insolence. But as these are incomparable examples of individual men, there is that other incomparable example of a public display of greatness. Cineas, the ambassador of king Pyrrhus whom I mentioned above, a man of outstanding talents and wisdom, when he was sent to Rome with vast gifts, having tried in vain first the Senate and afterwards, in order, all the other classes, finally approached the plebians, but also in vain. Finding absolutely no one who opened either his home or his mind to the royal gifts, he returned with all the gold that he had brought, himself feeling amazed. All of these examples, however, were tested either by an enemy king or an enemy people or by some kind of haughty donor. But Ptolemy the Egyptian king did not despise the gifts of the Roman Senate, nor Masinissa the gifts of a friendly king, nor finally did the Roman people itself, while admittedly a despiser of the gifts of enemies, scorn the inheritance and testament of the king of Pergamum whom it liked. It matters much with what spirit something is given and by whom, and just as certain kinds of contempt are fine so are others discourteous and insolent. I come as a friend and not as a tempter; nor, to confess the truth, am I giving you anything, but I am sharing with you what you yourself know has been held in common by us for a long time. And to avoid exaggerating with many words a very small gift, accept whatever it is in good spirit; especially because what it is or what kind it is neither the bearer nor anyone else really knows; and even I, if you would believe me, have forgotten. Farewell.

Fam. VI, 9.

To Philip, Bishop of Cavaillon.

I shall come to you because I feel that it is your desire and I shall bring along our Socrates who is so dedicated to your name. We shall come tomorrow, nor shall we shudder at the sight of the city although we shall be dressed in an unkempt and rustic manner. The day before yesterday we fled here hastily out of the bustling and noisy city with a wild leap as if we had jumped on to a shore from a damaged ship, with the purpose of concealing ourselves and enjoying some leisure and with clothes which appear to be most suitable for the country and for the winter. You order us to enter the city as we are: we shall obey, and all the more willingly because we are attracted by your very warm wishes. Nor shall we be unduly concerned over how we appear to others since we wish and hope that our minds will appear open and naked to you. You will not deny a favor to the wishes of your supporters, dear father, if you wish to have us as guests often, and that is that no elaborate preparation or banquet greet us but instead a friendly dinner.

Happily we bid you farewell. At the source of the Sorgue,

2 January, with a rural pen.

*To Barbato da Sulmona, a lamentation over the desolation of
his native land at the hands of the barbarians.*

Among the various cares with which I am beseiged, not the
least is what I imagine as I think about your situation; for
what is dearer to me than my Barbato, or sweeter? Love is an
uneasy affair, credulous, fearful, solicitous, noting all things
and dreading both inconsequential things, and things which
are certain. This is what I always feared, this is what I often
wrote, and this is what I used to say daily: such a detestable
deed could not remain unpunished, and this revenge is considerably more serious than I feared. So turn, oh God, your
anger against the perpetrators of crimes and strike the guilty
heads with a proper punishment. Spare the devoted ones, spare
the faithful. What did the innocent multitude deserve, what
did the sacred land of Ausonia deserve? See how now the
Italian dust is flying because of the advance of the barbarians,
and where we were once conquerors of peoples, we are now,
alas, the prey of conquerors. Either our sins have deserved
that punishment or some evil and gloomy constellation ha-
rasses us with its baleful light, or else (as I believe to be the
case) with the virtuous being confused with the wicked, we
are being punished for the crimes of others. But let it not be
said that I fear for all of Italy from which, rather, the rebels
will have something to fear as long as the tribunal power,
which has recently returned to the city, flourishes, and our
capital, Rome, is not ill. But a portion of Italy keeps me concerned, namely, the part formerly known as Magna Grecia,
including Abruzzi, Calabria, Puglia, and the Terra di Lavoro
now truly so called, and Capua once a powerful city, and
Naples now the queen of cities. Into these most delightful
lands an army from the roughest banks of the Danube is
rushing headlong, and a storm arising from the North covers
the serenity of our skies with foul clouds, a storm which I
fear will have broken forth with great thunder while I await
your answer. Now the entire situation is reported to have
reached a critical point; by now rumor has it that Sulmona
was trampled over by the first military attack and is now in

the power of the enemy. Alas, with what lamentation should I mourn that noble city, homeland of Naso and of yourself, seeing it occupied today by those among whom that great man considered exile worse than death? How miserable he must have been to have lamented not so much his exile as the place of his exile, and to have composed a lengthy book on those complaints. What would he have said had he foreseen the Danubian people and such men as are represented by the Sarmatian and Dacian archers ever storming over the snowy hills to seize his native land by force of arms. Towards these he set out by order of Caesar and was so upset that he could grieve over nothing else, curse nothing else, and speak of nothing else. What should I now think that you will say, dear brother, as you see those very things which bring tears to my eyes, and which he could not without consternation have imagined occurring in the future? Oh bones of Naso, more fortunate for being at least buried in a foreign land than if, buried with the honor of a monument in their homeland, they were being kept to be made sport of in our day! Now I would call more peaceful those tombs located between the Danube and the Bog than between the Liri and Volturno; because from those places the barbarians are fleeing in large numbers while they are swarming into these. But in following the grief of my mind I have surpassed my intent; and I would have proceeded further if this messenger had not called me back to my senses as he waited for me and repeatedly interrupted. So I return to where I left off.

I am greatly fearful for your safety, but I have no advice that I can confidently offer, nor assistance. Yet, because sometimes some men can do more than they believe they can, if you need any help from me make use of it as you please. I confess that I enjoy substantial favor with the Tribune, a man of humble background but of lofty mind and purpose, and I also enjoy the favor of the Roman people. Certainly out of no merit of my own, God has repaid me by replacing the hatred of evil men with the kindness of good men, not that I have done any harm to the former or any good to the latter, not because I have ceased being bad and am all good, but because I have determined to hate evildoers and to love good men. In truth, I often wished, if it were possible, to flee from the crowd of the former to the few members of the latter, and I still would want it that way if it were possible. If therefore my intercession with the previously mentioned Tribune and people could be of any help to you in the present danger, please rest assured that my mind and pen stand ready. Also in a region of Italy far from these troubles I have a house which is indeed small, but for two people having the same mind no house is too narrow. It is free from all harmful signs of wealth, but suffers neither poverty nor avarice, and is full of countless books. It is expecting only us, me to return from the West where it complains I have been for the past two years, and you from the East if destiny compels you and if it pleases you. Whatever else I can offer you beyond this, I do not possess. But you know the location of the house to which I invite you: that healthy location is free from fears, full of delights, and favorable for studies. Whatever plan you decide upon, may God lead to a happy conclusion. Meanwhile my fervent wish is that I have been wrongly fearful and that absence, as so often happens, has been responsible for increasing the fear of the devotee! For my mind will not rest until either I see you or through letters I hear that you are safe from these storms.

From Avignon, hastily and anxiously, 11 September.

To a friend, on the need for not despising true humility.

I beg you, do not scorn your friend so much because he is humble lest you sin against the beatitude which promises that humility will be exalted. There is indeed nothing less contemptible than true humility and nothing less to be honored and less worthy of respect than true pride. However, we are deceived by making minute distinctions in this matter as in many others. We call humble the worthless, the fainthearted and the cowardly while the high-minded we call proud. On the other hand we despise the truly humble because of their suspect timidity, and we worship the proud as if they were truly high minded. We should keep in mind what Sallust reports was said by Cato the Younger: "We lost the true names for things a long time ago." If, therefore, returning to the matter at hand, you maintain that your friend is as humble as he is, I urge you to beware lest you are despising that humility which is a very lofty virtue and most pleasing to Christ; and lest you appear to be what you never were, a victim of an insolent and unbecoming pride. For who, even of mediocre ability, having read both sacred and secular writings does not realize how much Christ, our master of humility, always loved humble things? To start from the beginning, what a humble birth he chose for himself whose very face is the source of the highest and greatest happiness! Could He not have been born from whatever noble line He wished, or could He not have ennobled the one He chose? But instead He despised fame and sought humility. "The twig emerged from the root of Jesse, and the flower sprang from its root." Under its shade kings now sit, peoples rest, and all of the world is refreshed with its odor. And indeed, what was this fruit of Jesse? Was it proud? Was it noble? His maternal ancestor was Ruth, a foreign woman, needy and widowed, who followed the footsteps of her childless mother-in-law beyond the boundaries of her fatherland and was the first to be admitted out of compassion into the fields of Boaz to gather the ears of corn behind the young reapers, and then as a result of nocturnal advances was promoted to the role of wife of the owner himself, whence the father of Jesse was begotten, a man of obscure name himself. Indeed who would have known Jesse himself except for his son David? And indeed who would have known anyone of them except because of Christ who was begotten from their root? How much Saul was accustomed to scorn their origin and with what anger, and how he used to call him the son of Isai and his servant, that Saul who was a haughty fellow-citizen and who admittedly was the offspring of a very obscure family from the lowest tribe of Israel, these things anyone can learn who reads the books of Kings. David himself, although possessing unusual virtues and outstanding talent, was but a very young shepherd when he was chosen by the Lord and freed from the flocks of sheep as he himself confesses. From following the ewes he was received into the kingship, and he tended Israel with the innocence of his heart. Was Moses perhaps more renowned when he saw that vision of the burning and unconsumed bush, or when, having become famous because of so many prodigious signs, he set forth to free the Israelites from the slavery of Egypt by the command of God? Certainly no king or prince was he who was chosen for such labor, but a humble shepherd, and what is even more marvelous, of a foreign flock. As for father Abraham himself and his son and grandson with whose names every corner of Scripture is full, and whose glory is so great that the Almighty received His name from them and wished to be called the God of Abraham, the God of Isaac, the God of Jacob, and use that same name for Himself when speaking about Himself, do you think that they were kings or tetrarchs? Indeed they were either farmers or shepherds. Sitting on base donkeys, surrounded by their flocks, they changed their dwellings with their children and wives. In this humility they deserved God as leader who then had no wish either to be so friendly with the most powerful and haughty kings of the Assyrians, or even to be known by them. Note how Jacob himself, from whom in sacred Scripture one sees how that extraordinary surname became more popular and more intimately associated with God, and who was famous not because of his pride of origin but because of his humility, returns from his long and demanding service with his father-in-law. He certainly does not return with a sceptre, crown, royal robe, a golden chariot, armed forces. Instead, secretly fleeing with the long lines of sheep and goats and oxen that had been gathered, he led away with him a large number of children and servants, and two wives and just as many concubines, the seed of countless peoples from whose womb descended the Twelve Tribes of Israel, and a so great a multitude of people whose women God rendered fertile in honor of his humility. Those things occurred in a way which on the surface made them appear contemptible, but in essence they were magnificent, for if they were to be understood only as they are recounted, who would not despise what they say?

But if temporal glory were personally superior in God's eye to humility, who would doubt in what direction that great love of God would have been much more inclined? Compare with these three aged men, who were so famous, together with all their flocks and wives, the three Roman leaders who were supported by immense armies: Scipio Africanus, who destroyed the strength of Hannibal and subjected powerful Carthage to the tributary yoke; Pompey the Great, who raised thunder in the North and in Asia and who filled his homeland not with milk but with gold, and who captured flocks, not of sheep but of kings, as he proceeded from the Red Sea to the Maeotic Marshes and the Rhiphaean mountains; Julius Caesar, who drove like lightning into Gaul and into Germany, and once having subdued the enemy finally turned his victorious spear against the organs of his homeland, and in a single battle in Thessaly defeated Rome herself, who then ruled over the gentiles and who contained within her the entire world. You perceive what this great inequality represented. The son of God who was about to be born of man could have decided to be born of these or to make those from whom he was born like the others, since he had created both. He could have made the founder of his lineage not David and the narrow limits of Judea, but Augustus ruling over the entire world, or He could have made David himself as great a prince as He made Augustus. He could have been born not in that narrow district of Bethlehem, but in Rome to which Judea was subject among the others, and in a golden bed rather than in a stable. And once born. He, who has heaven as his abode and to whom the earth and all abundance belong, could have been nourished not in deepest poverty but in the greatest pleasure, except that He scorns nobility and earthly delights (and would that He did not detest them!). Finally, He could have chosen as his successors and preachers of His name among the peoples, learned disciples, powerful princes, kings and orators and philosophers, rather than needy, unlearned, and rustic fishermen, except that He Himself is God who resists the arrogant but favors the humble, and needs neither our powers to act since his mere words are acts, nor our mortal eloquence for persuading: "For the discourse of God is alive and effective and more piercing than any double edged sword, and penetrating as far as the abode of the soul and of the spirit, and even of the joints and of the marrow, discerning even the thoughts and intentions of the heart." He had armed his disciples with such discourse when He dispersed them throughout the world to persuade mankind; armed not with consular robe, imperial crown, triumphant laurel crown, not with opinions of philosophers, not with gems of orators, not with subtleties of Sophists, not, in short, with the knowledge of words, as the Apostle says, lest the cross of Christ be made void. Among them were not a Caesar who commanded, not a Plato who taught, not an Aristotle who argued, not a Cicero who exhorted; but poor little men, feeble and unpolished, who never entered a school, or studied letters. These, however, among the swords of their persecutors and the teeth of beasts, and among flames and racks and tortures persuaded the people as they desired: that Christ God, born as man, suffered, descended to hell, arose from the dead, ascended into heaven, and will return to judge, and all the other truths that He had commanded who, as it is written, preferred the fools of the world and the weak in order to confound the strong, and who, though He had come to benefit all, chose, as Augustine says, that the fisherman profit the emperor rather than the emperor the fisherman, a fact that can be applied similarly to the orator and the philosopher.

And this occurred not in an age of ignorance and of super-
stition, but "when the arts and sciences had become firmly
rooted and when all those ancient errors had been removed
from the uncultivated life of men," and when long since
"men had already become more learned together with the
times themselves," than they had been in the age of Romulus
—writing about whose accepted divinity Cicero says in his
Republic and Augustine repeats in his that if hardly anyone
found fictions acceptable at that time, they would certainly
find them less so now, "for antiquity received fictitious fa-
bles, sometimes even absurd ones, whereas this cultivated age
rejects them, mocking those that could not possibly have
happened." If, as I said, in order to embellish the false divinity of Romulus, in which an already cultivated age was able
to believe, Cicero brought together arguments of considerable significance, saying that Rome had scarcely been founded
and that one of the Seven Hills was covered not with golden
roofs and marble walls but with thorny spaces, and was occupied with rustic thatched huts and smelled redolent with
the odor of shepherds; what must be said of the age of Christ
when Rome was already giving laws to the world and Augustus and Tiberius were ruling, under one of whom Christ
was born and under the other suffered? Between this time
and the age of Romulus the changes that occurred were
more wonderful than one might expect from the number of
years that had intervened. Not because the intervening time
was short, if indeed from the period when Romulus was
torn to pieces by the Roman Senate because of his insolence
at the Goat marshes until Christ was crucified by the Jews
because of our sins on the Mount of Olives, a little more
than seven hundred years, more or less, elapsed, if I am not
mistaken. Although Cicero says, "less than six hundred," he
was referring not to his time but to the age of Africanus and
of the others whom he has speak in that same book of the
Republic. Furthermore, between the murder of Cicero at
the time of Antonius and the Passion of Christ at the time
of Pilate, as close as I can guess, there intervened about seventy years or so. I would prolong this but your messenger
is looking over my shoulder and notices each stroke of the

pen and measures the delays between each, and often glancing at the doorway and the sky he sighs. I feel pity for him, having experienced what waiting means to the mind in haste, and I feel constrained to say before I should: love humility and farewell.

Fam. VII, 3.

*To his Socrates, a nocturnal vision, and that a calm poverty
ought to be preferred to an agitated wealth.*

I shall tell you about a dream I had last night. I seemed—
and I am uncertain as to why since I am not accustomed
either to think or to speak about such things—I seemed to
have found in that small field of mine that I own at the
source of the Sorgue, a treasure: it was a considerable pile of
ancient golden coins. We were taking a walk alone as is our
custom. I immediately called to you and pointed out the
find with my finger. We both stopped short, as will happen,
because of our joy and astonishment. As I stood there I remember recalling the words of Annaeus: "Avoid whatsoever
pleases the masses and those things which chance offers you;
remain suspicious and fearful of all good which is accidental:
both beast and fish are trapped by whatever raises their hope;
such gifts which you may think come to you through chance
are but traps." Deliberating over this, we joyfully and wor-
riedly hesitated for a little while. In short, it appeared to us
real insanity to disdain what is usually sought over land and
sea through great labors and dangers and was being offered
to us so simply. Soon we eagerly burdened ourselves with
gold, and silently and secretly carried it home after having
hidden temporarily those portions that could not be carried
in one load. We did this once, twice, and many more times,
always more greedily, and always, as is the nature of such
things, our anxiety and desire increased with the money.
Meanwhile an invisible murmur strikes our ears and our secret, revealed to no one, suddenly erupted by itself among the
multitude. Not long after this, some older lord of these parts
came forth claiming the treasure as rightfully his. We stood
firm. As a result there were first some lengthy and unpleasant
arguments, then contention and threats with insults always
added to the disputes as the lord argued bitterly in his own
behalf and we became highly indignant that such a gift of
favorable fortune found in our land should be snatched from
us. Thereupon several solutions were attempted and as many
plans made, at times proper and cautious, at others rash and

bitter as we were fired to resist not so much because of our own desire as because of the proud stubbornness of our inexorable opponent. At times, dragged from the peacefulness of the country to business in the city, and at times from our studies to take up needed weapons, we were constantly agitated by new storms of cares; at times in place of night-long efforts and most enjoyable research into new ideas there came night-long hatred and anger; finally the man turned from dispute to battle. The state of our minds being thus changed, we often felt sorry for having found the gold, and in our dreams we would philosophize as follows. "Where did we leave our serene and peaceful life? Who brought upon us these clouds of cares. Who pushed us into these storms? Were we not aware that in the possession of gold tribulation appears beautiful, and wretchedness appears splendid? Needs increase with wealth, and happiness flees with frugality." Large numbers of examples occurred to us of those who had been either unhappy in wealth or most happy in poverty. The useless wealth of Croesus and the fatal gold of Midas and the booty that was removed from the temples of Dionysius and Crassus were all scorned by us; while the happy and glorious poverty of Cincinnatus, of Regulus, of Curius, of Fabritius was praised. Great numbers of our own heroes came to mind who, naked, in solitude, burned by the sun and the cold, feeding upon roots of herbs and wild berries, with the sky above as their roof and with the earth as their bed, drank from the muddy streams with pleasure, walked along the rough and narrow path and, in the hope of a better homeland, completely despised all things mortal. However, the more examples of this kind came to mind, the more we felt sorry that we had not seen them in time but instead, as they say, had eyes in our back. Finally we reached the point where what kept us from wanting to abandon the undertaking was only the shame of unyielding. Already the risks of final battle were approaching when suddenly in the middle of the night, distressed by anger and fear, I awoke. A cold sweat covered my entire body. Thus, may God be my witness, I was weary of mind and body as if a serious and difficult matter had agitated me not while dreaming but while awake. It is not easy to say how happy I was to be freed not only of the treasure but of the anxieties, and that I possessed only enough to nourish myself without excess; and only what sufficed for life and not what afflicted it; and how I became rooted through a dream in that belief, which once awake I am convinced to be true, that wealth brings more harm than good to ambitious mortals. I finally got up at the regular hour (you know my custom) and after having recited my daily praises to God, I took up my pen as is my custom and began at once exposing in my waking state what had upset me in my sleep. And so I make you a partner in this lesson since you seem to be a partner in my dream.

Farewell and rid yourself of unnecessary desires if you wish to be happy.

14 January at dawn.

Fam. VII, 4.

To Giovanni Tricastrino, bishop and professor of theology.[1]

Mindful of your request and of my promise, I leave for, or rather (to avoid getting involved in the grammatical argument which Atticus brings up in his letters to Cicero) I am going to, Italy. I also know and recall that you asked me to put in order the works of Cicero himself and that you had often requested that I make some of them clear by introducing, as you are accustomed to say, notations in the form of sparks of light. Finally, so that your prayers might become truly irresistible you requested that the Roman Pontiff—who, aware of your dedication, had given you an assignment certainly worthy of your talent by entrusting the honorific custody of his library to you, just as once our rulers Julius Caesar and Caesar Augustus did with Marcus Varro, and with Pompeius Macer, respectively, and the Egyptian king Ptolemy Philadelphus did with Demetrius Phalerius—you requested that the Roman Pontiff, as I was saying, in some modest manner would indicate his position in this matter before I departed. What could I do? As the poem of some unknown poet says: "A request from a ruler is a violent kind of ordering and as powerful as if he were asking with a drawn sword." I shall obey if I can, for it is both necessary to obey him and delightful to please you, and likewise it is difficult to reject your requests and sacrilegious to disobey his orders. It all depends on this: how much good fortune I shall have in finding those corrected manuscripts that you seek. Being an expert in the faults of our century, you know what a lack there is of such books despite the fact that useless and unnecessary and indeed truly harmful and fatal riches continue to be sought after with so much trouble and toil. I shall devote whatever energy I may have and all my care to the search; and so that you may not accuse me of delaying, you ought to know that in an attempt to restore strength to my body which illness had depleted I have been staying in my solitude at the source of the Sorgue awaiting the temperate

1. Believed to be the librarian of Clement VI and a highly respected theologian.

weather of autumn and fearful of committing my still weak body to a long journey. When my strength has increased, God willing, and the heat has diminished, I shall take up the journey. Meanwhile I wish you could realize with what great pleasure I breathe solitary and free among the mountains, among the springs and rivers, among the books and the talents of the greatest men, and how together with the Apostle I project myself into those things which are before us, and try to forget those that are past, and not to see the present. Farewell.

Fam. VII, 5.

To his Lelius, on personal matters and on the disturbing rumors connected with the doings of the Tribune of Rome.

Time forbids me to write at great length, and sleep does not permit it. This is already the third night that I am sleepless. Still not free from my former worries, I am now burdened with new ones caused by my departure which indicate that there are many problems before me and behind me needing my attention. When I shall force myself to disdain all of them equally, which I have done in great part, only then shall I begin to enjoy some restful sleep like Virgil's Aneas who "when he was certain of his departure and when all preparations had been duly completed, enjoyed his sleep." So either I am wrong, or my long and uncertain deliberation is full of annoyance and toil; only the termination of doubt is the beginning of peace. One cannot say how the distressed mind exercised by aimless deliberation finds rest from the need for choice by arriving at a choice of one final position. Therefore when that happens I shall write at greater length. Now I speak half asleep and as if in a dream. I therefore embrace your excuse although superfluous; for I know that if distances between places are hateful to lovers, they are not with true friends. Wherever we shall be, we shall be together. Concerning your affair I shall do as you write, and as if I were doing it for myself. I shall expedite it in short order, for nothing I experience is more annoying than to drag out words. Being aware of this, I have never caused so much annoyance to friends, nor indeed shall I do so. I shall please them if I can; otherwise I shall try not to displease them. I shall consider composing the verses you request once my inspiration has been awakened at our Helicon, but without knowing how your notes which I had in my hands ten times somehow got away from me as I departed, leaving them behind. Search for them there and send them to me, although even without them I seem to know what I should be saying, if only I could come across a stopping place in a thick forest.

The copy of the letter of the Tribune which was sent me I have seen, read, and been amazed by; I know not what to answer. I recognize the fate of the fatherland, for wherever I turn I find reason and occasion for grief. Once Rome is torn to pieces what will happen to Italy? Once Italy is disfigured what would my life be? In this sorrow, which is both public and private, some will contribute wealth, others bodily strength, and still others power and advice. I see nothing that I can contribute except tears.

22 November, in transit.

To his Socrates, on his private affairs and his desire for moderation.

The gist of my affairs which I entrusted to your respected confidence I now repeat without removing or adding anything. In this I am not only determined but immovable in what I intend to do. If you remember my position it should be unnecessary to speak further about this affair. But so that you may know that I am not forgetful of myself, listen to what I have to say briefly. I have never been a seeker of great fortune whether because of modesty, pettiness, or, as some great men prefer to conceive it, magnanimity. I call truths to mind which even the multitude knows and for which you are my chief witness, sometimes praising me for them and sometimes censuring me, although because of the nature of the times in a very friendly way. To use your own words, I become too stubborn in whatever I undertake. This forces me to see that whenever I seek the reputation of the greatest consistency, I seem to attain the reputation and ill fame of obstinacy. However, thus far I have not been sorry for my decisions, since all kinds of heights are deeply suspect to me, and every ascent warns me of a descent. And I would much more easily and naturally incline toward associating with those who in the words of the poet, "inhabit the lowest valleys," than those who according to the same poet, "raised their city on the mountains." This being so, if my desired moderation which Horace rightly calls golden, should come to me as it was promised long ago, I accept it with gratitude and I shall admit that it was done for me in a most liberal way. But if that hateful and heavy burden of a major office is imposed upon me, I shall refuse it and push it away. I would rather be poor than upset, although with the way things are going and in my mental condition I may not be poor. These matters and others like them, and whatever else we used to discuss among ourselves along these same lines I beg you, who know me so well, to pass on to both friends and lords, and to the lord of lords when the time seems proper, even though they have never been hidden nor kept silent by me. But there are those upon whom the truth must often be forced in order to have it penetrate into their mind, and I am not surprised that it applies also to whatever you are about to say concerning me. I know I appear more distant from the customs of our age and from the opinions of the multitude, with which I disagree strongly, not only in many matters but especially in what we are discussing. But the strength of your mind and the eloquence of your speech will drive out the incredulity of your listeners. My Socrates has always been worthy of authority and of trust in whatever he discusses, but especially in speaking of the secret thoughts of his friend; and, what is more, one listens to many things more favorably coming from the mouth of a friend than from one's own mouth. Finally, so that no one should be amused at my simplicity, do not conceal the idea that true liberality is not difficult, slow, or troublesome; that it cares for nothing except the one it embraces and will be obedient only to him. It does not order but instead obeys; it satisfies wishes and does not restrict them. Therefore we know why offering vast amounts to someone who seeks only limited quantities is a kind of denial. Farewell.

25 November, in transit.

Fam. VII, 7.

To Nicholas, Tribune of the City of Rome,[1] indignation mixed with entreaties regarding the Tribune's changed reputation.

I confess that you have caused me recently to repeat often and with great pleasure the words that Cicero has Africanus speak: "What is this that fills my ears, so great and so sweet a sound it is?" For what is more suitable for the great splendor of your name than such joyful and frequent announcements of your accomplishments? How eagerly I participated in this is revealed in my book of exhortations dedicated to you, full as it is of my urging and my praise of you. Do not, I pray, cause me to say: "What is this great and sad sound that hurts my ears?" Do not, I beg you, disfigure with your own hands the very lovely appearance of your fame. No man has the right to demolish the foundations of your creations except you alone; you can overturn what you founded: the architect is the best demolisher of his own works. You know in what manner you climbed to glory; if you turn your steps backward you descend, the descent by nature is easier. For the path is very wide, and what the poet has to say does not apply only to those in the infernal regions: "Easy is the de-

1. Perhaps the most spectacular political figure of the fourteenth century. As a result of an uprising of the populace against the noble rulers of Rome he emerged a champion of the new democratic form of government, and was sent as emissary to Clement to request approval of the new government. His mission failed despite his eloquent pleading, but because of his enthusiasm for ancient and early Christian Rome and his desire to restore Rome's former power and glory, he and Petrarch became fast friends. Upon returning to Rome he worked for a revolutionary upheaval in government which occurred in 1347. In his haste to deprive the nobility of their powers and to display pomp and ceremony reminiscent of classical Rome, he soon began losing the support of his followers. By the end of 1347 he abdicated under pressure from papal troops. When his subsequent attempts to persuade the emperor to destroy the temporal power of the papacy failed, he was excommunicated by the Pope, brought to Avignon where he was imprisoned and charged with heresy. Eventually he regained the favor of the Pope and by 1354 re-entered Rome as a senator ruling in the name of the Pope. In the fall of the same year he was killed by a Roman mob. Of all the rulers of the time he alone stirred Petrarch's imagination to a near boiling point.

scent to Avernus." Only in the diversity of life do we differ from the desperate wretchedness of those in hell, because as long as we are here we fall but can rise, we descend but can ascend; on the other hand no one has been returned from there. What indeed is more maddening than a man who, being able to stand, falls because of his confidence in rising again? The fall from above is always more dangerous; and what, I ask you, is loftier than virtue and glory from whose inaccessible summit you contemplate our times? And you reached this summit so energetically and along such an unaccustomed path that I do not know anyone anywhere whose downfall may be more terrible. You must fix your steps more firmly so that you stand unmoved and avoid affording a spectacle at which your enemy would laugh and your friends mourn. A famous name is not sought freely, nor indeed is it preserved easily; "for it is great labor to guard a great fame." Permit me to use with you a short verse of mine, which I liked so much that I was not ashamed to extract it from my everyday letters and transfer it to my *Africa*. And also help me avoid the very troublesome necessity of being forced to terminate in satire the lyrical foundations of your praises in which I have been heavily engaged (as my pen itself can attest). And do not think that I have fallen into this subject by chance, or that I am speaking without knowledge. After I left your court, a number of letters from friends followed my departure in which the questionable turn of your affairs and stories of your reputation much different from the first accounts reached me. They say that you do not love the people as you used to but instead only the worst part of the people, that those are the ones you obey, cultivate, and admire. What more can I say except those words that Brutus wrote to Cicero: "Your condition and your fortune are shameful!" Will the world then see you move from a leader of good men to a follower of reprobates? Can the stars have so suddenly changed against us and God have become so hostile? Where now is that healthy genius of yours? Where, to employ my accustomed language, is that guiding spirit of good works with which you were believed to be in constant dialogue, since it was not considered possible for a man to achieve such great things otherwise?

Why however do I become so upset? Things will always go as eternal law decrees. I cannot change them, but I can flee from them. You have therefore freed me from a considerable task: I was hastening to you with all my heart, but I am changing direction for I certainly shall not see you as another person. For a long time farewell to you also, dear Rome; if what I hear is true I would rather visit the Indians or the Garamantes. Are these things not true? Oh how very different the end is from the beginning; oh ears of mine that are too sensitive! They had become accustomed to glorious reports and cannot suffer another kind. But perhaps what I am saying may be false. Would that it were really so; for never would I more willingly have been wrong. The credibility of the writer I do indeed consider great, but because of a number of signs I am also suspicious of a certain envy on his part, an envy which I know not whether to call noble or unfriendly. Therefore, although grief impels me to say many things, I shall nevertheless check the impulse which I certainly could not do except to console my anxiety with disbelief. May God assist me in this, and may He make it more joyful than it sounds, and rather afflict me with the falsehood of one friend than with disloyalty and shameful actions of the other. If indeed through evil customs it has come to pass that falsehood is considered a daily and common sin, the fact remains that through the centuries there has been no license, no custom, no freedom that could free from guilt the betrayer of his homeland. It is preferable therefore that he make a few days of mine sad by lying than that you make all my life sad by forsaking your homeland. If he transgressed with words, he will be cleansed with words. If yours is indeed a real crime—which I hope is not the case—with what remedies can you ever hope to abolish it? Yours will be eternal glory or eternal infamy. Wherefore, if (as I hope is not the case) you are perhaps overlooking your reputation, at least consider mine. You know what a tempest is hanging over my head and how great would be the crowd of censurers who would conspire against me if you begin to collapse. To use the words of the young man in Terence, "therefore, while there is time, weigh everything again and again." Consider with great zeal, carefully, I beg you, what you may be doing, shake yourself sharply, examine yourself without deceit to see who you are, who you have been, whence you came and where you go, where you are permitted to proceed with unobstructed liberty, what kind of person you have been, what title you have assumed, what hope of yours you have realized, and what you professed to be. You will see yourself not as the master of a state but as its servant.

From Genoa, 29 November.

Fam. VII, 8.

To Giovanni Aretino.[1]

All your wishes are coming true, dear friend. I rejoice therefore for the freedom of our homeland, for the glory of our rulers, for the quietness of your citizens, for the increase in religion, for the public joy, and particularly for your honor by whose hands an attractive serenity and a sweet peace has descended over a city which had up to now been agitated and gloomy. I also rejoice at the desired success of your family affairs. It is very rare to have large numbers of joyful things happen, for indeed fortune always spoils pleasant things with some mixture of unpleasant things. But if ever she desires to be fully propitious, she knows how to elicit in marvelous ways unhoped-for sweetness from the very bitterness of things. Often, therefore, softening and bending unyielding things, she turns into joy what seemed to be sorrow. The gifts of fortune are to be used and not relied upon. She is now certainly using her art. Therefore what do you wish me to say? I begin to rejoice not so much at the desired events but at our very misfortunes and difficulties, as, for example, the manner in which the great and manifold joyfulness of my mind was tempered by that single illness of your body, or the many and various obstacles in my way whose effects I now hope will enable both of us to return together to our homeland. Farewell.

1. Chancellor of the Gonzaga family, rulers of Mantua, whom Petrarch met in Avignon in 1350.

Fam. VII, 9.

That open enmity is to be preferred to concealed hatred.

A country proverb says: "To make a dog's bed requires great toil." If you were to ask the meaning of this proverb, it is that you do not know where to place the cushion because the dog when it is about to lie down turns this way and that. Trifling indeed was the thought of the man who first said this; nevertheless it is true, and the same may be said about many men as one says laughingly about the dog. For there are many for whom nothing is done properly; and they so repeatedly turn about that one cannot know on what side they may fall or what they desire. When you believe that you have pleased them, you discover that you have accomplished nothing; all your labor and all your indulgence is lost. If you offer them the pleasures of the city, they praise the frugality of the country; if you are drawn away from the city, they ask for the multitude and curse solitude; if you begin to talk with them, they become annoyed, and if you are silent, they become indignant. They long for those who are absent; they despise those who are present. And often they even hate friends. To stay away from such people at all times would be highly advisable. You understand what I would like, and it is useless for me to say any more. Nevertheless I shall say something more lest in my silence I offer you and your mild nature an opportunity for dissimulation. Why do you take so much trouble, dear man? You have met someone who is far different and unequal to you, so retreat from your laborious and useless attempt; in vain did you strive to win him over, you cannot be a friend against his will, but you can become a formidable opponent. The one he presently despises he will now begin to fear if you start to reveal your anger openly; and he will realize who it was that he inexplicably provoked with a spirit of ingratitude. Pursue the custom of doctors with this sick and infected man; I urge you to try the opposite of what is expected. Since gentleness has proven vain, perhaps sternness will be more effective and animosity more powerful than love. The one he spurns because of flattery, he will fear if you openly display some opposition. I have given you advice contrary to my custom, but suitable for the matter at hand. What else can you do for one who calls love a trap and thinks that kindness is fear? Farewell.

To Giovanni dell' Incisa, an apology and some thoughts on perishable hope.

Your letter, full of highly pleasing and sweet censure, reached me on the banks of the Po on the evening of March 23. Compare the day of arrival with the date of the letter and see if in that same space of time it might not have arrived from Egypt. Together with it came also letters from other friends and two who are not personally known to me but certainly illustrious young men, as you say, yet old men according to their writing. Would that our city had more of them whom it would not send into exile, or rather would at least permit their departure to bring luster to other Italian cities. But I shall pass over this inexhaustible and ancient complaint and instead turn to the letters. Almost all of them contained but one idea: I am accused of having turned to Cisalpine Gaul after my promise to come to Florence, as if I were a despiser of my native land, and as if I had deceived the expectation and desires of many people who were awaiting me there. I could answer this in many ways, and what I may answer to the letters of others I do not yet know. Although very busy I shall nevertheless respond in some manner to your request that I follow my inspiration and while holding pen in hand I let it say whatever emerges naturally. Certainly with the others, in order to equal their style of writing, I shall need the protection of the Muses. With you, however, toward whom everything of mine must be open and naked without any artificiality, I would not hide even this one thing: the difficulties of the journey, the plague of this year which has trampled and destroyed the entire world, especially along the coast, my grief, and, unless I am mistaken, the evil and unjust treatment of my homeland would not have turned me from my original journey since I had already completed the most difficult part of my effort, and had arrived at Genoa. This then is the truer and sounder reason, that, persuaded by the hope that I had conceived in my mind and fatefully dreamed, I did not think it possible that I could not bring you a happier outcome of our affairs. Therefore it gave me pleasure to wait until actual fact would succeed hope. I was already considering not only a hurried journey but a flight, and I already seemed to be about to cross the Alps of Bologna (I have called the Apennines by their common name of Alps) without any sense of fatigue. Indeed it was from there that I, unexpected although not unawaited, had decided to present myself to you and to my friends. It so happened that from there I primarily expected aid for the undertaking, with any delay in such aid being most dangerous since the greatest speed would not have sufficed. But what can I say? I know that things are solid and hopes empty; I know that whoever loses hope loses nothing—I said too little, for indeed he gains a great deal. Yet I speak as an expert when I say that just as nothing smaller than hope can be lost, in the same way there is nothing which is more troublesome. The reason is that often the things we hope for become more valued than the things we possess, and we often know by attaining them how much the flattering hope of possessions has deceived us. This is why every time hope disappears before the actual event, we consider ourselves afflicted by serious inconvenience. God therefore forestalled my plan and declared unnecessary the cares which I considered proper, so that being taught in such fashion I would recognize that the opinions of men are vain. But enough of this. I shall say nothing more on the progress of my legal disputes: the matter has been turned over to the Curia. I hope that the schemes of that thief are exposed. Nevertheless I am prepared for whatever happens: I shall rejoice as victor; if I am defeated I shall console myself as being on the side of defeated justice. This is not the first time I have been harassed in the games of fortune; and I have learned with what skills the wound of mortal hope is evaded. Let matters therefore go as they please, provided I am not moved, nor by heaven do I know where I ought to be moved. Certainly I can with a clear mind either pursue what is mine or abandon what I was never able to pursue. The philosopher's road is a short cut to wealth, and teaches not that wealth should be accumulated but that desires should be diminished. I determined to follow this course lest I should happen upon that difficult and troublesome journey of complex business matters from which God and the very condition of my nature withdrew me, as it were, by the hand. Let the results of legal action, therefore, be as they will. My poverty, which is not burdensome or base but more envied by many than I should like, will suffice for me. If it really befits me, as it seemed to Seneca, I am wealthy. Farewell.

7 April in Verona.

To the same correspondent, on the reputation of an expected friend.[1]

One would not believe how my cares have diminished and how much has been added to my delight by certain recent news which I have decided to share as briefly as possible with you since time and place prevent me from being too lengthy. I hear that our Francesco, who, after undergoing many misfortunes and dangers both on land and sea, fortunately is safe, is approaching and is already in Marseilles. And he is now first hastening, as they say, on the straight road to me and is complaining, I am sure, about the great length of the journey, using with justification those words of Virgil: "We follow the fleeing Italy and we are rolling in the waves." He thought he would find me in France but I was not able to bear that rabble of the Curia. The short jump into the homeland should be simple for him. I know that he certainly burns with a desire to see you, but, believe me (I would not write this to you if you could in any fashion subvert my plan), believe me, as I was saying, it is fortune that decides the plans of men. Between planning and doing, as the multitude says, there is a high mountain of difference. When he arrives here, which I hope will be shortly, I shall take him in my arms. Love is a powerful thing, and it believes nothing is forbidden to it. I shall appear to act within my rights if I hide him in my home like a rediscovered treasure, and shall take care that he does not slip away from me again so easily. I want to give you early notice of this so that you will bear it with greater resignation when it happens; for I shall not share him with you as readily as I am sharing news of his arrival. Friendship is much more rare and precious than gold. And, if I am somewhat more greedy than usual, let the value of the thing possessed excuse the insensibility of the possessor. I do not refuse you as a partner in the event, provided that we share it when it is

1. This and the following letter refer to a pending visit of Franceschino degli Albizzi, a relative of Petrarch.

present. Therefore if you would like to enjoy your portion of it, and indeed so that you might have not one but two parts, let your love make you come here. Farewell.

From the peaceful valley of Parma, with a rustic pen, on 10 April.

*To the same correspondent, a complaint over the death of an
expected friend.*

Alas, what has happened? What do I hear? Oh deceitful
hope of mortals, oh useless cares, oh precarious human condition! There is nothing peaceful for man, nothing stable, nothing safe: here we see the power of fortune, there the traps of
death, and there the flattery of the fleeing world: we wretched
mortals are best on every side, and surrounded by so many
pitfalls how dare we promise ourselves any happiness? Deceived so often, and so often made fools of, we know not how
to divest ourselves of the habit of hope and of a credulity
which has deceived us countless times. So great is the allure-
ment of happiness though proven false! How often do I say
to myself, "Alas, you madman, alas, you blind man so forgetful of your affairs, look carefully, take note, give heed, abide,
reconsider, and impress this like a fixed sign which remains
indelible; recall the many deceits you have suffered; do not
ever hope for anything or take fortune seriously: she is a liar,
she is fickle, capricious, untrustworthy; you have at one time
known her flattery and gentleness, but later you have seen her
bitterness. Now that you know this deadly monster, you need
no longer be taught by anyone. Take counsel from your own
experience and beware of engaging with her again; disdain
with equal vigor whatever she promises or denies and despise
with equal vigor whatever she bestows upon you or snatches
from you." I had determined to do this and had made up my
mind; but after such a manly decision, here I am again falling
prey like a woman and a silly man. Or should I have perhaps
said ridiculously or indeed tearfully? To others perhaps I may
appear ridiculous; to myself I appear deeply miserable and
wretched. After so many disappointments of my hopes, I had
brought my mind to hope again and to believe in this fleeting
and almost serene moment of a winter night and to count
upon the happiness of the following day rashly, confidently,
and imprudently. I dared to flatter my bothersome cares by
saying: "No, my dear Francesco will arive, my brother, my
friend, united to me no less by desire than by name, no less

through love than through blood; he will be arriving and has perhaps already arrived." So strongly did I concentrate on him that often I seemed to see him before my eyes though he was so distant by land and sea and, alas, I was never to see him again in this foreign exile. But following a habit of mine which is common to all lovers, I used to comfort myself over the delay and absence by imagining fictitious meetings and conversations and I used to deceive myself, as it turned out, with a certain pleasure. How often whenever some of my servants to whom he had become very dear because of his charming personality came to me to make some announcement, I felt as though I was already speaking with him; how often when anyone knocked at my door did I become restless and found those pastoral verses coming to my mind: "I do not know what certainty is: and Hylas is barking at my door. Should we believe it or is it that those who love fashion their own dreams?" Wretched lover that I was I fashioned such dreams for myself, I was tormented with such cares, I burned with such anxiety, and I fed myself on such tenuous hope like a hungry person feeding himself abundantly as he dreams. The barking of dogs, the voices of servants, the creaking of a moving hinge or the trampling of the pavement by the hoof of an animal, and any kind of noise in general would disturb me. How many times I hastily threw down books that I was reading or a pen that I was holding! How often I arose, leaped up, eager to see and to embrace my dear friend and most welcomed partner in my cares, not just a brother (to use the words of Tullius which I could make my own in this instance), but equal to a brother in his charm, to a son in his obedience, and to a parent in wise counsel. I know not whether I came to know him too late or indeed too quickly! For had I not started to love the man, I would not be shedding these tears because of his death.

For almost two years I have relied on his company and friendship, a time, alas, scarcely sufficient for conversation, not to say for friendship. I find comfort for my bereavement only in this, that we both eagerly made recompense for the brevity of time by our very strong and mortal devotion and affection and that whatever is pleasant and sacred in friendship which others enjoy over a long period of time we accomplished in a brief time; thus while our delight might have been longer lasting, certainly our mutual trust could not have been more pure or genuine nor our friendship closer. Fortune envied me my taste of the pleasure of life. I received many and great tokens of his trust both when well and when sick. These I stored in the innermost recesses of my mind as if in a safe; and I hope that he felt the same toward me and perhaps more so because nature disposed him for greater gentleness and kindness. Now however the memory of those days is both bitter and sweet for me. On the one hand it charms me, on the other it grieves me, nor am I sufficiently clear about whether I would prefer to have been known by him or not. For while it is a happy and pleasant thing to have had such a friend, it is a most unhappy and bitter thing to have lost him. Almost never have I examined anything as I now have myself, and I must confess not without shame that I find more feeling in me and less strength than I thought; for I used to think (and it was proper because of my wide reading and long experience in life) that I had hardened myself against all blows and injustices of fortune. Unhappily I was wrong: there was nothing softer than I, nothing weaker. I used to think, indeed I was certain, that I loved my Francesco most tenderly; for his love and obedience to me deserved this treatment. However, how much I loved him became clear too late, and I did not learn it until I had lost him. Now my torn mind grieves the more out of control, the more it perceives that it has lost more than it had thought. For this reason nothing upset me more than the unexpectedness of that which not only could happen but could not fail to happen: I had not considered the possibility of his being about to die. Indeed if there were any order in this torrent of human affairs, he ought not to have died before me, having been born after me. Added to this was my fervent and anxious expectation of his arrival about which I have already said much; for this he had himself promised tearfully at his last departure and had repeated in his letters. My Socrates had announced not merely his future arrival but his pending one saying that he was hastening out of France on a straight path to me in Italy.

Woe is me! Now I recall: having been happy and hopeful up to then I had a premonition of his pending departure and my approaching misery and that I would soon experience the loss of the best part of myself, and was trying to extend my very brief happiness not knowing what fortune would do to me. I used to say: "He will come to me before he goes to see his aged father and his sweet brothers and sisters. I shall hold out my hand and I shall hang on to him, nor will there be need for great strength, for I shall find in him a great help rather than resistance. The love which resides in him shall become part of me." He himself would often repeat that verse from Horace, "I would like to live with you and gladly die with you." But the hand which I had thought of holding out to him death has held out; and my saying to you in my brief letter yesterday that fortune decides the plans of men is interpreted far differently than I thought. Now that my hope is gone together with my twofold desire, what shall I do? Shall I indulge in tears and sighs and in place of my lost friend shall I embrace my sorrow incessantly? Or shall I strive to appease my mind and to escape from the echoing threats of fortune into the stronghold of my reason? The latter appears preferable, the former more pleasing; virtue drives me to one; feeling bends me to the other. And I am uncertain where I should turn or what I should chiefly follow, and it is bad for me to fall too often and to rise too often.

Oh wicked and ungodly Savona who involved me in these anxieties, what can I invoke that you deserve? You have taken away half my soul, and you have inexorably cut down a young man in the bloom of his life, amidst his growing excellence, when he was just beginning, and now you lie heavily upon the breast which my Francesco inhabited. He himself has departed notwithstanding your unwillingness; you have no control over him for you cover over only his body and my hope. For this what else should I wish you? May your hills extend in a curved arch so that in the form of a straight and harborless shore you afford an unfavorable port to ships. May your walls crumble as well as your man-made garrisons which you threw in the face of the wind and the waves. May the force of Syrtis and violence of Euripus be transported there, and the fury of Scylla and the blows of Charybdis and whatever other dangers exist under the vast sea. May Aeolus set loose his restless brothers, the South Wind and the others, which are accustomed to abusing your shores, so that while the entire world is calm perpetual storms might crash upon you alone. And may whatever either in the way of death or disease this pestilential year has spread through all the lands and seas flow upon you only; and may that plague that strikes others on an annual basis be with you eternally. And may the island of Sardinia and whatever there is anywhere under the impure heavens be cleansed; may the swamps be purified together with the sulfurous lakes and the deep, slimy marshes; and may the North become warm and Ethiopia become cool, and Africa become emptied of its serpents, and Hyrcania of its tigers, and the world of all its monsters and huge beasts, and may they all assemble in you from every part of the earth. And may the gloomy mists and the deadly waters and the inclement weather and the cold and the heat rage in you; in sum, with the final salvation of mankind may you alone perish and become the place of the dead, and the region of terror and fear, and the home of mourning and affliction. And may the pilgrim, the merchant, and finally your own citizens flee you, may the weary traveler from the highest peaks of the mountains despise you, and the disturbed sailor survey you from the deep and avoiding your infamous reefs, use his oars to hasten the work of his sails. Alas, where is my grief driving me? What am I saying? Or where am I? I, a mortal, lament so strongly over mortal things and I curse the innocent land which receives what is its due, when I know not where I myself will die and where on earth I shall return my remains. Therefore, dear brother, one must abstain from wailing and sighing and must begin praying in behalf of our brother who has gone ahead while we remain behind; that is more becoming to men. As for you, oh lovely city, which preserves my buried friend, returning finally to my true self, I express my gratitude because he would now perhaps lie in a strange land if you had not received him. The shortness of his life might have been indeed fated; and it is to your merit that my friend, although young, and yet already weary with cares, at least enjoys the repose of an Italian grave, a trifling consolation but highly desired by many illustrious men of the past. While I was hitherto desirous of seeing you to view your lands and their attractiveness; hereafter I shall much more willingly see you as the preserver of remains that are so dear to me, though it is a bitter pleasure. For if the death of her Pompey and his dreadfully mutilated body once so attracted his beloved wife to the sands of the Nile that she was unwilling to depart from there, why shall I not love the Italian shore which is the eternal abode of my dear friend? Hail, oh outstanding land, most faithful guardian of the remains of my brother; you taught me to weep more readily and to hope more sparingly. You, however, dear brother, snatched from me before your time, for whom I am grieving so deeply, farewell eternally; indeed I expected from you joy and consolation in these lands where we are continually dying, where there is no place either for joy or for comfort. I expect to enjoy all these things with greater certainty, God willing, and in greater amounts hereafter in the land of the living. But alas I am now proving what I read in Statius: "Speaking is sweet to those in misery." It is certainly so; for how many things I did not feel did I painfully pour forth impetuously rather than through rational judgment! Nor am I satisfied with speaking but instead become more excited and indeed know not how to stop: I shall therefore simply break off.

To Cardinal Giovanni Colonna, condolences on the deaths of his brothers and grandsons.

I shall freely confess (for although I may not be solvent I am a trusted debtor) that I owe you everything, certainly my talent and this little body that I inhabit as a pilgrim, and whatever external goods fall to my lot. For your palace contributed no less to my mind than to my body and to my destiny. Because I was brought up by you since my youth, grew up under you and was educated by you so far as the malevolence of intervening misfortunes or the mediocrity of my talent allowed, it is only right that I must persist in directing this pen, this hand and my mind, however humble, to the consolation and solace of your mind. I remember having done so to the best of my ability in other misfortunes of ours, and I do not believe that you have forgotten. In deed in this so serious, so unmanageable and deadly wound which death, not yet satisfied with our tears, has brought to us I have not yet found what to do, what to say, or even how to open my mouth. I collapsed in my misery at the first news of the event, and I was petrified as if at an unexpected crash of a thunderbolt. Then as soon as I could I began to collect the scattered arms of my reason and to lift my prostrate and collapsed mind. I requested the letter reporting the unhappy event of which I had sadly heard through the sorrowful announcement of that excellent man, Paganino Milanese, who rules the city. When the letter was shown me I read it with much weeping. But indeed everything in it seemed confused because of the ambiguities, and nothing could be learned with any deep certainty. The report had started at Orvieto; soon it spread to Florence and across the Apennines by means of the letters of certain clerics, which reached Bologna first; then, as always, they reached us with greater bulk and variations. In such doubt, I therefore (since nature does bring it about that those things we hear that displease us we hardly ever admit or completely accept) chose to predict happier news for myself. So did my sick mind run to the pleasantness of better hope. However, it was but the vanishing and fleeing happiness of a wretched dreamer. What more can I say? Although that hope steadily diminished with the subsequent arrival of new messengers, I was able to learn nothing of any certainty before the woeful letter of our Socrates reached me. And it was thus, amazing as it appears, that the calamities of the Tiber reached me from another world at the river Rhone. Because that letter indeed shut off any refuge for my hesitant hope, the limited power of reason, which I sometimes called forth for the comfort of my own mind and others, was crushed by the weight of tears and laments. However, I did not surrender, nor did I stop. How often, having succeeded in standing, I tried to write something! How often I brought out my books, tried to wipe off the mildew from my decaying talent, and entered like a sorrowful investigator into the most intimate recesses of my memory! In short I did everything in my power, but all in vain. I came across certain letters in prose and poetry which in response to the frequent visits of misfortune I had sent you in these last years, letters in which I was unable to find anything satisfactory not only for alleviating my anguish, or yours, but even to soothe it. It shamed me to repeat commonplaces so often, and yet because my talent had been exhausted by the earlier attempts, I did not have the strength to work out new ones. I did not, however, desist from trying to do something in the hope that perhaps some beginning might succeed beyond all expectation. I could show you three or four beginnings of letters different in styles and in almost any other way called for by the variety of events which my serious state of mind gave birth to. How I felt about these efforts may be seen by the oblique lines that my pen drew across them like so many wounds inflicted by their author and chastiser. Being entangled in these difficulties I resolved to remain silent and to commit my present grief to Christ, supreme consoler, for comfort and resolution.

I have said these things as an excuse for my silence. The fact that I am writing to you after so much time results not from a change in condition, but from the unexpected joy which of late certain recent letters of the same Socrates brought to my spirits which had become so obstinate in their grief that (according to the habit of wretched people) they had begun to find joy in their very grief. In those letters I became aware of the strength, greatness, and superiority of your mind amidst so many blows of misfortune, and I, who had borne my grief in silence, could not bear the overwhelming joy, nor avoid breaking out into pious tears and words seeing that what modesty, sorrow and respect had forbidden me vainly to attempt in empty words of advice had been accomplished by that heavenly Master to whom it is proper to render thanks not only for many other things but especially for the fact that He granted you, with all your experience in life's battles, exemplary fortitude and steadfastness. Therefore, having recomposed the condition of my weary heart and having calmed the flood of my tears which obscure the serenity of the mind the more violently they attack and destroy the appearance of truth, what else could I recommend to you or request from you, my grace and almost only supporter of my hope and that of many others, except that you must persist in your present manner and withstand the abuses of threatening fortune with a steadfast mind? And you must view the violent and arrogant laws of our nature with moderation: what we are, where we are, how long we will continue to be what we are or remain here from where we set out, what port we seek, among what reefs we navigate, how much sea we have traversed, how little remains, how much danger remains before the end, and how many there have been who having safely sailed the stormy waters perished at the entrance of the port or on the shore. Finally how heavy a yoke rests upon the children of Adam, not as on the necks of oxen for alternate hours and days, but truly always. No one enjoys immunity from this, or respite, from the day one emerges from the womb of one's mother as it is written, until the day of burial and return back to the mother of all. All we mortals are weighed down by the yoke which is as heavy as it is continuous, from which neither race, nor beauty, nor wealth, nor talent, nor eloquence, nor power can free us. Nor can arms, followers, friends, even armies, fleets, or troops accomplish this, but only patience, forbearance, and steadiness. One must call to mind what power fortune had over those who, embracing those perishable and fleeting favors of hers, submitted to her power. As for the rest, she tempts them, drives them and taunts them but does not overcome them. One should recall the examples offered by all ages, either of the wealth of very powerful people which she terminated, or of the kingdoms of very famous rulers she trampled upon, or of anything that in her rage she left intact anywhere since the beginning of the world.

There is not time to recount stories here, for I did so in other consolatory letters to you, and those that I could put together with any care are already known to you. Nor shall I behave abjectly or effeminately for I address neither a woman, child, nor an ordinary member of the flighty masses, but a strong man possessing always a lofty nature, now, as I hope, stronger than usual and greater because of the very misfortunes that have befallen him, a man marked by the repeated wounds of fortune, and with the strength of virtue greater than ever, and disdainful of her threats and battles. Furthermore I shall not apply charms and flattery to so many harsh misfortunes, nor make reference to the hope of grandchildren although even such hope, thanks to God's compassion on our destiny, may not be lacking. Instead I shall reveal you to yourself. I urge you to stop counting your reasons for mourning and to stop considering your losses; and turn your eyes cleansed by your tears, turn to those things that remain. Consider the condition of your family: the home of the Colonnas may have fewer columns than usual, but what difference does it make provided that the firm and solid foundation remains. Julius Caesar was alone in not having any brother or children, and in not knowing the name of his father. Nevertheless what that one man accomplished, everyone knows. I urge you to convince yourself of something that is most true. Fortune is least to be feared where she rages most strongly. She did all she could; in a short time she carried off your brothers and grandchildren and relations, and reduced a most flourishing family stock to a few members. Regard her fearlessly and full of noble stubbornness. Except for your magnanimous father there is now almost nothing left that she can strike. And just as nothing human has been intolerable for him, thus nothing unexpected can happen to him henceforth: he has left the boundary of mortal life far behind him. Indeed what other elder can you point out to me who can count so many years of life as he can count years of happiness and of glory? Indeed he would be the most fortunate of all who have lived in this age of ours had he departed somewhat earlier. Furthermore anxiety and fear are ordinarily for those minds who expect them; those who have already received their portion are safe. With how much comfort in fact will your fortitude supply him amidst the difficulties of his old age in which ruthless fortune has entangled him toward the end of life and from which nothing could disentangle him except his own power or the power of his surviving son! Let these things and others similar to them provide you with remedies for your present misfortune. The remaining suggestions which may appear remedies are really torments: they do not relieve, but rather aggravate. Death is not redeemed with tears nor is it overcome with weeping. It cannot be avoided, it can only be scorned. This is the only victory that can be enjoyed over this insurmountable and inevitable evil. I would say more except that I know that a mind which is erect and mindful of itself does not need a talkative consoler. Words do not raise up a man who is dejected and forgetful of his own nobility. Just continue what you have begun and behave inwardly with the good faith that you have revealed externally, unless a disturbed mind hide beneath a calm exterior. This was most dangerous to many, for while they disguised their upsets and behaved in public as though they were happy, they were dejected in their private rooms and wasted away in concealed grief. Such artifice is appropriate for an insane mind and labors only for one's own destruction. It is much safer to confess one's grief and to weep openly. Finally, to repeat something which I recall saying quite often and which is worthy of being said more often, you are located in a lofty position from which you cannot flee the sight and judgments and conversations of men; wherefore concern for your dignity and reputation should be greater. Among many injustices fortune deserves credit for having done this one good thing for you: she has provided great cause for praising you. Those who live among us and those who shall be born after us will have reason to admire you, to praise you, to hold you up as an example, and to admire the strength of your mind unbroken despite misfortunes and your noble dignity worthy of the true Roman spirit. Weeping continually over these things I bid you farewell.

Fam. VII, 14.

To Bruno di Firenze,[1] *that the judgment of love is blind.*

Your letter found me alone, or rather with only my cares as company. It was loaded with my praises, and although there was no one present I nevertheless blushed as I read it. The fact that it had followed in its content the testimony not of yourself or of another lover but of that very friendly elder took away some of the embarrassment. For to all those things that were either said therein or could be said along the same lines one could easily answer: the judgment of lovers is usually blind. As we find in Horace, Balbinus takes pleasure in Agna's polyp, while among the people there is the popular love story about the man who, overcome by the love of a one-eyed woman, was sent at length by his concerned parents to foreign shores, and having overcome his love after several years he returned to his country where by chance he met the woman he had loved so strongly. Suddenly shaken by the sad sight, he asked how she had happened to lose her eye. She answered, "I have hardly lost an eye; rather you have found yours." This was indeed plainly and admirably spoken. But let us not add further examples. If ever there were a lover, our elderly friend truly loves all his friends. With respect to any other matters, therefore, if you have any confidence in me, you ought to pay careful attention to him not as if he were Jupiter in Dodona or Apollo at Delphi, but as a particularly truthful man. Whenever his sweet and flattering words pertain to me whom he loves like a father, believe him sparingly except perhaps (and I am not certain whether this could happen to a wise man) insofar as to err and to be deceived are sometimes pleasant. As for the notable poem which was inserted into your letter, it would have received no reply, being sufficiently appreciated by the silent admiration of my heart, were it not for the great merits of your talent which radiates within the great cloud of ignorance of the multitude. You will therefore take in good part a brief poem, still in rough form, which you will receive under separate cover and which I

1. Florentine rhetorician and great admirer of Petrarch.

barely managed to compose since my mind has been so over-whelmed by grief. I send it to you not so much that it should be viewed as an answer, but rather lest there be no answer. Farewell.

To Luchino Visconti, lord of Milan,[1] *concerning learned princes.*

I found your letters just as I had hoped, indeed as I had not hoped. I am happy that this exchange has at last intervened between your excellence and my humbleness, and that such a stroke of luck has opened for me access to news of you. As for what the last part of your letter bids me do, I shall devote all my care to it and shall make a special effort, especially since such labor will rather be like pleasure. While the gardener devotes himself to herbs and plants, I devote myself to words and poetry by the inviting murmur of a stream which flows plaintively and divides a fruitbearing grove that branches out on the right and left. You will now taste the first fruits of such study. Perhaps such matters do not affect a mind that is involved in truly lofty cares, as is the custom these days. Nevertheless I know that those great rulers of state, Julius and Augustus Caesar, often found relaxation from the tasks of ruling and from the labors of wars in the tranquillity of our type of idleness, and their hands which were unbending in the use of the sword they directed from striking their enemy to counting syllables, and directing their voices, accustomed to thundering at opposing battle lines and usually heard among the sounds of trumpets and the din of battle, to the sweetness of poetic rhythms. I pass over Nero in order not to stain outstanding study and glorious names through the recollection of that monster. How dedicated to the Muses do we consider Hadrian whose efforts were so determined that he slackened not even when death was near? Unbelievable as it may appear he composed, at the threshold of death, some verses on the departure of the soul, verses which I would repeat here except that I trust they are known to you and to some of your friends. What shall I say about Marcus Antoninus who, when he ascended to power not through ambition but through his merits, retained his former name of philosopher and scorned his new title, believing that

1. Powerful head of the Visconti family, rulers of Milan, and a great admirer of Petrarch.

being a philosopher is considerably greater than being a ruler? The number of such examples is huge; and there is scarcely any prince who considered himself to be both a prince and a man without a background of letters. But the times have changed; kings of the earth have proclaimed war on letters; I believe they fear that they may befoul their gold and jewels with dark ink, but do not fear to possess a mind blind and shabby in its ignorance. But it is a serious and dangerous matter to offend with words a live and powerful prince; nor is there need for a long discourse to produce such offence: whoever lives badly is offended by the naked truth. The dead however are blamed with greater safety. As the Satirist says, "The fallen Achilles is dangerous to no one." Therefore it would be wise not to name the princes of our time who are enemies of letters. It is not safe to write against one who can proscribe, as Asinius Pollio, the great orator, says jestingly against Augustus Caesar; and I now follow his example completing my public indictment without revealing the names of the guilty ones. Almost all are guilty of the same error, and while none desires to follow those rulers friendly to letters whom I have cited above they imitate eagerly Licinius Caesar who (peasant type that he was) hated letters so much that he called them "poison and a public plague," words that are certainly not worthy of an emperor but of a peasant. It was not so with Marius who was likewise of peasant stock but, according to Cicero, truly a man whose involvements or the very nature of letters caused him to turn too late to studies, but he nevertheless loved learned men and especially poets whose talents he hoped some day would celebrate the glory of his deeds. And indeed what man is there, unless he is truly imbued with a rustic insensibility, who though he may not find great pleasure in letters, does not at least desire fame for himself which is never sought without virtue, and never preserved without letters? The memory of men is unstable; paintings are transitory; statues are perishable, and among the inventions of mortals nothing is more stable than letters. Whoever does not fear them, ought to esteem them, and those words of Claudian are true indeed: "Virtue enjoys having the Muses as witnesses; poetry loves whoever does things worthy of a poem." Indeed our contemporaries who do nothing except what is worthy of satire hate letters because they fear them. Therefore they all agree with Licinius and none with Marius nor with the others. Through an apathy the likes of which has never been seen, they allow themselves to be pilfered by plebeians of that very thing which they held most precious, and have slowly arrived at a point where now amidst their wealth they are feeling very serious poverty. And so those who marched into battle for a small amount of wealth or for a small corner of their kingdom abandoned the inestimable treasure left them by their ancestors and allowed foreigners to enter into the palace of the mind, and these in turn drove them away after depriving them not of their royal cloaks but of their heavenly endowment. As a result we see that royal disgrace in which the rabble is learned while kings are crowned asses, as a certain letter by a Roman emperor to the King of the Franks called them. You therefore, being a very great man of our time and lacking nothing in order to rule except the title of king, make it difficult for me to see which of the two views of rulers you adhere to, but I do hope for all the best from you. And thus, not to prolong this excessively, I have sent your excellency a brief poem, which I composed extemporaneously among those trees—a part of which you request in such a friendly manner. If I hear that it pleased you (for I seem to have some ability in that form), I shall appear much more liberal than you think and than my situation would seem to allow. Farewell.

13 March.

Fam. VII, 16.

To Jacopo Fiorentino,[1] that honest censure is to be preferred to false praise.

Your letters full of praises for me which I wish were deserved recently reached me and soothed my mind with a wonderful sweetness. I judged in them rather the affection that they reflected than the effect that they sought. If they were sent by anyone else I would judge them as jesting; but since they emerged from the purest depths of your mind I know that they do not intend to deceive. Would that they did not deceive themselves! Thus, because I am sure that everything you write appears true to you, I rejoice in your affection, and I have pity for your error. However, I would not wish you to err less, so pleased am I at seeming to you to be what I am not. I would prefer to be what I seem; but if this is denied from on high, do continue your friendly error. Indeed, although I was unable to keep myself from returning time and again to your letters, I yet felt that reading them was fraught with danger; for so seriously and elegantly and sweetly and, in short, persuasively did you write them that great care had to be taken lest anything which you expressed so easily should turn a reader into a believer. If you succeed in this you will have a companion in your belief; except that, though your error be generous and innocent, you would involve me in a ridiculous one. Therefore I determined, not without some difficulty, henceforth to turn my eyes away from those portions of your letters, and if hereafter you wish to make me a devoted and zealous reader of your letters I ask you to deal with me in a satirical fashion rather than in a typical one, for in this there is much room. If you tried to pay close attention, you will see in me many qualities that are questionable even to the eyes of a friend, qualities that cannot escape the censure even of a favorable tongue. I beg you devote yourself to this; turn your most eloquent pen this way; reveal me to myself; take

1. An ardent Florentine admirer of Petrarch in whose personal library Petrarch found many classics unknown to him, especially works of Cicero.

over the power of your tongue; seize, bind, strike, burn, cut, restrain all exaggeration, cut away all that is superfluous, and do not fear that you will cause me either to blush or to grow pale. A dismal drink drives away dismal illnesses. I am ill, who does not know it? I must be cured by more bitter remedies than yours; bitter things do not yield to sweet things but rather bitter things purge themselves in turn. If you want to be of benefit to me, write something that hurts me.

I have received together with the other things Cicero's oration in defense of Milo and thank you for it. This is not the first time that you have shown such kindness to me; I shall have it copied and shall return it. The comedy that you seek I confess I wrote at a very tender age with the title of *Philology*. It is now located at a great distance, but even if I had it with me this common friend of ours who will deliver this will make you understand what I think of it and the extent to which I consider it worthy of your ears and of other learned men. I wish you every happiness and well-being and hope that you will always remember me.

Padua, 25 March.

Fam. VII, 17.

To Giberto, grammarian of Parma,[1] *on the academic education of boys.*

Embrace with the strength of your paternal solicitude our young man who is in need of advice and who is troubled by the torments of his age. As you see, he has now arrived at the Pythagorean crossroads of his life; never will his prudence be less nor his danger greater. The left path indeed leads to hell, the right to heaven; but the former is easy, level, very wide, and worn through usage by many people, while the latter is steep, narrow, difficult, and marked with the footsteps of few men. It is not I who say this; but rather the Master and Teacher of all who say it: "Wide is the path that leads to perdition, and many are those who enter it; narrow is the road that leads to life, and few are those who find it." Indeed if our boy were to be abandoned to himself what do you think he would do? He will either follow the rumbling of the multitude in the manner of the blind, or he will take the paved road and, as is the nature of heavy bodies, will be borne downwards by his weight. I beg you, most excellent man, aid him, guide and sustain him in his heedlessness and in his wavering. Let him long to follow the right path with you as his leader; let him learn to ascend. This he will do more readily if you were to pay particular attention to him, and if the unusual medicine of your prudence were to relieve the disease of his youth. You know on what side he leans, and on what side he may be close to destruction; let him be supported on that side with a suitable protection. It is an ancient rule of doctors that opposites are cured with opposites. If he persists in joyfulness oppose it with something sad, and if he is reduced to sadness oppose it with something joyful. If his talent becomes blunted because of too much effort, like a clever farmer restore it by means of seasonal interruptions; if he becomes rusty through inaction, let exercise make him shine again. Let toil season his rest, and rest season his toil, and let his mind be refreshed at times through rest, and at times through action. Furthermore, differences of character are innumerable

1. A Florentine teacher for whom Petrarch had high regard.

and the remedies not only for the diseases of the body but also for the passions of the mind are diverse, so that what is injurious to one, is healthy for another. In this lies the central perception of the teacher. Youthful fear is soothed by friendship and flattery, haughtiness is restrained through threats and sternness; nor is there only one rule of scholastic discipline: unimportant things are to be punished with words, serious things with lashes, one person is to be encouraged with praises, another is to be restrained by shame, another is to be wearied with labor, while still another is to be tamed with the rod. To the generous mind one must give the drive of persistence, to the exhausted mind relief, to the despairing mind assistance, ardor to the lukewarm mind, a bridle to the precipitous mind, and spurs to the slow mind. I am burdening an expert with well-known things so that his memory may once again catch fire by being rubbed. A great portion of the liberal arts consists of things they hold in common, and sometimes we revisit familiar places more readily, while oftentimes we delight not so much in new songs as in well-known ones. To return to our subject, you must, against your will, give our boy a helping hand lest he fall or lest he take the wrong road. Teach him the great danger with which one advances, and then the great labor and the great expense with which one may retreat. Show him how much safer it is henceforth to follow the straight path than to turn off of it with the hope of returning, something that drove many men to destruction. Show him that falls are easy and always ready for anyone, while ascents require great strength, great effort, and much assistance. Show him that the dreams of the rabble are vain and that its opinions concerning all things and especially about passion are wrong. Show him that along the left road there is nothing except filth, darkness, brittleness, and perishable things; and that there is nothing on the right road except beauty, brightness, and immortal strength. Show him how much more appropriately what is written applies to those who follow that former road: "They foresake the right road and they wander through shadowy paths," or those other words: "Their roads are dark and slippery," and those others "The road of ungodly men is full of shadows; they know not to what depths they are sinking." These other words are indeed more appropriate for those traveling over the other road: "Their roads are beautiful and their paths peaceful," and those others: "The road of the just is without obstacles." And about both the same thing can be said: "The Lord knows the ways that are on the right; winding indeed are those that lie on the left." Nor were these words said to one people: "Behold I personally bequeath to you the way of life and the way of death." Make him reflect upon these things, make him see how reprehensible they are according to so many available examples, and how uncertain is the wandering through the tortuous windings of this brief life, whence death often overtakes those who are returning or are considering turning back. In short, as long as the affair remains wholesome and he is master of himself and has not assumed the yoke of sin, teach him how much easier it is to shun that yoke than to shake it off, and impose upon his tender ears as often as possible those poetic words: "By this path one goes to the stars"; and those other words: "This is the path we take to the Elysian Fields, but the one on the left is full of punishments for the evil and sends them to the ungodly Tartarus." In this a wise man of the Hebrews agrees with our poet when he says: "The road of sinners is composed of stones at the end of which there is but the infernal region and darkness and punishment." At his age let him become accustomed to such warnings and let him drink of these teachings. Just as fresh material readily takes on any form, it is also easy to impress upon an as yet unhardened mind whatever habit one wishes. Whenever one offers access to false notions they are more difficult to exclude. Pursue the matter therefore while an opportune time offers some chance of desired success; and be sure of this much, that by providing that boy with this kind of assistance you do more than if you were carefully to pour within him all the liberal arts at the same time. There is little question that knowledge of letters is a great thing, but the virtuous mind is greater, although a receptive student could hope to acquire both from you. You know how much talent can achieve, you know all the better for having experienced it. I know only one thing: it befalls a few to become men of letters, but it is possible for all to be good, providing they voluntarily subject themselves to good leaders. Knowledge is more fastidious indeed than virtue, since it may be more noble. The former deems worthy of itself only the talents of a few; the latter despises the mind of no one except of those who had previously despised her. Farewell.

Padua, 26 March.

Fam. VII, 18.

To Lancillotto di Piacenza,[1] *man of arms, on his multiple cares in writing letters to friends, and that love is not assuaged through poetry.*

Eager to write, my right hand clings to the pen but is uncertain of what to write, so overwhelmed have I been with the many and various messengers who reached me almost at the same time. From one side the Tiber seemed to interrupt me, from another the Arno, while from still another the Rhone. One informed me of the state of our unfortunate city and indeed of its destruction which I cannot hear without tears since it had such great merit in my eyes; another transmitted to me the complaints of certain gifted youths directed against me in different styles but with a single substance, that they were indignant and seriously disturbed by my having stopped off here when I was expected there, and asking why I so preferred this place to my native land, a question which has been the source of the greatest astonishment to many people. A third messenger delivered the letters of my friends in the Curia containing the substance of a mild, but nevertheless powerful censure of my silence over the distress of my distinguished friend (a silence I was hardly accustomed to keep in less important misfortunes and which I kept not by intent, but rather because of the stupor and sorrow that I felt at the fall of that very famous family). To which was I first to turn? I owed compassion to my Roman friends, explanations to my Florentine friends, and consolation to my transalpine friends. As I hesitated at this crossroads a fourth piece of news reached me. A certain person who was related to me in name and blood, but, even more important, very acceptable and dear to me in his love and in his respect for me, while hastening to France in order to visit me, was struck down by a death which has highly disturbed me since he succumbed to illness, to the rigors of the journey or the harshness of heaven which had forced him to stop off in Savona. With what words shall I console his aged father, the bereavement of his unhappy mother, or the soli-

1. A Lombard nobleman associated with the Visconti, and a strong admirer of Petrarch.

tude of his brothers and sisters when I cannot assuage my own tears? And so, caught in the rush of events, I did what I am accustomed to do in such cases, and as is the custom of my laziness: I determined to neglect all the misfortunes equally, and indeed, if possible, to forget them. While I was in such a condition your letter which arrived so unexpectedly removed my sluggishness and returned my abandoned and forsaken pen to my hand, so sweet was its seriousness and so serious its sweetness. Without question the fact that you included the title of my *Africa* among its contents forced me unwillingly to emit a sigh, for you are not alone in awaiting the conclusion of that work. For me indeed it would be simpler to count the sands of the sea and the stars of the heavens than all the obstacles envious fortune has put in the way of my labors. I myself await its end, uncertain as to whether I had spent sleepless nights utterly in vain or whether at least some joy, though late, is reserved for me for my labor. But if all goes well I shall see to it that no one will precede you in occupying the finest seats for this performance of my talents, of whatever sort it may be. I read the last portion of your letter smilingly; for it helps to know that one has such partners in one's ancient illness, and I am compelled to believe that it is not an ordinary happening when it occurs in such a subject. And indeed the comfort of vernacular poetry which, unless I am mistaken, you humorously request of me, I would say should rather be requested and expected of you if a troubled mind can be cured with words. But alas, what Horace says is all too true: "Do you hope that through these verses you can remove from your heart your heavy sorrows and passions and cares?" They rather increase and find nourishment. Therefore the cure for this illness lies elsewhere and Aesculapius, to tell the truth, was its discoverer. The herbs with which it is prepared, however, are certainly either not in your garden or are unknown to you or else you avoid using them because of their disagreeable taste. Farewell and please accept a remedy which I consider effective against all evils of our lives: examine with great care whatever tries to affect the condition of your mind. So, if you were delighted with the beginning, meditate on this ending.

Fam. VIII, 1.

To Stefano Colonna the elder,[1] a tearful consolation on the extremely harsh blows of fortune.

Alas, pitiable old man, alas, most enduring leader, what crime did you commit against Heaven, what did you do to be punished with so long a life? Not undeservingly were you called another Metellus; you were alike in all things, your fatherland, your family, your wealth and attractiveness, your unique and admirable qualities of body and mind, even your outstanding wife, fertile in noble offspring, your consular dignity, the highest command in the Roman army and your honors in conquests and victories, your lengthy old age and a constant good fortune up to the very end. If she has thus far dared to introduce adversity into your life, such as the many you endured in the famous persecutions, she did so in order to remove your noted harshness and to shed light on the dignity of your glory. Fortune continued being propitious to you until almost the hundredth year of your life; and you, likewise born a prince of this world and in the queen city of this world, were able to have your name listed among the very rare examples of the kind of happiness that could certainly be hoped for in this life, not as happened to Sophidius, that needy and lowly plowman who was declared happy by a lying oracle, but as would happen to the most glorious of all Roman leaders of our age in something I would certainly call most difficult and almost impossible, the very best relationship with fortune. Excluding the Arcadian foreigner, you could, as a Roman, sit more confidently with a Roman, as a prince with a prince, a Stefano with a Metellus. Aside from the superiority of your religion which admits of no comparison between pagan and Christian, he also had to yield to you at least in the number of brothers and children

1. An elder of the Colonna family and father of the various church dignitaries with whom Petrarch was friendly, he was deeply involved in Roman politics as a member of the Roman nobility. He was introduced to Petrarch in Avignon by his son Giacomo in 1330, and was highly respected by Petrarch. He eventually outlived all of his sons and reached the age of 100.

that you enjoyed. We read that he had no brother, while you had five, all outstanding men, and, to put it briefly, no less famous for their race and good fortune than for their virtues and glory. He had four sons, praetorians, consuls, censors, and triumphing generals. You had seven: one a Cardinal of the Roman church, another would have gone beyond the Cardinalship if he had arrived at a legal age, three bishops, and two generals who, to tell the truth, were almost equal in military glory to their father. He had three daughters while you had six, concerning whose conduct I would prefer to say nothing rather than to be brief. And, dear God, what a flourishing following of grandchildren and great grandchildren of either sex! What a joyful group, what a pleasant fellowship! Not to prolong this excessively, let us take your first grandson, Giovanni, born of your first son, who was indeed divine and a young man overflowing with that ancient and truly Roman nature whom you would admit to have fully deserved the surname "Colonna" which he acquired. Nor was he called 'of Colonna,' but indeed was referred to as only 'a Colonna,' a column on which most certainly the hopes of friends as well as of the vast and ancient family rested. He had already grown into another Marcellinus, being of the same age, the same strength of mind, the same power of body, as well as love of arms, fondness for horses, and skill in riding; he was also becoming daily another Marcellus and became even more famous than Marcellus. Such being the case, wherever the Roman names echoes you appeared to the multitudes even more fortunate than the most fortunate, if such a thing is possible, and more eminent than the very greatest. But wise men bid us to expect the end, as with that most fortunate king of the Lydians who was admonished by the advice of Solon; for the fact remains that death alone decides on human happiness and even more surprisingly on eternal happiness. No one therefore can be absolutely certain; happiness is a slippery matter. Do you wish that I consider you happy? Then die; the true witnesses of life are one's remains and one's tomb; prior to this, the higher your position the more serious your fall. You would have been the only true example of happiness in our day if your departure had been like the course of your life. There is no evil that is not encompassed in a long lifetime. A lifetime of many years is like a voyage of many days. One does not see only one star in heaven or only one storm on the seas; the rudder must be constantly turned and the sails must be constantly lowered, and often, and there is nothing more dangerous in sailing than having to turn them continually because of shifting winds. You can never expect to enjoy for long an undisturbed calmness either on the sea or in life; the appearance of things changes constantly, and often a very clear morning ends with a very cloudy evening. That famous sailor of Virgil says concerning the sea, "Are you asking me to ignore the appearance of a still sea and quiet waves, or to have faith in this monster?" This is what a wise man says to himself concerning life. The well-armed mind, prepared by constant meditation, fears nothing; infinite adversity casts down the unprepared mind anticipating nothing but joyful things. But I return to the changes in your fortune.

You long ago buried five of your brothers. Who is there who would not have been cast down by the fall of so many "columns?" You nevertheless remained unshaken, and as is appropriate for a great and unconquerable mind you transferred the entire burden of your household upon yourself alone. You then compensated for the irreparable damage with immortal fame, and you found consolation in the memory of its very great deeds; and a long succession of grandsons replaced your brothers. Meanwhile your beloved and dear wife was taken from you, "Fortunate in her death and not reserved for this grief." She was indeed much more fortunate in her death than the wife of Evander. It was to her that the previous citation referred; for an opportune death decreed that she should miss seeing the bitter destruction of only one son, but your wife the destruction of a great number of children. The oldest of your sons upon whom you relied heavily passed away. After you had gone through so much, the painful double blow struck you very hard but you nevertheless remained firm on the crumbling foundations. Then when the others achieved an enviable greatness and glittered in an astonishing light of success, you made your peace with fortune, and mingling the bitter with the sweet you soothed your longing for the dead with consolation over the survivors. Now the sorrow of the earlier losses had slowly been erased, and, as I said, in your new happiness you could have died happier than Metellus. Your long life makes you resemble Priam even more than Metellus, for while Metellus was buried by his loved ones, Priam buried his. A truly different state of affairs! Oh fierce fortune! It appeared as if you had not given sufficient proof of your fickleness, so you added to the ancient examples that of our beloved Stefano whom you deprived quickly and through various deaths of his children and grandchildren, and whom you have now changed from a most happy father to a spectacle of pitiable bereavement. Oh magnanimous man, oh remarkable Stefano, for a while you appeared so happy that you could not have ever again become unhappy, and you appeared so surrounded by loved ones that you could never have feared solitude, and so close to death that you could no longer fear the death of adolescent sons. You seemed to stand well beyond the danger of any weapon. But Fortune is not only an uncontrollable and cruel goddess, but rather a servant of the Lord and most energetic executrix of the divine will. She acts secretly in extraordinary and inconceivable ways, while her games are always as mysterious and varied as they are often sorrowful and tearful. There is little doubt that in this age of ours she has given no more perfect example of her fickleness. So insidious is she that I am inclined to believe she favored your glorious ascent in order to make herself known to the world, for having bestowed so much favor upon you, she felt that your defeat would be more remarkable and your fall from so high a position would be more terrible, for you could never have been so unhappy unless previously you had been extremely happy. The great number of such outstanding children makes your losses so much more remarkable. Alas, most bitter sweetness; alas, toilsome rest; alas, fatal blandishments! What is left for men to fear or desire to hold on to or avoid? It is vexatious not to have possessed anything that pleases; it is sad to have enjoyed transitory delights. You have lived too long, I admit; but it was appropriate so that you should die a wiser man. You could have considered fortune as something dependable if you had only perceived her other face. Oh you who have been cast about by many misfortunes, what do you expect me to say? Do not hope, do not despair; one is the mark of an inane spirit, the other of a weak one. And, indeed, I ask you, for what can you hope? More children? Another wife? Age is against you, for old age is as suitable for marriage as winter is for the harvests. An aged bridegroom is a ridiculous kind of joke. On the other hand, why despair? Of so many children you have none left; if you have yourself, it is sufficient. There is no greater wealth, no better position than to have one's mind under control. We can find one who had a hundred and fifteen children; Erotimus, a king of the Arabs, as astonishing as it may sound, is said to have had seven hundred. To be in possession of one's self happens to a few. Do you miss conversations with your children? Converse with yourself. To converse with others is possible for everyone, but to converse with one's self is reserved for a few. There are many things you can converse about with yourself, for you did many things in such a long life, the remembrance of which could be most pleasant. As Cato says in Cicero's works, "Not all can be Scipios or Maximi and enjoy the recollection of their assaults upon cities, or land and naval battles, or wars waged, or participation in triumphs." But you belong to that class of men whose recollections of their own accomplishments is a glorious joy. Recall what you did at home and in the service, what you suffered on land and sea, what labors and dangers you faced, what notable things happened to you. I believe that you will confess that even without ever having had children you would have been a great man and would have been happy though not with the happiness that comes from leisure. But you were not without children, and these happened to be such that it was just as difficult to lose them as it was most pleasing to have them. Add to this that nothing unforeseen has happened to you, for your wisdom was such that you foresaw not only those things that happened to you but all that could have happened; for nothing that is possible is inconceivable to the wise man, while all things unforeseen happen to fools.

I did not want to say all this; there is something greater in my mind about which I can refresh your memory with a single word, but so that you would not think that what I once heard from you does not stay with me, I shall speak at greater length. Recall then (the image of those days is always before my eyes) the time after I had worked with you in Rome ten years ago when we by chance happened to be alone one day at dusk, and were walking on that Via Lata which leads from your home to the Capitoline. We finally stopped where that road is crossed by another which descends from the hills to the Arch of Camillus and then down to the Tiber. While standing at that crossroads, we discussed many things about the state of your home and your household, since no one interrupted us, and since at that time it was being agitated by a very serious civil war despite its record of having proven more outstanding than others in confronting outside dangers. It so happened that mention was made of one of your sons with whom at that time you were angry, I believe, because of the evil tongues of troublemakers rather than because of a father's normal anger. But you favored me with your kindness, and you allowed me to do what you had never previously permitted others to do, to prevail upon you to have your son return into your graces. In any event, after you had complained about him to me in a friendly fashion, with a changed expression you finally added words more or less like these (not only do I remember the event, but my memory supplies me with the very words you used): "My son and your friend, whom you compel me to regard with fatherly affection, spewed forth many things against my old age which would much better have been left unsaid. But since I cannot deny your request, I shall, as they say, forgive and forget. After this day you will not notice a trace of anger either in my looks or in my words. There is only one thing I must mention, concerning which I wish to make you a witness for all time. Among the first accusations leveled against me was that I had become involved in more battles than I ought to, considering the dignity of my advanced age, and thereby would leave my children a legacy of hatred and of discord. I call God to witness that I have undertaken wars for no other reason than my love of peace. Both my advanced age and my spirit now growing cold in this bosom which is of the earth, and my long experience with human affairs make me eager for peace and quiet. On the other hand, I remain firm and determined not to turn my back to hardship. I would prefer a more peaceful existence, but if destiny ordains it I would prefer to go to my grave fighting than learning how to be a subservient old man. As for what they say concerning my legacy, I wish to answer only this (and I beg you to pay the closest attention to my words): Would that I could leave my children some kind of legacy, but contrary to my personal wish fate decreed otherwise; and—I say this with great sadness—the fact of the matter is that, contrary to the natural order, I shall be the heir of all my children." While you said these things you turned your tearful eyes away. Whether you said all this because of a foreboding or as a divine admonition I do not know, although the deified Vespasian is witness to the fact that rulers often do prophesy concerning their own children when he predicted the kind of death that one of his children was to suffer, and the assumption of imperial authority for both of them. I myself must confess that on that particular day I took your words lightly as if they had been spoken by chance or perhaps through anger, nor did I suspect that they could contain so much power of prophecy. When after a long period of time I saw that the prophecy was coming true, judging from the frequent deaths of your children, I spoke about the matter with my friends. Then it spread among the people. As a result Giovanni of venerable memory, of the Roman Cardinalate, and Prince of your family, with three of his brothers already dead, succeeded with his prayers in having me recount the entire matter to him. After I unwillingly did so, he said with a deep sigh, "Would that my father were not such an accurate prophet!" In that same year, because of the fatal misfortune to your first born and to your grandsons, he began ever more to fear your prophecy to the point where, I believe, overcome by his grief, he fulfilled the prediction of his father with his own recent death and with sorrowful but confident faith in its inevitability. Just as the entire matter appeared extraordinary to those who heard it, so it is dreadful and amazing to me more and more each day. I do not doubt that you remember all of it; but I recall it in such a way that I still seem to see that ancient marble tomb which stands at the corner and on which we rested with our elbows. I also see the expression on your face, and I seem to hear those words with my very ears. Such being the case, your misfortunes should not appear intolerable since you had foreseen them so much in advance; meditation arms the mind. What do you suffer that you did not know you would? No one deplores having begotten mortal children unless he is also mad and forgetful of his own mortality. We love to have children like to ourselves. But nothing belongs to us more than the innate condition of having to die which is common to all those who are born and which alone adheres inseparably to our bones and to our very marrow. Why then do men grieve for the death of their children? Certainly not because of the certain and acknowledged rights of nature but because of the unexpected arrival of death. As much as I can determine, what happened to you was neither unforeseen nor unknown. The primary cause for lamenting which involves the grief of an unexpected blow is thus removed. Consequently, either you subject your feelings to the divine power as do all learned and well-established men, and bear whatever happened to you as calmly as you foresaw it; or, since it is difficult to overcome the rights of nature, and if it was perhaps paternal love that caused you to utter a reluctant sigh, so much time has elapsed since you first began to mourn that now it is plausible to assume that your tears have dried. Grief diminishes with time, as does joy. If there is anything good in human passions, it is that none of them is perpetual. But since a great number of words do not appeal to doers of great things, I shall come to an end.

Just as the beginning of this letter, if natural feeling has so decreed, could be read by a sensitive father with moist eyes, so will it behoove a strong and indomitable man to read the end with dry eyes. I beg you, therefore, to collect your wits and with the greatest effort receive the assault of unbridled fortune. Whoever withstands the first assault will be victor. She overcomes most people with terror rather than with her power. But what am I doing? What I urge you to do I hope that you have already done. I implore and beg you to do this lest (since the mind is often more curious about things found only in the memory) you should slide into new miseries by recalling old ones, and by indulging excessively in your fatherly grief you should once again reopen the scars of your now closed wounds. Let those things slip away that one cannot bring back: whether they afflict you or delight you is in your power. The public calls you bereft of children, an old man, a wretched man. You must believe that the multitude is mad as usual, and that you are happy. You drank from both jars of fortune and know how they taste; pleasant things made you glad, but bitter things are making you cautious so that you may understand the degree to which favorable events ought to be trusted. You already knew all this, I believe; but you will not deny the fact that you never saw it more clearly. There are no more effective schools than those in which experience is teacher; what you had heard from many quarters you have now seen, and you have confirmed with your own eyes what your ears had told you. You now see that truth about which almost all mortals speak, that Fortune is nothing; you see that what the multitude calls happiness is but a myth; you lost that happiness, and you have found another which is more sound and enduring. You say, "And among so many sorrows what happiness can you be referring to?" What do you think I refer to except the kind that no one can take away from you if you do not wish? I refer to that happiness which is the opposite of the first one: to be content with what you have; to know that those things with which you seemed to be blessed were not yours; finally, having realized your error, to attain the truth though late; but before all else that the power of fortune need not be feared by humans. What more shall I say? I shall stop here. You entered this life naked, you shall exit naked; and you can scorn magnanimously what people call the mistress of human affairs; she has hurt you so much that she can hurt no more. What else can she be planning now, what else can she be threatening? She has emptied her quiver and stands disarmed; she no longer has arms to hurl at you nor do you, in what remains, have any point where you may be struck. Farewell.

8 September.

Fam. VIII, 2.

To Olimpio.[1]

There is nothing anywhere on this earth which can be called either happy or delightful as long as we live. I realize how improperly I may be speaking: I should really have said as long as we do not live; since when we do begin to live we shall know nothing except what is sweetest and most pleasant. Note that while I depart and return happily, I do not enjoy the highly desirable pleasure of seeing and conversing with you and that excellent friend of ours. I was scarcely able to contain my tears when I returned home today and learned that you both had been here at the same time and had crossed the Alps and suffered all the hardships of the roads in your desire to see me; and that having failed to find me, as though deprived of a great expectation, you had departed sadly. I learned all this from my servants and from your letters which you left among my books like pledges of undying devotion and like payment for your brief stay and assurances of your return. But since in adversity the wise man always turns to the brighter side of things, let us imagine that it was an act of heaven, and that by not having found me as you wished, your overwhelming desire to meet with your friend has not cooled, and that as a result of the irritation caused by my absence the joy we would have had perhaps for a few days will be compensated for by the delight of enjoying each other's company over a period of many years. However, she alone can accomplish this whose inflexible hardness often blunts the weak edge of human counsel. I for my part imagine it to be so, I think about it in this fashion, I hope for it, and in this hope I find rest from the many labors that besiege me. But because how I feel about this and what I would like to urge you to do require time, and in order to allow this messenger to hasten his departure, I am compelled to defer my thoughts to another time. Farewell.

5 May.

1. Mainardo Accursio of Florence, son of a famous jurist and one of Petrarch's earliest friends, to whom he also gave a classicizing name.

To the same correspondent, an exhortation to live together and to deliberate on the most appropriate place.

I waited most anxiously and still I have not found an available messenger or a day of leisure. Therefore, the ideas that I had conceived I shall now explain in part, but not indeed as I had conceived them, for I realize how much greater power an uninterrupted discourse possesses. You know how that greatest of all eastern rivers which is distinguished by its many riverbeds can become not only passable but contemptible as well. Let us therefore comply with the circumstances and let what is possible be pleasing when what is pleasing is not possible. Since my trust in the present messenger has hardly been tested, I shall, in order to allay your anxiety, pursue only that one portion of your letter in which you advise against a return to the mouth of the Sorgue. You seem to be deeply disturbed about this, and I understand why since I was unable to resist our dear Socrates who often called me there. Being finally convinced by his entreaties, I agreed to go provided the conditions involved assured a legitimate reason for settling there and no lack of the necessities of life (of the life, I might add, of my comrades and of the great numbers who are accustomed to meet with me; for my personal life is not only provided with all the necessities I need but I fear that it may be pampered by having too many such things). If this proved acceptable to him, I would gladly have gone along satisfied about all these matters. Furthermore, I knew that our great leader was located there as well as all of you whom death had spared for me, and so I was drawn by love of you as if by most powerful chains. Now everything has changed; the crowd of friends has departed as has our leader, and my Socrates is still there alone. Although by the inveterate power of habit he desires to remain there and to have all his friends and especially me there with him, he will never dare, with all hope gone forever, summon us into lands where all of us would be foreigners and strangers. Nor would it be appropriate for men who drag around mortal and perishable bodies to say what the happy souls deprived of their bodies say in Virgil: "We have no certain hope; we live in shadow and spend our time on the banks of rivers and meadows made fresh by streams." If such things sufficed, Vaucluse, where the Sorgue originates, could provide us all in abundance with clear streams, thatched homes and straw beds; but nature requires something more. The multitude considers philosophers and poets unyielding and inflexible, but it is wrong in this as in many other things, for they too are of flesh, preserve their humanity, and shun passions. There are, however, certain limits to the needs of philosophers and poets, limits which may be bypassed only with doubt and suspicion. As Aristotle says, "Nature by itself is insufficient for indulging in speculation; this requires a healthy body, food and other necessities." And as the Satirist says, "Cruel poverty cannot sing under the Pierian grotto or touch the Bacchic wand, without the support needed by the body night and day." There is great and universal agreement among learned men concerning the needs of philosophers and poets, but all are expressed in different ways. Therefore, to continue where I left off, Vaucluse would provide a pleasant lodging for some brief period of time as it did for me earlier, to help free us from the weariness of the passions of the cities. In the long run, however, it would neither assure nor provide for our needs. Without doubt we must look ahead not only at the long run but to the very end, so that we might avoid that impropriety which Seneca directs against the human species when he says: "Everyone gives thought to the parts of life, no one to the whole." Those are true words indeed and this is what precipitated our plan so that amidst such varied occupations (which are simultaneously lamentable and ridiculous), we not ignore where we are steering the ship of our fluctuating life. I know that Vaucluse would be a desirable residence especially in the summertime, and how that retreat proved ever more acceptable to me than to anyone else you may see in my ten years' stay there. But if I might boast to you (who are indeed like another me) without sounding as though I were bragging, I ask you this: aside from the peacefulness of the mountains and of the fountain and of the woods, what of any moment has happened in that place that could be considered, if not more outstanding, certainly more noteworthy than my residing there? I may even dare suggest that for many people that place is known as much for my name as for its certainly extraordinary spring. I have said all this so that no one will suspect that I am now rejecting that rustic place which I always found most suitable for my affairs, in which I often exchanged the cares of the city for rural relaxation, and which I tried to make famous, not only in the choice of the place itself, but in my rustic dwelling and, I hope, in the stronger mortar of my words and songs.

It is pleasing for me to recall that it was there that I started my *Africa* with such great energy and effort that now, as I try to apply the file to what I started, I seem to shudder at my boldness and at the great framework I laid. There also I completed a considerable portion of my letters in both prose and poetry and almost all of my *Bucolicum carmen* in such a brief period of time that you would be astounded if you knew. No other place ever offered more ease or greater incentives. That solitude gave me the courage to collect the most illustrious men of all kinds and all centuries into one work. There in separate volumes I started indicating those qualities that should be adopted and praised in the solitary life and in religious idleness. Finally, hoping to alleviate in those shady places that youthful fire which raged within me for so many years, as you well know, I often used to flee there during my youth as though to a secure fortress. But, alas, how incautious I was! Those very remedies became destructive; for my burning cares accompanied me and the fact that there was absolutely no help against the raging fire in so solitary a place made me burn even more hopelessly. Thus, the flames in my heart spread through my bones and filled those valleys and skies with a mournful, but, as some called it, pleasant tune. From all of this emerged those vernacular songs of my youthful labors which today I am ashamed of and repent, but are, as we have seen, most acceptable to those who are affected by the same disease. What else can I say? If anything I wrote anywhere else is compared with what I wrote there, that place in my judgment is superior to all others. That residence, therefore, is and will continue to be as long as I live most pleasing to me in the memory of my youthful concerns whose remnants I continue elaborating to this very day. Nevertheless, unless we deceive ourselves, a man should deal with things other than what youths deal with. At that age I saw these other things perhaps only indistinctly, and if I perceived them, the blindness of love hindered my judgment as did the foolishness of that age and the weakness of my insights. My respect for our leader was also a hindrance since I preferred remaining subject to him more than enjoying liberty, feeling indeed that without him neither liberty nor the joys of life could be realized. Now we have lost in almost a single shipwreck both him and whatever joy remains. Furthermore, and I can hardly add this without deep sighs, that laurel of mine which was once so green has been withered by the power of an unexpected storm, that laurel which made not only the Sorgue but the Durance dearer than the rushing Ticino. And the veil which covered my eyes has been lifted so that I can now see the difference between Vaucluse and Venusian territory, and the open valleys and spectacular hills of Italy with her very attractive and flourishing cities. I can also see the difference between the single river and source of the Sorgue and so many shining springs, so many rambling rivers, so many lakes full of fish, the two famous seas in the distance, which seem to fortify both shores of Italy with their curved and splendid windings, not to mention the rest of the natural beauties, and especially the talents and customs of the people which need not be mentioned here. And yet note how many first impressions cling to the mind and how much power is exerted in our affairs by force of habit. To open all the inlets of my heart to you in keeping with the laws of true friendship, I feel my emotions rebel against my reason in this matter, and I must confess that I sigh for that valley which I have just repudiated so strongly, and a strange love for that place still seems to haunt me. I have really gone on too long and have become aware of the murmurings of the waiting messenger, and so I shall simply say farewell.

18 May.

Fam. VIII, 4.

To the same correspondent, an exhortation for moderate goals, and for not deferring plans for a better life.

All love is naturally impatient and is eager for haste; and there is no speed which is not slow for a lover. I wrote many things to you yesterday, but since many things were still left and the mind burns to express them, and since no messenger was available, I turned to my servants. Weighing their sense of obedience, I turned first to my cook to show you how much I am a victim of my stomach, since I felt that I could spare him without discomfort or indeed great inconvenience. I speak about the cook who, as you know, was considered the most vile of servants among our ancestors and began to enjoy some esteem only after the conquest of Asia. Would that we had never conquered Asia so that it would never have conquered us with its pleasures! But let me get back to the main point. My cook then will become my traveler, and a farmer will act as my cook. You know that I find great delight in country food and that I agree with Epicurus only in his position regarding light nourishment, for he placed the apex of his much-praised pleasure in his gardens and in his vegetables. I often enjoy in my rustic living a pleasure which has become continuous for me while it can be only periodic for those who are delicate and refined. Is there hardly anybody so disgustingly proud who would not find it pleasant at least once a year to recline on grassy banks under the open sky or in the hut of a friendly shepherd despite the absence of overhanging gilded beams or heavy silverware to weigh down the table, or the lack of purple draperies adorning the marble walls? Is there anyone with such a vain thirst that he is repelled by any goblet not covered with precious stones or not having lions battling in a golden grove testifying to the workmanship of Polyclitus? Or indeed is there anyone with such a fancy hunger as to be unable at some time to enjoy a rustic meal despite the lack of exotic birds from Colchis, or a flatfish caught on foreign shores, or a pike traditionally considered the best of fish captured between the two bridges of the Tiber? These things, therefore, which are sometimes tried by gentle stomachs enticed by the rarity of the experience, have always been for me the bounty of nature, and if I were allowed to change I would always prefer this kind of living. I do not reject more sumptuous meals, but I prefer to have them very rarely and after long periods of time. Do not think that I have been speaking in vain since I ought to be speaking at length about something else. Please accept what I have said without concern for my inconvenience, and do not send my cook back to me before you have given serious thought to the heart of the problem we now face. I ask you to keep an open mind and not be stubborn. What I say to one I say to all and I wish that this letter if possible be disseminated by word of mouth among all our friends. If a messenger should be traveling westward from there I wish that it could be sent especially to our Socrates so that all might know the sensible things I say as well as the foolish ones. Much can indeed be said more loftily but, unless I am mistaken, not much that is more useful. But you will decide this for yourself. I shall proceed as I had planned. Avarice has this peculiar and ugly characteristic: it is insatiable, and while it promises things in the future it forbids their use in the present. This thirst for possessions is never satisfied by seeking more things but by coveting fewer things. You need not believe me but rather the philosophers who consider this the road to true riches. As for me, I have set a limit to my desires and I accept that poetic saying as though it were spoken by an oracle: the miser always lacks something. And so that I myself would not always lack something, I did what follows in that saying: I set a definite limit to my desires, a boundary that I reached long ago despite the blows of fortune. Nor shall I fear that my descendants accuse me of sloth; I live for myself and not for them and together with my friends I am master of my own affairs and not the agent of someone I do not yet know with any certainty. However, why do I toil so greatly for myself, since it pays to walk unimpeded on a rough road? Why do we now still think about useless and fatal burdens? Flaccus puts it elegantly when he says: "Do not restrict your long-range hope to a limited space." So that you would not think that he referred to a small proportion of life rather than to all of life, he says the same thing in another place: "A short life prohibits the assumption of long-range hope." It is so; he is not wrong; nothing is truer. For although we may divide in whatever way possible and with minute distinction the brief period of this life, and try to widen it into whatever subdivisions, and reduce all such subdivisions into a single group, and carefully put them together; and although you may mentally view the whole from the first to the last day of this very long life, you will often confess that the total of this very fleeting period of time is very brief. If we look behind and around us, we shall note that a good part of this period has already been taken from us. Let us therefore come together at the end of the road which without question is the roughest part; let us abandon all superfluous things and hold on to the necessary ones. Why do we procrastinate? Why do we delay? Day follows upon day and month upon month, "and the year rolls round on its own tracks," as Maro says most clearly; and in stopping, it simply begins over again without ever pausing to enjoy some rest. What therefore is the proper way for waiting or expecting the end? We have witnessed the white-haired companions of old age and we have received the messengers of death. What do we wait for? That our eyes become blind with old age, that our legs begin to tremble, that our backs begin to curve? Who is the astrologer that can be our guarantor of a long life? The fact is that whether it be Petosiris, or Neclepso, or Nigidius among others, and indeed truth itself, how mad will it nevertheless be to delay to the very last minute what could be done in a fair period of time and conveniently?

Either I know nothing at all with certainty, or it is true that unless we are men now we shall never be. Let no one flatter us, let no one beguile us with the name of young men. I grant that we are not decrepit; nor are we old men; but certainly we are not boys either. The time has come to leave behind youthful pursuits. Did I say, "the time has come?" Would that it had indeed and that it were not passing on! But believe me, it has passed on, and a great part of it is already behind us. I do not deny that there is some left: but if it too is not to slip by because of our sluggishness we must cope with it swiftly, otherwise we shall undergo what happens to almost all the multitude: namely, that by looking back at our youth and directing our minds and eyes to it we fall into the pit of old age, and lying there deluded, we lament the frailty of nature and the brevity of life and repeat too late the complaints of the writer Theophrastus which were magnificently rejected by Cicero and Sallust and Seneca. Why do we not seize whatever little remains to us and turn it to our advantage according to that opinion of Seneca which had previously been expressed by Cicero: "Let us hasten to do what is done by those who depart late and wish to compensate for the swiftness of time," so that we might attain even before the end of the road a truly happy life that has thus far escaped us? It is never too late to do what is beneficial. For although procrastination deserves censure, all attempts at improvement are worthy of praise. There is no doubt that what is good cannot be untimely: otherwise it could hardly be good if it ceases being timely, as we believe repentance to be for the dead, which would serve only to increase their misery. On the other hand, repentance is not ineffectual for old men. Let us not be ashamed of undertaking to do now what was proper to do sooner; let us rather be ashamed of the fact that we are not doing it even now. As our hair grows white it is shameful not to realize our wavering plans. Let us therefore begin right now and let us consider clearly in what state our affairs are, nor ours alone but of all mortals in general. I ask, what is the life of man except a short breath and a thin wisp of vapor? Let each man sense what a rotten, feeble, and frail body he inhabits. We pretend in the name of a long-standing common error, and though aware of our ignorance we imagine eagerly the close proximity of an eternity. That is the way it is: there is no one who considers himself as dying. Indeed there is no one who does not know that he is mortal, but each postpones the day of his death, which could be this very day, into the distant future. Thus the very thing whose presence we fear most, we confidently assume will always be absent, since there is nothing that is more ambiguously absent and nothing that can be present with greater suddenness.

Those words of Aristotle are unfamiliar to the wretched: "Those things which are at a great distance are not feared; all know that they will die but because death is not close, they do not worry." This is what that great man said in his *Rhetoric*. I, however, agree that men are not concerned about death, and I do not deny, as he says, that the cause is negligence. But I contend that his view is false, for what can be more false than to believe that death is at a great distance when the shortness of life itself shows that it is not too far away? That it is always threatening and hanging over our heads can be seen in the astonishing power of human misfortunes, in the inevitable accidents, and in their infinite variety. Therefore, men are not concerned about death not because it is remote but because they believe it to be so. If they knew how close it is (which they necessarily know otherwise they would not turn their eyes elsewhere), I believe that either they would begin to fear death or arm themselves with virtue in such a way that they would justly not fear her as the beginning of another life. Indeed nowadays whom do you find who does not grasp the hope of a long life without any concern for virtue; and though life may be very extensive for them, it is always short. At the end of their life, though their expectation is fixed and clear, it still fails them. I ask you to point out to me someone who does not expect to outlive his contemporaries? We arrange our thoughts and our actions in such a way as to believe that no one will be our heir and that we shall be the heirs of everyone, although meanwhile our heritage may have its claimers and both sides are clearly deceived. Let us free ourselves of this mockery, and if our reason does not move us, let examples do so since they are readily available and are brought to our attention despite our reluctance. Once seen, they settle deep within our hearts, and become most difficult to overlook unless we exercise an impious contempt and a fatal forgetfulness.

Do we wish to know what we are, and where we are going, and what end awaits us after our hesitations and evasions? Then let us consider others. One may not have the eyes of a lynx or the sight of that fellow who from the watch-tower in Lilybaeum saw the Punic fleet leave the port of Carthage. I ask you to look closer, at nearby Ostia, at our neighboring dwellings, and the very cities we inhabit. But I ramble too much. Let us return to our own households and dwellings; we shall see how suddenly whatever we held dearest on earth vanishes like a dream or like a shade from before our eyes. Friends who would have gladly died for us if the situation required caused our lives to become sad and too lonely with their death. They did not leave us here perpetually but preceded us as they hastened to the same end. They enjoyed their fate in time, let us enjoy ours, for as Flaccus says: "We all are forced toward the same end, and fate sooner or later empties the urn of all as she exits." As their turn came sooner, ours will come later, but with suddenness; there is no room for delay. How little it matters whether one dies old or young! If you consider the end of life which is the old age common to everyone, that saying is indeed true that no one dies who is not old. If you consider the opinions of men, no one dies who is not a child. But I shall bypass those things, for they present themselves in such large numbers that I could never cover them all. It grieves me that I am impeded by my tears from enumerating the intimate losses and the sweet promises that this sorrowful and fatal year, which has been the worst of the century, has deprived us of. I confess that there are only a few of you from all of the human race, with whom I would choose to live and die; nor would I exclude several others except for the fact that either marriage or business or age or other difficulties have separated them from us and forced us to love them from a distance. Nor indeed is it now a matter of superiors whose kindness may be considerable but whose presence can hardly be counted upon, for there stands in the way of mutual intimacy a disparity of fortune and that poison of friendship, pride, which prompts such superiors to be fearful of demeaning themselves and to expect to be worshipped rather than loved. What impedes us from completing together what remains of our life, however little that may be, through peace of mind and in the study of the arts, and, as Seneca says, "if we have lived on the waters (to) die in port?" What we formerly did obediently for one lord, shall we not dare do for ourselves while we are alive, or is it that our fondness for servitude was greater than our love of liberty? Although that kind of servitude might appear, if you like, more pleasing than liberty because the affection and lack of insolence on the part of that excellent man justified it, nevertheless to be under another, to obey another, to live with another, could have the appearance of a more distinguished servitude but certainly could never be the same as true liberty. Please note that now such liberty, although unseen, is possible for us, and we have become our own masters somewhat sooner than expected. Unless I am mistaken I feel I know the minds of all of us, though perhaps I do not know all the impediments involved. Yet I do feel that nothing which concerns you is hidden from me. We are not rulers of the land and sea, as Aristotle says, but this is not necessary for a happy life. We have, however, what should suffice for our modest spirits, being willing, as they are, to adjust to nature. But if we are individually self-sufficient, what can we suppose will happen to all of us when we can offer one another a hand and can satisfy whatever needs another may have? We have more than enough, believe me: and we shall have to fear envy rather than want. Why then are we waiting? Why are we divided by seas and mountains and rivers? In short why does not a single home unite us, who were once willingly united, unless it is because we flee any new and unusual things, and we consider it foolish to lay aside a promised hope and not to hear fortune beckoning us to her pursuits, even though it is much more foolish to disdain real and solid things than to place our hopes in vain shadows? I call upon not only my conscience but the present letter to bear witness to the fact that all the blame must fall on you and whoever may be slow in accepting my sound plan.

Why do you not hasten here when the chains which tied you down have now been loosened and cut; and please do not accuse me of pride because I seem to lead rather than follow. My mind is ready to do either. If there is a more suitable place anywhere for us to live I shall proceed to it immediately. I am not one accustomed to spurn any trustworthy advice. I believe there is no one who has greater trust or confidence in friends. But if this place is preferred in your judgment, which your letters seem to admit, what is now keeping you? Do not be tempted by ambition; it never is about to say "this is enough"; it always seems to want more. This is so especially because, as with oil and wine, so is it with time and life: the dregs lie in the bottom! To limit yourself to such dregs while neglecting what is closer to the surface is ridiculous. It is a custom of travelers to find lodging before night; I implore that we make similar plans and after many labors of the journey prepare ourselves finally for that eternal lodging. For this I offer you, oh brothers dearer to me than light, whatever resources I command or advice I can give, whatever delight or favor can be expected of me, whatever support from the things which are improperly called mine since they really belong to fortune, in short all of myself which I can do without pride, as well as my books, my gardens, and anything else I own. However, those things which are needed so badly in this human life of ours are not few, and while they might be expressly mentioned in a letter such as this, dignity forbids it. Finally, so that I might end with a vow and a prayer, may the consoling Holy Spirit inspire us to conspire at least in this, that while we desire to continue in this life, we may aspire to peace and tranquillity, and that we who have sighed all day may breathe normally at twilight. Farewell.

Fam. VIII, 5.

To the same correspondent, on the same matter.

I had scarcely sealed my earlier letter than, still not fully satisfied, the potential sweetness of our future which preoccupies my mind and thoughts caused me to take my tired pen in hand, and as the messenger lingered, in order not to lose the opportunity, I decided to push my idea even further. I enjoy speaking at greater length and trying to spur you with the same goads that I feel. If, therefore, we all seek a happy life—and there has never been any sect that disagrees with this in any way—although how to achieve such a life remains a basic problem for human curiosity; if, as I was saying, desire for happiness is inseparably joined to the soul that, though happiness may be lost, we do not really lose it nor can we lose it if we wished, nor would we want to lose it if we could; and if we know that happiness itself cannot be fulfilled here without the comfort of friends, why do we obstruct our enjoyment, and why does the slowness of particular ones hamper the good of all? As Seneca says, "Joy can indeed come to us from those we love even when absent, but it is slight and evanescent; their appearance and presence and conversation lead to enduring pleasure." We must, therefore, seize such happiness forthwith. For if some philosophers were so desirous of obscene pleasure that they considered it the greatest good, viewing it as mistress of human actions, they subordinated virtue itself to its service; who would be so inflexible as not to be attracted by honest pleasure which virtue and its companion, friendship, can offer? I ask you, what life is happier or gayer than the one spent with friends whose perfect love and mutual affection make all feel as one, bound as if with an indissoluble knot and a single mind in all things; with whom there is no disagreement, no secrets, but instead harmonious accord, serene brows, and a truthful and unstudied conversation, as well as a perfectly open mind? If such a life befalls us I shall desire nothing more; and if I shall see anywhere a usurer or a legacy hunter puffed up at the expense of another, he will provoke no envy on my part, and I shall indeed consider him very poor. As the Satirist said, "Let Nero possess all that he stole, let him keep his mountain of gold, but let him not love anyone nor let him be loved by anyone." When we have assembled in a single place—what is there that can prevent us from enjoying our future? If indeed you seem to approve this dwelling of mine (not undeservingly, for while perhaps it is not like the one possessed by King Latinus in Virgil, "august, huge, and having a hundred columns," it is certainly pleasant, solitary, healthy and fully capable of hospitality for a few who get along so well); if then the fates cause you to gather here—let us cast our anchor, and let us appear as though we had found our port. And if perchance the group of friends increases, drawn by the attractiveness of our life of ease, there is a more impressive house in the middle of the city which I keep empty for such an eventuality. I and all my household would fill only a very small part of that house, even though in my desire for solitude my household appears huge.

Please do not consider these words confining chains and believe that you will be restricted to one place. There will be on one side of us Bologna, mother of studies, in which we spent our early youth; and it will be pleasant, now that our thinking and our hair has changed, to see it again and to view the condition of that city and of our own minds with more mature judgment and, by comparison, to note how little we have truly progressed in our lives. There will be near the Po, Piacenza, the home of your venerable Antonnio which you manage, without spurning the mediocrity of the position after having turned down many more lucrative ones, since, as you usually say, you considered my nearness highly desirable. There you will be the host of all. If we would like to travel a little further, we shall have Milan close by, as well as Genoa, the former representing the glory of land-bound cities and the latter of maritime cities; the former having attractive lakes and rivers, the latter having its waters resounding and congested with sails. There we shall see huge Lake Lario with Como nearby from which the river Adda emerges; we shall see the Verbano which is called Lake Maggiore by its inhabitants and which the Ticino intersects. We shall see the Eupili from which the Lambro and the Sebino and the Oglio issue, and not far from there the Benaco from which breaks forth the Mincio, lakes that are very well-known to the public, but names that are not even known to the learned. We shall see overhanging the lakes the lofty and snowy Alps, a most pleasant spectacle in the summer, and forests which touch the stars, and resounding streams amidst the vaulted cliffs, and rivers crashing down from the mountains, and wherever you turn the singing of birds and the sound of springs. In the other region the Apennines tower, and the sea is below us. The Tritons will be present to our eyes as well as other monsters of the sea, and the din of Neptune will be in our ears, as will be the wailing of the stones and the plaints of the Nereids. We shall walk among all these things to which I am beyond belief attracted, and along the bending shores of the Tyrrhenian, free from biting and stinging cares; and that ever-desirable leisure which those noble friends, Scipio and Lelius, enjoyed in Gaieta after their military labors, we shall enjoy on the shores of Genoa after our poetic labors. If we ever have our fill of this part of the earth, Padua will offer an abode which is no less peaceful and suitable, where not the least part of our good fortune will be to enjoy the intimate friendship of that great man under whom that city, following a long series of hardships, has now recovered its breath. Here I shall name him with the deepest respect, Jacopo de Carrara, whom I would like to bring you to love and to cherish in your mind; for while virtue may be loved in every age it should be loved more in ours because it is rare. And there will be to one side of us a city, Venice, which I consider the most miraculous of all the ones I have seen—and I have seen almost all the ones of which Europe is most proud. There will also be its illustrious ruler who likewise deserves honorary mention, Andrea, a man acclaimed no less for his fondness for art and learning than for his distinguished handling of so great an office. And there will be Treviso, surrounded with fountains and rivers, the home and marketplace of delightful living. Thus, as often as monotony, the mother of tedium, overcomes us, there will be variety, the greatest medicine for boredom; and whatever annoyance steals upon us will be eliminated by an exchange of views and by traveling from place to place. I do not doubt that you see with what arms I am attacking you, with what arts I am pressing you, and how I am mixing womanly flattery with manly warnings. I shall do everything I can to persuade you: how sincerely I do so, I myself can testify. The outcome will show how effectively. I seem to have presented all that was in me; I could perhaps, had I wanted, have said this more eloquently, but excessive feeling often hinders eloquence. I have said as best I could what was in my mind, what you could understand, and I hope what you could approve. I beg you not to consider how I have said it but what I have said; a stammering friend gives better advice than an eloquent enemy. I do not know how to come to an end, and I feel I have gone further than I intended because of my zeal. This alone I shall not stop repeating, and it is something which you yourself leaned toward without my urging you: let us assemble forthwith in this place if this pleases all of us; otherwise choose a place which pleases you anywhere in the world—for I shall object to no area of the world, no foreign country. I shall put aside all my preferences and adopt yours. Whatever allows us to be together will be acceptable. Choose where we may live peacefully what remains of our life, where we may die calmly. Farewell, and do not allow any delay to interfere with sane advice.

19 May

Fam. VIII, 6.

To Friar Bartholomew of the order of Saint Augustine, Bishop of Urbino.[1]

You did what behooves your profession when you listed alphabetically in a huge volume all the sayings of Augustine; an accomplishment of great labor rather than of glory. In it I admire your intellect which, unless I am mistaken, reflects a talent that is inclined to greater things than the desire for public approval. As was fitting, the result has justified the effort. With it you have pleased the Roman Pontiff, Clement, a very learned but busy man, and thus appreciative of such compendia. As a result you were made Bishop of your native land and were made to expect even loftier rewards—although, according to the modesty of your mind and the humility of your religion, together with the attractiveness of your native land, I doubt that you could hope for anything loftier or more pleasing as honors for past accomplishments. And as you proceeded from this work to another, you were requested to do for Ambrose what you had done for Augustine. You will obey—having already started—and you will finish, I hope, with the same ease and happy outcome. Knowing you, I say you will obey not to achieve greater honor but to be of greater service. For although the desire for loftier status does not affect you since you are happy with your lot, nevertheless it befits the just man to be as grateful for unsought favors as he is for favors that are desired and sought, for nothing is of such import in the matter of rewards as the intention of a donor. But I return to your Augustine and to you. You requested that I send you some verses that can be appended at the end of that great work which you built with your sweat from the stones and mortar of that most opulent master, and which you prepared for our present Pontiff, but even more for posterity. I have prepared them since I wish to deny you nothing; and although my mind has been distracted from such work for a long time despite the

1. Bartolomeo Carusio, Augustinian friar who had taught theology at Paris and at Bologna where Petrarch had met him during his student days. His compendium of the works of St. Augustine earned him the Bishopric of Urbino from Clement VI.

anger of the Muses, and although I have been involved in many other cares, your request has called me back to them. I am herewith sending you, therefore, a few elegiac verses and a like number of hexameters, if you prefer them, all containing the same meaning. Make use of both or neither as you please; but you should know that they were dictated hastily and extemporaneously with your messenger actually assisting me in measuring the syllables so that none was so short which did not seem too long to him. Farewell.

To his Socrates, a tearful plaint concerning that unequaled plague which befell in their time.

Oh brother, brother, brother (a new kind of beginning for a letter, indeed an ancient one used by Marcus Tullius almost fourteen hundred years ago); alas dearest brother, what shall I say? Where shall I begin? Where shall I turn? Everywhere we see sorrow, on all sides we see terror. In me alone you may see what you read in Virgil concerning so great a city, for "on all sides there is cruel mourning, everywhere there is trembling and countless images of death." Dear brother, would that I had never been born or had died earlier! If I am compelled to wish this now, what do you think I would be saying if I had arrived at a truly old age? Oh would that I never reach that point. But I feel I shall, not because I shall live longer, but because I shall suffer a longer death. Indeed I know my destiny and I slowly understand what I am heading for in this troublesome and unhappy life. Alas, dear brother! I am deeply troubled from within and take pity on myself. What would anyone who hears these words say? "You who seem to offer comfort and aid to others, who had promised us things that were superior, who ought to have formed a thick skin from your constant misfortunes and to have become calloused against all the blows of fortune and hardened to something like a flintstone, see how weakly you bear your burdens, see how often you direct your frequent wailings to us. Where is that loftiness of soul which now especially should mark your profession? Where are the magnificent words, which, if intended rather to extol your genius than as advice for life, can be no more than empty sounds and curious charms for the ears? We expected from you a heroic poem, we get elegiac verses; we hoped for biographies of illustrious heroes, we are getting the story of your sorrow. What we considered letters are laments, where we sought ingenious combinations of words, new molds for language, and sweetly ordered rhetorical colors, we behold nothing but mournful exclamations and indignant tones and tear stains. And what will be the limit or the end if you want to deplore the fate of all mortals? One heart and one tongue would not suffice. Wretched man, you have undertaken a huge and troublesome task which is useless and implacable. You must seek another source for your tears; the recent and continually new causes of grief make it impossible for excessively tired, exhausted, and dried-up eyes to produce sufficient tears. Therefore, forgetful of yourself and dissatisfied with your own misery and illness which you incurred knowingly and willingly, what else are you doing but offering poison to your friends to whom you had promised a cure? Better that you should either cry alone or learn to bear mortal things with the equanimity of a mortal; and noting that not only you or your friends alone, but all living beings are being snatched away, it is time that you put an end to your useless complaining." There may be someone of quick temper who hates such gloomy recitals and will discard them or trample on them with biting scorn saying, "Go to the devil; if you are going to behave like a woman, at least do not prevent us from acting like men." I feel all of these things and none escapes me, dear brother. I realize that a man must either drive away grief or destroy it, or control it, or finally conceal it. But what can I do? I shall die if I cannot pour out my grief in tears and words. My one consolation is that whatever I shall have written, though weak and empty, will reach your hands not as if to a stranger's but as if to my own. Therefore I shall fear no greater shame while you read these things than I felt while I was writing them.

I shall not deny that I did feel some shame; for without the control of reason I felt my mind and my style pulled along with my feelings beyond what I intended, something I find most disturbing. But what I feel to be an even greater insult is that for a whole year and considerably more I have had little occasion, not, indeed, to do, but certainly to write anything worthy of a man as a result of fortune's thundering and storming on all sides. Because of this I may perhaps be excused by a benign judge if he were also to consider that I am bewailing not something inconsequential, but the 1348th year of the sixth age, which not only deprived us of our friends but the entire world of actual nations. If anyone escaped, the coming year is gathering its harvest so that whatever survived that storm is being pursued by death's sickle. How can posterity believe that there was once a time without floods, without fire either from heaven or from earth, without wars, or other visible disaster, in which not only this part or that part of the world, but almost all of it remained without a dweller? When was anything similar either seen or heard? In what chronicles did anyone ever read that dwellings were emptied, cities abandoned, countrysides filthy, fields laden with bodies, and a dreadful and vast solitude covered the earth? Consult the historians: they are silent; question the scientists: they are stupified; ask the philosophers: they shrug their shoulders, they wrinkle their brows and they order silence by holding their fingers to their lips. Will you believe such things, oh posterity, when we ourselves who see them can scarcely believe them and would consider them dreams except that we perceive them awake and with our eyes open and that after viewing a city full of funerals we return to our homes only to find them empty of our loved ones. Should we not indeed know that what we grieve over is indeed true? Oh happy generation of our great-grandsons who will not have known these miseries and perhaps will consider our testimony as fable! I do not deny that we deserve these things and even worse; but our ancestors also deserved them, and would that our descendants will not! Why is it, then, oh most blessed judge, why is it that the violence of your vengeance lies so extraordinary upon our times? Why is it that when guilt is not absent, examples of just punishment are lacking? We have sinned as much as anyone, but we alone are being punished. Alone, I say; for I dare assert that if the punishments of all the centuries, subsequent to that most famous ark that bore the remains of mortals over unformed seas, were compared to present ones, they would resemble delightful activities, games, and moments of ease. Nor is it fitting to compare these misfortunes to any wars, for in such wars there are many kinds of remedies, and ultimately the possibility of at least dying in a manly fashion. For to die well is an exceptional consolation for death. In the present case there is absolutely no remedy, and no comfort. Not knowing the cause and origin of our misfortune only adds to the extent of the disaster. For neither our ignorance nor indeed the plague itself is more troublesome than the nonsense and stories of certain men who profess to know everything, but really know nothing. Their mouths, accustomed to falsehoods, are finally silenced, and where at first they emitted their ignorance as is their custom, they finally remain closed with stupor. But let me return to my inquiry.

Is it not true that just as for wayfarers one part of the road produces a weariness that is admitted only upon reaching another part, so does it happen to us that Your mercy, oh Lord, gradually exhausted by human faults, and depressed by the continuing increase in such faults, finally can take no more, and must subside, and that You, like an ideal wayfarer unable to endure any more have cast us behind You and angrily turned away the eyes of Your mercy? But if this is so, we suffer punishment not only for our sins but for those of our fathers. I do not know whether we are worse than they, but certainly we are more wretched. Or is it perhaps true as is suspected by certain great minds that God cares not for mortal things? Let such madness not even enter our minds: if You did not care they would not be. What must be our opinion of those who attribute our welfare not to God but to nature, when we have been dedicated to the study of Your truths? Even Seneca calls most ungrateful those who through a change of name disguise a function of God, and through impious mockery deny what is owed to divine majesty. You certainly do care for us and our affairs, oh God, but the causes are concealed and unknown to us as to why we have been judged by You the most worthy of all centuries to be punished most harshly without there being any lessening of Your justice because it is hidden from us. For the depth of Your judgments is inscrutable and inaccessible to human senses. Therefore either we are really the worst of all, something which I would like to but dare not deny, or else we are being saved through these present evils by becoming more experienced and more pure for future blessings, or else there is something involved which we are simply unable to fathom. Yet, whatever the causes may be, however much you conceal them, the effects are most visible.

But to turn from public to private grief, the first part of the second year is hardly over since tearfully I left you crying at the mouth of the Sorgue as I returned to Italy. I am not asking you to consider a long period of time; consider simply these very few days and call to mind what we were and what we are. Where are our sweet friends now, where are their beloved faces, where are their soothing words, where is their mild and pleasant conversation? What thunderbolt destroyed all those things, what earthquake overturned them, what storm overcame them, what abyss absorbed them? We used to be a crowd, now we are almost alone. We must seek new friendships. But where or for what reason when the human species is almost extinct and the end, as I hope, is near? Why pretend, dear brother, for we are indeed alone. I believe that it was God's purpose to strip us of the sweet charms and impediments of this life so that we might now more freely desire the next life. See where we have arrived as a result of the sudden changes! We are now in a position to test that saying of Epicurus: "We represent a sufficiently large theater one for the other." To be truthful to each other, how long will we be able to say this? Or what soothsayer can indicate the extent to which we can have faith in the stability of such a reciprocal theater, when on the other hand we see the columns already shaking? About what can I in writing this be more certain concerning your life than you, in reading this, can be concerning mine? Man is too frail and proud an animal, he builds too securely on fragile foundations. See to what a small number we have been reduced from so large a group of comrades: and note that while we are speaking we ourselves are also fleeing and are vanishing in the fashion of shades, and in a moment of time one of us receives the news of the departure of the other and the survivor will in turn be following upon the footsteps of the other. What are we, therefore, dearest brother? What are we, indeed? Of what do we continue to be proud? Dismayed by his torments, Cicero says in one of his letters to Atticus, "What are we or how long shall we be attending to these things?" Indeed a brief but good question, if I am not mistaken. It is also a wholesome question, pregnant with useful advice in which the alert digger will discover a great deal about true humility and modesty and great contempt for fleeting things. I say, what are we? How heavy, how slow, how fragile is our body, how confused and how restless is our mind, how changeable and how uncertain and voluble is our destiny? How long shall we be concerned about these things? Very briefly. Cicero certainly meant nothing more by this than had he said: "How long shall we continue to be the very thing we are?" By heavens, certainly not long, since just as this very being of ours cannot last long, so can it actually cease as we utter these very words. Nor should it prove astonishing if this were to happen. Therefore, oh Marcus Tullius, you ask both questions well and seriously. But I ask you, where have you left the third question which is in fact more dangerous and more worthy of being asked? What shall we be after terminating our life here? An important and doubtful matter, indeed, but certainly neglected! Farewell.

Fam. VIII, 8.

To the same correspondent, on the same matter.

There remained here with me a very small number of remnants from the past year, and particularly a very famous, magnanimous and wise man, Paganino da Milano, who was most welcomed not only by me but by both of us after the many proofs of his worth. He had already begun to become for me another Socrates. He had begun to enjoy my trust and friendship almost as you did, as well as those privileges most enjoyed by friendship, the sharing in each other's misfortunes, the faithful sharing of secrets with a completely open heart. Indeed, how much he loved you, how he desired to see you whom he had indirectly gotten to know so well, how concerned he was for your life in this public disaster! I myself marveled at how an unknown man could be loved so strongly. He no sooner saw me sadder than usual than he would ask in a friendly but anxious manner: "What is the matter? What has happened? How is our friend?" When he heard that you were really well, he would lay his apprehension aside with an extraordinary joyfulness. This man (and I say this with copious tears and would be saying it with still more, except that I am protecting my eyes so exhausted from preceding misfortunes, and am reserving what remains of my tears for impending misfortunes), this man, I say, having been suddenly seized by the illness of the plague which is devastating the world, spent the evening with his friends and what remained of his ebbing life conversing with me and recalling our past friendship and relationship. He spent that night calmly amidst his excruciating pains, and was overtaken by a sudden death that morning. And in keeping with the fatal times, before three days were over, his children and all his family followed him. Go forth now, you mortals, rage, pant, toil, circle the earth and the seas to accumulate endless wealth and temporary glory. The life we live is but a sleep, and whatever occurs in it is very similar to a dream. Death alone breaks up the sleep and disperses the dreams. Oh, if only it were possible to awaken earlier! Farewell.

Fam. VIII, 9.

To the same correspondent, on the violent death of a friend.

I had not yet satisfied fortune for it had to attack me again with sharper weapons and had to add even the madness of wicked men to the wrath of God. Woe is me! I am now beginning to fail, and as with the terror that first attacks those who are about to undergo fears, I now tremble with a gloomy cold. I have reached the point where I now fear to recall and relate what must be said. I know what I am about to say but I do not dare begin, and I would most willingly be freed from these matters and from this subject, except that my grief draws my mind on as well as the need for relating what has happened, and indeed your very anxiety which perhaps causes you to laugh at my weeping since you do not know what has happened. This then is the way things have happened. Fortune had left us two friends. Although there are others, these were the ones with whom it appeared that we could complete what remained of our lives, God willing. I ask, what hindered us? Not wealth, not poverty, nor differences of inclination, nor that great enemy of friendship, business. We were four persons with a single mind. I therefore boasted that while antiquity could in very few of its periods scarcely boast of one or perhaps two such friendships, our age could shortly boast of a single household with two pairs of such friends. I said "pairs" improperly: for it was one, and not even one pair but a single mind shared by all, as I said, which believed that experience did not allow us to wander any longer. The first of these friends was of a nature that, aside from being a most pleasant colleague, he was also a sharer and partner in our studies. The other, though not participating in these studies, possessed characteristics that result from such studies—mainly, kindness, faith, generosity, and steadfastness. In short, though lacking in liberal training, he was aware of the wealth of the liberally educated mind and was an excellent man and friend. Within our group he was even more compatible than if, like all of us dedicated to the study of letters, he had elected to spurn those other things that are necessary to life, as the rest of us had done. He therefore represented the fourth member of our varied group most conveniently and almost as if willed by heaven. We appeared to be too happy. Most cruel fortune envied us and because she had not yet cast us all down as victims of the world's tragedy, she was indignant. Our friends set out together, and having left you at the Rhone river, they eagerly sought me in Padua as if I were an actual part of them. I have undertaken a truly sad and unhappy account. I seem to contradict myself in its words, nor can I restrain myself. But meanwhile, I know not how, I am seized by something I do not wish, if indeed I can wish unwillingly, and I am undergoing something miserable and deadly and yet pleasing to my mind. Weeping also has a certain kind of sweetness with which I have unhappily nourished myself in these days, and tormented myself, and in which I have taken pleasure. For unless I do find delight in it, who compels me to deal with these sorrowful things? But it is a delight more painful than any punishment, for while memory wrenches the mind, my grief diminishes. In any event, our two friends came together with excellent intention, with fate against them, with a miserable end in sight, and with one finally heading for Rome and the other for Florence. But why, dear friends, are you separated and where are you heading? Proceed more directly, go more safely. This is not the road to take: why did you seek out the Alps and the snows? "Love conquers all and you yielded to love." You were coming to see me: this was the catch, this was the chain with which almighty love was dragging you along, after having encircled and seized you, love to which heaven itself yields, and which the reluctant elements obey in turn. Thus one cannot ask you the reason for taking the longer road. You were being pulled, you were not proceeding on your own. Furthermore your destiny drove you on, as well as mine with which I had been acquainted for some time. There was no straighter road to destruction and to my perpetual grief.

Why, my dear Socrates, did fortune wickedly bring it about that I who had not moved a foot from my home in the space of a year, should have been absent at that very moment which kept us from seeing each other and drove them in constrenation and more rapidly into the trap of waiting death. They had certainly hastened up to that point, forgetful of all toil and of all other cares except for their one hope and desire, for it is natural that a greater passion absorbs a minor one. Their minds burned to see me personally and to discuss with me the plans for their future life. So they took up their journey once again and having arranged their affairs in their native land, they returned here so that, with the addition of yourself, we would live together until our death. If they had found me, their delay could perhaps have swayed the rigor of fortune. But had they perhaps changed their plan and had accomplished the business that they had in their native land through intermediaries, tempted by love, they would have settled down with me, and now (what indeed would have stopped it?) we would all be together enjoying that peace we have desired for such a long time. But we were held by the iron-like chains of fate, and mad fortune saw to it that I was absent. Therefore when they arrived here, having learned the truth from the travelers at the gate of the city, they proceeded sad and deeply dejected to my house. Why linger over details? They checked into every corner of the house and throughout the garden (for winter had begun to soften because of the approaching spring) sitting down periodically and filling the air with sighs. Although they could go elsewhere, they both slept for the night in my bed so that, in my opinion, the place which human frailty considers important for a necessary rest would become a source of trouble and groans for me. The following day they departed, leaving a letter in the house which disclosed their sadness and their intentions, a letter that as long as I live I shall hold amidst my dearest belongings as a recollection of sorrow and an dundying cause for tears.

A whole month had passed before I returned home unaware of all these things, and, having read the letter, I heard sorrowfully and with astonishment my housekeeper repeat what it said. But what was I to do? They had departed so long before that already I was expecting their return and, like a madman, was accusing them of negligence. After some time,

I sent one of my servants to Florence urging the friend who was closer to return, and adding that he send the same messenger to the other friend wherever he might be. To this one I had written a great many things during those days, but at that moment I dispatched a hortatory letter urging on his part the rather modest choice of electing either this or any other place, whichever showed itself more opportune for our affairs in addition to our love for a life of solitude and study. Since the letter concerned all of us equally, I added that it also be sent to you through him. Virgil certainly put it well, as he did so many things, when he said: "The mind of men is ignorant of destiny." The letter carrier departed, and I in the meantime imagined all kinds of pleasant things: "These would come from the East, he would come from the west; who was happier than I? Whose life could be more peaceful?" While indulging in such thoughts which were to double the bitterness of the approaching misfortune, my messenger, on the eighth day after he had departed, returned unexpectedly during a very intense storm, wet with rain and with tears. I turned to him and having shaken the pen from my hand, for he had appeared while I was writing, I cried out, "What news do you bring? Speak quickly." He interrupting his words with a sigh said, "I am a bearer of bad news. Your friends fell into the cruel hands of bandits on a summit of the Apennines."

"Alas," I said, "what happened? What are you telling me?" He continued sobbingly and this is a summary of what he said. Our Simpliciano, that most excellent and sincere man, who went first, walked into an ambush and was quickly overpowered, falling amidst the swords of his murderers. Soon Olimpio, aroused by the cries, hastened to his assistance and stood firm under the blows of the swords of ten or more would-be murderers. Having inflicted and received many wounds, he scarcely managed to escape alive by spurring on his horse. The robbers, without taking all the booty from the dead victim, fled so rapidly that weary of body and of spirit, they could easily have been captured by the farmers attracted by the uproar, except that certain so-called nobles, dashing down from the mountains, following a mild attack by their attendants, led the hard-pressed group and their bloody spoils into their hiding places. Olimpio was seen with his sword in hand wandering far off from there, but no more has been heard about him since.

The winds have brought with them a sad omen: I do not know whether I can bear lightly the news that both have been killed. I certainly know what I should do. Shutting my doors to all consolers, I ought to devote myself alone to my grief, and either lighten my mind with tears or oppress it, either lessen my desire for mourning or satisfy it, and I should show my concerns for my friends with tearful and wailing eyes because they have been seized by ungodly hands. I am now being tormented not by one but by three passions of the mind: hope, fear, and grief. And as though pierced with a like number of wounds on one side as on the other, I know not where my wounded heart inclines, and I am distracted and torn to pieces in an extraordinary and wretched manner by raging and contradictory anxieties and messengers. For I sent messengers out again, though in a different manner, and expected some kind of news concerning the one who had survived, but while there are many different reports from all sides, nothing certain has reached me. In such suspense and anxiety of mind, I keep a careful lookout on all roads and hold my breath at every loud noise. I have now gone fifteen days. If this period of time were to be weighed against the misfortunes of the many past years, I believe that it would easily outweigh them. I was tempted to go forth and not stop until I knew in what condition the survivor was, whatever it may have been, and (oh strange destiny!) to see the alpine and deserted grave of the other. Rumor has it that a great crowd not only from the surrounding towns but even from the city attended his burial with great compassion, with the farmers expressing their anger in loud voices and predicting many things which subsequently happened, such as the fact that when the road became impassable they could foresee only isolation for themselves and expensive and destructive wars in place of the handsome profits they enjoyed in lodging travelers. I believe that I too would have gone, and, driven by fate, I would have in all probability fallen into those same hands had not the time of year and my bad health restrained me. Not on that account am I any the less uncertain as to what to do, not knowing whether the mind should obey necessity or the desire for freeing myself of the chains that bind me. I say all these things so scrupulously, dear brother, so that you may understand all the details, even though without doubt you have learned about the general situation. I dislike intensely having my mind overwhelmed with countless waves tossing about the swift skiff of hope hither and yon on the changeable and swelling sea of rumors. This kind of life is for me no more pleasant than death, and I long for its end with my prayers and I detest any delay. Just recently we seemed to be young men, and now see how we have lived two years beyond our limit. This life is now approaching the maximum of tribulations because, while I begin to count the days in the manner of lovers, I am deeply astonished at your silence and feel some new suspicions arising within me. For I hear that that plague of last year which seemed to have ended, is again invading the banks of the Rhone, and I certainly hope that you are not dead! But what am I trying to do in my misfortune? Is my present misfortune insufficiently real and true, unless in my misery I also turn to fictitious and future ones? May God change all of this for the good so that as often as I am deceived by false hope I might once be deceived by a false fear.

Thus far, dearest Socrates, indulging in my grief in an undignified manner, I have unburdened my mind of its complaints as best I could. I had to do so in order not to crack under the weight of my misfortune. Forgive me, dear Socrates, and let others who may read this also forgive me. There are times when silence is noble; but others when words are necessary. Whatever death may do from now on I shall count not only my friends but myself among the dead, knowing that none of these things occur without the will of God, since He either orders them or permits them; I shall restrain my heavy and swollen soul and tongue from mourning, and I shall avoid being like those who do not consider it enough to excuse their sin without accusing the judgment of

God. And perhaps the last sun has not set for us and we may still be able to communicate either in writing or through conversation in the future. I join to this letter a copy of the letter to the Florentines concerning this great harm that has been done to their city, hoping that you might like it. Farewell, and try to preserve yourself for happier days so that we may see each other again on this earth if heaven does not forbid it.

22 June.

Fam. VIII, 10.

To the Florentines, an expression of indignation and complaint concerning the inhuman crimes perpetrated on their borders, and an exhortation to cultivate justice and guard their roads.

I have often on various occasions wanted to write you, oh distinguished citizens, concerning a variety of matters. I have in turn wanted to urge you to restrain yourselves, to spur you on, to complain about the loss of your liberty, and to congratulate you for its recovery. I have sometimes wanted to weep with you over the many and unpredictable storms that have swept over your state and faithfully to warn you of impending shipwrecks so that by doing so I might prove to you, since no other way existed, through words which at least give evidence of one's spirit, that although I was not a dweller in my homeland I was certainly devoted to it. But when I began to consider how far the humility of my studies were from your lofty concerns, I began to feel my pen slipping from my hands. Now, however, I am compelled to write, nor am I able to restrain myself, for a deep sorrow presses upon my mind and wrenches out of me words mixed with tears. Consider what has happened (something I knew nothing about until now and wish I had never known). A very pleasant and deservingly dear citizen of yours and friend of mine while returning from France to Florence, having gone through the many annoyances and dangers of such a long journey and finally approaching his beloved homeland, practically on the very threshold of his own door and of your gates, was cruelly killed, so to speak, in your very bosom. Oh unfortunate man, who bore so many tribulations in your younger years, and often traveled through unknown lands so that you might spend a peaceful and respected old age in your homeland! Where are you going? Alas, wretched friend unaware of your destiny and safer anywhere except in your homeland, where do you hasten, where are you rushing so pitiably? Those verses befit you which say, "your piety deceives heedless you," your piety about which Cicero says, "as great as it may be toward your acquaintances and neighbors, it will be even greater for your homeland." It was that piety which without doubt drew you on, being as attached as you are to your native soil. You are now returning there as an aged person having departed as a boy, and you are carrying back to that land that had frightened you as a child the remains of your weary life, desirous of burial in your place of birth and of a grave where you had crawled as a child. But, oh evil deed, oh inhuman savageness! The most ferocious of men, nay indeed, bloody and monstrous beasts, were awaiting you unsuspecting and unarmed in the middle of the road, that dreadful species of robbers unknown on Italian shores. They do not find satisfaction in gold, which is usually the supreme desire of robbers, but must skillfully draw your blood and prevent your highly desired return to your native land and reaching your place of burial. Oh unheard of thirst for blood! What more do you seek, you raging dogs? What more do you search for from a despoiled body? There certainly was no hatred of an unknown and innocent man, nor could one imagine it. If hunger for gold is the true cause of your evil deed, once your abominable desire has been fulfilled, return with your heavy booty to the caves and workshops of your crimes and go visit your hosts who eagerly await you there. Allow him to proceed barefooted. This would be sufficient. Nothing more is sought from you. He fell at the hands of robbers, but they too must have strongholds and are able to disdain without punishment heaven, Florence and justice. How could you fear a little man alone, weary and stunned, when your strong retreats were so close. Therefore, do not add fierceness to your greed: you have carried off anything that was of any value and could be turned to your use. Leave behind his soul which was so beneficial to himself and to his friends, but would be of no use to you. What do you consider savage, what are you thinking about, what are you trying to do? What is that madness of yours? What do your flashing swords seek, what do they want? Oh savage passion without hatred, without any expectation, slaughtering without fear a being who is sacred and similar to God, dip your lustful hands into his entrails and (something which even the more generous animals would not do) fall upon the mangled body and take delight in the foaming blood.

It shames me and makes me wretched, oh outstanding citizens, nor do these many laments emerge from a small spring of sorrow, nor indeed do I grieve more because such a misfortune befell such a friend than because so great a shame befell a state which was once so glorious. What will the people say? What will posterity think? That a harmless man who, as Lucan says, among the untamed people on the shores of the Rhone river, and through the desert sof the province of Arles than which there is nowhere any land more wild or desolate, and through the heart of the Alps beset not so much by snow or wandering travelers but at present by armed troops, did manage to travel along safely not only in daylight but in the dangers of the night, and yet was struck down in full daylight in Florentine territory like a sheep destined for an ungodly sacrifice. Oh eternal disgrace of our age, that there are to be found those who dared, almost in view of your city and of that formerly dreaded palace in which was the famous seat of your justice, tear to pieces one of your subjects as they pleased! Oh times, oh customs, one might exclaim with Tullius. Even as a child I used to hear my elders talk about the unusual virtues of all sorts possessed by that people, and their outstanding justice not only in civil suits but especially in these two things in which that most wise legislator, Solon, said was the basis of a true republic, namely, reward and punishment. If only one of these is missing, the state must limp along as if on the other foot, but if both are missing, it is utterly weakened and sluggish, with the virtue of good citizens becoming dull on the one hand, and, on the other, the badness of evil citizens taking fire. Your forefathers provided magnificently for both possibilities with skills truly worthy of their Roman origin which their fame had made renowned. Therefore, just as once those ancestors of ours, the Roman people, were powerful throughout the whole world, in the same manner did I conceive of the Florentines as having followed in the same footsteps to the extent it was granted by heaven. And they enjoyed an extraordinary amount of praise among all kinds of men and were able to maintain for a long time among the people of Tuscany a kind of voluntary pre-eminence although they carefully avoided even the name of empire. But what they lacked in arrogance and envy they gained in praise and glory. Their state was therefore not called a dominion but rather the aid and protector of neighbors, wherefore the flowering name of Florence was considered proper for it and given to it since in it visibly abounded the flower of all virtues and examples of glorious deeds. The fear of all the neighboring people for such a well-mannered people was mixed with love and respect. Not only in its own vicinity but in the furthest areas of Tuscany was this state feared as a mistress of justice. For how else could one explain that among the rocky and harsh hills, and on the parched soil, and without the assistance either of a maritime port or of a navigable river, its size increased in such a brief period of time (since of almost all cities of Italy, yours is the youngest) that it almost unbelievably surpassed all the largest neighboring ones, not only in reputation or in precious merchandise (which also was a kind of miracle), but in its most fortunate production of manly offspring? Being insufficiently large for all its offspring, did it not, again like a mother fill with its subjects almost every corner of the world? What, I ask, was the cause of this so great and sudden a growth especially because it had so many adversaries? There are some who say that the atmosphere which was most suitable for producing such offspring was the cause, thereby attributing to nature or to fate what really belongs to virtue. Others count among the causes the industry of your energetic people, their versatile minds, and a temper most suitable for all the arts. This may indeed not be wrong provided one recalls that it overlooks the first and greatest cause of all by saying nothing of their fondness for justice. That, I say, that alone is the true and primary cause of your growth. Without it neither the city itself nor the smallest home would either grow or even exist. Justice is the foundation of all cities on which, if one seeks the truth, your ancestors erected for you a most flourishing and powerful republic. If you allow this fact to be overlooked even through ignorance, what can you possibly expect other than a downfall?

Note that a band of infamous assassins appeared and (something that ought to have aroused the most widespread anger) ambushed a citizen of yours, an outstanding man, against whom it is believed they plotted from the day he left his home. They dared slay in your very midst, and they perpetrated under your very eyes on a public road and with cruel and intolerable insolence something that they would have feared even to think about in their very beds in the days of your forefathers. If you leave this crime unpunished, it will mean the end of your universal reputation, of your justice, and ultimately of your safety, of your liberty and of your glory. It will destroy the foundations from which you had sprung as high as the stars; and, dear God, by what hands they will be destroyed! A great portion of an offense is the violence of the perpetrator. A bunch of gallows-birds, murderers and cavemen, bestial in their nourishment but even more so in their hearts and in their ways, scarcely worthy of prison or chains or your hangman's rope, hasten to your bellies and ravenously feed upon the slaughter and blood of unfortunate people until they are full. They certainly would never have dared do this unless they had confidence either in your sluggishness or in their hiding places, a hope which would have proven completely useless to them if you, as was your custom, were truly men. I realize that fortune keeps you busy and preoccupied in times like these, but it does not scatter your forces nor weaken you to the point where you simply endure a few raging highwaymen freely circulating in your territories. True virtue rises higher and more clearly in adversity; and if I know your customs, nor has my opinion of you been wrong, you possess especially this one quality among the many that you have inherited from the Romans, namely, not to be cast down or crushed by the workings of fortune, but instead to let them exalt you and let your spirits spring forth in a more manly fashion amidst difficulties. I have become quite hopeful since hearing that, incensed by the atrocity of what has happened and inflamed with a noble indignation, you have turned to your usual arms of justice. If this is true, there is no place anywhere, I hope, no stronghold, no favor of wicked men that will turn the deserved thunderbolt of your wrath from the heads of the guilty.

I have indeed, illustrious men, spoken with you in a friendly fashion about many points concerning the loss of my dear and mourned friend over which I can be considered bitterly disturbed. But alas it has been in vain and too late! I realize that my loss cannot be recovered, not if I were to speak eternally with a thousand powerful tongues, or were to charm more sweetly than Orpheus the stone with my tearful plaints accompanied by the lyre. Never will my friend return to me. He entered upon a journey without return. It is now no longer a matter of his appearing again, but do not let your honor fall with him. His return is impossible, but maintaining your honor is very simple and within your power. To warn you that avengers of crimes do not look to the past but to the future is here not necessary. Of what benefit is it to concentrate on those things which cannot be undone? One must hasten to oppose such evils with their likes and contrain human rashness by means of frightful precedents. This is what produced that truly praised opinion of very learned men: "Punishments were invented not because evil exists, but to help avoid evil." Although such punishment is most appropriate because of the monstrous size of this crime, and although I can realistically expect it to be applied if I simply remain silent, I am nevertheless forbidden to demand it. Therefore let all these things I have said be understood as a reflection of my grief which by speaking out I am directing to friendly ears, and as a means of relieving my heavy heart of its weighty sadness, rather than as a means of inflaming your minds for bloody revenge. This would befit neither my profession nor my condition. I therefore declare (whatever I may say or have said) that I do not aspire to such vengeance, but rather request what I can ask in a more honorable fashion, namely, that mindful of your ancient glory and justice in which you flourished so uniquely, you do not allow them to perish in your day. And I beg even more firmly that at least your public roads over which there has always been much traveling both to your city and to the city of your ancestors, and over which there will now be even more traffic from every region since, as you know, we are about to celebrate the Jubilee, be purged of bandits and be open to pilgrims so that through justifiable apprehension they will not be compelled either to avoid undertaking the holy journey or to avoid taking the most direct route. Unless you see to this in a most expeditious manner (and I hope that you will be forward-looking), your reputation will be stained with eternal infamy. Among the first things, you must guarantee access to the pass over the Apennines where a greater number of travelers is expected. How I wish it had occurred to me to bring this to your attention earlier! The warning would perhaps have been more timely and the miserable fate of my unfortunate friend would not have provided others with a reason for being fearful. What was the reason for such a fear? Our age and our elders had always realized that the summit of the Apennines was naturally rough and demanding. Yet there was no place more safe for travelers nor more hospitable. What will happen, however, if the guardians become thieves and the dogs become wolves? When to the inherent terror of the woody mountain an external and additional fear is added, that entire tract of land will in a brief time be deserted by all and be viewed as more inhospitable than Mount Atlas or the Caucasian Mountains. Hasten to avoid this disgrace and this bane, oh powerful men; you see the rocks themselves still moist with your citizen's blood, which still has not dried. From this case learn how to provide for the safety of others. He who wishes to dry up streams must first dry up their source; he who wishes to destroy bandits must first insist that their protectors be rooted out. Go quickly, go happily back to what you began, and with the assistance of heaven destroy the foul hiding places of the criminals, and wipe this blot from before your eyes in order to leave to posterity the reputation for justice which you received from your fathers. God almighty will preserve you as victors and will protect you from so many evils in this world and keep you in a most happy state.

Parma, 2 June, hastily and deeply upset.

Bibliography

Bernardo, A. S. "Dramatic Dialogue in the Prose Letters of Petrarch." *Symposium* V (1951): 302–316.

———. "Dramatic Dialogue and Monologue in Petrarch's Works." *Symposium* VII (1953): 92–119.

———. "Letter-Splitting in Petrarch's *Familiares*." *Speculum* XXXIII (1958): 236–288.

———. "The Selection of Letters in Petrarch's *Familiares*." *Speculum* XXXV (1960): 280–288.

———. *Petrarch, Scipio and the 'Africa'*. Baltimore, 1962.

———. "Petrarch and the Art of Literature." In *Petrarch to Pirandello* (Toronto, 1973), 19–43.

Billanovich, G. *Lo Scrittoio del Petrarca*. Roma. 1947.

Bishop, M. *Petrarch and His World*. Indiana, 1963.

———. *Letters from Petrarch*. Indiana, 1966.

Bosco, U. *Francesco Petrarca*. Torino, 1946. 2nd ed., 1961.

———. "Francesco Petrarca." In *Letteratura italiana, I Maggiori* (Milano, 1956), 111–163.

Calcaterra, C. *Nella selva del Petrarca*. Bologna, 1942.

Cornell University Library. *Catalogue of the Petrarch Collection*. Bequeathed by Willard Fiske, compiled by Mary Fowler. Oxford University Press, 1916. Revised and updated, 1974.

Dotti, U. "La formazione dell'umanesimo nel Petrarca." *Belfagor* XXXIII (1968): 532–563.

———. *Francesco Petrarca Le Familiari, Libri I–IV* (Urbino, 1970). New edition, vol. I, *Libri I–V*, vol. II, *Libri VI–XI* (Urbino, 1974).

Fracassetti, G. *Francisci Petrarcae epistolae de rebus familiaribus et variae*. Florence, 1859.

———. *Lettere di Francesco Petrarca, delle cose familiari libri ventiquattro, Lettere varie libro unico*. Florence, 1863–1867.

———. *Lettere senili di Francesco Petrarca*. Florence, 1869.

Garin, E. *Italian Humanism*. Translated by Peter Munz. New York, 1965.

Girardi, M. "La 'Nuova data' scoperta dal Nolhac nelle vita del Petrarca." In *Atti e memorie della R. Accademia di scienze, lettere ed arti in Padova* VIII (1892).

Kraus, F. X. "Francesco Petrarca in seinem Briefwechsel." In *Deutsche*

Rundschau LXXXV (1895), and LXXXVI (1896). Italian translation by D. Valbusa, *Francesco Petrarca e la sua corrispondenza epistolare*, Florence, 1901.

Magrini, Diana. *Le epistole metriche di Francesco Petrarca*. Rocca S. Casciano, 1907.

Nolhac, P. de. *Pétrarque et l'humanisme*. Paris, 1907.

Pasquali, G. "Le 'Familiari' del Petrarca." In *Leonardo* IV (1933).

Petrarca, Francesco. *Prose*. Ed. G. Martellotti, P. G. Ricci, E. Carrara, and E. Bianchi. Vol. VII in the series *La Letteratura italiana, storia e testi* (Milano and Napoli, 1955).

———. *Book without a Name*. Translated by P. Zacour. Toronto, 1973.

Raimondi, E. "Correzioni medioevali, correzioni umanistiche e correzioni petrarchesche nella lettera VI del libro XVI delle 'Familiares'." In *Studi petrarcheschi* I (Bologna, 1948).

Robinson, J. H. and Rolfe, H. W. *Petrarch, the First Modern Scholar and Man of Letters*. New York and London, 1898.

Rossi, V. "Nell'intimità spirituale del Petrarca (con tre lettere inedite)." In *Nuova Antologia* CCLXXVIII (July, 1931).

———. "Sulla formazione delle raccolte epistolari petrarchesche." In *Annali della cattedra petrarchesca*, 1932.

———. *Francesco Petrarca, Le Familiari*. Florence, 1933–1942.

Sapegno, N. "Le lettere del Petrarca." In *La Nuova Italia* VII (1936).

———. *Il Trecento*. Milano, 1942.

Seigel, J. E. *Rhetoric and Philosophy in Renaissance Humanism*. Princeton, 1968.

Studi petrarcheschi. Bologna, 1948–1966.

Tatham, E. *Francesco Petrarca, His Life and Correspondence*. London, 1926.

Tonelli, L. "Le raccolte epistolari." In his *Petrarca* (Milan, 1930).

Wilkins, E. H. "A Chronological Conspectus of the Writings of Petrarch." In *Romanic Review* XXXIX (1948): 89–101.

———. "Letters Addressed to Petrarch." *MLN* LXV (1950): 293–297.

———. "The Miscellaneous Letters of Petrarch." *MLN* LXV (1950): 374–377.

———. "Petrarch and Giacomo de'Rossi." *Speculum* XXV (1950): 374–377.

———. *The Making of the 'Canzoniere' and Other Petrarchan Studies*. Roma: Edizioni di Storia e Letteratura, 1951.

———. *A History of Italian Literature*. Cambridge, Mass.: Harvard University Press, 1954.

———. *Studies in the Life and Works of Petrarch*. Cambridge, Mass.: The Medieval Academy of America, 1955.

———. *Petrarch at Vaucluse*. Chicago: The University of Chicago Press, 1958.

———. *Petrarch's Eight Years in Milan*. Cambridge, Mass.: The Medieval Academy of America, 1958.

———. "A Survey of the Correspondence between Petrarch and Francesco Nelli." In *Italia medioevale e umanistica* I (1958), 351–358.

———. *Petrarch's Later Years.* Cambridge, Mass.: The Medieval Academy of America, 1959.